The
Action Guide
to Government
Grants, Loans,
and Giveaways

The Action Guide to Government Grants, Loans, and Giveaways

The comprehensive guide to getting millions of dollars in grants, loan guarantees, loans, and other financial help from federal and state government sources

GEORGE CHELEKIS

A PERIGEE BOOK

Perigee Books
are published by
The Putnam Publishing Group
200 Madison Avenue
New York, NY 10016

Library of Congress Cataloging-in-Publication Data

Chelekis, George C.
    The action guide to government grants, loans, and giveaways / by George Chelekis.
        p.   cm.
    ISBN 0-399-51792-8
        1. Proposal writing for grants—United States. 2. Grants-in-aid—United
States—Directories. 3. Small business—United States—Finance—Directories.
4. Research grants—United States—Directories. 5. Government lending—United
States. I. Title.
HG177.5.U6C438   1993   92-38818 CIP
658.15′224—dc20

Cover design by Mike McIver
Cover photo © by Telegraph Colour Library/FPG

Printed in the United States of America
4   5   6   7   8   9   10

This book is dedicated to my mother who has helped me over the years; to my wife, Gwen, who has been incredibly supportive through thick and thin; to my daughter, Katie, who brings me joy every morning and night; and to Ron who helped me better understand business.

CONTENTS

****

10 CONTENTS

ACKNOWLEDGMENTS

****

Like my good friend, Maria Larsson, said in August, 1992, "I'll set the table, you cook the dinner." That's pretty much what happened in writing this book. Maria completed the most important task -- organizing the core research that facilitated my writing this book.

When Maria's assignment ended, Thelma Sharkey continued the fabulous job of research and directory verification on this book that she did on my earlier book, THE OFFICIAL GOVERNMENT AUCTION GUIDE (Crown Publishers, Inc.). Compared to an earlier version of THE ACTION GUIDE TO GRANTS, LOANS AND GIVEAWAYS, Thelma was worth six researchers. Michael Costello also spent many hours sifting through piles of directory materials to ensure that you have the most updated information.

As they wove together a directory, Cheryl Smith, Holly Schalter and Doc Paxton worked long hours into the waning days of September, 1992, typing and inputting this directory. Over five continuous days and sleepless nights, John Lux meticulously proofread and corrected each portion of the text and directory and then formatted this entire book on his Word Perfect version 5.1. I found John Lux to not only be useful with many of the investment banking areas of the text, but a godsend when it came to rolling up sleeves and doing the dirty work.

Throughout this, I wrote and re-wrote and tried to give you my best shot. I wanted you to have information that you could immediately use, not just another book that gathers dust and cobwebs on your shelf. In its present format, THE ACTION GUIDE TO GRANTS, LOANS AND GIVEAWAYS is an entirely different book from its predecessors; it bears no resemblance to the earlier book whatsoever, except in title.

A special thanks goes to the hundreds of government officials and employees who were interviewed about their areas of expertise. I was pleased to discover that there are many, many competent, courteous and efficient government employees. While there are many problems in government, it is a relief to find those who do their jobs and who really do care. I hope you run across and are helped by these fine men and women in the Small Business Administration, SCORE, Small Business Development Centers, Department of Commerce, Farmer's Home Administration, Department of Housing and Urban Development, Resolution Trust Corporation, Veterans Affairs, National Endowment for the Arts, and your local and state government offices.

It goes without saying that had it not been for Jane Gelfman, my literary agent, in creating this opportunity to help you, for Rena Wolner and John Duff at the Putnam Group and Perigee who gambled on me, this book would not, at this moment, be in your hands.

Finally, I would especially like to thank Linda Maxedon who was my main troubleshooter in bringing this book together and completed by its deadline. She has a way of finding resources and running logistics that would win over any entrepreneur.

Because of each person's commitment, support and dedication to see this book through each of its stages, its valuable information is now yours to read, enjoy and use to help improve your life.

FOREWORD

****

As Americans we are in an important time. The Federal Government has available to us hundreds of billions of dollars in government grants and loans programs. Yet, businesses struggle to find financing, researchers complain about federal spending cuts, and college students struggle to finance their educations. There has never been a better time for a comprehensive book on government grants and loans as this one.

Our economy needs the entrepreneur, the researcher, the educated individual, and our nation's artists. Without them, we, as a nation, grieve and scramble to stay on course with our international counterparts. Government grants and loans are available but it takes work to get them. THE ACTION GUIDE TO GOVERNMENT GRANTS, LOANS AND GIVEAWAYS can help you break through the bureaucratic maze and find the financing you need.

Nearly everyone has a project they would like funded. It may be the nonprofit organization, the small business startup, your child's education, a new idea you would like to research, the unwritten song or unpainted artwork. Our government understands these things and has set aside money to assist projects like these. But, finding these programs is not an easy task. Until now.

This book will take you through all the major federal and state government agencies that fund and assist the business person, the prospective homeowner, the real estate investor, college students, researchers, artists, and virtually anyone who has a worthwhile project. You will find out what you are eligible for and how to obtain funding. In this book, you will find dozens of government programs to assist you in achieving your goals.

If you are an entrepreneur, you will be amazed to discover the wonderful opportunities offered by the U.S. Small Business Administration, the U.S. Department of Commerce, your own state government, and other funding sources. Do you have a startup business? Do you want to export your product or service overseas? Do you want to expand your business? Government programs exist for nearly any dream you can think of.

If you are a prospective homeowner, you can turn to many federal and state government financing programs throughout the pages of this book. Four important federal government agencies not only have real estate available to sell you, but they also want to help you finance your new home. Your state is likely to have one or more grant or loan programs available to purchase or renovate your home.

If you are a college student, educator, researcher or scholar, there may be an abundance of government programs from which you can choose. Our government wants to upgrade our literacy level and programs are available for those who want a better education. Again, this book is loaded with these programs.

If you are an artist, you have come to the right place. Musicians, artists, sculptors, playwrights, philosophers, linguists, historians, writers, and others in the creative professions can find federal and state government money to bring their careers to fruition or help those callings along. As an added bonus, this book also contains private sector funding sources to help you, the artist.

THE ACTION GUIDE TO GOVERNMENT GRANTS, LOANS AND GIVEAWAYS is a virtual supermarket of government grant and loan information. Not only will you find a very complete guide on this vital and valuable topic, you have in your hands directory after directory to help speed your progress along.

Anyone who has ever thought about getting a government grant or loan needs to have this book in their personal library. I am very pleased that George Chelekis is sharing with the public his expertise and knowledge in the field of government grants and loans. No one in country could do a better job in putting together a book like this.

SONNY BLOCH
Author, Lecturer and
Broadcast Journalist

PREFACE

****

With this book my goal is to assist you, the reader, in achieving your own financial goals, whether personal or corporate, by introducing you to the world of Government Money. The idea of Government Money being lent or given out has gotten a bad reputation in the past twenty-five years. Defaulted Small Business Administration loans, Department of Housing and Urban Development scandals, Golden Fleece awards for ridiculous psychiatric and other "scientific research" programs, welfare cheats, shady Defense contract deals, food stamp abuses, non-payment of student loans and the like may have disabused honest taxpayers of the idea that Government Loans and Grants is a good thing.

Some even believe that the government practice of granting or lending money should be entirely eliminated. After all, the honest taxpayer should get upset. No one in their right mind would continue handing over money or investing in an activity that is insane, destructive or a criminal activity. In government, there are safeguards that eventually put the crook behind bars and official investigations that prevent those program abuses from continuing. Unfortunately, the taxpayer bears that cost as well as the funds lost or embezzled.

Strange as it may seem, the basic and fundamental purposes of Government Money, being lent or given out, were once not as confused as they are today. Look at the original intentions that our government leaders had when they postulated the government programs that appropriated these funds. You will be surprised, as I have been, to discover that many government programs were basically and vitally beneficial for our country.

Without Small Business Administration (SBA) loans millions of businesses would have never existed. Those businesses generate jobs and tax revenues, directly and indirectly, that make America's economy the largest in the world. Had the SBA never been created in the early 1950's many of those business owners and corporate founders might never have borrowed the money that engendered the prosperous decade of the 1960's.

The next time you visit your family doctor or chiropractor or another professional, ask him or her if a student loan helped pay for college and postgraduate training. A federal agency or his state's government may have helped provide him with a college education and a career. And, his career is providing you with a service which you greatly desire and need.

Ask a veteran if Government Money helped get him through college, taught him a valuable skill, lent him money to buy a home, or provided him with medical assistance and other benefits.

How many Americans would not own a home if it weren't for Government Money? You'd be surprised to know that Federal Government programs helped create the real estate industry we have today. Sure, you've probably read or heard about VA and HUD-repossessed homes for sale. Perhaps, some of you have even heard about Resolution Trust properties for sale. But, Federal Housing Authority money has helped millions of Americans own homes. Fannie Mae, and later Freddie Mac, continue to provide financing to keep the entire real estate market going.

This is Government Money at work. It influences our lives in many respects. When it is used properly and discreetly by the recipient, as this money is intended, Government Money helps fuel each sector of the economy. In areas where it is missing or has been abused, you will find a crisis in that area of government. But, the purpose of this book is not to expose the government agencies that may have been deceived or co-opted by criminal elements into funding destructive or despised government programs. Rather, this book exists to assist you in finding the money you need to launch a worthwhile project, start or expand a profitable business, get an education, or develop an artistic career.

Money, itself, may be the issue. Some consider money to be the fuel that keeps the great idea alive or the business machine going. Without money, books, such as the one you're reading, never get written, let alone printed and distributed so you can learn something new. Without money, the painting never gets painted, if only because the artist can not buy the art supplies or pay his rent or eat. Businesses neither get started nor stay around long enough to keep selling their goods and services without the fuel of money. Despite what you may have heard, money is not a bad thing to have in your pocket. Especially when you need it!

Unless one is born wealthy, marries into it, or has a knack and the stomach for counter-

feiting, he or she generally has to borrow it to bring into existence a good idea or keep it alive in the early (or even later) stages of its development. This can apply to the businessman and the artist alike. Some rare exceptions create wealth instantly.

They work hard and fast and know exactly what they are doing at all times in sequence and move from Point A to Point B in a flash. Even most of them, at some point, must borrow, if only for expansionary reasons. The rest of us are not that remarkable and struggle along, making mistakes, correcting them, and eventually getting it right. In the interim borrowed money or some sort of grant helps keep the shop owner or musician going.

After one has exhausted family and networking sources, the first place one usually thinks about, when borrowing money, is the bank. Think again. Banks are notoriously tight when it comes to a loan. We have all just gone through a decade of the spendthrift 1980's. Banks would have probably lent more money out if they could have printed their credit cards faster. You can look forward to an extremely tight decade for the rest of this century.

So, where can you get the cash you need to keep your business afloat, to start your business, for an expensive college education, to write your great novel, to launch a musical or artistic career, or whatever your dream may be? The Government. More specifically, one or more Federal government agencies, a state or local government program or a quasi-government funded source may be your only alternative to never getting started in the first place. Even the federal government depends on the banking industry for each agency's business, real estate and educations loan guaranty programs. Banks would be even more tight-fisted with funds if it weren't for those programs.

PURPOSE

The purpose of this book is to show you how and where to get money from the government for your business, your education, your home, or your artistic career. This book has been written primarily for the individual and with the individual in mind. Small sub-sections, within chapters, sometimes touch upon non-profit organizations. Many fine books exist to help these organizations obtain funding from private foundations. This is not one of those books; this book is for YOU, the individual business person, the individual student, the individual house shopper, or the individual student.

Every attempt has been made to obtain and study previous books on the subject and to provide you with the latest and most useful information. At the back of this book you will find a number of recommended books that can further assist you in obtaining a grant or loan.

This book is an attempt to give you a comprehensive guide that will help you work your way through the bureaucratic maze of obtaining government funding. Most of the research work has been completed. On occasion, you may need to update portions of this book, as telephone numbers or addresses change and as government agencies modify, add or delete programs. Used properly as a source work this book should last you many years.

Once you've received your Government Grant or Loan, please spend this money wisely. As a taxpayer you can appreciate the amount of work required of you just to receive enough income to pay your taxes. Congress approved funds for grants and loans from your tax payments. And they did so for the purpose of improving our country, not to give a frivolous spendthrift a free ride.

Let me know about any successes or difficulties you have with obtaining a government grant or loan. But, before you send me questions to answer, please take care that the material has not already been covered in this publication. You may also want to visit your local library for additional materials or current information. Start in your library's reference section with the current Catalog of Federal Domestic Assistance. This massive volume contains the federal domestic assistance programs for the most recent Fiscal Year. While you're at the library, look for some of the books I suggested you read at the end of this book. You can always write to me:

GEORGE CHELEKIS
c/o Perigee
200 Madison Avenue
New York, New York 10016

HOW TO USE THIS BOOK
****

Because of the nature of this book, I wanted to help prepare you for what follows. Some readers may wish to read this publication cover to cover. I find that flattering. However, that's not the way it was intended as I wrote it. Others may jump right into a particular government program without some of the important information that precedes it. That can become a fatal mistake and dash one's plans to participate in that program. Please do not jeopardize your ambition to obtain a grant or loan in this way. In an earlier work, THE OFFICIAL GOVERNMENT AUCTION GUIDE (Crown Publishers, Inc., New York), I recommended that auction goers prepare themselves for an auction by attending the inspection or preview period. Many ignore this advice and overpay at auctions. The same advice applies with this book -- prepare yourself before jumping into the details of the grant or loan program.

This book is broken down into four main sections, which you can use as a basic outline to help you get started. The first section, composed of Chapters 1 through 4, is really a long introductory section of the book. If you plan to apply for a business loan, then I would recommend you read Chapters 1, 3 and 4 before proceeding with Section Two. For grant seekers, study Chapters 1, 2 and 4 before proceeding with the rest of the book.

For businessmen I recommend you then examine the book's Table of Contents and de-termine specifically which program in Section Two is suitable for you. Are you a potential exporter? Read through Chapter 8. Do you need research funds for a business idea? Go to Chapter 10. Will you qualify for a minority program? Read Chapter 11. Is your business large enough to warrant venture capital? Have a look at Chapter 12. There are many different types of federally sponsored business programs available to you. The hardest part will be deciding which program is most suitable for you. The mainstay of Section Two is Chapter Five and it will probably be the most widely read chapter in this book. I suggest you read through this chapter as soon as you can after finishing Section One, as it may be helpful in directing you to other chapters within this section.

Section three comprises three separate and unrelated Areas. Chapters 13 through 17 are about real estate programs in which you may wish to participate if you are looking to buy a home or other property. There are both federally sponsored and financing programs available to you for your home purchase. Read through the beginnings of each chapter and get a feel for that chapter. Decide whether or not that program may be helpful to you; if not, move on to the next chapter. Each chapter has a special area that it concerns. In Chapter 13, I outline the basic programs available in the rest of the real estate group: Chapters 13 through 17.

Chapters 18 and 19 in Section Three discuss the different financial aid programs available within and outside the federal government. If you or your children are going to college and you desire financial assistance, then please read those chapters first.   Information in Chapter 18 and funding sources in Chapter 19 could help you or your children get a college education.

Artists and other creative individuals should read Chapters 20 and 21.   Many grant and financial assistance programs are available to writers, artists, musicians, actors and other creative professionals.   Federal, regional, state and private sources are included in these chapters.

Finally, Section Five is the concluding section of this book.   It incorporates additional reading materials that may help move you closer to your goals.   Most importantly, it includes a glossary of specialized terms used in this book.   You should refer to it whenever an unfamiliar word is used in the text.   If it is not found in the glossary, then please use a dictionary.   Reading habits have changed over the past half century and book readers don't look up and find the correct definition for the words they don't understand.   To better comprehend what you are reading in this text, please use the glossary in Section Five and your dictionary for words you do not clearly understand.   By doing this, you will find that you can use what you just read.   And, when it comes to borrowing or being granted money, that is pretty important.

Good luck in finding your program and obtaining government funding for your endeavor.   There is likely to be one or more government programs for which you qualify. Probably the only thing stopping you from obtaining a grant or loan is your failing to decide to do it ... and then following up on that decision!   Be sure and let me know how you do.

SECTION ONE:

INTRODUCTORY INFORMATION
****

1.

GET THE FACTS STRAIGHT

****

There are a few important points you should understand before contacting government agencies about their Grants and Loans programs. In an earlier version of this book I discovered that many readers had difficulties in distinguishing between a Grant and a Loan. Other readers found dealing with government bureaucrats a difficult task. Some took "no" for an answer all too quickly. Others sent applications to the wrong government agency. Some confused federal government programs with state program or even private funding sources. These were the main difficulties and we should clarify them here.

First, let me explain that fathoming some of these programs can generate confusion and can also put you to sleep. Reading the jargon in the Federal Budget or other government publications isn't easy for the layperson. Every effort has been made to simplify existing material so you can work with it.

However, you may be directed by one government agent, when investigating a particular program, to call a different government agency or a different section within that same agency. You may be sent material that is not covered in this book. If that does happen, I suggest you use a dictionary to define some of the terms used. When legal terms are scattered throughout the text of a program, turn to Black's Law Dictionary and find the correct definition for that word in there. Otherwise,

you'll probably find yourself disinterested in that particular program or, you will perhaps, even give up entirely on obtaining a grant or loan. And, that could be a shame -- since you might be eligible and qualify for funding from that program.

FREE MONEY?

Over the past few decades this phrase, Government Money, has come to mean "free money" to a large segment of the American population. You've heard it and so have I. "Government Money" has taken on a new definition created by our current "giveaway" society. In most cases, this really isn't free money. Even when it is given away, as with food stamps or welfare checks, money is created out of thin air, which then reduces our standard of living as a nation. Someone, somewhere, directly or indirectly, is able to buy a little less, spend a little less, and live less well.

Someone on welfare is rarely, if ever, leading a better life. The welfare, unemployment or food stamp "cheat" is not only hurting himself, he or she usually wastes the money in some way. Often, such persons find themselves in a deeper mess, by receiving money that isn't required to be repaid, than they would have been without the "public assistance."

Similarly, the crook running a scam with government real estate properties or those who commit SBA fraud are both headed for disaster and possibly a jail sentence. These individuals reduce our overall standard of living by making Government Money harder to come by: less money is given out, interest charges and carrying costs can be higher on loans, more strings are attached to grants, and so forth.

Money isn't free. I wonder how many people seriously believe that Government Money grows on those proverbial trees. It doesn't. Certainly, the way banks were handing out credit, through credit cards and consumer loans, during the 1970's and 1980's, it wouldn't be impossible for someone to evolve the strange idea that money is free. But, eventually all the pipers want to be paid.

Look at how you receive your paycheck to observe from where your income arrives. Money comes from someone exerting energy or creativity that results in goods or services produced and an equitable (or sometimes inequitable) interchange between the party selling these and another purchasing them.

Because such an exchange takes place, our federal, state and local governments receive, justly or unjustly, a percentage of that transaction, from nearly all the individuals and businesses that participated and/or benefited, directly and indirectly, in and from that transaction. From that revenue generated by that and hundreds of billions of these types of transactions, our elected politicians, in coordination with aides, supporters and "professional" government employees, elected, appointed or hired, determine how that income will be disbursed.

From the above we get what is called Government Money. A large portion of this money finds its way back into the society with the intention of helping Americans, and sometimes even non-Americans, increase the amount of transactions between themselves. That produces more tax revenues. The reason for that is so Americans can be prosperous and continue to vote for these same politicians.

For the past three decades politicians have taken short-cuts and deemed it necessary to directly purchase votes by appropriating money to individuals, and occasionally corporations, without an honest transaction taking place. However, we can't just blame the politicians. Some individuals and corporations looted the Treasury without those politicians even knowing about it. (Perhaps, it was because they were too busy writing "bad checks" on the Congressional bank.) But, because of this enormous Government Giveaway, the term, Government Money, has taken on the colloquial definition of "free money."

None of this implies that our current financial scene, between the private and public sectors, is fair. However, it is what we have to work with. Using Government Money in the way it was intended first starts with understanding what this phrase really means. Let's break it down into its elements.

GRANTS versus LOANS

The reason for the previous build-up is so that you correctly understand the difference between the two key words around which this book is written. Please note how these two words are different.

A) Government Grant: Money that you are given to pursue a project and produce something that is   beneficial for the greater good of the society. This money is not repaid in cash. It is repaid by the creation of an artistic product, an educational assistance or breakthrough, or a research endeavor that benefits the American public and humanity. A grant of cash fuels the artist, educator, organization or researcher and helps him or her produce something of value to the society. One is given cash, but does not repay with cash.

Please do not confuse this with "something for nothing." Artists, writers, poets, musicians, educators and researchers work hard in this society and are frequently paid a poor wage for the benefit they create for the rest of us.

B) Government Loan: Money that is lent to a business or individual to start-up or expand that business or to purchase real estate. Into that category can fall any aspect of the business, including research, development, marketing, manufacturing, working capital, and distribution. The government helps finance real estate purchases so that also falls into this category.

Quite simply, a grant is cash that is not repaid with cash. An applicant is given Government Money for a worthy project and, in return, develops that project. When talking about Government Money as a loan, the applicant receives cash and repays that money over a period of time, usually, but not always, with interest. Funds are lent to the business or applicant on the assumption that this enterprise or real estate will be well managed and bring a profit to the lender. That profit might be increased earnings for the business. It could also mean a definable monetary appreciation in the real estate. In either event, Government Money is lent out with the intention that you repay it.

Of course, there are a few gray areas. In some cases one can get a business grant for important research. There are federal and state programs for this. One student may receive a grant for his education while another will be lent funds, to be repaid at a later date. Every effort will be made in this book to distinguish between grants and loans, where there is any confusion. If there is still confusion in this area, please consult a dictionary.

LOAN GUARANTEES, DIRECT PAYMENTS AND INSURANCE

A loan guarantee is still a loan. Let's say you needed to borrow money from a bank, but the bank either didn't trust you or didn't feel you were a strong risk. That bank would ask that you find a more creditworthy person, usually a family member or friend, to co-sign a loan for you. The co-signer then bears the risk if you fail to repay. He or she is required to pay off the loan balance should you leave town or declare bankruptcy.

That is the nature of a personal guarantee. It is used most frequently by leasing companies, who lease equipment to new or unproven companies. They'll demand that the owner or one or more corporate officers sign a personal guarantee on the loan amount to purchase that equipment. That's the way it works on a government loan guarantee.

The Federal Government guarantees a private lender that a business or individual will repay the funds. When someone purchases real estate, they'll apply to a bank for the mortgage or loan and a government agency guarantees the bank that the funds will be repaid. This is one of the ways government real estate comes up for auction. The government loan guarantee facilitates the mortgage loan. When the individual or family defaults on that loan, the government is stuck with the tab and then resells the real estate property to recoup some or all of their loss.

It works this way in business. When Lee Iacocca made headlines in the 1970s That he was seeking government loan guarantees, he did so because private lenders were hesitant to lend Chrysler Corporation funds to stay in business. Banks and lending syndicates did not believe that Chrysler would, or could, repay the new money he was asking for.

Rather than allow this mammoth automaker to fail, thus laying off thousands of workers, the U.S. Government backed up Chrysler with a loan guarantee.

In most cases, loan guarantees are the main thrust of the government loan program. Most of the Small Business Administration (SBA) loans are, in reality, loan guarantees. Only in a small number of cases does the SBA lend money directly to a businesses or individual. Other government agencies work in a similar fashion -- they don't lend the money directly but, instead, guarantee the private lender against the loss.

Federal insurance is another type of Government Money. It can be insurance provided by a government agency or a private insurance company. One may an insurance premium or not, depending on the program and the coverage. Money is not paid to an individual or business but, instead, insurance is provided. Generally, such insurance is risky for most insurance companies, or has a high rate of payout, so the federal government performs this service.

Direct payments are a horse of a different color. They most resemble a grant. These involve programs that pay individuals or businesses money, which does not have to be repaid or is a payment for services rendered. Public assistance, food stamps, Social Security, Medicaid and other similar benefits fall into this category. Money is either directly given to an individual under a specific program or it is paid to a firm or institution for a service performed for individuals. A large number of Americans believe this redistribution of wealth is the only kind of Government Money. By now, you know this isn't true.

Now, that you understand the basic terms that breakdown and define Government Money, let's take up the next important step in obtaining your government grant or loan.

HOW TO DEAL WITH A GOVERNMENT EMPLOYEE

In civics textbooks and in other reading materials you were probably taught that government officials serve the people. From this we get the term "Government Servant." This can be taken too literally.

In an old Abbott and Costello comedy, there was a sketch where Bud Abbott refused to cooperate with a policeman and logically argued that if Bud was the taxpayer, the cop worked for him. That takes a lot of courage to say to a policeman, but it's basically true. However, the policeman is ALSO a taxpayer. Government employees work for the taxpayer, but they also perform their duties for ALL the taxpayers, not just one.

I've repeatedly interviewed government employees for other books, magazine articles, and other writings. Rarely have they been anything but helpful. Over the past year I needed information on everything from equipment leasing and computer floppy disks to chicken pox. When I telephoned the appropriate government agency for facts and figures, it was always done pleasantly, quickly and efficiently.

The underlying success of my obtaining useful information stemmed from my attitude. Had I telephoned a government agent, or anyone for that matter, and demanded this person drop everything he or she is doing and service me right now, I might have gotten a different response. Or been hung up on. "Hey, you, I wanna borrow Fifty Grand!" may not fly well with someone who's job it is to pick up phones and answer dumb questions all day long. If you don't believe this, try it. I can assure you that getting helping in raising that $50,000 is the last thing you'll see from that government agent.

Manners, courtesy, good cheer and a sincere interest in truly finding out how a program works, what paperwork you might have to file, how to go about obtaining or filing an application, what should be included and what shouldn't, and dozens of other similar questions can bring that government agent over to your side. Replace the "I-need- some-money-so-send-me-a-check-buddy" attitude with "Now, how do I go about doing this?" and you'll see some spectacular results.

There have been a number of classified advertisements, book-and-audio-tape seminar salesmen, and infomercials over the past few decades that have promised glorious and fantastic government giveaways. "Free" SBA money, Government Grants to buy commercial real estate, Government Money to bail a victim out of a tragedy, and so on. Good luck. I happen to have met some of those guys. One I know is now living overseas, a fugitive from several state attorney generals who would like to see him in a courtroom.

So, if you did call up a few government agents, realize they have also probably spoken to people who bought such book and tape packages. Then, you'll understand why the person on the other end of the phone sounds like he's strangling a scream. Put yourself in his shoes. How would you feel after receiving yet another, maybe even your 600th, phone call from someone demanding that you mail him a check for $150,000 because he's always wanted to start a hog farm in Arkansas? And, all because this young man heard on television about the wonderful money the government is giving away.

This is exactly what you are working against when you make a phone call to a government agency. How do you remedy it? Just be polite and interested in asking questions, not demanding money. There IS a lot of money government agencies disburse each year. But, you're not very likely to get it if you insist on barking orders to a government agent.

Let's close this section as simply as possible. Just treat the government agent in the same way you would want to be talked to, if you were answering that phone call. There's little more that anyone can say on the subject. But, there's a lot more to be said when a government agency rejects your grant or loan application. What do you do then?

BUT HE SAID "NO"

Wouldn't it be a wonderful world if every beautiful woman you met wanted to go out on a date with you? Or, conversely, if every fantastic man you ever knew fell in love with you and asked you to marry? Or every job you ever held was easy to do, paid beyond your wildest dreams, and was so much fun that you'd never even dream of taking a vacation? Or your car never broke down? Or when it did, the repairman failed to scratch his head and says "It's gonna cost a bundle"?

Well, it's not a perfect world. Just like you hear the word "no" when dealing with other aspects of your life, you are liable to hear "no," when it comes to inquiring about a particular government funding program or having your loan or grant application rejected. The secret is in how you react to that "no."

There's a guy I know. Let's call him "Joe." Joe gets turned down a lot, but he keeps on trucking. So what if Mr. NoCanDo rejects his loan application when Joe needs to borrow money? Joe just applies somewhere else. In fact, Joe applies to so many other places that he's eventually bound to get a "yes." By the way, Joe's pretty successful. Sure, he has his ups and downs, but overall he's ahead of the game.

Don't you have a little "Joe" in you? When contacting a government agency, you might discover they've just spent every last dime. Or the program stopped taking applications three months ago. Or worse yet, the program was cancelled.

Be persistent (while keeping that smile on your face). Ask if there is a similar program in that same department or section. Keep questioning him (politely) and find out if that sort of program was transferred to another department or another agency. The name of the program may have just been changed and a new employee, who hadn't heard about the previous one, just been hired. That "no" you just heard might just be a "yes" somewhere else. Maybe even right next door.

Apply to more than one place. Let's say you just read about the government program of your dreams and it's banging you right in your face. Alarm bells are going off. Smoking is blowing out of your nostrils and ears. It's a federal program and you qualify. In your mind that program has YOUR name written all over it. Mentally, you are spending the money, buying new equipment, hiring employees, refurnishing your office, and a hundred other wild ideas you've always wanted to try. And all this happens before you've made the phone call, let alone applied for the loan or grant. Great! Look some more. That's right. Try to find a few more programs just like that one. There might be another federal program that looks just as good. A little more searching could uncover one or two state programs that smell just as juicy as this federal "steak." Write them all down. Then, make your phone calls and applications. Being rejected by three and approved for one is better than applying for only one and getting a big and life-shattering "no" in your mailbox.

IS THIS THE RIGHT PLACE?

Did you ever walk into a room and everyone looks like a stranger? Cold, hard stares slice through your skin. Your palms sweat and your eyes blur as they glance at every person in the room. That's probably the wrong place to apply for a job or look for merriment. You definitely know you're not welcome here because it's not the right place.

That's the same way it is when you file an application for a loan or grant. Filing a grant application for submarine research when you want a business loan sounds ridiculous. It's just like trying to hammer a square block into a circular hole. The square doesn't fit the circle.

Again it's the same problem with the individual who thinks money to buy a farm is being given to him, as a grant, and not lent to him? What about the individual who applies to the wrong program entirely? On a different page he would have found the correct program.

The statistics on obtaining a government grant are roughly 10 percent or thereabouts. For every application filed one in ten are approved. Loan approvals can run as low as 1 percent and reach as high as around 60 percent.

By filing an application for a government program, for which you are ineligible, you become one of the nine in ten who are rejected. Now, please don't take this to mean that "all you have to do is file the right application with the right agency program and you'll get your grant or loan approved." The point I'm making is that you REDUCE your chances of approval by randomly or carelessly filing applications to programs for which you are ineligible. Not to mention that you're wasting a lot of postage money and your time.

Just like going to the wrong party, your application, like your presence, isn't going to be welcome. Originally, I thought it might be unnecessary to include this section. However, after speaking with various government agents, I realized that this carelessness is far more rampant than you might imagine. But then, you're not the one reading the grant and loan applications. The government agents are.

NO, THAT'S NOT BRAZIL

Someday, educational standards are going to return to where little Johnny knows where Iowa is located on the map. Knowing the difference between a state in the Union and a foreign country might be a troublesome task for many of our high school students, possibly even a few adults applying for a grant or loan. Let's clear up another problem some applicants have run into by doing a short political and geography lesson.

Most of us probably realize the United States of America (USA) is a country. As a whole that country is managed and run by the Federal Government. Each state in the USA has its own government. States are managed and run by a State Government. One of the reasons there are two types of governments, Federal and State, is because of money. And, more importantly who gets to spend that money and for what.

Here's how it works. The Federal Government taxes productive individuals to help pay for federal programs. State Governments also get to tax all individuals, directly or indirectly, so they can pay for their state programs.

For your purposes, it's important to understand which of these two governments is lending you the money. When you apply for a specific program, you should first determine whether or not it is a federal or state program. If it is a federal program, then the geographical restrictions are usually less limiting; nearly all US residents can participate in those programs (there are some federal programs which list out certain geographical stipulations).

To make matters confusing federal programs can also appropriate funds directly for state governments or organizations who then administer that money for the residents of those states. For instance, someone in Indiana might not be eligible for a program in Nebraska. More specifically, someone in Water-town, New York might be eligible for a private foundation grant if they met the criteria of that foundation AND lived in Watertown, New York. You're not going to find much leniency when a program specifies a residency requirement unless you meet it.

Again, that sounds silly. But, talk to those opening the magic envelopes and you would be surprised how many applicants try to fudge on some of these requirements, or aren't even aware of the restrictions. Just because you are an American citizen does not mean you are eligible for a business loan open only to residents of the state of Colorado.

In this same vein, a private foundation grant is not a federal or state government grant. Some private foundations have been included in this book as an alternative to a government grant. In some ways they DO belong in such a publication. Foundations are often set up as a method of avoiding

federal and state income tax. They are recognized by the Internal Revenue Service as a non-profit foundation. Money that would have gone to support other government programs has been legally removed from the political system and is now subject to the whims and policies of its trustees. Rather than have the government decide what money should be given to whom, private foundations have taken on that role. Like little dictators (or big ones such as the Ford Foundation), they decide which cause to support and which to ignore, which artistic endeavor or research program to fund and which artist or researcher to leave to his own devices. Nonetheless, they are not officially part of a federal or state government -- just little island monarchies, some benevolent and others dictatorial, with their own rules and regulations.

CONCLUSION

If the preceding comments have not been strong enough advice and caution against the frivolous abuse of Government Money, let me add the following statement. The Government, from which you are borrowing or being given money, is, for all practical purposes, broke. Broke might be too kind a word. If there were debtor prisons, the guard would have thrown away the key. A large percentage of your tax dollar does not go to using Government Money to fuel our economy but, instead, goes to pay the interest on the federal debt. Not to repay the debt. But, only to pay the INTEREST on the federal debt.

So, there's no free ride. No free lunch. No free Government Money. Every penny given as a government grant or lent out to a business is money that must be used wisely. Otherwise, there will come a day when these wonderful and generous government programs are going to cease.

We've all heard the horror stories of the Great Depression or seen old movies or old newsreels about this era. Many federal programs helped this nation recover from that economic catastrophe. Believe me, we do not want these government programs stopped.

Turning off the money pump, of intelligently appropriated government grants and loans will, indeed, bring about a Great Depression that will make the last one look like a mild downturn. Ask anyone who's received a Small Business Administration loan about how it helped provide him with a higher living standard and the number of employees he was able to provide with jobs. Ask an artist who's career was launched by a government grant.

Or the student who made it through college because of a student loan.

Many government programs that have endured from the last Great Depression are what got America OUT OF that economic catastrophe. Continued abuse of these valuable government programs might someday bring their end. When business transactions cease, our federal and state governments won't be able to raise funds for tax revenues. Any government less able to raise funds, or hampered as our federal and state governments are by the large share of our tax revenues being used to pay for past mistakes, is unlikely to continue appropriating funds for many of the programs described in this book. Governments will not be able to generate the minimum revenue necessary to run the government, let alone dole it out in bushels to those who might really need it and who could also generate jobs and tax revenues with it.

Government Money is granted or lent for a purpose. Before applying for such funding, please clarify for yourself what it is you are going to give back instead of take in for business that benefits the greater number of Americans is what such Government Money was originally intended for. So, please consider the overall value of your particular project before searching about for the right government program(s). After all, if you're a taxpayer, part of it is your money.

2.

WRITING A GRANT PROPOSAL
****

One's attitude is vital in writing a grant proposal. When it comes to asking for money, most individuals seem to have two entirely different reactions on this topic. There are those introverted personalities who, while usually competent in a technical or administrative capacity, treat a request for funding delicately. In fact, such a person is often downright embarrassed to ask for money.

On the other hand, there is what I call the "salesman" personality. This man or woman has no qualms or restraints in talking you into spending your last penny on a hot investment in South African gold mining share options. And, he or she will probably smile the entire way through the sales pitch.

Making a proposal to obtain a grant requires a little of both personalities. You need a pinch of humility with tempered dose of salesmanship. Most grant proposals fail because they do not convey an enthusiasm for one's project. How can you expect to persuade a grant review committee to endow funds for your project or program without its having an intrinsic excitement communicated in its writing?

As a reader how would you feel if I announced at this point that "even if you use this book, there is hardly a chance you'll ever obtain a grant or loan for your endeavor"? Stunned? Startled? You bet. Unless I imbue you with a high level of interest in this subject and leave you with an ardent desire to obtain a government grant or loan, you might not only stop reading this book, you may also forego any future urge to ever again apply for a government grant or loan.

In this same way, a grant writer must convey such an enthusiasm in his proposal that the exhilaration and intensity flies off the pages and persuades each committee member that the funds requested are, indeed, well-invested in this project. How can he or she convince an entire committee reviewing dozens, hundreds or thousands similar requests unless the grant writer is first convinced of the necessity for their program or project? He can't.

At the same time one can not simply write a grant proposal without also including the important technical details, inherent in any viable plan. The greater the number of vital technical details included in the proposal, the more organized they are in the presentation, and the way this information is sequentially released determines how a committee will review your proposal. The details of your proposal should, themselves, be your enthusiastic salesmen, each technical detail shouting the reason why the committee should approve your grant.

And, remember you are making a request. You are asking a group and its individual members for something. I'm sure we've all met those who confuse a request with a DEMAND. Courtesy and respect are important elements in a request. One can be enthusiastic in their request without becoming a boor. Your proposal's tone can exhibit excitement without being overbearing. Don't go too humble on your request or you'll sound like a street panhandler; overdo it and you'll come across like boiler room coin salesman.

So, you have two important elements which create the skeleton of your proposal: the tempered enthusiasm and the technical details. This component permeates your plan -- a little humility tempering an excitement for your project. In scrutinizing your particular grant proposal, one should test it amongst one's friends, family and peers by noting their level of excitement for your project once they finish reading it.

Attitude is the single most important aspect of a grant proposal, but without the "meat" of the proposal you're just left with bare bones and hot air. It's really the last thing we should be discussing in this chapter, but I wanted you in the proper frame of mind before getting into the technical details of a proposal. Once you've finished writing your first proposal and run it past the advice in this section. Is it selling anyone? Are the technical details of your proposal selling the reader? If they're not, find out where exactly it breaks down. It always does fall apart somewhere if it's not persuasive. The next section explains how to prevent that from occurring and how to correct that problem should you find your proposal unconvincing.

WHY YOU NEED A PLAN

One thing I've observed about this society is that it rarely, if ever, tolerates someone without a plan. Someone, flying by the seat of their pants, is an individual who is frowned upon by the rest of society. No matter how successful, his colleagues, friends, family, employees or associates are going to have this thought in the back of their minds or on the tip of their tongue: "He's flying but he's gonna fall."

In an decade of prosperity, most strong-willed, high energy level individuals can generally bully their way to success in an undertaking, if only for a short period of time. When the hard times arrive, these guys fall the hardest. What went wrong? They didn't have a plan.

Now, I'm not expecting you to write a total organization plan for the rest of your life -- it wouldn't hurt, though -- but a grant review committee will demand that you carefully explain the plan for your project or program. They will want you to organize your thoughts into details they can grasp and consider. A grant committee requires you to know how to implement your project. Nearly everyone has an idea of what they'd like to do. But, how many of those are dim thoughts? And, how few of those are carefully implementable programs?

ASSEMBLING YOUR PLAN

Creating a viable, doable plan is a deciding factor. Unless you've bribed a committee member to argue your case, your chances of success diminish with how small the bribe is, IF your plan can not be implemented. Executing your idea can fall apart on the absence of relatively few criteria, all which must be answered in your plan.

Let's take a hypothetical example, but one that is still practical. You plan to do a scientific research project. Are you qualified to oversee the research? If not, have you included those who are qualified to proceed with this research (and then also described your function and credentials for participating in this project)? The same factors would apply to the educator, the artist, or an activist.

In any grant proposal there exist restrictive guidelines that applicants must follow in order to have their project considered by a committee. A preparatory committee, panel, or individual weeds out those that ignore the guidelines, so that only serious proposals are reviewed.

One of your initial steps is to determine whether or not you or your organization meet the eligibility requirements. If there is doubt, request an application from the government agency or the private foundation and read the accompanying booklet describing the program. In this publication advice is given on eligibility requirements, criteria under which the proposal is considered, and other important details. Obtain it before writing your plan as this booklet will save you time should you not qualify for that program.

After reading through the guidelines of the program and really understanding it, you've then got to expand your project idea into a workable plan. This requires sequential thinking. Your goal is to move the idea from your mind into the physical environment.

The best way to do that is to sketch or draw out your project idea on a big piece of paper, from start to finish. For instance, draw a circle at one end of the paper and label that circle "NOW." On the other side of the sheet, sketch out what you would like your project to be doing in its production stage and what it would like. In between, you connect the two ends with a series of sketches moving from your current position on the sheet, through each level of development, to the other end of the paper.

On such a sketch you would answer a number of questions. These would include:

a) How many individuals would you need to hire for this project?

b) Where would the work be done?

c) What equipment would you need?

d) What other vital materials are necessary to achieve the project's goals?

e) How will this project be organized?

Once you have established this idea on paper so that it actually appears that you have the personnel, location, equipment, materials and organization to have the project functioning, you must now figure out two of the biggest problems we all face in life: Time and Money.

How long will it take for this project to be launched? And, how much is it going to cost to launch? Your proposal is deficient if it does not answer these questions. Using the questions (a) through (e) above, you must make two additional charts for yourself: a time chart and an expense chart.

Government and private grants expect to see a project successful and its ultimate goal achieved. Drop the idea of a "bottomless pocketbook" and endless funding for your project. A grant committee requires a time frame for completing the project and a carefully estimated cost projection. Think through your project in terms of stages.

How much money will be needed over a three-month period? During that time period, list out the expenses you will incur: labor, rent, equipment, materials. Call that Stage One. It might be the development or establish phase of your project. Similarly, evolve the balance of your project, in terms of cost and time, using the format of stages. Stage Two will cost this much, take this long; this is what it will pay for and the following objective will be accomplished. In this way YOU will know when the project will have been completed and how much the entire plan will cost to implement.

Once you've assembled this plan and satisfied yourself, run it by an accountant. Hire one for $100 or so in the off season (May through November) and have him review your grant sketch. What have you left out? He'll include costs, such as payroll taxes, legal fees, accountancy fees (of course), real estate taxes, utilities and telephone costs, insurance, and so forth. Your accountant may even show you where you can slash expenses.

Your final step in the assembly of the sketch is to then overestimate the time frame and the expense. It seems that everything can be done faster on paper than in real life. If a project looks like it can be completed over a sixth month period of time, give yourself a grace period of three additional months. Please realize that this advice is not intended to rip-off or deceive the grant committee. I have met far too many individuals who have no realistic grasp of time. Projects take longer to complete in real life than they do in the mental stage. Who wants their funding to run out because of a sudden and unexpected obstacle or upsetting surprise?

Many government agencies and private foundations require that you sign a legally binding contract to complete the project when the funding is approved. Some pay out funding in stages of project development and reports are required showing one's progress. Remember, you may be new to this game; it is very likely they aren't. So, please overestimate to prevent a later disappointment.

WRITING YOUR PLAN

One of the best ways to write something is to write it FOR someone. When writing a magazine article, a journalist is usually, if he's to be successful, writing to a particular audience, the type of reader who would be buying and reading that magazine. The same applies to a grant plan.

A grant writer should know who will be reading his or her plan, if that plan is to seriously considered by a committee. While you can't write for everyone or always know who will be reading your plan, it helps to know how it is scored. Government agencies give you points and generally evaluate you numeri-

cally, from your Social Security Number to your Draft Identification Number, and from how many points are held against you in passing your driver's test to the likelihood of an IRS audit.

If your application meets the basic requirements, there are several factors that you must still observe in order to increase your chances of approval. You are working with or against a yardstick when submitting your grant proposal, just as other, similar applicants are. For your proposal to shine above the rest, it should include the following elements. These are the main points a government agency will expect to see in grant proposals it generally approves.

1)   Your grant proposal must be clearly written and easy to under stand. Write in a style that is sinmple to grasp. Use words that you know and preferably in short sentences. Your verbs should be active, not passive.

2)   Organize your material. Use an outline with the key points high lighted and the details lined up in a logical order. Don't jump from one idea to the next without any bridge between them. If you are talking about apples, stick to apples until you have explained all that is necessary on them before introducing oranges. And, ensure that oranges logically follow apples, instead of pears.

3)   Carefully explain your idea. The committee members are likely to be experts in this field but I doubt they are mind readers. Don't assume they understand something. When in doubt, give a full description of your project -- in simple terms. A successful Broadway producer once said, "If you can't write it down on the back of your business card, I don't want to hear it." Now, it doesn't have to be that simple, but it

could. For instance, if you're trying to sell a "boy meets girl" movie idea, you might want to describe what kind of boy and girl, where, what event interferes with and/or facilitates their relationship, etc. Get the picture? Give a simple idea but illustrate it so that the committee understands what it is you really want to do.

4) Submit a COMPLETE application. Whether you are submitting an unsolicited grant proposal or not, your proposal should include all of the information requested by the government agency or private foundation. You may be asked to include specified materials, letters of agreements from researchers or others who will be assisting you, budgets, personnel profiles (or details), and so forth. Forms may have to be signed. It isimperative that you read an nderstand the guidelines and follow them to the letter before submitting your proposal. A grant application might be refused because all of the necessary signatures were not included. Yes, it could be something as simple as that. Follow the instructions and minimize your possibility of rejection.

5) Fulfill the need of the government agency. Each government agency grants funds on the basis of how a proposal helps them achieve their objectives. If unemployment has practically wiped out an entire community, your grant proposal for providing job training to those community members might receive a higher rating than one offers another project. Again, it depends on the government agency receiving your proposal. Read the program guidelines carefully. Telephone the agency and discuss your project idea with him or her before submitting your proposal.

6) Submit a cohesive and realistic proposal. A number of energized individuals always try to shoot for the moon in their ambitions. Great idea! But, one's proposal should not be offering a cure for cancer unless it systematically explains how a team of Nobel Prize winners will be jointly working on this cure. The proposal should fit in with the generally accepted practices of your field, unless they are innovative and you can prove, statistically, how your proposal would develop new territory within that field. Rarely does this occur. Cohesion is important in that one does not make a wild promise in one part of their proposal and offer a ludicrous solution at the end of it. In the same light, explain how you've carefully chosen your team and provide their credentials. The last thing any grant committee wants to see is an "only one" type of person winging it and demanding all the funds for himself. Your proposal's elements should fit it.

7) Include endorsements and testimonials in your proposal. In the businesss world these are known as references. Just as the personnel director wants to better understand your character and capacity to work, so does the grant committee wish to have it proven to them that you are capable of carrying out this project. Again, I'm sure each grant committee has seen its share of wild ideas. Someone with a great idea that just doesn't have the resources to deliver on it. If your idea holds water, then get a few credible authori-

ties to endorse you -- in a written letter on their letterhead -- and include those references with your proposal.

8)   Include a timetable to demonstrate how you plan to complete this project. If you are an educator and plan on providing specialized training to a particular community group, then your proposal should show when certain stages of that project will be completed and how much each stage will cost to complete. Any business owner knows the values of controls and checks (not the ones you cash). Explain in your proposal what safeguards you are providing, how the operation will be controlled, whether there will be an overseeing committee and what reports are to be filed with them and when. When and how much are important questions. If you are to receive funds, you must demonstrate the capacity for completing the project and indicate how that "investment" will be protected.

9)   Ensure that your proposal shows cost--effectiveness. How many times have you heard is this cost-effective? That simply means: Is it costing too much? Or it can mean: Can we do better elsewhere? If, for example, an inner city area is receiving a high share of welfare checks that is costing the government and taxpayers a certain figure, is your proposal going to create jobs in that area to remove those individuals from the welfare rolls? The same applies to the arts and research. For instance, does it really take $75,000 to produce that exhibition or can a clever cost-cutter bring it in for only $45,000? Face it, the government is in a serious monetary crisis. Cost-cutting is the byword for the rest of this century.

Show it in your grant proposal by producing a reasonable budget.

10)   Show leadership in your proposal. Government and private funders want to see competence. You must have achieved a certain level of credibility in each of the previous nine points, but you must also persuade them that you are capable and competent for this project. Once you've isolate the problem and proposed a solution, you must answer this question: Is this person the one who can carry out this plan? Your proposal must convey this ability to act. Leaders are decisive and can execute a series of steps to reach a final objective. Your plan must show this and by demonstrating that you can develop a proposal that sells others, you are, in fact, selling yourself. The above are the elements which must exist in your proposal. Depending on the approval practices and the scoring system of the grant committee, the more of the preceding points that you include in your proposal will determine your chances of being approved.

THE COMPLETE PROPOSAL

Packaging your grant proposal is similar to writing a college thesis or creating a business plan. Obtaining the requested finances is your passing grade with a government agency, a private foundation or an investor syndicate. There are several recommended approaches. I have composed a simple but effective packaging format. It will include many, but not all (depending on your proposal), of the following ingredients. I've listed them in the order you should present each item. When you've written your grant proposal, use each item below as a checklist to ensure you have accurately and closely followed this format.

1. Write a cover letter that introduces yourself and your organization on your letterhead with an address and contact telephone number. Summarize your grant request and provide these details: (a) the nature of your proposal, (b) the reason why you are making this proposal, (c) what objectives you expect to accomplish if your project is implemented, (d) a one sentence description of your project, (e) an explanation of who you or your organization is and what your experience is in this field, and (f) an offer to provide further information instantly, if required. Your cover letter should be one to two pages long. Edit as necessary to keep it short and concise.

2. Create a title page as you would any serious proposal. This is a simple one-page introduction to your proposal and provides a professional touch to any presentation. Include (a) the title of your proposal, (b) your name and address (or the organization's name and address), (c) the date you are submitting this proposal, and (d) the name of the government agency or foundation to whom you are submitting this proposal.

3. Create a table of contents outlining each of the section that follow it. Paginate each sheet in your proposal so that it corresponds with the page numbers shown in your table of contents. While a book may have chapters and sections within it, your proposal should show "headings" and "sub-headings." These can be numbered with a Roman number or Arabic number. Use the common outline format in your table of contents and have it correspond with each heading and section in your proposal.

4. If your proposal is lengthy, summarize it and include the key features of your proposal. Some government agencies may have you use their application form as the summary page and ask you to summarize the proposal in a space provided. Follow those instructions, but you may first want to summarize it on a separate sheet of paper and then revise the summary, as necessary, before including it on the application form. A summary can usually be written in 300 to 500 words.

5. Write an introduction. As with most books, this is usually the last part you'll write. However, it should included in this position of the sequence. An introduction is an expansion of your cover letter and should also restate those previously mentioned elements in a more developed format. Also, explain who and how many persons will specifically benefit by your project, where the project will be implemented, and carefully detail WHY your project is important right now. Make your introduction informative and timely. This is also the time to show how your or your organization is capable of performing the actions necessary to launch or complete this project.

6. State your project's goals and purposes and what will be accomplished. Write down exactly what your purpose is. Do not give a vague and generalized purpose or goal. For a training program, stating "to set up a training program" does not sell a grant committee on your project as effectively as "to

teach local residents vocational skills so they can get jobs." After you've stated your purpose, list out your objectives and number them. They should be written with specific achievements in mind, not broad, general statements. For instance, if you were going to climb a hill, you would state that (a) you were going to find a certain hill to climb and name that hill, (b) climb it on a specific date, (c) identify who would climb it with you, (d) identify that you will climb that hill to plant a tree, and (e) plant that tree on the top of that hill on a certain date so that the hill would attract tourists.

7.   Write an explanation of what problem is being solved. Obviously, there must be a problem that requires you to request funding. What is this problem? State it clearly. Include what you and other professionals believe caused this problem and how your project will help solve that problem. Provide statistics showing that this problem does, indeed, exist. Your local librarian can help point you to government publications or reference works that can assist you in locating and including this documentation in your proposal. Pad this section of your proposal with all the vital facts and figures that prove that such a problem exists. If you can't find them and have looked hard, you may need to question whether there really is a problem or not. Include letters describing this problem which you should obtain from local community leaders, professionals, politicians (where possible), and others who agree there is a problem and a definite need to solve it. Often, the local newspaper will have written articles about the problem. You can photocopy them at your local library and include clippings in this section. The stronger you demonstrate a NEED for a solution, by fully explaining that a problem exists, the greater your chances are of being considered for a grant. Many rejections don't develop the problem needed to be solved well enough.

8.   Fully describe what your program is and what its activities are or will be. An existing program, or experience in a previous similar project, increase one's chances of approval. Why? This section, with background information upon which to draw, will strengthen the practicality and workability of the grant proposal. If you have embarked upon a project and are short of funding or if you have an idea that has not yet been implemented, you are at a disadvantage to the existing organization. If I were an artist, who had yet to paint, and requested funding, I would be at a serious disadvantage compared to the accomplished, but financially struggling, artist. This is the "show-me" section of your proposal. The less your track record or experience in this area, the more carefully thought out your program activities section should be. A short-cut, if you do not have an existing program running, is to find a similar program and thoroughly investigate it. I do not mean copy it, but that comes pretty close. Find out how that organization runs and what it does. Before deciding how you'd do something differently, discover if they have already tried that and had it go flat. This is your game plan. Describe it fully if you have one. If not, find someone who does and follow it closely.

9.   Write a several page section showing who will be participating in this project. Who are they? What are their credentials? What will they be doing in this project? Is there a Board of Directors? An advisory board? What are their qualifications? Describe the management of the project and who will be hired and why and what their responsibilities will be. Include resumes or curriculum vitae in this section. You must show that you are organized fully to execute your plan.

10.   Write out a timetable as described earlier in this chapter. There are many ways of doing this. The linear one works best. Some things take longer than others so you will have to describe each activity of the project in a series of stages. Stage 1, Stage 2, etc. List out when each stage will be completed and how long it will take, from start to finish.

11.   Write out an evaluation plan. Government agencies often require that you collect and analyze data to justify the expense. You may be contractually liable for this function. This section is mandatory if there will be ongoing funding for a particular project or if later funding is required and to appropriated. A government agency may approve part of the funding and demand that evaluation reports are submitted to continue funding. You must plan out who will collect data, how it will be evaluated and make provisions to submit evaluation reports on a timely basis to the government agency or the private funder.

12.   Write out your budget and have it rigorously studied and evaluated by an accountant. Unless you are a qualified professional, hire one. You may even wish to work directly with an accountant to prepare your budget and ensure that it corresponds with your program activities section and earlier sections. Budgets are a touchy subject in Washington, DC, in state capitols around the country, and with private foundations. They WILL go over it with a magnifying glass. After all, you are asking for funding and your budget should demonstrate that you are a competent professional when it comes to money. That's all there is to it. Find the correct government agency or private foundation. Determine whether or not you can still apply for a grant with them. Obtain the recent guide lines and application form(s), write a grant proposal that follows the above procedure, and you have dramatically increased your chances of obtaining a government or private foundation grant.

CONCLUSION

There are a few more details, many of which can be obtained by reading the suggested materials at the end of this book. For instance, there are different categories of grant proposals. Some propose community services, others research and study or solve problems, many provide training and educational programs, and others ask for technical assistance. Arts and education grant programs are intensively covered in the balance of this book. Why not start looking for a government or private foundation grant right now?

3.

HOW TO WRITE A BUSINESS LOAN PROPOSAL
****

When asking to borrow money, every lender wants you to convince him how safe his loan to you really is. Few lenders are likely to stake money blindly into your venture or enterprise. Nearly all will expect to see a business plan that inspires them to invest and assures them their loan (and interest) will be repaid.

Have lunch, someday, with a few investment bankers and you'll soon find out that even the best business plans are riddled with gaps big enough to fly a Boeing 747 through. The horror stories you will hear from them lead you to believe that anyone trying to borrow money is an inveterate liar. Nonetheless, they expect to see a business plan. Most will review one with the attitude of "what's wrong with this one."

There are a few questions that astute investors and government agencies will ask about your business plan. You must provide this quantitative and qualitative data in your plan if you ever expect to see money.

Again, as with writing a grant a professional attitude must be evident throughout your business plan. As before use short sentences. A succinct and persuasive writing style must sell the government agency, venture capital group or investment banker on your idea. Your presentation must demonstrate that you are well-organized, have provided controls and safeguards for the unexpected in your business venture, and that your expectations are realistic.

While it is the presentation that relaxes the loan review committee, your plan must provide "hard details" if it is to succeed at all. Hot air and hyperbole can charm a few people some of the time, but only for a short time. Come up short on fully developing your idea or offer up inaccurate or unrealistic numbers in your budgeting and you will always wonder why none invest in your undertaking.

In repeated interviews with investors who raise money for businesses, I've isolated these three questions that must be answered in every aspect of your business plan.

1.   Will this idea fly at all and is this individual capable of transforming his idea into a profitable enterprise?

2.   How much it will it take for this entrepreneur's dream to become a profitable business and how long will it take to become profitable?

3.   Why hasn't someone else made this idea successful yet?

Of course, in the bank of every investor's mind is also this question: "What is this person hiding from me?" And also this one: "Will this enterprise fail and, if so, how will it fail?"

Government and private money is tight in the 1990's. Debt-laden consumers aren't carefree spenders since credit was tightened in early 1990. If consumers do not purchase goods and services, even the business selling only to another business eventually loses sales or profit margins. Business plans have to be more strongly written, offer stellar accounting, and include an unbeatable game plan to overcome investor and government agency obstacles and obtain the necessary funding.

Most successful business loan or venture capital applicants are past the early start-up stage. Many of their kinks have been worked out. Unless you've started a business, you might only have a small clue as to what I'm talking about. Generally, a successful business takes off because it fills a specific demand for its product or service. To launch one usually requires superb marketing skills, spectacular public relations or an astute advertising strategy. The most successful businesses incorporate all of the above. But, the greater number of businesses launched either spend too much selling their product or don't invest any funds in marketing. As the business expands, competition arrives, as it inevitably does, and reduces profit margins. By then, a company is overstaffed and making less money. It fails or stumbles. Most go out of business; the minority struggle along, reorganize and survive in a reduced state OR sell out to another with deeper pockets.

Investors, bankers and government agency loan committees know the above sequence cold. And, they expect you to guard against it as much as possible in your business plan. There's a reason for this.

THE BANKER MENTALITY

Hardly any banker, venture capitalist or government agency lends money these days without owing homage to the lending techniques based on the principles developed by the Rothschild family over the past three centuries. Since this family evolved into a European banking power, they have dominated or influenced, to a greater or lesser degree, the world-wide financial markets.

By understanding these principles someone seeking a business loan can better comprehend what is required of him or her in making a business loan application, whether one seeks funding from a government agency, a venture capital group, a public-private partnership corporation, or a bank. Because a large number of business loans are essentially bank loans guaranteed by the Small Business Administration or another government agency, one must first sell a bank's loan officer on your plan.

Banks hate rapid growth. A banker's first reaction to a business taking off to the stars is that the owners or management are, in some way, committing fraud. Too many companies have flown off to the stars in a hurry and never come back. Look where the Trump mentality of fast money landed the Donald. So, in any presentation demonstrate STEADY growth as opposed to big money fast.

A connection to credibility soothes a banker's nerves. If you can show that your business will be supplying AT&T or IBM or another similar household name, and can prove it, then lending officers will look at your business plan more favorably. This doesn't mean that's all you have to do, but this connection gives you a ring of authenticity. Please realize that most business plans are lucky to even mention who might be buying their product. So, doing this moves you to the head of the class.

Bankers also love money. You'll find out immediately just how much. It's mandatory that you hold your checking account at their bank. But, you can offer incentives by mentioning that your company will also keep its pension account at this branch, you will hold customer deposits at their bank, recommend their bank to your customers, and so forth. Bankers won't admit it but they love opening new accounts. It gives them greater leverage to lend out more money, builds asset base, etc.

Nonetheless, the key component when presenting a business plan and accompanying financial statements is RELIABILITY. The lender will ask "How reliable is this information?" You may not know this but bankers and other lenders compare your financials against industry reviews. Source-books and guides are at a lender's disposal to compare the consistency of your data against what is prevalent in your line of work. A quick flip through one of those will immediately determine whether or not you have "fudged" your figures, made an unrealistic projection, duplicated an existing market niche without covering any new territory, and so forth. There are a dozen ways your information can be disputed.

Fraudulent application is prevalent. Whole bodies of law have been written to protect investors against deceptive investment practices. Unless you are extremely clever and have a wealth of experience in the investment field, it is unlikely you will present any scheme or racket that has not been tried. For those of us who are more honest, preparing a loan proposal and plan requires rolling up our sleeves and doing some very hard and tedious work.

THE THREE CRITERIA

Rarely, if ever, will a business plan be approved without a financial statement. A lender often uses these three criteria in evaluating a loan request: liquidity, profitability, and capital. The latter is probably the most important. From the SBA to the venture capital group, a lender must see your own financial commitment to the project or business. Your commitment is often between 25 percent and 50 percent of the loan request. Capital with a capital "C" is what makes lenders say yes. Why would they want to sink their funds into it if you aren't putting a dime of your own in?

Or by finding additional financing elsewhere (like Aunt Jenny)?

So, most importantly, be prepared to bring additional funds to your project beyond what you might expect the government agency or venture capital group to provide you. Besides, you may request $125,000 but only receive $75,000. You might find an entire section of your request blue-lined and scratched. Lenders will expect that you are prepared for a rejection and that you will have made provisions for such a funding request cut.

Liquidity is also important. Basically, business liquidity gives the lender a snapshot of how likely you are to survive and whether or not your business is solvent. Most businesses expect to pay their bills by selling their inventory. An acid test ratio of determining business liquidity is done by computing how much cash it has on hand plus its current receivables and dividing that figure by its current liabilities. For example, let's say a business has $25,000 cash on hand, an additional $95,000 in receivables, and $120,000 in current liabilities. It's liquidity ratio is 1.0.

Lenders are usually pleased with such a ratio because most companies need to factor in their existing inventory to reach and exceed that 1.0 figure. Try it out on your business. Do your cash and receivables exceed your current liabilities? If they do, you are in great shape. And, you would probably be an excellent candidate for a business loan.

Another determining factor in your financials, that shows business liquidity, is "net sales to receivables." This shows the turnover of receivables. The higher this ratio just shows the number of times a year the receivables turn over and also demonstrates how successful or not a business is. The longer it takes to convert inventory into cash shows how much struggling the business is undergoing. Uncollected receivables can spell doom for a business. Either the collection department is non-functional or the company is producing a shoddy product.

Liquidity can also be determined by the "cost of goods sold to inventory." This will also show how many days it takes to sell goods. At fault here can be a company's marketing program, its corporate buyers, its production department, etc. The less turnover occurring within the business means the less demand consumers have for these goods.

A lender takes a hard look at liquidity because it shows high or low turnover. Turnover demonstrates demand for a product or service. A low turnover spells bad management, bad marketing, bad product or service, or that something is seriously wrong with the business. That raises a red flag and can prevent a loan request from being approved.

But, a company can create a high turnover just by haphazardly selling off assets and inventory in order to increase their liquidity. It's done in corporate America every week. One of the first measures Leveraged Buy Out sharks used was an asset sell-off to increase liquidity. Their principle was that the sum of the company's parts were more valuable that its whole. Undervalued companies were broken up and sold piecemeal to raise the company's liquidity level. But, what happened to the profits? And the jobs of companies that were closed down? Exactly!

Lenders will expect to see profitability. The strongest statement of profits are a high percentage of net profits after taxes compared to tangible net worth. Tangible net worth does not include goodwill, such as the name of the company, its trademarks, patents or copyrights. Net sales and fixed assets, less total debt, mainly determine net worth. The higher the company's net profits after taxes compared to the company's tangible net worth, the more agreeable the lender is providing financing.

THE IMPORTANCE OF A FINANCIAL STATEMENT

No company is likely to obtain financing without a legitimately prepared financial statement. One accountant I interviewed for a magazine article on corporate loan raising activities stated to me: "If I don't see audited financials, I advise my clients to forget about investing in that company." Why audited financials? Businessmen have been known to lie, that's why. An independent accountant actually inspecting the inventory, reviewing the books of the company and comparing what he sees and what window dressing he is show can make an intelligent endorsement of that business or not.

The time and costs involved in producing an audited financial statement can be expensive. An accountant may spend dozens of hours preparing an honest appraisal of the business, at a cost of $100 or more per hour. On a large company it may take him several weeks to follow generally accepted accounting practices and produce audited financials. However, if you are seriously committed to obtaining a large government or venture capital loan, it is likely that you will have to produce, or will be demanded that you produce, audited financials.

CONTENTS OF YOUR BUSINESS PLAN

As discussed in the preceding pages the financial statement is going to provide your lending agency with the strongest grasp of your business. Does that mean that an insolvent business will never attract financing? Not likely. In fact, the SBA loan program is required by law to only make or guarantee loans to those businesses that cannot obtain financing elsewhere. However, you must still write a business plan.

Business plan length can range from a few pages (under ten) or more than 100, depending on the loan request and the lender involved in the request. There is a good deal of similarity between a business grant proposal and a business loan proposal. The contents are about the same as a grant proposal (Chapter 2).

1. Cover letter. On your letterhead summarize your loan request with the key facts. Limit this to one or two pages.

2. Title Page. Create a title page on your letterhead or one that includes your company's name, address, telephone number, and president. Date this document.

3. Table of Contents. Create an outline of your business plan and use the Roman numeral format. The headings and sub-headings should refer to page numbers within the business plan and the table of contents should correctly correspond with those page numbers.

4. Summary. Concisely summarize your business plan so that you convey your company's current scene, business and marketing strategy, financial outlook and projections, and exactly what improvements new financing will bring to your company. Each of the above can be written in phases or stages. First, you describe who you are and what you produce (in detail), how you are generating new business, and a brief and honest financial snapshot of your business. That's Stage One. Then, you describe the next stage and what financing is needed to get you there. What will happen in Stage Two? De-

scribe that scene. And so on until you've demonstrated how the investors or government agency will get its investment and interest back.

5. Describe your company. Who are you? What do you do? How do you make your money? If you were at a cocktail party and were asked what your business was about, what would you say? That's what you would say here. Start with a brief description and then develop it from there. How long has it been around? What did it use to do as compared to now? What is the business objective? Market share? Competition? Do you generate most of your business through telephone sales or independently commissioned representatives? What are the credentials of the key managers? Include their resumes. This may be a ten page description or a two-pager, depending on the size of your company. Be complete and thorough in communicating what this business is. Make sure you know what it is first -- many people really can't name specifically what business they are in or to whom they are selling their product or service. I'm not kidding about this.

6. Write a detailed analysis of your segment of the market. Everyone is classified in a specific market whether they like it or not. Including this market analysis in your business plan is vital and shows the lender you know who your competition is and how your market segment is performing in relation to the rest of the economy. Statistics exist on your market segment. Got a question and need the data? Telephone the Commerce Department in Washington, D.C. and ask them for their specialist in your market. They

may have one or more experts who will mail or fax you current market data. Keep him on the phone and he'll give you estimates and other valuable data about your type of business that you probably never knew. All this helps you write a two-page or up to a fifty-page report on your market. Finding out about your local competition is also just as easy. Pull up a Dun and Bradstreet Report on them and see how well they're doing. Sorry, you probably won't be able to include that data in your business plan. However, you will be able to write intelligently about your competition.

7.   Write up a brief report on your product or service. Describe this product from an objective point of view. Give statistics, measurements, figures and facts. Don't load this section up with hyperbole. Explain pricing and how it compares with the rest of the market. Include safety requirements, production specifications, in what volume it's produced or delivered, and so on. Please also include expected product or service advancements or refinements (it can always be "new and improved").

8.   Describe your marketing plan. In today's "noisy" world, it's compulsory to have some sort of advertising or publicity campaign, just to be heard above the rest of the crowd. I've seen some incredible products never make it to the marketplace because its owner didn't have a clue as to how to market the product -- some even thought it a bad idea to advertise or publicize the product! Consult with a marketing specialist to help you develop a professional marketing plan. The marketing might include anything from radio and television talk show appearances to a strong direct mail campaign and everything in between.

9.   Describe your sales plan. Salesmen are a necessary evil. You need them to transport your product from the warehouse or showroom into a consumer's home. Explain in detail how you will be selling your product and how financing can be used to increase sales. This is the bottom line: Will your product move off the shelves and do so for a profit? Will you be using independent representatives or build your own sales team?

10.   Provide at least two to three years worth of financials, including a profit-and-loss statement and balance sheet. A three-year cash flow projection, based on the financing you require, helps strengthen your argument for a loan. Follow the advice found at the beginning of this chapter regarding a financial statement.

PRESENTATION OF THE BUSINESS PLAN

It doesn't hurt to spend a few dollars on a better quality paper on which to produce the business plan or to have it laser-printed, instead of typed. Having it professionally bound is also a plus. Use this rule of thumb in the presentation: the more professional the lender, the greater care you should pay to detail. A government agency may not be greatly impressed by a professional-looking business plan, but a large venture capital organization might.

Presenting your business plan in person or through a connection also helps bring you to the attention of the lender. In the book HOW TO WRITE A WINNING BUSINESS PLAN by Joseph R. Mancuso (Prentice-Hall, New

Jersey), one suggestion is made that does work and has been recommended elsewhere and throughout the industry. Mr. Mancuso suggests you locate an entrepreneur in your field who lives locally and who has just received funding by a venture capital group specializing in your type of product or service. By contacting that entrepreneur and showing him your business plan, you attempt to enlist his assistance in fine-tuning the proposal. Eventually, you become friends and persuade him, directly or indirectly, to having him show it to the venture capital group on your behalf. It is one roundabout way and does get you an in with that venture capital group. However, nothing replaces persistence and a long list of prospective lenders.

Another useful tip, suggested by John E. Lux, head of a small business venture capital group based in Florida, is to use "show and tell" in your presentation. Just as we brought our hobbies to class in third grade to show off, you should do the same at a presentation. Show your product in use. Let it sell itself. At one banker presentation, Lux had a lending office try to hammer a nail through his client's saw blade to prove a point. The saw blade dominated the nail and the bank financed that company.

YOUR CREDENTIALS

The main focus of any business plan is your willingness and capability to make the venture work. Anyone lending your business money, unless it is a very large one and incorporated and with an active board of directors, is basically lending YOU the money. They know that and will aim the spotlight on you.

It is important to put your best foot forward and argue the merits of your case, either by listing out your achievements or past experience in a venture or past performance in a similar business. You have got to persuade one or more individuals that you've got what it takes. This takes a little self-analysis. Before writing out this section of your business plan, inspect your past performance carefully. Discover what key components of a previous management team worked best with your personality. Are these same components evident in your current business plan?

Have you ever had experience in this line of work? What were the results? Show every scrap of valuable and logical piece of information that pertains to making you look like the candidate for the funding.

Inevitably, a credit report will be pulled on you. How is your credit rating? Have you ever declared bankruptcy? Don't hide it from the venture capital group or government agency if you are asked or if it is mandatory you answer on the application form. It may disqualify you but, on the other hand, it might not-- after all, more than 3 million individuals have declared bankruptcy since 1989 and many more are on the way to it. About 100,000 businesses failed in 1992 and approximately 80,000 in nearly every year before then.

When he looks at you, a lender will want to see consistency, character, competence and previous business or managerial experience. If your business has been operational for more than two years, the lender will want to see financial competence and a past ability to repay debts. Tell the truth when you create your business plan. It's less painful than a lie, even if it temporarily jeopardizes your funding.

RED FLAG CHECKLIST

John E. Lux of Lux Investor Services Corporation (Clearwater, Florida) specializes in raising capital for entrepreneurs by creating private placement offers for them. This is one form of venture capital funding which you might consider. Here are the criteria he and many others in the venture capital field use to eliminate candidates for business funding. Call John Lux at (813) 535-4655 if you pass all the points on the checklist and his firm might help finance your small business. Keep in mind, passing the test on all of them does not guarantee you funding. Having a strong product or service, a well-organized marketing plan and a proven management team is usually the acid test.

These are the red flags that will often stop you from obtaining funding not only with Mr. Lux with many venture capital groups and banks.

1. Too much of the loan is expected to pay off the company's debt.

2. Too little of the loan money is earmarked for increasing productivity.

3. Management salaries are unusually high.

4. The company is trying something they haven't done before.

5. The company is subject to price competition which will impact profit margins.

6. Track record of the company's management is questionable.

7. Raw material changes are subject to wild price fluctuations and the company can't hedge against them.

8. The company has an unresolved union problem.

9. The company is subject to government regulation that could ruin them.

10. The company has environmental liabilities.

11. The company has large lawsuits pending.

12. The company has had a recent change in accountants, management or directors.

13. The company's inventories have risen sharply.

14. Expenses (such as advertising costs) are being capitalized on the balance sheet instead of being taken from current income.

15. Company management remains idle in a losing situation when it should be taking corrective action.

If your company fits any of the above profiles, then please correct the problem before submitting a business plan. It's not definite that you will be rejected, but it is quite possible that you will. Always try to rectify the situation before proceeding. If you stop minding the store and try to solve the problem by obtaining funding, you may still not make the problem go away. More than likely, you'll waste your valuable managerial time by going off to chase down lenders. Sort of like chasing butterflies -- what do you do when you finally net one?

CONCLUSION

So, as they say in the Olympics, let the games begin. Now, go through the directory section and find the business or real estate program that best fits your needs. There's most assuredly one in there. Make your contacts, don't give up and win yourself a gold medal and a pot of gold.

4.

YOU CAN DO IT!
****

Your chances of obtaining a government grant or loan are better than you think. For instance, your chances of placing a winning bet in a horse race are usually around less than one in ten. The likelihood you'll come up with an ordinary full house in a hand of poker are one in 693. And, to pick the lucky number in roulette is about one in 38. Odds are 1 in 35 you would get a two or twelve on a single throw of the dice. How do government grants and loans compare?

Over a recent seven-year period, more than 15 percent of those businesses who applied for business research grants were approved. More than half of the loan applications for Small Business Administration (SBA) loan guarantees are approved each year; over the past five years over 58 percent of such applications received a loan. That adds up to over 105,000 SBA loan guarantee approvals between 1987 and 1992. And over 3,600 direct loans were approved by the Small Business Administration during that same period, approximately one in every five applications. SBA loans to small businesses have exceeded $3 billion each year for the past half decade.

Roughly 10 percent of the applications for a government grant obtain funding. Over a recent seven year period, more than 15 percent of those businesses who applied for business research grants were approved. More than 11 percent of grants to writers, magazines and publishers are approved. Over 30 percent of grants to television, film and radio producers

are approved. If you look at the numbers, the federal government is very generous, indeed.

Businesses have over $100 billion in grants, loans, and loan opportunities annually available to them. Add to this almost another $100 billion that states have aggregately appropriated to business investment in the form of grants and loans. And, this $200 billion investment in American businesses does not include the additional $360 billion in state and federal contract awards to businesses. More than ONE-HALF TRILLION DOLLARS is available to businesses on an average annual basis! More than 20 million government grants, loans, and contracts have been disbursed to businesses.

So, don't think that Uncle Sam and your state are holding back money from you. The numbers speak for themselves. That money is available. Here's what the Budget for Fiscal year 1993 says in Part One-22:

"Encouraging Entrepreneurship. The Budget includes proposals for tax incentives to increase investment in capital assets, R & D, and Enterprise Zones. These should be understood not merely as short-term economic stimuli. They are also part of a longer-term effort to reinvigorate American risk-taking, pioneering, and the entrepreneurial spirit.

That effort is to use government funding and incentives to build American business. Rather than wondering where and how you will raise capital for your much-needed expansion or start-up project, take advantage of the many resources found in this guide.

WASTED MONEY

The entire government grant and loan awards process has, in the past, gotten a bad rap from the media. It wasn't hard because not only were taxpayer dollars wasted but the projects funded just didn't make sense. Here's a few of examples of grants awarded by the National Science Foundation and other government agencies.

a. A government funded study on the effects of "scantily clad women" upon Chicago male drivers.

b. A $102,000 grant to determine whether goldfish would be more aggressive if they drank gin versus tequila.

c. A federal grant to the National Institute of Mental Health to study "social relationships" in a Peruvian brothel.

d. A grant made by the Department of Labor for $384,948 to find out the number of dogs, cats, and horses residing in Ventura County, California.

e. One government agency spent $27,000 to find out why convicts would want to escape from jail.

f. An experimental psychologist was given three grants totalling $500,000 to study why rats and monkeys clench their teeth.

g. One "sociologist" was granted $84,000 to study why people fall in love.

If these were all the silly and inane projects funded by government grants, it would probably be fine; even Congress is entitled to a few blunders every now and then. But, this ludicrous waste amounts to less than a microscopic tip of the proverbial iceberg. Ask not why we have a deficit, but ask instead why Congress and government agencies have been bullied by quacks and miscreants to fund such obvious waste of taxpayer dollars. Unfortunately, that's the way the system is set up.

But, there is hope. The greater the demand that pours in from the American public for worthy funding projects, in business, in the arts and in education, more funding will be appropriated for these projects. In the past government funded biological, chemical and psychological research programs have produced a drain on federal and state budgets. Writing letters to your Congressman, U.S. Senator and state legislators can and do produce funding cuts. However, overall, your response to existing programs increases that those programs be expanded. If only 10,000 applicants file for a particular business or art grant, and there is only a certain amount of funding available, then the normal percentages will get approved and that funding will stay about the same. IF 100,000 applicants try to obtain that same grant or loan, then the government agency WILL ask for additional funding. Wasted programs will be slashed and a larger sum will go to that program. So, show where your interest lies and apply for these important programs.

Let's make a concerted push to eliminate pointless human and animal experimentation by social "scientists" that are, in fact, front groups for drug and perfume manufacturers or other vested interest groups. Your taxpayer dollars are wasted on these destructive studies Take for example, one Clockwork Orange experiment I read about recently where teenage males were forced to watch pornographic movies while receiving electric shocks to their genitals. Is this why you pay taxes? Well, that's one of the "studies" funded by our government.

Congress and government agencies are responsive to the American public but they have to hear that "voice." Capitalizing on the existing funds appropriated for business, the arts, education, and productive research and aggressively applying for such funding translates into additional future dollars appropriated for these programs. And, of course, cuts in the preceding destructive programs. It's your money. You tell Congress and the government agencies how you want it spent. Filing an application, in this respect, is a more powerful action than casting a vote.

CHANGES IN GOVERNMENT GRANT AND LOAN PROGRAMS

Each year, government grant and loan programs are subject to additions, changes and deletions. The Fiscal Year 1993 budget proposed these changes and demonstrates the direction federal government is headed.

1. In the Veterans Affairs (VA) mortgage guaranty program, acquisition of foreclosures is expected to drop from 85 percent to 70 percent. However, the VA also proposes to increase the loan origination fee by 0.75 percent to 2.00 percent for a no downpayment loan and to require 2.50 percent fee and a 10 percent downpayment for second and subsequent uses of the VA program.

2. The Guaranteed Student Loan (GSL) program would be further strengthened. Federal cost would be reduced by lowering origination and servicing payments to lenders with high default rates. Students who borrow or receive other Federal student aid, such as Pell grants, would be subject to minimum performance standards so as to ensure that Federal student aid recipients are making satisfactory progress toward degree completion or certification.

3. Farm lending would be targeted to meet the needs of new and beginning farmers and those who are disadvantaged. Borrower eligibility would be limited to 7 years for direct loans and 10 years for loan guarantees. Expect a gradual shift away from direct loans as the decade progresses.

4. The Small Business Administration will continue its shift away from direct loans as well. Right now, the federal government is subsidizing bad loans -- about 19 percent of SBA loans default. The SBA will try to shift risk-sharing to banks, increasing the amount of risk financial institutions will bear from 15 percent to 25 percent. At the end of 1991, the SBA recorded over 91,000 loans outstanding, with a total exposure of $11.5 billion. At its current default rate, the SBA expects over $2 billion in bad loans.

In each of the above four categories you can observe how the federal government is inspecting problems it has experienced with wasted taxpayer funds. Efforts are being made to minimize future risk and tighten regulations. More stringent measures can be expected should the deficit crisis continue to deepen throughout the rest of the 1990's. Loans and grants won't be completely eliminated, they'll just be even harder to come by. Applicants will be demanded to be more exact and persuasive in their applications and proposals. Please use the materials in Chapters 2 and 3 when developing your grant or loan plan and proposal. Rejection is a painful experience, but it can be overcome with a professional attitude that shines through your proposals. The most competent, not necessarily the most connected, are generally approved.

EXAMPLES OF INDIVIDUALS AND COMPANIES THAT HAVE OBTAINED GOVERNMENT AND PRIVATE FUNDING

Norman C. Fawley received two federal grants (totalling $100,000) for an invention that strengthened natural gas cylinders and pipelines.

Chris Nguyen started his business of handmade eggrolls by raising $20,000 from private investors and a $40,000 Small Business Administration loan. His Lo-Ann Company commanded a 20 percent market share and his 1989 sales revenue reached $9 million before he sold his business to a larger company.

Charles Simic, winner of the 1990 Pulitzer Prize for Poetry, was previously awarded Creative Writing Fellowship grants, worth more than $10,000, from the National Endowment for the Arts.

Dennis Washington wanted to open a locomotive repair shop in Montana. He obtained a $10 million bank loan in cooperation with Montana's Coal Tax loan program.

Karakian Bedrosian got a government grant of $97,300 for inventing a technology that allows tomatoes to be shipped long distances without refrigeration.

Kalona Plastics applied to Iowa's Community Economic Betterment Association for plant expansion. The loan was approved on the basis that one person be hired for each $2,000 of the loan amount. Forty-six new jobs were created in the community.

The psGroup, a Michigan firm, received three research grants totaling $195,000 in exchange for three percent of the company's common stock.

Maurice W. Lee, Jr. got $75,000 to develop a quick-cooked hamburger that cooks in less than 30 seconds with no smoke, no chef, and no pre-heating of the grill and is faster than microwave.

Corporate Coachworks, of Springfield, Missouri, received a $1 million loan at 5.2% interest through Missouri's linked-deposit program. This program encouraged banks to reduce interest rates they charge to state businesses. In return the state of Missouri collateralized the loans with low-paying certificate of deposits.

Dorothy and Richard Watts, of Largo, Florida, bought their dream home in late 1991, as part of the federal Urban Homesteading program, for only $1. The house was renovated and restored with a 3 percent federal government loan and the Watts family will have twenty years to repay that loan. Had it not been for this federal program, they might still be renting instead of home-owners.

David Hicks obtained a $56,438 grant to develop NuCharge System, an electrical management system that reclaims energy from the car's momentum while slowing or stopping and which prevents drain on engine power and fuel efficiency.

JUST LIKE YOURSELF

Business owners, like yourself, apply for and get business grants and loans. Here is a sampling of the categories of small businesses that recently applied for and received a federal award:

a) Dry cleaners
b) Book stores and toy shops
c) Billiard parlor
d) Motels and resorts
e) Health clubs
f) Restaurants, caterers and pizza parlors
g) Bike shops
h) Hair designers
i) Interior design firms
j) Florists
k) Funeral parlors
l) Manufacturers
m) Food distributors
n) Clothing stores

These do not include all the categories but are just a small sample of the types of retail, manufacturing, service, and distributor enterprises that do receive government funding.

HOW MANY FEDERAL AWARDS ARE MADE?

The most cynical reader might think there is hardly any hope at all for him to receive government funding or assistance for his business. Here is a listing from the 1992 Catalog of Federal Domestic Assistance showing how many recent grants, loans, contracts, or assistance was provided to applicants, just from the Small Business Administration. The identification number for each program follows the name of the program. (FY represents Fiscal Year)

Economic Injury Disaster Loans (EIDL). 59.002
FY 1991: 1076 loans made
Early 1992: 394 loans made

Loans for Small Business (Business Loans 7(a) (11)). 59.003
FY 1991: 255 direct loans made

Business Development Assistance to Small Business. 59.005
FY 1991: 573,000 small businesspersons counseled and 483,800 enrolled in management training.

Minority Business Development (Section 8(a) Program). 59.006
FY 1991: 3,863 contracts awarded with a value of $4 billion

Management and Technical Assistance for Socially and Economically Disadvantaged Business. (7 (J) Development Assistance Program). 59.007.
FY 1991: 133 grants and cooperative agreements
FY 1992: 131 grants and cooperative agreements

Physical Disaster Loans. (7 (b) Loans (DL)). 59.008.
FY 1991: 11,375 loans
Early 1992: 3,801 loans

Procurement Assistance to Small Businesses. 59.009.
FY 1991: $90.5 million disbursed

Small Business Loans (Regular Business Loans -- 7(a) Loans). 59.012.
FY 1991: 17,323 loans approved

Local Development Company Loans (502 Loans). 59.013.
FY 1991: 38 loans approved

Bond Guarantees for Surety Companies (Surety Bond Guarantee). 59.016.
FY 1991: 7,544 bond guarantees issued

Handicapped Assistance Loans (HAL-1 and HAL-2). 59.021.
FY 1990: 105 direct loans approved

Service Corps of Retired Executives Association (SCORE). 59.026.
Since 1964 SCORE has responded to almost 3 million requests for assistance.

Veterans Loan Program (Veterans Loans). 59.038.
FY 1991: 204 loans approved

Certified Development Company Loans (504 Loans) 59.041.
FY 1991: 1,517 loans made

Business Loans for 8(A) Program Participants. 59.042.
FY 1990: 22 direct loans made

Women's Business Ownership Assistance. 59.043.
At present, training and counseling is being offered at 25 different sites.

Veterans Entrepreneurial Training and Counseling (VET Program). 59.044
FY 1990: 4 grants approved
FY 1991: 4 grants approved

There are hundreds of other federal programs and even more state programs available to applicants. The above has been used to demonstrate to you only that loans are, indeed, approved. When you run into your next naysayer, you can show him the above programs. These are just a handful.

So, what are you waiting for? Start looking through the directory in the remaining portion of this book. The sky's the limit if you want it to be.

SECTION TWO:

BUSINESS PROGRAMS
****

5.

THE SMALL BUSINESS ADMINISTRATION
****

Think of the Small Business Administration (SBA) as your rich uncle. While that uncle may be loaded and able to finance virtually any venture you'd want to start, he's not exactly dumb and ready to hand over his checking account to you. However, the SBA is loaded with financing and assistance programs. And, if you study this and the next few chapters you'll see the full range of the Small Business Administration's services available to you.

Whole books have been devoted exclusively to the Small Business Administration. Most deal with the most clear-cut aspect of the SBA and what it's known for: SBA Loans. Let's clarify that right now. The Small Business Administration rarely makes direct loans to individuals for starting or expanding a small business. But, there are loan guarantee and other programs that may be worthwhile finding out about.

It was a different story in 1953 when Congress passed the Small Business Act and created the Small Business Administration by doing so. As the successor to the Reconstruction Finance Corporation's small business loans program (a Great Depression business revitalization program), the SBA's basic purpose has been to finance, or guarantee loans for, those individuals who could not obtain funding elsewhere. It did. Money was lent out in bushels to small businessmen wanting to buy into the American dream.

Things didn't work out as planned. Businesses went under and the SBA got stuck with the tab. Underlying these business failures was the fact that those business owners didn't understand how to manage and run their companies.

Slowly, the SBA cleared out of the direct loan business. By 1958 Congress amended the original public law with the Small Business Investment Act, entrusting professional lenders to borrow money from the Small Business Administration and lend it out, along with their funds, to qualified small businesses. This loan program is discussed in Chapter 7 and directory information on contacting these investment companies is found there.

Because the SBA had a vested interest in keeping alive the American Dream -- that of being one's own boss, they persuaded Congress to appropriate funding to the Small Business Development Company (SBDC) program. These are programs organized in each state and run through local colleges and other institutions across America. Because it was found that throwing good taxpayer money into businesses didn't always work, SBDCs were created to help prepare the budding entrepreneur for the rigors of running a business. More on this is found in Chapter 6, as well as directory information on how to contact a local SBDC for loads of valuable free or low-cost assistance.

But, the main thrust of the SBA and this chapter is its involvement in financing, or

There were 15.6 million self-employed individuals in 1985. Small businesses create jobs. People that have jobs and are living well will vote for an incumbent president and re-elect their congressional leaders. So, the SBA, both the legislative and executive branches of the federal government have good reason to nurture and support small businesses throughout America.

SMALL BUSINESS ADMINISTRATION DIRECT LOANS

The Small Business Administration does make direct loans, but are only available with several restrictions. The maximum loan amount is $150,000 and are only available to applicants who are unable to secure an SBA loan guarantee. Before you can apply for an SBA direct loan, you must first try your local banker and fail to obtain a bank loan. If you live in a city with a population greater than 200,000, you must attempt to obtain financing from at least one other lender. And also fail a second time. With these strikes against you, there is a slim chance the SBA will make a direct loan for your business. Funds are nearly always tight. For many years the SBA has only made direct loans to those who meet these qualifications: businesses owned by Vietnam-era veterans, disabled veterans of any era, permanently handicapped individuals, those located in high unemployment areas or businesses owned in areas where there is a high percentage of low-income individuals.

It seems that those least probable to present an invigorating and persuasive business plan, are those most likely to be considered for an SBA direct loan. But wait, there's more! Imagine what a high unemployment area or an area predominantly inhabited by low-income individuals would look like. Now, add these additional restrictions: no SBA money can be earmarked for nonprofit enterprises, speculators in property, lending or investment enter-prises, gambling enterprises, and financing real property held for investment. (This is true for all SBA Loan programs, not just the direct loan program.)

Obviously, one past objective has been to ignore growth in the slums. It's not that I think the SBA should loosen up its regulations and finance Louie the loan shark or Ernesto's Pawn Shop or even the St. Eustacia's Bible Choir, but the SBA is not thinking in practical terms when it lists those qualifications and places unrealistic restrictions on who may qualify and who won't. It's out of touch with minority and disadvantaged America and hasn't used the clout provided it to make more Americans effective.

A look at the amount of funds lent out through this program can make one question why they just haven't eliminated it altogether, instead of perpetuating the hoax that there really is an SBA direct loan program. In the 1992 Catalog of Federal Domestic Assistance, please note, on pages 582-3, that the latest information about the 7(a)(11) program, also known as Loans for Small Business- 59.003, shows that in Fiscal Year 1991 only 255 direct loans were made. The average financial assistance in those programs was $67,694. Multiply those figures and you will discover that the SBA directly lent slightly more than $17 million to a mere 255 under qualified, handicapped and minority individuals. After having appeared on numerous talk shows across America, while promoting an earlier version of this book, many callers asked how they could participate in this particular program. Far more than 255 individuals called in to radio talk shows about this program. Yet, during the same year I was promoting that book, only that small number of individuals were awarded money under this program.

Ask anyone if they have a dream and you'll find someone talking about theirs. For many in high unemployment or low income areas they'd probably want some version of the good life. And that idea of the good life, in

America, usually comes from owning your business and providing a valuable product or service. Not from receiving a steady stream of public assistance checks and food stamps. If the Small Business Administration wanted to invigorate American business and make this country productive as a nation, then it should revitalize its direct loan program. Ask under-privileged, undereducated and under qualified Americans which they'd prefer: a welfare check and food stamps or owning and running their own business? I think the answer is obvious.

The SBA should open up its doors and use what it has learned over the past 40 years it has been in business, devoting time to expanding its direct loan program. Not making it less possible each year for someone to obtain one! It's time to dispense with a let-them-eat-cake attitude.

SMALL BUSINESS ADMINISTRATION LOAN GUARANTEES

Since there is hardly any direct financing available from the SBA, how is it involved in money lending? Using the preceding figures, please note on pages 587-8 of the Catalog of Federal Domestic Assistance the SBA 7(a) program, also known as Regular Business Loans. During Fiscal Year 1991 more than 17,000 loan guarantees were approved with a loan average of $192,126. That amounts to more than $3 billion!

On the positive side, if you are a business owner that has a solid business plan, has followed the guidelines and have collateral in the business you seek to finance through an SBA loan guarantee program, there is an enormous reserve of funds available. Annually, the Small Business Administration has been guaranteeing approximately $3 billion through its 7(a) program. If your bank refuses to lend your business money and is an SBA-participating bank, it will directly contact the Small Business Administration to guarantee your loan. That's the procedure.

While the SBA direct loan program has a ceiling of $150,000, loans guaranteed by the SBA have no limit. That doesn't mean the SBA will guarantee any loan amount; they won't. Through the SBA loan guarantee program, the most you can expect them to guarantee is $750,000 or 85% of the loan amount, whichever is less.

As was pointed out above, the loan average was slightly under $200,000. Having interviewed a number of SBA officials, I find that is the amount lenders prefer to work with. If you hope to borrow $50,000, forget it. Most won't bother unless the loan is at least $100,000. And, that is going to require a large financial commitment from you.

Besides having a stellar business plan, both the Small Business Administration and the lending institution want to see what kind of financial stake you have in the business. They will want to see a "reasonable" financial commitment from you. Expected investment in your own business may be for as little as 20 percent or reach as high as 50 percent, depending on whether yours is a startup or you are buying an existing business. Unquestionably, the greater your monetary interest in the company, the less the odds will be for a rejection. Demand for these loan guarantees last year was up thirty percent over the previous year.

THE MICRO LOAN PROGRAM

The Micro Loan program is a recent Small Business Administration development that could later change the nature of its lending practices. Because there has been such a high demand for its existing direct loan program and requirements have made approval extremely prohibitive the majority of potential applicants, the SBA started an experimental loan program. Before you rush to your local

SBA field office to apply for a Micro Loan, please remember that this loan program is still in its experimental stage. It has limited availability at this time.

In an interview with Tony O'Reilly, who oversees the Savannah SBA office's micro loan experiment, he believes the Small Business Administration is using this program to return to the money lending business. Somewhere in Washington, someone finally realized that the SBA had lost touch with smaller businesses, that its direct loan program was a little less than a drop in the bucket, and that a new loan program had to be implemented.

Here's how the Micro Loan program works. The Small Business Administration borrows at money at 6.75 percent interest and lends out the money to small businesses at an interest rate higher than prime, but not greater than prime plus four percent. The loan's maximum term is six years.

The reason for the SBA's return to direct lending in such a capacity is that small SBA loan guarantees generally start at $100,000. Most of the startup businesses that had approached the Small Business Administration were applying for such small amounts that banks weren't bothering with them. SBA Micro Loans are basically for startup small businesses because they have a loan ceiling amount of $25,000. The SBA is looking for an average loan portfolio amount of about $10,000.

For loans of less than $15,000 the applicant must first apply to a bank and strike out. If you are participating in this program, first get the rejection letter from the bank before pursuing your Micro Loan application. That will expedite your SBA loan request.

You will be required to show some form of collateral or personal capitalization for your business when applying for a Micro Loan. At present the SBA is expecting that you invest, from your own efforts, at least 20 percent of the total capitalization. For instance, if you approach the SBA for an $8,000 Micro Loan,

they will require that you have at least $2,000 already invested in the business. That form of personal capitalization in your business could include office equipment or tools and you might borrow the balance from your friends and family.

Keep in mind the SBA is still experimenting with this program and working out the kinks. At present there are 35 demonstration projects underway. Each is proposing, under the 7(a) program and SBA guidelines, variations of the loan package. Different types of projects are involved. Some, for example, are targeted for low-income areas. Loans may be for as little as $500. But, if the Micro Loan program rolls out, it could, indeed, create a small boom in home-based startup businesses across America. Many have nowhere else to turn for financing.

As you can see, the SBA is attempting to bring "seed money" into the environment. Remember, the SBA has a track record of heavy default activity, often on large loan amounts. So it is approaching this carefully. The Micro Loan program reinvents the original intention of the Small Business Administration. This experimental program makes local SBA offices, who are making these loans, intermediary lenders. The SBA borrows federal money and lends it out to private business people.

Unfortunately, at this writing there was no official literature on the SBA Micro Loan program. However, contact your local Small Business Administration office in this chapter's directory and have information about this vital program sent you.

SBA LOAN ELIGIBILITY REQUIREMENTS

Before applying for an SBA loan or loan guarantee, please determine whether or not your business is eligible. As mentioned earlier several types of business are not eligible. To that list the following are restricted:

a)Any business involved in the creation or distribution of ideas or opinions, such as newspapers, magazines and academic schools;

b)Any business engaged in speculation or investment in rental real estate.

Small businesses are, by law, the only ones the SBA can help. It defines a small business as one that is independently owned and operated, not dominant within its field, and falls into the size standards set by the Small Business Administration. Size standards are based on the average number of employees for the preceding 12 months or on sales volume averaged over a three-year period. Below are the maximum number of employees or maximum annual sales permitted by the Small Business Administration to be defined, by their standards, as a small business. This applies to both the direct loan and loan guarantee programs, as well as any related financing programs.

o Manufacturing: Maximum number of employees may range from 500 to 1,500, depending on the type of product manufactured.

o Wholesaling: Maximum number of employees may not exceed 100.

o Services: Average annual receipts may not exceed $3.5 to $14.5 million, depending on the industry.

o Retailing: Average annual receipts may not exceed $3.5 to $13.5 million, depending on the industry.

o Construction: General construction average annual receipts may not exceed $9.5 to $17 million, depending on the industry.

o Special trade construction: Average annual receipts may not exceed $7 million.

o Agriculture: Average annual receipts range from $1 to $3.5 million, depending on the industry.

While reading the above, you may have noticed that each business category was qualified by "depending on the industry." Please further clarify this stipulation by contacting your local SBA office and explaining your type of business.

CREDIT REQUIREMENTS

The Small Business Administration will require that you meet certain qualifications when evaluating your application. Additionally, you must pledge sufficient assets, usually between one-third and one-half, of the total assets needed to start the business. The two most important factors that will determine whether or not your loan is approved are:

a)How well-conceived, organized, and persuasive your business plan is or not, AND

b) How much collateral or financial stake you have in your business.

Aside from the above key requirements Small Business Administration literature outlines four broad, general characteristics they expect of a loan applicant. To apply you should:

o Be of good character.

o Demonstrate sufficient management expertise and the commitment necessary for a successful operation.

o Have enough funds -- including the SBA-guaranteed loan plus personal cash -- to operate the business on a sound financial basis. For new businesses, this includes sufficient resources to withstand start-up expenses and the initial operating phase when losses are likely to occur.

o Show that the past earnings record and probable future earnings will be sufficient to repay the loan in a timely manner.

As you can see, these are vague credit requirements. Let's take a look behind the official SBA literature to find out what these points really mean.

1. All SBA applicants must be of good character. That means that criminal records and other infractions are investigated thor-

oughly. Prior indictments and/or conviction will not necessarily disqualify your request, but you will be required to submit a set of fingerprints. This form and instructions are available from your local SBA office. Persons presently under indictment, incarcerated, on probation or on parole are ineligible to apply.

2. All SBA applicants must demonstrate sufficient management expertise. This means that business owners and its officers must show a track record of management and technical ability to reasonably assure the success of the business. In your business plan the SBA expects to see a resume of your business, technical and management skills and be persuaded that you have a history of sticking to something once it's been started.

3. All SBA applicants must have enough funds to operate the business on a sound financial basis. If you are starting a new business or purchasing an existing business and hope to borrow from the SBA, this means that you can practically forget getting 100 percent of your financing from the SBA. The borrower must have a reasonable personal down payment at stake, generally around 30 percent or more of the funds necessary. For a highly competitive business or those with high failure rates, such as a non-franchised restaurant, expect to invest up to 50 percent of your own funds.

In financing an existing business, each application is considered on a case-by-case basis and borrowers must have a reasonable amount of personal investment at stake, i.e. 20 to 30 percent of the amount requested. Negative net-worth situations caused by historical losses are rarely acceptable. The SBA will make comparisons to industry averages when considering your loan application.

4. All SBA applicants must show a repayment ability. This means that existing businesses must be able to show that the past earnings record and future prospects of the firm indicate ability to repay the loans and other fixed debt out of profits. A new busi-

ness proposal must be supported by a complete business plan along with a reasonable forecast of earnings for at least one year. Your entire plan must be supported by realistic market data not a fantasy projection. The SBA will compare your projection against industry averages.

Don't be discouraged by the above points. The SBA has had its fingers burned a few times lending out money. Like banks, they want to reassure themselves that you will repay your SBA loan. With a good business plan and enough other money behind you, either personal funds or borrowed from friends and family, getting an SBA loan guarantee, direct loan or Micro Loan is neither difficult nor a long drawn-out process.

USE OF SBA MONEY

Another prime concern of the SBA is how you plan to use the loan proceeds. They will extend financial assistance for one or more of the following reasons:

a) To furnish working capital

b) To purchase machinery, supplies or inventory

c) To purchase land or building, to fund new construction and/or to expand or convert existing facilities

d) For non-revolving lines of credit for seasonal inventory purchases and contract financing. Revolving credit is available for export related firms.

RED FLAGS will shoot up if you attempt to borrow money for certain reasons and your loan will be automatically declined. The SBA will not lend money for debt repayment, delinquent IRS withholding taxes or state sales tax or similar funds held in trust, for speculation purposes, for money lending or investment purposes (except under the SBIC and similar programs), for gambling, or for more pyramid sales plans.

APPLYING FOR AN SBA LOAN

While one can go about applying for an SBA loan in a variety of ways, as you could with any other type of loan, there's a right way and a wrong way. The Small Business Administration suggests the following procedure in applying for their loans or loan guarantees.

1. Visit, or call, a Commercial Loan Officer at your bank to find out exactly what is needed to apply for a commercial loan. Be sure you have all their forms and know what supplemental information is needed.

2. Assemble the required information, either through your own efforts or with the assistance of an outside source. A business plan outline may be used for your presentation. Be sure all the questions on the lender's forms are answered and supplemental information is provided. You may wish to contact a nearby Small Business Development Center or local SCORE office (see Chapter 6 for details and directory) for free counseling on your plan.

3. Make a second appointment with the Commercial Loan Officer to present your proposal and to discuss your plans. Don't expect an immediate credit decision. It will take at least two to five weeks for a decision IF you have furnished complete information, as requested by the loan officer.

4. If the loan is approved, there will be no need for SBA involvement. If the loan request is declined, try to provide other information or proposals to overcome the reasons for the rejection. Ask that the request be reconsidered with an SBA loan guarantee.

5. If the banker feels the loan could be given favorable consideration with SBA participation, he/she will give you an SBA loan package, which you must then add to the bank's application.

6. Complete and return the SBA loan package and the original bank's package to the bank. The bank will then deal directly with the SBA.

Processing of your SBA loan request does not begin until your loan is complete.

7. If your request for an SBA guaranteed loan is declined by the bank, you may be then eligible to apply for a direct loan.

LOAN AMOUNTS AND TERMS

On SBA direct loans the maximum amount is $150,000 to any one business or its affiliates. The SBA may guarantee 90 percent of a bank loan if the total amount is $155,000 or less. Loan guarantees in excess of $150,000 are limited to 85 percent. The SBA's maximum exposure is $750,000 but there is no ceiling to the amount a bank may lend you.

Banks like SBA loan guarantees. Because a certain portion of the loan is federally guaranteed, the bank can package up and re-sell a portion of that loan to investors at a profit. Then, the bank will use its funds to make other loans. If the business fails, the bank's exposure is minimal. Inventory, fixtures, equipment and other assets will be seized and sold at auction. The SBA, by guaranteeing the loan, will write a check to the bank to cover the bank's loss. It's a win-win situation for the bank.

The SBA has guidelines for loans against assets and these terms apply. Loan terms are determined by the "useful life" of the asset purchased and collateralized by the loan. Machinery, equipment, furniture and fixtures have terms of five to fifteen years, depending on what is being purchased. Limits on working capital loans and inventory loans are usually five to six years. But, real estate has terms of up to twenty-five years.

Interest rates on SBA guaranteed loans are negotiated between the borrower and the lender, subject to SBA maximums. Generally, interest rates for loans with maturities of seven years or more cannot exceed 2.75 percent over New York prime. Loans which mature in less than seven years cannot exceed 2.25 percent over New York prime. Interest rates on SBA direct loans are based on the cost of money to the Federal Government and are calculated quarterly.

SBA LENDER PROGRAMS

Many borrowers worry about how long it will take to get an SBA loan guarantee. Some have taken many months, others several weeks. There are speedier routes.

In an effort to reduce paperwork and streamline loan activity to small businesses, the Small Business Administration initiated the Certified Lenders Program (CLP) in 1979. Under the Certified Lenders Program, the lender performs an initial credit analysis of loan applications and then forwards them to the SBA for final approval.

A newer program was originated in recent years called the Preferred Lenders Program (PLP). Under this program the SBA delegates credit authority to the lender. Preferred lenders make final approvals on loan requests and then report them to the Small Business Administration, which guarantees up to 75 percent of the loan amount. PLP loans are guaranteed for a minimum of $100,000 and a maximum of $500,000. Interest rates are negotiable between the borrower and the lender. Preferred lenders can normally process loan requests in a matter of days.

How do you find out about them? You could try contacting your local banks to find out who are CLP or PLP lenders. In the long run that's probably a slow and inefficient method. The fastest and most rewarding way is to contact your local Small Business Development Center.

Why make that particular phone call or visit? They'll know who the CLP or PLP lenders in your area are and, more importantly, who are speediest lenders and also the most generous ones. See Chapter 6 for details.

SBA PROGRAMS FOR MINORITIES

The Small Business Administration offers special assistance to help minority-owned businesses grow. The SBA serves as the prime contractor for a share of all awards made by federal agencies and subcontract that work to firms owned by socially and economically disadvantaged Americans.

Contact your local SBA office to find management and technical assistance in your area through the 7(J) program. Special SBA-funded courses and training are available in business planning, accounting, and marketing to socially and economically disadvantaged firms and firms located in areas with a surplus labor pool. The SBA also provides loans to eligible minority-owned businesses. Individual business owners who want help should contact the local SBA office and ask for SBA Form 641, Request for Counseling.

Minorities can find additional assistance through their state economic development offices (see Chapter 9) or one can find a local minority enterprise association through a national association (see Suggested Reading in Section Five). For instance, the National Business League is the oldest African-American Business Trade Organization in the United States (it is actually 12 years older than the U.S. Chamber of Commerce). You can contact them for assistance:

NATIONAL BUSINESS LEAGUE
1629 K Street, N.W.
Suite 605
Washington, DC 20006
Telephone: (202) 466-5483
Fax: (202) 466-5487

Your local SBA office may also direct you to local Specialized Small Business Investment Companies, which the SBA licenses and regulates, and who may provide you with venture capital. See Chapter 7 for additional details.

NATIVE AMERICANS

Small Business Administration programs do not specifically provide for Native Americans. Because of the layout of this book, these have been included here, rather than omitted from it. The Indian Financing Act of 1984 (Public Law 94-449) and 1988 (Public Law 100-422) were added to augment and expand original legislation assisting Native Americans. These laws are the basis for providing funds to Indian tribes, Indian organizations, and individual Indians for economic development projects and business ventures.

These funds are administered by the Division of Financial Assistance, Bureau of Indian Affairs (BIA), and are available in the form of direct loans, loan guarantees, and non-reimbursable grants. In addition to these specific forms of financial assistance, management and technical assistance is to be made available to loan and grant applicants for the preparation of project funding applications and/or administration of funds awarded.

Native Americans may contact the following Bureau of Indian Affairs Area Credit Offices for further details:

Aberdeen Area Office
Federal Building
115 4th Avenue, S.E.
Aberdeen, South Dakota 57401-4382
Telephone: (605) 226-7381

Albuquerque Area Office
P.O. Box 26567
Plaza Maya Building
615 1st Street, N.W.
Albuquerque, New Mexico 87125-6567
Telephone: (505) 766-3155

Anadarko Area Office
P.O. Box 368
Anadarko, Oklahoma 73005
Telephone: (405) 247-2432

Billings Area Office
316 N. 26th Street
Billings, Montana 59101
Telephone: (406) 657-6392

Eastern Area Office
Suite 260/Mailroom
3701 N. Fairfax Drive
Arlington, Virginia 22203
Telephone: (703) 235-1303

Juneau Area Office
P.O. Box 25520
Juneau, Alaska 99802-5520
Telephone: (907) 586-7061

Minneapolis Area Office
331 Second Ave., So.
3rd Floor
Minneapolis, Minnesota 55401
Telephone: (612) 373-1181

Muskogee Area Office
101 N. 5th Street
Muskogee, Oklahoma 74401-6206
Telephone: (918) 687-2377

Navajo Area Office
P.O. Box 1060
Gallup, New Mexico 87305

Phoenix Area Office
One No. First Street
P.O. Box 10
Phoenix, Arizona 85004
Telephone: (602) 379-6624

Portland Area Office
911 N.E. 11th Avenue
Portland, Oregon 97232-4169
Telephone: (503) 231-6716

Sacramento Area Office
Federal Office Building
2800 Cottage Way
Sacramento, California 95825
Telephone: (916) 978-4704

SBA HELP FOR WOMEN

Special Small Business Administration programs are available for women who own at least 51 percent of their business. The SBA's Office of Women's Business Ownership was established by Executive Order of the President in 1979 in response to Congressional findings
"recognizing the many obstacles facing women entrepreneurs and the need to aid and stimulate women's business enterprise."

On October 26, 1988, President Reagan signed into law special assistance to women business owners. Because of this women business owners can take advantage of a wide range of services and resources, including pre business workshops, technical information, credit conferences and programs that promote women business owners in federal procurement.

This legislation also extended equal credit opportunities for women entrepreneurs in obtaining business loans. And, this has been supported with technical assistance and financial conferences, such as "Meet the Lender", "Selling to the Federal Government," and Financial Planning."

Each SBA office has a women's representative who can talk with you about resources that are available and provide guidance on how to access them. Find your state listing below and call the regional coordinator for women's programs. She/he will direct you to your local women's representative.

ME, VT, MA, NH, CT, RI . (617) 451-2040
NY, NJ, PR, VI . . . . (212) 264-1450
PA, DE, MD, VA, DC, WV (215) 962-3710
NC, SC, KY, TN, GA, AL,
MS, FL . . . . (404) 347-2797
MN, WI, MI, OH, IN, IL . . (312) 353-0357
NM, TX, OK, AR, LA . . . . (214) 767-7611
KS, MO, IA, NE . . . . (816) 426-3316
MT, ND, SD, WY, UT, CO (303) 294-7020
CA, NV, AZ, HI . . . . (415) 744-6402
WA, OR, ID, AK . . . . (206) 553-5676

You can also telephone the national office of the SBA's Women's Business Ownership: (202) 205-6673.

The Women's Entrepreneurial Training Network links new and long-term successful women business owners in ongoing relationships. This is a mentor program that matches women business owners who are in a startup phase with more experienced and successful women business owners. They can meet up to four hours monthly for a year and help iron out business difficulties or to network for sales opportunities.

Contact your local SBA office found at the end of this chapter for additional details, further assistance and newly released programs.

SBA PROGRAMS FOR VETERANS

The Small Business Administration also makes special efforts to help veterans get into business or expand existing businesses through workshops, long-term entrepreneurial training, and personal guidance from veterans affairs specialists located in SBA field offices.

Direct business loans are also available, though in limited quantity, to Vietnam-era and disabled veterans. You are eligible if you served for a period of more than 180 days, during any part of that term between August 5, 1964 and May 7, 1975, and were discharged other than dishonorably with a service-related disability; if you have at least 30 percent compensatory disability; or if you receive disability discharge payments.

Additionally, the veteran must own at least 51 percent of his company, manage or run the actual daily operations of the business, demonstrate that he or she can successfully manage the company, and prove that the loan cannot otherwise be obtained. As with all Small Business Administration loans, the veteran must also have a financial stake in the business.

There is a Veterans Affairs Officer in each Small Business Administration office who acts as your contact point for loans, workshops and other assistance. Telephone or visit your nearest SBA office in the directory at the end of this chapter.

SBA ASSISTANCE FOR THE HANDICAPPED

The Small Business Administration has two programs available to assist handicapped persons called Handicapped Assistance Loans (HAL). HAL-1 provides assistance to the handicapped via assistance loans to nonprofit organizations. HAL-2 directly assists small businesses owned or started up by the handicapped.

HAL-1 funding is limited to working capital or construction of facilities; it may not be used for training, education, housing or other supportive services for the handicapped. HAL-2 assistance may be used for construction, expansion or conversion of facilities; to purchase building, equipment or materials; and for working capital. About $12 million is annually appropriated for this assistance.

LOCAL DEVELOPMENT COMPANIES: SBA (502) LOANS

The Small Business Administration helps businesses indirectly through Local Development Company (LDC) loans. An LDC is a corporation chartered for the purpose of helping foster economic growth in a local community. Funds are lent to the LDC who, in turn, finances small businesses who wish to acquire land or buildings and for modernizing, renovating or restoring existing facilities and sites.

An LDC can also be named a Certified Development Company (CDC) in your area. The CDC raises capital by selling 100 percent SBA-guaranteed debentures to private investors. State lending authorities can also participate in these ventures. Many promote heavily to outside industries to move industry into their communities and provide jobs for their residents. For each project the local development company bears 10 percent of the project cost and another 50 percent must be provided by a private lender. SBA funding is provided on a progress basis.

You should contact your local SBA office, in the directory at the end of this chapter, to find out about the availability of an LDC or CDC in your area.

EXPORT ASSISTANCE

The Small Business Administration is heavily encouraging exports through various programs and is eager to help you export your products. Through their Office of International Trade the SBA provides counseling by international trade experts and international attorneys. They offer training sessions and publications that can assist you in cracking the export marketplace. In coordination with the U.S. Department of Commerce, the SBA links U.S. firms with potential foreign buyers through its Matchmaker Trade Missions. International SCORE executives are also available in local areas (see Chapter 6) to assist you in exporting.

Firms having trouble securing conventional financing for export purposes and get backing from the SBA. The International Trade Loan Guarantee program offers loan guarantees to finance to U.S.-based facilities or equipment for producing goods or services for export. An Export Revolving Line of Credit (ERLC) finances a firm with working capital and inventory to help them sell their product overseas.

Further details are available in Chapter 8 and from your local SBA office in the directory at the end of this chapter.

THE SMALL BUSINESS INSTITUTE

The Small Business Institute (SBI) program gives small business owners an opportunity to receive intensive management counseling from qualified college-level business students working under expert faculty guidance. It was established by the SBA in 1972 and helps about 7,000 businesses every year. To date, SBIs have advised more than 140,000 businesses, has provided 350,000 students with "real world" experience in applying business skills, and has involved 6,000 professors in the economic development of their community.

All small business owners/managers are eligible to participate. Any accredited four-year college or university can contact the SBA about becoming an SBI school. There are more than 500 SBIs under contract in every state, the District of Columbia, Guam, Puerto Rico and the Virgin Islands. Services include training and educational programs, advisory services, publications, financial programs and contract assistance. The Agency also offers specialized programs for women business owners, minorities, veterans, international trade and rural development.

The students meet frequently over the course of a full university term (or longer) with the small business owner to identify and solve specific management problems. SBI counseling focuses on the full range of management problems and solutions, including market studies, accounting systems, personnel policies, production design, product line diversification, exporting and expansion feasibility, and strate-

gy. The program also involves SCORE (the Service Corps of Retired Executives), whose volunteers frequently advise SBI teams and offer followup counseling to clients.

OTHER SBA PROGRAMS

The Small Business Administration also helps small businesses secure their fair share of the billions of dollars in federal contracts awarded each year. It works closely with all federal agencies by monitoring and increasing both the dollar value and percentage of prime and subcontract awards to small firms. Through the Procurement Automated Source System (PASS) the SBA electronically brings the resumes of qualified small businesses to the desks of thousands of government procurement officials and large government prime contractors throughout the U.S.

There are additional loan guarantee programs available for small businesses. Small construction businesses can turn to the SBA for Small General Contractor Loan Guarantees. Firms facing seasonal business increases can apply for Seasonal Line of Credit Guarantees. Companies that make, install, sell or service energy equipment and technology may apply for SBA Energy Loan Guarantees. Firms involved in pollution control and reduction could turn to the SBA for a Pollution Control Loan Guarantee.

If your firm is involved in technology research and innovation, you may be eligible for a Small Business Innovation Research grant. More on these in Chapter 10.

THE SMALL BUSINESS IS IMPORTANT

Where would America be without small businesses? They create almost two out of every three new jobs, produce about 40 percent of the gross national product, and invent more than half the nation's technological innovations. Small businesses employ 75 percent of all American workers. The SBA recognizes the numbers game; after all, there are more than 20 million small companies throughout America. And, many are on the cutting edge of technology, services and exports to help America enter the 21st century.

The Small Business Administration recognizes this and champions the cause of small business before Congress, the Executive Branch, state governments, and with financial, educational, professional and trade organizations. Today, the SBA has financing and training available through SBA offices in every state, the District of Columbia, the Virgin Islands, and Puerto Rico.

Please use the Directory following the list of the Small Business Administration-funded programs immediately after this text. Find your local Small Business Administration office and pay them a visit. While there pick up your free copy of the Small Business Startup Kit.

If you experience any difficulties in understanding these programs, want additional details without visiting the SBA, or wish to contact the SBA headquarters directly, please call the SBA ANSWER DESK at 1- 800-827--5722 (also known as 1-800-U-ASKSBA). There are between nine and eleven taped messages you can hear 24 hours, seven days a week. Information is available on starting your own business, financing a business, obtaining counseling and training, local services and assistance, minority small businesses, veterans assistance, women's business assistance, international trade and procurement assistance.

An SBA representative can also help answer your questions if you call Monday through Friday, between 8:30 a.m. and 5:00 p.m.

SMALL BUSINESS ADMINISTRATION PROGRAMS

59.002 Economic Injury Disaster Loans (EIDL)

OBJECTIVES: To assist business concerns suffering economic injury as a result of certain Presidential, SBA, and/or Department of agriculture declared disaster.
TYPES OF ASSISTANCE: Direct Loans, Guaranteed/Insured Loans (including Immediate Participation Loans).
APPLICANT ELIGIBILITY: Must be a small business concern, small agricultural cooperative or a nursery victim of drought as defined in SBA rules and regulations. Must furnish evidence of the cause and extent of economic injury claimed. Must be unable to obtain credit elsewhere. Must be located within declared disaster area.
BENEFICIARY ELIGIBILITY: Small businesses and agricultural cooperatives.
APPLICATION PROCEDURE: Applications are filed with nearest available SBA disaster area office or special disaster office. One copy of SBA Form 5 and Form 1368 are provided for this purpose.
RANGE OF APPROVAL/DISAPPROVAL TIME: From 14 to 90 days.
REGULATIONS, GUIDELINES, AND LITERATURE: 13 CFR Part 123; 'Economic Injury Disaster Loans for Small Business'; DAD-3.
HEADQUARTERS OFFICE: Office of Disaster Assistance, Small Business Administration, 409 3rd Street, SW., Washington DC 20416. Telephone: (202) 205-6734.

59.003 Loans for Small Businesses (Business Loans 7(A)(11)

OBJECTIVES: To provide direct loans to small businesses owned by low-income persons or located in any area having a high percentage of unemployment, or having a high percentage of low income individuals. (Guaranteed Loans, including Immediate Participation Loans are provided under program 59.0-12.)

TYPES OF ASSISTANCE: Direct Loans; Advisory Services and Counseling.

APPLICANT ELIGIBILITY: Creditworthy individuals with income below basic needs or businesses located in areas of high unemployment or businesses located in areas with a high percentage of low income individuals, which have been denied the opportunity to acquire adequate business financing through normal lending channels on reasonable terms. The business must be independently owned and operated, and not dominant in its field and must meet SBA business size standards. Generally, for manufacturers, the range is from 500 to 1,500 employees, depending on the industry; for wholesalers, up to 500 employees is allowed; retailers and service concerns having revenues up to $13.5 million for retailers and $14.5 million for services; agricultural enterprises having gross sales not exceeding gross sales of $0.5 million to $3.5 million.

BENEFICIARY ELIGIBILITY: Creditworthy individuals with income below basic needs or small businesses located in areas of high unemployment, or businesses located in areas with a high percentage of low income individuals.

APPLICATION PROCEDURE: Applications are filed in the field offices serving the territory in which the applicant's business is located.

RANGE OF APPROVAL/DISAPPROVAL TIME: Approximately 20 days from date of application acceptance.

REGULATIONS, GUIDELINES, AND LITERATURE: 'SBA-Business Loans from the SBA,' OPC-6.

HEADQUARTERS OFFICE: Director, Loan Policy and Procedures Branch, Small Business Administration, 409 3rd St., SW., Washington, DC 20416. Telephone: (202) 205-6570.

59.005 Business Development Assistance to Small Business

OBJECTIVES: To help the prospective as well as the present small business person improve skills to manage and operate a business.

TYPES OF ASSISTANCE: Advisory Services and Counseling; Dissemination of Technical Information; Training.

APPLICANT ELIGIBILITY: Existing and potential small business persons and, in some cases, members of community groups are eligible. A small business is one independently owned and operated, and not dominant in its field. Generally for manufacturers, average employment not in excess of 500; wholesalers, average employment not in excess of 100; retail and services concerns, revenues not over $3,500,000, and agricultural enterprises, gross annual sales not over $500,000. Veterans are eligible for all programs.

BENEFICIARY ELIGIBILITY: Small business persons, veterans, community groups.

APPLICATION PROCEDURE: Personal or written application to SBA field offices.

REGULATIONS, GUIDELINES, AND LITERATURE: 'Business Development - Building Excellence in Enterprise'; 13 CFR 129.

HEADQUARTERS OFFICE: Associate Administrator for Business Initiatives, Education and Training, Small Business Administration, 409 3rd Street, SW.,Washington DC 20416. Telephone: (202) 205-6665.

59.006 Minority Business Development (Section 8(a) Program)

OBJECTIVES: To foster business ownership by individuals who are both socially and economically disadvantaged; and to promote the competitive viability of such firms by providing such available contract, financial, technical and managerial assistance as may be available to assist the firms to achieve competitive viability.

TYPES OF ASSISTANCE: Provision of Specialized Services.

APPLICANT ELIGIBILITY: Firms applying for 8(a) program participation must meet certain requirements which include, but not limited to:

(a) status as a small business; (b) at least 51 percent unconditional ownership, control and management of the business by and American citizen(s) determined by SBA to be socially or economically disadvantaged, or by an economically disadvantage Indian Tribe, Alaska Native Corporation, or Native Hawaiian Organization and (c) demonstrated potential for success. Absent evidence to the contrary, the following individuals are presumed to be socially disadvantaged: African Americans, Hispanic Americans, Native Americans, Asian Pacific Americans, and Subcontinent Asian Americans. Individuals who are not members of the named groups may establish their social disadvantage on the basis of clear and convincing evidence of personal disadvantage stemming from color, national origin, gender, physical handicap, long term residence in an environment isolated from the American society, or other similar cause beyond the individual's control. Economic disadvantage must be demonstrated on a case-by-case basis.

BENEFICIARY ELIGIBILITY: Socially and economically disadvantaged individuals; economically disadvantaged Indian Tribes including Alaska Native Corporations; Economically disadvantaged Native Hawaiian organizations.

APPLICATION PROCEDURE: Written application to SBA District offices. Application forms, detailed instructions, and if necessary, assistance in completing applications are available at those offices.

RANGE OF APPROVAL/DISAPPROVAL TIMES: Ninety days.

REGULATIONS, GUIDELINES, AND LITERATURE: SBA Rules and Regulations, 13 CFR Section 124.

HEADQUARTERS OFFICE: Office of AA/MSB&COD, Small Business Administration, 409 3rd Street, SW, Washington, DC 20416. Telephone: (202) 205-6410.

59.007 Management and Technical Assistance for Socially and Ecnomically Disadvantaged Businesses.
(7(J) Development Assistance Program)

OBJECTIVES: To provide management and technical assistance through qualified individuals, public or private organizations to 8(a) certified firms and other existing or potential businesses which are economically and socially disadvantaged; business operating in areas of high unemployment or low income; firms owned by low-income persons; or participants in activities authorized by Sections 7(i), 7(j) and 8(a) of the Small Business Act.

TYPES OF ASSISTANCE: Project Grants (Cooperative Agreements).

APPLICANT ELIGIBILITY: State and local governments, educational institutions, public or private organizations, Indian tribes and individuals that have the capability to provide the necessary assistance, as described in each program solicitation announcement.

BENEFICIARY ELIGIBILITY: Socially and economically disadvantaged persons; businesses which are owned and operated by economically and socially disadvantaged; participants in the 8(a) program, (59.006) or businesses operating in low-income or high-unemployment areas, or firms owned by low-income individuals.

APPLICATION PROCEDURE: Application proposal forwarded to Assistant Regional Administrator for Minority Small Business and Capital Ownership Development -- SBA Regional Office for appropriate area. This program is subject to the provisions of OMB Circular No. A-110.

RANGE OF APPROVAL/DISAPPROVAL TIMES: Variable.

REGULATIONS, GUIDELINES, AND LITERATURE: Fact sheet upon request.

Headquarters Office: Associate Administrator For Minority Small Business and Capital Ownership Development, 409 3rd Street, SW, Washington, DC 20416. Telephone: (202) 205-6423.

59.008 Physical Disaster Loans (7(b) Loans (DL))

OBJECTIVES: To provide loans to the victims of designated physical type disasters for uninsured losses.

TYPES OF ASSISTANCE: Direct Loans; Guaranteed/Insured Loans (including Immediate Participation Loans).

APPLICANT ELIGIBILITY: Must have suffered physical property loss as a result of a disaster which occurred in an area designated as eligible for assistance by the President or SBA. Must demonstrate an ability to repay the loan. Individuals, business concerns, charitable and nonprofit organizations are eligible to apply for assistance.

BENEFICIARY ELIGIBILITY: Individuals, business concerns, charitable and nonprofit organizations.

APPLICATION PROCEDURE: Application is made on a standard form for either a home or business type loan and filed in a single copy with the nearest available SBA Disaster Area office or special disaster office. Only one copy required.

RANGE OF APPROVAL/DISAPPROVAL TIME: From 14 to 90 days depending on complexity of case and availability of resources.

REGULATIONS, GUIDELINES, AND LITERATURE: 13 CFR Part 123; 'Physical Disaster Business Loans,' DAD-2; Disaster Loans for Homes and Personal Property,'DAD-1.

HEADQUARTERS OFFICE: Office of Disaster Assistance, Small Business Administration, 409 3rd Street, SW, Washington, DC 20416. Telephone: (202) 205-6734

59.009 Procurement Assistance to Small Business

OBJECTIVES: To assist small business in obtaining a 'fair' share of contracts and subcontracts for Federal Government Supplies and services and a 'fair' share of property sold by the Government.

TYPES OF ASSISTANCE: Provision of Specialized Services.

APPLICANT ELIGIBILITY: Existing and potential small businesses. A small business is a business entity organized for profit, with a place of business located in the United States and which makes a significant contribution to the U.S. economy through payment of taxes and/or use of American Products, materials and/or labor. Generally for manufacturers, average employment not in excess of 500; wholesalers, average employment not in excess of 500; general construction, revenues not over $17,000,000; special trade, revenues not over $3,500,000; and agricultural enterprises, gross annual sales not over $500,000.

APPLICATION PROCEDURE: Forms to obtain necessary assistance are provided by SBA field offices.

REGULATIONS, GUIDELINES, AND LITERATURE: Title 13, Code of Federal Regulations, Part 125; 'U.S. Government Purchasing and Sales Directory,' available from the Superintendent of Documents, Government Printing Office, Washington DC 20402; and 'Procurement Assistance' and 'Small Business Pooling, Defense Production Research and Development' pamphlets available from SBA offices (See listing of field offices in Appendix !V of the Catalog.)

Headquarter Office: Associate Administrator for Procurement Assistance, Small Business

Administration, 409 3rd Street, SW, Washington, DC 20416. Telephone:(202) 205-6460.

OBJECTIVES: To establish privately owned and managed investment companies, which are licensed and regulated by the U.S. Small Business Administration; to provide equity capital and long term loan funds to small businesses; and to provide advisory services to small businesses.

TYPES OF ASSISTANCE: Direct Loans; Guaranteed/Insured Loans; Advisory Services and Counseling.

APPLICANT ELIGIBILITY: Any chartered small business investment company having a combined paid-in capital and paid-in surplus of not less than $2,500,000 ($1,500,000 for SSBICs), having qualified management, and giving evidence of sound operation, and establishing the need for SBIC financing in the geographic area in which the applicant proposes to operate.

BENEFICIARY ELIGIBILITY: Individual businesses (single proprietorship, partnership or corporation) which satisfy the established criteria of a small business. SSBICs beneficiary must also be a business owned and operated by socially or economically disadvantaged individuals.

APPLICATION PROCEDURE: Request information and appropriate forms from SBA District or Regional office. Complete application requirements and submit with application fee payment of $5,000 to SBA headquarters office.

RANGE OF APPROVAL/DISAPPROVAL TIME: From 90 to 120 days.

REGULATIONS, GUIDELINES, AND LITERATURE: 13 CFR chapter I, part 107.

HEADQUARTERS OFFICE: Director, Office of Operations, Investment Division, Small Business Administration, 409 3rd Street, SW, Washington, DC 20416. Telephone: (202) 6510.

OBJECTIVES: To provide guaranteed loans to small businesses which are unable to obtain financing in the private credit marketplace, but can demonstrate an ability to repay loans granted. Guaranteed loans to low income business owners or businesses located in areas of high unemployment, nonprofit sheltered workshops and other similar organizations which produce goods or services; to small businesses being established, acquired or owned by handicapped individuals; and to enable small businesses to manufacture, design, market, install, or service specific energy measures.

APPLICANT ELIGIBILITY: Small business which is independently owned and operated and not dominant in its field. Generally, size standards for manufacturers range from 500 to 1,500 employees, depending on industry; for wholesalers up to 500 employees is allowed, retailers and service concerns having revenues of $3,500,000 and in certain cases up to $14,500,000, may be considered small; and depending upon the type of industry, agricultural enterprises have size standards for $5000,000 to $3,500,000 in annual receipts.

BENEFICIARY ELIGIBILITY: Small businesses including those owned by low-income and handicapped individuals, or located in high unemployment areas.

APPLICATION PROCEDURE: Applications are filed by the participating lender in the field office serving the territory in which the applicant's business is located. Where the participating lender is in another territory, applications may be accepted and processed by the field office serving that territory, provided there is mutual agreement between the two field office involved. (See listing of field offices in Appendix IV of the Catalog.)

RANGE OF APPROVAL/DISAPPROVAL TIME: From 1 to 20 days from date of application acceptance, depending on type of loan and type of lender program.

REGULATION, GUIDELINES AND, LITERATURE: 'SBA Business Loans from the SBA,' OPC-6.

HEADQUARTERS OFFICE: Director, Loan Policy and Procedures Branch, Small Business Administration, 409 3rd Street, SW, Washington, DC 20416. Telephone: (202) 205-6570.

OBJECTIVES: To make Federal loans to local development companies to provide long-term financing to small business concerns located in their areas. Local development companies are corporations chartered for the purpose of promoting economic growth within specific areas.

TYPES OF ASSISTANCE: Guaranteed/Insured Loans.

APPLICANT ELIGIBILITY: Loans are available to local development companies which are incorporated under general State corporation statute, either on a profit, or nonprofit basis, for the purpose of promoting economic growth in a particular community within the State.

BENEFICIARY ELIGIBILITY: Potential beneficiaries are small businesses independently owned and operated for a profit and not dominant in their fields. More specific criteria defining a small business are established by the Small Business Administration.

APPLICATION PROCEDURE: Application must be made on SBA From 1244 for Local(502) Development Company loans and requirements set forth thereon must all be fully complied with by the local development company (borrower) and the small business being assisted.

RANGE OF APPROVAL/DISAPPROVAL TIME: From 20 to 30 days from the date of acceptance of an application.

REGULATIONS, GUIDELINES, AND LITERATURE: 'Loans to Local Development Companies, 'OPI-17; 'Key Features of SBA's Principal Lending Programs, 'OPI-7. 'Long--Term Financing Through the Secondary Market of the U.S. Small Business Administration, SBA-475.

HEADQUARTERS OFFICE: Office of Rural Affairs and Economic Development, Small Business Administration, 409 3rd Street, SW, Washington, DC 20416. Telephone: (202) 205-6485.

59.021 Handicapped Assistance Loans (HAL-1 and HAL-2)

OBJECTIVES; To Provide direct loans for nonprofit sheltered workshops and other similar organizations that produce goods and services; and to assist in the establishment, acquisition, or operation of a small business owned by handicapped individuals. (Guaranteed Loans, including Immediate Participation Loans, are provided under program 59.012.)

TYPES OF ASSISTANCE: Direct Loans.

APPLICANT ELIGIBILITY: For nonprofit organizations (Hal-1), must be organized under the laws of the state, or of the United States as an organization operating in the interests of handicapped individuals and must employ handicapped individuals for not less that 75 percent of the work-hours required for the direct production of commodities or in the provision of services which it renders. For HAL-2 (small business concerns), must be independently owned and operated, not dominant in its field, meet SBA size standards, and be 100 percent owned by handicapped individuals. Handicap must be of such a nature as to limit the individual in engaging in normal competitive business practices without SBA assistance.

BENEFICIARY ELIGIBILITY: Nonprofit organizations, small businesses.

APPLICATION PROCEDURE: Applications are filed in the field office serving the territory in which the applicant is located.

RANGE OF APPROVAL/DISAPPROVAL TIME: Approximately 20 days from date of acceptance of application.

REGULATIONS, GUIDELINES, AND LITERATURE: Fact Sheet 'Handicapped Assistance Loans, 'Part 120, Sba Rules and Regulations.

HEADQUARTERS OFFICE: Director, Loan Policy and Procedures Branch, Small Business

Administration, 409 3rd Street, SW, Washington, DC 20416. Telephone: (202) 205-6570.

59.038 Veterans Loan Program (Veterans Loans)

OBJECTIVES: To provide loans to small businesses owned by Vietnam era and disabled veterans.
TYPES OF ASSISTANCE: Direct Loans.
APPLICANT ELIGIBILITY: Must be a small business concern as described in SBA regulations. Small business concerns must be owned (a minimum of 51 percent) by an eligible veteran(s). Management and daily operation of the business must be directed by one or more of the veteran owners of the applicant whose veteran status is used to qualify for the loan. Vietnam-era veterans who served for a period of more than 180 days, any part of which was between August 5, 1964, and May 7, 1975, and were discharged other than dishonorably. Disabled veterans of any era with a minimum compensable disability of 30 percent or a veteran of any era who was discharged for disability. Veterans status may be used only once to obtain a loan under this program.
BENEFICIARY ELIGIBILITY: Small business concerns.
APPLICATION PROCEDURE: Applications are filed in the field office serving the territory in which the applicant's business is located.
RANGE OF APPROVAL/DISAPPROVAL TIME: Approximately 20 days from date of acceptance of application.
REGULATIONS, GUIDELINES, AND LITERATURE: Fact Sheet 'Business Loans for Vietnam-Era and Disabled Veterans. 'Part 122 Subpart E, SBA Rules and Regulations.
HEADQUARTERS OFFICE: Director, Loan Policy and Procedures Branch, Small Business Administration, 409 3rd Street, SW, Washington, DC 20416. Telephone: (202) 205-6570.

59.041 Certified Development Company Loans (504 Loans)

OBJECTIVES: To assist small business concerns by providing long term financing for fixed assets through the sale of debentures to private investors.
TYPES OF ASSISTANCE: Guaranteed/Insured Loans.
APPLICANT ELIGIBILITY: Certified Development Companies must be incorporated under general State corporation statute, on a nonprofit basis, for the purpose of promoting economic growth in a particular area.
BENEFICIARY ELIGIBILITY: Small businesses independently owned and operated for profit. More specific criteria defining a small business are established by the small Business Administration.
CREDENTIALS/DOCUMENTATION: To become a Certified Development Company (CDC), the applicant should include the following information: (1) name and address of applicant; (2) type of CDC, State or local; (3) area of operation; (4) list of members or stockholders with address, occupation and telephone number; (5) list of officers and directors; (6) SBA Form 1081 on all officers, directors, and staff; (7) certified statement that no member or stockholder controls more than 10 percent of the voting control; (8) resume on each officer and director; (9) the name of each individual who provides the CDC with the professional staff capability; (10) if contracted out, a copy of the contract is required to be submitted to SBA; (11) proof of compliance of representatives from the following groups; local government, private sector lending institution, community organization and business concern; (12) an organization chart and operating plan (13) a flow chart on the CDC (evaluating, packaging, processing, closing and servicing functions); (14) address and description of the place of business, telephone number and financial statement; (15) the CDC's

charter and certified by-laws; (16) articles certified by the State; and (17) a resolution of the Board of Directors certified by a corporate officer in which a company resolves to become a CDC, naming the person who is authorized to execute all documents.

APPLICATION PROCEDURE: Applications must be made on SBA Form 1244 and requirements set forth thereon must be fully complied with by the Certified Development Company and the small business being assisted.

RANGE OF APPROVAL/DISAPPROVAL TIME: Within 15 working days after formal acceptance of application.

REGULATIONS, GUIDELINES, AND LITERATURE: SBA Rules and Regulation, Section 108.503; Section 108.504 and Section 108.505; Certified Development Company Program - Program Guide.

HEADQUARTERS OFFICE: Office of Rural Affairs and Economic Development, Small Business Administration, 409 3rd Street, SW., Washington, DC 20416. Telephone: (202) 205-6485

59.042 Business Loans for 8(A) Program Participants (8(A) Program Loans)

APPLICATION PROCEDURE: Applications are filed by the loan applicant (direct loans) or by the participating financial institution (guaranteed loans) in the field office serving the territory in which the applicant's business is located. Where the participating bank is in another territory, applications may be accepted and processed by the field office serving that territory, provided there is mutual agreement between the two field offices involved. (See listing of SBA field offices in Appendix IV of the Catalog.)

RANGE OF APPROVAL/DISAPPROVAL TIME: Approximately 20 days from date of application acceptance, depending on type of loan.

REGULATIONS, GUIDELINES, AND LITERATURE: 13 CFR Chapter 1, Part 122; Federal Register Volume 54, Number 170, September 5, 1989.

HEADQUARTERS OFFICE: Director, Loan Policy and Procedures Branch, Small Business Administration, 409 3rd Street, SW, Washington, DC 20416. Telephone: (202) 205-6570.

59.043 Women's Business Ownership Assistance

OBJECTIVES: To promote the legitimate interest of small business concerns owned and controlled by women and to remove, in so far as possible, the discriminatory barriers that are encountered by women in accessing capital and other factors of production.

TYPES OF ASSISTANCE: Project Grants (Cooperative Agreements or Contracts).

APPLICANT ELIGIBILITY: Profit or nonprofit organizations having experience in training and counseling business women effectively. Educational institutions, State and local governments, and SBA-funded Small Business Development Centers are not eligible.

APPLICATION PROCEDURE: Applications are accepted in accordance with and up to the data specified in the Program Announcement issued annually, usually in the first half of the year. In addition to properly completed application for Federal Assistance: (Standard forms 424, 424A, and 424B), application procedures require a written proposal addressing all items of the selection criteria published in the Program Announcement. All application/proposals are submitted to the SBA Office of Procurement and Grants Management, 5th Floor, 409 3rd Street, SW, Washington, DC 20416

RANGE OF APPROVAL/DISAPPROVAL: Within 120 days from filing deadline.

REGULATIONS, GUIDELINES, AND LITERATURE; Assistance to individuals or enterprises eligible under the Women's Business

Ownership Act of 1988, Federal Register, 54 FR 50466.

HEADQUARTERS OFFICE: Small Business Administration, Office of women's Business Ownership, 409 3rd Street, SW, Washington, DC 20416. Telephone: (202)205-6673. Contact Harriet Fredman.

59.044 Veterans Entreprenurial Training and Counseling (VET Program)

OBJECTIVES: To design, develop, administer, and evaluate an entrepreneurial and procurement training and counseling program for U.S. veterans.

TYPES OF ASSISTANCE: Project Grants (Cooperative Agreements).

APPLICANT ELIGIBILITY: Nonprofit volunteer organizations having the capabilities necessary to provide effective services. The grantee may subcontract with another entity having the technical qualifications for providing some specialized services.

BENEFICIARY ELIGIBILITY: Veterans starting and managing a business, and their dependents.

RANGE OF APPROVAL/DISAPPROVAL TIME: Within time frame specified in the program announcement (usually 60 days after closing date).

REGULATIONS, GUIDELINES, AND LITERATURE: Fiscal year 1991 Program Announcement is to be published in the Federal Register. Contact Federal Agency for more information.

HEADQUARTERS OFFICE: Assistant Director, Office of Veteran Affairs, Small Business Administration, 6th Floor, 409 3rd Street, SW, Washington, DC 20416. Telephone: (202) 205-6773. Contact: Reginald Teamer or William Truitt.

SMALL BUSINESS ADMINISTRATION

FIELD OFFICES

Regional Offices

CALIFORNIA

71 Stevenson St.
20th Floor
San Francisco, CA
94105-2939
(415) 744-6429
Regional Office

COLORADO

999 18TH Street,
N. Tower, Suite 701
Denver, CO 80202
(303) 294-7186
Regional Office

GEORGIA

1375 Peachtree St., NE
5th Floor
Atlanta, GA 30367-6102
(404) 347-2797
Regional Office

ILLINOIS

300 S. Riverside ST.
1975 -South
Chicago, IL 60504-1593
(312) 353-5000
Regional Office

MASSACHUSETTS

155 Federal Street
9th Floor
Boston, MA 02110
(617) 451-2023
Regional Office

MISSOURI

911 Walnut Street, 13th Floor
Kansas, City, MO 64106
(816) 426-3608
Regional Office

NEW YORK

26 Federal Plaza
NY, NY 10278
(212) 264-7772

TEXAS

8625 King George Drive
Building C
Dallas, TX 75235-3391
(206) 553-5676
Regional Office

DISTRICT OFFICES

ALABAMA

2121 8th Ave. N.
Suite 200
Birmingham, AL
35203-2398
(205)731-1344
District Office

ALASKA

22 W. 8th Ave.
Room A36
Anchorage, AK 99513-7559
(917) 271-4022
District Office

ARIZONA

2828 N. Central Ave
Suite 800
Phoenix, AZ 85004
(602) 640-2316
District Office

ARKANSAS

2120 Riverfront Dr.
Suite 100
Little Rock, AR 72202
(501) 324-5871
District Office

CALIFORNIA

2719 N. Air Fresno Dr.
Suite 107
Fresno, CA 93727
(209) 487-5189
District Office

330 N. Grand Blvd.
Suite 109
Glendale, CA 91203-2304
(213) 894-2956
District Office

880 Front Street
Suite 4-S-29
San Diego, CA 92188
(619) 557-5440
District Office

221 Main Street
4th Floor
San Francisco, CA
94105-1988
(415) 744-6804
District Office

901 W. Civic Center Drive
Suite 160
Santa Ana, CA 92703-2352
(714) 836--2494
District Office

COLORADO

721 19th Street
Room 407
Denver, CO 80201-0660
(303) 844-2607
District Office

CONNECTICUT

330 Main St., 2nd Floor
Hartford, CT 06106
(201) 240-4700
District Office

DELAWARE

920 N. King St.
Suite 412
Wilmington, DE 19801
(302) 573-6295
District Office

DISTRICT OF COLUMBIA

1111 18th St. NW
6th Floor
Washington, DC 20036
(202) 634-1500
District Office

FLORIDA

1320 S. Dixie Hwy.
Suite 501
Coral Gables, FL 33146
(305) 536-5521
District Office

GEORGIA

1720 Peachtree Rd. NW
6th Floor
Atlanta, GA 30309
(404) 347-4749
District Office

HAWAII

300 Ala Moana Blvd.
Room 2213
Honolulu, HI 96850-4981
(801) 541-2990
District Office

IDAHO

1020 Main Street
Suite 290
Boise, ID 83702
(208) 334-1696
District Office

ILLINOIS

500 W. Madison
Suite 1250
Chicago, IL 60661-2251
(312) 353-4528
District Office

INDIANA

429 N. Pennsylvania St.
Suite 100
Indianapolis, IN
46204-1873
(317) 226-7272
District Office

IOWA

373 Collins Road NE
Room 100
Cedar Rapids, IA
52402-3147
(319) 393-8630
District Office

210 Walnut Street
Federal Bldg.
Des Moines, IA 50309
(515) 284-4762
District Office

KANSAS

100 E. English St.
Suite 510
Wichita, KS 67202
(316) 269-6616
District Office

KENTUCKY

600 Dr. Martin Luther
King Jr. Place, Rm. 188
Louisville, KY 40202-2254
(502) 582-5971
District Office

LOUISIANA

1661 Canal Street
Suite 2000
New Orleans, LA 70112
(504) 589-6685
District Office

MAINE

40 Western Avenue
Room 512
Augusta, ME 04330
(207) 622-8378
District Office

MARYLAND

10 N. Calvert Street
Third Floor
Baltimore, MD 21202
(301) 962-4392
District Office

MASSACHUSETTS

10 Causeway Street
Room 265
Boston, MA 02222-1093
(617) 565-5590
District Office

MICHIGAN

477 Michigan Avenue
Room 515
Detroit, MI 48226
(313) 226-6075
District Office

MINNESOTA

100 North 6th Street
Suite 610-C
Butler Square
Minneapolis, MN 55403-1563
(612) 370-2324
District Office

MISSISSIPPI

101 W. Capitol Street
Suite 400
Jackson, MS 39201
(601) 965-5325
District Office

MISSOURI

323 West 8th Street
Suite 501
Kansas City, MO 64105
(816) 374-6762
District Office

815 Olive Street
Room 242
St. Louis, MO 63101
(314) 539-6600
District Office

MONTANA

Federal Bldg
Drawer#10054
Helena, MT
59626
(406) 449-5381
District Office

NEBRASKA

11145 Mill Valley Road
Omaha, NE 68154
(402) 221-3604
District Office

NEVADA

301 E. Stewart Ave
PO Box 7527
Las Vegas, NV 89125-7527
(702) 388-6611
District Office

NEW HAMPSHIRE

143 N. Main St.
PO Box 1257
Concord, NH 03302-1257
(603) 225-1400
District Office

NEW JERSEY

60 Park Place
4th Floor
Newark, NJ 07102
(201) 645-2434
District Office

NEW MEXICO

625 Silver Avenue SW
Suite 320
Albuquerque, NM 87102
(505) 766-1870
District Office

NEW YORK

26 Federal Plaza
Room 3100
New York, NY 10278
(212) 264-4354
District Office

NORTH CAROLINA

200 N. College St.
Suite A-2015
Charlotte, NC 28202
(704) 344-6563

NORTH DAKOTA

657 Second Avenue North
Room 218 Federal Bldg.
Fargo, ND 58108-3086
(701) 239-5131
District Office

OHIO

1240 E. 9th Street
Room 317
Cleveland, OH 44199
(216) 522-4180
District Office

2 Nationwide Plaza
Suite 1400
Columbus, OH 43215
(614) 469-6860
District Office

OKLAHOMA

200 NW 5th Street
Suite 670
Oklahoma City, OK 73102
(405) 231-4301
District Office

OREGON

222 SW Columbia St.
Suite 500
Portland, OR 97201-6605
(503) 326-2682
District Office

PENNSYLVANIA

SBA
475 Allendale Road
Suite 201 King of Prussia, PA 19406
(215) 962-3700
District Office

960 Penn Avenue
5th Floor
Pittsburgh, PA 15222
(412) 644-2780
District Office

PUERTO RICO

150 Carlos Chardon Avenue
Room 691
Hato Rey, PR 00918-1729
(809) 766-5572
District Office

RHODE ISLAND

380 Westminster St.
Room 511
Providence, RI 02903
(401) 528-4561
District Office

SOUTH CAROLINA

1835 Assembly Street
Room 358
Columbia, SC 29201
(808) 765-5376
District Office

SOUTH DAKOTA

101 S. Main Avenue
Suite 101
Sioux Falls, SD 57102-0527
(605) 330-4231
District Office

TENNESSEE

50 Vantage Way
Suite 201
Nashville, TN 34228-1500
(615) 736-7176
District Office

TEXAS

1100 Commerce Street
Room 3C-36
Dallas, TX 75242
(214) 767-7643
District Office

10737 Gateway West Blvd.
Suite 320
El Paso, TX 79935
(915) 540-5586
District Office

222 E. Van Buren Street
Suite 500
Harlingen, TX 78550
(512) 427-8533
District Office
9301 SW Fwy
Suite 550
Houston, Tx 77074
(713) 953-6255
District Office

1611 Tenth Street
Suite 200
Lubbock, TX 79401
(806) 743-7462
District Office

7400 Blanco Road
Suite 200
San Antonio, Tx 78216
(512) 229-4535
District Office

UTAH

125 S. State Street
Room 2237
Salt Lake City, UT
84138-1195
(801) 524-5800
District Office

VERMONT

87 State Street
Room 205
Montpelier, VT 05602
(802) 828-4474
District Office

VIRGINIA

400 N. 8th Street
Room 3015
Richmond, VA 23240
(804) 771-2617
District Office

WASHINGTON

915 Second Avenue
room 1792
Seattle, WA 98174-1088
(206) 553-5534
District Office

WEST VIRGINIA

168 West Main Street
5th Floor E.
Clarksburg, WV 26301
(304) 623-5631
District Office

WISCONSIN

212 E. Washington Avenue
Room 213
Madison, WI 26301
(304) 623-5631
District Office

WYOMING

100 East "B" Street
Room 4001
Casper, WY 82601
(307) 261-5761
District Office

BRANCH OFFICES

CALIFORNIA

660 J . Street, Rm. 215
Sacramento, CA
95814-2413
(916) 551-1426
Branch Office

GUAM

Pacific Daily News Building
Room 508
Agana, Guam 96910
(671) 472-7277
Branch Office

ILLINOIS

511 W. Capitol Street
Suite 302
Springfield, IL 62704
(217) 492-4416
Branch Office

MICHIGAN

228 W. Washington St.
Suite 11
Marquette, MI 49855
(906) 225-1108
Branch Office

MISSISSIPPI

One Hancock Plaza
Suite 1001
Gulfport, MS 39501-7758
(601) 863-4449
Branch Office

MISSOURI

620 S. Glenstone Street
Suite 110
Springfield, MO
65802-3200
(417) 864-7670
Branch Office

NEW YORK

111 W. Huron Street
Room 1311
Buffalo, NY 14202
(716) 846-4310
Branch Office

333 East Water Street
4th Floor
Elmira, NY 14901
(607) 734-8130
Branch Office

35 Pinelawn Road
Room 102E
Melville, NY 11747
(516) 454-0750
Branch Office

100 State Street
Room 410
Rochester, NY 14614
(716) 263-6700
Branch Office

OHIO

525 Vine Street
Suite 870
Cincinnati, OH 45202
(513) 684-2814
Branch Office

PENNSYLVANIA

100 Chestnut Street
Room 309
Harrisburg, PA 17101
(717) 782-3840
Branch Office

20 N. Pennsylvania Avenue
Room 2327
Wilkes-Barre, PA 18702
(717) 826-6497
Branch Office

TEXAS

606 N. Caranca
Suite 1200
Corpus Christi, TX 78476
(512) 888-3331
Branch Office

819 Taylor Street
Room 8A-32
Fort Worth, TX 76102
(817) 334-3777
Branch Office

WEST VIRGINIA

550 Eagan Street
Room 309
Charleston, WV 253301
(304) 347-5220
Branch Office

WISCONSIN

310 W. Wisconsin Avenue
Suite 400
Milwaukee, WI 53203
(414) 291-3941
Branch Office

POSTS OF DUTY

ARIZONA

300 W. Congress Street
Room 7H-Box FB-33
Tucson, AZ 85701-1319
(602) 670-6715
Post of Duty

CALIFORNIA

6477 Telephone Rd.
Suite 10
Ventura, CA 93003-4459
(805) 642-1866
Post of Duty

FLORIDA

501E. Polk Street
Suite 104
Tampa, FL 33602-3945
(813) 228-2594
Post of Duty

5601 Corporate Way
Suite 402 W. Palm Beach, FL
33407-2044
(407) 689-3922
Post of Duty

GEORGIA

52 North Main Street
Room 225
Statesboro, GA 30458
(912) 489-8719
Post of Duty

LOUISIANA

500 Fannin Street
Room 8A-08
Shreveport, LA 71101
(318) 676-3196
Post of Duty

NEVADA

50 S. Virginia Street
Room 238
Reno, NV 89501
(702) 784-5268
Post of Duty

NEW JERSEY

2600 Mt. Ephrain Avenue
Camden, NJ 08104
(609) 757-5183
Post of Duty

NEW YORK

Leo O'Brian Bldg. Rm 815
Clinton & Pearl Streets.
Albany, NY 12207
(518) 472-6300
Post of Duty

TEXAS

300 East 8th Street
Suite 520
Austin, TX 78701
(512) 482-5288
Post of Duty

505 E. Travis
Room 103
Marshall, TX 75670
(903) 935-5257
Post of Duty

VIRGIN ISLANDS

4C & 4D Est Sion Farm
Room 7
St. Croix, VI 00820
(809) 778-5380
Post of Duty

Veterans Drive
Room 210
St. Thomas, VI 00801
(809) 774-8530
Post of Duty

DISASTER AREA OFFICES

360 Rainbow Blvd. S.
3rd Floor
Niagara Falls, NY 14303-1192
(716) 282-4612

One Baltimore Pl.
Suite 300
Atlanta, GA 30308
(404) 347-3771

4400 Amon Carter Blvd.
Suite 102
Ft. Worth, TX 76155
(817) 885-7600

1825 Bell Street
Suite 208
Sacramento, CA 95825
(916) 978-4578

OMB Approval No. 3245-0091
Expiration Date: 11-30-93

U.S. SMALL BUSINESS ADMINISTRATION

REQUEST FOR COUNSELING

A. NAME OF COMPANY	B. YOUR NAME (Last, First, Middle)	C. TELEPHONE (H) (B)

D. STREET	E. CITY	F. STATE	G. COUNTY	H. ZIP

I. TYPE OF BUSINESS (Check one)
1. ☐ Retail   4. ☐ Manufacturing
2. ☐ Service   5. ☐ Construction
3. ☐ Wholesale 6. ☐ Not in Business

J. BUS. OWNSHP./GENDER
1. ☐ Male
2. ☐ Female
3. ☐ Male/Female

K. VETERAN STATUS
1. ☐ Veteran
2. ☐ Vietnam-Era Veteran
3. ☐ Disabled Veteran

L.
- INDICATE PREFERRED DATE AND TIME FOR APPOINTMENT
  DATE _____ TIME _____
- ARE YOU CURRENTLY IN BUSINESS? YES ____ NO ____
- IF YES, HOW LONG? _____
- TYPE OF BUSINESS (USE THREE TO FIVE WORDS)
  _____

M. ETHNIC BACKGROUND
a. Race:
1. ☐ American Indian or Alaskan Native
2. ☐ Asian or Pacific Islander
3. ☐ Black
4. ☐ White

b. Ethnicity:
1. ☐ Hispanic Origin
2. ☐ Not of Hispanic Origin

N. INDICATE, BRIEFLY, THE NATURE OF SERVICE AND/OR COUNSELING YOUR ARE SEEKING
_____
_____

O.
- IT HAS BEEN EXPLAINED TO ME THAT I MAY USE FURTHER SERVICES SPONSORED BY THE U.S. SMALL BUSINESS ADMINISTRATION   YES _____ NO _____
- I HAVE ATTENDED A SMALL BUSINESS WORKSHOP   YES _____ NO _____
- CONDUCTED BY _____

P. HOW DID YOU LEARN OF THESE COUNSELING SERVICES?
1. ☐ Yellow Pages   3. ☐ Radio   5. ☐ Bank   7. ☐ Word-of-Mouth
2. ☐ Television   4. ☐ Newspapers   6. ☐ Chamber of Commerce   8. ☐ Other _____

Q. SBA CLIENT (To Be Filled Out By Counselor)
1. ☐ Borrower   2. ☐ Applicant   3. ☐ 8(a) Client   4. ☐ COC   5. ☐ Surety Bond

R. AREA OF COUNSELING PROVIDED (To Be Filled Out By Counselor)

1. Bus. Start-Up/Acquisition	5. Accounting & Records	9. Personnel
2. Source of Capital	6. Finan. Analysis/Cost Control	10. Computer Systems
3. Marketing/Sales	7. Inventory Control	11. Internat'l Trade
4. Government Procurement	8. Engineering R&D	12. Business Liq./Sale

I request business management counseling from the Small Business Administration. I agree to cooperate should I be selected to participate in surveys designed to evaluate SBA assistance services. I authorize SBA to furnish relevant information to the assigned management counselor(s) although I expect that information to be held in strict confidence by him/her.

I further understand that any counselor has agreed not to: (1) recommend goods or services from sources in which he/she has an interest and (2) accept fees or commissions developing from this counseling relationship. In consideration of SBA's furnishing management or technical assistance, I waive all claims against SBA personnel, SCORE, SBDC and its host organizations, SBI, and other SBA Resource Counselors arising from this assistance.

SIGNATURE AND TITLE OF REQUESTER	DATE

FOR USE OF THE SMALL BUSINESS ADMINISTRATION

RESOURCE	DISTRICT	REGION

PLEASE READ DETACH AND RETAIN FOR YOUR RECORDS

STATEMENTS REQUIRED BY LAW AND EXECUTIVE ORDER

Federal executive agencies, including the Small Business Administration (SBA), are required to withhold or limit financial assistance, to impose special conditions on approved loans, to provide special notices to applicants or borrowers and to require special reports and data from borrowers in order to comply with legislation passed by the Congress and Executive Orders issued by the President and by the provisions of various inter-agency agreements. SBA has issued regulations and procedures that implement these laws and executive orders, and they are contained in Parts 112, 113, 116, and 117, Title 13, Code of Federal Regulations Chapter 1, or Standard Operating Procedures.

Freedom of Information Act (5 U.S.C. 552)
This law provides, with some exceptions, that SBA must supply information reflected in agency files and records to a person requesting it. Information about approved loans that will be automatically released includes, among other things, statistics on our loan programs (individual borrowers are not identified in the statistics) and other information such as the names of the borrowers (and their officers, directors, stockholders or partners), the collateral pledged to secure the loan, the amount of the loan, its purpose in general terms and the maturity. Proprietary data on a borrower would not routinely be made available to third parties. All requests under this Act are to be addressed to the nearest SBA office and be identified as a Freedom of Information request.

Right to Financial Privacy Act of 1978 (12 U.S.C. 3401)
This is notice to you as required by the Right to Financial Privacy Act of 1978, of SBA's access rights to financial records held by financial institutions that are or have been doing business with you or your business, including any financial institutions participating in a loan or loan guarantee. The law provides that SBA shall have a right of access to your financial records in connection with its consideration or administration of assistance to you in the form of a Government loan or loan guaranty agreement. SBA is required to provide a certificate of its compliance with the Act to a financial institution in connection with its first request for access to your financial records, after which no further certification is required for subsequent accesses. The law also provides that SBA's access rights continue for the term of any approved loan or loan guaranty agreement. No further notice to you of SBA's access rights is required during the term of any such agreement.

The law also authorizes SBA to transfer to another Government authority any financial records included in an application for a loan, or concerning an approved loan or loan guarantee, as necessary to process, service or foreclose on a loan or loan guarantee or to collect on a defaulted loan or loan guarantee. No other transfer of your financial records to another Government authority will be permitted by SBA except as required or permitted by law.

Flood Disaster Protection Act (42 U.S.C. 4011)
Regulations have been issued by the Federal Insurance Administration (FIA) and by SBA implementing this Act and its amendments. These regulations prohibit SBA from making certain loans in an FIA designated floodplain unless Federal flood insurance is purchased as a condition of the loan. Failure to maintain the required level of flood insurance makes the applicant ineligible for any future financial assistance from SBA under any program, including disaster assistance.

Executive Orders -- Floodplain Management and Wetland Protection (42 F.R. 26951 and 42 F.R. 26961)
The SBA discourages any settlement in or development of a floodplain or a wetland. This statement is to notify all SBA loan applicants that such actions are hazardous to both life and property and should be avoided. The additional cost of flood preventive construction must be considered in addition to the possible loss of all assets and investments in future floods.

Occupational Safety and Health Act (15 U.S.C. 651 et seq.)
This legislation authorizes the Occupational Safety and Health Administration in the Department of Labor to require businesses to modify facilities and procedures to protect employees or pay penalty fees. In some instances the business can be forced to cease operations or be prevented from starting operations in a new facility. Therefore, in some instances SBA may require additional information from an applicant to determine whether the business will be in compliance with OSHA regulations and allowed to operate its facility after the loan is approved and disbursed.

Signing this form as borrower is a certification that the OSA requirements that apply to the borrower's business have been determined and the borrower to the best of its knowledge is in compliance.

Civil Rights Legislation
All businesses receiving SBA financial assistance must agree not to discriminate in any business practice, including employment practices and services to the public, on the basis of categories cited in 13 C.F.R., Parts 112, 113 and 117 of SBA Regulations. This includes making their goods and services available to handicapped clients or customers. All business borrowers will be required to display the "Equal Employment Opportunity Poster" prescribed by SBA.

Equal Credit Opportunity Act (15 U.S.C. 1691)
The Federal Equal Credit Opportunity Act prohibits creditors from discriminating against credit applicants on the basis of race, color, religion, national origin, sex, marital status or age (provided that the applicant has the capacity to enter into a binding contract); because all or part of the applicant's income derives from any public assistance program, or because the applicant has in good faith exercised any right under the Consumer Credit Protection Act. The Federal agency that administers compliance with this law concerning this creditor is the Federal Trade Commission, Equal Credit Opportunity, Washington, D.C. 20580.

Executive Order 11738 -- Environmental Protection (38 F.R. 25161)
The Executive Order charges SBA with administering its loan programs in a manner that will result in effective enforcement of the Clean Air Act, the Federal Water Pollution Act and other environmental protection legislation. SBA must, therefore, impose conditions on some loans. By acknowledging receipt of this form and presenting the application, the principals of all small businesses borrowing $100,000 or more in direct funds stipulate to the following:

1. That any facility used, or to be used, by the subject firm is not cited on the EPA list of Violating Facilities.

2. That subject firm will comply with all the requirements of Section 114 of the Clean Air Act (42 U.S.C. 7414) and Section 308 of the Water Act (33 U.S.C. 1318) relating to inspection, monitoring, entry, reports and information, as well as all other requirements specified in Section 114 and Section 308 of the respective Acts, and all regulations and guidelines issued thereunder.

3. That subject firm will notify SBA of the receipt of any communication from the Director of the Environmental Protection Agency indicating that a facility utilized, or to be utilized, by subject firm is under consideration to be listed on the EPA List of Violating Facilities.

Debt Collection Act of 1982   Deficit Reduction Act of 1984 (31 U.S.C. 3701 et seq. and other titles)
These laws require SBA to aggressively collect any loan payments which become delinquent. SBA must obtain your taxpayer identification number when you apply for a loan. If you receive a loan, and do not make payments as they come due, SBA may take one or more of the following actions:

-Report the status of your loan(s) to credit bureaus
-Hire a collection agency to collect your loan
-Offset your income tax refund or other amounts due to you from the Federal Government
-Suspend or debar you or your company from doing business with the Federal Government
-Refer your loan to the Department of Justice or other attorneys for litigation
-Foreclose on collateral or take other action permitted in the loan instruments.

Immigration Reform and Control Act of 1986 (Pub. L. 99-603)
If you are an alien who was in this country illegally since before January 1, 1982, you may have been granted lawful temporary resident status by the United States Immigration and Naturalization Service pursuant to the Immigration Reform and Control Act of 1986 (Pub. L 99-603). For five years from the date you are granted such status, you are not eligible for financial assistance from the SBA in the form of a loan or guaranty under section 7(a) of the Small Business Act unless you are disabled or a Cuban or Haitian entrant. When you sign this document, you are making the certification that the Immigration Reform and Control Act of 1986 does not apply to you, or if it does apply, more than five years have elapsed since you have been granted lawful temporary resident status pursuant to such 1986 legislation.

Lead-Based Paint Poisoning Prevention Act (42 U.S.C 4821 et seq.)
Borrowers using SBA funds for the construction or rehabilitation of a residential structure are prohibited from using lead-based paint (as defined in SBA regulations) on all interior surfaces, whether accessible or not, and exterior surfaces, such as stairs, decks, porches, railings, windows and doors, which are readily accessible to children under 7 years of age. A "residential structure" is any home, apartment, hotel, motel, orphanage, boarding school, dormitory, day care center, extended care facility, college or other school housing, hospital, group practice or community facility and all other residential or institutional structures where persons reside.

U.S. Small Business Administration
APPLICATION FOR BUSINESS LOAN

Individual	Full Address

Name of Applicant Business	Tax I.D. No. or SSN

Full Street Address of Business	Tel. No. (inc. A/C)

City	County	State	Zip	Number of Employees (Including subsidiaries and affiliates)

Type of Business	Date Business Established	At Time of Application _____

Bank of Business Account and Address	If Loan is Approved _____
	Subsidiaries or Affiliates (Separate from above) _____

Use of Proceeds: (Enter Gross Dollar Amounts Rounded to the Nearest Hundreds)	Loan Requested		Loan Requested
Land Acquisition		Payoff SBA Loan	
New Construction/ Expansion Repair		Payoff Bank Loan (Non SBA Associated)	
Acquisition and/or Repair of Machinery and Equipment		Other Debt Payment (Non SBA Associated)	
Inventory Purchase		All Other	
Working Capital (Including Accounts Payable)		Total Loan Requested	
Acquisition of Existing Business		Term of Loan - (Requested Mat.)	_____ Yrs.

PREVIOUS SBA OR OTHER FEDERAL GOVERNMENT DEBT: If you or any principals or affiliates have 1) ever requested Government Financing or 2) are delinquent on the repayment of any Federal Debt complete the following:

Name of Agency	Original Amount of Loan	Date of Request	Approved or Declined	Balance	Current or Past Due
	$			$	
	$			$	

ASSISTANCE   List the names(s) and occupations of any who assisted in the preparation of this form, other than applicant.

Name and Occupation	Address	Total Fees Paid	Fees Due
Name and Occupation	Address	Total Fees Paid	Fees Due

PLEASE NOTE: The estimated burden hours for the completion of this form is 19.8 hours per response. If you have any questions or comments concerning this estimate or any other aspect of this information collection please contact, Chief Administrative Information Branch, U.S. Small Business Administration, Washington, D.C. 20416 and Gary Waxman, Clearance Officer, Paperwork Reduction Project (3245-0016), Office of Management and Budget, Washington, D.C. 20503.

ALL EXHIBITS MUST BE SIGNED AND DATED BY PERSON SIGNING THIS FORM

BUSINESS INDEBTEDNESS: Furnish the following information on all installment debts, contracts, notes, and mortgages payable. Indicate by an asterisk(*) items to be paid by loan proceeds and reason for paying same (present balance should agree with the latest balance sheet submitted).

To Whom Payable	Original Amount	Original Date	Present Balance	Rate of Interest	Maturity Date	Monthly Payment	Security	Current or Past Due
Acct. #	$		$			$		
Acct. #	$		$			$		
Acct. #	$		$			$		
Acct. #	$		$			$		

MANAGEMENT (Proprietor, partners, officers, directors all holders of outstanding stock - <u>100% of ownership must be shown</u>). Use separate sheet if necessary.

Name and Social Security Number and Position Title	Complete Address	% Owned	*Military Service From	To	*Race	*Sex

*This data is collected for statistical purpose only. It has no bearing on the credit decision to approve or decline this application.

THE FOLLOWING EXHIBITS MUST BE COMPLETED WHERE APPLICABLE . ALL QUESTIONS ANSWERED ARE MADE A PART OF THE APPLICATION.

For Guaranty Loans please provide an original and one copy (Photocopy is Acceptable) of the Application Form, and all Exhibits to the participating lender. For Direct Loans submit one original copy of the application and Exhibits to SBA.

1. Submit SBA Form 912 (Personal History Statement) for each person e.g. owners, partners, officers, directors, major stockholders, etc.; the instructions are on SBA Form 912.

2. If your collateral consists of (A) Land and Building, (B) Machinery and Equipment, (C)Furniture and Fixtures, (D) Accounts Receivable (E) Inventory, (F) Other, please provide an itemized list (labeled Exhibit A) that contains serial and identification numbers for all articles that had an original value greater than $500. Include a legal description of Real Estate offered as collateral.

3. Furnish a signed current personal balance sheet (SBA Form 413 may be used for this purpose) for each stockholder (with 20% or greater ownership), partner, officer, and owner. Social Security number should be included on personal financial statement. It should be as of the same date as the most recent business financial statements. Label this Exhibit B.

4. Include the statements listed below: 1,2,3 for the last three years; also 1,2,3, 4 as of the same date, which are current within 90 days of filing the application; and statement 5, if applicable. This is Exhibit C (SBA has Management Aids that help in the preparation of financial statements.) All information must be <u>signed and dated</u>.

1. Balance Sheet   2. Profit and Loss Statement
3. Reconciliation of Net Worth
4. Aging of Accounts Receivable and Payable
5. Earnings projects for a least one year where financial statements for the last three years are unavailable or where requested by District Office.
   (If Profit and Loss Statement is not available, explain why and substitute Federal Income Tax Forms.)

5. Provide a brief history of your company and a paragraph describing the expected benefits it will receive from the loan. Label it Exhibit D.

6. Provide a brief description similar to a resume of the education, technical and business background for all the people listed under Management. Please mark it Exhibit E.

APPLICANT'S CERTIFICATION

By my signature I certify that I have read and received a copy of the "STATEMENTS REQUIRED BY LAW AND EXECUTIVE ORDER" which was attached to this application. My signature represents my agreement to comply with the approval of my loan request and to comply, whenever applicable, with the hazard insurance, lead-based paint, civil rights or other limitations in this notice.

Each Proprietor, each General Partner, each Limited Partner or Stockholder owning 20% or more, and each Guarantor must sign. Each person should sign only once.

Business Name _____

_____ By _____
Date   Signature and Title

_____
Date   Signature

_____
Date   Signature

_____
Date   Signature

_____
Date   Signature

ALL EXHIBITS MUST BE SIGNED AND DATED BY PERSON SIGNING THIS FORM

7. Do you have any co-signers and/or guarantors for this loan? If so, please submit their names, addresses, tax Id Numbers, and current personal balance sheet(s) as Exhibit F.

8. Are you buying machinery or equipment with your loan money? If so, you must include a list of equipment and cost as quoted by the seller and his name and address. This is Exhibit G.

9. Have you or any officer of your company ever been involved in bankruptcy or insolvency proceedings? If so, please provide the details as Exhibit H. If none, check here: ☐ Yes ☐ No

10. Are you or your business involved in any pending lawsuits? If yes, provide the details as Exhibit I. If none, check here: ☐ Yes ☐ No

11. Do you or your spouse or any member of your household, or anyone who owns, manages, or directs your business or their spouses or members of their households work for the Small Business Administration, Small Business Advisory Council, SCORE or ACE, any Federal Agency, or the participating lender? If so, please provide the name and address of the person and the office where employed. Label this Exhibit J. If none, check here: ☐ Yes ☐ No

12. Does your business, its owners or majority stockholders own or have a controlling interest in other businesses? If yes, please provide their names and the relationship with your company along with a current balance sheet and operating statement for each. This should be Exhibit K.

13. Do you buy from, sell to, or use the services of any concern in which someone in your company has a significant financial interest? If yes, provide details on a separate sheet of paper labeled Exhibit L.

14. If your business is a franchise, include a copy of the franchise agreement and a copy of the FTC disclosure statement supplied to you by the Franchisor. Please include it as Exhibit M.

CONSTRUCTION LOANS ONLY

15. Include a separate exhibit (Exhibit N) the estimated cost of the project and a statement of the source of any additional funds.

16. Provide copies of preliminary construction plans and specifications. Include them as Exhibit O. Final plans will be required prior to disbursement.

DIRECT LOANS ONLY

17. Include two bank declination letters with your application. (In cities with 200,000 people or less, one letter will be sufficient.) These letters should include the name and telephone number of the persons contacted at the banks, the amount and terms of the loan, the reason for decline and whether or not the bank will participate with SBA.

EXPORT LOANS

18. Does your business presently engage in Export Trade? Check here: ☐ Yes ☐ No

19. Do you have plans to begin exporting as a result of this loan? Check here: ☐ Yes ☐ No

20. Would you like information on Exporting? Check here: ☐ Yes ☐ No

AGREEMENTS AND CERTIFICATIONS

Agreements of non-employment of SBA Personnel: I agree that if SBA approves this loan application I will not, for at least two years, hire as an employee or consultant anyone that was employed by the SBA during the one year period prior to the disbursement of the loan.

Certification: I certify: (a) I have not paid anyone connected with the Federal Government for help in getting this loan. I also agree to report to the SBA office of the Inspector General, Washington, D.C. 20416 any Federal Government employee who offers, in return for any type of compensation, to help get this loan approved.

(b) All information in this application and the Exhibits are true and complete to the best of my knowledge and are submitted to SBA so SBA can decide whether to grant a loan or participate with a lending institution in a loan to me. I agree to pay for or reimburse SBA for the cost of any surveys, title or mortgage examinations, appraisals credit reports, etc., performed by non-SBA personnel provided I have given my consent.

(c) I understand that I need not pay anybody to deal with SBA. I have read and understand SBA Form 159 which explains SBA policy on representatives and their fees.

(d) As consideration for any Management, Technical, and Business Development Assistance that may be provided, I waive all claims against SBA and its consultants.

If you make a statement that you know to be false or if you over value a security in order to help obtain a loan under the provisions of the Small Business Act, you can be fined up to $5,000 or be put in jail for up to two years, or both.

If Applicant is a proprietor or general partner, sign below.

By:_____

Date

If Applicant is a Corporation, sign below:

Corporate Name and Seal   Date

_____

By:_____

Signature of President

Attested by:_____

Signature of Corporate Secretary

SBA Form 4 (12-91) Previous Edition is Obsolete

6.

SMALL BUSINESS DEVELOPMENT CENTERS AND SCORE

****

If you have a business idea, whether it is for a service, a new product, an invention, expansion of your current business, saving your business from failure, there are Small Business Development Centers and SCOREs throughout your state waiting to help you. Your tax dollars finance the various business services they offer. And they're worth making a visit to.

After the Small Business Administration was created by the Small Business Act of 1953, Congress and the SBA soon realized that the SBA borrowers didn't know how to start and operate a business enterprise. Many SBA-financed businesses had failed by the 1970's, because of managerial incompetence, and the solution was to create training and educational programs to help business men and women learn how to properly run a business.

Thus, Small Business Development Centers came about. Logically, the SBA turned to public and private institutions of higher education as bases for Small Business Development Centers (SBDC). Virtually any college could be a seat for an SBDC. Your SBDC works with local Chambers of Commerce, Trade Associations, local businessmen and others to provide you with managerial expertise to start a business or stay in business.

The SBA funds SBDCs for the purpose of assisting current and potential small business owners and entrepreneurs in getting started and expanding their business. In 1992 the SBA appropriated more than $60 million

to fund these SBDCs, an increase of $5 million from a year earlier.

Small Business Development Centers are organized on a state level so they can stay in touch with local concerns. There are 56 SBDCs located in 49 states, the District of Columbia and Puerto Rico. Nationwide, there are more than 600 SBDC service centers, with one probably located in or near your hometown.

A local SBDC is likely to offer a full schedule of training seminars above all else. One look at their seminar schedule will show you the breadth of their assistance. You can get professional training in raising finances, marketing, salesmanship, accounting and taxes, credit, collections, bookkeeping and payroll, insurance, and nearly everything you wanted to know to start a business from your local Small Business Development Center. Practically everything you'd want to learn about the export business to making a business plan presentation is covered in the courses they offer. Quite a few of their programs are free. The rest cost as little as $20.

These business seminars generally discuss start-up and financing. That's the main concern of entrepreneurs today: How do I get started? And, that's what these sessions help answer for you. Usually, registration is limited to a small number of participants and have additional SBDC counselors to help you hands-on with some of the topics. Those can include developing a business plan, analyzing financial statements, controlling the business and developing a financial statement. You will find these to be informative and entertaining. The thrust of such SBDC seminars is to address the major causes of small business failures and how to spot and overcome problems.

But, there are more services available from your local SBDC than just a training seminar. There are more than fifty SBA booklets, fliers, video tapes, pamphlets and documents available, either at no charge or for a small fee, through an SBDC. For example, if your an inventor and want trademark protection, your local SBDC can provide you with the necessary patent disclosure documents. Or, you can obtain a sample invention/marketing contract to avoid being taken advantage fraudulent marketers. You can get loads of information, from buying a franchise and finding affordable health coverage to controlling your cash flow to planning your company's budget. Also, SBDCs will often analyze your financial plan to find its flaws and help you correct them.

Contact your state's SBDC office in the directory for further assistance and use of these services.

SCORE

SCORE is the acronym for the Service Corps of Retired Executives. SCORE works differently from an SBDC, but often in conjunction with them. For instance, many of the SBDC seminars, courses and workshops are conducted by SCORE. This is a non-profit organization also funded by the Small Business Administration and receives about $2 million annually, with which to operate its offices.

SCORE is composed of retired professionals and help act as counselors to launch your business idea or help expand it. Nationwide there are 750 SCORE offices staffed by more than 13,000 volunteers. On average, a typical SCORE counselor has about 35 years of business experience.

Contacting a SCORE counselor is not a one-time visit. He or she will stay with you and help guide you through the pitfalls of starting up and staying in business. Often, SCORE will try to match you up with someone who is familiar with your business. Such "connections" are invaluable to a business startup.

One familiar theme about the country at SCORE seminars is STARTING RIGHT. If you are struggling to launch your business or just scuffling to keep yours above water, then you might consider this workshop. At it you'll learn how to plan your business, the legal structures available to you, how to keep business records, getting business insurance, learning how to do financial planning, where to find capital to finance your business, key data about licensing and taxes, and how to market your business. Contact your local SCORE office about seminar details.

SCORE not only offers training courses but personalized attention. Your SCORE counselor will help you prepare your business plan, can guide you carefully through many of the difficult steps, and may answer troubling questions you may have. Remember, these were once successful business owners in the field you are now endeavoring to break into. They have volunteered their breadth of expertise and knowledge to assist your business. It's something worth taking advantage of.

Got a question? Ask your SCORE counselor. Contact the SCORE nearest you from the directory that follows the SBDC directory. If your city is not included in this directly, contact SCORE's national headquarters for a nearby location:

National SCORE Office
1825 Connecticut Avenue NW
Washington, DC 20009
Telephone: (202) 653-6279

OR

Small Business Administration
Office of Business Development
409 3rd Street SW
Washington, DC 20416
Telephone: (202) 205-7414

OR

THE SBA ANSWER DESK (1-800-827-5722)
can direct you to nearby SCORE and SBDC offices.

SMALL BUSINESS DEVELOPMENT CENTERS DIRECTORY

Alabama
John Sandefur
State Director
Alabama SBDC Consortium
University of Alabama at Birmingham
Medical Towers Building
1717 11th Avenue, Suite 419
Birmingham, AL 35294
PHONE: (205) 934-7260
FAX: (205) 934-7645

Alaska
Jan Fredericks
State Director
Alaska Small Business Development Center
University of Alaska Anchorage
430 W. Seventh Avenue, Suite 110
Anchorage, AK 99501
PHONE: (907) 274-7232
FAX: (907) 274-9524

Arizona
Dave Smith
State Director
Arizona SBDC Network
9215 N. Black Canyon Highway
Phoenix, AZ 85021
PHONE: (602) 943-2311
FAX: (602) 371-8637

Arkansas
Paul E. McGinnis
State Director
Arkansas Small Business Development
 Center
University of Arkansas at Little Rock
100 South Main , Suite 401
Little Rock, AR 72201
PHONE: (501) 324-9043
FAX: (501) 324-9049

California
Patrick Valenzuela
Interim Director
California Small Business Development
 Center
801 K St., 17th Floor, Suite 1700
Sacramento, CA 95814
PHONE: (916) 324-5068
FAX: (916) 322-5084

Colorado
Rick Garcia
State Director
Colorado Small Business Development
 Center
Colorado Office of Business Development
1625 Broadway, Suite 1710
Denver, CO 80202
PHONE: (303) 892-3809
FAX: (303) 892-3848

Connecticut
John P. O'Connor
State Director
Connecticut Small Business Development
 Center
University of Connecticut
368 Fairfield Road, U-41, Rm 422
Storrs, CT 06269-2041
PHONE: (203) 486-4135
FAX: (203) 486-1576

Delaware
Linda L. Fayerweather
State Director
Delaware Small Business Development
 Center
University of Delaware
Purnell Hall, Suite 005
Newark, DE 19716-2711
PHONE: (302) 831-2747
FAX: (302) 831-1423

District of Columbia
Nancy A. Flake
State Director
District of Columbia SBDC
Howard University
6th and Fairmont St. N.W., Room 128
Washington, DC 20059
PHONE: (202) 806-1550
FAX: (202) 806-1777

Florida
Jerry G. Cartwright
State Director
Florida Small Business Development Center
 Network
University of West Florida
Building 76, Rm 231
Pensacola, FL 32514
PHONE: (904) 474-3016
FAX: (904) 474-2030

Georgia
Hank Logan
State Director
Georgia Small Business Development
 Center
University of Georgia
Chicopee Complex, 1180 East Broad Street
Athens, GA 30602-5412
PHONE: (706) 542-5760
FAX: (706) 542-6776

Hawaii
Janet M. Nye
State Director
Hawaii Small Business Development Center
 Network
523 W. Lanikaula Street
Hilo, HI 96720
PHONE: (808) 933-3515
FAX: (808) 933-3683

Idaho
Ronald R. Hall (Ron)
State Director
Idaho Small Business Development Center
Boise State University
1910 University Drive
Boise, ID 83725
PHONE: (208) 385-1640
FAX: (208) 385-3877

Illinois
Jeff Mitchell
State Director
Illinois Small Business Development Center
Department of Commerce & Community
 Affairs
620 East Adams St., 6th Floor
Springfield, IL 62701
PHONE: (217) 524-5856
FAX: (217) 785-6328

Indiana
Stephen G. Thrash (Steve)
Executive Director
Indiana Small Business Development
 Centers
Economic Development Council
One North Capitol, Suite 420
Indianapolis, IN 46204
PHONE: (317) 264-6871
FAX: (317) 264-3102

Iowa
Ronald A. Manning (Ron)
State Director
Iowa Small Business Development Center
Iowa State University
137 Lynn Avenue
Ames, IA 50010
PHONE: (515) 292-6351
FAX: (515) 292-0020

Kansas
Thomas H. Hull (Tom)
State Director
Kansas Small Business Development
 Centers
Wichita State University
1845 Fairmount
Wichita, KS 67260-0148
PHONE: (316) 689-3193
FAX: (316) 689-3647

Kentucky
Janet S. Holloway
State Director
Kentucky Small Business Development
 Center
Center for Business & Economics Building
225 Business & Economics Building
University of Kentucky
Lexington, KY 40506-0034
PHONE: (606) 257-7668
FAX: (606) 258-1907

Louisiana
John P. Baker
State Director
Louisiana Small Business Development
 Center
Northeast Louisiana University
College of Business Administration
700 University Avenue
Monroe, LA 71209-6435
PHONE: (318) 342-5506
FAX: (318) 342-5510

Maine
Charles Davis
State Director
Maine Small Business Development Center
University of Southern Maine
96 Falmouth Street
Portland, ME 04103
PHONE: (207) 780-4420
FAX: (207) 780-4810

Maryland
Woodrow McCutchen
State Director
Maryland Small Business Development
 Center
Dept. of Economic & Employment Development
217 East Redwood Street, 10th Floor
Baltimore, MD 21202
PHONE: (410) 333-6996
FAX: (410) 333-6609

Massachusetts
John F. Ciccarelli
State Director
Massachusetts Small Business Development
 Center
University of Massachusetts-Amherst
Room 205, School of Management
Amherst, MA 01003
PHONE: (413) 545-6301
FAX: (413) 545-1273

Michigan
Norman J. Schlafmann (Norm)
State Director
Michigan Small Business Development
 Center
2727 Second Avenue
Detroit, MI 48201
PHONE: (313) 577-4848
FAX: (313) 577-4222

Minnesota
Randall Olson (Randy)
State Director
Minnesota Small Business Development
 Center
Department of Trade & Economic
 Development
150 East Kellogg Blvd., 900 American
 Center Bldg.
St. Paul, MN 55101
PHONE: (612) 297-5770
FAX: (612) 296-1290

Mississippi
Raleigh H. Byars
Executive Director
Mississippi Small Business Development
 Center
University of Mississippi
Old Chemistry Building, Suite 216
University, MS 38677
PHONE: (601) 232-5001
FAX: (601) 232-5650

Missouri
Max E. Summers
State Director
Missouri Small Business Development
 Center
University of Missouri
300 University Place
Columbia, MO 65211
PHONE: (314) 882-0344
FAX: (314) 884-4297

Montana
Evan McKinney
State Director
Montana Small Business Development
 Center
Montana Department of Commerce
1424 Ninth Avenue
Helena, MT 59620
PHONE: (406) 444-4780
FAX: (406) 444-2808

Nebraska
Robert E. Bernier (Bob)
State Director
Nebraska Business Development Center
University of Nebraska at Omaha
60th & Dodge Sts., CBA Room 407
Omaha, NE 68182
PHONE: (402) 554-2521
FAX: (404) 554-3747

Nevada
Sam Males
State Director
Nevada Small Business Development Center
University of Nevada, Reno
College of Business Administration-032
Room 411
Reno, NV 89557-0100
PHONE: (702) 784-1717
FAX: (702) 784-4337

New Hampshire
Helen M. Goodman
State Director
New Hampshire Small Business
 Development Center
University of New Hampshire
108 McConnell Hall
Durham, NH 03824
PHONE: (603) 862-2200
FAX: (603) 862-4468

New Jersey
Brenda Hopper
State Director
New Jersey Small Business Development
 Center
Rutgers University Graduate School of
Management
180 University Avenue
Newark, NJ 07102
PHONE: (201) 648-5950
FAX: (201) 648-1110

New Mexico
Randy W. Grissom
State Director
New Mexico Small Business Development
 Center
Santa Fe Community College
P.O. Box 4187
Santa Fe, NM 87502-4187
PHONE: (505) 438-1362
FAX: (505) 438-1237

New York
James L. King (Jim)
State Director
New York Small Business Development
 Center
State University of New York
SUNY Central Plaza, S-523
Albany, NY 12246
PHONE: (518) 443-5398
FAX: (518) 465-4992

North Carolina
Scott R. Daugherty
Executive Director
North Carolina Small Business
 Development Center
University of North Carolina
4509 Creedmore Road, Suite 201
Raleigh, NC 27612
PHONE: (919) 571-4154
FAX: (919) 571-4161

North Dakota
Walter Kearns (Wally)
State Director
North Dakota Small Business Development
 Center
University of North Dakota
118 Gamble Hall, UND, Box 7308
Grand Fork, ND 58202
PHONE: (707) 777-3700
FAX: (701) 777-5099

Ohio
Holly Schick
State Director
Ohio Small Business Development Center
77 South High Street
P.O. Box 1001
Columbus, OH 43226
PHONE: (614) 466-2711
FAX: (614) 466-0829

Oklahoma
Grady L. Pennington
State Director
Oklahoma Small Business Development
 Center
Southeastern Oklahoma State University
P.O. Box 2584, Station A
Durant, OK 74701
PHONE: (405) 924-0277
FAX: (405) 924-7071

Oregon
Edward Cutler, Ph.D. (Sandy)
State Director
Oregon Small Business Development Center
Lane Community College
99 West 10th Avenue, Suite 216
Eugene, OR 97401
PHONE: (503) 726-2250
FAX: (503) 345-6006

Pennsylvania
Gregory L. Higgins (Greg)
State Director
Pennsylvania Small Business Development
 Center
The Wharton School, University of
 Pennsylvania
444 Vance Hall,
3733 Spruce Street
Philadelphia, PA 19104-6374
PHONE: (215) 898-1219
FAX: (215) 573-2135

Puerto Rico
Jose M. Romaguera
Executive Director
Puerto Rico Small Business Development
 Center
University of Puerto Rico
P.O. Box 5253 College Station
Mayaguez, PR 00681
PHONE: (809) 834-3590
FAX: (809) 834-3790

Rhode Island
Douglas H. Jobling (Doug)
State Director
Rhode Island Small Business Development
 Center
Bryant College
150 Douglas Pike
Smithfield, RI 02917
PHONE: (401) 232-6111
FAX: (401) 232-6416

South Carolina
John M. Lenti
State Director
Small Business Development Center
University of South Carolina
1710 College Street
Columbia, SC 29208
PHONE: (803) 777-4907
FAX: (803) 777-4403

South Dakota
Donald D. Greenfield (Don)
State Director
South Dakota Small Business Development
 Center
University of South Dakota
414 East Clark
Vermillion, SD 57069
PHONE: (605) 677-5272
FAX: (605) 677-5427

Tennessee
Kenneth J. Burns (Ken)
State Director
Tennessee Small Business Development
 Center
Memphis State University
Bldg. 1, South Campus
Memphis, TN 38152
PHONE: (901) 678-2500
FAX: (901) 678-4072

Texas-Dallas
Ms. Marty Jones
Region Director
North Texas-Dallas SBDC
Bill J. Priest Institute for Economic
 Development
1402 Corinth Street
Dallas, TX 75215
PHONE: (2414) 565-5833
FAX: (214) 565-5857

Texas-Houston
Betsy J. Gatewood
Regional Director
Univ. of Houston SBDC
University of Houston
601 Jefferson, Suite 2330
Houston, TX 77002
PHONE: (713) 752-8444
FAX: (713) 752-8484

Texas-Lubbock
Craig Bean
Region Director
N.W. Texas Small Business Development
 Center
Texas Tech University
2579 S. Loop 289, Suite 114
Lubbock, TX 79423
PHONE: (806) 745-3973
FAX: (806) 745-6207

Texas-San Antonio
Robert M. McKinley (Bob)
Regional Director
UTSA South Texas Border SBDC
UTSA Downtown Center
801 South Bowie Street
San Antonio, TX 78205
PHONE: (512) 224-0791
FAX: (512) 222-9834

Utah
David A. Nimkin
Executive Director
Utah Small Business Development Center
102 West 500 South, Suite 315
Salt Lake City , UT 84101
PHONE: (801) 581-7905
FAX: (801) 581-7814

Vermont
Norris A. Elliott
State Director
Vermont Small Business Development
 Center
Suite 13 One Blair Park
Williston, VT 05495-9404
PHONE: (802) 878-0181
FAX: (802) 878-0245

Virgin Islands
Soloman S. Kabuka
State Director
UVI Small Business Development Center
University of the Virgin Islands
P.O. Box 1087
St. Thomas, VI 00804
PHONE: (809) 776-3206
FAX: (809) 775-3756

Virginia
Dr. Robert D. Smith (Bob)
State Director
Virginia Small Business Development
 Center
1021 East Cary Street, 11th Floor
Richmond, VA 23219
PHONE: (804) 371-8253
FAX: (804) 371-8185

Washington
Lyle M. Anderson
State Director
Washington Small Business Development
 Center
Washington State University
245 Todd Hall
Pullman, WA 99164-4727
PHONE: (509) 335-1576
FAX: (509) 335-0949

West Virginia
Eloise Jack
State Director
West Virginia Small Business Development
 Center
GOCID
1115 Virginia Street East
Charleston, WV 25301
PHONE: (304) 348-2960
FAX: (304) 558-0127

Wisconsin
William Pinkovitz (Bill)
State Director
Wisconsin Small Business Development
 Center
University of Wisconsin
432 North Lake Street, Room 423
Madison, WI 53706
PHONE: (608) 263-7794
FAX: (608) 262-3878

Wyoming
Jim Glover
State Director
WSBDC/State Network Office
111 West Second, Suite 416
Casper, WY 82601
PHONE: (307) 235-4825
FAX: (307) 473-7243

Associate Members
Anne Hope
Director
St. Mary's University Business Development
 Center
Suite 58, 201 Brownlow Avenue
Dartmouth, Nova Scotia
Canada, B3B 1W2
PHONE: (902) 468-2992
FAX: (902) 468-3894

Legislative Counsel
Allen Neece
Thomas Cator (Tom)
Neece, Cator, Barnicle & Associates
1050 17th Street, N.W. Suite 810
Washington, DC 20036
PHONE: (202) 223-8607
FAX: (202) 223-8608

Project Consultant
Warren Purdy
Marketing Services Associates
P.O. Box 8781
Portland, ME 04103
PHONE: (207) 780-4866
FAX: (207) 780-4810

Membership Services Office
Mike May
Membership Services Director
ASBDC
1313 Farnam, Suite 132
Omaha, NE 68182-0472
PHONE: (402) 595-2387
FAX: (402) 595-2388

SBDC Connection
Tim Dixon
Acting Director
SBDC Connection
Small Business Development Center
University of Georgia
Chicopee Complex
1180 East Broad Street
Athens, GA 30602
PHONE: (800) 633-6450
FAX: (706) 542-6776
     (706) 542-2737

7.

SMALL BUSINESS INVESTMENT COMPANIES
****

Since 1958, when Congress passed the Small Business Investment Act, government has worked with private investors to supply equity capital, long-term loans and management assistance to qualifying small businesses. SBICs are private investment companies that use a combination their own capital and government funds to help fund small businesses. An SBIC must be licensed by the SBA to qualify for long-term government-backed loans, which are, in turn, lent out to your business.

When an SBIC borrows money from the SBA to lend it out to your business, it does so for profit-making purposes. While one SBIC may wish to invest in your business as a partner, another might make a straight loan. Some do both. But, because SBICs are a hybrid of private and government money, they must abide by the rules and regulations set by the SBA. Small businesses that are at least 51 percent owned by socially or economically disadvantaged persons, for example, can receive preferential assistance from Specialized SBICs, also known as Section 301 (d) SBICs or Minority Enterprise Small Business Investment Companies (MESBICs). MESBICs were created in 1969, during the turmoil of the civil rights movement, to serve only those small businesses that qualify as per the above stipulation.

SBICs, since their inception, have invested more than $9 billion to over 65,000 businesses. Because an SBIC is also investing its own money, along with government money, into the venture, their track record is better than the national average, as measured by increases in assets, sales, profits and new employment.

SBICs are not limited to specific types of investments. Each have their specialties and preferences for industry categories. Some pursue small businesses launching a new product or service. Others may only invest in companies where that SBIC's management is familiar with that product or service field. Contact as many different SBICs as possible to determine whether there is interest from them in investing in your product or service. There is not set industry preference for an SBIC.

Because SBICs are overseen by the Small Business Administration, the same rules apply as with the SBA. The SBA defines a small company as one with net worth of $6 million or less and its average net income of less than $2 million for the preceding two years. This suffices for most readers; however, if you are in an industry where these standards are too low, there are alternative size standards available, such as an employment standard or amount of annual sales. In any event, please discuss any questions you may have, with the SBIC you contact, concerning your size and these standards.

CONTACTING A SMALL BUSINESS INVESTMENT COMPANY

If you wish to participate in a loan or joint venture with an SBIC, contact the ones nearest you first. While not always the case, they generally prefer to invest or loan money to nearby, rather than distant, businesses. Some also have offices throughout your region; others have branches nationally. It also saves in telephone calls and personal visits to select those closest to home.

Don't make your first phone call the moment you realize your till is dry. Plan in advance. An SBIC is not an automated teller machine or a fast checking cashing store. Just as you will want to investigate them, the SBIC will carefully research your business before investing a dime.

SBICs will scrutinize your business plan so a thorough presentation is required. According to SBA materials and in materials presented by SBICs, there are seven points they will need to see in your presentation. For the most part, these have been covered in Chapter 3. However, be sure your presentation follows the guidelines below and includes each of these points, as these pertain specifically to SBICs.

IDENTIFICATION
o   The name of the business as it appears on the official records of the state or community in which it operates.
o   The city, county, and state of the principal location and any branch offices or facilities.
o   The form of business organization and, if a corporation, the date and state of incorporation.

PRODUCT/SERVICE
o   A description of the business performed, including the principal products sold or services rendered.

o   A history of the general development of the products and/or services during the past five years (or since inception).
o   Information about the relative importance of each principal product or service to the volume of the business and to its profits.

PRODUCT FACILITIES AND PROPERTY
o   Description of real and physical property and adaptability to other business ventures.
o   Description of technical attributes and production facilities.

MARKETING
o   Detailed information about your business's customer base, including potential customers. Indicate the percentage of gross revenue generated by your five largest customers.
o   A marketing survey and/or economic feasibility study.
o   A description of the distribution system by which you provide products or services.

COMPETITION
o   A descriptive summary of the competitive conditions in the industry in which your business is engaged, including your concern's position relative to its largest and smallest competitors.
o   A full explanation and summary of your business's pricing policies.

MANAGEMENT
o   Brief resumes of the business's management personnel and principal owners, including their ages, education, and business experience.
o   Banking, business, and personal references for each member of the management and for the principal owners.

FINANCIAL STATEMENTS

o   Balance sheets and profit and loss statements for the last three fiscal years or from your business's inception.

o   Detailed projections of revenues, expenses, and net earnings for the coming year.

o   A statement of the amount of funding you are requesting and the time requirement for the funds.

o   The reasons for your request for funds and a description of the proposed uses.

MORE ABOUT SBICs

No set policy determines how quickly an SBIC will move in making an investment in your business. You should be able to instantly get a yes or no from an SBIC. But, then it may take weeks or months for them to completely study your business or plan before acting. Generally, an SBIC will invest more of its own money than government money in an enterprise (a MESBIC might invest less of its piggybank and use more government money). Therefore, they will give you a thorough inspection.

MESBICs have minimum loan maturities of four years. SBIC loans mature in not less than five years. Loans are generally for five to seven years although some are extended over a 20-year period.

Because an SBIC wants to generate capital gains, it will probably want to purchase some of your company stock. If it lends you funds, they may ask for rights to buy your stock at a later, prearranged date. Take it for granted they will act in their best interests -- after all, not only is much of their own money, but they also have the SBA looking over their shoulder. You're still getting a good deal when working with an SBIC. For instance, one industry study shows that for each SBIC dollar invested in a business two MORE dollars become available from commercial banks or other institutions. That kind of leverage comes in handy.

SBIC DIRECTORY

SMALL BUSINESS INVESTMENT COMPANIES - MINORITY ORIENTED

REGION I

MASSACHUSETTS

Argonauts MESBIC Corp. (The)
929 Worchester Road
Framingham, MA 01701
PHONE: (508) 820-3430

New England MESBIC, Inc.
530 Turnpike Street
North Andover, MA 01845
PHONE: (508) 688-4326

Transportation Capital Corp.
45 Newbury Street, Suite 207
Boston, MA 02116
PHONE: (617) 536-0344
(Main office in New York)

REGION II

NEW JERSEY

Capital Circulation Corp.
2035 Lemoine Avenue, 2nd Floor
Fort Lee, NJ 07024
PHONE: (301) 947-8637

Formosa Capital Corp.
1037 Route 46 East, Unite C-208
Clifton, NJ 07013
PHONE: (201) 916-0016

Rutgers Minority Investment Co.
92 New Street
Newark, NJ 07102
PHONE: (201) 648-5287

Transpac Capital Corp.
1037 Route 46 East
Clifton, NJ 07013
PHONE: (201) 470-8855

Zaitech Capital Corp.
1037 Route 46 East, Unit C-201
Clifton, NJ 07013
PHONE: (201) 365-0047

NEW YORK

American Asian Capital Corp.
130 Water Street, Suite 6-L
New York, NY 10005
PHONE: (212) 442-6880
Avdon Capital Corp.
1413 Avenue J
Brooklyn, NY 11230
PHONE: (718) 692-0950

CVC Investors & Management Corp.
210 Canal Street, Suite 607
New York, NY 10013
PHONE: (212) 964-2480

Concord Finance Corp.
221 Canal Street, Suite 204
New York, NY 10013
PHONE: (212) 233-5059

East Coast Venture Capital, Inc.
313 West 53rd Street, 3rd Floor
New York, NY 10019
PHONE: (323) 245-6460

Elk Associates Funding Corp.
600 Third Avenue, 38th Floor
New York, NY 10016
PHONE: (212) 972-8550

Empire State Capital Corp.
170 Broadway, Suite 1200
New York, NY 10038
PHONE: (212) 513-1799

Equico Capital Corp.
135 West 50th Street, 11th Floor
New York, NY 10020
PHONE: (212) 641-7650

Esquire Capital Corp.
1328 Broadway, Suite 646
New York, NY 10001
PHONE: (516) 462-6946

Exim Capital Corp.
9 East 40th Street
New York, NY 10016
PHONE: (212) 683-3375

Fair Capital Corp.
210 Canal Street, Suite 607
New York, NY 10013
PHONE: (212) 964-2480

First Pacific Capital Corp.
59-11 56th Street
Maspeth, NY 11378
PHONE: (829) 386-1895

Flushing Capital Corp.
137-80 Northern Blvd.
Flushing, NY 11354
PHONE: (718) 961-1552

Freshstart Venture Capital Corp.
313 West 53rd Street, 3rd Floor
New York, NY 10019
PHONE: (212) 265-2249

Hanham Capital Corp.
110 East 42nd Street, Room 1612
New York, NY 10017
PHONE: (212) 697-0622

Hop Chung Capital Investors, Inc.
185 Canal Street, Room 303
New York, NY 10013
PHONE: (212) 219-1777

Ibero American Investors Corp.
104 Scio Street
Rochester, NY 14604
PHONE: (716) 262-3440

Intercontinental Capital Funding Corp.
432 Park Avenue South, Suite 1307
New York, NY 10016
PHONE: (212) 689-2484

International Paper Cap. Formation, Inc.
Two Manhattanville Road
Purchase, NY 10577
PHONE: (914) 397-1578
(Main office in Tennessee)

Jardine Capital Corp.
109 Lafayette Street, Unit 204
New York, NY 10013
PHONE: (212) 941-0993

Manhattan Central Capital Corp.
1255 Broadway, Room 405
New York, NY 10001
PHONE: (212) 684-6411

Medallion Funding Corp.
205 East 42nd Street, Suite 2020
New York, NY 10017
PHONE: (212) 682-3300

Minority Equity Capital Co., Inc.
42 West 38th Street, Suite 604
New York, NY 10018
PHONE: (212) 768-4240

Monsey Capital Corp.
125 Route 59
Monsey, NY 10952
PHONE: (914) 425-2229

New Oasis Capital Corp.
114 Liberty Street, Suite 304
New York, NY 10006
PHONE: (212) 349-2804

Pan Pac Capital Corp.
121 East Industry Court
Deer Park, NY 11729
PHONE: (516) 586-7653

Pierre Funding Corp.
605 Third Avenue
New York, NY 10016
PHONE: (212) 490-9540

Situation Ventures Corp.
56-20 59th Street
Maspeth, NY 11378
PHONE: (718) 894-2000

Square Deal Venture Capital Corp.
766 North Main Street
New Square, NY 10977
PHONE: (914) 354-7917

Transportation Capital Corp.
60 East 42nd Street, Suite 3115
New York, NY 10165
PHONE: (212) 697-4885

Triad Capital Corp. of New York
960 Southern Blvd.
Bronx, NY 10459
PHONE: (212) 589-6541

Trico Venture, Inc.
1413 Avenue J
Brooklyn, NY 11230
PHONE: (718) 692-0950

Trusty Capital, Inc.
350 Fifth Avenue, Suite 2026
New York, NY 10118
PHONE: (212) 736-7653

United Capital Investment Corp.
60 East 42nd Street, Suite 1515
New York, NY 10165
PHONE: (212) 682-7210

Venture Opportunities Corp.
110 East 59th Street, 29th Floor
New York, NY 10022
PHONE: (212) 832-3737

Watchung Capital Corp.
153 Centre Street, Room 206
New York, NY 10013
PHONE: (212) 431-5427

Yusa Capital Corp.
622 Broadway
New York, NY 10012
PHONE: (212) 420-4810

Yuzary Capital Funding, Ltd.
386 Park Avenue South
Suite 1101
New York, NY 10016
PHONE: (212) 545-9011

Zenia Capital Corp.
3901 Main Street, Suite 210
Flushing, NY 11354
PHONE: (718) 461-1778

PUERTO RICO

North America Investment Corp.
P.O. Box 1831
Hato Rey Station, PR 00919
PHONE: (809) 754-6178

REGION III

D.C.

Allied Financial Services Corp.
1666 K Street N.W., Suite 901
Washington, DC 20006
PHONE: (202) 331-1112

Broadcast Capital, Inc.
1771 N Street N.W., Suite 421.
Washington, DC 20036
PHONE: (202) 429-5393

Consumers United Capital Corp.
2100 M Street N.W.
Washington, DC 20037
PHONE: (202) 872-5262

Fulcrum Venture Capital Corp.
2021 K Street N.W., Suite 210
Washington, DC 20006
PHONE: (202) 833-9580

Minority Broadcast Investment Corp.
1200 18th Street N.W.
Suite 705
Washington, DC 20036
PHONE: (202) 293-1166

MARYLAND

Security Financial & Investment Corp.
7720 Wisconsin Avenue, Suite 207
Bethesda, MD 20814
PHONE: (301) 951-4288

Syncom Capital Corp.
8401 Colesville Road, #300
Silver Spring, MD 20910
PHONE: (301) 608-3207

PENNSYLVANIA

Alliance Enterprise Corp.
1801 Market Street, 3rd Floor
Philadelphia, PA 19103
PHONE: (215) 977-3925

Greater Philadelphia Venture Capital Corp.,
Inc.
920 Lewis Tower Building
225 South 15th Street
Philadelphia, PA 19102
PHONE: (215) 732-3415

Salween Financial Services, Inc.
228 North Pottstown Pike
Exton, PA 19341
PHONE: (215) 524-1880

VIRGINIA

Continental SBIC
4141 North Henderson Road
Suite 8
Arlington, VA 22203
PHONE: (703) 527-5200

East West United Financial Co.
815 West Broad Street
Falls Church, VA 22046
PHONE: (703) 237-7200

REGION IV

ALABAMA

Alabama Capital Corp.
16 Midtown Park East
Mobile, AL 36606
PHONE: (205) 476-0700

Alabama Small Business Investment Co.
1732 5th Avenue North
Birmingham, AL 35203
PHONE: (205) 324-5234

FJC Growth Capital Corp.
200 West Court Square, Suite 750
Huntsville, AL 35801
PHONE: (205) 922-2918

FLORIDA

Allied Financial Services Corp.
Executive Office Center, Suite 305
2770 North Indian River Blvd.
Vero Beach, FL 32960
PHONE: (407) 778-5556
(Main office in D.C.)

Business Assistance Center-MESBIC, Inc.
6600 N.W. 27th Avenue
Miami, FL 33247
PHONE: (305) 693-5919

Pro-Med Investment Corp.
AmeriFirst Bank Building, 2nd Floor S.
18301 Biscayne Blvd.
N. Miami Beach, FL 33160
PHONE: (305) 933-5858
(Main office in Texas)

Venture Group, Inc.
5433 Buffalo Avenue
Jacksonville, FL 32208
PHONE: (904) 353-7313

GEORGIA

First Growth Capital, Inc.
4630 Chambers Road
Macon, GA 31206
PHONE: (912) 781-7131

Renaissance Capital Corp.
161 Spring Street, N.W.
Suite 815
Atlanta, GA 30303
PHONE: (404) 658-9061

KENTUCKY

Equal Opportunity Finance, Inc.
420 Hurstbourne Lane, Suite 201
Louisville, KY 40222
PHONE: (502) 423-1943

MISSISSIPPI

Sun-Delta Capital Access Center, Inc.
819 Main Street
Greenville, MS 38701
PHONE: (601) 335-5291

TENNESSEE

Chicakasaw Capital Corp.
67 Madison Avenue
Memphis, TN 38147
PHONE: (901) 523-6404

International Paper Capital Formation, Inc.
6400 Poplar Avenue
Memphis, TN 38197
PHONE: (901) 763-6282

Tennessee Equity Capital Corp.
1102 Stonewall Jackson Court
Nashville, TN 37220
PHONE: (615) 373-4502

Tennessee Venture Capital Corp.
P.O. Box 3001
Nashville, TN 37219
PHONE: (615) 244-6935

Valley Capital Corp.
100 W. Martin Luther King Blvd.
Chattanooga, TN 37402
PHONE: (615) 265-1557

West Tennessee Venture Capital Corp.
P.O. Box 300
Memphis, TN 38101
PHONE: (901) 527-6091

REGION V

ILLINOIS

Amoco Venture Capital Co.
200 East Randolph Drive
Mail Code 3905A
Chicago, IL 60601
PHONE: (312) 856-6523

Chicago Community Ventures, Inc.
25 East Washington Blvd.
Suite 2015
Chicago, IL 60603
PHONE: (312) 726-6084

Combined Fund, Inc. (The)
915 East Hyde Park Blvd.
Chicago, IL 60615
PHONE: (312) 363-0300

Neighborhood Fund, Inc. (The)
1950 East 71st Street
Chicago, IL 60649
PHONE: (312) 753-5670

Peterson Finance & Investment Co.
3300 West Peterson Avenue
Suite A
Chicago, IL 60659
PHONE: (312) 539-0502

Tower Ventures, Inc.
Sears Tower, BSC 43-50
Chicago, IL 60684
PHONE: (312) 875-0571

MICHIGAN

Dearborn Capital Corp.
P.O. Box 1729
Dearborn, MI 48121
PHONE: (313) 337-8577

Metro-Detroit Investment Co.
30777 Northwestern Highway
Suite 300
Farmington Hill, MI 48018
PHONE: (313) 851-6300

Motor Enterprises, Inc.
General Motors Building/Room 15-134
3044 West Grand Blvd.
Detroit, MI 48202
PHONE: (313) 556-4273

Mutual Investment Co, Inc.
21415 Civic Center Drive
Mark Plaza Building, Suite 217
Southfield, MI 48076
PHONE: (313) 357-2020

MINNESOTA

Capital Dimensions Ventures Fund, Inc.
Two Appletree Square, Suite 335
Minneapolis, MN 55425
PHONE: (612) 854-3007

Milestone Growth Fund, Inc.
2021 East Hennepin Avenue
Suite 155
Minneapolis, MN 55413
PHONE: (612) 378-9363

OHIO

Cactus Capital Company
870 High Street, Suite 216
Worthington, OH 43085
PHONE: (614) 436-4060

Center City MESBIC, Inc.
40 South Main Street
Dayton, OH 45402
PHONE: (513) 461-6164

Rubber City Capital Corp.
1144 East Market Street
Akron, OH 44316
PHONE: (216) 796-9167

WISCONSIN

Future Value Ventures, Inc.
250 East Wisconsin Avenue
Suite 1875
Milwaukee, WI 53202
PHONE: (414) 278-0377

REGION VI

ARKANSAS

Capital Management Services, Inc.
1910 North Grant Street
Suite 200
Little Rock, AR 72207
PHONE: (501) 664-8613

Power Ventures, Inc.
829 Highway 270 North
Malvern, AR 72104
PHONE: (501) 332-3695

LOUISIANA

SCDF Investment Corp.
P.O. Box 3885
Lafayette, LA 70502
PHONE: (318) 232-3769

TEXAS

Chen's Financial Group, Inc.
6671 Southwest Freeway, Suite 505
Houston, TX 77074
PHONE: (713) 772-8868

Evergreen Capital Co., Inc.
6161 Savoy Drive, Suite 1225
Houston, TX 77036
PHONE: (713) 789-0388

MESBIC Financial Corp. of Houston
811 Rusk, Suite 201
Houston, TX 77002
PHONE: (713) 228-8321

MESBIC Ventures, Inc.
12655 N. Central Expressway
Suite 710
Dallas, TX 75243
PHONE: (214) 991-1597

Minority Enterprise Funding, Inc.
17300 El Camino Real, Suite 107-B
Houston, TX 77058
PHONE: (713) 488-4919

North Texas MESBIC, Inc.
Box 832673
Richardson, TX 75083
PHONE: (214) 991-8060

Pro-Med Investment Corp.
17772 Preston Road, Suite 101
Dallas, TX 75252
PHONE: (214) 380-0044

United Oriental Capital Corp.
908 Town & Country Blvd.
Suite 310
Houston, TX 77024
PHONE: (713) 461-3909

REGION IX

CALIFORNIA

ABC Capital Corp.
27 North Mentor Avenue
Pasadena, CA 91106
PHONE: (818) 355-3577

Allied Business Investors, Inc.
428 South Atlantic Blvd., Suite 201
Monterey Park, CA 91754
PHONE: (818) 289-0186

Ally Finance Corp.
9100 Wilshire Blvd., Suite 408
Beverly HIlls, CA 90212
PHONE: (213) 550-8100

Asian American Capital Corp.
1251 West Tennyson Road
Suite 4
Hayward, CA 94544
PHONE: (415) 887-6888

Astar Capital Corp.
429 South Euclid Avenue, Suite B
Anaheim, CA 92802
PHONE: (714) 490-1149

Bentley Capital
592 Vallejo Street, Suite 2
San Francisco, CA 94133
PHONE: (415) 2362-2868

Best Finance Corp.
4929 West Wilshire Blvd.
Suite 407
Los Angeles, CA 90010
PHONE: (213) 937-1636

Calfsafe Capital Corp.
245 East Main Street, Suite 107
Alhambra, CA 91801
PHONE: (818) 289-3400

Charterway Investment Corp.
222 South Hill Street, Suite 800
Los Angeles, CA 90012
PHONE: (213) 687-8539

Continental Investors, Inc.
8781 Seaspray Drive
Huntington Beach, CA 92646
PHONE: (714) 964-5207

Equitable Capital Corp.
855 Sansome Street
San Francisco, CA 94111
PHONE: (415) 434-4114

Far East Capital Corp.
123 South Figueroa Street
Los Angeles, CA 90012
PHONE: (213) 253-0599

First American Capital Funding, Inc.
10840 Warner Avenue, Suite 202
Fountain Valley, CA 92708
PHONE: (714) 965-7190

Helio Capital, Inc.
One Wilshire Building
624 South Grand Avenue, Suite 2700
Los Angeles, CA 90017
PHONE: (213) 721-8053

Branch Office
6263 Randolf Street
Commerce, CA 90040
PHONE: (213) 728-6637

LaiLai Capital Corp.
223 East Garvey Avenue, Suite 228
Monterey, CA 91754
PHONE: (818) 288-0704

Magna Pacific Investments
700 North Central Avenue, Suite 245
Glendale, CA 91203
PHONE: (818) 547-0809

Myriad Capital, Inc.
328 South Atlantic Blvd., Suite 200A
Monterey Park, CA 91754
PHONE: (818) 570-4548

New Kukje Investment Co.
3670 Wilshire Blvd., Suite 418
Los Angeles, CA 90010
Phone: (213) 389-8679

Opportunity Capital Corp.
39650 Liberty Street, Suite 425
Fremont, CA 94538
PHONE: (415) 651-4412

Positive Enterprises, Inc.
1166 Post Street, Suite 200-S6
San Francisco, CA 94109
PHONE: (415) 885-6600

RSC Financial Corp.
P.O. Box 544
Ojai, CA 93024
PHONE: (805) 646-2925

San Joaquin Business Investment Group,
 Inc.
1900 Mariposa Mall, Suite 100
Fresno, CA 93721
PHONE: (209) 233-3580

South Bay Capital Corp.
18039 Crenshaw Blvd., Suite 203
Torrance, CA 90504
PHONE: (213) 515-1712

Vinh An Capital Investment, Inc.
9191 Bolsa Avenue, Suite 116
Westminster, CA 92683
PHONE: (714) 895-3218

Western General Capital Corp.
13701 Riverside Drive, Suite 328
Sherman Oaks, CA 91423

HAWAII

Pacific Venture Capital, Ltd.
222 South Vineyard Street
PH1
Honolulu, HI 96813
PHONE: (808) 521-6502

DIRECTORY

SMALL BUSINESS INVESTMENT COMPANIES

ALABAMA

FIC Growth Capitol Corp. (SSBIC)
200 West Court Square, #750
Huntsville, AL 35801
PHONE: (205) 922-2918
FAX: (205) 922-2909

First SBIC of Alabama
16 Midtown Park East
Mobile, AL 36606
PHONE: (205) 476-0700

ARIZONA

First Commerce and Loan, LP
2806 North Camino Prin.
Tucson, AZ 85715
PHONE: (602) 298-2500
FAX: (602) 745-6112

Valley National Investors, Inc.
201 North Central, #900
Phoenix, AZ 85004
PHONE: (602) 261-1577
FAX: (602) 261-1734

ARKANSAS

Capital Management Services, Inc.
1910 N. Grant, #200
Little Rock, AR 72207
PHONE: (501) 664-8613

Power Ventures, Inc. (SSBIC)
829 Highway 270 North
P.O. Box 518
Malvern, AR 72104
PHONE: (501) 332-3695
FAX: (501-337-4393

Southern Ventures, Inc.
605 Main Street, #202
Arkadelphia, AR 71923
PHONE: (501) 246-9627
FAX: (501) 246-2182

CALIFORNIA

BankAmerica Capital Corp.
(formerly First SBIC of CA/Security Pacific
  Capital Corp.)
650 Town Center Drive, 17th Floor
Costa Mesa, CA 92626
PHONE: (714) 556-1964
FAX: (714) 546-8021

Branch Office
2400 Sand Hill Road, #101
Menlo Park, CA 94025
PHONE: (415) 424-8011
FAX: (415) 324-6830

Branch Office
Pasadena Office
650 Town Center Drive, 17th Floor
Costa Mesa, CA 92626
PHONE: (818) 304-3451
FAX: (818) 440-9931

Bank America Ventures, Inc.
c/o BankAmerica Capital Corp.
555 California Street, 12th Floor
San Francisco, CA 94104
PHONE: (415) 933-3001
FAX: (415) 622-4714

Bentley Capital (SSBIC)
592 Vallejo Streeet, #2
San Francisco, CA 94133
PHONE: (415) 398-8209
FAX: (415) 398-8209

Continental Investors, Inc. (SSBIC)
8781 Seaspray Drive
Huntington Beach, CA 92646
PHONE: (714) 964-5207
FAX: (415) 963-3785

DSC Ventures IL LP
20111 Stevens Creek Blvd., #130
Cupertino, CA 95014
PHONE: (408) 252-3800
FAX: (408) 252-0527

Far East Capital Corp. (SSBIC)
123 S. Figueroa Street
Los Angeles, CA 90012
PHONE: (213) 253-0563
FAX: (213) 253-0566

First American Capital Funding, Inc. (SSBIC)
10840 Warner Avenue, #202
Fountain Valley, CA 92708
PHONE: (714) 965-7190
FAX: (714) 965-7193

First SBIC of California
(See BankAmerica Capital Corp.)

Helio Capital, Inc. (SSBIC)
624 S. Grand Avenue,, #2700
Los Angeles, CA 90017
PHONE: (213) 721-8053
FAX: (213) 622-3582

Opportunity Capital Corp. (SSBIC)
39650 Liberty Street, #425
Fremont, CA 94538
PHONE: (510) 651-4412
FAX: (510) 651-4415

San Joaquin Business Investment Group (SSBIC)
1900 Mariposa Mall, #100
Fresno, CA 93721
PHONE: (209) 233-3580
FAX: (209) 233-3709

San Joaquin Capital Corp.
P.O. Box 2538
Bakersfield, CA 93303
PHONE: (805) 323-7581
FAX: (805) 323-7365

Security Pacific Capital Corp.
(See BankAmerica Capital Corp.)

Sundance Venture Partners, LP
10600 N. De Anza Blvd., #215
Cupertino, CA 95014
PHONE: (408) 257-8100
FAX: (408) 257-8111

Branch Office
Sunwestern Investment Group
12520 High Bluff Drive, #265
San Diego, CA 92130
PHONE: (619) 259-8100
FAX: (619) 259-0470
(Main office in Texas)

VK Capital Company
50 California Street, 24th Floor
San Francisco, CA 94111
PHONE: (415) 391-5600
FAX: (415) 397-2744

CONNECTICUT

Capital Resource Co. of Connecticut, LP
2558 Albany Avenue
West Hartford, CT 06117
PHONE: (203) 3236-4336
FAX: (203) 232-8161

Financial Opportunities, Inc.
174 South Road
Enfield, CT 06082
PHONE: (203) 741-9727
FAX: (203) 741-9786

First New England Capital LP
255 Main Street
Hartford, CT 06103
PHONE: (203) 728-5200
FAX: (203) 549-2528

RFE Capital Partners, LP
36 Grove Street
New Canaan, CT 06840
PHONE: (203) 966-2800
FAX: (203) 966-3109

Small Business Investment Co. of Connecticut
965 White Plains Road
Trumbull, CT 06611-4502
PHONE: (203) 261-0011
FAX: (203) 452-9699

DISTRICT OF COLUMBIA

Allied Capital Corp.
1666 K Street N.W., #901
Washington, DC 20006
PHONE: (202) 331-1112
FAX: (202) 659-2053
(Allied Financial Services Corp. (SSBIC) ,
Allied Investment Corp. and Allied Investment
Corp. II under Allied Capital Corp. management)

Legacy Fund (The
1400 34th Street N.W.
Washington, DC 20007
PHONE: (202) 659-1100
FAX: (202) 342-7474

FLORIDA

Florida Capital Ventures, Ltd.
111 E. Madison Street, #2650
Tampa, FL 33602
PHONE: (813) 229-2294
FAX: (813) 229-2028

J & D Financial Corp.
12747 Biscayne Blvd.
N. Miami, FL 33181
PHONE: (305) 893-0300
FAX: (305) 891-2338

Quantum Capital Partners, Ltd.
4400 Northeast 25th Avenue
Ft. Lauderdale, FL 33308
PHONE: (305) 776-1133

Venture Groupe, Inc. (SSBIC)
5433 Buffalo Avenue
Jacksonville, FL 32208
PHONE: (904) 353-7313

GEORGIA

North Riverside Capital Corp.
50 Technology Park/Atlanta
Norcross, GA 30092
PHONE: (404) 446-5556
FAX: (404) 446-8627

Renaissance Capital Corp. (SSBIC)
161 Spring Street N.W., #815
Atlanta, GA 30303
PHONE: (404) 658-9061
FAX: (404) 658-9064

HAWAII

Bancorp Hawaii SBIC, Inc.
P.O. Box 2900 (22T)
Honolulu, HI 96846
PHONE: (808) 537-8012
FAX: (808) 521-7602

Pacific Venture Capital, Ltd. (SSBIC)
222 South Vineyard Street, #PH-1
Honolulu, HI 96813-2445
PHONE: (808) 521-6502
FAX: (808) 521-6541

ILLINOIS

Alpha Capital Venture Partners, LP
Three First National Plaza, #1400
Chicago, IL 60602
PHONE: (312) 372-1556
FAX: (312) 726-3690

Amoco Venture Capital Co. (SSBIC)
200 E. Randolph Drive-MC 3905A
Chicago, IL 60601
PHONE: (312) 856-6523
FAX: (312) 856-3060

Chicago Community Ventures, Inc. (SSBIC)
25 East Washington Street, #2015
Chicago, IL 60603
PHONE: (312) 726-6084
FAX: (312) 726-0167

Continental Illinois Venture Corp.
231 South LaSalle Street
Chicago, IL 60697
PHONE: (312) 828-7483
FAX: (312) 987-0887

First Capital Corp. of Chicago
Three First National Plaza, #1330
Chicago, IL 60670
PHONE: (312) 732-5400
FAX: (312) 732-4098

Heller Equity Capital Corp.
500 West Monroe Street
Chicago, IL 60661
PHONE: (312) 441-7200
FAX: (312) 441-7378

Tower Ventures, Inc. (SSBIC)
Sears Tower, BSC 23-27
Chicago, IL 60684
PHONE: (312) 875-0583
FAX: (312) 906-0164

Walnut Capital Corp.
Two North LaSalle Street, #2410
Chicago, IL 60602
PHONE: (312) 346-2033
FAX: (312) 346-2033

INDIANA

Circle Ventures, Inc.
26 North Arsenal Avenue
Indianapolis, IN 46201
PHONE: (317) 636-7242
FAX: (317) 637-7581

1st Source Capital Corp.
P.O. Box 1602
South Bend, IN 46634
PHONE: (219) 235-2180
FAX: (219) 235-2719

IOWA

InvestAmerica Venture Group, Inc.
101 2nd Street S.E., #800
Cedar Rapids, IA 52401
PHONE: (319) 363-8249
FAX: (319) 363-9683

KANSAS

Kansas Venture Capital, Inc.
6700 Antioch Plaza, #460
Overland Park, KS 66204
PHONE: (913) 262-7117
FAX: (913) 262-3509

KENTUCKY

Equal Opportunity Finance, Inc. (SSBIC)
420 S. Hurstbourne Pkwy., #201
Louisville, KY 40222-8002
PHONE: (502) 423-1943
FAX: (502) 423-1945

LOUISIANA

Premier Venture Capital Corp.
451 Florida Street
Baton Rouge, LA 70801
PHONE: (504) 389-4421
FAX: (504) 332-4299

MASSACHUSETTS

BancBoston Ventures, Inc.
100 Federal Street, 31st Floor
Boston, MA 02110
PHONE: (617) 434-2442
FAX: (617) 434-1383

LRF Capital LP
189 Wells Avenue, #4
Newton, MA 02159
PHONE: (617) 965-4100
FAX: (617) 964-5318

Media/Communications Partners
75 State Street, #2500
Boston, MA 02109
PHONE: (617) 345-7200
FAX: (617) 345-7201
(Advent Atlantic Captial Co. LP, Avent Industrial Capital Co. LP, Advent V Capital Co. LP, Chestnut St. Partners Inc., Chestnut Capital International II LP and Mezzanine Capital Corp. are all under Media/Communications Partners and TA Communications management)

Branch Office
Norwest Venture Capital
50 Milk Street, 20th Floor
Boston, MA 02109-5097
PHONE: (617) 426-9143
FAX: (617) 426-5294
(Main office in Minnesota)

Pioneer Ventures LP
60 State Street
Boston, MA 02109
PHONE: (617) 742-7825
FAX: (617) 742-7315

Southern Berkshire Investment Corp.
P.O. Box 669
Sheffield, MA 01257
PHONE: (413) 229-3106
FAX: (413) 229-8857

MICHIGAN

Mutual Investment Co., Inc. (SSBIC)
21415 Civic Center Drive, #217
Southfield, MI 48076
PHONE: (313) 357-2020

White Pines Corp.
2929 Plymouth Road, #210
Ann Arbor, MI 48105
PHONE: (313) 747-9401
FAX: (313) 747-9704

MINNESOTA

Milestone Growth Fund, Inc. (SSBIC)
2021 E. Hennepin Avenue, #155
Minneapolis, MN 55413
PHONE: (612) 378-9363
FAX: (612) 378-9361

Northland Capital Venture Partnership
613 Missabe Building
277 West First Street
Duluth, MN 55802
PHONE: (218) 772-0545
FAX: (218) 722-7241

Norwest Venture Capital
2800 Piper Jaffray Tower
222 South Ninth Street
Minneapolis, MN 55402-3388
PHONE: (612) 667-1650
FAX: (612) 667-1660
(Norwest Venture Partners and Norwest Equity
Partners IV under same management)

Shared Ventures, Inc.
6550 York Avenue S., #419
Minneapolis, MN 55435
PHONE: (612) 925-3411
FAX: (612) 925-4054

MISSOURI

Bankers Capital Corp.
3100 Gillham Road
Kansas City, MO 64109
PHONE: (816) 531-1600

Capital For Business, Inc.
11 South Meramec, #800
St. Louis, MO 63105
PHONE: (314) 746-7427
FAX: (314) 746-8739

Branch Office
InvestAmerica Venture Group, Inc.
#2724-Commerce Tower
911 Main Street
Kansas City, MO 64105
PHONE: (816) 842-0114
(Main office in Iowa)
(MorAmerica Capital Corp. under Invest
America management)

United Missouri Capital Corp.
P.O. Box 419226
Kansas City, MO 64141
PHONE: (816) 556-7333
FAX: (816) 556-7143

NEW JERSEY

Bishop Capital, LP
500 Morris Avenue
Springfield, NJ 07081
PHONE: (201) 376-0345
FAX: (201) 376-6527

Capital Circulation Corp. (SSBIC)
2035 Lemoine Avenue
Fort Lee, NJ 07024
PHONE: (201) 947-8637
FAX: (201) 585-1965

The CIT Group/Venture Capital, Inc.
650 CIT Drive
Livingston, NJ 07039
PHONE: (201) 740-5429
FAX: (201) 740-5555

ESLO Capital Corp.
212 Wright Street
Newark, NJ 07114
PHONE: (201) 242-4488
FAX: (201) 643-6062

Fortis Captial Corp.
333 Thornall Street, 2nd Floor
Edison, NJ 08837
PHONE: (908) 603-8500
FAX: (908) 603-8250

Rutgers Minority Investment Co. (SSBIC)
180 University Avenue, #300
Newark, NJ 07105
PHONE: (201) 648-5627
FAX: (201) 648-1110

Tappan Zee Capital Corp.
201 Lower Notch Road
Little Falls, NJ 07424
PHONE: (201) 256-8280
FAX: (201) 256-2841

Unicorn Ventures II, LP
6 Commerce Drive
Cranford, NJ 07016
PHONE: (908) 276-7880
FAX: (908) 276-5635

NEW MEXICO

Albuquerque Small Business Investment Co.
P.O. Box 487
Albuquerque, NM 87103
PHONE: (505) 247-4089
FAX: (505) 843-6912

NEW YORK

American Commercial Capital Corp.
310 Madison Avenue, #1304
New York, NY 10017
PHONE: (212) 986-3305
FAX: (212) 983-4585

Argentum Capital Partners
405 Lexington Avenue, 54th Floor
New York, NY 10174
PHONE: (212) 949-6262
FAX: (212) 949-8294

BT Capital Corp.
280 Park Avenue, 32 West
New York, NY 10017
PHONE: (212) 454-1903
FAX: (212) 454-2421

Barclays Capital Investors Corp.
222 Broadway
New York, NY 10038
PHONE: (212) 412-6796
FAX: (212) 412-6780

CIBC Wood Gundy Ventures
425 Lexington Avenue
New York, NY 10017
PHONE: (212) 856-3713
FAX: (212) 697-1544

CMNY Captial, LP
135 East 57th Street
New York, NY 10022
PHONE: (212) 909-8428
FAX: (212) 980-2630
(CMNY Capital II, LP under same management)

Chase Manhattan Capital Corp.
One Chase Manhattan Plaza, 7th Floor
New York, NY 10081
PHONE: (212) 552-3554
FAX: (212) 552-2807

Chemical Venture Capital Associates
270 Park Avenue, 5th Floor
New York, NY 10017-2070
PHONE: (212) 270-3220
FAX: (212) 270-2327

Citicorp Investments, Inc.
399 Park Avenue, 6th Floor
New York, NY 10043
PHONE: (212) 559-7194
FAX: (212) 758-7285

Citicorp Venture Capital, Ltd.
399 Park Avenue, 6th Floor
New York, NY 10043
PHONE: (212) 559-1118
FAX: (212) 758-7285

ELK Associates Funding Corp. (SSBIC)
600 Third Avenue, #3810
New York, NY 10016
PHONE: (212) 972-8550
FAX: (212) 983-0751

First Wall St., SBIC, LP
44 Wall Street, 24th Floor
New York, NY 10005
PHONE: (212) 495-4890
FAX: (212) 269-1438

Fortis Capital Corp.
One Penn Plaza, #1521
New York, NY 10119
PHONE: (212) 629-6900

Fundex Capital Corp.
525 Northern Blvd.
Great Neck, NY 11021
PHONE: (516) 466-8550
FAX: (516) 466-0180

Genesee Funding, Inc.
100 Corporate Woods, 3rd Floor
Rochester, NY 14623
PHONE: (716) 272-2334
FAX: (716) 272-2396

Harvest Ventures, Inc.
767 Third Avenue, 7th Floor
New York, NY 10017
PHONE: (212) 838-7776
FAX: (212) 593-0734
(ASEA-Harvest Partners II, 767 LP under
Harvest management)

IBJS Capital Corp.
One State Street
New York, NY 10004
PHONE: (212) 858-2522
FAX: (212) 858-2768

InterEquity Capital Corp.
220 Fifth Avenue, 10th Floor
New York, NY 10001
PHONE: (212) 779-2022
FAX: (212) 779-2103

J.P. Morgan Investment Corp.
60 Wall Street, 14th Floor
New York, NY 10260
PHONE: (212) 483-2323
FAX: (212) 837-5032

M & T Captial Corp.
One M & T Plaza, 12th Floor
Buffalo, NY 14240
PHONE: (716) 842-5881
FAX: (716) 842-4436

Medallion Funding Corp. (SSBIC)
205 East 42nd Street, #2020
New York, NY 10017
PHONE: (212) 682-3300
FAX: (212) 983-0351

Minority Equity Captial Co., Inc. (SSBIC)
42 West 38th Street, #604
New York, NY 10018
PHONE: (212) 768-4240
FAX: (212) 768-4246

NatWest USA Capital Corp.
175 Water Street, 25th Floor
New York, NY 10038
PHONE: (212) 602-1200
FAX: (212) 602-2149

North American Funding Corp. (SSBIC)
177 Canal Street
New York, NY 10013
PHONE: (212) 226-0080

Norwood Venture Corp.
1430 Broadway, #1607
New York, NY 10018
PHONE: (212) 869-5075
FAX: (212) 869-5331

Pan Pac Capital Corp. (SSBIC)
121 East Industry Court
Deer Park, NY 11729
PHONE: (516) 586-7653

R & R Financial Corp.
1370 Broadway, 2nd Floor
New York, NY 10018
PHONE: (212) 790-1468
FAX: (212) 356-0900

Rand SBIC, Inc.
1300 Rand Building
Buffalo, NY 14203
PHONE: (716) 853-0802
FAX: (716) 854-8480

Sterling Commercial Capital, Inc.
175 Great Neck Road, #408
Great Neck, NY 11021
PHONE: (516) 482-0781
FAX: (516) 487-0781

TLC Funding Corp.
660 White Plains Road
Tarrytown, Ny 10591
PHONE: (914) 332-5200
FAX: (914) 332-5660

Transportation Capital Corp. (SSBIC)
60 East 42nd Street, #3115
New York, Ny 10165
PHONE: (212) 697-4885
FAX: (212) 949-9836

TSG Ventures, Inc. (SSBIC)
135 West 50th Street, #1170
New York, NY 10020
PHONE: (212) 641-7650
FAX: (212) 641-7657

Vega Capital Corp.
720 White Plains Road
Scarsdale, NY 10583
PHONE: (914) 473-8550
FAX: (914) 472-8553

Venture Opportunities Corp. (SSBIC)
110 East 59th Street, 29th Floor
New York, NY 10022
PHONE: (212) 832-3737
FAX: (212) 223-4912

Winfield Capital Corp.
237 Mamaroneck Avenue
White Plains, NY 10565
PHONE: (914) 949-2600
FAX: (914) 949-7195

Zenia Capital Corp. (SSBIC)
39-01 Main Street, #210
Flushing, NY 11354
PHONE: (718) 461-1778
FAX: (718) 461-1835

OHIO

A. T. Capital Corp.
900 Euclid Avenue, T-11
Cleveland, OH 44115
PHONE: (216) 737-3080
FAX: (216) 737-3177

Center City MESBIC, Inc. (SSBIC)
1400 Miami Valley Tower
Dayton, OH 45402
PHONE: (513) 226-0457
FAX: (513) 222-7035

Clarion Capital Corp.
1801 East 9th Street, #1520
Cleveland, OH 44114
PHONE: (216) 687-1096
FAX: (216) 694-3545

National City Capital Corp.
1965 East 6th Street, #400
Cleveland, OH 44114
PHONE: (216) 575-2491
FAX: (216) 575-3355

Society Venture Capital Corp.
127 Public Square, 4th Floor
Cleveland, OH 44114-1306
PHONE: (216) 689-5776
FAX: (216) 689-3204

OKLAHOMA

Alliance Business Investment Co.
One Williams Center, #200
Tulsa, Ok 74172
PHONE: (918) 584-3581
FAX: (918) 582-3403

OREGON

Northern Pacific Capital Corp.
P.O. Box 1658
Portland, OR 97207
PHONE: (503) 241-1255
FAX: (503) 299-6653

U.S. Bancorp Capital Corp.
111 S.W. Fifth Avenue, T-15
Portland, OR 97204
PHONE: (503) 275-5860
FAX: (503) 275-7565

PENNSYLVANIA

CIP Capital, Inc.
300 Chester Field Parkway
Malvern, PA 19312
PHONE: (215) 251-5074
FAX: (215) 651-5930

Branch Office
BankAmerica Capital Corp.
P.O. Box 412
Washington, PA 15301
PHONE: (412) 223-0707
FAX: (412) 223-8290
(Main office in California)

Enterprise Venture Capital Corp. of PA
551 Main Street, #303
Johnstown, PA 15901
PHONE: (814) 535-7597
FAX: (814) 535-8677

Fidelcor Capital Corp.
123 South Broad Street, #7MBO
Philadelphia, PA 19109
PHONE: (215) 985-3722
FAX: (215) 985-7282

Greater Philadelphia Venture Captial Corp.
(SSBIC)
225 South 15th Street, #920
Philadelphia, Pa 19102
PHONE: (215) 732-1666

Meridian Capital Corp.
455 Business Center Drive, #200
Horsham, PA 19044
PHONE: (215) 957-7520
FAX: (215) 957-7521

PNC Capital Corp.
PNB Building, 19th Floor
Pittsburgh, PA 15222
PHONE: (412) 762-2238
FAX: (412) 762-7568

PUERTO RICO

North America Investment Corp. (SSBIC)
P.O. Box 1831, Hato Rey Station
San Juan, PR 00919
PHONE: (809) 751-6177/8
FAX: (809) 754-6181

RHODE ISLAND

Domestic Capital Corp.
815 Reservoir Avenue
Cranston, RI 02910
PHONE: (401) 946-3310
FAX: (401) 943-6708

Fleet Equity Partners
111 Westminster Street
Providence, RI 02903
PHONE: (401) 278-6770
FAX: (401) 278-6387
(NYSTRS/NV Capital and New England
Capital Corp. under same management)

Old Stone Capital Corp.
One Old Stone Square, 11th Floor
Providence, RI 02903
PHONE: (401) 278-2559
FAX: (401) 278-2558

Richmond Square Capital Corp.
One Richmond Square
Providence, RI 02906
PHONE: (401) 521-3000
FAX: (401) 751-3940

TENNESSEE

Chickasaw Capital Corp. (SSBIC)
67 Madison Avenue, 3rd Floor
Memphis, TN 38103
PHONE: (901) 523-6470

Valley Capital Corp. (SSBIC)
#212 Krystal Building
100 West Martin Luther King Blvd.
Chattanooga, TN 37402
PHONE: (615) 265-1557
FAX: (615) 265-0619

TEXAS

AMT Capital Ltd.
8204 Elmbrook, #101
Dallas, TX 75247
PHONE: (214) 905-9757
FAX: (214) 907-9761

Banc One Capital Partners
300 Crescent Court, #1600
Dallas, TX 75201
PHONE: (214) 979-4360
FAX: (214) 979-4355

Capital Southwest Venture Corp.
12900 Preston Road, #700
Dallas, TX 75230-1314
PHONE: (214) 233-8242
FAX: (214) 233-7362

Catalyst Fund, Ltd. (The)
3 Riverway, #770
Houston, TX 77056
PHONE: (713) 623-8133
FAX: (713) 523-0143

Enterprise Capital Corp.
515 Post Oak Blvd., #310
Houston, TX 77035
PHONE: (713) 621-9444
FAX: (713) 621-9503

HCT Capital Corp.
4916 Camp Bowie Blvd., #200
Fort Worth, TX 76107
PHONE: (817) 763-8705

Houston Partners SBIP, Ltd.
401 Louisiana
Capital Center Penthouse
Houston, TX 77002
PHONE: (713) 222-8600
FAX: (713) 222-8932

Jiffy Lube Capital Corp.
P.O. Box 2967
Houston, TX 77252
PHONE: (713) 546-4100
FAX: (713) 546-4154

MESBIC Ventures, Inc. (SSBIC)
12655 N. Central Expressway, #710
Dallas, TX 75002
PHONE: (214) 991-1597
FAX: (214) 991-6467

NationsBanc Capital Corp.
1401 Elm Street, #4764
Dallas, TX 75202
PHONE: (214) 508-5050
FAX: (214) 508-5060
(Central Texas SBI Corp. under same
management)

North Texas MESBIC, Inc. (SSBIC)
12770 Coyt Road, #525
Dallas, TX 75251
PHONE: (214) 991-8060
FAX: (214) 991-8061

SBI Capital Corp.
P.O. Box 570368
Houston, TX 77257-0368
PHONE: (713) 975-1188
FAX: (713) 975-1302

Sunwestern Investment Group
12221 Merit Drive, #1300
Dallas, TX 75251
PHONE: (214) 239-5650
FAX: (214) 701-0024
(Mapleleaf Capital, Ltd., Sunwestern Capital,
Ltd., and Sunwestern Ventures, Ltd. under
same management)

UNCO Ventures, Inc.
520 Post Oak Blvd., #130
Houston, TX 77027
PHONE: (713) 622-9595
FAX: (713) 622-9007

VIRGINIA

Dominion Capital Markets Corp.
213 Jefferson Street
Roanoke, VA 24011
PHONE: (703) 563-6156
FAX: (703) 563-7679

East West United Investment Co. (SSBIC)
815 West Broad Street
Falls Church, VA 22046
PHONE: (703) 237-7200

Ewing & Co.
801 Main Street, #401
Richmond, VA 23219
PHONE: (804) 780-2094
FAX: (804) 780-2098

Rural America Fund, Inc.
Woodland Park
2201 Cooperative Way
Herndon, VA 22071-3025
PHONE: (703) 709-6750
FAX: (703) 709-6779

Branch Office
Walnut Capital Corp.
8300 Boone Blvd., #780
Vienna, VA 22182
PHONE: (703) 448-3771
(Main office in Illinois)

WASHINGTON

Branch Office
Norwest Venture Capital
777 108th Avenue N.E., #2460
Bellevue, WA 98004-5117
PHONE: (206) 646-3444
FAX: (206) 646-3448
(Main office in Minnesota)

WISCONSIN

Banc One Venture Corp.
111 East Wisconsin Avenue
Milwaukee, WI 53202
PHONE: (414) 765-2274
FAX: (414) 765-2235

Bando McGlocklin Capital Corp.
13555 Bishops Court, #205
Brookfield, WI 53005
PHONE: (414) 784-9010
FAX: (414) 784-3426

Capital Investments, Inc.
744 North 4th Street, #540
Milwaukee, WI 53203
PHONE: (414) 273-6560
FAX: (414) 273-0530

Future Value Ventures, Inc. (SSBIC)
250 East Wisconsin Avenue, #1875
Milwaukee, WI 53202
PHONE: (414) 278-0377
FAX: (414) 278-7321

M & I Ventures Corp.
770 North Water Street
Milwaukee, WI 53202
PHONE: (414) 765-7800
FAX: (414) 765-7850

Branch Office
InvestAmerica Venture Group, Inc.
600 East Monroe Street
Milwaukee, WI 53202
PHONE: (414) 276-3839
(Main office in Iowa)

Polaris Capital Corp.
11270 West Park Place, #320
Milwaukee, WI 53224
PHONE: (414) 359-3040
FAX: (414) 359-3059

8.

FEDERAL EXPORT ASSISTANCE
****

One way to expand one's market is to reach beyond U.S. borders and sell to foreign countries. Going global opens not just new horizons, but it also doors to a great deal of federal and state government assistance. (For purposes of clarity, this chapter will only discuss federal financing and assistance programs; available state offices may be found in the directory at the end of this chapter.

There's a lot of money and customers outside of the United States. Between 1986 and 1990, U.S. merchandise exports contributed more than 40 percent to the rise in Gross National Product (GNP). In 1990 along, nearly 84 percent of the U.S. GNP growth was due to exports, which totaled a record high of $394 billion. Until you have sold your products or services overseas, as I have, you won't really grasp the enormity of the customer base available to purchase your products or services. If you were able to sell your product or service to the majority of working adults in the United States, your marketing might only reach 110 million households. But, that's just a fraction of your potential market reach.

Compare that figure to the entire global community and your current domestic marketing is reaching LESS THAN THREE PERCENT of your potential customers. Let's put that in practical terms. Say you owned a grocery store. How would you feel if you were only allowed to sell to three percent of the people in your neighborhood? Please notice that I didn't say that these were buyers,

just possible customers. Of course, out of that three percent, not all of those would-be buyers. Your grocery store would soon shrink to nothing.

Let's describe this same situation another way. Pretend you own a grocery store in a small town. For years, you only serviced local customers. Imagine a freeway built nearby and your grocery store is near the ramp. How would you feel if you were prevented from selling to anyone but your local customer base? Or, stopped from selling to customers in communities across your state. I'd be pretty upset, wouldn't you? But, that's how Americans have held themselves back in doing business, for decades, while foreign corporations have assaulted the American public with their products.

Keeping that grocery store analogy in mind, let's say you were still restricted to selling your wares to the local community AND suddenly other grocery stores popped up around your store and began selling to the additional customers provided by the new freeway and any tourists who happened to come along. Wouldn't you get a bit angry? Let's make it worse: imagine if those new grocery stores started cutting prices and slowly your existing customers started shopping at your competitors' stores. Now, wouldn't you draw the line there? No?

Well, follow it a step further. Not only are your competitors looting your customer base, through deep price discounting, but their bosses back home are financing any losses your competition might incur through tax incentives YOUR local government is providing them. In fact, your competition is being financing, not only by their government but yours as well. Still haven't thrown in the towel?

Let's add to this misery yet another problem. The competition is making a killing, living off your customer base and being financed by your friends and enemies alike. But, that's not enough. Now, your competition has manipulated the currency used to buy your services so that buying your merchandise costs more. Conversely, buying their wares costs less. Within a short period of time any profit you are making evaporates because your capacity to buy inventory to stock your shelves now costs more. Your lifestyle deteriorates. Still hanging in there?

Finally, the competition starts embarrassing you publicly to the last vestiges of your customer base. Now, even your customers wonder, quietly and aloud, whether you should be closed down completely. While this is going on, your competition cheaply buys up the real estate around your store, pays your suppliers more than you do, and thus bars you from restocking your inventory. You have nothing left to sell. You close your doors and go on some sort of government handout.

Too ugly to face? Well, that pretty much sums up the existing scenario with regards to the U.S. manufacturing climate. Too broad a paint stroke? Look ahead. It's been happening to the United States since the 1960's. If it weren't true, then why has the federal government instituted a ton of new export financing and assistance programs? Why have the states set up trade councils?

There is a war going on right now in the global economy as each country scrambles for currency by attempting to out-think and out-produce its competition. Currencies fluctuate wildly throughout every year. Price swings against a country smash its buying power and wreck the nation's overall lifestyle. Trade deficits and how to overcome them are the order of the day. And, a trade deficit can only be reduced by exporting more than a country is importing. Japan, Taiwan, the Arab nations, and several Pacific Rim countries have accumulated such wealth that annual revenues alone would make Midas blush. Europe, Latin America, Africa and Asia can either be your competition or your customer base or both. There is no idle spectating from the sidelines.

For your business to survive at all into the next generation, you must export your products and services overseas and sell them effectively to a broader customer base. The rest of the world operates on that strategic plan. And, if you're not, your business will eventually shrivel and cease. At that point your best-case scenario is being bought out by a foreign competitor rather than having him squash your business like an annoying bug.

THE U.S. DEPARTMENT OF COMMERCE

The Japanese have MITI (Ministry for International Trade and Industry) and that government agency has cleverly all but co-opted the global economy to serve its country. The U.S. has the Department of Commerce. While not as powerful as MITI, the Commerce Department can still help you compete. The first step an exporter should take is to contact the local state office of your nearest U.S. Department of Commerce. Why? Because they have dozens of financing and assistance programs. Use the Department of Commerce to supply you with the ammunition necessary to win the export war. Each billion dollars in U.S. exports creates approximately 19,000 to 25,000 new jobs.

Just as the Small Business Administration (see Chapter 5) has its domestic sphere of influence, the Department of Commerce has clout to assist your overseas pursuits. There are sixty-seven Department of Commerce district and branch offices throughout the United States and Puerto Rico. They form the domestic arm of the U.S. and Foreign Commercial Service (US&FCS). These offices provide export information and professional counseling to prospective exporters. Each district office is headed by a director and supported by trade specialists and other staff. Branch offices usually have one trade specialist.

Commerce Department professionals counsel U.S. companies on the steps involved in exporting, help them assess the export potential of their products, target markets where they might sell, and locate and check out potential overseas partners. Through its worldwide network of international business experts, district offices can probably answer any question you might have or put you in touch with someone who can. Here's a sampling of the services or information your local Commerce Department district office may provide you with:

o international trade opportunities abroad,

o foreign markets for U.S. products or services,

o services to locate and evaluate overseas buyers and representatives,

o financial aid to exporters,

o international trade exhibitions,

o export documentation requirements,

o foreign economic statistics,

o U.S. export licensing and foreign nation import requirements, and

o export seminars and conferences,

o free initial consultation with an international attorney through the Export Legal Assistance Network (ELAN)

In addition, most district offices also maintain business libraries containing the latest reports and other publications of interest to exporters. Data bases at district offices provide trade leads, foreign business contacts, in-depth country market research, export-import trade statistics and other valuable information.

THE NATIONAL DATA BANK: YOUR EXPORT CONNECTION

The National Data Bank (NTDB) was established by the Omnibus Trade and Competitiveness Act of 1988 to provide "reasonable public access" to export promotion and international economic information. The NTDB is your one-stop source for the best international trade and export data from 15 federal government agencies.

The NTDB brings you this wealth of information using the latest in information technology Compact Disc-Read Only Memory (CD--ROM). Each month's disc contains the complete Data Bank and two software programs to simplify access and retrieval. You can use the NTDB CD-ROM on any IBM compatible with at least 512K of memory, and ISO 9660 (standard) CD-ROM reader, and Microsoft CD-ROM extensions (version 2.0 or higher). The monthly NTDB CD-ROM is entirely self-contained and requires no additional space on your hard drive.

For further information about the National Data Bank, write or telephone:

THE NATIONAL TRADE DATA BANK
U.S. Department of Commerce
Economics and Statistics Administration
Office of Business Analysis
HCHB Room 4885
Washington, DC 20230
(202) 377-1986

INTERNATIONAL TRADE ADMINISTRATION

At U.S. Commerce Department district and branch office you will find trade specialists who will counsel you on the steps you will need to take to export. The International Trade Administration (ITA) in Washington, a branch of the U.S. Commerce Department oversees the trade specialists in these offices. Business people call ITA "the best kept secret in Washington", because of its many and varied export services. ITA has as its chief responsibility the promotion of U.S. exports. Through each district office you have access to all assistance available from industry and country desk officers in Washington, as well as commercial officers in foreign countries where you wish to export.

These country desk officers are located in ITA's International Economic Policy unit and can provide you with excellent information on trade potential in specific countries. Every country in the world has a country desk officer assigned to it. These specialists can look at the needs of an individual U.S. firm wishing to sell in a particular country in the full context of that country's overall economy, trade policies, and political situation.

Desk officers keep up-to-date on the economic and commercial conditions in their assigned countries. Each collects information on the country's regulations, tariffs, business practices, economic and political developments, trade data and trends, market size, and growth. These desk officers keep tabs on the country's potential as a market for U.S. products, services, and investments.

Aside from export counseling ITA has the following export services available:

o Market Research on foreign countries

o Agent/Distributor Service to find you foreign representatives to sell your product overseas

o Commercial News USA, a monthly magazine, to promote your product to over 110,000 overseas agents

o Comparison Shopping that provides firms with key marketing and representative information

o Foreign Buyer Program to meet qualified foreign purchasers of your product or service

o Gold Key Service to help orient you to a country when you visit there

o Trade Opportunities Program (TOP) to provide you with current sales leads in foreign countries

o World Traders Data Report to evaluate potential trading partners

o Overseas Catalog and Video-Catalog Shows to expose your product abroad without a personal visit there

o Overseas Trade Missions to meet with foreign business and government officials

o Overseas Trade Fairs to meet potential customers face to face and to also evaluate competition o Matchmaker Events to match you with a representative or prospective joint-venture/licensee partner during an overseas visit

o Trade Information Center for information on all federal government export assistance programs

o The Export Yellow Pages available free at ITA district offices

U.S. EXPORT-IMPORT BANK

The Export-Import Bank (Eximbank) is an independent U.S. government agency. Its mission is to provide loans, guarantees and insurance to finance the purchase of U.S. goods and services in foreign countries.

For example, Eximbank finances a wide variety of American environment exports ranging from engineering services to the completion of the feasibility study for a combined-cycle power plant, to design and construction services for a large public sector waste-water treatment facility, to pollution control equipment and to clean, energy-efficient technologies for industrial and manufacturing companies in the private sector. Since 1979, Eximbank has supported over 40 renewable energy projects around the world, representing $1.5 billion in U.S. goods and services.

Open for business in 145 countries, Eximbank provides most of its financing support to developing countries. There are only two basic requirements for obtaining Eximbank financing. First, the product or service being financed must be manufactured or originate in and be exported from, the United States. Second, there must be a reasonable assurance of repayment.

Eximbank does not give preferential treatment to any U.S. product, company or industry, nor does it set aside specific sums of money in support of certain countries or regions. Instead, Eximbank responds to specific requests for financing from foreign buyers and American exporters. In 1991, Eximbank supported a total of nearly $12 billion in guarantees, loans and insurance to finance U.S. exports to 129 countries. Over the past 58 years, Eximbank has helped finance more than $220 billion in U.S. exports.

Eximbank offers the following programs:

o Preliminary Commitment Financing

o Working Capital Guarantees

o Export Loan Guarantees

o Direct Loans

o Intermediary Export Loans

o New-to-Export Insurance Policies

o Umbrella Insurance Policies

o Bank Letter of Credit Insurance Policy

o Financial Institution Buyer Credit Insurance Policies

o Short-Term and Medium Single-Buyer and Multi-Buyer Insurance Policies

o Lease Insurance Policies

Because there can be risks in selling overseas Eximbank has undertaken a major effort to reach more small business exporters. Eximbank works to reduce risks for your small business exporting needs. Recently, Eximbank has begun providing better financing facilities and services to small business exporters, increasing the value of these facilities and services and authorizing greater funding to support small business exports.

Good news for west coast exporters. Eximbank has established a west coast office to serve exporters in California, Arizona, Nevada, Oregon, Washington and Idaho. For program information, counseling and training support, write or call:

WEST COAST OFFICE
EXPORT-IMPORT BANK OF THE UNITED STATES
Suite 9103
11000 Wilshire Boulevard
Los Angeles, California 90024
Telephone: (310) 575-7425
Fax: (310) 575-7428

Eximbank loan working capital loan guarantees cover 100 percent of the principal interest on working capital loans extended by commercial lenders to eligible U.S. exporters. The program assists small businesses in obtaining crucial working capital to fund their export activities. These loans my be used for pre-export activities such as the purchase of inventory, raw materials, the manufacture of a product, or marketing. Eximbank requires the working capital loan to be secured with inventory of exportable goods, accounts receivable, or by other appropriate collateral.

Eximbank provides to two types of loans:

a) Direct loans to foreign buyers of U.S. exports and
b) intermediary loans to fund responsible parties that extend loans to foreign buyers of U.S. capital and quasi-capital goods and related services.

Direct loans of any size and long-term loans to intermediaries (more than $10 million OR over 7 years repayment) are offered at the lowest interest rate permitted under the current international arrangement for the market and term. Medium-term intermediary loans (less than $10 million AND 7 years) are structured as "standby" loan commitments. The intermediary may borrow against the remaining undis-

bursed loan at any time during the term of the underlying debt obligation.

Eximbank's guarantees provides repayment protection for private sector loans to creditworthy buyers of U.S. capital equipment and related services. The guarantee is available alone or may be combined with an intermediary loan. Most guarantees provide comprehensive coverage of both political and commercial risks, but political-risks-only coverage is available. The guarantee covers 100 percent of principal and interest.

Repayment term guidelines for Eximbank--supported financing are as follows for capital goods sales:

Contract Value	Maximum Term
$75,000 or less	2 years
$75,001 - $150,000	3 years
$150,000 - $300,000	4 years
$300,001 and over	5-10 years

Loans for projects and large product acquisitions, such as aircraft, are eligible for longer terms while lower unit value items such as automobiles and appliances receive shorter terms.

Eximbank has begun City/State cooperative ventures to give potential exporters local access to Eximbank programs, saving them the time and cost of travel to Washington, DC. Potential borrowers are assisted by area residents trained in Eximbank programs and familiar with local business and economic conditions. This allows Eximbank to service more small business exporters better. At this writing City/State Eximbank programs were operating in 19 states, 2 cities and the Commonwealth of Puerto Rico (see directory at the end of this chapter for local contact address and telephone numbers). For additional details about the City/State program, contact Eximbank's Marketing Division (202) 566-4490.

For further information from Eximbank, telephone their EXPORT FINANCING HOTLINE:

Toll-Free: 1-800-424-5201
Telephone: (202) 566-4423
Electronic Bulletin Board: (202) 566-4490

You may also write to:

U.S. Export-Import Bank
811 Vermont Avenue N.W.
Washington, DC 20571

SMALL BUSINESS ADMINISTRATION

The Small Business Administration has important business programs for exporters. Many were covered in Chapter 5 but this section calls for additional details on two of the programs with regards to exporting.

The International Trade Loan Program helps small businesses engaged in or prepared to engage in international trade. Loans are made through lending institutions under the U.S. Small Business Administration's (SBA) Guaranty Loan Program. As with the 7(a) Loan Guaranty Program strict guidelines must be followed. However, there are two additional requirements for borrowers.

a) You must demonstrate in what way your business is adversely affected by import competition. This is done with financial statements and narrative describing how directly competitive imported products have caused a decline in your firm's competitive position, i.e. reductions in sales, production, profitability and/or underutilization of capacity; and,
b) Your business plan must persuade the SBA who the loan proceeds will significantly expand existing export markets or develop new export markets.

The plan should include a profit and loss projection and a narrative rationale.

The SBA can guarantee up to $1.25 million, less the amount of SBA's guaranteed portion of other loans outstanding to the borrower under the SBA's regular lending program. The guaranteed portion of loans for facilities and equipment is limited to $1 million, and the SBA's share of loans is limited to $250,000. The working capital portion of this loan will be administered according to the provisions of the SBA's Export Revolving Line of Credit (ERLC). Only collateral located in the United States (including its territories and possessions) will be acceptable under this program. Maturities of loans for facilities or equipment may extend to the 25-year maximum applicable to most SBA programs. But, the working capital portion of loans, under ERLC provisions, have a three year provision.

To help small businesses obtain short-term financing to sell their products and services abroad, the SBA created the Export Revolving Line of Credit Program (ERLC), which was mentioned above. This program guarantees repayment to a lender in the event an exporter defaults. By reducing a lender's risks, the ERLC provides incentive for lenders to finance small business exporters' working capital needs. The ERLC only protects the lender from default by the exporter, not the exporter if a foreign buyer should default. Lenders and exporters must determine whether foreign receivables need credit risk protection.

ERLC funding can be used only to finance labor and materials needed for manufacturing, to purchase goods or services for export, to develop foreign markets or to finance foreign accounts receivable. If the primary purpose is to develop or penetrate foreign markets, a traditional SBA 7(a) guaranteed loan may be more appropriate.

Applicants can have other SBA loans in addition to an ERLC, but the SBA cannot guarantee more than $750,000 in loans to any one borrower, unless it is through the International Trade Loan Program. However, you can increase the loan guarantee by securing a co-guaranty from the Export-Import Bank (see previous section in this chapter).

ERLC loan maturity is based on the applicant's business cycle, but cannot -- together with renewals -- exceed 36 months. Maturities are usually for one year with options to renew at the discretion of SBA and the lender. Requests for renewals must be made through the lender not more than 45 nor less than 30 days prior to maturity. Lenders may charge a commitment fee (equal to 0.25 percent of the loan amount with a $200 minimum) but it cannot be levied until after the SBA approves the ERLC. Initial guaranty fees must be paid by the lender but may be charged to the borrower upon approval of the ERLC by the SBA. Additional guaranty fees are paid by the borrower at the time a renewal is requested.

Applicants must submit a cash flow projection showing anticipated monthly activity and cash balances for the entire term of the ERLC. After the SBA approves the ERLC, borrowers must also submit monthly progress reports to the lender. You should request that your lender seek SBA participation only when the lender won't make a direct loan. The same provision found under a normal SBA Loan Guarantee program applies here as well. Collateral for an ERLC is required under the same stipulations as an International Trade Loan.

Another SBA exporting assistance program is the Export Legal Assistance Network (ELAN). As with the U.S Commerce Department offices, your local SBA office can direct you to an international trade attorney for a free initial consultation. This is done through an agreement with the Federal Bar Association and your local Commerce or SBA district office.

For further export assistance, contact your local SBA office at the end of Chapter 5 or telephone the Small Business Administration's Answer Desk: 1-800-U-ASK-SBA. You may also write or call to the SBA International Trade Office:

U.S. SMALL BUSINESS ADMINISTRATION
Office of International Trade
6th Floor
409 - 3rd Street S.W.
Washington, DC 20416
(202) 205- 6720

DEPARTMENT OF AGRICULTURE

The export promotion efforts of the U.S. Department of Agriculture (USDA) are centered in the Foreign Agricultural Service (FAS). FAS provides financial support for U.S. agricultural exports through the Commodity Credit Corporation. Firms may obtain information on financial programs and other programs availability from the USDA by writing or telephoning:

U.S. DEPARTMENT OF AGRICULTURE
FOREIGN AGRICULTURAL SERVICE
Room 4649-S
Washington, DC 20250-1000
(202) 382-9498

DEPARTMENT OF STATE

The State Department and Foreign Service professionals provide businesses, including producers of services and farm products, with unique insights into problems of foreign marketing and doing business abroad. They direct administration of Commerce Department programs for exporters in more than 82 countries where no Commerce personnel are available and they will brief prospective exporters and investors on political and economic conditions in foreign countries.

When you require this information in making a planning or project decision, please contact a State Department country desk officer and specify the country you wish to find out about. Telephone: (202) 647-1942

You may also contact the Bureau of Economic and Business Affairs by writing to:

Office of Commercial, Legislative and Public
 Affairs
Bureau of Economic and Business Affairs
U.S Department of State
Room 6822
Washington, DC 20520

OVERSEAS PRIVATE INVESTMENT CORPORATION

The Overseas Private Investment Company (OPIC) has its roots in the Marshall Plan, which was established in 1948 to channel U.S. economic and technical strength into the rebuilding of war-torn Europe. At the time, the plan offered insurance against the risk of getting stuck with a non-convertible currency. By the 1950's the Marshall Plan's insurance aspect was restructured to supplement direct aid programs for the world's developing countries, and expanded to include protection against expropriation and war risk.

In 1961, under President Kennedy, the insurance program was transferred to the newly established Agency for International Development (AID), whose main purpose was government-to-government assistance, i.e. foreign aid. Coverage was broadened to include revolution and insurrection insurance and AID was given authority for a loan guaranty program for U.S. investors.

By late 1969 the business aspect of the original investment plan had been obscured and the government decided to create a new agency that would be responsive to private business and provide effective support for American investors entering the international marketplace. OPIC began operations in 1971 to serve that purpose.

Today, OPIC is an independent, financially self-supporting corporation, fully owned by the U.S. Government with offices in Washington, DC. It provides political risk insurance and financing to American companies interested in doing business in developing and emerging countries. OPIC facilitates private investments in less developed nations. It also offers specialized insurance and financing services for U.S. service contractors and exporters operating in the developing world.

OPIC is a profit-making agency and has recorded a positive net income for every year of operations. It has long since returned its initial start-up appropriation of $106 million to the U.S. Treasury and its reserves stood at $1.6 billion at the end of fiscal year 1991. It conducts its operations in line with standard principles of prudent business and risk management. It annually has more than $2.4 billion in insurance assistance available.

Aside from high risk insurance, which was a key purpose of its predecessors, OPIC makes available medium to long-term financing for overseas investment projects through loan guarantees and/or direct loans. OPIC's all-risk loan guarantees, issued to U.S. lending institutions on behalf of U.S. investors, typically range from $2 million to $25, but can be as large as $50 million. An estimated $185 million are available through its loan guarantee program. OPIC's direct loans, reserved for overseas investment projects involving small and medium-sized companies, range from $500,000 to $6 million. OPIC will participate in up to 50 percent of the total project cost for a new venture and up to 75 percent of the total cost of an expansion. An estimated $23 million are available annually for direct loans.

For more information on other OPIC programs, such as its fee-based advisory services, regular investment missions, the OPIC Opportunity Bank, the Investment Information Service, and/or its periodic seminars and conferences, please contact:

Overseas Private Investment Corporation
 (OPIC)
Suite 400
1100 New York Avenue NW
Washington, DC 20527
Toll-Free: (800) 424-OPIC
Telephone: (202) 336-8799
            (202) 336-8680

AGENCY FOR INTERNATIONAL DEVELOPMENT

The Agency for International Development (AID) administers most of the foreign economic assistance programs for the federal government. AID offers U.S. exporters the chance to compete in the sales of goods or services supplied to foreign countries under loans and grants made by AID. If you export commodities, your business can benefit from two programs: the Commodity Import Programs and Project Procurements. Under both of these programs the countries purchase directly from you.

For more information about these programs, write or telephone the Office of Business Relations:

Commodities . . . . (703) 875-1590
Technical Assistance
Service . . . . (703) 875-1551

Agency for International Development (AID/
 USDBU)
Department of State Building
320 21st Street N.W.
Washington, DC 20523

TRADE AND DEVELOPMENT PROGRAM

The Trade and Development Program (TDP) is an independent U.S. Government agency that primarily funds feasibility studies for public/private sector projects in developing countries. TDP finances studies mainly in large-scale energy generation and conservation, infrastructure, mineral development, agribusiness, and basic industrial facilities. One major purpose of TDP funding is to help U.S. engineering/planning firms win major consulting contracts overseas. For additional information please write or call:

Trade and Development Program
Room 304, SA 16
Department of State
Washington, DC 20523-1602
(703) 875-4357

U.S. TRAVEL AND TOURISM ADMINISTRATION

The U.S. Travel and Tourism Administration (USTTA) promotes U.S. export earnings through trade in tourism. Ask any high profile tourist city or resort about the importance of foreign travellers. USTTA stimulate foreign demand, helps to remove barriers, increases the number of small- and medium-size travel businesses, provides timely data, and forms marketing partnerships with private industry and state and local governments.

U.S. destinations and suppliers of tourism services interested in the overseas promotion of travel to the United States should telephone USTTA at (202) 377-4003.

NATIONAL INSTITUTE OF STANDARDS AND TECHNOLOGY (NIST)

If you wish to find out about foreign standards and certification systems or other foreign requirements for your products or services, then NIST. This government agency maintains a GATT Hotline with a recorded announcement on the latest notifications of proposed foreign regulations that may affect your export business. To listen to this recorded announcement, updated weekly, telephone: (301) 975-4041. Call or write NIST at:

NCNSI
National Institute of Standards and Technology (NIST)
Administration Building
Gaithersburg, Maryland 20899

Telephone: (301) 975-4040
                              (301) 975-4038
                              (301) 975-4036

There are two non-governmental organizations that can assist you with additional information. Telephone:

American National Standards Institute: (212) 642-4900
American National Metric Council: (202) 857-0474

U.S. TRADE REPRESENTATIVE

The Office of the U.S. Trade Representative (USTR) is an agency of the Executive Office of the President. The USTR is the President's chief advisor on trade, coordinates trade policy within the U.S. government, is the principal negotiator of trade agreements, and is responsible for administering some of the laws to prevent unfair trade practices.

To file a complaint about unfair trade practices or seek relief because of them, contact the USTR's office at:

Office of the United States Trade Represen tative
600 17th Street, N.W.
Washington, DC 20501
(202) 395-3230

TRADE PROMOTION COORDINATING COMMITTEE

Finally, in order to assist U.S. firms when competing against foreign behemoth trade ministries, that subsidize and sponsor their nation's penetration into another country's marketplace, President Bush created the Trade Promotion Coordinating Committee (TPCC) for the purpose of bringing together all the resources of the federal government to serve Americans in exporting their products and services overseas.

The TPCC conducts export conferences, coordinates trade events and missions that cross-cut federal agencies, and operates an export information center that can help exporters find the right federal program to suit their needs. The TPCC's Trade Information Center was designed to assist and guide exporters through the assistance programs of 19 federal agencies. This committee is chaired by the Secretary of Commerce and is comprised of:

U.S. Department of State
U.S. Department of the Treasury
U.S. Department of Defense
U.S. Department of the Interior
U.S. Department of Agriculture
U.S. Department of Commerce
U.S. Department of Labor
U.S. Department of Transportation
U.S. Department of Energy
Office of Management and Budget
Office of the U.S. Trade Representative

Council of Economic Advisers
Environmental Protection Agency
Small Business Administration
Export-Import Bank of the United States
Overseas Private Investment Corporation
U.S. Trade and Development Program
U.S. Information Agency

If you haven't found the desired solution or financing by this point from the preceding programs in this chapter, or if you are a new-to-export company, then please call the Trade Information Center's hotline:

1-800-USA-TRADE

PRIVATE SECTOR INVOLVEMENT

Additional assistance can be obtained at little or no cost from private, multinational corporations and non-profit organizations.

AT&T, DHL, Delta Airlines, KPMG Peat Marwick, Berlitz and other multinational corporations have underwritten and operate THE EXPORT HOTLINE, a fax information retrieval system designed to help U.S. companies learn more about worldwide markets. The database contains up-to-date information on 50 key industries in 68 foreign countries. You can access this free service from anywhere in the United States 24 hours a day. Call 1-800-USA-XPORT to receive your free starter kit. Once you've filed your application, you can obtain information as often as you'd like. The information is free and you only pay for the cost of the fax transmission to your fax machine.

The Small Business Foundation of America operates the Export Opportunity Hotline. You can find out who needs your product, how to find them, how to ship it and more. They'll provide you with low-cost access to comprehensive research reports on over 140 countries and introduce you to over 1,000 new business opportunities and sales leads daily. This hotline service is operated with the cooperation of a number of trade associations, government agencies and private companies. Call or write them:

THE SMALL BUSINESS FOUNDATION OF AMERICA
1155 15th Street NW
Washington, DC 20005
1-800-243-7232
(202) 223-1103

Other private sector organizations that focus on export and trade issues are:

o   U.S. Council for International
         Business
         1212 Avenue of the Americas
         New York, New York 10036
         (212) 354-4480

o   American Association of Exporters
         and Importers
         30th Floor
         11 West 42nd Street
         New York, New York 10036
         (212) 944-2230

o   Federation of International Trade
         Associations
         1851 Alexander Bell Drive
         Reston, Virginia 22091
         (703) 391-6108

o   World Trade Centers Association
         Suite 7701
         One World Trade Center
         New York, New York 10048
         (212) 313-4600

o   International Trade Facilitation
          Council
       Suite 205
       350 Broadway
       New York, New York 10013
       (212) 925-1400

o   National Customs Brokers and
          Forwarders Association of America
       Suite 1153
       One World Trade Center
       New York, New York 10048
       (212) 432-0050

o   Export Managers Association of
          California
       Suite A761
       110 East 9th Street
       Los Angeles, California 90079
       (213) 821-1388

EXPORT ASSISTANCE DIRECTORY

For additional export assistance contact these
government offices in the directory section of
this chapter.

DIRECTORY OF FEDERAL EXPORT ASSISTANCE

A.   Department Of Commerce
B.   Small Business Administration
C.   Export-Import Bank
D.   Department of Agriculture
E.   Overseas Private Investment Corp.
F.   Department of State
G.   Department of Treasury
H.   Agency for International
          Development
I.   Office of the U.S. Trade
          Representative

A.   DEPARTMENT OF COMMERCE

THE U.S. Department of Commerce can
provide a wealth of information to exporters.
The first step an exporter
should take is to contact the nearest Department of Commerce district office, which can
help guide the exporter to the right person or
office.

Phone Area Code: 202
U.S. and Foreign Commercial Service
Office of Domestic Operations,
Room 3810 . . . 377-4767

Export Promotion Services
Office of Export Marketing Programs,
Room 1322 (trade show and trade mission
information 377-4231

Office of International Operations
Regional Directors for
Africa, Near East and South Asia
Room 1223 377-4836

East Asia and Pacific,
Room 1223 377-8422

Europe,
Room 3130 377-1599

Western Hemisphere,
Room 3130 377-2736
Fax (Europe and Western
Hemisphere) 377-3159
Fax (AnESA and EAP) 377-5179

Trade Development

Product/Service Specialists

Aerospace, Room 2130 377-2835
Automotive Affairs and Consumer Goods
Room 4324 377-0823

Basic Industries,
Room 4045 377-0614

Export Trading Company Affairs,
Room 1800 377-5131

Services,
Room 1128A 377-5261

Textiles and Apparel,
Room 3100 377-3737

International Economic Policy

Eastern Europe Business Information
Center 377-2645
Latin America/Caribbean Business
Information Center 377-0703
Gulf Reconstruction Center 377-5767

Country desk officers can provide specific country information relating to international trade. The following is a list of telephone numbers for each country's desk officer.

Country	Phone (202)
Afghanistan	377-2954
Albania	377-4915
Algeria	377-4652
Angola	377-5148
Anguilla	377-2527
Argentina	377-1548
Aruba	377-2527
ASEAN	377-3875
Antigua/Barbuda	377-2527
Australia	377-3647
Austria	377-2920
Bahamas	377-2527
Bahrain	377-5545
Baltics Republic	377-3952
Bangladesh	377-2954
Barbados	377-2527
Belgium	377-5373
Belize	377-2527
Benin	377-4388
Bermuda	377-2527
Bhutan	377-2954
Bolivia	377-2521
Botswana	377-5148
Brazil	377-3871
Brunei	377-3875
Bulgaria	377-4915
Burkina Faso	377-4388
Burma (Myanmar)	377-3875
Burundi	377-5149
Cambodia	377-3875
Cameroon	377-5149
Canada	377-3101
Cape Verde	377-4388
Caymans	377-2527
Central Africa Rep.	377-5149
Chad	377-5149
Chile	377-1548
Colombia	377-1659
Comoros	377-4564
Congo	377-5149
Costa Rica	377-2527
Cuba	377-2527
Cyprus	377-3945
Czechoslovakia	377-4915
Denmark	377-3254
D'Jibouti	377-4564
Dominica	377-2527
Dominican Rep.	377-2527
East Caribbean	377-2527
Ecuador	377-1659
Egypt	377-4441
El Salvador	377-2527
Equatorial Guinea	377-5149
Ethiopia	377-4564
European Community	377-5276
Finland	377-3254
France	377-8008
Gabon	377-5149
Gambia	377-4388
Germany	377-2435
	377-2841

Ghana	377-4388	Morocco	377-5545
Greece	377-3945	Mozambique	377-5148
Grenada	377-2527	Namibia	377-5148
Guadeloupe	377-2527	Nepal	377-2954
Guatemala	377-2527	Netherlands	377-5401
Guinea	377-4388	Netherland Antilles	377-2527
Guinea-Bissau	377-4388	New Zealand	377-3647
Guyana	377-2527	Nicaragua	377-2527
Haiti	377-2527	Niger	377-4388
Honduras	377-2527	Nigeria	377-4388
Hong Kong	377-2462	Norway	377-4414
Hungary	377-4915	Oman	377-5545
Iceland	377-3254	Pacific Islands	377-3875
India	377-2954	Pakistan	377-2954
Indonesia	377-3875	Panama	377-2527
Iran	377-5545	Paraguay	377-1548
Iraq	377-4441	People's Rep.	
Ireland	377-5401	of China	377-3583
Israel	377-4652	Peru	377-2521
Italy	377-2177	Philippines	377-3875
Ivory Coast	377-4388	Poland	377-4915
Jamaica	377-2527	Portugal	377-3945
Japan	377-2425	Puerto Rico	377-2527
Jordan	377-1860	Qatar	377-5545
Kenya	377-4564	Romania	377-2645
Korea	377-4957	Rwanda	377-5149
Kuwait	377-1860	Sao Tome & Principe	377-5149
Laos	377-3875	Saudi Arabia	377-4652
Lebanon	377-1860	Senegal	377-4388
Lesotho	377-5148	Seychelles	377-4564
Liberia	377-4388	Sierra Leone	377-4388
Libya	377-5545	Singapore	377-3875
Luxembourg	377-5373	Somalia	377-4564
Macao	377-3583	South Africa	377-5148
Madagascar	377-4564	Spain	377-4508
Malawi	377-5148	Sri Lanka	377-2954
Malaysia	377-3875	St. Barthelemy	377-2527
Maldives	377-2954	St. Kitts-Nevis	377-2527
Mali	377-4388	St. Lucia	377-2527
Malta	377-3748	St. Martin	377-2527
Martinique	377-2527	St. Vincent-Grenadines	377-2527
Mauritania	377-4564	Sudan	377-4564
Mauritius	377-4564	Suriname	377-2527
Mexico	377-4464	Swaziland	377-5148
Mongolia	377-3583	Sweden	377-4414
Montserrat	377-2527	Switzerland	377-2920

Syria	377-1860
Taiwan	377-4957
Tanzania	377-5148
Thailand	377-3875
Togo	377-4388
Trinidad & Tobago	377-2527
Tunisia	377-1860
Turkey	377-2177
Turks & Caicos Islands	377-2527
Uganda	377-4564
United Arab Emirates	377-5545
United Kingdom	377-3748
Uruguay	377-1548
USSR	377-4655
Venezuela	377-4303
Vietnam	377-3875
Virgin Islands (UK)	377-2527
Virgin Islands (US)	377-2527
Yemen, Rep. of	377-1860
Yugoslavia	377-4915
Zaire	377-5149
Zambia	377-5148
Zimbabwe	377-5148

Bureau of Export Administration

Office of Export Licensing

Exporter Counseling Division,
Room 1099
(Exporting licensing, controls,
etc.) 377-4811

Office of Antiboycott Compliance,
Room 3886 377-2381

Minority Business Development Agency

Office of Program Development
Room 5093 377-3237

B. SMALL BUSINESS ADMINISTRATION

All export programs administered through the Small Business Administration (SBA) are available through SBA field offices . More information about the programs
can be obtained through

Small Business Administration Office of
 International Trade
409 Third Street, S.W., 6th Floor
Washington, DC 20416 202-205-6720

C. EXPORT-IMPORT BANK

Export-Import Bank
811 Vermont Avenue, N.W.
Washington, DC 20571

Area Code: 202

Export Financing Hotline 566-8860

Export Trading
Company Assistance 566-8944

Engineering Division 566-8802

D. DEPARTMENT OF AGRICULTURE

U.S. Department of Agriculture
14th Street and Independence
 Avenue, S.W.
Washington, DC 20250

E. OVERSEAS PRIVATE INVESTMENT CORPORATION

Overseas Private Investment Corp.
7th Floor
1129 20th Street, N.W.
Washington, DC 20527
202-336-8680

F. DEPARTMENT OF STATE

U.S. Department of State Commercial Coordinators:

Bureau of Economic and Business Affairs
Commercial Coordinator 202-647-1942

Bureau of African Affairs
Commercial Coordinator 202-647-3503

Bureau of Inter-American Affairs
Commercial Coordinator 202-647-2066

Bureau of East Asian and Pacific Affairs
Commercial Coordinator 202-647-4835

Bureau of Near Eastern and South Asian
Commercial Coordinator 202-647-9583

Bureau of European and Canadian Affairs
Commercial Coordinator 202-647-2395

Bureau of International Communications
and Information Policy 202-647-5832

G. DEPARTMENT OF THE TREASURY

U.S. Department of The Treasury
15th Street and Pennsylvania
Avenue. N.W.
Washington, DC 20220

U.S. Customs Strategic
Investigation Division
(Exodus Command
Center) 202-927-1184

H. AGENCY FOR INTERNATIONAL DEVELOPMENT

Agency for International
Development
Department of State Building
320 21st Street, N.W.
Washington, DC 20523

I. OFFICE OF THE U.S. TRADE REPRESENTATIVE

Office of the United States Trade
Representative
Winder Building
60017th Street, N.W.
Washington, DC 20506

Area Code: 202

General Counsel 395-3150
Private Sector Liaison 395-6120
Argricultural Affairs & Commodity
Policy 395-6127
The Americas Trade Policy 395-6135
Europe & Mediterranean 395-4620
General Agreement on Tariffs &
Trade (GATT) 395-6843
Pacific, Asia &
North-South Policy 395-3430

STATE AND LOCAL SOURCES OF ASSISTANCE

ALABAMA

U.S. Department of Commerce
US & FCS District Office
3rd Floor, Berry Building
2015 2nd Avenue North
Birmingham, AL 35203
(205) 731-1331
Fax: (205) 731-0076

U.S. Small Business Administration
2121 8th Avenue, North, Suite 200
Birmingham, AL 35203-2398
(205) 731-1344
Fax: (205) 731-1404

Alabama Development Office
International Development Office
State Capitol
401 Adams Avenue
Montgomery, AL 36130
(205) 242-0400

Alabama International Trade Center
University of Alabama, Tuscaloosa
P.O. Box 870396
Tuscaloosa, AL 35487-0396
(205) 348-7621
Fax: (205) 348-6974

North Alabama International Trade Association
Madison County Courthouse, 7th Floor
Huntsville, AL 35801
(205) 532-3505
Fax: (205) 532-3704

Department of Planning & Economic Development
Madison County Courthouse, 7th Floor
Huntsville, AL 35801
(205) 532-3505
Fax: (205) 532-3704

Center for International Trade & Commerce
250 North Water Street, Suite 131
Mobile, AL 36602
(205) 433-1151
Fax: (205) 438-2711

Alabama World Trade Association
250 North Water Street, Suite 131
Mobile, AL 36602
(205) 433-3171
Fax: (205) 438-2711

Alabama Export Council
2015 2nd Avenue North, Suite 302
Birmingham, AL 35203
(205) 731-1331

Birmingham Area Chamber of Commerce
International Department
P.O. Box 10127
Birmingham, AL 35202
(205) 323-5461
Fax: (205) 324-2320

ALASKA

U.S. Department of Commerce
US & FCS District Office
World Trade Center
4021 Tudor Center Drive, Suite 319
Anchorage, AK 99508-5916
(907) 271-6237
Fax: (907) 271-6242

U.S. Small Business Administration
222 West 8th Avenue, Suite 319
Anchorage, AK 99513-7559
(907) 271-4022
Fax: (907) 271-4545

Alaska Department of Commerce
& Economic Development
International Trade Division
3601 C Street, Suite 798
Anchorage, AK 99503
(907) 561-5585
Fax: (907) 561-4557

World Trade Center Alaska/Anchorage
World Trade Center
4201 Tudor Center Drive, Suite 320
Anchorage, AK 99508-5916
(907) 561-1516
Fax: (907) 561-1541

Alaska Center for International Business
World Trade Center
4201 Tudor Center Drive, Suite 120
Anchorage, AK 99508-5916
(907) 561-2322
Fax: (907) 586-3744

Alaska Chamber of Commerce-Juneau
310 Second Street
Juneau, AK 99801
(907) 586-2322
Fax: (907) 586-3744

Alaska Chamber of Commerce-Anchorage
801 B Street, Suite 405
Anchorage, AK 99501
(907) 278-2722
Fax: (907) 278-6643

Anchorage Chamber of Commerce
437 E Street, Suite 300
Anchorage, AK 99501-2365
(907) 272-2401
Fax: (907) 272-4117

Fairbanks Chamber of Commerce
First National Center
100 Cushman Street
Fairbanks, AK 99707
(907) 452-1105

ARIZONA

U.S. Department of Commerce
US&FCS District Office
230 North First Avenue, Room 3412
Phoenix, AZ 85025
(602) 379-3285
Fax: (602) 379-4324

U.S. Small Business Administration
Central and One Thomas, Suite 800
2828 North Central Avenue
Phoenix, AZ 85004-1025
(602) 379-3732

U.S. Small Business Administration
300 West Congress, Box FB33
Tucson, AZ 85701
(602) 670-6715

Arizona Department of Commerce
International Trade & Investment Division
3800 North Central Avenue, Suite 1500
Phoenix, AZ 85012
(602) 280-1371

Foreign Trade Zone No. 48
7800 South Nogales Highway
Tucson, AZ 85706
(602) 741-1940

Arizona World Trade Association
34 West Monroe, Suite 900
Phoenix, AZ 85003
(602) 254-5521

ARKANSAS

U.S. Department of Commerce
US & FCS District Office
Room 811, Savers Building
320 West Capitol
Little Rock, AR 72201
(501) 324-5794
Fax: (501) 324-7380

U.S. Small Business Administration
Little Rock Field Office
Room 600, Savers Building
320 West Capitol
Little Rock, AR 72201
(501) 324-5871

Marketing Division
Arkansas Industrial Development Commission
1 Capitol Mall
Little Rock, AR 72201
(501) 682-7690
Fax: (501) 682-7691

The World Trade Center
c/o Marketing Division
Arkansas Industrial Development Commission
1 Capitol Mall
Little Rock, AR 72201
(501) 682-7690

Export Finance Office
Arkansas Development Finance Authority
100 South Main
Little Rock, AR 72201
(501) 682-5909

Arkansas International Center
University of Arkansas at Little Rock
2801 South University
Little Rock, AR 72204
(501) 569-3282

Mid-South International Trade Association
P.O. Box 888
100 South Main, Room 438
Little Rock, AR 72201
(501) 374-1957
Fax: (501) 375-8317

Arkansas Small Business Development
 Center
100 South Main, Room 401
Little Rock, AR 72201
(501) 324-9043

CALIFORNIA

U.S. Department of Commerce
US & FCS District Office
11000 Wilshire Blvd., Suite 9200
Los Angeles, CA 90024
(213) 575-7104
Fax: (213) 575-7220

U.S. Department of Commerce
US &F CS District Office
250 Montgomery Street, 14th Floor
San Francisco, CA 94104
(415) 705-2300
Fax: (415) 705-2299

U.S. Department of Commerce
US & FCS District Office
6363 Greenwich Drive, Suite 145
San Diego, CA 92701
(619) 557-5395
Fax: (619) 557-6176

U.S. Department of Commerce
US & FCS District Office
Suite #1, 116-A West 4th Street
Santa Ana, CA 92701
(714) 836-2461
Fax: (714) 836-2330

U.S. Department of Commerce
Bureau of Export Administration
5201 Great America Parkway, Suite 226
Santa Clara, CA 95050
(408) 748-7450
Fax: (408) 748-7470

U.S. Small Business Administration
2719 N. Air Fresno Drive
Fresno, CA 93727-1547
(209) 487-5189

U.S. Small Business Administration
330 North Brand Blvd., Suite 190
Glendale, CA 91203-2304
(213) 688-2956
Fax: (213) 894-5665

U.S. Small Business Administration
880 Front Street, Room 4-S-29
San Diego, CA 92188
(619) 557-7252

U.S. Small Business Administration
(District Office)
211 Main Street, 4th Floor
San Francisco, CA 94105-1988
(415) 744-6801

U.S. Small Business Administration
901 West Civic Center Drive, Suite 160
Santa Ana, CA 92703
(714) 836-2494
Fax: (714) 836-2528

California State World Trade Commission
1121 L Street, Suite 310
Sacramento, CA 95814
(916) 324-5511
Fax: (916) 324-5791

California State World Trade Commission
Office of Export Development
One World Trade Center, Suite 990
Long Beach, CA 90831-0990
(213) 590-5965
Fax: (213) 590-5958

California Export Finance Office
425 Market Street, Suite 2838
San Francisco, CA 94105
(415) 557-9812
Fax: (415) 557-7770

California Export Finance Office
107 South Broadway, Suite 8039
Los Angeles, CA 90012
(213) 620-2433
Fax: (213) 620-6102

California Chamber of Commerce
International Trade Department
1201 K Street, 12th Floor
P.O. Box 1736
Sacramento, CA 94111
(916) 444-6670

California Council for International Trade
700 Montgomery Street, Suite 305
San Francisco, CA 94111
(415) 788-4127

California Department of Food & Agriculture
Agriculture Export Program
1220 N Street, Room 104
Sacramento, CA 95814
(916) 322-4339
Fax: (916) 324-1681

Economic Development Corporation
  of Los Angeles County
6922 Hollywood Blvd., Suite 415
Los Angeles, CA 90028
(213) 462-5111
Fax: (213) 462-2228

Long Beach Area Chamber of Commerce
International Business Association
One World Trade Center, Suite 350
Long Beach, CA 90853
(213) 436-1251
Fax: (213) 436-7088

Century City Chamber of Commerce
International Business Council
1801 Century Park East, Suite 300
Century City, CA 90067
(213) 553-4062

Los Angeles Chamber of Commerce
International Commerce Division
404 South Bixel Street
Los Angeles, CA 90017
(213) 629-0602
Fax: (213) 629-0708

San Diego Chamber of Commerce
402 West Broadway, Suite 1000
San Diego, CA 92101
(619) 232-0124

San Francisco Chamber of Commerce
San Francisco World Trade Association
465 California Street
San Francisco, CA 94104
(415) 392-4511

The Greater Los Angeles World Trade
  Center Association
One World Trade Center, Suite 295
Long Beach, CA 90831-0295
(213) 495-7070
Fax: (213) 495-7071

Citrus College Center for International
  Trade Development
363 South Park Avenue, Suite 105
Pomona, CA 91766
(714) 629-2223
Fax: (714) 622-4217

Riverside Community College Center for
  International Trade Development
1760 Chicago Avenue, Building K
Riverside, CA 92507
(714) 276-3400

Custom Brokers & Freight Forwarders
  Association
303 World Trade Center
San Francisco, CA 94111
(415) 536-2233

Export Managers Association of California
124 East Olympic Blvd., Suite 517
Los Angeles, CA 90015
(213) 627-0634

International Marketing Association of
  Orange County
CA State Fullerton
Marketing Department
Fullerton, CA 92634
(714) 773-2223

Santa Clara Valley World
  Trade Association
P.O. Box 611208
San Jose, CA 95161
(408) 998-7000

Valley International Trade Association
(San Fernando Valley)
1323 Carmelina Avenue, Suite 214
Los Angeles, CA 90025
(213) 207-1802

World Trade Association of Orange County
1 Park Plaza, Suite 150
Irvine, CA 92714
(714) 549-8151

World Trade Association of San Diego
6363 Greenwich Drive, Suite 140
San Diego, CA 92122
(619) 453-4605

San Mateo County Economic Development
 Association
951 Mariners Island Blvd., Suite 200
San Mateo, CA 94404
(415) 345-8300
Fax: (415) 345-6896

San Jose Center for International Trade
 and Development
50 West San Fernando Street, Suite 900
San Jose, CA 95113
(408) 277-4060
Fax: (408) 277-3615

Santa Clara Chamber of Commerce
P.O. Box 387
Santa Clara, CA 95052
(408) 970-9825
Fax: (408) 970-8864

COLORADO

U.S. Department of Commerce
US & FCS District Office
World Trade Center Denver
1625 Broadway, Suite 680
Denver, CO 80202
(303) 844-3246
Fax: (303) 844-5651

U.S. Small Business Administration
U.S. Customhouse, Room 454
721 19th Street
Denver, CO 80202
(303) 844-3984

International Trade Office of Colorado
Governor's Office of Economic Development
World Trade Center Denver
1625 Broadway, Suite 680
Denver, CO 80202
(303) 892-3850

Colorado Department of Agriculture,
 Markets Division
700 Kipling
Lakewood, CO 80215
(303) 239-4114

Colorado International Capital Corporation
1981 Blake Street
Denver, CO 80202
(303) 297-2605
CO Toll Free: (800) 877-2432

Rocky Mountain World Trade Center
 Association
World Trade Center Denver
1625 Broadway, Suite 680
Denver, CO 80202
(303) 592-5760

Greater Denver Chamber of Commerce
1445 Market Street
Denver, CO 80202
(303) 534-8500

Colorado Springs Chamber of Commerce
P.O. Drawer B
Colorado Springs, CO 80901
(719) 635-1551

International Business Association
 of the Rockies
10200 West 44th Avenue, Suite 304
Wheat Ridge, CO 80033
(303) 422-7905

Export Legal Assistance Network
(303) 922-7687   Federal Bar Association
(303) 844-3984   Small Business Administration
(303) 844-3246   Department of Commerce

Note: The above network is an agreement that
allows a small firm to receive an initial, free
consultation with an attorney to discuss legal
issues and concerns relating to international
trade.

CONNECTICUT

U.S. Department of Commerce
US & FCS District Office
Federal Building, Room 610-B
450 Main Street
Hartford, CT 06103
(203) 240-3530
Fax: (203) 844-5651

U.S. Small Business Administration
33 Main Street
Hartford, CT 06106
(203) 240-4670

International Division
Department of Economic Development
865 Brook Street
Hartford, CT 06067-3405
(203) 258-4256

DELAWARE

U.S. Department of Commerce
US & FCS District Office
(See Philadelphia, PA)

U.S. Small Business Administration
920 King Street, Room 412
Wilmington, DE 19801
(302) 573-6295

Delaware Development Office
Box 1401
Dover, DE 19903
(302) 736-4271
Fax: (302) 736-5749

Delaware Department of Agriculture
2320 South DuPont Highway
Dover, DE 19901
(302) 736-4811
Fax: (302) 697-6287

Delaware State Chamber of Commerce
One Commerce Center, Suite 200
Wilmington, DE 19801
(302) 655-7221

Delaware-Eastern Pennsylvania Export
 Council
475 Allendale Road, Suite 202
King of Prussia, PA 19406
(215) 962-4980
Fax: (215) 951-7959

World Trade Center Institute (Delaware)
Dupont Building, Suite 1022
Wilmington, DE 19899
(302) 656-7905
Fax: (302) 656-2145

DISTRICT OF COLUMBIA

U.S. Department of Commerce
US & FCS Branch Office
 (See listing for Gaithersburg, MD)

World Trade Center, Washington, DC
1101 King Street, Suite 700
Alexandria, VA 22314
(703) 684-6630

Office of International Business
Government of the District of Columbia
1250 Eye Street, N.W., Suite 1003
Washington, DC 20005
(202) 727-1576

Washington/Baltimore Regional Association
1129 20th Street, N.W., Suite 202
Washington, DC 20036
(202) 861-0400

FLORIDA

U.S. Department of Commerce
US & FCS District Office
Federal Building, Suite 224
51 S.W. First Avenue
Miami, FL 33130
(305) 536-5267
Fax: (305) 536-4765

U.S. Department of Commerce
US & FCS Branch Office
c/o Clearwater Chamber of Commerce
128 North Osceola Avenue
Clearwater, FL 34615
(813) 461-0011
Fax: (813) 449-2889

U.S. Department of Commerce
US & FCS Branch Office
c/o University of Central Florida
RM 346, CEBA II
Orlando, FL 32816
(407) 648-6235

U.S. Department of Commerce
US & FCS Branch Office
Rm 401, Collins Building
107 West Gaines Street
Tallahassee, FL 32304
(904) 488-6469
Fax: (904) 487-1407

U.S. Small Business Administration
7825 Bay Meadows Way, Suite 100-B
Jacksonville, FL 32256-7504
(904) 443-1900
Fax: (904) 443-1980

U.S. Small Business Administration
1320 South Dixie Highway, Suite 501
Coral Gables, FL 33146
(305) 536-5521
Fax: (305) 536-5058

U.S. Small Business Administration
501 East Polk Street, Suite 104
Tampa, FL 33602
(813) 228-2594
Fax: (813) 228-2111

Division of International Trade
  and Development
Florida Department of Commerce
Collins Building, Room 366
Tallahassee, FL 32399-2000
(904) 488-6124
Fax: (904) 487-1407

Tampa Bay International Trade Council
P.O. Box 420
Tampa, FL 33601
(813) 228-7777
Fax: (813) 223-7899

World Trade Center Miami
One World Trade Plaza, Suite 1800
80 S.W. 8th Street
Miami, FL 33130
(305) 579-0064
Fax: (305) 536-7701

Office for Latin American Trade
Florida Department of Commerce
2701 LeJeune Road, Suite 330
Coral Gables, FL 33134
(305) 442-6921
Fax: (305) 442-6931

GEORGIA

U.S. Department of Commerce
US & FCS District Office
Plaza Square North
4360 Chamblee Dunwoody Road, #310
Atlanta, GA 30341
(404) 452-9101
Fax: (404) 452-9105

U.S. Department of Commerce
US & FCS District Office
Room A-107
120 Barnard Street
Savannah, GA 31401
(912) 944-4204
Fax: (912) 944-4241

U.S. Small Business Administration
1720 Peachtree Road, N.W., 6th Floor
Atlanta, GA 30309
(404) 347-4749
Fax: (404) 347-4745

U.S. Small Business Administration
52 North Main Street, Room 225
Statesboro, GA 30458
(912) 489-8719

Department of Industry, Trade
and Tourism
Suite 1100
285 Peachtree Center Avenue
Atlanta, GA 30303
(404) 656-3545
Fax: (404) 656-3567

International Trade Division
Division of Marketing
Department of Agriculture
19 Martin Luther King Jr Drive
Room 330
Atlanta, GA 30334
(404) 656-3740
Fax: (404) 656-9380

HAWAII

U.S. Department of Commerce
US & FCS District Office
40 Ala Moana Blvd.
P.O. Box 50026
Honolulu, HI 96850
(808) 541-1782
Fax: (808) 541-3435

U.S. Small Business Administration
2213 Federal Building
300 Ala Moana Blvd., Box 50207
Honolulu, HI 96850
(808) 541-2987

Department of Business, Economic
Development & Tourism
Business Development & Marketing Division
P.O. Box 2359
Honolulu, HI 96804
(808) 548-7719

Chamber of Commerce of Hawaii
World Trade Association
735 Bishop Street
Honolulu, HI 96813
(808) 531-4111

Economic Development Corporation
of Honolulu
1001 Bishop Street, Suite 735
Honolulu, HI 96813
(808) 545-4533

Also served by the Honolulu District Office:

AMERICAN SAMOA

Office of Development Planning
Territory of American Samoa
Pago Pago, American Samoa 96799
(684) 633-5155
Fax: (684) 633-4195

Guam Chamber of Commerce
P.O. Box 283
Agana, Guam 96910
(671) 472-6311
Fax: (671) 472-6202

COMMONWEALTH OF THE NORTH-ERN MARIANA ISLANDS

Department of Commerce & Labor
Commonwealth of the Northern Mariana
 Islands
Saipan, MP 96950
(670) 322-8711
Fax: (670) 234-7151

IDAHO

U.S. Department of Commerce
US & FCS District Office
2nd Floor, Joe R. Williams Building
700 West State Street
Boise, ID 83720
(208) 334-3857
Fax: (208) 334-2783

U.S. Small Business Administration
1020 Main Street, Suite 290
Boise, ID 83702
(208) 334-1696

Idaho Department of Commerce
International Business Division
700 West State Street, 2nd Floor
Boise, ID 83720
(208) 334-2470
Fax: (208) 334-2783

Department of Agriculture
International Marketing Division
2270 Old Penitentiary Road
P.O. Box 790
Boise, ID 83701
(208) 334-2227
Fax: (208) 334-2170

District Export Committee
Boise Area Chamber of Commerce
P.O. Box 2368
Boise, ID 83701
(208) 344-5515

ILLINOIS

U.S. Department of Commerce
US & FCS District Office
55 East Monroe Street, Room 1406
Chicago, IL 60603
(312) 353-4450
Fax: (312) 886-8025

U.S. Department of Commerce
US & FCS Branch Office
IIT-Rice Campus
201 East Loop Drive
Wheaton, IL 60187
(708) 353-4332

U.S. Department of Commerce
US & FCS Branch Office
P.O. Box 1747
515 North Court Street
Rockford, IL 61110-0247
(815) 363-4347
Fax: (815) 987-8122

U.S. Small Business Administration
Business Development Office
500 West Madison, Suite 1250
Chicago, IL 60606
(708) 353-4578

U.S. Small Business Administration/SCORE
500 West Madison, Suite 1250
Chicago, IL 60606
(708) 353-4528

U.S. Small Business Administration
511 West Capitol, Suite 302
Springfield, IL 62704
(217) 492-4416

International Business Division
IL Department of Commerce &
Community Affairs
100 West Randolph Street, Suite 3-400
Chicago, IL 60601
(312) 814-7166

Illinois Department of Agriculture
Division of Marketing & Promotion
State Fairgrounds
P.O. Box 19281
Springfield, IL 62794-9291
(217) 782-6675

Automotive Exporters Council
463 North Harlem Avenue
Oak Park, IL
(708) 524-1880

Carnets
U.S. Council for International Business
1930 Thoreau Drive, Suite 101
Schaumburg, IL 60173

Central Illinois Exporters Association
302 East John Street, Suite 202
Champaign, IL 61820
(217) 333-1465

Chicago Association of Commerce
 and Industry
World Trade Division
200 North LaSalle Street
Chicago, IL 60616
(312) 580-6928

Chicago Convention & Tourism Bureau
McCormick Place on the Lake
Chicago, IL 60616
(312) 567-8500

Chicago Council on Foreign Relations
116 South Michigan Avenue, 10th Floor
Chicago, IL 60603
(312) 726-3860

Chicago Midwest Credit Management
 Associations
315 South Northwest Highway
Park Ridge, IL 60068
(708) 696-3000

City of Chicago
Economic Development Commission
1503 Merchandise Mart
Chicago, IL 60654
(312) 744-2622

City of Chicago
Department of Economic Development
International Division
24 East Congress Parkway, 7th Floor
Chicago, IL 60605
(312) 408-7485

Custom Brokers & Freight Forwarders
 Association of Chicago, Inc.
P.O. Box 66584/AMF O'Hare
Chicago, IL 60666
(708) 678-5400

Foreign Credit Insurance Association
19 South LaSalle Street, Suite 902
Chicago, IL 60603
(312) 641-1915

Foreign Trade Zones
U.S. Customs Service
Warehouse Desk
610 South Canal Street
Chicago, IL 60607
(312) 353-5822

Illinois District Export Council
55 East Monroe Street, Room 1406
Chicago, IL 60603
(312) 353-4450

Illinois Export Council
321 North Clark Street, Suite 550
Chicago, IL 60610
(312) 793-4982

Illinois Export Development Authority
321 North Clark Street, Suite 550
Chicago, IL 60610
(312) 793-4995

Illinois International Port District
3600 East 95th Street
Chicago, IL 60617
(312) 646-4400

Illinois Manufacturers' Association
209 West Jackson Blvd., Suite 700
Chicago, IL 60606
(312) 922-6575

Illinois State Chamber of Commerce
International Trade Division
20 North Wacker Drive, Suite 1960
Chicago, IL 60606
(312) 372-7373

Illinois World Trade Center Association
321 North Clark Street, Suite 550
Chicago, IL 60610
(312) 793-4982

International Trade Association of
Greater Chicago
P.O. Box 454
Elk Grove Village, IL 60009
(708) 980-4109

International Trade Club of Chicago
203 North Wabash, Suite 1102
Chicago, IL 60601
(312) 368-9197

International Visitors Center
520 North Michigan Avenue, Suite 522
Chicago, IL 60611
(312) 645-1836

Library of International Relations
77 South Wacker Drive
Chicago, IL 60606
(312) 567-5234

Mid-America International Agri-Trade
 Council (MIATCO)
820 Davis Street, Suite 212
Evanston, IL 60201
(708) 866-7300

Overseas Sales & Marketing Association
 of America, Inc.
P.O. Box 37
Lake Bluff, IL 60044
(708) 234-1760

World Trade Council of Northern IL
515 North Court Street
Rockford, IL 61103
(815) 987-8128

INDIANA

U.S. Department of Commerce
US & FCS District Office
One North Capitol, Suite 520
Indianapolis, IN 46204-2227
(317) 226-6214
Fax: (317) 226-6139

U.S. Small Business Administration
429 North Pennsylvania Street, Suite 100
Indianapolis, IN 46204
(317) 226-7272

Indiana District Export Council
One North Capitol, Suite 520
Indianapolis, IN 46204-2227
(317) 226-6214
Fax: (317) 226-6139

Indiana Department of Commerce
International Trade Division
One North Capitol, Suite 700
Indianapolis, IN 46204-2248
(317) 232-3527

Indiana Chamber of Commerce
One North Capitol, Suite 200
Indianapolis, IN 46204-2248
(317) 264-3100

World Trade Committee
Fort Wayne Chamber of Commerce
826 Ewing Street
Fort Wayne, IN 46802
(219) 424-1435

World Trade Club of Indiana, Inc.
One North Capitol Street, Suite 200
Indianapolis, IN 46204-2248
(317) 264-3100

Tri-State World Trade Council
Old Post Office Place
100 N.W. 2nd Street, Suite 202
Evansville, IN 47708
(812) 425-8147

Michiana World Trade Club
P.O. Box 1715-A
South Bend, IN 46634
(219) 289-7323

Forum for International Professional
Services
One North Capitol, Suite 200
Indianapolis, IN 46204-2248
(317) 264-3100

Indiana-ASEAN Council, Inc.
One American Square, Box 82017
Indianapolis, IN 46282
(317) 685-1341

IOWA

U.S. Department of Commerce
US & FCS District Office
817 Federal Building
210 Walnut Street
Des Moines, IA 50309
(515) 284-4222
Fax: (515) 284-4021

U.S. Department of Commerce
US & FCS Branch Office
424 First Avenue, N.E.
Cedar Rapids, IA 52401
(319) 362-8418
Fax: (319) 398-5228

U.S. Small Business Administration
373 Collins Road, N.E.
Cedar Rapids, IA 52402
(319) 393-8630
Fax: (319) 393-7585

U.S. Small Business Administration
794 Federal Building
210 Walnut Street
Des Moines, IA 50309
(515) 284-4422
Fax: (515) 284-4572

Iowa Department of Economic Development
Bureau of International Marketing
200 East Grand Blvd.
Des Moines, IA 50309
(515) 242-4743
Fax: (515) 242-4749

Iowa Department of Agriculture
 and Land Stewardship
International Trade Bureau
Wallace Building
Des Moines, IA 50319
(515) 281-5993
Fax: (515) 242-5015

Northeast Iowa Small Business Development
770 Town Clock Plaza
Dubuque, IA 52001
(319) 588-3350
Fax: (319) 557-1591

Siouxland International Trade Association
Sioux City Chamber of Commerce
101 Pierce Street
Sioux City, IA 51101
(712) 255-7903
Fax: (712) 258-7578

Iowa-Illinois International Trade Association
Davenport Chamber of Commerce
112 East Third Street
Davenport, IA 52801
(319) 322-1706
Fax: (319) 322-2251

International Trade Bureau
Cedar Rapids Area Chamber of Commerce
424 First Avenue, N.E.
Cedar Rapids, IA 52401
(319) 398-5317
Fax: (319) 398-5228

International Traders of Iowa
P.O. Box 897
Des Moines, IA 50309
(515) 245-5284
Fax: (515) 245-5286

Northeast Iowa International Trade Council
Regional Economic Development Center
Hawkeye Institute of Technology
1501 East Orange Street
Waterloo, IA 50704
(319) 296-2320
Fax: (319) 296-2874

Top of Iowa Trade Forum
Regional Economic Development Center
North Iowa Community College
500 College Drive
Mason City, IA 50401
(515) 421-4353
Fax: (515) 424-2011

KANSAS

U.S. Department of Commerce
US & FCS Branch Office
151 North Volutsia
Wichita, KS 67214-4695
(316) 269-6160
Fax: (316) 262-5652

U.S. Small Business Administration
110 East Waterman Street
Wichita, KS 67202
(316) 269-6571

Kansas Department of Commerce
400 S.W. 8th, Suite 500
Topeka, KS 66603-3957
(913) 296-4027

International Trade Council
P.O. Box 1588
Manhattan, KS 66502
(913) 539-6799

Kansas District Export Council
c/o Sunflower Manufacturing Company
Box 628
Beloit, KS 67420
(913) 738-2261

World Trade Council of Wichita
Wichita State University
Barton School of Business, MBMT-IB
Campus Box 88
Wichita, KS 67208
(316) 689-3176

KENTUCKY

U.S. Department of Commerce
US & FCS District Office
U.S. Post Office & Courthouse
Building, Room 636-B
601 West Broadway
Louisville, KY 40202
(502) 582-5066
Fax: (502) 582-6573

U.S. Small Business Administration
600 Federal Place, Room 188
Louisville, KY 40201
(502) 582-5971

Office of International Marketing
Kentucky Cabinet for Economic Develop-
 ment
Capitol Plaza Tower, 24th Floor
Frankfort, KY 40601
(502) 564-2170

Louisville/Jefferson County Office
 for Economic Development
200 Brown & Williamson Tower
401 South Fourth Avenue
Louisville, KY 40202
(502) 625-3051

Kentucky District Export Council
601 West Broadway, Room 636-B
Louisville, KY 40202
(502) 582-5066

Kentuckiana World Commerce Council
P.O. Box 58456
Louisville, KY 40258
(502) 583-5551

Bluegrass International Trade Association
P.O. Box 24074
Lexington, KY 40524
(606) 272-6656

Northern Kentucky International
 Trade Association
7505 Sussex Drive
Florence, KY 41042
(606) 283-1885
Fax: (606) 283-8178

Kentucky World Trade Center
410 West Vine Street, Suite 290
Lexington, KY 40507
(606) 258-3139
Fax: (606) 233-0658

University of Louisville
School of Business
Louisville, KY 40292

University of Kentucky
Patterson School of Diplomacy
Lexington, KY 40506

LOUISIANA

U.S. Department of Commerce
US & FCS District Office
432 World Trade Center
2 Canal Street
New Orlean, LA 70130
(504) 589-6546
Fax: (504) 586-2337

U.S. Small Business Administration
1661 Canal Street, Suite 2000
New Orleans, LA 70114-2890
(504) 589-6685

Office of Commerce & Industry
Louisiana Department of
 Economic Development
P.O. Box 94185
Baton Rouge, LA 70804-9185
(504) 342-9232
Fax: (504) 342-5389

Chamber of Commerce/New Orleans
 and the River Region
301 Camp Street
New Orleans, LA 70130
(504) 527-6900

International Business Council
 of North Louisiana
c/o Shreveport Chamber of Commerce
P.O. Box 20074
Shreveport, LA 71120
(318) 667-2510

International Trade Center
(Small Business Administration Office)
University of New Orleans-Lakefront
 Campus
New Orleans, LA 70148
(504) 286-6978

World Trade Center of New Orleans
Executive Offices, Suite 2900
2 Canal Street
New Orleans, LA 70130
(504) 529-1601
Fax: (504) 529-1691

Le Centre International de Lafayette
P.O. Box 4017-C
Lafayette, LA 70502-4017
(318) 268-5474

Small Business Development Center
Northeast Louisiana University
Monroe, LA 71209
(318) 342-1224

MAINE

U.S. Department of Commerce
US & FCS Branch Office
77 Sewall Street
Augusta, ME 04330
(207) 622-8249
Fax: (207) 626-9156

U.S. Small Business Administration
40 Western Avenue, Room 512
August, ME 04333
(207) 622-8378

State Development House
State House, Station 59
Augusta, ME 04333
(207) 289-2656

MARYLAND

U.S. Department of Commerce
US & FCS District Office
413 U.S. Customhouse
40 South Gay Street
Baltimore, MD 21202
(301) 962-3560
Fax: (301) 962-7813

U.S. Department of Commerce
US & FCS Branch Office
c/o National Institute for
 Standards and Technology
Building 411
Gaithersburg, MD 20899
(301) 975-3904

U.S. Small Business Administration
Equitable Building
10 North Calvert Street
Baltimore, MD 21202
(301) 962-2235

Maryland International Division
World Trade Center
7th Floor
Baltimore, MD 21202
(301) 333-4295

Maryland Chamber & Economic Growth
 Associates
111 South Calvert Street, Suite 2220
Baltimore, MD 21202
(301) 837-6068

Maryland Chamber & Economic Growth
 Associates
275 West Street, Suite 400
Annapolis, MD 21401

Foundation for Manufacturing
 Excellence, Inc.
Catonsville Community College
800 South Rolling Road
Baltimore, MD 21228
(301) 455-4919

Eastern Baltimore Area Chamber of
 Commerce
2 Dunmanway
Suite 238, Dunkirk Building
Dundalk, MD 21222
(301) 282-9100

Greater Baltimore Committee
Legg Mason Tower
111 South Calvert Street, Suite 1500
Baltimore, MD 21202
(301) 727-2820

Office of Economic Development
Anne Arundel County
Arundel Center
Annapolis, MD 21401
(301) 280-1122

Office of Economic Development
Prince George's County
9200 Basil Court, Suite 200
Landover, MD 20785
(301) 386-5600

Baltimore County Economic
 Development Commission
400 Washington Avenue
Courthouse Mezzanine
Towson, MD 21204
(301) 887-8000

Office of Economic Development
Montgomery County
Executive Office Building
101 Monroe Street, Suite 1500
Rockville, MD 20850
(301) 762-6325

Howard County Office of
 Economic Development
3430 Court House Drive
Ellicott City, MD 21043
(301) 313-2900

World Trade Center Institute
401 East Pratt Street, Suite 1355
Baltimore, MD 21202
(301) 516-0022

Montgomery County High-Tech Council,
 Inc.
51 Monroe Street, Suite 1701
Rockville, MD 20850
(301) 762-6325

Maryland Small Business Development
 Center
(Central Maryland)
1414 Key Highway
Baltimore, MD 21230
(301) 234-0505

International Visitors Center
The World Trade Center, Suite 1353
Baltimore, MD 21202
(301) 837-7150

Washington/Baltimore Regional Association
1129 20th Street, N.W., Suite 202
Washington, DC 20036
(202) 861-0400

MASSACHUSETTS

U.S. Department of Commerce
US & FCS District Office
World Trade Center, Suite 307
Boston, MA 02110-2071
(617) 565-8563
Fax: (617) 565-8530

U.S. Small Business Administration
155 Federal Street, 9th Floor
Boston, MA 02110
(617) 451-2047

U.S. Small Business Administration
1550 Main Street
Springfield, MA 01103
(413) 785-0268

Massachusetts Department of Commerce
 & Development
Office of Economic Affairs
100 Cambridge Street, 13th Floor
Boston, MA 02202
(617) 727-3206

Office of International Trade
100 Cambridge Street, Suite 902
Boston, MA 02202
(617) 367-1830

Massachusetts Department of Food
 and Agriculture
100 Cambridge Street
Boston, MA 02202
(617) 727-3018

Massachusetts Port Authority (MASSPORT)
Foreign Trade Unit
World Trade Center, Suite 321
Boston, MA 02210
(617) 439-5560

International Business Center of New England
World Trade Center, Suite 323
Boston, MA 02210
(617) 439-5280

Smaller Business Association of New England, Inc.
69 Hickory Drive
Waltham, MA 02254-9117
(617) 890-9070

Associated Industries of Massachusetts
441 Stuart Street, 5th Floor
Boston, MA 02116
(617) 262-1180

Metro South Chamber of Commerce
60 School Street
Brockton, MA 02401
(508) 586-0500

Central Berkshire Chamber of Commerce
60 West Street
Pittsfield, MA 01201
(413) 499-4000

Chamber of Commerce of Attleboro Area
42 Union Street
Attleboro, MA 02703
(508) 222-0801

Fall River Area Chamber of Commerce
P.O. Box 1871
200 Pocasset Street
Fall River, MA 02722
(508) 676-8226

Greater Boston Chamber of Commerce
600 Atlantic Avenue
Boston, MA 02110
(617) 227-4500

North Central Massachusetts Chamber
 of Commerce
110 Erdman Way
Leominster, MA 01453
(508) 840-4300

Greater Gardner Chamber of Commerce
55 Lake Street
Gardner, MA 01440
(508) 1780

Greater Lawrence Chamber of Commerce
264 Essex Street
Lawrence, MA 01840
(508) 686-0900

Greater Springfield Chamber of Commerce
1350 Main Street, Third Floor
Springfield, MA 01103
(413) 787-1542

New Bedford Area Chamber of Commerce
P.O. Box G-827, 794 Purchase Street
New Bedford, MA 02742
(508) 999-5231

North Suburban Chamber of Commerce
7 Alfred Street
Woburn, MA 01801
(617) 933-3499

Metro West Chamber of Commerce
1671 Worcester Street, Suite 201
Framingham, MA 01701
(508) 879-5600

South Shore Chamber of Commerce
36 Miller Stile Road
Quincy, MA 02169
(617) 479-1111

Waltham/West Suburban Chamber of
 Commerce
500 Main Street
Waltham, MA 02154
(617) 894-4700

Watertown Chamber of Commerce
101 Walnut Street, P.O. Box 45
Watertown, MA 02272-0045
(617) 926-1017

Worcester Area Chamber of Commerce
33 Waldo Street
Worcester, MA 01608
(508) 753-2924

MICHIGAN

U.S. Department of Commerce
US & FCS District Office
1140 McNamara Building
Detroit, MI 48226
(313) 115-3650
Fax: (313) 226-3657

U.S. Department of Commerce
US & FCS Branch Office
300 Monroe Avenue, N.W., #406A
Grand Rapids, MI 49503
(616) 456-2411
Fax: (616) 456-2695

U.S. Small Business Administration
515 McNamara Building
Detroit, MI 48226
(313) 226-6075
Fax: (313) 226-4769

U.S. Small Business Administration
300 South Front
Marquette, MI 49855
(906) 225-1108
Fax: (906) 225-1109

Office of International Development
Michigan Department of Commerce
Law Building, 5th Floor
Lansing, MI 48909
(517) 373-6390
Fax: (517) 335-2521

Michigan Export Development Authority
Michigan Department of Commerce
Law Building, 5th Floor
Lansing, MI 48909
(517) 373-6390
Fax: (517) 335-2521

Michigan Department of Agriculture
Office of International Trade
P.O. Box 30017
Lansing, MI 48909
(517) 373-1054
Fax: (517) 335-2521

City of Detroit
Community & Economic Development
 Dept.
150 Michigan Avenue
Detroit, MI 48226
(313) 224-6533
Fax: (313) 224-4579

Detroit/Wayne County Port Authority
174 Clark Street
Detroit, MI 48209
(313) 841-6700
Fax: (313) 841-6705

Michigan State Chamber of Commerce
Small Business Programs
200 North Washington Square, Suite 400
Lansing, MI 48933
(517) 371-2100
Fax: (517) 371-7224

Ann Arbor Chamber of Commerce
211 East Huron, Suite 1
Ann Arbor, MI 48104
(313) 665-4433
Fax: (313) 995-7283

Greater Detroit Chamber of Commerce
600 West Lafayette Blvd.
Detroit, MI 48226
(313) 964-4000
Fax: (313) 964-0531

Downriver Community Conference
15100 Northline
Southgate, MI 48195
(313) 283-8933
Fax: (313) 281-3418

Flint Area Chamber of Commerce
708 Root
Flint, MI 49503
(313) 232-7101
Fax: (313) 233-7437

Greater Grand Rapids Chamber of Commerce
17 Fountain Street, N.W.
Grand Rapids, MI 49503
(616) 459-7221
Fax: (616) 771-0318

Kalamazoo Chamber of Commerce
128 North Kalamazoo Mall
Kalamazoo, MI 49007
(616) 381-4000
Fax: (616) 343-0430

Macomb County Chamber of Commerce
10 North Avenue, P.O. Box 855
Mt. Clemens, MI 48043
(313) 463-1528

Muskegon Areat Chamber of Commerce
1065 Fourth Street
Muskegon, MI 49441
(616) 722-3751

Greater Port Huron-Marysville Chamber
of Commerce
920 Pine Grove Avenue
Port Huron, MI 48060
(313) 985-7101

Greater Saginaw Chamber of Commerce
901 South Washington
Saginaw, MI 48606
(517) 752-7161
Fax: (517) 752-9055

Cornerstone Alliance
P.O. Box 428
Benton Harbor, MI 49023
(616) 925-0044
Fax: (616) 925-4471

Detroit Custom Brokers & Foreign Freight
Forwarders Association
1237-45 First National Building
Detroit, MI 48226
(313) 961-4130

Michigan Manufacturers Association
124 East Kalamazoo
Lansing, MI 48933
(517) 372-5900
Fax: (517) 372-3322

Business & International Furniture
Manufacturers Association
2335 Burton, S.E.
Grand Rapids, MI 49506
(616) 243-1681
Fax: (616) 243-1011

Michigan District Export Council
c/o Arthur Anderson & Company
400 Renaissance Center, Suite 2500
Detroit, MI 48243
(313) 568-9210

Kalamazoo International Trade Council
(KITCO)
128 North Kalamazoo Mall
Kalamazoo, MI 49007
(616) 382-5966

Central Business District Association
700 Penobscot Building
Detroit, MI 48226
(313) 961-1403
Fax: (313) 961-9547

President's Export Council
c/o ASC, Inc.
One Sunroof Center
Southgate, MI 48195
(313) 285-4911
Fax: (313) 246-0500

Port Huron Trade Center
511 Ford Street, Suite 530
Port Huron, MI 48060
(313) 982-3510

World Trade Center
150 West Jefferson Avenue
Detroit, MI 48226
(313) 965-6500
Fax: (313) 965-1525

International Business Centers
Michigan State University
6 Kellogg Center
East Lansing, MI 48824-1022
(517) 353-4336
Fax: (517) 336-1009

West Michigan World Trade Association
17 Fountain Street, N.W.
Grand Rapids, MI 49503
(616) 771-0319
Fax: (616) 771-0318

World Trade Club of Detroit
600 West Lafayette Blvd.
Detroit, MI 48226
(313) 964-4000
Fax: (313) 964-0531

MINNESOTA

U.S. Department of Commerce
US & FCS District Office
110 South 4th Street, Room 108
Minneapolis, MN 55401-2227
(612) 348-1638
Fax: (612) 348-1650

U.S. Small Business Administration
100 North 6th Street, Suite 610C
Minneapolis, MN 55403-1504
(612) 370-2324
Fax: (612) 370-2303

Minnesota Export Finance Authority
30 East 7th Street, Suite 1000
St. Paul, MN 55101-4902
(612) 297-4659
Fax: (612) 296-3555

Minnesota Trade Office
30 East 7th Street, Suite 1000
St. Paul, MN 55101-4902
(612) 297-4222
Fax: (612) 296-3555

Minnesota World Trade Center Corporation
30 East 7th Street, Suite 400
St. Paul, MN 55101-4901
(612) 297-1580
Fax: (612) 297-4812

Minnesota Word Trade Association
P.O. Box 24341
Apple Valley, MN 55124
(612) 441-9261

MISSISSIPPI

U.S. Department of Commerce
US & FCS District Office
300 Woodrow Wilson Blvd., Suite 328
Jackson, MS 39213
(601) 965-4388
Fax: (601) 965-5386

U.S. Small Business Administration
101 West Capitol Street, Suite 400
Jackson, MS 39201
(601) 965-4378

U.S. Small Business Administration
One Hancock Plaza, Suite 1001
Gulfport, MS 39501
(601) 863-4449

Mississippi Department of Economic
 & Community Development
P.O. Box 849
Jackson, MS 39205
(601) 359-3552

Mississippi Department of Agriculture
 and Commerce
P.O. Box 1609
Jackson, MS 39205
(601) 961-4725

International Trade Club of Mississippi, Inc.
P.O. Box 16673
Jackson, MS 39236
(601) 366-0331

MISSOURI

U.S. Department of Commerce
US & FCS District Office
7911 Forsyth Blvd., Suite 610
St. Louis, MO 63105
(314) 425-3302
Fax: (314) 425-3381

U.S. Department of Commerce
US & FCS District Office
601 East 12th Street, Room 635
Kansas City, MO 64106
(816) 426-3141
Fax: (816) 426-3140

U.S. Small Business Administration
1103 Grand Avenue, 6th Floor
Kansas City, MO 64106
(816) 374-6760

U.S. Small Business Administration
620 South Glenstone, Suite 110
Springfield, MO 65802
(417) 864-7670

U.S. Small Business Administration
815 Olive Street, Second Floor
St. Louis, MO 63101
(314) 539-6600

Export Development Office
Missouri Dept. of Economic Development
P.O. Box 118
Jefferson City, MO 65102
(314) 751-4855

Missouri Department of Agriculture
International Marketing Division
P.O. Box 630
Jefferson City, MO 65102
(314) 751-5611

Missouri District Export Council
7911 Forsyth Blvd., Suite 610
St. Louis, MO 63105
(314) 425-3306

Mid America District Export Council
 (MADEC)
601 East 12th Street, Room 635
Kansas City, MO 64106
(816) 426-3141

International Trade Club of Greater
 Kansas City
920 Main Street, Suite 600
Kansas City, MO 64105
(816) 221-1462

World Trade Club of St. Louis, Inc.
135 North Meramec Avenue, 5th Floor
St. Louis, MO 63105
(314) 725-9605

MONTANA

U.S. Department of Commerce
US & FCS Branch Office
2nd Floor, Joe R. Williams Building
700 West State Street
Boise, ID 83720
(208) 334-3857
Fax: (208) 334-2783

U.S. Small Business Administration
301 South Park, Room 528
Helena, MT 59626-0054
(406) 449-5381

U.S. Small Business Administration
2525 Fourth Avenue North, 2nd Floor
Billings, MT 59101
(406) 657-6567

Department of Commerce
International Trade Division
1424 Ninth Avenue
Helena, MT 59620-0401
(406) 444-3923

NEBRASKA

U.S. Department of Commerce
US & FCS District Office
11133 O Street
Omaha, NE 68137
(402) 221-3664
Fax: (402) 221-3668

U.S. Small Business Administration
11145 Mill Valley Road
Omaha, NE 68137
(402) 221-3604

International Division
Nebraska Dept. of Economic Development
P.O. Box 94666
301 Centennial Mall South
Lincoln, NE 68509
(402) 471-3111

Omaha Chamber of Commerce
International Affairs
1301 Harney Street
Omaha, NE 68102
(402) 346-5000

Midwest International Trade Association
P.O. Box 37402
Omaha, NE 68137
(402) 221-3664

NEVADA

U.S. Department of Commerce
US & FCS District Office
1755 East Plumb Lane, Room 152
Reno, NV 89502
(702) 784-5203
Fax: (702) 784-5343

U.S. Small Business Administration
301 East Stewart Street
Las Vegas, NV 89125
(702) 385-6611

U.S. Small Business Administration
50 South Virginia Street, Room 238
Reno, NV 89505
(702) 388-5268

Commission on Economic Development
Capitol Complex
Carson City, NV 89710
(702) 687-4325

Economic Development Authority of
 Western Nevada
5190 Neil Road, Suite 111
Reno, NV 89502
(702) 829-3700

Latin Chamber of Commerce
P.O. Box 7534
Las Vegas, NV 89125-2534
(702) 385-7367

Nevada Development Authority
3900 Paradise Road, Suite 155
Las Vegas, NV 89109
(702) 791-0000

Nevada District Export Council
1755 East Plumb Lane, Suite 152
Reno, NV 84502
(702) 784-5305

NEW HAMPSHIRE

U.S. Department of Commerce
US & FCS District Office
(See listing for Boston, MA)

U.S. Small Business Administration
55 Pleasant Street, Room 211
Concord, NH 03301
(603) 244-4041

New Hampshire Department of Resources
 & Economic Development
Office of Industrial Development
172 Pembroke Street, P.O. Box 856
Concord, NH 03301
(603) 271-2591

NEW JERSEY

U.S. Department of Commerce
US & FCS District Office
3131 Princeton Pike
Building 6, Suite 100
Trenton, NJ 08648
(609) 989-2100
Fax: (609) 989-2395

U.S. Department of Commerce
US & FCS District Office
c/o Bergen Community College
368 Paramus Road
Paramus, NJ 07632
(201) 447-9624

U.S. Small Business Administration
60 Park Place, 4th Floor
Newark, NJ 07102
(201) 645-6065

World Trade Association of New Jersey
c/o Schering-Plough International
27 Commerce Drive
Cranford, NJ 07016
(908) 709-2632

New Jersey Division of International Trade
Dept. of Commerce & Economic Development
153 Halsey Street
Newark, NJ 07102
(201) 648-3518

New Jersey Small Business Development
Center-International Trade (NJSBDC)
Rutgers, the State University
Graduate School of Management
180 University Avenue
Newark, NJ 07102
(201) 648-5950

Raritan Valley Community College
International Education Program
P.O. Box 3300
Somerville, NJ 08876
(908) 526-1200, ext. 312

NEW MEXICO

U.S. Department of Commerce
US & FCS Branch Office
625 Silver, S.W., 3rd Floor
Albuquerque, NM 87102
(505) 766-2070
Fax: (505) 766-1057

U.S. Small Business Administration
625 Silver, S.W., 3rd Floor
Albuquerque, NM 87102
(505) 766-1879
Fax: (505) 766-1057

Trade Division
State of New Mexico
Economic Development & Tourism Dept.
1100 St. Francis Drive
Joseph M. Montoya Building
Santa Fe, NM 87503
(505) 827-0307
Fax: (505) 827-0263

New Mexico Department of Agriculture
Marketing and Development Division
Box 30005, Dept. 5600
Las Cruces, NM 88003
(505) 646-4929
Fax: (505) 646-3303

New Mexico Small Business
Development Center Network
P.O. Box 4187
Santa Fe, NM 87502-4187
(505) 438-1362
Fax: (505) 438-1237

New Mexico International Trade Council
P.O. Box 25381
Albuquerque, NM 87125-5831
(505) 821-2318
Fax: (505) 821-2318

Greater Albuquerque Chamber of Commerce
International Trade Committee
P.O. Box 25100
Albuquerque, NM 87125
(505) 764-3700
Fax: (505) 247-9140

Albuquerque Hispano Chamber of Commerce
International Trade Committee
1600 Lomas Street, N.W.
Albuquerque, NM 87104
(505) 842-9003
Fax: (505) 764-9003

NEW YORK

U.S. Department of Commerce
US & FCS District Office
1312 Federal Building
111 West Huron Street
Buffalo, NY 14202
(716) 846-4191
Fax: (716) 846-5290

U.S. Department of Commerce
US & FCS Branch Office
111 East Avenue, Suite 220
Rochester, NY 14604
(716) 263-6480
Fax: (716) 325-6505

U.S. Department of Commerce
US & FCS District Office
Federal Office Building, Room 3718
26 Federal Plaza
New York, NY 10278
(212) 264-0600
Fax: (212) 264-1356

U.S. Department of Commerce
US & FCS Associate Office
216 C.E.D.C.
Jamestown Community College
Jamestown, NY 14701
(716) 665-6066

U.S. Small Business Administration
26 Federal Plaza, Room 3100
New York, NY 10278
(212) 264-4355

U.S. Small Business Administration
35 Pinelawn Road, Room 102E
Melville, NY 11747
(516) 454-0750

U.S. Small Business Administration
100 South Clinton Street, Room 1071
P.O. Box 7317
Syracuse, NY 13260-7317
(315) 423-5383

U.S. Small Business Administration
111 West Huron Street, Room 1311
Buffalo, NY 14202
(716) 846-4301

U.S. Small Business Administration
333 East Water Street
Elmira, NY 14901
(607) 734-8130

U.S. Small Business Administration
445 Broadway, Room 2368
Albany, NY 12207
(518) 472-6300

U.S. Small Business Administration
100 State Street, Room 601
Rochester, NY 14614
(716) 263-6700

International Division
New York State Department of
 Economic Development
1515 Broadway, 51st Floor
New York, NY 10036
(212) 827-6100

International Division
New York State Department of
 Economic Development
111 East Avenue, Suite 220
Rochester, NY 14604
(716) 325-1944

International Division
New York State Department of
 Economic Development
16 Hawley Street
Binghampton, NY 13901
(607) 773-7813

International Division
New York State Department of
 Economic Development
333 East Washington Street
Syracuse, NY 13202
(315) 428-4097

Canada-United States Trade Center
State University of NY at Buffalo
130 Wilkeson Quadrangle
Buffalo, NY 14261
(716) 636-2299

Southern Tier World Commerce Association
c/o School of Management
State University of NY at Binghampton
P.O. Box 6000
Binghampton, NY 13902-6000
(607) 77762342

American Association of Exporters
and Importers
11 West 42nd Street
New York, NY 10036
(212) 944-2230

Foreign Credit Insurance Association
40 Rector Street, 51st Floor
New York, NY 10006
(212) 306-5000

National Association of Export Companies
747 Middle Neck Road
Great Neck, NY 11024
(516) 487-0700

World Trade Institute
One World Trade Center
New York, NY 10048
(212) 466-4044

Syracuse International Trade Council
Greater Syracuse Chamber of Commerce
572 South Salina Street
Syracuse, NY 13202
(315) 470-1883

U.S. Council of the International
Chamber of Commerce
1212 Avenue of the Americas
New York, NY 10036
(212) 354-4480

Albany-Colonie Regional Chamber
of Commerce
518 Broadway
Albany, NY 11207
(518) 434-1214

Greater Buffalo Area Chamber of Commerce
107 Delaware Avenue
Buffalo, NY 14202
(716) 852-7100

Long Island Association, Inc.
80 Hauppauge Road
Commack, NY 11725
(516) 499-4400

International Business Council of the
Rochester Area Chamber of Commerce
55 St. Paul Street
Rochester, NY 14604
(716) 454-2220

New York Chamber of Commerce & Industry
One Battery Park Place
New York, NY 10009
(212) 493-7500

Buffalo World Trade Association
P.O. Box 39
Tonawanda, NY 14150
(716) 877-1452

Long Island Association, Inc.
World Trade Club
Legislative & Economic Affairs
80 Hauppauge Road
Commack, NY 11725
(516) 499-4400

Mohawk Valley World Trade Council
P.O. Box 4126
Utica, NY 13540
(315) 826-3600

Tappan Zee International Trade Association
One Blue Hill Plaza, Suite 812
Pearl River, NY 10965-1575
(914) 735-7040

Westchester County Association, Inc.
World Trade Club of Westchester
235 Mamaroneck Avenue
White Plains, NY 10605
(914) 948-6444

World Trade Club of New York, Inc.
28 Vesey Street, Suite 230
New York, NY 10007
(212) 435-8335

Western NY International Trade Council
P.O. Box 1271
Buffalo, NY 14240
(716) 852-7160

Western NY Economic Development Corp.
Liberty Building, Suite 717
424 Main Street
Buffalo, NY 14202
(716) 856-8111

NORTH CAROLINA

U.S. Department of Commerce
US & FCS District Office
324 west Market Street, Room 203
P.O. Box 1950
Greensboro, NC 27402
(919) 333-5345
Fax: (919) 333-5158

U.S. Small Business Administration
222 South Church, Suite 300
Charlotte, NC 28202
(704) 371-6563

NC Department of Economic & Community
 Development-International Division
430 North Salisbury Street
Raleigh, NC 27611
(919) 733-7193

North Carolina Department of Agriculture
P.O. Box 27647
Raleigh, NC 27611
(919) 733-7912

North Carolina World Trade Association
P.O. Box 28271
Raleigh, NC 27611
(919) 794-4327

Research Triangle World Trade Center
1007 Slater Road, Suite 200
Morrisville, NC 27560
(919) 549-7467

North Carolina Port Authority Headquarters
North Carolina Maritime Building
2202 Burnett Blvd., P.O. Box 9002
Wilmington, NC 28402
(919) 763-1621
Outside NC: (800) 334-0682

North Carolina Small Business and
 Technology Development Center
4509 Creedmoor Road, Suite 201
Raleigh, NC 27612
(919) 733-4643

NORTH DAKOTA

U.S. Department of Commerce
US & FCS District Office
(See listing for Omaha, NE)

U.S. Small Business Administration
657 2nd Avenue North, Room 218
Fargo, ND 58108
(701) 237-5771

International Trade Division
North Dakota Department of Economic
 Development & Finance
1833 East Expressway
Bismarck, ND 58504
(701) 224-2810

Fargo Chamber of Commerce
321 North 4th Street
Fargo, ND 58108
(701) 237-5678

OHIO

U.S. Department of Commerce
US & FCS District Office
9504 Federal Building
550 Main Street
Cincinnati, OH 45202
(513) 684-2944
Fax: (513) 684-3200

U.S. Department of Commerce
US & FCS District Office
668 Euclid Avenue, Room 600
Cleveland, OH 44114
(216) 522-4750
Fax: (216) 522-2235

U.S. Small Business Administration
1240 East 9th Street, Room 317
Cleveland, OH 44199
(216) 552-4180

U.S. Small Business Administration
85 Marconi Blvd.
Columbus, OH 43215
(614) 469-6860

U.S. Small Business Administration
5028 Federal Office Building
550 Main Street, Room 5028
Cincinnati, OH 45202
(513) 684-2814

International Trade Development OFfice
37 North High Street
Columbus, OH 43215
(614) 221-1321

State of Ohio Department of Development
International Trade Division
77 South High Street
P.O. Box 1001
Columbus, OH 43266
(614) 466-5017

Greater Cincinnati Chamber of Commerce
Export Development and World
 Trade Association
441 Vine Street, 300 Carew Tower
Cincinnati, OH 45202
(513) 579-3122

Columbus Area Chamber of Commerce
Economic Development
37 North High Street
Columbus, OH 43215
(614) 221-1321

Dayton Area Chamber of Commerce
Chamber of Plaza
5th and Main
Dayton, OH 45402

Columbus Council on World Affairs
Two Nationwide Plaza, Suite 705
Columbus, OH 43215
(614) 249-8450

Cleveland World Trade Association
Greater Cleveland Growth Association
200 Tower City Center
50 Public Square
Cleveland, OH 44113
(216) 621-3300

Dayton Council on World Affairs
Wright Brothers Branch
P.O. Box 9190
Dayton, OH 45409
(513) 229-2319

Miami Valley International Trade
Association
P.O. Box 291945
Dayton, OH 45429
(513) 439-9465

International Business & Trade Association
of Akron Regional Development Board
One Cascade Plaza, 8th Floor
Akron, OH 44308
(216) 376-5550

Toledo Area International Trade Association
Toledo Area Chamber of Commerce
218 Huron Street
Toledo, OH 43604
(419) 243-8191

Stark International Marketing
Greater Canton Chamber of Commerce
229 Wells Avenue, N.W.
Canton, OH 44703
(216) 456-9654

Youngstown Area Chamber of Commerce
200 Wick Building
Youngstown, OH 44503
(216) 744-2131

OKLAHOMA

U.S. Department of Commerce
US & FCS District Office
6601 Broadway Extension
Oklahoma City, OK 73116
(405) 231-5302
Fax: (405) 841-5245

U.S. Small Business Administration
200 N.W. 5th Street, Suite 670
Oklahoma City, OK 73102
(405) 231-4301

Oklahoma Department of Commerce
International Trade & Investment Division
6601 Broadway Extension
Oklahoma City, OK 73116
(405) 841-5220

Oklahoma Department of Agriculture
Market Development Division
2800 Lincoln Blvd.
Oklahoma City, OK 73105
(405) 521-3864

Oklahoma State Chamber of Commerce
4020 Lincoln Blvd.
Oklahoma City, OK 73105
(405) 424-4003

Oklahoma City Chamber of Commerce
Economic & Community Development
One Santa Fe Plaza
Oklahoma City, OK 73102
(405) 278-8900

Oklahoma District Export Council
6601 Broadway Extension
Oklahoma City, OK 73116
(405) 231-5302

Metropolitan Tulsa Chamber of Commerce
Economic Development Division
616 South Boston Avenue
Tulsa, OK 74119
(918) 585-1201

Oklahoma City International
Trade Association
P.O. Box 1936
Oklahoma City, OK 73101
(405) 943-9590

Tulsa World Trade Association
616 South Boston Avenue
Tulsa, OK 74119
(918) 585-1201

Small Business Development Center
6420 S.E. 15th Street
Midwest City, OK 73110
(405) 733-7348

Center for International Trade Development
Oklahoma State University
Hall of Fame and Washington
Stillwater, OK 74078
(405) 744-7693

OREGON

U.S. Department of Commerce
US & FCS District Office
One World Trade Center
121 S.W. Salmon, Suite 242
Portland, OR 97204
(503) 326-3001
Fax: (503) 326-6351

U.S. Small Business Administration
International Trade Program
One World Trade Center
121 S.W. Salmon, Suite 210
Portland, OR 97204
(503) 274-7482

Department of Economic Development
International Trade Division
One World Trade Center
121 S.W. Salmon, Suite 300
Portland, OR 97204
(503) 229-5625

Oregon Department of Agriculture
One World Trade Center
121 S.W. Salmon, Suite 240
Portland, OR 97204
(503) 229-6734

International Trade Institute
One World Trade Center
121 S.W. Salmon, Suite 230
Portland, OR 97204
(503) 725-3246

World Trade Center Portland
One World Trade Center
121 S.W. Salmon, Suite 250
Portland, OR 97204
(503) 464-8888

Central Oregon International Trade Council
2600 N.W. College Way
Bend, OR 97701
(503) 385-5524

Mid-Willamette Valley Council
of Governments
105 High Street, S.E.
Salem, OR 97301
(503) 588-6177

Pacific Northwest International
Trade Association
200 S.W. Market, Suite 190
Portland, OR 97201
(503) 228-4361

Portland Chamber of Commerce
221 N.W. 2nd Avenue
Portland, OR 97209
(503) 228-9411

Southern Oregon International
Trade Council
290 N.E. "C" Street
Grants Pass, OR 97526
(503) 474-0762

Willamette International Trade Center
1059 Willamette, Room 209
Eugene, OR 97401
(503) 686-0195

PENNSYLVANIA

U.S. Department of Commerce
US & FCS District Office
475 Allendale Road, Suite 202
King of Prussia, PA 19406
(215) 962-4980
Fax: (215) 951-7959

U.S. Department of Commerce
US & FCS District Office
2002 Federal Building
1000 Liberty Avenue
Pittsburgh, PA 15222
(412) 644-2850
Fax: (412) 644-4875

Delaware-Eastern Pennsylvania
District Export Council
475 Allendale Road, Room 202
King of Prussia, PA 19406
(215) 962-4980
Fax: (215) 951-7959

U.S. Small Business Administration
475 Allendale Road, Suite 201
King of Prussia, PA 19406
(215) 962-3815
Fax: (215) 962-3795

U.S. Small Business Administration
Branch Office
100 Chestnut Street, Suite 309
Harrisburg, PA 17101
(717) 782-3840

U.S. Small Business Administration
Branch Office
20 North Pennsylvania Avenue
Wilkes-Barre, PA 18701
(717) 826-6495

U.S. Small Business Administration
District Office
960 Pennsylvania Avenue, 5th Floor
Pittsburgh, PA 15222
(412) 644-2780

Pennsylvania Department of Commerce
Bureau of International Development
433 Forum Building
Harrisburg, PA 17120
(717) 783-5107

Pennsylvania Department of Agriculture
Bureau of Markets
2301 North Cameron Street
Harrisburg, PA 17110
(717) 783-3181
Fax: (717) 234-4560

Economic Development Council
 of Northwestern Pennsylvania
1151 Oak Street
Pittston, PA 18640
(717) 655-5581
Fax: (717) 654-5137

Technology Development and
 Education Corporation
4516 Henry Street
Pittsburgh, PA 15213
(412) 687-2700

Western Pennsylvania District
Export Council
1000 Liberty Avenue, Room 2002
Pittsburgh, PA 15222
(412) 644-2850

American Society of International
 Executives, Inc.
15 Sentry Parkway, Suite 1
Blue Bell, PA 19422
(215) 540-2295
Fax: (215) 540-2290

Berks County Chamber of Commerce
P.O. Box 1698
645 Penn Street
Reading, PA 19603
(215) 376-6766
Fax: (215) 376-6769

Delaware County Chamber of Commerce
602 East Baltimore Pike
Media, PA 19063
(215) 565-3677
Fax: (215) 565-1606

Delaware River Port Authority
World Trade Division
Bridge Plaza
Camden, NJ 08101
(215) 925-8780 ext. 2264
Fax: (09) 964-8106

International Business Forum
1520 Locust Street
Philadelphia, PA 19102
(215) 732-3250
Fax: (215) 732-3258

Lancaster Chamber of Commerce & Industry
Southern Market Center
100 South Queen Street, P.O. Box 1558
Lancaster, PA 17603-1558
(717) 397-3531
Fax: (717) 293-3159

Lehigh University Small Business
 Development Center
International Trade Development Program
30 Broadway
Bethlehem, PA 18015
(215) 758-4630
Fax: (215) 758-5205

Montgomery County Department
 of Commerce
#3 Stoney Creek Office Center
151 West Marshall Road
Norristown, PA 19401
(215) 278-5950
Fax: (215) 278-5944

Northern Tier Regional Planning
 and Development Commission
507 Main Street
Towanda, PA 18848
(717) 265-9103
Fax: (717) 265-7585

Pennsylvania State University Small
Business Development Center
Export Development Program
 of South Central Pennsylvania
Middletown, PA 17057
(717) 948-6069
Fax: (717) 249-4468

Greater PA Chamber of Commerce
1346 Chestnut Street, Suite 800
Philadelphia, PA 19107
(215) 545-1234
Fax: (215) 875-6700

Philadelphia Industrial Development Corp.
123 South Broad Street, 22nd Floor
Philadelphia, PA 19109
(215) 875-3508
Fax: (215) 790-1537

University of Scranton Small
 Business Development Center
415 North Washington Avenue
Scranton, PA 18510
(717) 961-7577
Fax: (717) 961-4053

SEDA-Council of Governments
Timberhaven Road, #1
Lewisburg, PA 17838
(717) 524-4491
Fax: (717) 524-9190

Wharton Export Network
Wharton School
University of Pennsylvania
3733 Spruce Street, 413 Vance Hall
Philadelphia, PA 19104
(215) 898-4187
Fax: (215) 898-1299

Wilkes College Small Business
 Development Center
Hollenbeck Hall
192 South Franklin Street
Wilkes-Barre, PA 18766

Clarion University of Pennsylvania
Small Business Development Center
Dana Still Building
Clarion, PA
(814) 226-2060
Fax: (814) 226-2636

Duquesne University
Small Business Development Center
Rockwell Hall, Room 10
600 Forbes Avenue
Pittsburgh, PA 15282
(412) 434-6233
Fax: (412) 434-5072

Gannon University
Small Business Development Center
University Square
Erie, PA 16541
(814) 871-7714
Fax: (814) 871-7383

Greater Pittsburgh World Trade Association
3 Gateway Center, 14th Floor
Pittsburgh, PA 15222
(412) 392-4500
Fax: (412) 392-4520

Indiana University of Pennsylvania
Small Business Development Center
202 McElhaney Hall
Indiana, PA 15705
(412) 357-2929
Fax: (412) 357-5743

North Central Pennsylvania Regional
 Planning & Development Commission
P.O. Box 488
Ridgeway, PA 15853
(814) 722-6901
Fax: (814) 722-1552

SMC/Pennsylvania Small Business
1400 South Braddock Avenue
Pittsburgh, PA 15218
(412) 371-1500
Fax: (412) 371-0460

Southern Alleghenies Commission
541 58th Street
Altoona, PA 16602
(814) 252-3595
Fax: (814) 949-6505

St. Francis College
Small Business Development Center
Schwab, Suite A-2
Loretto, PA 15940
(814) 472-3200
Fax: (814) 472-3154

St. Vincent College
Small Business Development Center
Latrobe, PA 15650
(412) 537-4572
Fax: (412) 537-4554

Southwestern Pennsylvania
Economic Development District
12300 Perry Highway
Wexford, PA 15090
(412) 935-6122
Fax: (412) 935-6888

Greater Willow Grove Chamber
 of Commerce
603 North Easton Road, P.O. Box 100
Willow Grove, PA 19090
(215) 657-2227
Fax: (215) 657-8564

Erie Area Chamber of Commerce
1006 State Street
Erie, PA 16501
Fax: (814) 459-0241

Women's International Trade Association
P.O. Box 40004
Philadelphia, PA 19106
(215) 922-6610
Fax: (215) 922-0784

World Trade Association of Philadelphia
P.O. Box 58640
Philadelphia, PA 19110
(215) 988-0711

York Area Chamber of Commerce
13 East Market Street
York, PA 17401
(717) 848-4000
Fax: (717) 843-8837

PUERTO RICO

U.S. Department of Commerce
US & FCS District Office
U.S. Federal Building, Suite G-55
150 Carlos Chardon Avenue
Hato Rey, PR 00918-1738
(809) 766-5555

U.S. Small Business Administration
U.S. Federal Building, Suite 691
150 Carlos Chardon Avenue
Hato Rey, PR 00918-1729
(809) 766-5572

Puerto Rico Department of Commerce
Box 4275
San Juan, PR 00936
(809) 721-3290

PR Economic Development Administration
G.P.O. Box 2350
San Juan, PR 00936
(809) 758-4747

Puerto Rico Chamber of Commerce
Box 3789
San Juan, PR 00904
(809) 721-6060

Puerto Rico Manufacturers Association
Box 2410
Hato Rey, PR 00919
(809) 759-9445

Puerto Rico/Virgin Islands
 District Export Council
U.S. Federal Building, Suite G-55
150 Carlos Chardon Avenue
Hato Rey, PR 00918-1738
(809) 766-5555

Virgin Islands Department of Economic
 Development & Agriculture
Commissioner of Commerce
P.O. Box 6400
St. Thomas, VI 00801
(809) 774-8784

RHODE ISLAND

U.S. Department of Commerce
US & FCS Branch Office
7 Jackson Walkway
Providence, RI 02903
(401) 528-5104
Fax: (401) 528-5067

U.S. Small Business Administration
380 Westminster Mall
Providence, RI 02903
(401) 528-4562

Department of Economic Development
7 Jackson Walkway
Providence, RI 02903
(401) 277-2601

SOUTH CAROLINA

U.S. Department of Commerce
US & FCS District Office
1835 Assembly Street, Suite 172
Columbia, SC 29201
(803) 765-5345
Fax: (803) 253-3614

U.S. Department of Commerce
US & FCS Branch Office
JC Long Building
9 Liberty Street
Charleston, SC 29424
(803) 724-4361

South Carolina District Export Council
1835 Assembly Street, Suite 172
Columbia, SC 29201
(803) 765-5345

U.S. Small Business Administration
Strom Thurmond Federal Building, #172
Columbia, SC 29201
(803) 765-5376

International Division
SC State Development Board
P.O. Box 927
Columbia, SC 29202
(803) 737-0400
Fax: (803) 737-0481

South Carolina State Ports Authority
P.O. Box 817
Charleston, SC 29402
(803) 577-8100
Fax: (803) 577-8616

Jobs-Economic Development Authority
1201 Main Street, Suite 1750
Columbia, SC 29201
(803) 737-0079
Fax: (803) 737-0016

Charleston-Trident Chamber of Commerce
P.O. Box 975
Charleston, SC 29402
(803) 577-2510
Fax: (803) 723-4853

Greater Greenville Chamber of Commerce
P.O. Box 10048
Greenville, SC 29603
(803) 242-1050
Fax: (803) 282-8549

Greater Columbia Chamber of Commerce
P.O. Box 1360
Columbia, SC 29202
(803) 733-1110
Fax: (803) 733-1149

Small Business Development Center
College of Business
University of South Carolina
Columbia, SC 29208
(803) 777-5118
Fax: (803) 777-4403

Low Country International Trade Association
P.O. Box 159
Charleston, SC 29402
(803) 724-3566
Fax: (803) 724-3400

Midlands International Trade Association
P.O. Box 1481
Columbia, SC 29202
(803) 822-5039
Fax: (803) 822-5147

Pee Dee International Trade
 Association (Florence)
P.O. Box 669
Hartsville, SC 29550
(803) 383-4507 ext. 42
Fax: (803) 332-8003

Western South Carolina International
 Trade Association
P.O. Box 2081
Greenville, SC 29602-2081
(803) 574-9540
Fax: (803) 574-9566

SOUTH DAKOTA

U.S. Department of Commerce
US & FCS District Office
(See listing for Omaha, NE)

U.S. Small Business Administration
101 South Main Avenue, Suite 101
Sioux Falls, SD 57102
(605) 336-2980

South Dakota Governor's Office
 of Economic Development
Export, Trade & Marketing Division
Capitol Lake Plaza
Pierre, SD 57501
(605) 773-5032

Rapid City Area Chamber of Commerce
P.O. Box 747
Rapid City, SD 57709
(605) 343-1774

Sioux Falls Chamber of Commerce
127 East 10th Street
Sioux Falls, SD 57101
(605) 336-1620

TENNESSEE

U.S. Department of Commerce
US & FCS District Office
Parkway Towers, Suite 1114
404 James Robertson Parkway
Nashville, TN 37219-1505
(615) 736-5161

U.S. Department of Commerce
US & FCS Branch Office
Falls Building, Suite 200
22 North Front Street
Memphis, TN 38103
(901) 544-4137

U.S. Department of Commerce
US & FCS Branch Office
301 East Church Avenue
Knoxville, TN 37915
(615) 549-9268

U.S. Small Business Administration
50 Vantage Way, Suite 201
Nashville, TN 37228-1500
(615) 741-5870

Tennessee Export Office
Department of Economic and
 Community Development
7th Floor, Rachel Jackson Building
Nashville, TN 37219
(615) 741-5870

Tennessee Department of Agriculture
Ellington Agricultural Center
P.O. Box 40627, Melrose Station
Nashville, TN 37294
(615) 360-0160

Tennessee Small Business
Development Center
International Trade Center
Memphis, TN 38152
(901) 678-4174

Tennessee Export Council
Suite 114, Parkway Towers
404 James Robertson Parkway
Nashville, TN 37219-1505
(615) 736-7771

World Trade Center-Chattanooga
1001 Market Street
Chattanooga, TN 37402
(615) 752-4316

Chattanooga World Trade Council
1001 Market Street
Chattanooga, TN 37402
(615) 752-4302

East TN International Commerce Council
P.O. Box 2688
Knoxville, TN 37901
(615) 637-4550

Memphis World Trade Club
P.O. Box 3577
Memphis, TN 38173-0577
(901) 345-5420

World Affairs Council of Memphis
577 University
Memphis, TN 38112
(901) 523-6764

Mid-South Exporters' Roundtable
P.O. Box 3521
Memphis, TN 38173
(901) 523-4420

Middle Tennessee World Trade Council
P.O. Box 198073
Nashville, TN 37219-8073
(615) 736-6223

TEXAS

U.S. Department of Commerce
US & FCS District Office
1100 Commerce Street, Room 7A5
Dallas, TX 75242
(214) 767-0542
Fax: (214) 767-8240

U.S. Department of Commerce
US & FCS District Office
2625 Federal Building
515 Rusk Street
Houston, TX 77002
(713) 229-25783
Fax: (713) 229-2203

U.S. Department of Commerce
US & FCS Branch Office
P.O. Box 12728
816 Congress Avenue
Austin, TX 78701
(512) 482-5939
Fax: (512) 320-9674

U.S. Small Business Administration
300 East 8th Street, Room 520
Austin, TX 78701
(512) 482-5288

U.S. Small Business Administration
7400 Blanco, Suite 20
San Antonio, TX 78216
(512) 229-4551

U.S. Small Business Administration
400 Mann Street, Suite 403
Corpus Christi, TX 78401
(512) 888-3301

U.S. Small Business Administration
1100 Commerce Street, Room 3C36
Dallas, TX 75242
(214) 767-0496

U.S. Small Business Administration
819 Taylor Street, Room 8A32
Ft. Worth, TX 76102
(817) 334-5613

U.S. Small Business Administration
222 East Van Buren Street, Room 500
Harlingen, TX 78550
(512) 427-8533

U.S. Small Business Administration
505 East Traves, Room 103
Marshall, TX 75670
(903) 935-5257

U.S. Customs Service
P.O. Box 61050
DFW Airport, TX 75261
(214) 574-2170

Texas Department of Agriculture
Export Services Division
P.O. Box 12847, Capitol Station
Austin, TX 78711
(512) 463-7624

Texas Department of Commerce
Office of International Trade
P.O. Box 12728, Capitol Station
816 Congress
Austin, TX 78711
(512) 472-5059

Texas Department of Commerce
Export Finance
P.O. Box 12728, Capitol Station
816 Congress
Austin, TX 78711
(512) 320-9662

South Texas District Export Council
515 Rusk Street, Room 2625
Houston, TX 77002
(713) 229-2578

North Texas District Export Council
1100 Commerce Street, Room 7A5
Dallas, TX 75242
(214) 767-0496

City of Dallas Office of International Affairs
City Hall 5EN
Dallas, TX 75201
(214) 670-3319

Foreign Credit Insurance Association
600 Travis, Suite 2860
Houston, TX 77002
(713) 227-0987

Dallas/Fort Worth Airport Board
P.O. Box DFW
DFW Airport, TX 75261
(214) 574-3079

Export Assistance Center
Greater Austin Chamber of Commerce
P.O. Box 1967
111 Congress, Suite 10
Austin, TX 78767
(512) 322-5695

International Committee
P.O. Box 1967
Austin, TX 78767
(512) 322-5695

Austin World Affairs Council
P.O. Box 5912
Austin, TX 78763
(512) 469-0158

Port of Beaumont
P.O. Drawer 2297
Beaumont, TX 77704
(409) 835-5367

Brownsville Economic Development Council
1600 East Elizabeth
Brownsville, TX 78520
(512) 541-1183

Brownsville Minority Business
 Development Center
2100 Boca Chica Tower, Suite 301
Brownsville, TX 78521-2265
(512) 546-3400

Brownsville Navigation District
P.O. Box 3070
Brownsville, TX 78523-3070
(512) 831-4592

Cameron County Private Industry Council
285 Kings Highway
Brownsville, TX 78521
(512) 542-4351

Texas Information & Procurement Service
601 Jefferson, Suite 2330
Houston, TX 77002
(713) 752-8477

Port of Corpus Christi Authority
P.O. Box 1541
Corpus Christi, TX 78403
(512) 882-5633

Corpus Christi Area Economical Development
Corp. and Corpus Christi Small Business
 Development Center
1201 North Shoreline, P.O. Box 640
Corpus Christi, TX 78403-0640
(512) 883-5571

Council for South Texas Economic
 Progress (COSTEP)
1701 West Business Highway 83
Texas Commerce Bank, Suite 600
McAllen, TX 78501
(512) 682-1201

Greater Dallas Chamber of Commerce
1201 Elm Street, Suite 2000
Dallas, TX 75270
(214) 746-6739

Fort Worth Chamber of Commerce
777 Taylor, Suite 900
Fort Worth, TX 76102
(817) 336-2491

Port of Houston Authority
111 East Loop North
Houston, TX 77029
(713) 670-2400

International Small Business
 Development Center
P.O. Box 58299
Dallas, TX 75258
(214) 653-1777

International Trade Association of
Dallas/Fort Worth
P.O. Box 58035
Dallas, TX 75258
(214) 748-3777

International Trade Resource Center
P.O. Box 581249
Dallas, TX 75258
(214) 653-1113

McAllen Minority Business
 Development Center
1701 West Business Hwy., Suite 1023
McAllen, TX 78501
(512) 687-5224

North Harris County College
Small Business Development Center
20000 Kingwood Drive
Kingwood, TX 77339
(713) 359-1624

Port of Port Arthur
Box 1428
Port Arthur, TX 77641
(409) 983-2011

San Antonio World Trade Center
118 Broadway, Suite 600
P.O. Box 1628
San Antonio, TX 78205
(512) 978-7601

San Antonio World Trade Association
118 Broadway, Suite 640
San Antonio, TX 78205
(512) 229-9036

International Trade Center
 Greater San Antonio Chamber of Commerce
P.O. Box 1628
San Antonio, TX 78296
(512) 229-2113

Greater Houston Partnership, World
 Trade Division
1100 Milam Building, 25th Floor
Houston, TX 77002
(713) 658-2408

U.S. Chamber of Commerce
4835 LBJ Freeway, Suite 750
Dallas, TX 75244
(214) 387-0404

Dallas Council on World Affairs
P.O. Box 58232
Dallas, TX 75258
(214) 748-5663

UTAH

U.S. Department of Commerce
US & FCS District Office
324 South State Street, Suite 105
Salt Lake City, UT 84111
(801) 524-5116
Fax: (801) 524-5886

U.S. Small Business Administration
125 South State Street, Room 2237
Salt Lake City, UT 84138
(801) 524-5800

Utah Economic & Industrial
 Development Division
324 South State Street, Suite 201
Salt Lake City, UT 84111
(801) 538-8700

Salt Lake Area Chamber of Commerce
Export Development Committee
175 East 400 South, 6th Floor
Salt Lake City, UT 84111
(801) 364-3631

World Trade Association of Utah
324 South State Street, Suite 105
Salt Lake City, UT 84111
(801) 524-5116

Salt Lake County Inland Port
2001 South State Street, Suite S-2100
Salt Lake City, UT 84109
(801) 468-3246
Fax: (801) 468-3684

VERMONT

U.S. Department of Commerce
US & FCS District Office
(See listing for Boston, MA)

U.S. Small Business Administration
87 State Street, Room 204
Montpelier, VT 05602
(802) 229-0538

Agency for Development and
 Community Affairs
Pavillion Office Building
109 State Street
Montpelier, VT 05602
(802) 828-3221

VIRGINIA

U.S. Department of Commerce
US & FCS District Office
Suite 8010
400 North 8th Street
Richmond, VA 23240
(804) 771-2246
Fax: (804) 771-2390

U.S. Small Business Administration
P.O. Box 10126
400 North 8th Street
Richmond, VA 23240
(804) 771-2765

VA Department of Economic Development
2 James Center
P.O. Box 798
Richmond, VA 23206-0798
(804) 371-8100

Virginia Department of Agriculture
Office of International Marketing
1100 Bank Street, Suite 915
Richmond, VA 23219
(804) 786-3953

Virginia Port Authority
600 World Trade Center
Norfolk, VA 23510
(804) 771-2765

Virginia Chamber of Commerce
9 South Fifth Street
Richmond, VA 23219
(804) 644-1607

Virginia District Export Council
P.O. Box 10190
Richmond, VA 23240
(804) 771-2246

International Trade Association
 of Northern Virginia
P.O. Box 2982
Reston, VA 22090

Piedmont World Trade Council
P.O. Box 1374
Lynchburg, VA 24505
(804) 528-7511

WASHINGTON

U.S. Department of Commerce
US & FCS District Office
3131 Elliott Avenue, Suite 290
Seattle, WA 98121
(206) 553-5615
Fax: (206) 553-7253

U.S. Department of Commerce
US & FCS Branch Office
Box 625
West 808 Spokane Falls Blvd.
Spokane, WA 99201
(509) 456-2922
Fax: (509) 458-2224

U.S. Small Business Administration
915 Second Avenue, Room 1792
Seattle, WA 98174
(206) 553-8405
Fax: (206) 553-8635

U.S. Small Business Administration
Farm Credit Building, 10th Floor
Spokane, WA 99204
(509) 353-2424
Fax: (509) 353-2829

WA State Department of Trade and
 Economic Development
2001 6th Avenue, Suite 2600
Seattle, WA 98121
(206) 464-7143
Fax: (206) 464-7222

WA State Department of Agriculture
406 General Administration Building
Olympia, WA 98504
(206) 753-5046

Export Assistance Center of Washington
2001 Sixth Avenue, Suite 1700
Seattle, WA 98121
(206) 464-7123

WA State International Trade Fair
1020 First Interstate Center
Seattle, WA 98104
(206) 682-6900
Fax: (206) 682-6190

Trade Development Alliance for
 Greater Seattle
One Union Square, 12th Floor
Seattle, WA 98101
(206) 389-7301
Fax: (206) 389-7288

Inland Northwest World Trade Council
P.O. Box 1124
Spokane, WA 99210
(509) 456-3243
Fax: (509) 458-2224

Spokane International Coordinating Council
City Hall, Room 650
West 808 Spokane Falls Blvd.
Spokane, WA 99201
(509) 456-3243

Washington Council on International Trade
Suite 350, Fourth & Vine Building
Seattle, WA 98121
(206) 443-3826
Fax: (206) 443-3828

World Affairs Council
515 Madison Street, Suite 501
Seattle, WA 98104
(206) 682-6986

World Trade Club of Seattle
P.O. Box 21488
Seattle, WA 98111
(206) 624-9586

World Trade Center, Tacoma
3600 Port of Tacoma Road
Tacoma, WA 98424
(206) 383+9474
Fax: (206) 926-0384

International Trade Institute
North Seattle Community College
9600 College Way North
Seattle, WA 98103
(206) 527-3732
Fax: (206) 527-3734

WEST VIRGINIA

U.S. Department of Commerce
US & FCS District Office
405 Capitol Street, Suite 809
Charleston, WV 25301
(304) 347-5123
Fax: (304) 347-5408

U.S. Small Business Administration
District Office
P.O. Box 1608
Clarksburg, WV 26302-1608
(304) 623-5631
Fax: (304) 623-0023

U.S. Small Business Administration
Branch Office
550 Eagan Street
Charleston, WV 25301
(304) 347-5220
Fax: (304) 347-5350

Governor's Office of Community
 & Industrial Development
Internation Development Division
Room 517, Building #6
1900 Washington Street, East
Charleston, WV 25305
(304) 348-2234
Fax: (304) 348-0449

Institute for International
Trade Development
Marshall University
1050 Fourth Avenue
Huntington, WV 25755-2131
(304) 696-6271
Fax: (304) 696-6880

West Virginia Chamber of Commerce
P.O. Box 2789
Charleston, WV 25330
(304) 342-1115
Fax: (304) 342-1130

West Virginia Export Council
P.O. Box 26
Charleston, WV 25321
(304) 347-5123
Fax: (304) 347-5408

West Virginia Manufacturers Association
405 Capitol Street, Suite 503
Charleston, WV 25301
(304) 342-2123
Fax: (304) 342-4552

WISCONSIN

U.S. Department of Commerce
US & FCS District Office
Room 596
517 East Wisconsin Avenue
Milwaukee, WI 53202
(414) 297-3473
Fax: (414) 297-3470

U.S. Small Business Administration
212 East Washington Avenue, Room 213
Madison, WI 53703
(608) 264-5261

U.S. Small Business Administration
500 South Barstow Street, Room 17
Eau Claire, WI 54701
(715) 834-9012

U.S. Small Business Administration
310 West Wisconsin Avenue, Room 400
Milwaukee, WI 53203
(414) 291-3941

Wisconsin Department of Development
123 West Washington Avenue
Madison, WI 53702
(608) 266-1767

Small Business Development Center
602 State Street
Madison, WI 53703
(608) 263-7766

Milwaukee Association of Commerce
756 North Milwaukee Street
Milwaukee, WI 53202
(414) 273-3000

Central Wisconsin World Trade Association
P.O. Box 803
Stevens Point, WI 54481
(715) 346-2728

Northeastern Wisconsin World
Trade Association
213 Nicolet Blvd.
Neenah, WI 54956
(414) 722-7758

Madison World Trade Association
P.O. Box 7900
Madison, WI 53707
(608) 222-3484

Milwaukee World Trade Association
756 North Milwaukee Street
Milwaukee, WI 53202
(414) 273-3000

Western Wisconsin World
Trade Association
P.O. Box 1425
Eau Claire, WI 54702
(715) 232-2311

South Central Wisconsin World
 Trade Association
Small Business Development Center
University of Wisconsin-Whitewater
2000 Carlson Hall
Whitewater, WI 53190
(414) 472-3217

WYOMING

U.S. Department of Commerce
US & FCS District Office
(See listing for Denver, CO)

U.S. Small Business Administration
100 East B Street, Room 4001
Casper, WY 82602
(307) 261-5761

Department of Commerce
Division of Economic & Community
 Development
Herschler Building, 2nd Floor West
Cheyenne, WY 82002

Department of Commerce
International Trade Office
Herschler Building, 2nd Floor West
Cheyenne, WY 82002

9.

STATE GRANTS, LOANS AND ASSISTANCE
****

Your state probably has money waiting for you. But, they won't send it to you unless you contact them first. No one will. Nearly each state has one or more active business programs to assist you in launching or expanding your business. Why? Because they know that new businesses provide jobs and increase tax revenues. Logically, the more businesses thriving in a state, the higher the employment, less redistribution of wealth to the indigent, and more tax dollars to spend on education, the arts, and, of course, paying off their state's indebtedness. A booming business climate keeps the politicians in office. Or, it helps launch them into the national spotlight, like Michael Dukakis' presidential bid in 1988. (The fact that he lost badly in his bid is missing the point; that he was able to make a bid, at all, came from a then-prospering business climate in his state.)

While states copy federal and each other's programs, every state has different kinds of money and assistance available. Because each state has different predominant industries or commerce, from Wall Street and investment banking to manufacturing, high technology or farming, they have different needs to fulfill for their resident enterprises.

Modifications are made annually in many state programs. Amounts granted for research and development and loan guarantees to launch new businesses or attract existing businesses to a state invariably change. Not only are some new programs added, but old or corruption-tainted programs dropped. Some, like the Massachusetts Technology Development Corporation, have become quasi-public companies, once financed by federal and state grants, but are now self-sufficient and profitable.

TYPES OF ASSISTANCE

State government programs can include these types of financial programs.

1. State Loan Guarantees. These are similar to the Small Business Administration's 7(a) program.

2. State Export Loans and assistance. Each state has one or more offices whose mission it is to promote the exportation of products manufactured in that state. States vary in the degree in which they assist exporters (see Chapter 8 for directory information on state export contacts).

3. State Interest rate subsidies. Some states, such as Missouri, will subsidize the interest rate a bank charges on your loan. The state uses its clout and deposits a large amount of money into a Certificate of Deposit. Happy to work with the state, your bank slices

the interest rate on your business loan and saves you thousands of dollars.

4.   State Department of Commerce assistance. Each state has a department of commerce that helps small businesses develop. A variety of assistance programs can include funding, business publications, research and licensing assistance and preparing business plans or business checklists to launch your enterprise.

5.   State specialty loans and grants. These may include industrial revenue bonds for building or purchasing a factory or heavy equipment; or offer loans to agricultural, high technology or energy conservation businesses. Some offer loans to inventors to assist them in developing and marketing new products Nearly all states offer financial and educational assistance to minorities and women and reserve money for economically disadvantaged groups.

6.   Local Government Loans. Money may be obtained from your local government to help you start or expand your business.

7.   Community Development Block Grants. Money is given to cities and counties to rehabilitate existing commercial buildings. Grants can go as high as $500,000 for this purpose and benefit local businesses and industries.

8.   Enterprise zone tax incentives. Firms can obtain varying tax credits that reduce specific taxes or exempt them from certain state taxes. In Florida these credits can add up to $200,000 per firm by reducing corporate income tax, property tax and sales tax.

This above list is by no means inclusive of all state loans, grants and assistance. Check your state for applicable programs found in the directory immediately following the text of this chapter. For additional programs not covered here visit your local library and ask for these publications.

a) The National Directory of State Agencies. (Bethesda, Maryland: National Standards Association) Updated annually.

b) The State Executive Directory. (Washington, D.C.: Carroll Publishing) Updated triannually.

c) The Book of the States. (Lexington, Kentucky: Council of State Governments) Update biennially.

d) National Association of State Development Agencies. Directory of Incentives for Business Investment: A State-by-State Guide. (Washington, D.C.: Urban Institute Press)

The latter (d) can help you locate hard-to-find programs, otherwise not covered in this chapter. Now, let's look at different programs found in two dissimilar states.

MASSACHUSETTS TECHNOLOGY DEVELOPMENT CORPORATION

Think about this for a moment. One state conceived of a state-operated venture capital company with the expressed purpose of investing in small technology-based companies that could not obtain financing elsewhere. In 1978 a law was enacted creating the Massachusetts Development Corporation (MTDC). For about ten years it was subsidized, in part, on grants from the U.S. Department of Commerce and the Commonwealth of Massachusetts, for more than $8 million.

Its mission was to leverage private investment in Massachusetts early-stage technology companies. They soon discovered that while these firms had business owners who were experienced in their technology, many were not proficient business managers. So, part of

MTDC's strategy included increasing the visibility and successful presentation of these companies to potential investors.

Where is today?   Still being subsidized? Absolutely not. Not only has it launched 56 new high technology businesses, but it now has assets in excess of $11 million. This state business financing program is probably THE most successful in the nation. It is one that other states should emulate in every way possible (Connecticut already has with their Connecticut Innovations). Here's why:

a)   Through 1991 MTDC has invested $17.7 million in 56 Massachusetts corporations.

b)   These investments have returned an annual average of 16 percent (which is then reinvested in other companies).

c)   These companies have, in turn, created 5,000 jobs in Massachusetts.

d)   Those 5,000 jobs have paid workers $186 million.

e)   From that $52 million has been paid out for federal taxes;

f)   And $9.6 million has been paid in Massachusetts state taxes.

In this instance, the federal government invested a little less than $3 million and got back $52 million, a return of more than 1700-%. Massachusetts invested over $5 million and kept 5,000 workers off unemployment while nearly doubling their money back on state taxes. Not bad at all! A few more government programs like this one and the federal deficit would be licked in our lifetimes!

MTDC has also made a few bum mistakes. Seven of the 56 failed and four paid back the investment without a worthwhile profit. However, 45 did succeed. Of those eight went public and five were purchased by larger companies. That's not bad considering that venture capital firms traditionally see about one-third of their investment go up in smoke. Percentage-wise MTDC has proven itself.

If you are a Massachusetts resident and have a business plan that fits under the MTDC profile, then I highly recommend you contact this quasi-government agency. They receive about 350 proposals annually, but only five to seven meet MTDC criteria for investment. Avoid disappointment and send away for their literature before submitting your business proposal.

Here are the key characteristics that MTDC is looking for in your company:

a)   Your company is located in, or agree to locate in, Massachusetts.

b)   The company's business must be technology based, and its principal products or services must be sufficiently innovative to provide a competitive advantage.

c)   The business expansion which MTDC's investment would help to finance must product a significant growth in employment.

d)   The company must be able to demonstrate that it has been unable to secure from conventional sources sufficient capital on affordable terms to finance its expansion.

e)   The company must be able to show the prospect of a high rate of return on investment.

If you feel your business qualifies for such funding, then please contact them.

MASSACHUSETTS TECHNOLOGY DEVELOPMENT CORPORATION
148 State Street
Boston, MA 021209
Telephone: (617) 723-4920
Fax: (617) 723-5983

THE IOWA PRODUCT DEVELOPMENT CORPORATION

The Iowa Product Development Corporation (IPDC) is a seed capital investment program providing financial assistance for businesses to launch innovate products and services into national and international markets. Its mission is to support qualified entrepreneurs in need of financial assistance when such assistance cannot be acquired from conventional sources due to risk levels inherent in new products, young and untested companies, and unproven markets. IPDC supports businesses which are capable of high growth and of providing substantial returns on invested funds. It seeks to promote creation of new jobs in firms that can make a significant contribution to the Iowa's communities.

IPDC, in six years of operation, has invested in forty companies with financial assistance ranging from $5,000 to nearly $500,000. It distilled those forty from more than one thousand inquiries and applications for lending assistance. IPDC is strictly interested in yielding a profitable financial return on the programs in which it invests.

Being from the Midwest, Iowans are generally cautious and skeptical of new ideas. So companies hoping to obtain IPDC financial assistance must first pass through a series of stages.

Stage One is the Initial Project Introduction and Review. Any person may submit a proposed project to IPDC staff by calling the office, arranging an office appointment, or preferably by submitting a brief written summary. Initial staff review will base their decision whether or not to proceed beyond this stage, depending on these criteria:

o Is this a well-defined product or service which is ready or nearly ready for commercial introduction and which reflects a promising innovation?

o Is there a national or international opportunity, based on knowledge of specific customers and their needs?

o Is the project's manager experienced with the product and its intended customers?

o Is there evidence of an entrepreneurial vision and commitment which holds promise for company growth, job creation, and significant community impact?

Stage Two is reserved for those who pass the first test and are then invited to make a formal application. IPDC will counsel the entrepreneur on developing a complete application and business concept plan conforming to IPDC requirements. Your business concept plan would include sufficient documentation to describe:

1. That the innovative product, process, or service works, or that there is convincing evidence that it will work after routine prototype assembly steps have been completed; that is has a distinct advantage over products or services currently used by intended customers; that the product concept would not be easily copied by potential competitors.

2. That surveys, trade journals, or other reliable sources show that the target market has need for and will accept a new product from the company; that customer purchasing decisions are made by people willing to buy from a new company; and will occur within a time period that can be accommodated by the applicant's resources; that the effective systems for marketing, sales, distribution, and product support can be developed within the financial and managerial resources of the company; that there is long-term market growth

potential for the applicant's product or service, or for others that it may introduce in the future.

3. That the applicant has the basic skills required to operate the proposed business and recognizes the need to obtain other assistance where appropriate to achieve business goals; that previous experience provides the applicant with knowledge of how the product will be received by its customers; that the applicant's specialized knowledge would permit the product to command substantial profit margins or marketing advantages; that reference and credit checks would reveal the type of person likely to be well received by customers, lenders, and others with whom he or she must do business.

4. That the business concept plan includes current and historical financial statements, with lists of all stockholders, debt sources and terms; that projections of future income, cashflow, and balance sheets are based on sound, documented assumptions; that there is an opportunity to produce growth in revenues and earnings that will yield satisfactory returns to IPDC and other participating investors; that there are capable outside directors and other advisors in place to support this project.

Those are the basic stages that most fail to pass in working with IPDC. Over time, they have discovered that those who pass muster and complete Stage Two have usually been counseled by the local Small Business Development Center (see Chapter 6).

By Stage Three most would-be Iowan entrepreneurs have either turned to another form of financing or given up on their project and returned to growing corn or raising hogs. If your has gotten this far, your presentation is ready for the IPDC Board of Directors who meet monthly to discuss such business concept plans. At this point you will pay a minimum of $100 to make the formal application. Fees are based on $100 or 0.025% of the amount requested, whichever is greater.

An Investment Committee appointed by the IPDC Board of Directors will investigate your plan. The Board may also authorize an initial exploratory investment for professional market research, prototype evaluation, product testing, and other activities necessary for confirmation of a complete and credible business plan. Funding commitments at this exploratory stage may bring you between $5,000 and $50,000, but are subject to repayment as part of any subsequent IPDC investment in your business.

At Stage Four, when the complete investigation confirms that the project may provide an acceptable investment risk and when a fully documented business plan has been completed, the IPDC Board of Directors may authorize funding to launch a commercial venture. They won't give it to you all once. The funding agreement will often include a sequence of performance measures to be met as each increment of financial assistance is released. IPDC funding at this stage may range from $100,000 to $500,000.

The IPDC now becomes the venture capitalist. Their funding is typically in the form of a subordinated debenture or preferred stock, both convertible to common stock. Other common contract provisions include signing away proprietary rights in your product and non-voting participation in the company's board of directors.

Finally, in a post-funding stage, the IPDC maintains frequent contact with the company to monitor progress and to support company operations. You will be required to file quarterly reports of financial conditions and other performance measures, with an annual audit or review by public accountants. Why? Because IPDC, like any other venture capital company, realizes it takes between five and ten years for a new business to reach sustaining profitability. Usually, the entrepreneur calls upon IPDC to provide additional financing, often to bail him out of serious trouble.

If you're game, try them out. They receive hundreds of proposals each year but only fund between six and ten new business projects; that's less than five percent of all funding requests. At worst, they'll refer you to other sources. For further information, write or call:

THE IOWA PRODUCT DEVELOPMENT CORPORATION
200 East Grand Avenue
Des Moines, Iowa 50309
(515) 242-4860

OTHER STATES

While other states don't have such a gem to show off, many have similar programs and successes.   While yours may not be a technology-based company, it may still find funding. There are probably more opportunities available than you realize. States would be in far more dire straits if they only financed minorities, veterans, women and techno-nerds. There's a world of financial and managerial assistance for your business open to you in your state. Use it.

In the directory which follows, find your state and start calling applicable government agencies that could begin helping your business get the help needs the moment someone answers the telephone.

STATE ASSISTANCE DIRECTORY

ALABAMA

Division of Vocational Services
5106 Gordon Persone Bldg.
50 North Ripley Street
Montgomery, AL 36130
(205) 242-9111

Technology Assistance Partnership
Science, Technology and Energy Division
Alabama Department of Economic and
 Community Affairs
P.O. Box 250347
Montgomery, AL
(205) 242-5425

Business Council of Alabama
Alabama Development Office
State Capitol
Mongomery, AL 36130
(205) 242-0400

ALASKA

Department of Commerce and Economic
 Development
Division of Business Development
333 Willoughby Ave.
9th Floor
Anchorage, AK 99503
(907) 563-2165

Department Of Commerce and Economic
 Development
P.O. Box 110804
Juneau, AK 99811
(907) 465-2017

Yarmon Investments
5th Avenue, #440
Anchorage, AK 99501
(907) 276-4466

Alaska Industrial Development and Export
 Authority (AIDEA)
480 West Tudor Road
Anchorage, AK 99503
(907) 561-8050

State Executive Director
Agricultural Stabilization and Conservation
 Service
800 W. Evergreen, Suite 216
Palmer, AK 99645
(907) 745-7892

Alaska Department of Natural Resources
Division of Agriculture
P.O. Box 949
Palmer, AK 99645-0949

Department of Community and Regional
 Affairs
Rural Development Fund
949 East 36th Avenue, Suite 400
Anchorage, AK 99507
(907) 269-4500

Loan Officer
Alaska Energy Authority
P.O. Box 190869
701 East Tudor Road
Anchorage, AK 99519-561-7877

Community Enterprise Development
 Corporation (CDEC)
1577 C Street, Suite 304
Anchorage, AK 99501
(907) 274-5400

Railbelt Community Development Corporation
619-Warehouse Avenue
Anchorage, AK 99501
(907) 277-5161

Alaska Commercial Fishing and Agricultural
 Bank (CFAB)
P.O. Box 92070
Anchorage, AK 99503
(907) 276-2007

State Executive Director
Alaska State ASCS Office
634 South Bailey, Suite 102
Palmer, AK 99645
(907) 271-4022

Child Care Programs Coordinator
Department of Community and Regional
 Affairs
Rural Development Fund
949 East 36th Avenue, Suite 400
Anchorage, AK 99058
(907) 269-4500

Office of Industrial Trade
Department of Commerce and Economic
Development
3601 C Street, Suite 798
Anchorage, AK 99503
(907) 561-5585

Community Development Program
Cooperative Extension Service
2221 East Northern Lights Blvd.
Suite 132
Anchorage, AK 99508-4143
(907) 276-2433

Cooperative Extension Service
University of Alaska
Fairbanks, AK 99701-271-7246
(907) 474-7246

State Conservationist
Soil Conservation Service
201 East 9th Avenue, Suite 300
Anchorage, AK 99501-3687
(907) 271-2424

Department of Natural Resources
Division of Agriculture
P.O. Box 949
Palmer, AK 99645-0949
(907) 745-7200

4420 Airport Way
Fairbanks, AK 99709
(907) 451-2780

Department of Economic and Community
 Development
Division of Tourism
P.O. Box E
Juneau, AK 99811
(907) 465-2012

Department of Environmental Conservation
Division of Environmental Quality
P.O. Box O
Juneau, AK 99811
(907) 465-5260

Economic Development Administration
Old Federal Building
605 West Fourth Avenue, Room G-80
Anchorage, AK 99513
(907) 271-2272

Community Information Exchange
1029 Vernon Avenue Northwest, Suite 710
Washington, D.C. 20005
(202) 628-2981

Community Enterprise Development
 Corporation
Minority Business Development Center, Inc.
1011 East Tudor Road, Suite 210
Anchorage, AK 99503
(907) 274-5400

Alaska Business Development Center, Inc.
143 East 9th Avenue, Suite 250
Anchorage, AK 99501
(907) 279-7427

Fairbanks Native Association
Manpower and Training
Native Business Center
310 First Avenue
Fairbanks, AK 99701
(907) 456-2311

ARIZONA

Arizona Department of Economic
 Development
Department of Commerce
3800 N. Central
Phoenix, AZ 85012
(602) 280-1300

Arizona Business Connection
(602) 280-1480

Business Finance Unit
Arizona Office of Economic Development
Department of Commerce
3800 N. Central
Phoenix, AZ 85012
(602) 280-1341

Economic Development Administration
(602) 379-3750

First Interstate Equity Corporation
100 West Washington Street
Phoenix, AZ
(602) 528-6647

Rocky Mountain Equity Corporation
2525 E. Camelback, Suite 275
Phoenix, AZ 85016
(602) 955-6100

Sundance Venture Partners, LP
Main Office: Menlo Park, CA
400 E. Van Buren
Phoenix, AZ 85004
(602) 252-3441

Arizona Business Connection
Arizona Department of Commerce
3800 N. Central, Suite 1400
Phoenix, AZ 85012
(602) 280-1480

ARKANSAS

Arkansas Industrial Development
 Commission
One State Capital Mall
Little Rock, AR 72201
(501) 682-1121

Coordinator, Small Business Programs
Arkansas industrial Development Commis-
sion
One State Capitol Mall, Room 4C300
Little Rock, AR 72201-8023
(501) 682-5800

Arkansas Industrial Development Commission
Community Development Commission
One State Capitol Mall
Little Rock, AR 72291
(501) 682-5275

Arkansas Development Finance Authority
100 Main Street, Suite 200
Little Rock, AR 72201-8023
(501) 682-5960

Arkansas Industrial Development
 Commission
Community Development Commission
One State Capitol Mall
Little Rock, AR 72291
(501) 682-1211

Enterprise Zone Program
(501) 682-7310

Community Assistance Division
Community Development Block Grants
(501) 682-5193

Arkansas Science and Technology Authority
100 Main Street, Suite 450 (Technology
 Center)
Little Rock, AR 72201
(501) 324-9006

Small Business Investment Capital, Inc.
10003 New Benton Hwy.
P.O. Box 3627
Little Rock, AR 72203
(501) 455-6599

Southern Ventures, Inc.
605 Main Street, Suite 202
Arkadelphia, AR 71923
(501) 246-9627

Arkansas Capital Corporation
800 Pyramid Place
221 West Second Street
Little Rock, AR 72201
(501) 374-9247

Minority Business Development Division
(501) 682-1060

Small Business Division
(501) 682-5275

Office of Employment and Training Service
Employment Security Division
P.O. Box 2981
Little Rock, AR 72203
(501) 682-5227

Arkansas Industrial Development
 Corporation
One State Capital Mall
Little Rock, AR 72201
(501) 682-5275

Small Business Division
(501) 682-5275

Marketing Division
(501) 682-7781

Motion Picture Development Office
(501) 682-7676

Research Section
(501) 682-2301

Arkansas Inventors Congress
P.O. Box 411
Dardanelle, AR 72834
(501) 229-4515

Arkansas Science and Technology Authority
100 Main Street, Suite 450 (Technology
 Center)
Little Rock, AR 72201
(501) 324-9006

Small Business Institutes:
Arkansas College, Batesville
(501) 843-1224
Arkansas State University, Jonesboro
(501) 972-3517
Arkansas Tech University, Russellville
(501) 968-0537
Harding University, Searcy
(501) 279-4552
Henderson State University, Arkadelphia
(501) 246-5511
Southern State University, Magnolia
(501) 235-4375
University of Arkansas, Fayetteville
(501) 575-5148
University of Arkansas, Little Rock
(501) 569-8852
University of Arkansas, Monticello
(501) 460-1041
University of Arkansas, Pine Bluff
(501) 543-8030
University of Arkansas, Conway
(501) 450-3190
University of the Ozarks, Clarksville
(501) 754-3839

Business and Industrial Institute
Westark Community College
P.O. Box 3649
Fort Smith, AR 72913
(501) 785-7311

Center for Economic Development
Economic Development Assistance Program
Arkansas State University
P.O. Box 2110
State University, AR 72467-2110
(501) 972-3850

Economic Development Districts
Economic Development Administration
5th & Gaines, Room 2509
Little Rock, AR 72201
(501) 324-5637

White River Planning and Development
 District
P.O. Box 2396
Batesville, AR 72501
(501) 793-5233

Western Arkansas Planning and Development District
623 garrison Avenue
P.O. Box 2067
Fort Smith, AR 72901
(501) 741-5404

Northwest Arkansas Development District
P.O. Box 190
Harrison, AR 72601
(501) 741-5404

West Central Arkansas Planning and Development District
P.O. Box 1558
Hot Springs, AR 71901
(501) 624-1036

East Arkansas Planning and Development
 District
P.O. Box 1403
Jonesboro, AR 72401
(501) 932-3957

Central Arkansas Planning and Development
 District
112 N.E. Front Street
P.O. Box 187
Lonoke, AR 72086
(501) 676-2721

Southeast Arkansas Economic Development
 District
P.O Box 6806
Pine Bluff, AR 71601
(501) 536-1971

Entrepreneurial Service Center
College of Business Administration
University of Arkansas
Fayetteville, AR 72701
(501) 575-2856

Tourism Development Section
Arkansas Department of Parks and Tourism
One State Capital Mall
Little Rock, AR 72201
(501) 682-5240

CALIFORNIA

California Department of Commerce
801 K Street, Suite 1700
Sacramento, CA 95814
(916) 322-1394

Office of Small Business
(916) 324-5056

Office of Local Development
(916) 324-8211

OBD Field Office
200 East Del Mar Drive
Suite 204
Los Angeles, CA 90005
(818) 568-9856

OBD Field Office
111 N. Market street
Suite 815
San Jose, CA 95113
(408) 277-9799

Small Business Advocate
1120 N Street, Room 2101
Sacramento, CA 95814
(916) 322-0467

California Commission for Economic Devel-
 opment
Office of the Lieutenant Governor
State Capitol, Room 1028
Sacramento, CA 95814
(916) 445-8994

California Department of Commerce
801 K Street, Suite 1700
Sacramento, CA 95814
(916) 324-8211

Major Corporate Projects
(916) 322-5665

California Statewide Certified Development
 Corporation
129 C Street
Davis, CA 95616
(916) 756-9310

AMF Financial,Inc.
4330 La Jolla Village Drive
Suite 110
San Diego, CA 92122
(619) 546 0167

BNP Venture Capital Corporation
3000 Sand Hill Road
Building 1, Suite 125
Menlo Park, CA 04025
(415) 854-8001

Citicorp Venture Capital, Inc.
(Main Office: New York, N.Y.)
2 Embarcadero Place
220 Geny Road, Suite 203
Palo Alto, CA 94303
(415) 424-8000

Developers Equity Capital Corporation
1880 Century Park East, Suite 311
Los Angeles, CA 90067
(310) 277-0330

Draper Associates, A California LP
c/o Timothy C. Draper
400 Seaport Ct.
Suite 25
Redwood City, CA 94063
(415) 599-9000

Hall, Morris Drufba
5000 Birch Street
Suite 10100
Newport Beach, CA 92660

First SBIC of California
650 Town Center Drive, 17th Floor
Costa Mesa, Ca 92626
(714) 556-1964

First SBIC of California
(Main Office Costa Mesa, CA)
155 North Lake Avenue, Suite 938
(415) 424-8011

GC&H Partners
One Maritime Plaza, 20th Floor
San Francisco, CA 94110
(415) 981-5252

Hamco Capital Corporation
One Bush Street, 18th Floor
San Francisco, CA 94104
(415) 576-3635

Imperial Ventures, Inc.
9920 South La Cienega Blvd.
P.O. Box 92991; L.A. 90009
Inglewood, CA 90301
(310) 417-5491

Jupiter Partners
600 Montgomery Street, 35th Floor
San Francisco, CA 94111
(415) 421-9990

Marwit Capital Corporation
180 Newport Center Drive, Suite 200
Newport Beach, CA 92660
(714) 640-6234

Merrill Pickard Anderson & Eyre I
2480 Sand Hill Rd.
Menlo Park, CA 94025
(415) 854-8600

Metropolitan Venture Company, Inc.
4021 Rosewood Avenue, 3rd Floor
Los Angeles, CA 90004
(213) 666-9882

New West Partners II
4350 Executive Drive, Suite 206
San Diego, CA 91212
(619) 457-0723

Ritter Partners
150 Isabella Avenue
Atherton, CA 94025
(415) 854-1555

San Joaquin Capital Corporation
1415-18th Street, Suite 306
P.O. Box 2538
Bakersfield, CA 93301
(805) 323-7581

Seaport Ventures, Inc.
525 B Street, suite 630
San Diego, CA 92101
(619) 232-4069

Jeremiah Corp.
3000 Sand hill Road
Building 4, #130
Menlo Park, CA 94025
(415) 854-8100

Union Venture Corporation
45 South Figueroa Street
Los Angeles, CA 90071
(213) 236-4092

VK Company
11661 San Vicente Blvd., Suite 709
Los Angeles, CA 90049
(310) 820-2970

Wells Fargo Business Retirement
420 Montgomery Street, 9th Floor
San Francisco, CA 94163
(415) 396-2059

Westamco Investment Company
8929 Wilshire Blvd., Suite 400
Beverly Hills, CA 90211
(310) 652-8288

California World Trade Commission
Export Finance Office
107 south Broadway, Suite 8039
Los Angeles, CA 90012
(213) 557-3007

California Capital Small Business Development Corporation
926 J Street, Suite 1500
Sacramento, CA 95814
(916) 442-1729

California Coastal Rural Development
 Corporation
Five East Gabilan Street, Suite 218
Salinas, CA 93902
(408) 424-1099

Bay Area Development Corporation
3932 Harrison Street
Oakland, CA 94611
(510) 652-5262

Hancock Urban Development Corporation
3540 Wilshire Blvd., Suite 215
Los Angeles, CA 90010
(213) 382-4300

Pacific Coast Regional Urban Development
 Corporation
3810 Wilshire Blvd., Suite 1910
Los Angeles, CA 90010

California Southern
600 B Street, Suite 2200
San Diego, CA 92189
(619) 232-7771

Valley Small Business Development Corporation
2344 Tulare street, Suite 302
Fresno, CA 93721
(209) 268-0166

Office of Small and Minority Business
Department of General Services
1808 14th Street, Suite 100
Sacramento, CA 95814
(916) 322-5060

California Department of Commerce
801 K Street, Suite 1700
Sacramento, CA 95814
(916) 322-1398

Office of Small Business
(916) 324-1295

Office of Business Development
(916) 322-5665

Office of Local Development
(916) 322-3597

Office of Economic Research
(916) 324-5853

Office of Foreign Investment
(916) 327-0583

CompTech
200 East Del Mar Avenue
Suite 204
Pasadena, CA 91005
(213) 568-9660

California Film Association
6922 Hollywood Boulevard
Suite 660
Hollywood, CA 90028
(213) 736-2465

Western Association of Venture Capitalists
3000 Sand Hill Road
Building 1 , Suite 190
Menlo Park, CA 94025
(415) 854-1322

COLORADO

Office of Business Development
1625 Broadway, Suite 1710
Denver, CO 80202
(303) 892-3840

Office of Economic Development
1625 Broadway, Suite 1710
Denver, CO 80202
(303) 892-3840

Colorado Housing and Finance Authority
 (CHFA)
1981 Blake Street
Denver, CO 80202
(303) 297-2605

Colorado Department of Local Affairs
1313 Sherman Street, #518
Denver, CO 80203
(303) 866-2771

Colorado Agricultural Development Authority
 (CADA)
1525 Sherman Street, Room 406
Denver, CO 80302
(303) 239-4124

Northwest Investment Services
1700 Broadway
Denver, CO 80274
(303) 863-6329

Colorado Development Companies (CDC)
Pikes Peak Regional Development Corporation
1826 East Platte Avenue, Suite 101
Colorado Springs, CO 80909
(719) 471-2044

Community Economic Development of
 Colorado
1111 Osage Street, Suite 110
Denver, CO 80204
(303) 893-8989

Denver Urban Economic Development of
 Colorado
303 West Colfax Avenue, Suite 1025
Denver, CO 80204
(303) 296-5400

SCEDD Development Company
P.O. Box 1900
212 West 13th
Pueblo, CO 81003
(719) 545-8680

Colorado Department of Local Affairs
1313 Sherman Street # 518
Denver, CO 80203
(303) 866-2771

Colorado Venture Management
4845 Pearl East Circle, Suite 300
Boulder, CO 80301
(303) 892-3840

Department of Transportation
Office of Small and Disadvantaged Business
 Utilization
Minority Business Resource Center
400 7th Street, N.W.
Washington, D.C. 20590
(202) 366-2582

Minority Business Office
Office of Economic Development
1625 Broadway, Suite 1710
Denver, CO 80202
(303) 892-3840

National Minority Supplier
Development Council, Inc.
Business Consortium Fund
(212) 944-2430

Department of Economic Development
1625 Broadway, Suite 1710
Denver, CO 80202
(303) 892-3840

Colorado Community College and Occupational Education System
1391 North Speer Blvd., Suite 600
Denver, CO 80204
(303) 620-4000

Governor's Job Training Office
1391 North Speer Blvd., Suite 400
Denver, CO 80204
(303) 758-5020

Colorado Division of Employment and
 Training
600 Grant Street, Suite 900
Denver, CO 80203
(303) 837-3900

CU Business Advancement Centers BAC's)
4700 Walnut Street, Suite 101
Boulder, CO 80301
(303) 444-5723

CONNECTICUT

Office of Small Business Services
Department of Economic Development
865 Brooks Street
Rocky Hill CT   06067
(203) 258-4295

Connecticut Development Authority
Business Development Division
217 Washington Street
Hartford, CT 06106
(203) 258-7800

Innovation, Inc.
845 Brook Street
Rocky Hill, CT 06067
(203) 258-4305

Connecticut Department of Economic
 Development
865 Brooks Street
Rocky Hill, CT 06067
(203) 258-4275

AB SBIC Inc.
275 School House Road
Cheshire, CT 06410
(203) 272-0203

All State Venture Capital Corporation
The Bishop House
32 Elm Street, P.O. Box 1629
New Haven, CT 06506
(203) 787-5029

Capital Impact Corporation
10 Middle Street, 16th Floor
Bridgeport, CT 06601
(203) 384-5670

Capital Resource Co. of Connecticut
699 Bloomfield Avenue
Bloomfield, CT 06002
(203) 236-4336

Dewey Investment Corporation
85 Charter Oak Street
Manchester, CT 06040
(203) 649-0654

First Connecticut SBIC
1000 Lafayette Blvd.
Suite 805
Bridgeport, CT 06604
(203) 366-4726

First New England Capital, LP
255 Main Street
Hartford, CT 06106
(203) 293-3333

Marcon Capital Corporation
49 Riverside Avenue
Westport, CT 06880
(203) 226-6893

Northeastern Capital Corporation
209 Church Street
New Haven, CT 06510
(203) 966-2800

RFE Capital Partners, LP
36 Grove Street
New Canaan, CT 06840

SBIC of Connecticut, Inc.
1115 Main Street
Bridgeport, CT 06603
(203) 261-0011

Connecticut Small Business
 Development Center
University of Connecticut
School of Administration
368 Fairfield Road
Box-U-41, Room 422
Storrs, CT 06269-2041
(203) 486-4135

DELAWARE

Delaware Development Office
99 Kings Highway
P.O. Box 1401
Dover, DE 19903
(302) 739-4271

Delaware Development Office
Carvel State Office Building
820 North French Street
Wilmington, DE 19801
(302) 577-3156

BDP Capital Ltd.
103 Springer Street
3411 Silverside Road
Wilmington, DE 19810
(302) 234-1849

Morgan Investment Corporation
902 Market Street
Wilmington, DE 19801
(302) 651-2500

Delaware Development Corporation
99 Kings Highway
P.O. Box 1401
Dover, DE 19903
(302) 739-4271

Wilmington Chamber of Commerce
City County Building
800 French Street
Wilmington, DE 19801

(302) 571-4169

New Castle County Economic Development
 Corporation
704 King Street
1st federal Plaza
Suite 536
Wilmington, DE 19801
(302) 656-5050

Wilmington Economic Development Corporation
605A Market Street Mall, Suite 306
Wilmington, DE 19801
(302) 571-9088

Sussex County Department of Economic
 Development
Sussex County Courthouse
P.O. Box 589
Georgetown, DE 19947
(302) 855-7770

Central Delaware Economic Development
9 Lockerman Street
Treadway Towers, Suite 2-B
P.O. Box 576
Dover, DE 19903
(302) 571-6028

Minority Business Development Agency
6th Floor, City/County Building
800 French Street Wilmington, DE 19801
(302) 571-4169

Delaware State Chamber of Commerce
One Commerce Center, Suite 200
Wilmington, DE 19801
(302) 655-6294

Division of Facilities Management/Energy
 Office
Margaret M. O'Neill Building
P.O. Box 1401
Dover, DE 19903
(302) 739-5644

Delaware Development Office
Carvel State Office Building
P.O. Box 8911
Wilmington, DE 19801
(302) 577-6262

Governor's International Trade Council
Carvel State Office Building
P.O. Box 8911
Wilmington, DE 19801
(302) 577-3160

Delaware Department of Agriculture
2320 South duPont Highway
Dover, DE 19901
(302) 739-4811

Container Port of Wilmington
P.O. Box 1191
Wilmington, DE 19899
(302) 652-6644

DISTRICT OF COLUMBIA

Office of Business and Economic Development
717 14th Street, N.W., 10th Floor
Washington, DC 20005
(202) 727-6600

Office of Business and Economic Development
Financial Services Division
717 14th Street, N.W., 10th Floor
Washington, DC 20005
(202) 727-6600

Economic Development and Finance Corporation
1111 18th Street, N.W., 6th Floor
P.O. Box 1993
Washington, DC 20036
(202) 634-7838

Allied Investment Corporation
1666 K Street, NW, Suite 901
Washington, DC 20006
(202) 331-1112

American Security Capital Corporation, Inc.
730 15th Street, NW
Washington, DC 20005
(202) 624-5573

Venture Capital Company
1801 K Street, NW
Washington, DC. 20006
(202) 955-8188

Washington DC Minority Business
 Development Center
1133 15th Street, NW
Suite 1120
Washington, DC 20005
(202) 785-2886

Minority Business Opportunity Commission
2000 14th Street, NW, Room 324
Washington, DC 20009
(202) 939-8780

The Greater Washington Ibero-American
 Chamber of Commerce
2100 M Street, NW, Suite 607
Washington, DC 20037
(703) 535-2100

Washington District Small Business
 Administration
1111 18th Street, NW, 6th Floor
P.O. Box 1993
Washington, DC 20036
(202) 634-7838

Office of Job Services
Department of Employment Services
500 C Street, NW
Washington, DC 20001
(202) 639-1601

Office of Business and Economic
 Development
717 14th Street, NW, 10th Floor
Washington, DC 20005
(202) 727-6600

Business and Permit Center
Department of Consumer and Regulatory
 Affairs
614 H Street, NW, Room 100
Washington, DC 20001
(202) 727-7100

George Washington University Small Business Legal Clinic
National Law Center
720 20th Street, NW, Suite SL-101
Washington, DC 20052
(202) 994-7463

Washington District Small Business Administration
1111 18th Street, NW, 6th Floor
P.O. Box 1993
Washington, DC 200036
(202) 634-7838

FLORIDA

Bureau of Business Assistance
Department of Commerce
107 W. Gains St.
Collins Building, Room 443
Tallahassee, FL 32399-2000
(904) 488-9357

Business Services Section
1-800-342-0771

Industry and Retention Program
(904) 488-9360

Bureau of Economic and Community Assistance
Florida Department of Community Affairs
2740 Centerview Drive
Rhyne Building
Tallahassee, FL 32299-2000
(904) 4883581

Florida First Capital Finance Company
c/o Florida Department of Commerce
Bureau of Business Assistance
107 W. Gains Street
Collins Building
Tallahassee, FL 32399-2000
(904) 488-9357

Florida Department of Commerce
Bureau of Business Assistance
Business Finance Section
107 W. Gains Street
Tallahassee, FL 32399-2000
(904) 488-9357

Economic Development and Commercial
 Revitalization
Bureau of Community Assistance
2740 Centerview Drive
Rhyne Building
Tallahassee, Fl 332399-2000
(904) 488-3581

Allied Investment Corporation
(Main Office: Washington, DC)
Executive Office center, Suite 305
2770 N. Indian River Blvd.
Vero Beach, FL 32960
(407) 778-5556

Florida Capital Ventures, Ltd.
111 Madison Street, 26th Floor
Tampa, Fl 33602
(813) 229-2294

J & D Capital Corporation
12747 Biscayne Blvd.
North Miami, Fl 33181
(305) 893-0300

Mariner Venture Capital Corporation
2300 W. Glades Road
Suite 440 West Tower
Boca Raton, FL 33431
(407) 394-3066

Market Capital Corporation
1102 North 28th Street
P.O. Box 33667
Tampa, FL 33631
(813) 247-1357

Quantum Capital Partners, Ltd.
Main Office: New York, N.Y.
4400 NE 25th Ave.
Ft. Lauderdale, FL 33308
(305) 570-6231

Sigma Capital Corporation
1515 N. Federal Highway, Suite 210
Boca Raton, FL 33432
(407) 368-9783

Western Financial Capital Corporation
Main Office: Dallas, TX
AmeriFirst Bank building, 2nd Floor S
18301 Biscayne Blvd.
N. Miami Beach, FL 33160
(305) 933-5858

Community and Business Loan Program
410 SE First Avenue
Room 214, Federal Building
Gainesville, FL 32601
(904) 338-3440

Central Florida Areawide Development
 Corporation
490 East Davidson Street
Bartow, FL 33830
(813) 534-7138

North Central Florida Areawide Development Company, Inc.
235 South Main Street, Suite 205
Gainesville, FL 32601
(904) 336-2199

Jacksonville Local Development Company,
 Inc.
128 East Forsyth Street
Florida Theatre Building, Suite 600
Jacksonville, FL 32202
(904) 630-1914

Miami Citywide Development, Inc.
DuPont Plaza Center
300 Biscayne Blvd. Suite 614
Miami, FL 33131
(305) 358-1025

Miami-Dade Business Development Corporation
300 Southwest 12th Avenue, Suite A
Miami, FL 33130
(305) 541-0457

Orlando Neighborhood Improvement Corporation, Inc..
455 south Orange Avenue
Orlando, FL 32801
(407) 246-2522

St. Petersburg Certified Development Corporation
475 Central Ave.
St. Petersburg, FL 33701
(813) 892-5108

Florida First Capital Finance Corporation,
 Inc.
Department of Commerce
426 Collins Building
107 West Gaines Street
Tallahassee, FL 32399-2000
(904) 487-0466

Tampa Urban Economic Development
 Corporation
Office of Urban Development
306 East Jackson Street, 7th Floor E
P.O. Box 3330
Tampa, Fl 33601-3330
(813) 223-8418

Orlando Neighborhood Improvement Corporation, Inc.
455 South Orange Avenue
Orlando, FL 32801
(407) 246-2522

St. Petersburg Certified Development Corporation
475 Central Avenue
St. Petersburg, FL 33701
(813) 892-5108

Florida First Capital Finance Corporation,
 Inc.
Florida Department of Commerce
426 Collins Building
108 West Gaines Street
Tallahassee, FL 32399-2000
(904) 487-0466

Tampa Bay Economic Development Corporation
Office of Urban development
306 East Jackson Street, 7th Floor East
P.O. Box 3300
Tampa, FL 33601-3330
(813) 223-8418

Coconut Grove Local Development Corporation, Inc.
3582 Grand Avenue
P.O. Box 75
Coconut Grove, FL 33133
(305) 446-3095

Liberia Economic and Social Development
Corporation, Inc.
1190 Sheridan Street
Dania, FL 33004
(305) 921-2371

Central Florida Community Development
Corporation, Inc.
520 North Ridgewood Avenue, Suite B
Daytona Beach, Fl 32014
(904) 258-7520

Deerfield Beach Community Development
Corporation, Inc.
13 Southwest Tenth Street
Deerfield Beach, FL 33441
(305) 427-4692

United Gainesville Community Development Corporation, Inc.
P.O. Box 2518
Gainesville, FL 32602
(904) 764-1728

Community Economic Development Council, Inc.
8911 Devenshire Blvd.
Jacksonville, FL 32208
(904) 764-1728

New Washington Heights Community Development Conference, Inc.
1600 Northwest Third Avenue
Miami, FL 33136
(305) 573-8217

Northeast Miami Chamber of Commerce,
Inc.
8281 Northeast Second Avenue
Miami, FL 33138
(305) 895-7182

Martin Luther King Community Development Operation, Inc.
6166 Northwest Seventh Avenue
Miami, FL 33127
(305) 757-7652

Miami Beach Development Corporation,
Inc.
1205-Drexel Avenue, 2nd Floor
Miami beach FL 33139
(305) 538-1010

Community Equity Investments, Inc.
302 North Barcelona Street
Pensacola, FL 32501
(904) 433-5619

Community and Economic Development
Organization of Gasden Cty, Inc.
215 West Jefferson Street, Suite 2
Quincy, FL 32351
(904) 627-7565

Seminole Employment Economic Development Corporation, Inc.
1011 South Sanford Avenue
P.O. Box 2076
Sanford, FL 32771
(407) 323-4360

Metro-Broward Black Business Investment
Corporation
1415 East Sunrise Blvd., Suite 102
Ft. Lauderdale, FL 33304
(305) 465-3143

First Coast Black Business Investment
 Corporation
101 East Union Street, Suite 309
Jacksonville, FL 32202
(904) 634-0543

Business Assistance Center
6600 Northwest 27th Avenue
Miami, FL 33147
(305) 693-3550

Black Business Investment Fund of Central
 Florida
Landmark Building#655
315 Robinson Street
Orlando, FL 32801
(407) 649-4780

Palm Beach County Black Business Investment Corporation
Barnett Bank Building, Suite 301
2001 Broadway
Riviera Beach, FL 33404
(305) 895-7182

Tampa Bay Black Business Investment
 Corporation
315 East Kennedy Blvd.
Tampa, FL 33602
(813) 223-8381

Florida Department of Transportation
Minority Programs Office
Hayden Burns Building, Room 260
Tallahassee, FL 32399-0450
(904) 488-3145

Minority Construction Program
Florida Board of Regents
Florida Education Center. Room 1601
Tallahassee, FL 32399-1950
(904) 488-5251

Minority Business Enterprise Assistance
 Office
Department of Managers Services
Knight Building
Koger Executive Center, Suite 201
2737 Centerview Drive
Tallahassee, FL 32399-0100
(904) 487-0915

Ft. Lauderdale MBDC
3500 North State Road 7
Suite 407
Ft. Lauderdale, FL 33319
(305) 485-5333

Jacksonville MBDC
333 North Laura Street, Suite 465
Jacksonville, FL 32202-3508
(904) 353-3826

MBDC District Office
51 Southwest 1st Avenue, Room 1314
Box 25
Miami, FL 33130
(305) 535-5054

Miami MBDC
100 Northwest 78 Avenue, Suite 301
Miami, FL 33126
(305) 591-7355

Orlando MBDC
132 East Colonial Drive, Suite 211
Orlando, FL 32801
(407) 422-6234

Tampa/St. Petersburg MBDC
4601 W. Kennedy Street, Suite 200
Tampa, FL 33609
(813) 289-8824

Florida Regional Minority Purchasing Council, Inc.
7900 Northeast Second Avenue, Suite 202
Miami, FL 33138

(305) 536-5521

Greater Florida Minority Development
 Council,Inc.
120 University Park Drive, Suite 170
Winter Park, FL 32792-4419
(407) 679-4147

Small and Minority Business Advocate
Florida Department of Commerce
503 Collins Building
Tallahassee, FL 32399-2000
(904) 487-4698

Industry Services Training Program
Division of Vocational Services
Florida Department of Education
Florida Education Center, Room 1102
Tallahassee, FL 32399-0400
(904) 487-1040

Economic Development and Industry Pro-
 grams
State Board of Community Colleges
Florida Department of Education
Florida Education Center, Room 1314
Tallahassee, FL 32399-0667
(904) 487-4943

Bureau of Job Training
204 Atkins Building
1320 Executive Center Drive
Tallahassee, FL 32399-0667
(904) 488-9250

Florida Department of Commerce
Bureau of Business Assistance
107 W. Gains St.
Collins Building
Tallahassee, FL 32399-2000
(904) 487-4698

Venture Capital Clubs
(904) 488-9357

Community Development Section
(904) 488-3957

Business Finance Section
(904) 488-9357

Bureau of International Trade and Development
Florida Department of Commerce
331 Collins Building
Tallahassee, FL 32399-2000
(904) 487-1399

Bureau of Economic Analysis
Florida Department of Commerce
305-Collins Building
Tallahassee, FL 32399-2000
(904) 487-2568

STAC
University of Florida
Progress Center
One Progress Blvd., Box 24
Alachua, FL 32615
(904) 462-3913

Florida Atlantic University
NASA/STAC
1515 West Commercial Bank
Ft. Lauderdale, FL 33039
(305) 351-4104

University of North Florida
STAC/College of Business
Building 11, Room 2163
4567 St. John's Bluff South
Jacksonville, FL 32216-6699
(904) 646-2487

Florida International University
STAC/College of Engineering
Miami, FL 33199
(305) 348-3039

University of Central Florida
STAC/College of Engineering
Box 25000, CEBA 1< Room 319
Orlando, FL 32816
(407) 823-5826

University of West Florida
STAC/SBDC
Pensacola, FL 32504
(904) 474-2908

University of South Florida
STAC/College of Engineering
ENG-118, Trailer #3
Tampa, FL 33260-5350
(813) 974-4222

Florida Atlantic University
Small Business Development Center
International Trade Center
P.O. Box 3091
Boca Raton, FL 33431-0090
(407) 367-2273

Department of Management Services
Division of Purchasing
2737 Centerview Drive
Knight Building. Room 220
Tallahassee, FL 32399-0950
(904) 474-2908

Statewide Contracts Register
(904) 477-3016

GEORGIA

Georgia Department of Community Affairs
1200 Equitable Building
100 Peachtree Street
Atlanta, GA 30303
(404) 656-6200

Georgia Chamber of Commerce
1280 South CNN Center
Atlanta, GA 30303
(404) 223-2271

Department of Administrative Services
West Tower, Room 1302
100 Peachtree Street, NW
Atlanta, GA 30334
(404) 656-6315

Georgia Department of Community Affairs
1200 Equitable Building
100 Peachtree Street, NW
Atlanta, GA 30303
(404) 656-6200

Revolving Loan Fund Programs
(404) 656-4143

Investor's Equity, Inc.
945 E. Paces Ferry Road, Suite 1753
Atlanta, GA 30326
(404) 266-8300

North Riverside Capital Corporation
50 Technology Park/Atlanta
Norcross, GA 30092
(404) 446-5556

Business Development Corporation of Georgia
4000 Cumberland Parkway, Suite 1200 A
Atlanta, GA 30339
(404) 434-0273

Georgia Development Authority
Agricultural Loan Division
P.O. Box 1979
Atlanta, GA 30301
(404) 493-5700

Georgia Department of Natural Resources
Historic Preservation Section
205 Butler Street, SE
Atlanta, GA 30334

(404) 656-2840

Georgia Residential Finance Authority
60 Executive Parkway, South
Suite 250
Atlanta, GA   30329
(404) 679-0662

Economic Development Administration
Atlanta Regional Office
1365 Peachtree Street, NE, Suite 750
Atlanta, GA   30309
(404) 730-3004

Certified Development Company of Northeast Georgia
305 Research Drive
Athens, GA 30610
(706) 369-5650

Atlanta Local Development Corporation
230 Peachtree Street, NW
Suite 1650
Atlanta, GA   33030
(404) 658-7000

The Business Growth Corporation of Georgia
4000 Cumberland Parkway, Suite 11200-A
Atlanta, GA   30339
(404) 434-0273

CSRA Local Development Corporation
2123 Wrightsboro Road
P.O. Box 2800
Augusta, GA   30904
(706) 737-1823

Fulton County Certified Development Corporation
10 Park Place South, Suite 305
Atlanta, GA   30303
(404) 572-2429

McIntosh Trail Area Development Corporation
P.O. Drawer A
Barnesville, GA   30204
(706) 358-3647

Coastal Area District Development Authority
P.O. Box 1917
127 F Street
Brunswick, GA   31521
(912) 264-7315

Sowega Economic Development Corporation
30 East Broad Street
P.O. Box 346
Camilla, GA   31730
(912) 336-5617

Consolidated of Columbus
P.O. Box 1430
Columbus, GA   31993
(706) 571-4886

Lower Chattachoochee Development Corporation
P.O. Box 1908
Columbus, GA   31994
(706) 571-5571

Community Economic Development Corporation
P.O. Box 1340
Columbus, GA   31993
(706) 571-4886

Middle Flint Area Development Corporation
P.O. Box 6
Ellaville, GA   31806
(912) 937-2561

Heart Of Georgia Area Development Corporation
501 Oak Street
Eastman, GA 31023
(912) 374-4771

Georgia Mountains Regional Economic
Development Corporation
1010 Ridge Road
Gainesville, GA 30501
(404) 536-3431

Troup County Local Development Corporation
900 Dallas Street
La Grange, GA 31240
(706) 883-1658

Development Corporation of Middle
Georgia
661 Mulberry Street, Suite 600
Macon, GA 31201
(912) 751-6160

Oconee Area Development Corporation
P.O. Box 707
Milledgeville, GA 31061
(912) 453-4328

Savannah Certified Development Corporation
P.O. Box 1917
Brunswick, GA 35121
(912) 264-7376

Southeast Georgia Development Corporation
3395 Harris Road
Waycross, GA 31503
(912) 285-6097

South Georgia Area Development Corporation
327 West Savannah Avenue, P.O. Box 1223
Vldosta, GA 31601
(912) 333-5277

Venture Capital Network of Atlanta
230 Peachtree Street, NW, Suite 1810
Atlanta, GA 30303
(404) 894-1076

Georgia Capital Network
Georgia Tech Advanced Technology Development Center
430 10th Street NW, Suite N-116
Atlanta, GA 30318
(404) 894-5344

Small and Minority Business Coordinator
Georgia Department of Administrative
Services
200 Piedmont Avenue South
Suite 1302, West Floyd Building
Atlanta, GA 30334
(404) 656-6315

Office of Minority Business Development
1180 East Broad Street
Athens, GA 30602
(706) 369-9132

Minority Business Development Agency
401 W. Peachtree, Suite 1930
Atlanta, GA 30308
(404) 730-3300

Georgia Department of Labor
Job Training Division
Suite 650, Sussex Place

148 International Boulevard
Atlanta, GA 30303
(404) 656-7392

Chamber of Commerce
233 Peachtree St. Suite 200
Atlanta, GA 303033
(404) 223-2285

Georgia Department of Community Affairs
1200 Equitable Building
100 Peachtree Street
Atlanta, GA 30303
(404) 656-6200

Agricultural Affairs Department
Georgia Power Co.
270 Peachtree, 5th Floor
Atlanta, GA 30303
(404) 526-7320

TRI Regional Office
117 Whispering Pines Rd.
Albany, GA 31707
(912) 430-4188

GTRI Regional Office
Suite 307
1054 Clausen Rd.
Augusta, GA 30907
(706) 737-1420

GTRI Regional Office
P.O. Box 1196 31521
1227 F Street
Brunswick, GA 31520
(912) 262-2346

GTRI Regional Office
P.O. Box 676
201 Tanner Street
Carrollton, GA 30117
(404) 836-6675

GTRI Regional Office
P.O. Box 8965 31908
3575 Macon Rd
Suite 23
Governor's Place
Columbus, GA
(706) 568-2482

GTRI Regional Office
P.O. Box 1244
405 N. Peterson Ave,
Douglas, GA 315333
(912) 384-4151

GTRI Regional Office
P.O. Box 4620 31040-4620
1205 Bellvue Ave.
Bellvue Place
Suite B
Dublin, GA 31021
(912) 275-6543

GTRI Regional Office
P.O. Box 3015 30503
200 Main Street
Suite 108
Hunt Tower
Gainesville, GA 31201
(404) 535-5728

GTRI Regional Office
P.O. Box 5105 31208
990-B Riverside Drive
Macon, GA 31021
(912) 751-6190

GTRI Regional Office
216 N. Main Street
Madison, GA 30650
(706) 295-6008

GTRI Regional Office
1 Reservation Street
Rome, GA 31406
(912) 921-5510

Economic and Marketing Services Branch
(404) 894-3851

Georgia Productivity and Quality Center
(404) 894-6101

Economic Development Laboratory

(404) 894-3830

Southeastern Trade Adjustment Assistance
Center
(404) 894-3858

Energy Resources Branch
(404) 894-3412

Environmental Science and Technology Laboratory
(404) 894-3412

Georgia Procurement Assistance Center
(404) 894-6121

Georgia Department of Industry, Trade, and
Tourism
P.O. Box 1776
Atlanta, GA 30301
(404) 656-3557

Trade Division
(404) 656-3571

Advanced Technology Development Center
Georgia Institute of Technology
430 10th Street,NW
Suite N-116
Atlanta, GA 30318
(404) 894-3575

Quick Start
Technical and Adult Education
Suite 660
1 CNN Center
Atlanta, GA 30303-2705

Vietnam Veterans Leadership Program
825 Fairfield Drive
Marietta, GA 30068
(404) 565-8444

HAWAII

Small Business Information Service
Department of Business and Economic
Development
P.O. Box 2359
Honolulu, HI 96804
(808) 586-2360

Department of Business, Economic Development and Tourism
220 South King Street
P.O. Box 2359
Honolulu, HI 96804
(808) 586-1518

Hawaii Capital Loan Program
Grosvenor Center
Mauka Tower, Suite 1900
737 Bishop Street
Honolulu, HI 96813
(808) 586-2577

State Department of Agriculture
1428 South King Street
Honolulu, HI 96814
(808) 973-9551

Bancorp Hawaii SBIC
111 South King Street, Suite 1060
Honolulu, HI 996813
(808) 537-8111

Honolulu Minority Business Development
Center
Pacific Tower, Suite 2900
1001 Bishop Street
Honolulu, HI 96813-3652
(808) 531-6232

Alu Like Business Development Center
33 South King Street, Suite 311
Honolulu, HI 96813
(808) 524-1225

Alu Like Molokai Island Center
P.O. Box 392
Kaunakakai, HI 96748
(808) 533-53393

Alu Like Hawaii Island Center
P.O. Box 606
Hilo, HI 96720
(808) 961-2625

Department of Labor and Industrial Relations
830 Punchbowl Street, Room 316
Honolulu, HI 96813
(808) 586-9060

WorkHawaii
715 South King Street, Suite 500
Honolulu, HI 96813
(808) 523-4102

Kauai Community College
3-1902 Kaumuali Highway
Lihue, HI 96766
(808) 245-8210

Hawaii State Employment Service
2064 Wells Street, Suite 108
Wailuku, HI
(808) 242-5232

Hawaii State Employment Service
180 Kinoole Street
Hilo, HI 96720
(808)933-4481

Department of Business Economic Development and Tourism
Grosvenor Center
Mauka Tower, Suite 1900
Honolulu, HI 96813
(808) 586-2406

Small Business Center
The Chamber of Commerce of Hawaii
735 Bishop Street Honolulu, HI 96813-4897
(808) 586-8831

Economic Development Corporation of Honolulu (EDCH)
1001 Bishop Street
Pacific Tower
Suite 735
Honolulu, HI 96813
(808) 545-4533

Hawaii Island Economic Development Board (HIEDB)
First Federal Building
75-5737 Kuakini Highway, #206
Kailua-Kona, HI
(808) 329-4713

HIEDB
1999 Ainoala Drive
Hilo, HI 96724
(808) 959-0108

Kauai Economic Development Board (KEDB)
4370 Kukui Grove Street, #211-C
Lihue, HI 96766
(808) 245-6692

Maui Economic Development Board, Inc. (MEDB)
300 Ohukai Rd. #301
Kihlihei, HI 96766
(808) 245-2300

Small Business Hawaii
811-A Cooke Street Honolulu, HI 96813
(808) 533-2183

Pacific Business Center Program (PBCP)
College of Business Administration
University of Hawaii
2404 Maile Way, 4th Floor
Honolulu, HI 96813
(808) 956-6286

IDAHO

Idaho Department of Commerce
Economic Development Division
700 West State Street, Room 108
Boise, ID 83720-2700
(208) 334-2470

Idaho Department of Commerce
Economic Development Division
700 West State Street, Rm 108
Boise, ID 83720
(208) 334-2470

Panhandle Area Council, Inc.
11100 Airport Drive
Hayden, ID 83835
(208) 772-0584

Clearwater Economic Development Association
1626 B Sixth Avenue North
Lewiston, ID 83501
(208) 746-0015

Treasure Valley Certified Development
Corporation/Ida-Ore Planning and Develop-
 ment Association
7270 Potomac Drive
Boise, ID 83704
(208) 322-7033
Region IV Development Corporation/Reg ion
IV Development Association
P.O. Box 1844 Twin Falls, ID 83303
(208) 736-3064

Eastern Idaho Development Corporation
Southeast Idaho Council of Governments
ISU Business & Technology Center
1651 Alvin Ricken Drive
Pocatello, ID 83201
(208) 356-4524

Community & Business Programs
Farmers Home Administration
3232 Elder
Boise, ID 83720
(208) 334-1521

Economic Development Districts or Mayor or
 Association of Idaho Cities
3314 Grace
Boise, ID 83703
(208) 344-8594

Disadvantaged Business Enterprise
110 North 27th
Boise, ID 83702
(208) 344-0150

State of Vocational Education
LBJ Building 650 W. State Street
Boise, ID 83720
(208) 334-3214

State of Idaho
Department of Employment
317 Main Street
Boise, ID 83735(208) 334-6100

Idaho Department of Commerce
Economic Development Division
700 West State Street
State House Mail
Boise, ID 83720-2700
(208) 334-2470

ILLINOIS

Small Business Assistance Bureau
Illinois Department of Commerce and
 Community Affairs
State of Illinois Center
100 W. Randolph Street, Suite 3-400
Chicago, IL 60601
(312) 814-7179

Small Business Advocate
(312) 814-7179

Small Business Assistance Bureau
Illinois Department of Commerce and
 Community Affairs
State of Illinois Center
100 W. Randolph Street, Suite 3-400
Chicago, IL 60601
(312) 814-7179

Alpha Capital Venture Partners, LP
Three First National Plaza, 14th Floor
Chicago, IL 60602
(312) 214-3440

Business Ventures, Inc.
20 N. Wacker Drive, Suite 1741
Chicago, IL 60606
(312) 346-1580

Continental Illinois Venture Corporation
209 South LaSalle Street
Mail: 231 South LaSalle Street
Chicago, IL 06060
(312) 828-8023

First Capital Corporation of Chicago
Three First National Plaza, Suite 1330
Chicago, IL 60670
(312) 732-5400

Heller Equity Capital Corporation
200 North LaSalle Street, 10th Floor
Chicago, IL 60601
(312) 621-7200

Walnut Capital Corporation
208 South LaSalle Street
Chicago, IL 60604
(3312) 346-2033

Illinois Department of Revenue
(217) 782-3128

Small Business Assistance Bureau
Illinois Department of Commerce and
 Community Affairs
State of Illinois Center
100 W. Randolph Street, Suite 3-400
Chicago, IL 60601
(312) 814-3263

Industrial Training Program
(217) 785-6006

Illinois Department of Commerce and
 Community Affairs
State of Illinois Center
100 W. Randolph Street, Suite 3-400
Chicago, IL 60601 (312) 814-7179

International Business Division
(312) 814-7176

Small Business Utility Advocate
(217) 814-6107

Industrial Development Support Service
Springfield
(217) 785-6167

Industrial Development Support Service
Chicago
(312) 814-2335

Commerce Community Affairs
Springfield
(217) 782-6861
Chicago
(312) 814-6619
Marion
(618) 997-4371

TEL-DCCA Information System
1-800-835-3222

INDIANA

Indiana Department of Commerce
One North Capitol, Suite 700
Indianapolis, IN 46204-2288
(317) 232-8888

Indiana Statewide Certified
 Development Corp.
8440 Woodfield Crossing, Suite 315
Indianapolis, IN 46240
(317) 469-6166

Cip Venture Partners
210 North Illinois Street, Suite 1950
Indianapolis, IN 46204
(317) 237-2350

Department of Economic Development
City of Fort Wayne
429 N. Pennsylvania, #100
Indianapolis, IN 46204-1873
(317) 427-1127

1st Source Capital Corporation
100 N. Michigan Street
Mail: P.O. Box 1602, South Bend 46634
South Bend, IN 46601
(219) 235-2180

Circle Ventures, Inc.
3228 East 10th Street
Indianapolis, IN 46201
(317) 636-7242

Metro Small Business Assistance Corporation
306 Civic Center Complex
1 NW Martin Luther King Blvd.
Evansville,IN 47708
(812) 426-5867

Indiana Institute for New Business Ventures, Inc.
One North Capital, Suite 1275
Indianapolis, IN 46204-2806
(317) 264-2820

Metro Small Business Assistance Corporation
306 Civic Center Complex
1 NW Martin Luther King Blvd.
Evansville, IN 47708
(812) 426-5857

Greater Bloomington Chamber of Commerce
116 West 6th Street, Suite 100
P.O. Box 1302
Bloomington IN 47402
(812) 336-6361

Mount Vernon Venture Capital Company
P.O. Box 40177
Indianapolis, IN 46240
(317) 469-5888

Heritage Venture Partners, II, Ltd.
135 N. Pennsylvania, #2380
Indianapolis, IN 46204
(317) 635-5696

CID Venture Partners
201 Illinois Street, #1950
Indianapolis, IN 46204
(317) 237-2350

Indiana Department of Commerce
Office of Minority and Women Business
 Development Division
One North Capitol, Suite 501
Indianapolis, IN 46204-2288
(317) 232-8820

Department of Economic Development
City of Fort Wayne
840 City-County Building
Fort Wayne, IN 46802
(219) 427-1127

Home Business Network
2625 North Meridian Street
Indianapolis, IN 46208
(317)353-1818

Indiana Department of Commerce
One North Capitol, Suite 700
Indianapolis, IN 46204-2288
(317) 232-8888

Department of Employment and Training
 Services
10 North Senate
indianapolis, IN 46204
(317) 232 7670

Inventors and Entrepreneurs Society of
 Indiana
Purdue University Calumet
P.O. Box 2224
Hammond, IN 46323
(219) 989-2400

Indiana Department of Commerce
One North capitol
Suite 700
Indianapolis, IN 46204-2288

Federal Marketing Development Division
(317) 264-5600

Office of Business Ombudsman
(317) 232-8913

Business Development Marketing Division
(313 232-8888

International Trade Development Office
(317) 232-8888

Agriculture Division
(317)232-8770

Business Development Division
(317) 232-8888

Partners in Contracting Corporation
8139 Kennedy Avenue
Highland, IN 46322
(219) 923-8181

Small Business Development Corp.
One North Capitol, Suite 1060
Indianapolis, IN 46202
(317) 264-2820

Entrepreneurs Alliance
P.O. Box 509161
Indianapolis, IN 46250-9161
(317) 843-1655

School of Business, Room 510
Indiana State University
Terre Haute, IN 478009
(812) 237-3232

Indiana Memorial Union 662
Indiana University
Bloomington IN 47405

Civil Engineering Building G175
Purdue University
West Lafayette, IN 47907
(317) 494-6258

Krannert Graduate School of Management
Purdue University
West Lafayette, IN 47907
(317) 494-9876

Indiana Business Modernization and Technology Corp.(IBMT)
One North Capitol, Suite 925
Indianapolis, In 46294
(317) 635-3058

IOWA

Iowa Department of Economic Development
200 east Grand Avenue
Des Moines, IA 50309
(515) 242-4700

Small Business Division
Iowa Department of Economic Development
200 East Grand Avenue
Des Moines, IA 50309
(515) 242-4750

Division of Job Training
(515) 242-9810

Bureau of Business Grants and Loans
(515) 242-4819

Community Development Block Grant:
(515) 242-4831

Community Development Block Grants:
(515) 242-4837

Bureau of Housing and Community Development
(515) 242-4837

Export Trade Assistance Program
(515) 242-4729

President, Iowa Product Development Corp.
  (IPDC)
200 East Grand Avenue
Des Moines, IA 50309
(515) 284-4422

MorAmerica Capital Corporation
800 American Building
Cedar Rapids, IA 52401
(319) 363-8249

Targeted Small Business
Bureau of Business
Division of Financial Assistance
Iowa Department of Economic Develop-
  ment
200 East Grand
Des Moines, IA 50309
(515) 242-4819

Bureau of Business
(515) 242-4721

Iowa Procurement Outreach Center
c/o Kirkwood Community College, Bldg. 9
6301 Kirkwood Blvd.
P.O. Box 2068
Cedar Rapids, IA 52406
(319) 398-5665

Bureau of State Programs
Division of Job Training
Department of Economic Development
200 East Grand Avenue
Des Moines, IA 50309
(515) 242-4774

Department of Economic Development
200 East Grand Avenue
Des Moines, IA 50309
(515) 242-4774

KANSAS

First-Stop Clearinghouse
Existing Industry Development Division
Kansas Department of Commerce
400 SW 8th Street, 5th floor
Topeka, KS 66603-3597
(913) 296-5298

Regional Advocates
SBA-Region VII Office
911 Walnut, Suite 1300
Kansas City, MO 64106
(913) 296-5298

Kansas Department of Commerce
400 SW 8th Street, 5th Floor
Capitol Tower Building
Topeka, KS 66603-3957
(913) 296-5298

Community Development Division
(913) 296-3004

Enterprise Zones
(913) 296-3485

Low Income Housing Tax Credits
(913) 296-3485

Business Tax Bureau
Kansas Department of Revenue
Docking State Office Building, 3rd Floor
P.O. Box 12001
Topeka, KS 66612-2001
(913) 296-2461

Kansas Technology Enterprise Corporation
 KTEC
112 West 6th Street, Suite 400
Topeka, KS 66603
(913) 296-5272

Pooled Money Investment Fund
P.O. Box 2608
Topeka, KS 66601-2608
(913) 296-3372

Kansas Development Finance Authority
Landon State Office Building, Suite 113
900 S.W. Jackson Street
Topeka, KS 66612

Kansas Association of Certified Development
 Companies
P.O. Box 1116
Dodge City, KS 67801
(316) 227-6406

Kansas Venture Capital, Inc.
One Townsite Plaza
Bank IV Tower, Suite 825
Topeka, KS 66603
(913) 233-1368

Kansas Venture Capital, Inc.
(Main Office: Topeka, KS)
6700 Antioch Plaza
Suite 200
Overland Park, KS 66204
(913) 482-1221

Business Development Division
Economic Development Administration
Suite 201, Grant Building
611 E. Sixth Street
Austin, TX 78701
(913) 271-2700

Office of Minority Business
Existing Industry Development Division
Kansas Department of Commerce
400 SW 8th Street, 5th Floor
Topeka, KS 66603-3957
(913) 296-3805

Assistant Regional Administration for MSB
 -COD
Small Business Administration- Region VII
 Office
911 Walnut, 13th Floor
Kansas City, MO 64106
(816) 426-3516

Department of Human Resources
401 Topeka Boulevard
Topeka, KS 66603
Job Service
(913) 296-5317

Job Service Administration
(913) 296-5317

Older Workers Programs Administrator
Kansas Department of Aging
Docking State Office Building, Room 122S
Topeka, KS 66612-1500
(913) 296-4986

Job Training Coordinator
Industrial Development Division
Kansas Department of Commerce
400 SW 8th Street, Suite 500
Topeka, KS 66603-3957
(913) 296-3483

Job Training Partnership Act (JTPA)
(919) 296-3588

Business and Industry Institute
Johnson County Community College
12345 College at Quivera Road
Averland Park, KS 66210
(913) 469-8500

Wichita State University
Brennan Hall, 2nd Floor, Box 148
Wichita, KS 67208-1595
(316) 689-3193

Kansas Department of Commerce
400 SW 8th Street, Suite 500
Topeka, KS 66603-3957
(316) 296-3483

Travel & Tourism Development Office
(913) 296-7091

Trade Promotion
(913) 296-4027

Division of Purchases
Department of Administration
Landon State Office Building, Room 102
Topeka, KS 66612
(913) 296-2376

FACTS
State Board of Agriculture
148 Waters
Manhattan, KS 66506
(913) 532-6958

Center for Economic Development and
 Business Research
Wichita State University
Box 48
Topeka, KS 67208
(316) 689-3225

Center for Entrepreneurship
Devlin Hall Wichita State University
Wichita, KS 67208
(316) 689-3000

College of Architecture and Design
Seaton Hall
Kansas State University
Manhattan, KS 66506
(913) 532-595

BETA
Space Technology Center
University of Kansas
2291 Irving Hill Drive, Campus West
Lawrence, KS 66045
(913) 864-2447

Engineering Extension Program
133 Ward Hall, Kansas State University
Manhattan, KS 66506
(913) 532-6026

Institute for Economic Development
Pittsburg State University
Pittsburg, KS 66762
(316) 231-7000 ext. 4920

Kansas State University Cooperative Extension
  Service
Kansas State University
Umberger Hall, Room 311
Manhattan, KS 66506
(913) 296-7987

Kansas Board of Agriculture
Marketing Division
901 S. Kansas Ave.
Topeka, KS 66612-1281
(913) 296-3736

KENTUCKY

Business Information Clearinghouse
Cabinet of Economic Development
Department of Economic Development
Department of Existing Business and Industry
Capital Plaza Tower, 22nd Floor
Frankfort, KY 40601
(502) 564-4252

Division of Research & Planning
(502) 564-4886

Kentucky Development Finance Authority
  (KDFA)
Capital Plaza Tower
24th Floor
Frankfort, KY 40601
(502) 564-4554

Commonwealth Small Business Development
  Corporation (CSBDC)
Capital Tower, 24th Floor
Frankfort, KY 40601
(502) 564-4320

Cabinet for Economic Development
Office of Business and Technology
Capital Plaza Tower, 24th Floor
Frankfort, KY 40601
(502) 564-7670

Cabinet for Economic Development
2300 Plaza Office Tower, 24th Floor
Frankfort, KY 40601
(502) 564-4252

Mountain Ventures, Inc.
London Bank & Trust Building
362 Old Whitley Rd.
London, KY 40741
(606) 864-5175

Wilbur Venture Capital Corporation
(Main Office: Tucson, AZ)
400 Fincastle Building
3rd & Broadway
Louisville, KY 40202
(502) 585-1214

Kentucky Department of Local Government
Division of Community Programs
Capital Plaza Tower, 2nd Floor
Frankfort, KY 40601
(502) 564-2382

Farmers Home Administration
711 Corporate Plaza, Suite 200
Lexington, KY 40503
(606) 334-7300

Economic Development Administration (EDA)
711 Corporate Administration (EDA)
Lexington, KY 40503
(606) 233-2596

Barren River Area Development District
(502) 781-2381

FIVCO Area Development District
(606) 739-5191

Buffalo Trace Area Development District
(606) 564-6840

Lincoln Trail Area Development district
(502) 769-2393

Northern Kentucky Area Development
 District
(606) 283-1885

Kentucky River Area Development District
(606) 436-3158

Pennyrile Area Development District
(502) 886-9484

Urban County Economic Development
 Office
(606) 272-6651

Cumberland Valley Area Development
 District
(606) 864-7391

Louisville And Jeffersonn County Economic
 Development Office
(502) 266-6084

Purchase Area Development District
(502) 247-7171

Green River Area Development District
(502) 926-4433

Gateway Area Development District
(606) 674-6355

Lake Cumberland Area Development District
 trict
(502) 866-4200

Commonwealth Venture Capital Fund
Office of Financial Management and Economic Analysis
261 Capital Annex
Frankfort, KY 40601
(502) 564-2924

Kentucky Heights Investment Corporation
 (KHIC)
362 Old Whitely Rd.
P.O. Box 1783
London, KY 40601
(606) 864-5175

The Cumberland Fund
433 Chestnut Street
Berea, KY 40403
(606) 986-2373

Louisville & Jefferson County Economic
 Development Office
401 South Forth Avenue
Suite 200
(502) 625-3051

Equal Opportunity Finance, Inc.
420 S. Hurstbourne Pkwy, # 201
Louisville, KY 40222-8002
(502) 423-1943

Kentucky Cabinet for Economic Development
Capital Plaza Tower
Frankfort, KY 40601
(502) 564-2064

Kentuckiana Minority Supplier Development Council (KMSDC)
Louisville Chamber of Commerce
One Riverfront Plaza
Louisville, KY 40402
(502) 625-0135

Louisville Minority Business Development Center (LMBDC)
611 W. Main
Louisville, KY
(502) 589-6232

Kentucky Cabinet for Economic Development
Capital Plaza Tower
Frankfort, KY 40601
(502) 564-2021

Department of Existing Business and Industry
(502) 564-7140

Small Business Division
(502) 564-4252

Craft Marketing Branch
(502) 564-8076

Research and Planning Division
(502) 564-4886

Site and Building Evaluation Branch
(502) 564-7140

Office of Business Technology
(502) 564-7670

College of Business and Economics
University of Kentucky
Lexington, KY 40506
(502) 257-1571

Kentucky Society of CPAs
310 West Liberty Street
Louisville, KY 40202
(502) 589-9239

Division of Purchases
Department of Administration
Capitol Annex Building, Room 354
Frankfort, KY 40601
(502) 564-4510

Secretary of State
Capitol Building
Frankfort, KY 40601
(502) 564-2848

Center for Entrepreneurship and Technology
School of Business, University of Louisville
Louisville, KY 40292
(502) 588-7854

Center for Small Business
Louisville Chamber of Commerce
One Riverfront Plaza
Louisville, KY 40202
(502) 452-8282

Entrepreneur Society- SBDC
20001 Newburg Road
Louisville, KY 40205
(502) 452-8282

Jefferson Community College
Community Education Division
109 East Broadway
Louisville, KY 40402
(502) 582-5973

University of Kentucky
465 East High Street, Suite 109
Lexington, KY 40507-1941
(606) 257-7666

Ashland Small Business Development Center
Boyd-Greenup County Chamber of Commerce Building
P.O. Box 830-207 15th Street
Ashland, KY 41105-0830
(606) 329-8011

Western Kentucky University
Bowling Green Small Business Development Center
245 Grise Hall
Bowling Green KY 42101
(502) 745-2901

Southeast Community College
Southeast Small Business Development Center
Room 113 Crisman Hall
Cumberland, KY 40823
(606) 589-4514

University of Kentucky
Elizabethtown Small business Development Center
238 West Dixie Avenue
Elizabeth, KY 42701
(502) 765-6737

North Kentucky University
North Kentucky Small Business Development Center
BEP Center 463
Highland Heights, KY 41076
(606) 572-6524

Hopkinsville Small Business Development Center
Pennyrile Area Development District
300 Hammond Drive
Hopkinsville, KY 42240
(502) 886-8666

Bellarmine College
Small Business Development Center
School of Business
2001 Newburg Road
Louisville, KY 40205
(502) 452-8282

University of Louisville
Small Business Development Center
Center for Entrepreneurship & Technology
School of Business
Belknap Campus
Louisville KY 40292
(502) 588-7854

Morehead State University
Small Business Development Center
Butler Hall
Morehead KY 40351
(606) 783-2895

Murray State University
West Kentucky Small Business Development Center
College of Business and Public Affairs
Murray, KY 42071
(502) 762-2856

Owensboro Small Business Development Center
3860 US Highway 60 West
Owensboro, KY 42301
(502) 926-8085

Pikeville Small Business Development
  Center
222 Hatcher Court
Pikeville, KY 41501
(606) 432-5848

Eastern Kentucky University
South Central Small Business Development
  Center
107 West Mt. Vernon St.
Somerset, KY 42501
(606) 678-5520

LOUISIANA

Louisiana Department of Economic Development
101 France Street, Suite 115
P.O. Box 95185
Baton Rouge, LA 70804-9185
(504) 342-3000

Community Development Division
Louisiana Department of Commerce and
  Industry
P.O. Box 94185
Baton Rouge, LA 70804-9184
(504) 342-3000

Louisiana Department of Economic Development
101 France Street Suite 115
P.O. Box 94185
Baton Rouge, LA 70804-91285
(504) 342-5358

Capital for Terrebonne, Inc.
27 Austin Drive
Houma, LA 70360
(504) 838-3930

Louisiana Economic Development Corpora-
  tion
Department of Economic Development
P.O. Box 94185
Baton Rouge, LA 70804-9285
(504) 342-5675

Division of Minority and Women's Business
  Enterprise
Department of EconomIc Development
P.O. Box 94185
Baton Rouge, LA 70804-9185
(504) 342-5373

Development Division
Office of Commerce and Industry
Department of Economic Development
P.O. Box 94185
Baton Rouge, LA 70804-9185
(504) 342-5893

Office of Commerce and Industry
Department of Economic Development
P.O. Box 94185
Baton Rouge, LA   04185
(504) 342-5385

Market Analysis and Planning
(504) 342-5385

Directory of Louisiana Manufacturers
(504) 342-5385

Office of Trade, Finance and Development
(504) 342-4320

MAINE

Department of Economic and Community
  Development
State House Station #59
193 State Street
Augusta, ME 04333
(207) 287-2656

Department of Economic and Community
 Development
State House Station #59
Augusta, ME 04333
(207) 289-3153

Finance Authority of Maine
83 Western Avenue
P.O. Box 049
Augusta, ME 04332-0949
(208) 623-3263

Maine Capital Corporation
Seventy Center Street
Portland, ME 01401
(207) 772-1001

Farmers Home Administration
444 Stillwater Ave., Suite 2
P.O. Box 405
Bangor, ME 04402-0405
(207) 990-9120

Economic Development Administration
Department of Commerce
40 Western Avenue
Augusta, ME 04330
(207) 622-8271

Androscoggin Valley Council of Governments
70 Court Street
Auburn, ME 04210
(207) 783-9186

Coastal Enterprises, Inc.
P.O. Box 268
Wiscasset, ME 04578
(207) 882-7552

Eastern Maine Development Corporation
1 Cumberland Place, #300
Bangor, ME 04401
(207) 942-6389

Northern Kennebec Regional Planning
 Commission
7 Benton Avenue
Winslow, ME 04902
(207) 873-0711

Northern Maine Regional Planning Commission
P.O. Box 779
Caribou, ME 04736
(207) 498-8736

Lewiston/Auburn Economic Growth Council
P.O. Box 1188
Lewiston, ME 04243
(207) 784-0161

Maine Department of Transportation
Division of Equal Opportunity/Employee
 Relations
State House #6
Augusta, ME 04333
(207) 287-3576

Maine State Department of Labor
Bureau Training Program
State House Station #55
Augusta, ME 04333
(207) 287-3377

Maine State Department of Agriculture
 Food and Rural Resources
State House Station #28
Augusta, ME 04333
(207) 287-3871

State Department of Marine Resources
Bureau of Marine Development
State House #21
Augusta, ME 04333
(207) 624-3871

Maine Department of Economic and Community Development
State House Station #59
Augusta, ME 04333
(207) 287-2656

Maine Procurement Assistance Center
1 Cumberland Place, #300
Bangor, ME 04401
(207) 942-6389

Finance Authority of Maine (FAME)
83 Western Avenue
P.O. Box 949
Augusta, ME 04330

Maine Procurement Assistance Center
1 Cumberland Place, #300
40 Western Avenue
Bangor. ME 04401
(207) 622-6389

Finance Authority of Maine (FAME)
83 Western Avenue
P.O. Box 949
Augusta, ME 04330
(207) 623-3263

Maine Procurement Assistance Center
1 Cumberland Place 300
Bangor, ME 04401
(207) 942-6389

MARYLAND

Maryland Business Assistance Center
217 East Redwood Street. 10th Floor
Baltimore, MD 21202
(800) 834-7232

Maryland Industrial Division of Finance Authority (MIDFA)
217 East Redwood Street
Suite 2244
Baltimore, MD 21202
(410) 333-4236

Maryland Small Business Development Financing Authority (MSBDFA)
(410) 333-6975

Development Credit Fund, Inc,
2530 N. Charles Street. Suite 200
Baltimore, MD 21218
(410) 467-7500

Community Financing Group
Department of Economic and Employment Development
Redwood Tower, 217 East Redwood
Baltimore, MD 21210
(410) 333-4304

Maryland Division of Business Development
217 East Redwood Street 10th Floor
Baltimore, MD 21202
(410) 333-6975

Department of Economic and Employment Development
217 East Redwood street
Baltimore, MD 21202
(410) 333-6975

Maryland Energy Financing Administration
(410) 333-6975

City of Baltimore
Small Business Administration
10 North Calvert
Baltimore, MD 21202
(410) 962-2233

Washington District Small Business Administration
1111 18th Street, NW., 6th Floor
P.O. Box 1993
Washington, DC 20036
(202) 634-7838

Jupiter Investments, Inc.
5454 Wisconsin Avenue
Chevy Chase, MD 20815
(301) 656-0626

Maryland National
502 Washington Avenue
Towson, MD 21204
(301) 821-7666

Maryland Small Business Development
Financing Authority
(410) 333-4270

Baltimore Small Business Administration
10 North Calvert
Baltimore, MD 21202
(410) 962-2233

Washington District Small Business Administration
1111 18th Street, NW, 6th Floor
P.O. Box 1993
Washington, DC 20036
(202) 634-7838

Office of Business Assistance
Office of Employment Training
1100 North Eutaw Street, Room 304
Baltimore, MD 21201
(410) 333-5367

Maryland Division of Business Assistance
217 East Redwood Street
10th Floor
Baltimore, MD 21202
(410) 333-6975

Division of Business Resources
Maryland Department of Economic and
Employment Development
217 East Redwood Street
Baltimore, MD 21202
(410) 333-0988

Department of Human Resource
Office of Child Care Licensing and Regulation
500 East Lombard Street
Suite 312
Baltimore, MD 21202
(410) 333-0988

Maryland Division Business Assistance
217 East Redwood Street 10th Floor
Baltimore, MD 21202
(410) 333-6975

Baltimore Small Business Administration
10 North Calvert
Baltimore, MD 21202
(301) 962-2233

Maryland Small Business Development
Center
Department of Economic and Employment
Development
217 East Redwood Street, 10th Floor
Baltimore, MD 21202
(410) 222-6975

Baltimore Economic Development Corporation
Central Region Small Business Development Center
1414 Key Highway
Baltimore, MD 21218
(410) 234-0505

Cecil County College
Eastern Region Small Business Development Center
107 Railroad Avenue
Elkton, MD 21921
(410) 392-3366

Western Maryland Community College
  Consortium
Small Business Development Center
c/o Potomac Edison Company
Downsville Pike
Hagerstown, MD 21740
(310) 790-2800

Charles Community College Southern Region Small Business Development Center
235 Smallwood Village Center
Waldorf, MD 20601
(301) 932-4155

MASSACHUSETTS

Massachusetts Dept. of Business Development
100 Cambridge Street
Boston, MA 02202
(617) 727-3206

Community Development Finance Corporation
10 P.O. Square
Suite 1090
Boston, MA 02109
(617) 482-9141

Massachusetts Economic Stabilization Trust
  Fund
One Ashburton Place, Room 1413
Boston, MA 02108
(617) 727-8158

Massachusetts Business Development Corp-
  poration
One Liberty Square, 2nd Floor
Boston MA 02109
(617) 350-8877

Massachusetts Capital Resource Company
400 Boylston Street
Boston, MA 02116
(617) 536-3900

Massachusetts Industrial Finance Agency
75 Federal Street
Boston, MA 02110
(617) 451-2477

Massachusetts Government Land Bank
One Court Street, Suite 200
Boston, MA 02108
(617) 727-8257

Massachusetts Product Development Corporation
55 union Street
Boston, MA 02108
(617) 727-1133

CDAG Program Director
Division of Communities Development
Executive Office of Communities and De
  velopment
100 Cambridge Street
Boston, MA 02202
(617) 727-7180

Economic Development Set Aside Program
(617) 727-7001

Farmers Home Industries
451 West Street
Amherst, MA 01002
(413) 253-4300

Community Development Finance Corporation
10 P.O. Square
Suite 1090
Boston, MA 02116
(617) 482-8151

Advent Atlantic Capital Company, LP
75 State Street
Suite 2500
Boston, MA 02109
(617) 345-7200

Advent IV Capital Company
75 State Street
Suite 2500
Boston, MA 02109
(617) 345-7200

Advent Industrial Capital Company, LP
75 State Street, Suite 200
Boston, MA 02109
(617) 345-7200

Advent V Capital Company
75 State Street, Suite 2500
Boston, MA 02109
(617) 345-7200

Atlas II Corporation
1 International Place
Boston, MA 02110
(617) 951-9920

BancBoston Ventures, Inc.
100 Federal Street
Mail: P.O. Box 2016 Stop 10-31-08
Boston, MA 02110
(617) 434-2442

Bever Capital Corporation
1 International Place
Boston, MA 02110
(618) 051-9920

Boston Hambro Capital Company
160 State Street, 9th Floor
Boston, MA 02109
(617) 523-7767

Business Achievement Corporation
1172 Beacon Street, Suite 209
Boston, MA 02161
(617) 965-0550

Chestnut Capital International II LP
75 State Street, Suite 2500
Boston, MA 02109
(617) 345-7200

Chestnut Street Partners, Inc.
75 State Street, Suite 2500
Boston, MA 02109
(617) 345-7200

First Capital Corporation of Chicago
(Main Office: Chicago, IL)
One Financial Center, 27th Floor
Boston, MA 02111
(617) 457-2500

First United SBIC, Inc.
135 Will Drive
Canton, MA 02021
(617) 828-6150

LRF Capital, LP
189 Wells Avenue, Suite 4
Newton, MA 02159
(617) 964-0049

Mezzanine Capital Corporation
75 State Street
Suite 2500
Boston, MA 02109
(617) 345-7200

Milk Street Partners, Inc.
75 State Street
Suite 2500
Boston, MA 02109
(617) 345-7200

Monarch-Narragansett Ventures, Inc.
One Financial Plaza, 12th Floor
Springfield, MA 01102
(413) 781-3000

Northeast SBI Corporation
16 Cumberland Street
Boston, MA 02115
(617) 267-3983

Orange Nassau Capital Corporation
1 International Place
Boston, MA 02110
(617) 267-3893

Pioneer Ventures, LP
60 State Street Boston, MA 02109
(517) 742-7825

Corporate Finance
One Federal Street, 30th Floor
Boston, MA 02211
(617) 556-4700

Southern Berkshire Investment Corporation
P.O. Box 669
Sheffield, MA 01257
(413) 229-3106

UST Capital Corporation
40 Court Street
Boston, MA 02108
(617) 726-7137

Vadus Capital Corporation
1 International Place
Boston, MA 02110

Office of Community Planning and Development Division
Department of Housing and Urban Development
10 Causeway Street, 3rd Floor
Boston, MA 02222
(617) 727-8690

Executive Office of Communities and Development
18th Floor, 100 Cambridge Street
Boston, MA 02202
(617) 727-8690

Massachusetts Technology Development Corporation
148 State Street, 94th Floor
Boston, MA 02109
(617) 723-4920

The Thrift Fund
50 Congress Street, Suite 515
Boston, MA 02109
(617) 227-0404

State Office of Minority and Women and Business Assistance
Department of Commerce
100 Cambridge Street
Boston, MA 02109
(617) 723-4920

State Office of Minority and Women Business Assistance
Department of Commerce
100 Cambridge Street
Boston, MA 02202
(617) 727-8692

New England Trade Adjustment Assistance Center
120 Boyston Street
Boston, MA 02108
(617) 727-0506

Community Economic Development Assistance Corporation
8 Winter Street
Suite 800
Boston, MA 02222-1093
(617) 565-5590

MICHIGAN

Michigan Business Ombudsman
P.O. Box 30107
525 W. Ottawa
5th Floor Law Building
Lansing, MI 48909
(517) 373--6241

Michigan Department of Commerce
P.O. Box 30107
5th Floor Office Building
Lansing, MI 48909
(517) 373-2727

Michigan Strategic Fund
P.O. Box 30234
Lansing, MI 48909
(5170 335-2139

BIDCO Program
(517) 373-7550

Tax Exempt Bonds
(517) 373-7550

Taxable Bonds
(517) 373-7550

Capital Access Program
(517) 373-4330

Seed Capital Funds
(517) 373-7551

MERRA
1200 Sixth Street
Suite 328
Detroit, MI 48226
(313) 964-5030

Michigan Certified Development Corporation
525 W. Ottawa
Lansing, MI 48909
(517) 373-6378

Michigan Department of Commerce
P.O. Box 30225
525 W. Ottawa
Lansing, MI
(517) 373-0933

Michigan Department of Commerce
525 W. Ottawa
P.O. Box 30225
Lansing, MI 48909
(517) 335-4720

Minority Business Enterprise
1200 6th Street
20th Floor
Detroit, MI 48226
(517) 373-4720

Bureau of Employment Training/Community Services
Michigan Department of Labor
P.O. Box 30015
Lansing, MI 48909
(517) 335-5853

Technical Business Services Office
Department of Commerce
Law Building
Lansing, MI 48909
(517) 335-4720

MINNESOTA

Minnesota Small Business Assistance Office
900 American Center Building
150 East Kellogg Boulevard
St. Paul, MN 55101
(612) 296-3871

Minnesota Department of Trade and Economic Development
500 Metro Square
121 7th Place E
St. Paul, MN 55101-2146
(612) 296-5005

Community Development Corporation Program
(612) 297-1363

Opportunities Minnesota Incorporated (OMNI)
(612) 296-5005

Rural Development Program
(612) 296-9090

Minnesota Public Facilities Authority
(612) 296-4704

Capital Access Program
(612) 297-1391

Tourism Loan Program
(612) 338-7722

Recycling Financial Assistance
(612) 649-5750

Minnesota Technology, Inc.
International Center II, Suite 1250
900 Second Avenue South
Minneapolis, MN 56601
(218) 755-3825

Indian Affairs Council
1819 Bemidji Avenue
Bemidji, MN 55403
(612) 370-2324

Northwest Minnesota Initiative Fund
4 West Office Building, # 310
P.O. Box 975
Bemidji, MN 56601
(218) 290-2057

Midwest Minnesota Initiative Fund
204 Ordean Building
424 West Superior Street
Duluth, MN 55802
(218) 723-4040

West Central Minnesota Initiative Fund
Norwest Bank
220 West Washington, Suite 205
Fergus Falls, MN 56537
(218) 739-2239

Southwest Minnesota Initiative Fund
163 Ninth Avenue
Granite Falls, MN 56241
(612) 564-3060

Central Minnesota Initiative Fund
585 East Broadway
P.O. Box 59
Little Falls, MN 56345
(612) 632-9255

Southeast Minnesota Initiative Fund
540 West Hill Circle
Owatonna, MN 55060
(507) 455-3215

Metropolitan Economic Development Association
2021 East Hennepin Avenue
Suite 370
Minneapolis, MN 55413
(612) 378-0361

Emerging Small Business Clearing House
1121 Glenwood Avenue North
Minneapolis, MN 55405
(612) 374-5161

Minnesota Chippewa Tribe
Indian Business Development Center
P.O. Box 217
Cass Lake, MN 56633
(612) 335-8583

Minnesota Minority Purchasing Council
2021 East Hennepin Avenue
Suite 370
Minneapolis, MN 55413(612) 378-0361

St. Paul Women's Venture
2324 University Avenue #200
St. Paul, MN 55114
(612) 646-3808

Minnesota Small Business Assistance Office
900 American Center Building
150 East Kellogg Boulevard
St. Paul, MN 55101
(612) 296-3871

Minnesota Department of Labor and Industry
Division of Voluntary Apprenticeship
443 Lafayette Road
St. Paul, MN 55101
(612) 296-2371

Minnesota Technical Assistance Program
1313 5th Street SE
Suite 207
Minneapolis, MN 55414
(612) 627-4646

Minnesota Trade Office
1000 World Trade Center
30 East 7th Street
St. Paul, MN 55101-4902

Minnesota Small Business Assistance Office
900 American Center Building
1150 East Kellogg Boulevard
St. Paul, MN 55101
(612) 296-3871

Minnesota Project Innovation
Supercomputer Center, Suite M100
1200 Washington Avenue S.
Minneapolis, MN 55415
(507) 637-2344

Minnesota Inventors Congress
610-C Butler Square Building
100 North Sixth Street
Minneapolis, MN 55403
(612) 370-2324

MISSISSIPPI

Mississippi Department of Economic and
 Community Development
P.O. Box 849
1200 Walter Sillers Building
Jackson, MS 39205
(601) 359-3449

Communications and Advertising Division
(601) 359-3593

Small Business Advocate
(601) 359-3552

Mississippi Department of Economic and
 Community Development
P.O. Box 849
1200 Walter Sillers Building
Jackson, MS 39205
(601) 359-3449

First Jackson Century
Jackson, MS 39201
(601) 965-4378

Mississippi Department of Economic and
 Community Development
P.O. Box 849
1200 Walter Sillers Building
Jackson, MS 32905
(601) 359-3449

Mississippi State Department of Education
Office of Vocational Technical Education
Special Federal Program JPTA
P.O. Box 771
Jackson, MS 39205-0771

Mississippi Department of Economic and
 Community Development
P.O. Box 849
1200 Walter Sillers Building
Jackson, MS 32905
(601) 359-3449

MISSOURI

Missouri Business Assistance Center
Department of Economic Development
P.O. Box 118
Jefferson City, MO 65102
(314) 751-4241

Federal Information Center
Federal Building
601 East 12th Street
Kansas City, MO 64106
1-800-829-1040

Department of Economic Development
P.O. Box 118
Jefferson City, MO 65102
1-800-523-1434

Bankers Capital Corporation
3100 Gilham Road
Kansas City, MO 64109
(816) 531-1600

Capital for Business, Inc.
1000 Walnut
18th Floor
Kansas City, MO 64106
(816) 234-2357

Capital for Business, Inc.
(Main Office: Kansas City, MO)
11 South Meramec, Suite 800
St. Louis, MO 63105
(314) 854-7427

MBI Venture Capital Investors, Inc.
850 Main Street
Kansas City, MO 64105
(816) 471-1700

Midland Capital Corporation
One Petticoat Lane, Suite 110
1020 Walnut Street
Kansas City, MO 64106
(816) 471-8000

MorAmerica Capital Corporation
(Main Office: Cedar Rapids, IA)
911 Main Street, Suite 2724A
Commerce Tower Building
Kansas City, MO 64105
(816) 842-0114

United Missouri Capital Corporation
1010 Grand Avenue
Mail: P.O. Box 419226
Kansas City, MO 64173
(816) 860-7333

Missouri Department of Economic Development
P.O. Box 118
Jefferson City, MO 65102
(314) 751-3237

Division of Job Development and Training
221 Metro Drive
Jefferson City, MO 65109
(314) 751-4750

Missouri Department of Economic Development
P.O. Box 118
Jefferson City, MO 65102
(314) 751-4982

MONTANA

Department of Commerce
1424 Ninth Avenue
Helena, MT 59620
(406) 444-3923

Business Assistance Division
(406) 444-3923

Business Development Division
(406) 444-3814

Business Information System (BIS)
(404) 444-2787

Small Business Advocacy and Licensing
1-800-221-8015 (MT)

Board of Investments
Office of Development Finance
Capitol Station
Helena, MT 59621-0125
(406) 442-1970

Renaissance Capital Ltd. Partnership
2815 Montana Avenue
Billings, MT 59101
(406) 248-6771

The Glacier Springs Company
P.O. Box 399
Black Eagle, MT 59414
(406) 727-7500

Southwest Montana Development Corp.
305 West Mercury
Butte, MT 569701
(406) 723-4349

Montana Progress Capital Corporation
9 Third Street North
Suite 205
Great Falls, MT 59401
(406) 761-7978

First Montana Capital Corporation
310 West Spruce Street
Missoula, MT 59802
(406) 721-8300

Local Government Assistance Division
Department of Commerce
Cogswell Building, Room C-211
Helena, MT 59620
(406) 444-3757

Department of Agriculture
Agriculture/Livestock Building
Capitol Station
Helena, MT 59620-0201
(406) 444-2402

Water Development Bureau
Department of Natural Resources and Conservation
1520 East 6th Avenue
Helena, MT 59620-2301
(406) 444-6668

Montana Science and Technology Alliance
46 North Last Chance Gulch, Suite 2B
Helena, MT 59620
(406) 449-2778

DBE Program Specialist
Civil Rights Bureau
Montana Department of Highways
2701 Prospect Avenue
Helena, MT 59620
(406) 444-7906

Research, Safety and Training Division
Department of Labor and Industry
P.O. Box 1728
Helena, MT 59624
(406) 444-4525

Department of Commerce
1424 Ninth Avenue
Helena, MT 59620

Marketing Assistance and Montana Product
 Promotion
(406) 444-4392
(406) 444-4127

Promotion Division
(406) 444-2654

Business Development Division
(406) 444-3923

International Trade
(406) 444-3923

Department of Agriculture
Agricultural Development Division
Agricultural/Livestock Building
Capitol Station
Helena, MT 59620
(406) 444-2402

Cooperative Extension Service
Montana State University
101 Taylor Hall
Bozeman, MT 59717
(406) 994-6648

University Technical Assistance Program
Montana State University
402 Roberts Hall
Bozeman, MT 59717
(406) 994-3812

National Center for Appropriate Technology
P.O. Box 3838
Butte, MT 59702
(406) 494-4572

Procurement & Printing Division
Division of Administration
Room 165, Mitchell Building, Capitol
 Station
Helena, MT 59620
(406) 444-2575

Research Bureau
Department of Revenue
Sam Mitchell Building
Room 419
Helena, MT 59620
(406) 444-3526

NEBRASKA

Department of Economic Development
P.O. Box 94666
301 Centennial Mall South
Lincoln, NE 68509-4666
(402) 471-3782

Nebraska Investment Finance Authority
Gold's Galleria
1033 O Street
Suite 218
Lincoln, NE 68508
(402) 434-3900

Department Of Economic Development
P.O. Box 94666
301 Centennial Mall South
Lincoln, NE 68509
(402) 471-3119

Existing Business Assistance Division
(402) 471-4167

United Financial Resources Corporation
6211 L Street
P.O. Box 1131
Omaha, NE 68101
(402) 734-1250

Nebraska Economic Development Corporation
(NEDC)
2631 O Street
Lincoln, NE 68510
(402) 475-2795

Farmers Home Administration
Federal Building, Room 308
100 Centennial Mall North
Lincoln, NE 68508
(402) 437-5556

Nebraska Research and Development
 Authority
NBC Center, Suite 780
Lincoln, NE 68508
(402) 475-5109

Nebraska Venture Capital Network
1313 Farnam, Suite 132
Omaha, NE 68182-0248
(402) 346-5000

Northeast Nebraska Venture Capital Network
405 Madison Avenue
Norfolk, NE 68701
(402) 371-4862

Office of Operations
Minority Business Development Agency
Department of Commerce
14th and Constitution Avenue, NW
Washington, DC 20230
(202) 377-2366

Office of Women's Business Partnership
Small Business Administration
11145 Mill Valley Road
Omaha, NE 68154
(402) 221-3604

Minority Business Development Agency
Department of Commerce
Communications Division, Room 6708
Washington, DC 20230
(202) 377-1936

Nebraska Department of Education
P.O. Box 94987
301 Centennial Mall South
Lincoln, NE 68509-4987
(402) 4710-2435

Nebraska Department of Labor
P.O. Box 95004
550 South 16th Street
Lincoln, NE 68509-5004
(402) 471-9000

Nebraska Association of Farmworkers
 (NAF):
Lincoln . . . . (402) 476-6341
Grand Island . . . . (308) 382-3956
North Platte . . . . (308) 534-2630
                                1-800-662-2904

Omaha . . . . (402) 734-4100
Scottsbluff . . . . (308) 632-5831

Operation Able of Southeast Nebraska
129 North 10th Street, Room 332
Lincoln, NE 68508-3548

Existing Business Assistance Division
Nebraska Department of Economic Development
P.O. Box 94666
301 Centennial Mall South
Lincoln, NE 68509
(402) 471-3780

Department of Economic Development
P.O. Box 94666
301 Centennial Mall South
Lincoln, NE 68509
(402) 471-3111

Existing Business Assistance Division
(402) 471-3782

International Commerce
(402) 471-2941

Material Division
Nebraska Department of Administrative
 Services
P.O. Box 94847
301 Centennial Mall South
Lincoln, NE 68509-4847
(402) 471-2401

Agriculture Promotion and Development
 Division
Nebraska Department of Agriculture
P.O. Box 94947
301 Centennial Mall South
Lincoln, NE 68509-4947
(402) 471-4876

Division of Safety
Nebraska Department of Labor
P.O. Box 95024
301 Centennial Mall South
Lincoln, NE 68509-5024
(402) 471-2239

Nebraska Energy Office
9th Floor
P.O. Box 95085
Lincoln, NE 68509-5085
(402) 471-2867

Nebraska Gasohol Committee
P.O. Box 94922
301 Centennial Mall South
Lincoln, NE 68509-4922
(402) 471-2941

University of Nebraska
200 CBA
Lincoln, NE 68588-0406
(402) 472-2334

Extension Service:
Panhandle Center, Scottsbluff
(308) 632-1230

West Central Center, North Platte
(308) 532-3611

Northeast Center, Concord
(401) 584-2261

South Central Center, Clay Center
(402) 762-3535

Southeast Center, Lincoln
(402) 472-3674

Extension Administration, Lincoln
(402) 472-2966

Food Processing Center
Food Technical Assistance
(402) 472-5833

Food Marketing Assistance
(402) 472-5832

International Center for Franchise Studies
(402) 472-3353

Nebraska Center for Entrepreneurship
1237 R Street
Suite 203
Lincoln, NE 68558-0226
(402) 472-3353

NEVADA

State of Nevada Commission on Economic
 Development
Capitol Complex
Carson City, NV 89710
(702) 687-4325

Small Business Advocate
Nevada Office of Community Services
400 W. King, Suite 400
Carson City, NV 89710
(702) 687-4990

Nevada Commission of Economic Development
Capital Complex
Carson City, NV 89710
(702) 687-4325

Nevada Department of Commerce
1665 Hot Springs Road
Carson City, NV 89710
(702) 687-4250

Department Commission of Economic Development
Capital Complex
Carson City, NV 89710
(702) 687-4325

Nevada State Development Corporation
350 S. Center Street
Suite 310
Reno, NV 89501
(702) 323-3625

Farmers Home Administration
Nevada Development Corp.
350 South Center Street
Suite 310
Reno, NV 89501
(702) 323-3625

Nevada Commission of Economic Development
3770 Howard Hughes Parkway #295
Las Vegas, NV
(702) 486-7282

Nevada Commission of Economic Development
Capital Complex
Carson City, NV 89710
(702) 687-4325

Job Training Partnership Act
(702) 687-4310

Western Nevada Community College
Ofc. of Business & Education Partnerships
2201 West Nye Lane
Carson City, NV 89701
(702) 887-3049

Northern Nevada Community College
Adult Basic Education/Occupational Education
901 Elm Street
Elko, NV 89801
(702) 738-8493

Clark County Community College
Center for Business and Industry Training
3200 East Cheyenne Avenue
Las Vegas, NV 89030
(702) 643-6060

Truckee Meadows Community College
Institute for Business and Industry Services
401 West Second Street
Reno, NV 89503
(702) 829-9000

Nevada Development Authority
3900 Paradise Road, Suite 155
Las Vegas, NV 89109
(702) 791-0000

Economic Development Authority of Western Nevada
5190 Neil Road, Suite 111
Reno, NV 89510
(702) 829-3700

Nevada Commission of Economic Development
Northern Nevada Regional Manager
Capital Complex
5151 South Carson Street
Carson City, NV 89710
(702) 687-4325

Commission on Economic Development
Nevada World Trade Council
Capital Complex
Carson City, NV 89710
(702) 687-4235

Nevada Commission on Economic Development
Nevada World Trade Council
3770 Howard Hughes Parkway, Suite 295
Las Vegas, NV 89158
(702) 486-7282

Department of Commerce
1665 Hot Springs Road
Carson City, NV 89710
(702) 885-4250

Nevada Commission on Tourism
Capital Complex
Carson City, NV 89710
(702) 687-4322

NEW HAMPSHIRE

Office of Business and Industrial Development
Director, Division of Economic Development
172 Pembroke Road
P.O. Box 856
Concord, NH 03302-0856
(603) 271-2591

Office of Business and Industrial Development
Division of Economic Development
P.O. Box 856
Concord, NH 03302-0856
(603) 271-2591

Business Finance
4 Park Street, Room 302
Concord, NH 03301
(603) 271-2391

Concord Community Development Corporation (Merrimac County)
45 Airport Road P.O. Box 664
Concord, NH 03301

Granite State Economic Development Corporation
126 Daniel Street
P.O. Box 1491
Portsmouth, NH 03801
(603) 436-0009

Northern Community Investment Corporation
P.O. Box 904
St. Johnsbury, VT 05819
(802) 748-5101

Granite State Capital, Inc.
10 Fort Eddy Road
Concord, NH 03301
(603) 228-9090

Farmers Home Administration
141 Main Street P.O. Box 588
Montpelier, VT 05602
(802) 828-4472

New Hampshire Office of State Planning
2 1/2 Beacon Street
Concord, NH 03301
(603) 271-2155

Economic Development Administration
Federal Building
55 Pleasant street
Concord, NH 03301
(603) 225-1624

New Hampshire Port Authority
555 Market Street
Box 506
Portsmouth, NH 03801
(603) 436-8500

Public Service of New Hampshire (PSNH)
1000 Elm Street Manchester, NH 03102
(603) 669-4000

Northern Community Investment Corporation (NCIC)
P.O. Box 904
St. Johnsbury, VT 05819
(802) 748-5101

NETAAC (New England Trade Adjustment
Assistance Center)
620 Statler Office Building
Boston, MA 02116
(617) 542-2395

Office of Business and Industrial Development
Division of Economic Development
172 Pembroke Road, P.O. Box 856
Concord, NH 03302-0856
(603) 271-2591

New Hampshire Job Training Councils
64 B Old Suncook Road
Concord, NH 03301 (603) 228-9500

New Hampshire Department of Employment Security
32 South Main Street
Concord, NH 03301 (603) 224-3311

Bureau of Vocational-Technical Education
New Hampshire Department of Education
State Office Park South
101 Pleasant Street
Concord, NH 03301
(603) 271-3186

Office of Industrial Development
Division of Economic Development
P.O. Box 856
Concord, NH 03302
(603) 271-2591

Wiggin and Nourie
P.O. Box 808
Manchester, NH 03105
(603) 669-2211

New Hampshire International Trade Association
P.O. Box 239
Portsmouth, NH 03802
(603) 431-6128

New Hampshire Small Business Development Center
108 McConnell Hall
Durham, NH 03824
(603) 862-2200

Research Office
Horton Social Science Center
University of New Hampshire
Durham, NH 03824
(603) 862-3750

NETAAC (New England Trade Adjustment
Assistance Center)
620 Statler Office Building
Boston, MA 02116
(617) 542-2395

Waste Management Division
NH Department of Environmental Services
6 Hazen Drive
Concord, NH 03301
(603) 271-2900

NEW JERSEY

Office of Small Business Assistance
Department of Commerce and Economic
Development
20 West State Street, CN 835
Trenton, NJ 08625
(609) 292-3860

Office of Business Advocacy
Department of Commerce and Economic
 Development
20 West State Street, CN 823
Trenton, NJ 08625
(609) 292-0700

New Jersey Economic Development Authority
Capital Place One
200 S. Warren Street, CN 990
Trenton, NJ 08625
(609) 292-1800

New Jersey Urban Development Corp.
Capital Place One
200 S. Warren Street
CN 834
Trenton, NJ 80625
(609) 633-1100

Office of Urban Enterprise Zones
New Jersey Department of Commerce and
 Economic Development
20 W. State Street
CN 829
Trenton, NJ 08625
(609) 292-1912

Bishop Capital, LP
500 Morris Avenue
Springfield, NJ 07081
(201) 376-1595

ESLO Capital Corporation
212 Wright Street
Newark, NJ 07114
(201) 242-4488

First Princeton Capital Corporation
Five Garrett Mountain Plaza
West Paterson, NJ 07424
(201) 278-8111

Monmouth Capital Corporation
125 Wycoff Road
Midland National Bank Bldg.
P.O. Box 335
Eatontown, NJ 07724
(908) 542-4927

Tappan Zee Capital Corporation
2091 Lower Notch Road
Little Falls, NJ 07424
(201) 256-8280

Unicorn Ventures II, LP
6 Commerce Drive
Cranford, NJ 07016
(908) 276-7880

Unicorn Ventures, Ltd.
Commerce Drive,
Cranford, NJ 07016
(908) 276-7880

New Jersey Commission on Science &
 Technology
122 West State Street CN 832
Trenton, NJ 08625
(609) 984-1671

New Jersey Commission on Science and
 Technology
20 West State Street, CN 832
Trenton, NJ 08625-0832
(609) 984-1671

Casino Reinvestment Development Authority
1301 Atlantic Ave., 2nd Floor
Atlantic City, NJ 08401
(609) 347-0500

Office of Technology Assistance
Department of Commerce and Economic
 Development
Division of Development for Small Busi-
nesses and Women and Minority
 Businesses
20 West State Street, CN 835
Trenton, NJ 08625-0835
(609) 292-3860

Set-Aside and Certification Office
CN 835
Trenton, NJ 08625
(609) 984-9834

Employment and Training Service
New Jersey Department of Labor
Labor Building, Room 703
Trenton, NJ 08625
(609) 292-5005

Division of International Trade
153 Halsey Street, 5th Floor
P.O. Box 47024
Newark, NJ 07102
(201) 648-3518

Trade Adjustment Assistance Center
Economic Development Authority
Capital Place One
200 S. Warren Street, CN 990
Trenton, NJ 08625
(609) 292-0360

NEW MEXICO

Department of Economic Development
Joseph Montoya Building
1100 St. Francis Drive
P.O. Box 20003
Santa Fe, NM 87503
(505) 827-0300

State Investment Council
Ark Plaza, Suite 203
2025 South Pacheco Street
Santa Fe, NM 87505
(505) 827-6226

Securities Division
Regulation and Licensing Department
725 St. Michaels Drive
Santa Fe, NM 87501
(505) 827-7140

State Board of Finance, DFM
131 S. Capitol Street
Batan Memorial Building, Room 203
Santa Fe, NM 87503
(505) 827-4980

New Mexico Taxation and Revenue Department
Revenue Division, Returns Processing Bureau
P.O. Box 630
Santa Fe, NM 87509-0630
(505) 827-0700

Albuquerque SBIC
501 Tijeras Avenue NW
P.O. Box 487
Albuquerque, NM 87103
(505) 247-0145

New Mexico Industry Development Corporation
300 San Mateo NE, Suite 185
Albuquerque, NM 87108
(505) 246-6000

New Mexico Business Development Corporation
6001 Marble NE
Suite 6
Albuquerque, NM 87110
(505) 848-4548

Farmers Home Administration
Room 3414, Federal Building
517 Gold Ave., SW
Albuquerque, NM 87102
(505) 766-2462

New Mexico Housing Authority
Joseph Montoya Building
P.O. Box 20003
1100 St. Francis Drive
Santa Fe, NM 87503
(505) 827-0258

Economic Development Department
Pinion Building
Suite 358
1220 South St. Francis Drive
Santa Fe, NM 87501
(505) 827-5886

Department of Economic Development
Joseph Montoya Building
1100 St. Francis Drive, Room 2150
Santa Fe, NM 87503
(505) 827-0425

Associated Southwest Investors Corporation
6400 Uptown Blvd. NE, Suite 580 W
Albuquerque, NM 87110
(505) 881-0066

Department of Economic Development &
 Tourism
Joseph Montoya Building
P.O. Box 20003
1100 St. Francis Drive
Santa Fe, NM 87501
(505) 827-0300

Business Plan Development
(505) 827-0271

New Mexico Technet
4100 Osuna NE, Suite 103
Albuquerque, NM 87109
(505) 345-6555

Rio Grande Technology Foundation
P.O. Box 1369
Albuquerque, NM 87103
(505) 766-1879

NEW YORK

Small Business Division
Department of Economic Development
One Commerce Plaza
Albany, NY 12245
(518) 474-7756

Small Business Division
Department of Economic Development
1515 Broadway
New York, NY 10036
(212) 827-6100

Business Opportunity Center
1-800-STATE NY
1-800-782-8369

New York State Urban Development Corporation
1515 Broadway
New York, NY 10036
(212) 930-0356

Targeted Investment Program
(212) 930) 0320

Regional Economic Development Partnership
 Program (REDPP)
(212) 930-0297

New York State Department of Economic
 Development
One Commerce Plaza
Albany, NY 12245
(518) 474-1131

Agricultural Wastewater Loan Program
(518) 473-6291

Economic Development Zones
(518) 473-6930

New York Job Development Authority
 (JDA)
6095 Third Avenue
New York, NY 10158
(212) 818-1700

New York State Science & Technology
 Foundation
99 Washington Avenue, Suite 1730
Albany, NY 12210
(518) 473-9741

New York State Department of Agriculture
 & Markets
Division of Agricultural Support Services
One Winners Circle, Capital Plaza
Albany, NY 12235
(518) 457-7076

New York State Energy Research Development Authority
Two Rockefeller Plaza
Albany, NY 12223
(518) 465-6251

New York State Environment Facilities
 Corporation (NYBDC)
50 Wolf Road
Albany, NY 12207
(518) 463-2268

767 Limited Partnership
767 Third Avenue
New York, NY 10017
(212) 838-7776

ASEA Harvest Partners II
767 Third Avenue
New York, NY 10017
(212) 838-7776

American Commercial Capital Corporation
600 Third Avenue
Suite 3810
New York, NY 10016
(212) 986-3305

Amev Capital Corporation
One World Trade Center, Suite 5001
New York, NY 10048
(212) 323-9800

Argentum Capital Partners, LP
405 Lexington Avenue
New York, NY 10017
(212) 495-1784

Atlanta Investment Company, Inc.
655 Park Avenue
New York, NY 10019
(212) 956-9100

BNY One Capital Corporation
48 Wall Street
New York, NY 10286
(212) 495-1784

Hambro International Capital Company
650 Madison Avenue
New York, NY 10022
(212) 223-7400

Bridger Capital Corporation
645 W. Madison Avenue, Suite 1010
New York, NY 10022
(212) 888-4004

Chase Manhattan Capital Corporation
1 Chase Manhattan Plaza, 23rd Floor
New York, NY 10081
(212) 552-3581

Chemical Venture Corporation
270 Park Avenue, 5th Floor
New York, NY 10017
(212) 270-3220

Citicorp Investments, Inc.
399 Park Avenue
New York, NY 10043
1-800-624-4675

Citicorp Venture Capital, Ltd.
399 Park Avenue, 6th Floor
New York, NY 10043

Creditanstalt Capital Corporation
245 Park Avenue
New York, NY 10167
(212) 856-1050

Edwards Capital Company
Two Park Avenue, 20th Floor
New York, NY 10016
(212) 686-5449

Fifty-Third Street Ventures, LP
155 Main Street
Cold Spring, NY 10516
(914) 265-4244

First Wall Street SBIC, LP
44 Wall Street
New York, NY 10005
(212) 495-4890

Fundex Capital Corporation
525 Northern Blvd.
Great Neck, NY 11021
(516) 466-8551

Genesee Funding, Inc.
100 Corporate Woods
Rochester, NY 14623
(716) 272-2332

Hanover Capital Corporation
315 East 62nd Street, 6th Floor
New York, NY 10021
(212) 980-9670

IBJS Capital Corporation
One State Street, 8th Floor
New York, NY 1004
(212) 858-2000

M&T Capital Corporation
One M&T Place
Buffalo, NY 14240
(716) 842-5881

MH Capital Investors, Inc
270 Park Avenue
New York, NY 12201
(212) 270-3222

NYBDC Capital Corporation
41 State Street
P.O. Box 738
Albany, NY 12201
(518) 463-2268

NatWest USA Capital Corporation
175 Water Street
New York, NY 10038
(212) 602-1200

Norwood Venture Capital Fund, Inc.
1430 Broadway Suite 1607
New York, NY 10018
(212) 869-5075

Preferential Capital Corporation
380 Lexington Avenue
New York, NY 10017
(212) 661-9030

R&R Financial Corporation
1430 Broadway
New York, NY 10018
(212) 356-1400

Rand SBIC, Inc.
1300 Rand Building
Buffalo, NY 14203
(716) 853-0802

Small Business Electronics Corporation
1220 Peninsula Blvd.
Hewlett, NY 11557
(516) 374-0743

TLC Funding Corporation
660 White Plains Road
Tarrytown, NY 10591
(914) 332-5200

Vega Capital Corporation
720 White Plains Road
Scarsdale, NY 10583
(914) 472-8550

WFG Harvest Partners, Ltd.
767 Third Avenue
New York, NY 10017
(212) 838-7776

Winfield Capital Corporation
237 Mamaroneck Avenue
White Plains, NY 10605
(914) 949-9420

HUD Regional Office
26 Federal Plaza
New York, NY 10278-0068
(212) 264-8068

New York State Urban Development Corporation Director
Minority and Women Revolving Loan Fund
1515 Broadway
New York, NY 10036
(212) 930-0452

Division of Minority and Department of Economic Development
State Capitol, Room 235
Albany, NY 12224
(518) 474-1238
1515 Broadway, 52nd Floor
New York, NY 1036
(212) 930-9000

Job Training Partnership Council
Alfred E. Smith State Office
17th Floor
Albany, NY 12225
(518) 474-6014

Department of Economic Development Regional Offices
Albany . . . . (518) 432-2697
Binghamton . . . . (607) 773-7813
Brooklyn . . . . (718) 596-4120
Buffalo . . . . (716) 856-8111
Jericho . . . . (516) 349-1266
Kingston . . . . (914) 331-6415
Ogdensburg . . . . (315) 393-3980
Plattsburgh . . . . (518) 561-5642
Rochester . . . . (716) 325-1944
Syracuse . . . . (315) 428-4097
White Plains . . . . (914) 428-8000
Utica . . . . (315) 793-2366

New York State Urban Development Corporation
1515 Broadway
New York, NY 10036
(212) 930-0297

New York State Department of Labor
Harriman State Office Campus Building 12
Albany, NY 12240
(518) 457-6820

Apprentice Training Office, Room 140
(518) 457-6820

Principal Occupational Analyst, Room 171
(518) 457-1988

TJTC Unit, Room 238
(518) 457-2513

Liability and Determination Section
(518) 457-5807

New York State Education Department
Bureau of Economic Development Coordi-
nation
One Commerce Plaza
Albany, NY 12234
(518) 474-5506

New York State Office of Business Permits
& Regulatory Assistance
Permit Coordinator
Alfred E. Smith Building, 17th Floor
Albany, NY 12225
(518) 474-8275

Department of Economic Development
One Commerce Plaza
Albany, NY 12224
(518) 473-1325
1515 Broadway
New York, NY 10036
(212) 827-6150

Ombudsman Program
(212) 827-6150

Domestic Attraction Group
(518) 473-1325

Division for Small Business
Albany
(518) 474-7756
New York
(212) 827-6150

International Division
(212) 827-6200

Governor's Hasidic and Orthodox Task
Force
(212) 827-6117

New York State Environment Facilities
Corporation
509 Wolf Road
Albany, NY 12205
(518) 457-4138

New York State Science and Technology
Foundation
99 Washington Avenue, Suite 1730
Albany, NY 12210
(518) 473-9746

NORTH CAROLINA

North Carolina Department of Economic
and Community Development
Business Industrial Development
430 North Salisbury Street
Raleigh, NC 27611
(919) 733-4151

Business License information
NC Department of the Secretary of State
301 West Jones Street
Raleigh, NC 27603
(919) 733-0641

Finance Center
(919) 790-2731

North Carolina Technological Development
Authority
430 North Salisbury Street
Raleigh, NC 27611
(919) 990-8558

Finance Center
(919) 790-2731

North Carolina Technological Development
Authority
430 North Salisbury Street
Raleigh, NC 27611
(919) 990-8558

Heritage Capital Corporation
2000 Two First Union Center
Charlotte, NC 28282
(704) 372-5404

NCNB SBIC Corporation
One NCNB Plaza, T05-2
Charlotte, NC 28255
(704) 386-5583

NCNB Venture Company, LP
One NCNB Plaza, T-39
Charlotte, NC 28255
(704) 386-5723

North Carolina Department of Economic
and Community Development Division of
Community Assistance
1307 Glenwood Ave., Suite 250
Raleigh, NC 27605
(919) 733 2850

North Carolina Enterprise Corporation
P.O. Box 20429
Raleigh, NC 27619
(919) 781-2691

North Carolina Biotechnology Center
79 Alexander Drive
P.O. Box 13547
Research Triangle Park, NC 27709-3547

Institute of Private Enterprise
University of North Carolina
The Kenan Center, 498A
Chapel Hill, NC 27514
(919) 962-8201

North Carolina Department of Economic
Training and Community Development
Division of Employment and Training
11 Seaboard
Raleigh, NC 28202-2173
(919) 733-6383

North Carolina Department of Commerce
Finance Center
430 North Salisbury Street
Raleigh, NC 27611
(919) 733-5297

North Carolina Employment Security Commission
P.O. Box 25903
Raleigh, NC 27611
        OR
700 Wade Ave.
Raleigh, NC 27605
(919) 733-3098

North Carolina Rural Economic Development Center
4 N. Blount Street
Raleigh, NC 27601
(919) 821-1154

North Carolina Department of Commerce
430 North Salisbury Street
Raleigh, NC 27611
(919) 733 4151

Buyer/Supplier Exchange
(919) 733-4151

A and T State University
Agriculture Extension Program
P.O. Box 21928
Greensboro, NC 27420
(919) 27603-1337

NORTH DAKOTA

Center for Innovation and Business Devel-
opment
Box 8103, University Station
University of North Dakota
Grand Forks, ND 58202
(701) 777-3132

North Dakota Economic Finance Corp.
1833 E. Bismarck Expressway
Bismarck, ND 58504
(701) 221-5300

Bank of North Dakota (BND)
700 East Main Avenue
Box 5509
Bismarck, ND 58202-5509
(701) 224-5600

Export-Import Bank Working Capital Guarantee
(701) 746-5674

Export-Import Bank Medium and Long Term Loans
(710) 224-5674

Export Credit Insurance
(701) 224-5674

Office of Urban Development
122 South 5th Street
Room 233
Grand Forks, ND 58201-1518
(701) 746-2545

Office of Intergovernmental Assistance
State Capitol
Bismarck, ND 58505
(701) 224-2094

Governor's Office
State Capitol
Bismarck, ND 58505
(701) 224-3722

Agricultural Products Utilization Commission
600 East Boulevard
6th Floor
Bismarck, ND 58505
(701) 224-4760

North Dakota Tax Commissioner
State Capitol
Bismarck, ND 58505
(701) 224-2770

Fargo-Cass County Economic Development Corporation
321 North 4th Street
P.O. Box 2443
Fargo, ND 58108
(701) 237-6132

State Director
Farmers Home Administration
Third and Rosser Avenues
Bismarck, ND 58501
(701) 250-4781

Economic Development Administration
P.O. Box 1911
Bismarck, ND 58502
(701) 250-4321

Capital Dimensions Inc.
400 East Broadway
Suite 420
Bismarck, ND 58501
(701) 222-0995

Women Business Development Administration
Native American Business Development Administration
Department for Economic Development and Finance
1833 East Bismarck Expressway
Bismarck, ND 58504
(701) 221-5300

Governors Employment Training Forum
P.O. Box 2736
Bismarck, ND 58501
(701) 224-2792

North Dakota Economic Development Commission
1833 E. Bismarck Expressway
Bismarck, ND 58504
(701) 221-5300
(701) 221-5302

Center For Innovation and Business Development
Box 8103, University Station
University of North Dakota
Grand Forks, ND 58202
(701) 777-3132

NDSU Extension Service
North Dakota State University
P.O. Box 5437
Fargo, ND 58105
(701) 237-7394

Home-Based Business Program
(701) 237-7256

Farm and Ranch Management
(701) 237-7393

Grand Forks Development Foundation
202 North 3rd Street, Suite 300
Grand Forks, ND 58203
(701) 780-9915

North Dakota Micro Business Marketing
 Alliance
400 E. Broadway
Bismarck, ND 58203
(701) 224-8869
(701) 667-2008

OHIO

Ohio Department of Development
P.O. Box 1001
Columbus, OH 43266-0101
(614) 644-8748

One-Stop Business Permit Center
(614) 644-8748
1-800-248-4040

Business Advocacy Center
1-800-345-0hio

Small and Developing Business Division
Ohio Department of Development
77 S. High Street
P.O. Box 1001
Columbus, OH 43266-0101
(614) 466-2718

Ohio Department of Development
P.O. Box 1001
Columbus, OH 43266-0101
(614) 446-5420
1-800-282-1085

Pooled Bond Program
(614) 644-5645

Office of Local Government Services
(614) 466-2285

Office of Industrial Development
(614) 466-4551

International Trade Division
(614) 466-5017

Ohio Thomas Edison Program
(614) 466-5867

Small Business Innovation Research Program
(614) 466-8758
1-800-282-1085

Ohio Coal Development Program
(614) 466-3465

Ohio Statewide Development Corporation
(614) 466-5043

Minority Development Financing Commission
(614) 644-7708

Public Affairs Office
Treasurer of the State
Ohio State House, First Floor
Columbus, OH 43215
(614) 446-8851
1-800-228-1102

Clarion Capital Corporation
Ohio Savings Plaza, Suite 1520
1801 E. 9th Street
Cleveland, OH 44114
(216) 687-1096

Gries Investment Corporation
1500 Statler Office Tower
1127 Euclid Ave.
Cleveland, OH 44115
(216) 861-1146

National City Capital Corporation
1965 E. 6th Street, Suite 400
Cleveland, OH 44114
(216) 575-2491

Society Venture Capital Corporation
127 Public Square, 4th Floor
Cleveland, OH 44114
(216) 689-5776

Minority Development Financing Commission
Ohio Department of Development
P.O. Box 1001
Columbus, OH 43266-0101
(614) 644-7708

Minority Small and Business Assistance
 Program
(614) 446-5700

Minority Management and Technical Services
 ices
(614) 446-5700

Minority Contract Procurement Services
(614) 446-5700

Women's Business Resource Program
(614) 446-4945

Ohio Department of Development
P.O. Box 1001
Columbus, OH 43266-0101

Ohio Bureau of Employment Services
145 S. Front Street
Columbus, OH 43215
(614) 644-7138

Veteran's Job Training Act
(614) 466-3817

Job Training Partnership/Ohio Division
Ohio Bureau of Employment Services
145 South Front Street
Columbus, OH 43215
(614) 446-6000

Ohio Department of Development
P.O. Box 1001
Columbus, OH 43266-0101
(614) 446-2711
1-800-282-1085

International Trade Division
(614) 466-5017

Ohio Technology Transfer Organization
(614) 466-3086

Ohio Data User Center
(614) 466-2115

Small Business Innovation Research Program (SBIR)
(614) 466-5867

Buy Ohio Program
(614) 752-7393

Division of Travel and Tourism
(614) 466-8844
1-800-BUCKEYE

OKLAHOMA

Teamwork Oklahoma
6601 Broadway Extension
Oklahoma City, OK 73126-0980
(405) 843-5236

Oklahoma Department of Commerce
Five Broadway, Executive Park
6601 Broadway Extension
Oklahoma City, Ok 73116-8214
(405) 841-9770
(405) 841-5259

Oklahoma Development Finance Authority
301 NW 63rd
Suite 225
Oklahoma City, Ok 73116

Oklahoma Industrial Finance Authority
301 NW 63rd
Oklahoma City, OK 731116
(405) 842-1145

Office of the State Treasurer
Room 217, State Capitol Building
Oklahoma City, OK 73105
(405) 521-4301

Alliance Business Investment Company
One Williams Center
Suite 2000
Tulsa, OK 74172
(918) 584-3581

HUD Regional Office
Murray Federal Building
200 NW Fifth Street
Oklahoma City, OK 73102-3202
(405) 231-4181

Oklahoma Department of Commerce
6601 Broadway Extension
Oklahoma City, OK &3116-8214
(405) 843-9770
1-800-443-OKLA

Community Affairs and Development Division
(405) 841-9326

Research and Planning Division
(405) 841-5156

Capital Resources Division
(405) 841-5139

Farmers Home Administration
USDA Agriculture Building
Stillwater, OK 74074
(405) 624-4294

Venture Capital Exchange
Enterprise Development Center
University of Tulsa
600 South College Avenue
Tulsa, OK 74104
(918) 631-2684

Energy and Seed Fund
Oklahoma Department of Commerce
Capital Resources Division
6601 Broadway Extension
Oklahoma City, OK 73116
(405) 843-9770 ext.161

McGowan Investment Company
P.O. Box 270008
4300 Highline
Oklahoma City, OK
(405) 946-9706

ML Oklahoma Venture Partners, LP
211 North Robinson
One Leadership Square
Oklahoma City, OK 73102
(405) 270-1800

OKC Innovation Center
101 Park Avenue
Suite 500
Oklahoma City, OK 73102
(405) 235-3217

Davis Venture Partners, LP
One Williams Center
Suite 2000
Tulsa, OK 74172
(918) 584-7272

TSF Capital Corporation
2415 East Skelly Drive
Suite 102
Tulsa, OK 74105
(918) 747-2600

Western Venture Capital Corporation
4880 South Lewis
P.O. Box 702680
Tulsa, OK 74170
(918) 744-6275

Venture Capital Club
Tri-County Business Assistance Center
P.O. Box 3428
Bartlesville, OK 74006
(918) 333-3422

The Oklahoma Venture Forum
P.O. Box 2176
Oklahoma City, OK 73101-2176
(405) 636-9736

Oklahoma Private Enterprise Forum
Metropolitan Tulsa Chamber of Commerce
616 South Boston
Tulsa, OK 74119
(918) 585-1201

Oklahoma Department of Commerce
Small Business Division
6601 Broadway Extension
Oklahoma City, OK 73116-8214
(918) 585-1201

Women-Owned Business Assistance Program
(405) 841-5242

Oklahoma Department of Commerce
Employment Training Division
6601 Broadway Extension
Oklahoma City, OK 73116-8214
(405) 843-9770
1-800-443-OKLA

Oklahoma Business Assistance Network
1500 W. 7th
Stillwater, OK 75074
(405) 377-2000

Oklahoma Department of Commerce
6601 Broadway Extension
Oklahoma City, OK 73116-8214
(405) 843-9770
1-800-443-6552

Community Affairs and Development Division
(405) 841-9326

Small Business Division
(405) 841-5235

Capital Resources Division
(405) 841-5142

International Division
(405) 841-5215

Capital Resources Division
(505) 841-5138

Research and Planning Division
(405) 521-1601
1-800-522-8555

Business Development Division
(405) 841-5266

Community Affairs and Development Division
(405) 841-9326

Oklahoma Center for The Advancement of
Science and Technology (OCAST)
205 NW 63rd, Suite 305
Oklahoma City, OK 73116-8209
(405) 848-2633

Rural Enterprises
10 Waldren Dr.
Durant, OK 74701
(405) 924-5094

Office of Business and Economic Development
University of Oklahoma 1000Asp
314 Buchanan Hall
Norman, OK 73019
(405) 325-5627

OREGON

Department of Economic Development
775 Summer Street NE
Salem, OR 97310
Business Development Division
(503) 373-1225

Small Business Program
(503) 373-1200

Oregon Economic Development Department
775 Summer St. NE
Salem, OR 97310
(503) 373-1240

Community Development Section
(503) 378-3732

Business Development Section
(503) 373-1225

Oregon Economic Development Department
Ports Division/International Trade Division
1 World Trade Center
121 SW Salmon Street, Suite 300
Portland, OR 97204
(503) 229-5625

Portland Development Commission
1120 SW 5th, Suite 1102
Portland, OR 97204
(503) 796-5300

Oregon Department of Energy
625 Marion Street NE
Salem, OR 97310
(503) 373-1033

Oregon State Treasury
159 State Capitol
Salem, OR 97310
(503) 378-4111

Northern Pacific Capital Corporation
1201 SW 12th Avenue, Suite 608
Mail: P.O. Box 1658
Portland, OR 97205
(503) 241-1255

U.S. Bancorp Capital Corporation
111 SW 5th Avenue, Suite 1570
Portland, OR 97204
(503) 275-5860

Oregon Resource and Technology Development Corporation (ORTDC)
1934 NE Broadway
Portland, OR 97232
(503) 282-4462

Department of Environmental Quality
Management Services Division
811 SW Sixth Avenue
Portland, OR 97204
(503) 229-6022
1-800-452-4011

Office of Minority, Women & Emerging Small Business (OMWESB)
155 Cottage Street, NW
Salem, OR 97201-6605
(503) 326-2682

Work Force Development Section
Partnership Division
(503) 378-2285

Job Training Partnership Administration
(503) 378-1995

Workplace Training for Key Industries
(503) 378-2285

Oregon Department of Education
Job Development and Training Section
700 Pringle Parkway SE
Salem, OR 97310-0290
(503) 358-3584

Bureau of Labor and Industries
Apprenticeship and Training Division
1400 SW Fifth
4th Floor
Portland, OR 97201
(503) 731-4072

Oregon Office of Educational Policy and Planning
225 Winter Street, NE
Salem, OR 97310
(503) 378-8420
1-800-237-3710

Employment Division
875 Union Street, NE
Salem, OR   97311
(503) 378-8420

Small Business International Trade Program
One World Trade Center
121 SW Salmon Street
Suite 210
Portland, OR 97204
(503) 274-7482

International Trade Division
(503) 229-5625

Community Initiatives Section
(503) 373-1200

International Trade Institute
One World Trade Center
121 SW Salmon, Suite 230
Portland, OR 97204
(503) 725-3246

Port of Portland
700 NE Multnomah
Portland, OR 97232
(503) 231-5000

Oregon International Port of Coos Bay
326 Front Street
Coos Bay, OR 97420
(503) 267-7678

International Trade Administration
Dept. of Commerce/Foreign Commercial
 Service
1200 SW Third
Suite 240
Portland, OR 97204
(503) 326-3001

Department of Agriculture
Agricultural Development Division
121 SW Salmon
Suite 240
Portland, OR 97204
(503) 229-6734

Advanced Science and Technology Institute
 (ASTI)
University of Oregon
318 Hendricks Hall
Eugene, OR 97403
(503) 346-3189

    OR

Advanced Science and Technology Institute
Oregon State University
Corvallis, OR 97331
(503) 737-0671

Oregon Marketplace
618 Lincoln
Eugene, OR 97401
(503) 343-7712

Policy and Research Section
Partnership Division
Oregon Economic Development Department
775 Summer Street, NE
Salem, OR 97310
(503) 378-2286

PENNSYLVANIA

Bureau of Small Business Appalachian
 Development
461 Forum Bldg.
Harrisburg, PA 17120
(717) 783-5700

Office of Enterprise Development
461 Forum Building
Harrisburg, PA 17120
(717) 783-5700

Small Business Advocate
(717) 783-2525

Government Response Team
Commonwealth of PA
Department of Commerce
439 Forum Building
Harrisburg, PA 17120
(717) 787-8199
(717) 787-6500

Pennsylvania Treasury Department
Room 129, Finance Building
Harrisburg, PA 17120
(717) 787-2520

Nursing Home Loan Agency
Room 460
Forum Building
Harrisburg, PA 17120
(717) 783-8523

Revenue Bond and Mortgage Program
Room 466
Forum Building
Harrisburg, PA 17120
(717) 783-1108

Office of Technology Department
Forum Building
Harrisburg, PA 17120
(717) 787-4147

Challenge Grants Division
Executive Director North East Tier BFTC
125 Goodman Drive
Lehigh University
Bethlehem, PA 18015
(215)-758-5200

Executive Director
BFTC of Southern Pennsylvania
University City Science Center
3624 Market Street
Philadelphia, PA 19104
(215) 387-2255

President
BFTC of Western Pennsylvania
4516 Henry Street
Suite 103
Pittsburgh, PA 15213
(412) 681-1520

President
BFTC of Central/Northern Pennsylvania
5th Floor, Rider Building
120 South Burrowes Street
University Park, PA 16801
(814) 863-0532

Enterprise Venture Cap. Corp. of Pennsylvania
551 Main Street, Suite 303
Johnstown, PA 15901
(814) 535-7597

Erie SBIC
32 West 8th Street, Suite 615
Erie, PA 16501
(814) 453-7964

Fidelcor Capital Corporation
Witherspoon Building, 6th Floor
123 South Broad Street
Philadelphia, PA 19109
(215) 985-3722

First SBIC of America
P.O. Box 512
Washington, PA 15301
(412) 223-0707

Meridian Capital Corporation
Horsham Business Center, Suite 200
455 Business Drive
Horsham, PA 19044
(215) 957-7520

Meridian Venture Partners
The Fidelity Court Building
259 Radnor-Chester Road
Radnor, PA 19087
(215) 293-0210

PNC Capital Corporation
Pittsburgh National Building
Fifth Avenue and Wood Street
Pittsburgh, PA 15222
(412) 762-2248

Pennsylvania Minority Business Authority
1712 State Office Building
1400 Spring Garden Street
Philadelphia, PA 19130

Pennsylvania Minority Business Authority
461 Forum Building
Harrisburg, PA 17120
(717) 783-1127
(717) 783-1128

Pennsylvania Minority Business Development Authority
Room 461, Forum Building
Harrisburg, PA 17120
(717) 783-1127

Economic Development Partnership
Bureau of Job Training Partnership
Labor and Industry Building
7th and Foster
Harrisburg, PA 17120
(717) 787-8944

Government Response Team
Pennsylvania Department of Commerce
439 Forum Building
Harrisburg, PA 17120
(717) 787-7190

Office of International Development
Room 464
Forum Building
Harrisburg, PA 17120
(717) 787-7190

PENNTAP
Pennsylvania Department of Commerce
Pennsylvania State University
248 Calder Way, Suite 306
University Park, PA 16801
(814) 865-0427

Director
Governor's Response Team
Room 439
Forum Building
Harrisburg, PA 17120
(717) 787-6500

Office of Technology Development
Pennsylvania Department of Commerce
352 Forum Building
Harrisburg, PA 17120
(717) 787-4147

RHODE ISLAND

Good Neighbor Alliance Corp.
1664 Cranston Street
Cranston, RI 02920
(401) 467-2880

Rhode Island Department of Economic
 Development (RIDED)
7 Jackson Walkway
Providence, RI 02903
(401) 277-2601

Rhode Island Department of Economic
 Development (RIDED)
7 Jackson Walkway
Providence, RI 02903
(401) 277-2601

Newport
(401) 849-9889

Bristol County
(401) 245-0750

Domestic Capital Corporation
15 Reservoir Drive
Cranston, RI 02910
(401) 946-3310

Fairway Capital Corporation
285 Governor Street
Providence, RI 02906
(401) 861-4600

Fleet Venture Resources, Inc.
111 Westminster Street
Providence, RI 02903
(401) 278-6770

Moneta Capital Corporation
285 Governor Street
Providence, RI 02903
(401) 861-4600

Old Stone Capital Corporation
One Old Stone Square
11th Floor
Providence, RI 02903
(401) 278-2559

Richmond Square Capital Corporation
1 Richmond Square
Providence, RI 02906
(401) 521-3000

Wallace Capital Corporation
170 Westminster Street, Suite 1020
Providence, RI 02903
(401) 273-9191

Business Development Company Financing
(401) 351-3036

Governors Office of Energy Assistance
(401) 277-3370

RISE
(401) 277-2678

Department of Administration
Rhode Island Division of Taxation
1 Capital Hill
Providence, RI 02908
(401) 277-3050

RI Department of Environmental Management
 (RIDEM)
9 Hayes Street
Providence, RI 02908
(401) 277-3434

Technical Assistance:
Bristol . . . . (401) 253-7010
Central Falls . . . . (401) 728-3270
Cranston . . . . (401) 461-1000
Cumberland . . . . (401) 728-2400
East Providence . . . . (401) 434-3311
Newport . . . . (401) 846-9600
North Providence . . . . (401) 232-0900
Pawtuckett . . . . (401) 728-0500
Warwick . . . . (401) 738-2000
West Warwick . . . . (401) 822-9215
Westerly . . . . (401) 596-7355
Woonsocket . . . . (401) 762-6400

Department of Economic Development
7 Jackson Walkway
Providence, RI 02903
(401) 277-2601

Rhode Island Department of Employment
 and Training
101 Friendship Street
Providence, RI 02903
(401) 277-2090

Workforce 2000
100 North Main Street
5th Floor
Providence, RI 02903
(401) 277-6700

Rhode Island Department of Economic
 Development
7 Jackson Walkway
Providence, RI 02903
(401) 277-2601

Brown University Venture Forum
Box 1949
Providence, RI 02912
(401) 863-3528

University of Rhode Island
Ballentine Hall
Kingston, RI 02881
(401) 792-1000

Sea Grant Advisory Services
(401) 792-6842

Business and Economic Research Center
(401) 792-2549

Labor Research Center
(401) 792-2239

Institute for International Business
(401) 792-4372

Center for Pacific-Basin Capital Markets
 Research
(401) 729-5105

MBA Job Bank
(401) 792-2337

Research Institute for Telecommunications and
Information Marketing
(401) 792-5065

SOUTH CAROLINA

South Carolina State Development Board
P.O. Box 927
1201 Main Street
Columbia, SC 29202
(803) 737-0400

Industry-Business and Community Services
(803) 734-1400

South Carolina State Development Board
P.O. Box 927
Columbia, SC 29202
(803) 737-0400

South Carolina Jobs/Economic Development Authority
1201 Main Street, Suite 1750
Columbia, SC 29201
(803) 737-0079

Business Development Corporation
Suite 225, Enoree Building
Koger Center
111 Executive Drive
Columbia, SC 29221
(803) 798-4064

Charleston Capital Corporation
111 Church Street
P.O. Box 328
Charleston, SC 24902
(803) 723-6464

Reedy River Ventures
233 N. Main Street, Suite 350
P.O. Box 17526
Greenville, SC 29606
(803) 232-6198

Governors Office of Small and Minority
Business Assistance
1205 Pendleton Street
Room 437
Columbia, SC 29201
(803) 734-0657

South Carolina Jobs/Economic Development Authority
1201 Main Street, Suite 1750
Columbia, SC 29201
(803) 737-0079

South Carolina State Development Board
P.O. Box Columbia, SC 29202
(803) 737-0400

Lander College
Small Business Development Center
P.O. Box 6143
Greenwood, SC 29646
(803) 227-6110

Hilton Head Small Business Development
Center
Suite 300, Kiawah Bldg.
10 Office Park Road
Hilton Head Island, SC
(803) 785-3995
(803) 777-0333

South Carolina State College
Small Business Development Center
School of Business Administration
Orangeburg, SC 29117
(803) 536-8445

Winthrop College
Small Business Development Center
School of Business Administration
119 Thurmond Building
Rock Hill, SC 29733
(803) 323-2283

Spartanburg Chamber of Commerce
Small Business Development Center
P.O. Box 1636
Spartanburg, SC 29304
(803) 594-5081

SOUTH DAKOTA

Governors Office of Economic Development
711 East Wells Avenue
Capitol Lake Plaza
Pierre, SD 57501-3369
(605) 773-5032

Governors Office of Economic Development
711 East Wells Avenue
Capitol Lake Plaza
Pierre, SD 57501
(605) 773-5032
1-800-872-6190

State Investment Council
4009 West 49th
Suite 300
Sioux Falls, SD 57106-3784
(605) 335-5023

Minority Business Office
Governors Office of Economic Development
Capitol Lake Plaza
Pierre, SD 57501
(605) 773-5072

South Dakota Department of Labor
420 South Roosevelt
P.O. Box 4730
Aberdeen, SD 57402-4730
(605) 622-2302

Department of Labor
Private Industry Council
Kneip Building
Pierre, SD 57501
(605) 773-5017

Labor Market Information Center
P.O. Box 4730
420 South Roosevelt
Aberdeen, SD 57402-4730
(605) 622-2314

School of Business-USD
414 East Clark Street
Vermillion, SD 57069
(605) 677-5287

Governors Office of Economic Development
Capitol Lake Plaza
Pierre, SD 57501
(605) 773-5032

Export, Trade and Marketing Division
(605) 773-5735

Promotion of Agricultural Products
(605) 773-3375

TENNESSEE

Office of Small Business
Department of Economic and Community Development
Rachel Jackson State Office Building
320 Sixth Avenue North
Nashville, TN 37243-0405
(615) 741-2626

Department of Economic and Community
 Development
Rachel Jackson State Office Building
320 North Sixth Avenue North
Nashville, TN 37243-0404
(615) 741-6671
1-800-342-1340

Program Management Section
(615) 741-6201

Financial Resources, Inc.
2800 Sterick Building
Memphis, TN 38103
(901) 527-9411

Tennessee Valley Authority (TVA)
400 W. Summit Hill Drive
O.H.C. 28
Knoxville, TN 37902
(615) 632-3148

Tennessee Technology Foundation
P.O. Box 23184
Knoxville, TN 37922-1184
(615) 694-6772

Office of Minority Business Enterprise
Department of Economic and Community
 Development
Rachel Jackson Building
7th Floor
320 Sixth Avenue North
Nashville, TN 37243-0405

Department of Economic and Community
 Development
Industrial Training Service
Suite 660
Volunteer Plaza
500 James Robertson Parkway
Nashville, TN 37243-0406
(615) 741-1746
1-800-342-8472
1-800-251-8594

Private Industry Council
100 North Main Street
Memphis, TN 38103
(901) 576-6536

Department of Economic and Community
 Development
Rachel Jackson State Office Building
320 Sixth Avenue North
Nashville, TN 37243
(615) 741-1888

Office of the Security of State
James K. Polk Building
18th Floor
Nashville, TN 37243-0306
(615) 741-0531

TEXAS

Texas Department of Commerce
Texas Market Place
P.O. Box 12728
Austin, TX 78711
(512) 472-5059

Texas Department of Commerce
P.O. Box 12728
Austin, TX 78711
Community Development Block Grant
(512) 320-9649

Texas Enterprise Zone Program
(512) 320-9592

Texas Rural Economic Development Fund
(512) 320-9649

Texas Exporters Loan Guarantee Program
(512) 320-9662

Eximbank Working Capital Guarantee
(512) 320-9662

Texas Export Credit Umbrella Insurance
 Program
(512) 320-9662

Agriculture Finance Office
Department of Agriculture
P.O. Box 12847
Austin, TX 78711
(512) 463-7476

Linked Deposit Program
(512) 463-7476

TylerSeed/Venture Growth Fund
P.O. Box 2004
Tyler, TX 75710
(903) 593-2004

Alliance Business Investment Company
(Main Office: Tulsa, OK)
911 Louisiana
One Shell Plaza
Suite 3990
Houston, TX 77002
(713) 224-8224

Brittany Capital Company
7557 Rambler Street
Suite 108
2424 LTV Tower
Dallas, TX 75231
(214) 363-1341

Business Capital Corporation
4809 Cole Avenue
Suite 250
Dallas, TX 75205
(214) 522-3739

Capital Southwest Venture Corporation
12900 Preston Road
Suite 700
Dallas, TX 75230
(214) 233-8242

Cagharter Venture Group, Inc.
2600 Citadel Plaza Drive
Suite 600
Houston, TX 77008
(713) 863-0704

Citicorp Venture Capital, Ltd.
(Main Office: New York, NY)
2001 Ross
Suite 3050, LBJ 117
Dallas, TX 75201
(214) 880-9670

Simmons & Co. Int.
4900 Republic Bank center
700 Louisiana
Houston, TX 77002
(713) 236-9999

Enterprise Capital Corporation
515 Post Oak Blvd.
Suite 310
Houston, TX 77027
(713) 621-9444

PCA Investment Company
San Felipe Plaza
Suite 850
Houston, TX 77507
(713) 781-2857

First City Corp. Finance
1001 Main Street, 15th Floor
Houston, TX 77002
(713) 658-5421

Ventex Management, Inc.
1000 Louisiana, 7th Floor
Suite 1110
Houston, TX 77002
(713) 659-7870

Ford Capital, Ltd.
1445 Ross Ave.
Suite 3500
Dallas, TX 75202
(214) 855-4247

Houston Partners, SBIP
Capital Center Penthouse, 8th Floor
401 Louisiana
Houston, TX 77002
(713) 222-8600

Jiffy Lube Capital Corporation
700 Milam
P.O. Box 2967
Houston, TX 77252
(713) 546-8910

MVenture Corporation
1717 Main Street, 7th Floor
7th Momentum Place
Dallas, TX 75201
(214) 939-3131

Aspen Capital Ltd.
55 Waugh Street
Suite 710
Houston, TX 77007
(713) 880-4494

Nations Banc Capital Corp.
1401 Elm Street
Suite 4764
Dallas, TX 77007
(214) 508-5050

Rust Capital Ltd.
200 Norwood Tower
114 West 7th Street
Austin, TX 78701
(512) 482-0806

SBI Capital Corporation
6305 Beverly Hill Lane
Mail: P.O. Box 570368; Houston, TX 77257
Houston, TX 77057
(713) 975-1188

South Texas SBIC
120 South Main Street
P.O. Box 1698
Victoria, TX 77902
(512) 373-5151

Sunwest Capital, Ltd.
3 Forest Plaza
12221 Merit Drive
Suite 1300
Dallas, TX 75251
(214) 239-5650

Texas Commerce Investment Company
Texas Commerce Bank Bldg., 30th Floor
712 Main Street
Houston, TX 77002
(713) 236-4719

Western Financial Capital Corporation
1729 Preston Road, Suite 300
Dallas, TX 75252
(214) 380-0044

Austin Business Development Center
Grant Thornton
310 Congress Ave.
Austin, TX 78701
(512) 476-9700

Brownsville Minority Business Development
 Center
2100 Boca Chica
Suite 301
Brownsville, TX 78520
(512) 546-3400

Corpus Christi Minority Business Development Center
Cara, Inc.
3649 Leopard Street
Suite 524
Corpus Christi, TX 78469
(512) 887-7961

Dallas/Ft. Worth Minority Business Development Center
Grant Thornton
1445 Ross Avenue
Dallas, TX 75202
(214) 855-7373

Houston Minority Business Development Center
Grant Thornton
2800 CitiCorp Center
1200 Smith Street
Houston, TX 77002
(713) 650-3831

Laredo Minority Business Development Center
2801 E. Montgomery
Laredo, TX 78403
(512) 725-5177

Lubbock, Midland, Odessa Minority Business Development Center
1220 Broadway, #509
Lubbock, TX 74901
(806) 762-6232

McAllen Minority Business Development Center
Cara, Inc.
1701 West Bus. Highway 83, #1108
McAllen, TX 78501
(512) 224-1945

San Antonio Minority Business Development Center
University of Texas at San Antonio
Economic Development Center
San Antonio, TX 78207
(512) 224-1945

Texas Department of Commerce
Work Force Development Division
P.O. Box 12728
Austin, TX 78711
(512) 320-9800

Texas Capital Network
8716 North Mopac
Suite 200
Austin, TX 78711
(512) 794-9398

Pan Handle Small Business Corp.
1800 South Washington, Suite 110
Amarillo, TX 79102
(806) 372-5151

Southwest Venture Forum
Southern Methodist University
Box 333
Dallas, TX 75275-0333
(214) 692-3326

MIT Enterprises Forum of Dallas-Fort Worth, Inc.
625 Digital Drive
Suite 107
Plano, TX 75075
(214) 741-8700

Longview Venture Club
Longview Chamber of Commerce
P.O. Box 472
Longview, TX 75606
(903) 237-4000

Northwest Texas Small Business Development Center
2579 South Loop 289
Suite 114
Lubbock, TX 79423
(806) 745-3973

Ventex Group, Inc.
14785 Omicron Drive
San Antonio, TX 78245
(512) 677-6000

Central Texas Venture Capital Group
Greater Waco Chamber of Commerce
P.O. Drawer 1220
Waco, TX 76703
(817) 752-6551

MIT Enterprise Forum
P.O. Box 61385
Houston, TX 77208-1385
(713) 237-2590

Texas Department of Commerce
P.O. Box 12728
Austin, TX 78711
(512) 472-5059

Office of Business Finance
(512) 320-9634

Business Development Division
(512) 320-9699

Tourism Division
(512) 462-9191

UTAH

Heber M. Wells Building, First Floor
160 East 300 South
Salt Lake City, UT 84113-3330
(801) 530-4848

Utah Small Business Development Center
102 W. 500 South
Suite 315
Salt Lake City, UT 84101-2315
(801) 581-7905

Weber County
Weber County Capital Development Company
2404 Washington Blvd., #1000
Ogden, UT 84401
(801) 629-7119

Utah County
Central Utah Certified Development Company
2696 N. University Avenue
Suite 240
Provo, UT 84604
(801) 374-1025

Utah Technology Finance Corporation
185 S. State
Suite 208
Salt Lake City, UT 84111
(801) 364-4346

Utah Venture Fund I
419 Wakara Way
Salt Lake City, UT 84108
(801) 583-5922

Department of Commerce
350 E. 500 Street, Suite 101
Salt Lake City, UT 84111
(801) 328-8181

Office Job Training for Economic Development
Department of Community and Economic Development
324 S. State
Suite 200
Salt Lake City, UT 84111
(801) 538-8700

Business and Economic Specialist
USU Cooperative Extension
Logan, UT 84322-3505
(801) 750-2284

Utah Association of Certified Public
 Accountants
455 East 400 South
Suite 202
Salt Lake City, UT 84111
(801) 359-3533

Utah Public Society of Public Accountants
451 East 300 South
Salt Lake City, UT 84111
(801) 363-1776

Lawyer Referral Service
645 South 200 East
Salt Lake City, UT 84111-3834
(801) 531-9075

Utah State BAR
645 South 200 East
Salt Lake City, UT 84111-3834
(801) 531-9077

Attorney Referral Service
141 West Haven Avenue
Salt Lake City, UT 84115
(801) 485-6023

Utah Trial Lawyers Association
141 West Haven Avenue
Salt Lake City, UT 84115
(801) 531-7514

Mountain West Venture Group
50 South Main Street
P.O. Box 210
Salt Lake City, UT 84144
(801) 521-8900

Metro Utah, Inc.
6150 State Office Building
Salt Lake City, UT 84114
(801) 538-3055

Utah Supplier Development Council
151 Annex Building
University of Utah
Salt Lake City, UT 84112
(801) 581-8169

Procurement Outreach
(801) 538-8790

International Marketing Program
(801) 538-8737

Rural Marketing Program
(801) 538-8780

Urban Marketing Program
(801) 538-8800

Business Expansion & Retention Program
(801) 538-8775

Bureau of Economic and Business Research
401 Kendall D. Graff Building
University of Utah
Salt Lake City, UT 84112
(801) 581-6333

VERMONT

Vermont Economic Development Department
109 State Street
Montpelier, VT 05609
(802) 828-3221

Vermont Agency of Development and
 Community Affairs
109 State Street
Montpelier, VT 05609
(802) 223-7226

Agency of Development and Community
Affairs
109 State Street
Pavilion Office Building
Montpelier, VT 05602-9990

Job Development Zones
(802) 828-3221

Department of Housing and Community Affairs
(802) 828-3217

Public Facilities Division
(802) 244-8744

Vermont Housing Finance Authority
P.O. Box 408
Burlington, VT 05402-0408
1-800-748-5101

Northern Community Investment Corporation
20 Main Street
P.O. Box 904
St. Johnsbury, VT 05819
(802) 748-5101

Queneska Capital Corporation
123 Church Street
Burlington, VT 05401
(802) 865-1806

Minority Assistance Program
City Hall, Room 32
Church Street
Burlington, VT 05401
(802) 865-7144

Women Small Business Project
City Hall
Room 32
Church Street
Burlington, VT 05401
(802) 865-7144

Agency of Development and Community
Affairs
Economic Development Department
109 State Street
Pavilion Office Building
Montpelier, VT 05602-9990
(802) 828-3221

Department of Employment and Training
P.O. Box 488
5 Green Mountain Drive
Montpelier, VT 05602
(802) 828-4000

Department of Labor and Industry
120 State Street
Montpelier, VT 05602

Division of Apprenticeship
(802) 828-2157

Vermont Occupational Safety and Health
Act
(802) 828-2765

Vermont Department of Employment and
Training
P.O. Box 488
Montpelier, VT 05602
(802) 828-4000

Agency of Economic and Community Affairs
109 State Street
Pavilion Office Building
Montpelier, VT 05602-9990

Economic Development Department
(802) 828-3221

Vermont Dept. of Travel & Tourism
(802) 828-3236

Department of Forest, Parks and Recreation
 Forestry Division
103 South Main Street
Building 10 South
Waterbury, VT 05676
(802) 244-8716

VIRGINIA

Department of Economic Development
Office of Small Business
P.O. Box 798
Richmond, VA 23206-0798
(804) 371-8252

Virginia Employment Commission Economic Information Services Division
703 East Main Street
P.O. Box 1358
Richmond, VA 23211
(804) 786-3047

Virginia Small Business Financing Authority
 (VSBFA)
1021 E. Cary Street
P.O. Box 798
Richmond, VA
(804) 371-8254

Virginia Department of Housing and Community Development
205 N. Fourth Street
Richmond., VA 23219-1747
(802) 371-7061

Community Development Block Grants
(802) 371-7061

Department of Economic Development
P.O. Box 798
Richmond, VA 23206-0799
(804) 371-8100

Crestar Capital, LP
901 E. Cary Street
Suite 1212
Richmond, VA 23219
(804) 780-2094

Dominion Capital Markets Corporation
213 South Jefferson Street
Roanoake, VA 24011
(703) 563-6156

Metropolitan Capital Corporation
7110 Rainwater Place
Lorton, VA 22709
(703) 550-8530

Sovran Funding Corporation
Sovran Center
6th Floor
One Commercial Plaza
P.O. Box 600
Norfolk, VA 23510
(804) 441-4041

Walnut Capital Corporation
(Main Office: Chicago, IL)
8300 Boone Boulevard, Suite 780
Vienna, VA 22182
(703) 448-3771

VEDCORP, Inc.
951 East Byrd Street, Suite 940
Richmond, VA 23219
(802) 771-2765

Norfolk Business Development Center
355 Crawford Pkwy., Suite 608
Portsmouth, VA 23704
(804) 399-0888

Governors Employment and Training Department
4615 W. Broad Street
Commonwealth Building
Richmond, VA 23230
(804) 367-9800

Department of Economic Development
Workforce Services
James Center
1021 E. Cary
Richmond, VA 23219
(804) 371-8120

Center for Innovative Technology
2214 Rock Hill Road
Suite 600
Herndon, VA 22071
(703) 689-3000

Department of General Services
Division of Purchases and Supply
P.O. Box 1199
Richmond, VA 23209-1199
(804) 786-5494

Department of Economic Development
P.O. Box 798
Richmond, VA 23206-0798
(804) 371-8100

Office of Small Business
(804) 371-8252

Virginia Port Authority
600 World Trade Center
Norfolk, VA 23510
(804) 683-8000

Secondary Road Division of the Department
 of Transportation
State Secondary Roads Engineer
1401 East Broad Street
Richmond, VA 23240
(804) 771-2765

WASHINGTON

Business Assistance Center
Department of Trade and Economic Development
2110 6th Avenue
Suite 2700
Seattle, WA 98121
(206) 464-6282

Washington State Business
 Assistance Center
919 Lakeridge Way
Suite A
Olympia, WA 98502
(206) 753-5632
1-800-237-1233

Department of Community Development
9th and Columbia Building
MS: GH-51
Olympia, WA 98504-4151
(206) 586-8974
1-800-562-5677

Department of Trade and Development
2001 Sixth Avenue
Suite 2700
Seattle, WA 98121
(206) 464-6282

Washington State Business Assistance
 Center
Department of Trade and Economic Devel-
 opment
919 Lakeridge Way SW
Suite A
Olympia, WA 98502
(206) 464-6282

Washington Economic Development
 Finance Authority
(206) 389-2560

Washington State Energy Office
809 Legion Way SE
MS: FA-11
Olympia, WA 98504
(206) 956-2000

Export Assistance Center Of Washington
 (EACW)
2001 Sixth Avenue
Suite 1700
Seattle, WA 98121
(206) 464-7123

Department of Revenue
G.A. Building
MS: AX-02
Olympia, WA 98504
(206) 753-3171

Capital Resource Corporation
1001 Logan Building
Seattle, WA 98101
(206) 623-6550

Norwest Growth Fund, Inc.
(Main Office: Minneapolis, MN)
P.O. Box 21693
Seattle, WA 98111
(206) 746-1973

Seafirst Capital Corporation
Columbia Seafirst Center
701 Fifth Avenue
P.O. Box 34997
Seattle, WA 98124
(206) 358-3000

Grant Building
Room 201
611 East Sixth Street
Austin, TX 78701
(512) 482-5461

Economic Development Administration
Jackson Federal Building
915 Second Avenue
Room 1856
Seattle, WA 98174
(206) 553-4731

Washington State Business Assistance
 Center
Department of Trade and Economic Devel-
 opment
919 Lakeridge Way SW
Suite A
Olympia, WA 98502
(206) 586-4852

Office of Minority and Women's Business
 Enterprises (OWMBE)
406 South Water Street
MS-FK-11
Olympia, WA 98504-4611
(206) 753-9693

State Board of Community College Education
319 East Seventh Avenue
MS: FF-11
Olympia, WA 98504
(206) 753-0878

Employment Security Department
605 Woodview Drive SE
MS: KG-11
Olympia, WA 98504-5311
(206) 438-5116

Employment Security Department
212 Maple Park
MS: KG-11
Olympia, WA 98504-5311
(206) 438-5116

Targeted Jobs Tax Credit
(206) 586-3321

Work Force for Training & Coordinating
 Board
Building 17
Airdustrial Park
MS: AX-22
Olympia, WA 98504-0622
(206) 753-5439

Department of Trade and Economic Development
101 G.A. Building
MS: AX-13
Olympia, WA 98504-0613
(206) 753-5600

Department of Labor and Industry
Office of Information and Assistance
1-800-LISTENS

Business License Service
Department of Licensing
405 Black Lake Boulevard
Olympia, WA 98504
(206) 586-2786
1-800-562-8203

Corporation Division
Office of the Secretary of State
505 East Union Avenue
Olympia, WA 98504
(206) 753-7115

Washington Public Ports Association
P.O. Box 1518
Olympia, WA 98507
(206) 943-0760

Washington Business Assistance Center
919 Lakeridge Way SW
Suite A
Olympia, WA 98502-9917
(206) 664-9501
1-800-237-1233

Department of Trade and Economic Development
2001 Sixth Avenue
Suite 2700
Seattle, WA 98121
(206) 464-6282

Site Selection
(206) 464-6282

Business Retention
(206) 464-6282

Film and Video Office
(206) 464-7148

Export Information
(206) 464-7143

CINTRAFOR
College of Forest Resources
AR-10
University of Washington
Seattle, WA 98195
(206) 543-8684

Department of Community Development
Ninth & Columbia Building
MS: GH-51
Olympia, WA 98504-4151
(206) 586-8984

Washington State Energy Office
809 Legion Way SE
MS: FA-11
Olympia, WA 98504
(206) 956-2069

Washington Technology Center
University of Washington Campus Office
FH-10
Seattle, WA 98195
(206) 545-1920

WEST VIRGINIA

West Virginia Development Office
State Capitol Complex
Charleston, WV 25305
(304) 558-4010

West Virginia Economic Development
 Authority (WVEDA)
Building 6, Room 525
State Capitol Complex
Charleston, WV 25305
(304) 558-3650

West Virginia State Tax Department
State Capitol
Room W-300
Charleston, WV 23505
(304) 558-2500

West Virginia Development Office
State Capitol, M-146
Charleston, WV 25305
(304) 558-0400

West Virginia Development Office
Room 517, Building 6
Capitol Complex
Charleston, WV 25305
(304) 558-2234

WISCONSIN

Department of Development
123 West Washington Avenue
P.O. Box 7970
Madison, WI 53707
(608) 266-1018

Permit Information Center
1-800-HELP-BUS

Small Business Advocate
(608) 266-1018

Wisconsin Housing and Economic Development Authority
1 South Pinckney Street
P.O. Box 1728
Madison, WI 53701-1728
(608) 266-0976
(608) 266-2297

Department of Development
123 W. Washington Avenue
P.O. Box 7970
Madison, WI 53707
(608) 266-1018

Banc One Venture Corporation
111 East Wisconsin Avenue
Milwaukee, WI 53202
(414) 765-2274

Bando McGlocklin Capital Corporation
13555 Bishops Court, Suite 205
Brookfield, WI 53005
(414) 784-9010

Capital Investments, Inc.
Commerce Building, Suite 540
744 North Fourth Street
Milwaukee, WI 53203
(414) 273-6560

M&I Ventures Corporation
770 North Water Street
Milwaukee, WI 53202
(414) 765-7910

MorAmerica Capital Corporation
(Main Office: Cedar Rapids, IA)
600 East Mason Street
Milwaukee, WI 53202
(414) 276-3839

Polaris Capital Corporation
One Park Plaza
11270 W. Park Place, Suite 320
Milwaukee, WI 53224
(414) 359-3040

Wisconsin Community Capital, Inc.
1 South Pinckney Street
Suite 500
Madison, WI 53703
(608) 256-3441

Wisconsin Business Development Finance
 Corporation
P.O. Box 2727
Madison, WI 53701
(608) 258-8830

Northwest Regional Planning Commission
302 Walnut Street
Spooner, WI 54801
(715) 635-2197

Impact Seven
Route 2, Box 8
Turtle Lake, WI 54889
(715) 986-4171

First Commercial Financial Corporation
330 South Executive Drive #204
Brookfield, WI 53005
(414) 786-0699

Venture Investor of Wisconsin, Inc.
University Research Park
565 Science Drive
Suite A
Madison, WI 53711
(414) 272-4400

Bureau of Minority Business Development
P.O. Box 7970
Madison, WI 53707
(608) 267-9550

Minority Business Development Fund
(608) 266-8380

Minority Business Recycling Development
 Program
(608) 266-8380

Wisconsin Housing and Economic Development Authority
1 Pinckney Street
#500
P.O. Box 1728
Madison, WI 53701-1728
(608) 266-0976
(608) 266-7884

Future Value Ventures, Inc.
622 North Water Street
#500
Milwaukee, WI 53202
(414) 278-0377

Milwaukee County Department of Public
 Works & Transportation
907 North 10th Street
#311
Milwaukee, WI 53233
(414) 278-5248

City of Milwaukee-Minority Business Enterprise Program
200 East Wells Street #102
Milwaukee, WI 53202
(414) 278-5553

Milwaukee Economic Development Corporation
809 North Broadway
P.O. Box 324
Milwaukee, WI 53201
(414) 233-5812

Wisconsin Department of Transportation
Disadvantaged Business Program
4802 Sheboygan Avenue, Room 951
Madison WI 53707
(608) 266-6961

Wisconsin Women Entrepreneurs
1126 South 70th Street, Suite 106
Milwaukee, WI 53214
(414) 475-2436

Department of Industry, Labor and Human
 Relations
201 E. Washington Avenue
Madison, WI 53701
(608) 266-5370

Department of Development
123 West Washington Avenue
P.O. Box 7970
Madison, WI 53707
(608) 266-1018

Board of Vocational, Technical and Adult
 Education
310 Price Place
P.O. Box 7874
Madison, WI 53707
(608) 266-1207

Bureau of Apprenticeship Standards
DILHR
P.O. Box 7972
Madison, WI 53707
(608) 266-3133

Department of Development
123 West Washington Avenue
P.O. Box 7970
Madison, WI 53707
(608) 266-1018

Bureau of International Development
(608) 266-1480

Entrepreneurial Networking Program
(608) 266-8525

Wisconsin Film Office
(608) 267-3686

Wisconsin Rural Development Center
P.O. Box 504
Black Earth, WI 53515
(608) 767-2539

Center for Innovation and Development

School of Industry and Technology
(715) 232-2565

UW-Stout
(715) 232-1686

Wisconsin Innovation Service Center
402 McCutchan
Whitewater, WI 53190
(414) 472-1365

Marquette University
College of Engineering
(414) 288-6720

Medical College of Wisconsin
MCW Research Foundation
(414) 257-8219

Milwaukee School of Engineering
Applied Technology Center
(414) 277-7324

UW Madison
Biotechnology Transfer Office
(608) 262-8606

Engineering Industrial Relations
(608) 262-5215

Office of Industrial Research and Technology
 Transfer
(608) 229-5000

Wisconsin Center for Manufacturing and
 Productivity
(608) 262-6426

Council of Small Business Executives (Cosbe)
756 North Milwaukee Street
Milwaukee, WI 53202
(414) 273-3000

WYOMING

Division of Economic Community Development
Department of Commerce
Herschler Building
2 West
Cheyenne, WY 82002
(307) 777-7284

Division of Economic & Community Development
Department of Commerce
Barrett Bldg.
4th Floor
Cheyenne, WY 82002
(307) 777-7284

Office of the State Treasurer
State Capitol
Cheyenne, WY 82002
(307) 777-7408

Wyoming Industrial Development Corporation
P.O. Box 3599
Casper, WY 82602
(307) 234-5251

Western Research Institute
Box 3395
University Station
Laramie, WY 82701
(307) 721-2327

Job Training Program Employment Service Division
Department of Employment
P.O. Box 2760
Casper, WY 82602
(307) 235-3280

Division of Economic & Community Development
Dept. of Commerce
Barrett Bldg.
4th Floor
2301 Central Avenue
Cheyenne, WY 82002
(307) 777-7284

Community College Resources
Community College Commission
Herschler Bldg.
Cheyenne, WY 82002
(307) 777-7763

Institute of Business & Management Services
Barrett Bldg.
4th Floor North
2301 Central Avenue
Cheyenne, WY 82002
(307) 777-6412

Marketing Division
Department of Agriculture
2219 Carey Avenue
Cheyenne, WY 82002
(307) 777-7321

Department of Labor & Statistics
Herschler Bldg.
Cheyenne, WY 82002
(307) 777-7261

Representative MTDC Investments

While MTDC does not target specific industry groups, the following will provide a good illustration of the diversity of its investments:

Computer Software and Services

*Access Technology, Inc. .... Natick
*Aspen Technology, Inc. .... Cambridge
*Business Research Corporation. .... Boston
CimTelligence Corporation .... Lexington
COLLEGE COUNSEL, Inc. .... Natick
Digital Techniques, Inc. .... Burlington
IMC Systems Group, Inc. .... Waltham
**Interleaf, Inc. .... Cambridge
Powersoft Corporation .... Burlington
Symbiotics, Inc. .... Cambridge
Technology Integration, Inc. .... Bedford

Computer Equipment and Peripherals

Augment Systems, Inc. .... Bedford
**Display Components, Inc. .... Westford
Graftel Systems, Inc. .... Wilmington
MicroTouch Systems, Inc. .... Wilmington
Reflection Technology, Inc. .... Waltham
SKY Computers, Inc. .... Chelmsford
**Xylogics, Inc. .... Bedford

Industrial Automation Systems and Equipment

*Aeonic Systems, Inc. .... Billerica
Aseco Corporation .... Marlboro
Icon Corporation .... Woburn
IVS Incorporated .... Concord
Kronos Incorporated .... Waltham
Proconics International, Inc. .... Wilmington
Tytronics, Inc. .... Waltham
**Vitronics Corporation .... Newmarket, NH†
XRL, Inc. .... Canton

Biomedical Investments

*AMDEV, Inc. .... Danvers
Endogen, Inc. .... Boston
EXOS, Inc. .... Burlington
Laser Engineering, Inc. .... Milford
Optical Micro Systems, Inc. .... North Andover
StatSpin Technologies .... Norwood

Telecommunications and Data Communications

AT/Comm, Inc. .... Marblehead
*Chromatic Technologies, Inc. .... Franklin
Fotec, Inc. .... Boston
MultiLink, Inc. .... Lynnfield
Voicetek Corporation .... Chelmsford
**Zoom Telephonics .... Boston

Material Science and Related Systems

*Crystal Systems, Inc. .... Salem
**Spire Corporation .... Bedford

Advanced Defense Systems and Products

Millitech Corporation .... So. Deerfield
**Pacer Systems, Inc. .... Billerica

Environmental Management

*/**Cambridge Analytical Associates, Inc. .... Boston

*Exit Strategy Completed - Acquisition/Buyback
**Exit Strategy Completed - Initial Public Offering
†Previously Newburyport, MA

10.

THE SMALL BUSINESS INNOVATION RESEARCH PROGRAM
****

How would you like Uncle Sam to fund your research and development? Under the Small Business Innovation Research Program (SBIR) it could happen. The Small Business Innovation Development Act of 1982 (P.L. 97-219, amended by P.L. 99-443) requires federal government agencies with the largest research and development (R & D) budgets to a reserve a specified amount of their extramural R & D budgets for an SBIR Program. This legislation was intended to:

o stimulate technological innovation;
o use small business to meet federal research and development needs;
o increase private sector commercialization of innovations derived from federal research and development;
o foster and encourage participation by minority and disadvantaged persons in technological innovation.

The Small Business Administration was designated to coordinate and monitor the government-wide activities of the SBIR program and report on its results annually to Congress. At this writing eleven federal government agencies are participating in this program. They support small business research in important scientific and engineering areas to encourage the conversion of that R & D into commercial applications to benefit Americans. You can contact the applicable fe-

deral agency, or all of them, to find out more about each one's SBIR Program by either telephoning or writing your local SBA office (see Chapter 5) or the national office overseeing this program at:

SMALL BUSINESS ADMINISTRATION
OFFICE OF INNOVATION, RESEARCH AND TECHNOLOGY
409 - 3rd Street S.W.
Washington, DC 20416
Telephone: (202) 205-6450
                      (202) 205-7777

The SBA publishes the SBIR Pre-Solicitation Announcement, a quarterly publication describing the SBIR in detail. This publication contains all the pertinent facts on current and upcoming SBIR solicitations.
The following agencies of the Federal Government participate in the SBIR program:

Department of Agriculture
Department of Commerce
Department of Defense
Department of Education
Department of Energy
Department of Health and Human Services
Department of Transportation
Environmental Protection Agency
National Aeronautics and Space Administration

National Science Foundation
Nuclear Regulatory Commission

Each of the above Federal agencies designate topics upon which SBIR proposals will be sought, release at least one SBIR solicitation annually, receive and evaluate SBIR proposals, and award funding agreements competitively that are based on technical and scientific merit and cost effectiveness as well as meeting the agency's needs and requirements.

HOW TO PARTICIPATE IN THIS PROGRAM

Each participating government agency invites small business firms to submit research proposals under their program solicitations. You can read about these in the Commerce Business Daily (available at your local public library or Chamber of Commerce) when they are released; or, you can also contact the federal agencies directly (as described previously) and ask for their program solicitation entitled "Small Business Innovation Research Program" for that Fiscal Year.

The government agency will encourage business firms, usually with strong scientific capabilities, to participate. The agency you contact is looking for proposals containing advanced concepts related to important scientific problems and opportunities that could lead to significant public benefit if the research is successful.

If you feel your business firm qualifies and your research matches the program solicitation, then you should apply for funding under the SBIR program. The program is broken up into three phases.

THE THREE PHASE PROGRAM

Phase I: The objective of this phase is to establish the technical merit and feasibility of proposed research or R & D efforts and to determine the quality of performance of the small business awardee organization prior to funding further federal support. In this phase you may be awarded up to $50,000 to pay for further research for a period normally not to exceed six months.

Phase II: This phase permits you to continue the research or R & D efforts initiated in Phase I. Funding will be based on the results of Phase I and the scientific and technical merit of the Phase II proposal. Only Phase I awardees are eligible to apply for Phase II funding. Phase II proposals may be submitted only after the Phase I contract has expired. In this phase your award can be up to $500,000 to pay for further research for a period normally not to exceed two years.

The third phase requires the small business to pursue with non-federal funds the commercialization of the Phase I and Phase II research results (see Chapter 11 for Venture Capital Sources). In some federal agencies, Phase III may involve non-SBIR funding or production contracts for products or processes intended for use by the United States Government.

PROGRAM AVAILABILITY

To apply your firm must qualify as a small business under this definition:

1.   The business is organized for profit, independently owned and operated, not dominant in the field of operation in which it is proposing, and has its principal place of business located in the United States.

2.   The business is at least 51 percent owned, or in the case of a publicly owned business, at least 51 percent of its voting stock is owned by United States citizens or lawfully admitted permanent resident aliens.

3.   The business, including its affiliates, has less than 500 employees and meets other regulatory requirements. Business concerns include, but are not limited to, any individual, partnership, corporation, joint venture, association, or cooperative.

The number of Phase I awards given annually vary. Each federal agency sets aside a limited number of awards. For instance, the United States Department of Agriculture has earmarked 40 Phase I awards for Fiscal Year 1993. The National Institutes of Health has approximately 36 Phase I awards available for that Fiscal Year. Over the next several years the Small Business Administration anticipates that total Phase I and Phase II awards will average approximately $500 million annually.

PROPOSAL PREPARATION INSTRUCTIONS AND REQUIREMENTS

Your SBIR Phase I proposal should be less than 25 single-spaced standard size (8.5" by 11") pages, including the cover sheet, cost breakdown, and all enclosures or attachments. Use the cover sheet provided for you by the government agency, also known as the PHASE I PROPOSAL COVER SHEET. Fill it out completely.

The agency will also provide you with an Abstract Form where you may describe your research project. Include this as the second page of your proposal.

On the third page of your proposal, discuss the following elements in this order and with these headlines.

1.   Identification and Significance of the Problem or Opportunity. Provide a clear statement of the specific technical problem or opportunity addressed.

2.   Technical Objectives. State the specific objectives of the Phase I effort, including the technical questions it will try to answer to determine the feasibility of the proposed approach.

3.   Work Plan. Provide a detailed plan for the R & D to be carried out, including the experimental design, procedures, and protocols to be used. This plan should address the objectives and the questions stated in (2) above. The methods to be used to achieve each objective or task should be discussed in detail.

4.   Related Research or R & D. Describe significant research or R & D that is directly related to the proposal, including any conducted by the principal investigator/project manager or by the proposing firm. Describe how it relates to the proposed effort, and any planned coordination with outside sources. The principal investigator/project manager must persuade the Phase I reviewers of his or her awareness of recent significant research or R & D conducted by others in the same scientific field.

5.   Relationship with Future R & D.
a. State the results expected from the proposed approach.
b. Discuss the significance of the Phase I effort in providing a foundation for Phase II.

6.   Potential Commercial Applications. Briefly describe why the proposed

project appears to have potential commercial applications.

7. Key Personnel and Bibliography of Directly Related Work. Identify key personnel, including their directly related education, experience, and bibliographic information. If a person's resume or curriculum vitae is extensive, use a summary that focuses on the most relevant experience or publications. Provide dates and places of employment and some information about the nature of each position or professional experience. Identify each key personnel's current or most recent position.

8. Consultants. Involvement of consultants in the planning and/or research stages of the project is permitted. If such involvement is intended, it should be described in detail. If consultants are to be used, attach appropriate letters from each individual confirming his/her role in the project.

9. Facilities and Equipment. Indicate where the proposed research will be conducted. One of the performance sites must be at the location of the organization making the proposal. Describe the facilities to be used; identify the location; and briefly describe their capacities, pertinent capabilities, relative proximity, and extent of availability to the project. Include clinical, computer, and office facilities of business and those of any other performance sites to be used in the project. List the important equipment items already available for this project, noting location and pertinent capabilities of each.

In your next section you must provide information on any active funding through contracts, grants, and cooperative agreements from public or private sponsors; any contract proposals and grant and cooperative agreements pending review or funding; and, contract proposals and grant and cooperative agreement applications about to be submitted. Include ALL pertinent details about these contracts, grants and cooperative agreements.

Finally, your proposal must include a budget. Fortunately, each federal agency includes a government form that asks for the details and cost of each item. You will find the three (or more) vital forms when you receive the official SBIR Program Solicitation from the federal agency. They are in the appendix section at the end of the booklet.

THE EVALUATION PROCESS

Contract proposals are evaluated by a panel of experts selected for their competence in the relevant scientific and technical fields. Their task is to evaluate your proposal for scientific and technical merit and to perform a concept review. It rates proposals and makes specific recommendations related to the scope, direction and/or conduct of the proposed research, and for those proposals recommended for award. The panel also provides a commentary about the funding level, fee and duration of the proposed contract project.

An award may only be made if the proposal has been recommended as technically acceptable by the evaluation panel. However, proposals recommended as acceptable are not automatically funded.

The following factors and the weight they carry are used to determine the technical acceptability of your proposal.

FACTORS	WEIGHT
The soundness and technical merit of the proposed approach.	40%
Qualifications of the proposed principal investigator, supporting staff and consultants.	30%
The potential of the proposed research for technological innovation.	20%
Adequacy and suitability of the facilities and research environment.	10%

ADDITIONAL INFORMATION

Payments on Phase I contract awards are made on a monthly advance basis.

A final report is required of all Phase I contractors. It should include a detailed description of the project objectives, the activities that were carried out, the results obtained, and an in-depth discussion of whether such results provided a foundation for a Phase II effort. An original and five copies of this report must be submitted to the contracting officer not later than the expiration date of the Phase I contract.

Information contained in unsuccessful proposals will remain your property. However, the federal agency may retain copies of all proposals. Public release of information in any proposal will be subject to existing statutory and regulatory requirements. Please carefully mark any confidential or privileged information or trade secrets.

Small business firms may normally retain the principal worldwide patent rights to any invention developed with government support. Under existing regulations, the government receives a royalty-free license for federal government use, reserves the right to require the patent holder to license others in certain circumstances, and requires that anyone exclu-sively licensed to sell the invention in the United States must normally manufacture it substantially in the United States.

Further details about a federal agency's requirements may be found in the program solicitation guide. You may contact the participating federal agencies after receiving your quarterly SBIR Pre-Solicitation Announcement.

INVENTORS:
THE ENERGY-RELATED INVENTIONS PROGRAM

There is a federal program, different and separate from the SBIR Program, for inventors. The Federal Nonnuclear Energy Research and Development Act of 1974 (Public Law 93-577) established a comprehensive national program for research and development of all potentially beneficial energy sources and utilization technologies. While this program is conducted by the Department of Energy, the legislation directs the National Institute of Standards and Technology (NIST) to evaluate all promising nonnuclear energy-related inventions, particularly those submitted by independent inventors and small companies for the purpose of obtaining direct grants for their development from the Department of Energy.

The purpose of the Energy-Related Inventions Program is to help independent inventors obtain Federal assistance in developing and commercializing their inventions. NIST evaluates the inventions and recommends those considered sufficiently promising to the Department of Energy (DOE) for support. DOE determines whether and how the recommended inventions should be supported and takes the necessary support action. DOE expects to support almost all NIST-recommended inventions. The average grant or contract award is about $70,000 although some awards have exceeded $100,000.

Submit your invention with the correct government form, NIST-1019, called the ENERGY-RELATED INVENTION EVAL-UATION REQUEST. Include a written disclosure of your invention. You should describe it in full and include drawings of this device (they need not be professionally done). Your invention does not have to be patented before you make your submission. Claims should be set forth clearly, pointing how the invention is unique, how performance and costs are advantageous over similar items on the market or in development, and how the invention will affect national energy objectives. The basis of any claims made must be included; these could include calculations or test data. Don't submit a model or sample of your invention unless the NIST requests one during the evaluation. The NIST will NOT test your invention.

If your submission is acceptable, First-Stage evaluation is conducted in which brief technical opinions are obtained, usually independent from the Office of Energy-Related Inventions' staff evaluators. The staff engineer, assigned to your submission, will then review and integrate those opinions and make a decision as to your invention's potential. If the invention is rated as "promising", a Second-Stage evaluation is conducted and a formal report prepared. If the second evaluation confirms that the invention is promising, then disclosure and evaluation results are forwarded to the Office of Inventions and Innovative Programs with a recommendation of government support. Getting through both stages of the evaluation process can take between 16 and 32 weeks.

After you have passed muster with the NIST, the DOE will assign your invention to an invention coordinator within the Office of Invention and Innovative Programs. The coordinator will asks you to submit a preliminary proposal describing the dollar amount of support you are seeking and the work needed to complete your invention.

The invention description and your preliminary proposal will be reviewed by those in the DOE technical program most closely related to your invention. Their review will determine whether your preliminary proposal is a technically valid way of developing your invention and if the costs are reasonable and commensurate with the potential benefits.

The invention coordinator will weigh the NIST conclusions, your preliminary proposal, the review by the DOE technical program, and the availability of funds in arriving at feasible options for supporting your invention.

Then, the DOE is prepared to offer one-time-only assistance. The grant is decided on the basis of individual merit and need. While the primary method of support is a grant award, assistance has also included contracts and testing of the invention at one of the DOE facilities or through arrangements with a non-profit technology innovation center.

DOE also has an agreement with the Small Business Administration (see Chapter 5) to give particular attention to loan requests from inventors recommended under this program in order to meet capital needs, such as production tooling. Contact your local Small Business Administration office for details.

For further information about this program write to:

OFFICE OF ENERGY-RELATED INVEN-TIONS
NATIONAL INSTITUTE OF STANDARDS AND TECHNOLOGY
GAITHERSBURG, MARYLAND 20899

SBIR DIRECTORY OF FEDERAL AGENCIES

Contact these federal agencies to find out about their SBIR programs.

DEPARTMENT OF AGRICULTURE
Dr. Charles F. Cleland
Director, SBIR Program
Cooperative State Research Service
Room 320, Aerospace Center
901 D Street, S. W.
Washington, DC 20250-2200
Telephone: (202) 401-4002

DEPARTMENT OF COMMERCE
Mr. Edward V. Tiernan
SBIR Program Manager
U.S. Department of Commerce
Suitland Professional Center
SPC, Room 307
Suitland, Maryland 20233
Telephone: (301) 763-4240

DEPARTMENT OF DEFENSE
Mr. Robert Wrenn
SBIR Program Manager
U.S. Department of Defense
OSD/SADBU
The Pentagon -- Room 2A340
Washington, DC 20301-3061
Telephone: (703) 697-1481

DEPARTMENT OF EDUCATION
Mr. John Christensen
SBIR Program Coordinator
U.S. Department of Education
Room 602D
555 New Jersey Avenue, N.W.
Washington, DC 20208
Telephone: (202) 219-2050

DEPARTMENT OF ENERGY
Dr. Samuel J. Barish
SBIR Program Manager - ER-16
Washington, DC 20585
Telephone: (301) 903-3054

DEPARTMENT OF HEALTH AND HUMAN SERVICES
Mr. Richard Clinkscales
SBIR Program Manager
Office of the Secretary
U.S. Department of Health
 and Human Services
Washington, DC 20201
Telephone: (202) 245-7300

DEPARTMENT OF TRANSPORTATION
Dr. George Kovatch
SBIR Program Director, DTS-22
U.S. Department of Transportation
Research and Special Programs Administration
Volpe National Transportation
Systems Center
55 Broadway, Kendall Square
Cambridge, Massachusetts 02142-1093
Telephone: (617) 494-2051

ENVIRONMENTAL PROTECTION AGENCY
SBIR Program Manager
Research Grants Staff (RD-675)
Environmental Protection Agency
401 M Street, S.W.
Washington, DC 20460
Telephone: (202) 260-7899

NATIONAL AERONAUTICS AND
SPACE ADMINISTRATION
Mr. Harry Johnson
Program Director, SBIR Office - Code CR
National Aeronautics and Space
Administration Headquarters
300 E Street, S.W.
Washington, DC 20546
Telephone: (202) 358-1989

NATIONAL SCIENCE FOUNDATION
SBIR Program Manager
National Science Foundation-V-502
1800 G Street, N.W.
Washington, DC 20550

NUCLEAR REGULATORY COMMIS-
SION
Ms. Marianne M. Riggs
SBIR Program Representative
Program Management, Policy
Development and Analysis Staff
U.S. Nuclear Regulatory Commission
Washington, DC 20555
Telephone: (301) 492-3625

U.S. DEPARTMENT OF AGRICULTURE

SMALL BUSINESS INNOVATION RESEARCH

PHASE I AND PHASE II

PROJECT SUMMARY*

APPENDIX B
OMB Approved 0524-0025
Expires 4/95

FOR USDA USE ONLY			
Program Office	Solicitation No.	Proposal No.	Topic No.

TO BE COMPLETED BY PROPOSER	
Name and Address of Firm	Name and Title of Principal Investigator(s)

Title of Project (80-character maximum)

Technical Abstract (200-word limit)

Anticipated Results/Potential Commercial Applications of Research (100-word limit)

Keywords to Identify Technology/Research Thrust/Commercial Application (8-word maximum)

*The Project Summary must be suitable for publication by USDA in the event of an award. *Do not include proprietary information on this page.*

DEPARTMENT OF HEALTH AND HUMAN SERVICES
SMALL BUSINESS INNOVATION RESEARCH PROGRAM
PHASE I PROPOSAL COVER SHEET

Solicitation No. PHS 92-1

TOPIC NO.	PROJECT TITLE

SUBMITTED BY *(Firm name, address, and telephone number)*	YEAR FIRM FOUNDED
	NO. OF EMPLOYEES *(Include all affiliates)*

NOTICE TO OFFERORS

The offeror organization and the principal investigator are jointly responsible for the accuracy and validity of all the administrative, fiscal and scientific information in the proposal. Deliberate withholding, falsification or misrepresentation of information could result in a determination of non-responsibility [FAR 9.104-1(d)] which would preclude an award to the offeror. In addition, sanctions such as suspension, debarment and criminal penalties could apply.

CERTIFICATIONS

YES   NO

☐   ☐   1. The above organization certifies that it is a small business and meets the definition stated in this Solicitation.

☐   ☐   *2. The above organization certifies that it qualifies as a minority and disadvantaged small business as defined in this Solicitation.

☐   ☐   *3. The above organization certifies that it qualifies as a woman-owned small business as defined in this Solicitation.

☐   ☐   4. The above organization certifies that more than one-half of the principal investigator's time will be spent in the employ of the firm.

☐   ☐   5. The above organization certifies, pursuant to FAR 52.223-5, incorporated in this Solicitation, that it will provide a drug-free workplace.

*   Capture of this information is strictly for statistical purposes.

YES   NO

☐   ☐   1. If this proposal does not result in an award, is the Government permitted to disclose the title and abstract of your research project, and the name, address and telephone number of the corporate official of your firm, to organizations that may be interested in contacting you for further information or possible investment?

☐   ☐   2. This proposed project involves human subjects. *(See instructions in Solicitation)*

☐   ☐   3. This proposed project involves vertebrate animals. *(See instructions in Solicitation)* If YES, identify by common names

and circle primates._____

NOTICE OF PROPRIETARY INFORMATION

The information identified by asterisks (*) on pages _____ of this proposal constitutes trade secrets or information that is commercial or financial and confidential or privileged. It is furnished to the Government in confidence with the understanding that such information shall be used or disclosed only for evaluation of this proposal; provided that, if a contract is awarded as a result of or in connection with the submission of this proposal, the Government shall have the right to use or disclose information herein to the extent provided by law. This restriction does not limit the Government's right to use the information if it is obtained without restriction from another source.

PRINCIPAL INVESTIGATOR/PROJECT MANAGER		CORPORATE OFFICIAL	
NAME		NAME	
SIGNATURE	DATE	SIGNATURE	DATE
TITLE		TITLE	
PHONE NO. *(Include area code)*		PHONE NO. *(Include area code)*	

ABSTRACT OF RESEARCH PLAN

NAME, ADDRESS AND TELEPHONE NUMBER OF OFFEROR ORGANIZATION

TITLE OF PROJECT

KEY PROFESSIONAL PERSONNEL ENGAGED ON PROJECT

NAME	POSITION TITLE	ORGANIZATION

ABSTRACT OF RESEARCH PLAN: State the proposal's long-term objectives and specific aims, making reference to the health-relatedness of the project, and describe concisely the methodology for achieving these goals. Summarize the results that are expected during Phase I, the implications of the proposed approach for Phase II, and the potential for technological innovation and commercial application. Avoid summaries of past accomplishments and the use of the first person. If abbreviations or acronyms are used, provide complete spelling of such words when they appear for the first time in the abstract.

The abstract is meant to serve as a succinct and accurate description of the proposed work when separated from the application. Since abstracts of funded applications may be published by the Federal Government, proprietary information should not be included. DO NOT EXCEED 200 WORDS.

Provide keywords (8 maximum) to identify the research or technology.

Provide a brief summary of the potential commercial applications of the research.

INSTRUCTIONS TO OFFERORS

1. The purpose of this form is to provide a standard format by which the offeror submits to the Government a summary of incurred and estimated costs (and attached supporting information) suitable for detailed review and analysis. Prior to the award of a contract resulting from this proposal the offeror shall, under the conditions stated in FPR 1-3.807-3 be required to submit a Certificate of Current Cost or Pricing Data (See FPR 1-3.807-3(h) and 1-3.807-4).

2. In addition to the specific information required by this form, the offeror is expected, in good faith, to incorporate in and submit with this form any additional data, supporting schedules, or substantiation which are reasonably required for the conduct of an appropriate review and analysis in the light of the specific facts of this procurement. For effective negotiations, it is essential that there be a clear understanding of:

    a. The existing, verifiable data.

    b. The judgmental factors applied in projecting from known data to the estimate, and

    c. The contingencies used by the offeror in his proposed price.

In short, the offeror's estimating process itself needs to be disclosed.

3. When attachment of supporting cost or pricing data to this form is impracticable, the data will be described (with schedules as appropriate), and made available to the contracting officer or his representative upon request.

4. The formats for the "Cost Elements" and the "Proposed Contract Estimate" are not intended as rigid requirements. These may be presented in different format with the prior approval of the Contracting Officer if required for more effective and efficient presentation. In all other respects, this form will be completed and submitted without change.

5. By submission of this proposal the offeror grants to the Contracting Officer, or his authorized representative, the right to examine, for the purpose of verifying the cost or pricing data submitted, those books, records, documents and other supporting data which will permit adequate evaluation of such cost or pricing data, along with the computations and projections used therein. This right may be exercised in connection with any negotiations prior to contract award.

FOOTNOTES

1. Enter in this column those necessary and reasonable costs which in the judgment of the offeror will properly be incurred in the efficient performance of the contract. When any of the costs in this column have already been incurred (e.g., on a letter contract or change order), describe them on an attached supporting schedule. Identify all sales and transfers between your plants, divisions, or organizations under a common control, which are included at other than the lower of cost to the original transferror or current market price.

2. When space in addition to that available in Exhibit A is required, attach separate pages as necessary and identify in this "Reference" column the attachment in which the information supporting the specific cost element may be found. No standard format is prescribed; however, the cost or pricing data must be accurate, complete and current, and the judgment factors used in projecting from the data to the estimates must be stated in sufficient detail to enable the Contracting Officer to evaluate the proposal. For example, provide the basis used for pricing materials such as by vendor quotations, shop estimates, or invoice prices; the reason for use of overhead rates which depart significantly from experienced rates (reduced volume, a planned major re-arrangement, etc.); or justification for an increase in labor rates (anticipated wage and salary increases, etc.). Identify and explain any contingencies which are included in the proposed price, such as anticipated costs of rejects and defective work, or anticipated technical difficulties.

3. Indicate the rates used and provide an appropriate explanation. Where agreement has been reached with Government representatives on the use of forward pricing rates, describe the nature of the agreement. Provide the method of computation and application of your overhead expense, including cost breakdown and showing trends and budgetary data as necessary to provide a basis for evaluation of the reasonableness of proposed rates.

4. If the total cost entered here is in excess of $250, provide on a separate page the following information on each separate item or royalty or license fee: name and address of licensor; date of license agreement; patent numbers, patent application serial numbers, or other basis on which the royalty is payable; brief description, including any part or model numbers of each contract item or component on which the royalty is payable; percentage or dollar rate of royalty per unit; unit price of contract item; number of units; and total dollar amount of royalties. In addition, if specifically requested by the contracting officer, a copy of the current license agreement and identification of applicable claims or specific patents shall be provided.

5. Provide a list of principal items within each category indicating known or anticipated source, quantity, unit price, competition obtained, and basis of establishing source and reasonableness of cost.

CONTINUATION OF EXHIBIT A – SUPPORTING SCHEDULE AND REPLIES TO QUESTIONS II AND V.

CONTRACT PRICING PROPOSAL *(RESEARCH AND DEVELOPMENT)*		
	PAGE NO.	**NO. OF PAGES**

NAME OF OFFEROR	SUPPLIES AND/OR SERVICES TO BE FURNISHED *(Title of Proposed Effort)*	
HOME OFFICE ADDRESS		

DIVISION(S) AND LOCATION(S) WHERE WORK IS TO BE PERFORMED	TOTAL AMOUNT OF PROPOSAL $	GOV'T SOLICITATION NO.

DETAIL DESCRIPTION OF COST ELEMENTS

1. DIRECT MATERIAL *(Itemize on Exhibit A)*	EST COST ($)	TOTAL EST COST[1]	REFERENCE[2]
a. PURCHASED PARTS			
b. SUBCONTRACTED ITEMS			
c. OTHER–*(1)* RAW MATERIAL			
(2) YOUR STANDARD COMMERCIAL ITEMS			
(3) INTERDIVISIONAL TRANSFERS *(At other than cost)*			
TOTAL DIRECT MATERIAL			

2. MATERIAL OVERHEAD[3] *(Rate   %X$ base=)*

3. DIRECT LABOR *(Specify)*	ESTIMATED HOURS	RATE/ HOUR	EST COST ($)		
Principal Investigator					
TOTAL DIRECT LABOR					

4. LABOR OVERHEAD *(Specify Department or Cost Center)*[3]	O.H. RATE	X BASE=	EST COST ($)		
TOTAL LABOR OVERHEAD					

5. SPECIAL TESTING *(Including field work at Government installations)*	EST COST ($)		
TOTAL SPECIAL TESTING			

6. SPECIAL EQUIPMENT *(If direct charge) (Itemize on Exhibit A)*			

7. TRAVEL *(If direct charge) (Give details on attached Schedule)*	EST COST ($)		
a. TRANSPORTATION			
b. PER DIEM OR SUBSISTENCE			
TOTAL TRAVEL			

8. CONSULTANTS *(Identify–purpose–rate)*	EST COST ($)		
TOTAL CONSULTANTS			

9. OTHER DIRECT COSTS *(Itemize on Exhibit A)*			
10. TOTAL DIRECT COST AND OVERHEAD			
11. GENERAL AND ADMINISTRATIVE EXPENSE *(Rate % of cost element Nos.)*			
12. ROYALTIES[4]			
13. TOTAL ESTIMATED COST			
14. FEE OR PROFIT			
15. TOTAL ESTIMATED COST AND FEE OR PROFIT			

This proposal is submitted for use in connection with and in response to *(Describe RFP, etc.)*

and reflects our best estimates as of this date, in accordance with the Instructions to Offerors and the Footnotes which follow.

TYPED NAME AND TITLE	SIGNATURE	
NAME OF FIRM		DATE OF SUBMISSION

EXHIBIT A–SUPPORTING SCHEDULE *(Specify. If more space is needed, use reverse.)*

COST EL NO.	ITME DESCRIPTION *(See footnote 5.)*	EST COST *($)*

I. HAS ANY EXECUTIVE AGENCY OF THE UNITED STATES GOVERNMENT PERFORMED ANY REVIEW OF YOUR ACCOUNTS OR RECORDS IN CONNECTION WITH ANY OTHER GOVERNMENT PRIME CONTRACT OR SUBCONTRACT WITHIN THE PAST TWELVE MONTHS?

☐ YES ☐ NO *(If yes, identify below.)*

NAME AND ADDRESS OF REVIEWING OFFICE AND INDIVIDUAL	TELEPHONE NUMBER/EXTENSION

II. WILL YOU REQUIRE THE USE OF ANY GOVERNMENT PROPERTY IN THE PERFORMANCE OF THIS PROPOSED CONTRACT?

☐ YES ☐ NO *(If yes, identify on reverse or separate page.)*

III. DO YOU REQUIRE GOVERNMENT CONTRACT FINANCING TO PERFORM THIS PROPOSED CONTRACT?

☐ YES ☐ NO *(If yes, identify.):* ☐ ADVANCE PAYMENTS ☐ PROGRESS PAYMENTS OR ☐ GUARANTEED LOANS

IV. DO YOU NOW HOLD ANY CONTRACT *(Or, do you have any independently financed (IR&D) projects)* FOR THE SAME OR SIMILAR WORK CALLED FOR BY THIS PROPOSED CONTRACT?

☐ YES ☐ NO *(If yes, identify.):*

V. DOES THIS COST SUMMARY CONFORM WITH THE COST PRINCIPLES SET FORTH IN AGENCY REGULATIONS?

☐ YES ☐ NO *(If no, explain on reverse or separate page.)*

See Reverse for Instructions and Footnotes

11.

MINORITY BUSINESS DEVELOPMENT AGENCY
****

One of the great American business myths is that minorities cannot successfully manage enterprises. Census Bureau statistics beg to differ. In 1987, there were more than 1.2 million minority firms in the United States generating 77.8 billion dollars in gross receipts and with 836,483 employees. That is more than the Gross National Product of many small countries around the world.

Minority-owned firms now account for approximately nine percent of the total number of individual proprietorships, partnerships and subchapter S corporations in the United States and four percent of gross receipts. The number of minority firms grew by over 63 percent from 1982 to 1987. The growth rate for Black firms was 37.6 percent; 80.5 percent for Hispanic firms; 57.5 percent for Native American firms; and 89.3 percent for Asian and Pacific Islander firms.

These firms are geographically concentrated in a few states and metropolitan areas. California has the largest number of minority-owned firms, 27 percent of the businesses and almost one-third of the gross sales receipts. Texas follows with 13 percent of the minority firms and 9 percent of the gross sales receipts. The largest metropolitan area concentrations are Los Angeles-Long Beach, California with 142,580 minority firms; New York City with 78,886 firms; Miami-Hialeah with 55,712 firms; Washington, DC with 39,408 firms; and Houston with 37,516 firms.

Most of the minority-owned enterprises are small, just as are the majority of small businesses in America. But, more than 8,000 firms had more than $1 million in gross sales receipts and over 400 firms had more than 100 employees. To continue the five year increase in number of minority-owned firms and a greater share of the gross sales receipts by those firms, the Minority Business Development Agency (MBDA) is doing its part in assisting small minority enterprises.

The MBDA was established in 1969 by Executive Order and its role was expanded in 1971. MBDA was initially called the Office of Minority Business Enterprise (OMBE) and went through a name change in 1979 to the Minority Business Development Agency.

MBDA is part of the United States Department of Commerce and is the only federal agency created specifically to foster the establishment and growth of minority-owned businesses in America. MBDA has its headquarters in Washington, DC where all activities are planned, developed, coordinated and evaluated. It has six regional offices (Atlanta, Chicago, Dallas, New York, San Francisco, and Washington, D.C.) which oversee assistance services for their zones.

Through MBDA's approximately 100 Minority Business Development Centers, located in areas with the largest concentration of minority populations and the largest number of minority businesses, minority entrepreneurs can find management and technical assistance services to start, expand or manage a business. MBDA also lobbies Federal, state and local government agencies, as well as major corporations, to increase their purchases from minority-owned firms.

Minority Business Development Centers (MBDCs) are MBDA-funded organizations, which offer a wide range of business services to minority entrepreneurs, and are the heart of the MBDA direct assistance program. MBDCs are staffed by business specialists who have the knowledge and practical experience needed to run successful, profitable businesses. MBDCs are operated by profit or non-profit organizations, state or local government agencies, American Indian tribes or educational institutions. They are selected on a competitive basis with the federal government providing a percentage of each MDBC's project cost, with the MBDC, itself, providing the balance.

Services you will find at a MBDC include business planning for start-ups and expansions; marketing to help sell your company's products and services; financial planning to assure adequate financing for business ventures; loan packaging to acquire capital with which to finance business activity; bid estimating and surety bonding for construction projects; management counseling to operate personnel, accounting and inventory systems.

In the aftermath of the Los Angeles riots (May, 1992) MBDA's presence in that area helped implement a four point emergency business relief assistance strategy. This included:

1. Management and technical assistance, specifically loan packaging and general accounting;
2. Private/public sector minority business contracting support;
3. Franchising support in conjunction with the International Franchise Association (IFA);
4. Leadership development/support.

MBDA also distributed more than 2,000 Emergency Business Assistance flyers to riot victims. Their business consultants interviewed more than 1,700 minority business victims and helped assemble 400 loan packages worth $12 million, of which $760,000 was submitted to the U.S. Small Business Administration for disaster lending assistance.

NATIONAL FRANCHISE INITIATIVE

Because the minority community comprises more than one-fifth of the American population, yet owns only three percent of the franchised business, the MBDA has established the National Franchise Initiative. Its purpose is to promote a climate for accelerated growth in minority franchise ownership. To achieve that goal the MBDA has begun the following activities:

o   Building private- and public-sector alliances, with the Small Business Administration, the Department of Labor, the Federal Trade Commission, and the International Franchise Association.

o Conducting promotion and outreach activities to publicize franchising to the minority community.
o Conducting in-depth orientation seminars to selected cities for the purpose of educating prospective franchisees about the benefits and risks of franchising.
o Providing specialized franchise assistance.

The MBDA expects to increase minority awareness of franchising as a viable business option through this initiative. As a result it expects to increase minority participation in franchising and create more job opportunities and employment in this business category.

THE AMERICAN INDIAN PROGRAM

Despite the Native American's access to a wealth of natural resources, such as 50 million acres of land; an abundance of oil, gas, coal and uranium; and valuable water and fishing rights, American Indians are at the bottom of virtually every social and economic statistical indicator. Why is there such a disparity between an enormous potential for wealth and actual poverty? These are the four reasons cited by the MBDA:

o Lack of American Indian control over their resources;
o Leasing of American Indian resources to non-Indian enterprises;
o Lack of business knowledge; and
o Lack of capital.

The American Indian Program (AIP) addresses these problems through its organization network and seeks to establish economic self-determination for individuals and tribes. They hope to accomplish this by:

1. Providing management and technical assistance;
2. Identifying financial and other types of business resource opportunities;
3. Identifying market and capital opportunities;
4. Developing and maintaining inventories of resource opportunities; and
5. Using other federal agency resources through interagency agreements with the U.S. Department of Health and Human Services' Administration for Native Americans and the U.S. Department of Interior's Bureau of Indian Affairs (see Chapter 5 for the Native American direct loan and loan guarantee program through the Bureau of Indian Affairs).

Two tangible initiatives have already begun. Because Western art and American Indian crafts are both a novelty and collectible merchandise in Europe and Asia, one program has begun promoting for outside investment and trade opportunities. Five selected Indian tribes form the test program to identify overseas export opportunities and facilitate sales in international markets.

The second program call for the establishment of a non-profit institute to increase domestic and export sales of American Indian handicrafts and expand the northern Arizona American Indian crafts industry. This institute will market its crafts domestically through an annual catalog targeting retail customers outside of the southwestern United States. Export marketing will be directed to overseas wholesale distributor markets.

For additional information or to participate in the American Indian Program, please telephone or write to:

Joe Hardy, Coordinator
American Indian Program
Office of Program Development
Minority Business Development Agency
Room 5096
14th and Constitution Avenue, N.W.
Washington, DC 20230
Telephone: (202) 377-3261

OTHER MINORITY BUSINESS DEVELOPMENT AGENCY PROGRAMS

MBDA has penetrated into many areas to assist minority enterprises. They work to increase the amount of products and services purchased from minority firms. For example, PROFILE is a computer data file designed to match minority-owned firms with actual contract opportunities. This system contains descriptive information on construction, manufacturing, service and research firms. You may register your firm in PROFILE, free of charge, at any Minority Business Development Center. Government and private industry use PROFILE to identify minority-owned firms that can provide the products and services they need.

The Legislative and Intergovernmental Affairs (LIA) office within the MBDA lobbies Congress to further MBDA's goals. It also has an ongoing liaison strategy of involving key congressional committees, majority and minority trade and industry associations, and key intergovernmental units. These units include state, county and municipal minority business advocates, other federal agencies and state offices on Capitol Hill.

The MBDA's Research Program identifies market-based development needs of minority-owned firms. This program primarily develops resources, both national and local, necessary for business growth. Their strategy is to identify the financial, human, social and capital resources available in the public and private sectors and assess the extent to which they are or are not being effectively used for minority business development.

The Minority On-Line Information Service (MOLIS) is a pilot effort funded by MBDA. This service is intended to advance the development of human potential by strengthening the capacity of Historically Black Colleges and Universities (HBCUs). It is part of a multi-agency effort to expand opportunities of federally funded research and development and training projects to minority educational institutions. In an interagency agreement with the Department of Energy (DOE) and the White House Initiative for Historically Black Colleges and Universities (WHI/HBCUs), MBDA has implemented a cooperative effort to promote the expansion of industrial research and development and accelerate the commercial application of new technologies. This will be done by improving critical information of the institutions' educational, research, faculty and student capabilities.

MBDA established a Quality Council and appointed a Quality Improvement Manager as part of its Total Quality Management (TQM) program. This is part of an overall strategy to improve intra-agency management and thus provide better service downline to the MBDCs. As a result minority-owned firms can benefit from expert top management administration and operations.

The Cities in Schools Program (CISP) is a continued initiative to promote entrepreneurship within selective local urban educational systems. MBDA provides financial support to CISP, currently operating out of 309 educational sites across the U.S. Through this program, at-risk students receive exposure guidance and training to promote entrepreneurship, to lower the school dropout rates, reduce teen pregnancy, increase educational upward mobility and reduce reliance on public assistance as a way of life. At-risk students will be tutored and offered curriculum and exposure to basic business and economics. CISP student learn about the development and operation of small business.

For additional information about MBDA's programs, please write or telephone:

U.S. Department of Commerce
Minority Business Development Agency
Room 5073
Communications Division
Washington, DC 20230
Telephone: (202) 377-1936

MBDA REGIONAL OFFICES

ATLANTA
Carlton Eccles
MDA Regional Director
401 West Peachtree Street, N.W.
Suite 1715
Atlanta, GA 30308-3516
(404) 730-3300
FTS 880-3300

Rodolfo Suarez
MBDA Miami District Officer
51 SW First Ave.,
Room 1314, Box 25
Miami, FL 33103
(305) 536-5054
FTS 350-5054

CHICAGO
David Vega
MBDA Regional Director
55 East Monroe St.
Suite 1440
Chicago, IL 60603
(312) 353-0182
FTS 353-0182

DALLAS
Melda Cabrera
MBDA Regional Director
1100 Commerce Street
Room 7B23
Dallas, TX 75242
(214) 767-8001
FTS 729-8001

NEW YORK REGION
John Inglehart
MBDA Regional Director
26 Federal Plaza
Room 3720
New York, NY 10278
(212) 264-3262
FTS 264-3262

Shelley Schwartz
MBDA Boston District Officer
10 Causeway St., Room 418
Boston, MA 02222-1041
(617) 565-6850
FTS 835-6850

SAN FRANCISCO REGION

Xavier Mena
MBDA Regional
221 Main Street
Room 1280
San Francisco, CA 94105
(415) 744-3001
FTS 484-3001

Rodolfo Guerra
MBDA Los Angeles District Officer
977 North Broadway, Suite 201
Los Angeles, CA 90012
(213) 894-7157
FTS 798-7157

WASHINGTON REGION
Georgina Sanchez
MBDA Regional Director
14th & Constitution Ave., N.W.
Room 6723
Washington, DC 20230
(202) 377-8275
FTS 467-0504

Alfonso Jackson
MBDA Philadelphia District Officer
600 Arch ST., Room 10128
Philadelphia, PA 19106
(215) 597-9263
FTS 597-9236

MINORITY BUSINESS DEVELOPMENT CENTERS

ATLANTA MBDC
75 Piedmont Ave., NE, Suite 256
Atlanta, GA 30303
404-586-0973

AUGUSTA MBDC
1394 Laney Walker Blvd.
Augusta, GA 30901-2796
706-722-0994

BIRMINGHAM MBDC
2100 16th Ave., S., Suite 304
Birmingham, AL 35205
205-930-9254

CHARLESTON MBDC
77 Grove St.
Charleston, SC 29403
803- 722-3618

CHARLOTTE MBDC
700 East Stonewall St., Suite 360
Charlotte, NC 28202
704-334-7522

CHEROKEE IBDC
Alquoni Rd., Box 1200
Cherokee, NC 28719
704-252-2516

CHEROKEE IBDC
70 Woodfin Place, Suite 305
Asheville, NC 28801
704-252-2516

COLUMBIA MBDC
2230-B Taylor St.
Columbia, SC 29204
803-779-5905

COLUMBUS MBDC
P.O. Box 1696
Columbia, SC 31902-1696
706-324-4253

FAYETTEVILLE MBDC
114-1/2 Anderson St.
Fayetteville, NC 28302
919-483-7513

GREENVILLE/SPARTANBURG MBDC
211 Century Plaza Dr., Suite 100-D
Greenville, SC 29607
803-271-8753

JACKSON MBDC
5285 Galaxie Drive, Suite A
Jackson, MS 39206
601-362-2260

JACKSONVILLE MBDC
218 W. Adams, Suite 300
Jacksonville, FL 32202-3508
904-353-3826

LOUISVILLE MBDC
611 West Main St., 4th Floor
Louisville, KY 40202
502-589-6232

MEMPHIS MBDC
5 North Third St., Suite 2020
Memphis, TN 38103
901-527-2298

MIAMI/FT. LAUDERDALE MBDC
1200 NW 78th Ave., Suite 301
Miami, FL 33216
305-591-7355

MOBILE MBDC
801 Executive Park Drive, Suite 102
Mobile, AL 36606
205-471-5165

MONTGOMERY MBDC
770 S. McDonough St., Suite 209
Montgomery, AL 36104
205-834-7598

NASHVILLE MBDC
14 Academy Place, Suiet 2
Nashville, TN 37201-2026
615-255-0432

ORLANDO MBDC
132 E. Colonial Dr., Suite 211
Orlando, Fl 32801
407-422-6234

RALEIGH/DURHAM MBDC
817 New Bern Ave., Suite 8
Raleigh, NC 27601
919-833-6122

SAVANNAH MBDC
31 W. Congress Stl, Suite 201
Savannah, GA 31401
912-236-6708

TAMPA/ST. PETERSBURG MBDC
4601 W. Kennedy Blvd., Suite 200
Tampa, FL 33609
813-289-8824

WEST PALM BEACH MBDC
2001 Broadway, Suite 301
Riviera beach, FL 33404
407-863-0895

CHICAGO 1 MBDC
35 Wacker Dr., Suite 922
Chicago, Il 60601
312-977-9190

CHICAGO 2 MBDC
130 E. Randolf
One Prudential Plaza, Suite #700
Chicago, IL 60601
312-565-4710

CINCINNATI MBDC
1821 Summit Road, Suite 111
Cincinnati, OH 45327-2810
513-679-6000

CLEVELAND MBDC
601 Lakeside, Suite 335
Cleveland, OH 44114
216-664-4150

DAYTON MBDC
1818 W. 3rd St.
Dayton, OH 45417
513-263-6232

DETROIT MBDC
269 13 N. Western Hwy,. Suite 400
Southfield, MI 48034
313-262-1967

GARY MBDC
567 Broadway
Gary, IN 46402
219-883-5802

INDIANAPOLIS MBDC
4755 Kingsway Dr., Suite 103
Indianapolis, IN 46205
317-257-0327

KANSAS CITY MBDC
1101 Walnut St., 15th Floor
Kansas City, MO 64106-2143
816-471-1520

MILWAUKEE MBDC
1442 N. Farwell, Suite # 500
Milwaukee, WI 53202
414-289-3422

MINNEAPOLIS MBDC
2021 E. Hennepin Ave., Suite LL 35
Minneapolis, MN 55413
612-331-5576

MINNESOTA IBDC
Leech Lake Reservation
P.O. Box 217
Cass Lake, MN 56633
218-335-8583

ST. LOUIS MBDC
500 Washington Ave., Suite 1200
St. Louis, MO 63101
314-621-6232

ALBUQUERQUE MBDC
718 Central Ave., SW
Albuquerque, NM 87102
505-846-7114

AUSTIN MBDC
301 N. Congress Ave., Suite 1020
Austin, TX 78701
512-476-9700

BATON ROUGE MBDC
2036 Wooddale Blvd., Suite D
Baton Rouge, LA 70806
504-924-0186

BROWNSVILLE MBDC
2036 Boca Chica Blvd., Suite 301
Brownsville, TX 78521-2265
512-546-3400

CORPUS CHRISTI MBDC
3649 Leopard St., Suite 514
Corpus Christi, TX 78404
512-887-7961

DENVER MBDC
930 W. 7th Ave.
Denver, CO 80204
303-623-5660

EL PASO MBDC
6068 Gateway East, Suite 200
El Paso, TX 79905
915-774-0626

HOUSTON MBDC
1200 Smith St., Suite 2870
Houston, TX 77002
713-650-3831

LARECO MBDC
2801 E. Montgomery, Ste., #210
Laredo, TX 78043
512-725-5177

LITTLE ROCK MBDC
One Riverfront Place, Suite 740
North Little Rock, AR 72114
501-372-7312

LUBBOCK/MIDLAND/ODESSA MBDC
1220 Broadway, Suite 509
Lubbock, TX 79401
806-762-6232

MCALLEN MBDC
1701 W. Bus. Hwy. 83, Suite 306
Mcallen, TX 78501
512-687-5224

NEW MEXICO IBDC
P.O. Box 3256
3939 San Pedro, N.E., Suite D
Albuquerque, NM 87190-3256
505-532-5400

NEW ORLEANS MBDC
1001 Howard Ave., Suite 2305
New Orleans, LA 70113
504-523-5400

NORTH DAKOTA IBDC
3315 University Dr.
Bismarck, ND 58504-7596
701-255-6859

OKLAHOMA CITY MBDC
1500 NE 4th St., Suite 101
Oklahoma City, OK 73117
405-235-0430

OKLAHOMA IBDC
5727 Garnett, Suite C
Tulsa, OK 74146
918-250-5950

SALT LAKE CITY MBDC
350 East 500 South, Suite 101
Salt Lake City, UT 84111
801-328-8181

SAN ANTONIO MBDC
801 S. Bowie
San Antonio, TX 78205
512-224-1945

SHREVEPORT MBDC
820 Jordan St., Suite 105
Shreveport, LA 71101
318-226-4931

TULSA MBDC
240 East Apache St.
Tulsa, OK 74106
918-592-1995

BOSTON MBDC
98 N. Washington
Boston, MA 02114
617-723-7900

BROOKLYN MBDC
16 Court St., Room 1903
Brooklyn, NY 11241
718-522-5880

BUFFALO MBDC
570 E. Delavan Ave.
Buffalo, NY 14211
716-895-2218

CONNECTICUT MBDC
410 Asylum St., Ste 243
Hartford, CT 06103
203-246-5371

MANHATTAN MBDC
51 Madison Ave., Suite 2212
New York, NY 10010
212-779-4360

MAYAGUEZ MBDC
70 West Mendez Vigo
P.O. Box 3146 Marina Station
Mayaguez, PR 00681
809-833-7783

NASSAU/SUFFOLK MBDC
150 Broad Hollow Road, Suite 304
Melville, NY 11747
516-549-5454

NEW BRUNSWICK MBDC
100 Jersey Ave., Bldg. D, Suite 3
New Brunswick, NJ 08901
908-249-5511

NEWARK MBDC
60 Park Place, Suite 1404
Newark, NJ 07102
201-623-7712

PONCE MBDC
19 Salud St.
Ponce, PR 00731
809-840-8100

QUEENS MBDC
110-29 Horace Harding Expwy.
Corona, NY 11368
718-699-2400

ROCHESTER MBDC
350 North Street
Rochester, NY 14605
716-232-6120

SAN JUAN MBDC
122 Eleanor Roosevelt Ave.
Hato Rey, PR 00918
809-753-8484

VIRGIN ISLANDS MBDC
81-AB Kronprindsen Gade, 3rd Floor
P.O. Box 838
St. Thomas, VI 00804
809-774-7215

VIRGIN ISLANDS MBDC
35 King Street Christensted
St. Croix, VI 00820
809-774-6334
All mail for the MBDC in ST. Croix
should be forwarded to the MBDC
in St. Thomas.

ALASKA MBDC
1577 C St. Plaza, Suite 304
Anchorage, AK 99501
907-274-5400

ANAHEIM MBDC
6 Hutton Centre Dr., Suite 1050
Santa Ana, CA 92707
714-434-0444

ARIZONA IBDC
953 E. Juanita Ave
Mesa, AZ 85204
602-831-7524

ARIZONA IBDC
2070 East Southern Ave.
Tempe, AZ 85282
602-945-2635

BAKERSFIELD MBDC
218 South H St., Suite 103
Bakersfield, CA 93304
805-837-0291

CALIFORNIA IBDC
9650 Flair Dr., Suite 303
El Monte, CA 91731-3008
818-442-3701

FRESNO MBDC
2300 Tulare St., Suite 210
Fresno, CA 93721
209-266-2766

HONOLULU MBDC
1132 Bishop St., Suite 1000
Honolulu, HI 96813
808-531-6232

LAS VEGAS
2860 E. Flamingo Rd., Suite K
Las Vegas, NV 89121
702-892-0151

LOS ANGELES 1 MBDC
1000 Wilshire Blvd., Suite 700
Los Angeles, CA 90017
213-627-1717

LOS ANGELES 2 MBDC
601 South Figueroa St., Suite 1370
Los Angeles, CA 90017
213-488-4949

OXNARD MBDC
451 W. Fifth St.
Oxnard, CA 93030
805-483-1123

PHOENIX MBDC
432 N. 44th St., Suite 354
Phoenix, AZ 85008
602-225-0740

PORTLAND MBDC
8959 SW Barbur Blvd., Suite 102
Portland, OR 97219
503-245-9253

RIVERSIDE MBDC
Vanir Tower
#290 No.D St., Suite 303
San Bernadino, CA 92401
714-386-5266

SACRAMENTO MBDC
1779 Tribute Road, Suite J
Sacramento, CA 95815
916-649-2551

SALINAS MBDC
14 Maple St., Suite D
Salinas, CA 95815
408-422-8825

SAN DIEGO MBDC
7777 Alvardo Rd., Suite 310
La Mesa, CA 91941
619-688-6232

SAN JOSE MBDC
150 Almaden Blvd., Suite 600
San Jose, CA 95113
408-275-9000

SANTA BARBARA MBDC
3887 State St., Suite 23
Santa Barbara, CA 93105
805-687-8899

SEATTLE MBDC
155 NE 100th Ave., Suite 401
Seattle, WA 98125
206-525-5617

STOCKTON MBDC
305 N. El Dorado St., Suite 305
Stockton, CA 95202
209-467-4774

TUSCON MBDC
1200 North El Dorado Pl., Ste. F-670
Tucson, AZ 85715
602-721-1187

BALTIMORE MBDC
301 N. Charles, St., Suite 902
Baltimore, MD 21201
410-752-7400

NEWPORT NEWS MBDC
6060 Jefferson Ave., Suite 6016
Newport News, VA 23605
804-245-8743

NORFOLK MBDC
125 North 8th St., 4th Floor
Phildelphia, PA 19106
215-629-9841

PITTSBURGH MBDC
Nine Parkway Center, suite 250
Pittsburgh, PA 15220
412-921-1155

RICHMOND MBDC
3805 Cutshaw Ave., Suite 402
Richmond, VA 23230
804-355-4400

WASHINGTON MBDC
1133-15th St., Suite 1120
Washington, DC 20005
202-785-2886

12.

VENTURE CAPITAL SOURCES
****

I have not seen it any newspaper or television polls, but to nearly any entrepreneur I've mentioned the phrase, Venture Capitalist, screws up their face. To a businessman a venture capital investor conjures up visions of a shark devouring his business. Yet, the number of venture capital companies seems to grow each decade. And, the number of entrepreneurs chasing them for cash swells just as fast.

Now, you might ask: why is a chapter on Venture Capital Sources being included in a book about government grants and loans? That's easy to answer. Here's why: In order to obtain a Small Business Administration Loan Guarantee or some other form of federal or state government financing, the government agency is inevitably going to want to see some form of private lending commitment to your business.

Call this the "Herd of Sheep" theory or whatever similar metaphor comes to mind. Lenders, like lemmings, follow the crowd. Sometimes the flock wanders to high ground and safety while other times that same crowd all rush into the ocean, playing follow the leader. The one common denominator is not whether they think their backing will succeed or fail, but whether there are enough of them in the group funding you. Misery loves company, especially when it comes to a business, which they've invested in, that fails. If lenders feel anything at all, it's feeling safety in numbers. Getting four to jointly finance you

is probably easier than selling just one venture capital firm on your idea.

A warning is appropriate here. Venture capital sources don't waste their time with small fry. The amount of time spent on a $150,000 loan proposal is about the same it takes to work over a $1 million or $5 million proposal. However, if you like to think big, have the energy and resources for the task, and own a terrific earth-shattering idea (and it is organized into a stellar business plan with easy to understand and dynamic financials), then go for venture capital. And, nail down that financing by also getting one or more forms of government backing.

Rarely have I come across a spirited entrepreneur who isn't utterly convinced that his business idea is likely to score a home run. In reality few are going to alter the world much. But, if yours really shows promise, talk it up and see how long it holds water. What, you say? It's my little secret and if anyone else finds out about it . . . . Unfortunately, that's exactly the problem. An even more rare event than the electrifying new business idea is the theft of that brilliant idea and its subsequent implementation by a friend or colleague. Most are mired in their own daily worries and upsets with as little get go as the dreamer of the dream. Getting that vision organized, financed and launched takes more than a hard day's work tilling soil. Rejection from all sides is the more likely hazard. And that's what happens to a lot of entrepreneurial dreams.

Persistence is the key. Finding out from your closest friends is going to give you the feedback you absolutely need to discover whether or not your idea has flaws. Put it under a microscope with those least likely to run off with your idea. What's wrong with it? Hear them out first. Contact a professional and pay him to review your plan. Demand that he list out what's wrong with it. Work that out. Then, if it's as bright as when you thought it up, and you've organized it into a business plan, then and only then, approach a venture capital source. These guys play for blood and get bombarded with dozens (or more) "revolutionary" business ideas every day.

Aside from other questions you will ever be asked by a venture capital firm or other lending institution, the key ones are going to boil down to these:

A. What is your product (or service)?
B. Who is your market, i.e. who is going to buy this product?

If you can succinctly answer the above two questions and document them thoroughly so as to persuade even your most skeptical critic, then you stand a greater chance of getting your foot in the door with a venture capital firm.

PRIVATE PLACEMENT

Let's say you don't have that kind of idea. The amount of money you're asking for it less than $1 million, perhaps even less than $100,-000. One idea that's caught on with business startups and smaller existing businesses is the private placement source.

Someone involved in private placement is often less ambitious than the venture capital source. Instead of only looking at million dollar deals, this sort of investment firm is probably looking at raising anywhere from $25,000 to $300,000 for a solid business idea. However, just like the venture capital source, the private placement dealmaker wants a good idea that will eventually take your firm public, i.e. sold through a public offering as an Over the Counter stock or better.

Private placements are a stranger to all but the most sophisticated investors. In short, this method has been a way for the largest public corporations to quietly raise money, either for large acquisitions or expansion. The primary reason they would make a private placement offering is to keep their names out of the newspapers and financial magazines. SEC regulations don't require the usual release of financial information in a restricted deal.

But, that's for the big guys. For smaller companies the private placement deal is just another packaging technique. An investment firm raises funds for you, convinces a bank loan officer to throw in some cash, and you've got financing to run your business. Add to that an SBA loan guarantee and your venture is off and running. The idea of a private placement is to get a small firm large enough so that it can be registered with the SEC and publicly offered to even more investors.

Few companies doing private placement offerings succeed, although many do raise seed money. Most fail because they are entirely speculative in nature or have some other type of disability: poor management team, heavy debt load, lawsuits, etc. Those that have a great product or service, energetic managers and key executives and properly market their product survive the startup phase and go public.

Finding a firm specializing in private placements is not easy. You can contact your local brokerage house about the feasibility of having one done for your business. Occasionally, such firms advertise in the *Wall Street Journal* for small businesses who need to raise funds. One that has been raising steady deals for companies throughout the nation is Lux Investors Services Corporation (813-535-4655).

WHAT A VENTURE CAPITAL FIRM WANTS

No, a venture capitalist doesn't want your first born child. That's probably not enough. He wants more. A venture capitalist, if he's still offering money, has a track record that includes, on average, watching between thirty and forty percent of his investments turn sour. That's right, three or four out of every ten ideas that do pass scrutiny still go belly up. So, a venture capital firm won't settle for a straight loan. More often, if a loan is made, it will be on the provision that he will later get a healthy percentage of stock in your company. Most entrepreneurs err in thinking they can offer him a small amount of shares. Sure, that will happen. But, only if your product is comparable to the personal computer, the fax machine, or some other revolutionary new product that does have potential to create a billion dollar industry.

Usually, a venture capital source will want your entire company, if he thinks it's a great idea. But, he'll settle for less -- say forty to forty-five percent of your stock, convertible from a loan at a later date. Many will take less, though, because, if you're smart, you will have packaged up your loan to include more than one investor. So, in the long run, if you can settle with the shirt still on your back and fifty-one percent of the shares, be happy.

Oh, that's the other thing they want. Participation. A good deal of it. Nothing makes a venture capital firm more interested in your deal than others jumping into it. The more the merrier. If you've masterminded a brilliant business plan, you'll probably be turning away investor money. And, then you won't need government backing.

One secret to success is getting one venture capital firm that might be interested into thinking that you've got other funding lined up. I'm not suggesting you lie to him. But, if you've got someone else lined up and intrigued, get the second one to verbally commit that he will join you as well, provided you obtain the earlier funding. This is the Hollywood method of raising capital or even getting stars to pledge to a film deal. Get one investor or movie star to agree to the movie idea and then use that clout to sign up the others.

Another way to get interest to provide realistic earnings projections on your business idea that shows the venture capital source will get back an annual return on his investment of between 40 and 60 percent. Returns of less than 40 percent, compounded annually, aren't strong enough to attract venture capital. Many average around forty-five percent; that's barely enough to make up for the "dogs" some firms invest in.

Promise a compounded annual return greater than 60 percent and you might get carted off in a straight jacket for the nearest asylum. It's just not credible to most venture capital firms that a start up business idea can produce that much that fast. And, if you've an existing business, they will expect to see your financials. And, Lord help the business owner who's fudged on those figures. Even if your venture can produce 100 percent or 500 percent returns, bring them down to earth in your financial projections. If you remember the banker mentality mentioned in Chapter 3, one of my recommendations was that bankers like to see steady growth. Fast growth scares them. Too many problems happen too quickly when a business takes off. Personnel problems, inventory deficiencies, bad press, customer complaints, cash flow shortages, and so forth. Ask anyone who's business took off about what happened to their personal life. Until you've been there, you will never know what I'm talking about. Venture capital firms have been there and, believe me, they want to see realistic projections.

YOUR IDEA

While there are many important books written on obtaining venture capital funding and each of these have brilliant tips and suggested procedures, nothing works like a great idea. I've recommended further books on the subject at the end of this book. Joseph Mancuso's books are probably the most valuable on the subject of writing business plans and raising venture capital. He has an on-hands grasp of the subject and a tremendous depth of experience.

However, no matter how much you read and how brilliantly you prepare, nothing works as well as a great idea. Most ideas don't cut the mustard because they aren't thoroughly thought through. The dreamer didn't get past the fantasy stage. Possibly, he or she failed to look around them and discover whether or not the marketplace actually needed such a product or service. Perhaps, it was too good and was just ahead of its time. Or, more likely, it had been tried and the idea died a quiet death elsewhere. Some venture capital firms won't invest if the market is too narrow. Others might come back to your idea later, when the timing is better.

Alas, your business lives or dies on how well you have developed your idea. For example, many earlier authors wrote books on government auctions. If one inspected the subject closely, it wouldn't have taken much of a genius to discover that at least twenty different authors took a stab at this subject. However, when I wrote an earlier version of THE OFFICIAL GOVERNMENT AUCTION GUIDE (Crown Publishers), I sold more than $20 million worth of books in less than 18 months. In reviewing the top bestsellers of 1989 I discovered that my auction book had been one of the year's highest grossing books, nearly on par with one of Stephen King's or Danielle Steele's bestsellers! My success was in the way I packaged and marketed my book. No one else had tried doing it the way I did.

So, your idea might need a little tinkering. Use your friends and family to work out the kinks. It might be a brilliant idea but it's packaging needs a professional makeover. Use your resources in the planning stage. That extra work, time and expense won't let you down later. The wrong time and place to find out that your business plan won't work or that your idea is old hat is during your business plan's presentation in a venture capital source's office. Nothing is more intimidating to an entrepreneur than being laughed at by a roomful of potential investors. Especially when you know they're right and your idea is a loser. Don't let it happen to you.

A QUICK ROUNDUP OF U.S. VENTURE CAPITAL FIRMS

In 1977 the total amount of venture capital available in the United States was less than $3 billion. By the end of the 1980's that figure grew to more than $30 billion -- a 1000 percent increase in thirteen years. Venture capitalists have been managing more deals, and larger deals, than ever before.

In the past, offering $250,000 on a deal was commonplace. But because their staff command huge salaries or demand participation in deals that will add another million dollars to their portfolio, many venture capital firms won't touch deals that tiny these days. They work on the principle that if the idea is that great, then why isn't this guy asking for three or four million dollars?

Also, many venture capitalists went for the fast bucks in leveraged buyouts, where large corporations were purchased and their parts profitably sold off. Others turned to new industries, like biotechnology investments, or jumped on the bandwagon of rapid-growth service businesses. These brought home the bacon, warehouses full of it. The little guys with the also-ran idea got shoved off to the side.

Today, venture capital firms want to a certain amount of annual deals and set minimum figures they want to invest. Let's say they have $50 million for investment that year and they only want to do 25 deals. That means their average deal is going to come in around $2.5 million. Rarely does that average dip below a million or two per investment.

To approach such companies takes a lot of patience. Weeding out the mammoth investors, unless you've got the idea and plan, can be just as tedious for you as it is for them, as they similarly dig out deals that don't make sense for them. Persistence in finding the right investment partner does, however, pay off for the lucky businessman who's stock just went public and he or she joins the millionaire's circle.

NATIONAL VENTURE CAPITAL ASSOCIATION

The National Venture Capital Association (NVCA) was started in 1973 and has a membership of 200 professional venture capital organizations. As a nonprofit organization it was founded for the purpose of fostering a broader understanding of the importance of venture capital to the vitality of the U.S. economy. This association is also interested in stimulating the flow of capital to young companies.

Professional venture capital firms invest capital to launch new businesses and to finance the growth of a young company through its startup phase. NVAC members may not be full time venture capitalists, but must have as their primary business the development of venture capital. Each member must represent capital funds and utilize a professional approach before and after making an investment. NVAC members must operate out of an office located in the United States and must be investing from a dedicated U.S. based venture capital pool of funds of at least $1 million.

Here's a look at some of the more familiar names from the thousands of companies that venture capital firms have helped start and develop over the past two decades:

Apple Computer	Sun Microsystems
Federal Express	Compaq Computer
Cray Research	Genetech
Digital Equipment	Intel
Lotus	McDonnell Douglas
Wang Computers	Microsoft
Seagate Technology	Control Data
ROLM	

For further details from this national venture capital association, please write or telephone:

National Venture Capital Association
Daniel T. Kingsley, Executive Director
1655 North Fort Myer Drive,
Suite 700
Arlington, Virginia 22209
Telephone: (703) 528-4370
Fax: (703) 351-5268
                        or (703) 525-8841

THE WESTERN ASSOCIATION OF VENTURE CAPITALISTS (WAVC)

The Western Association of Venture Capitalists (WAVC) is a nonprofit association whose approximately 120 member firms represent virtually all professionally managed venture capital in the United States. These firms are organized to provide financial and business development assistance to entrepreneurial companies.

The goal of WAVC, and other similar venture capital associations, is to encourage public policy that supports the creation of new entrepreneurial companies, especially in the high technology industries. They are determined to pursue policies that will encourage long term investment of "high risk" capital in new companies developing innovative technologies, and that provide commensurate financial rewards for successful entrepreneurs and investors.

WAVC member firms basically seek to finance these types of business companies: electronics, healthcare, instrumentation, computers, software, telecommunications and biotechnology. They've helped create 2,000 new California companies. Here are a few examples of WAVC member investments:

o   AmGen: Biotechnology products that inhibit viral infections and stimulate cell growth.

o   Apple Computer: Personal computers and software for home and business.

o   Genentech: Biotechnology products for medicine, agriculture and industry.

o   Intel: Microprocessors for consumer, business, and scientific products.

o   ROLM: Communications systems for business and government.

o   Sun Microsystems: High performance engineering workstations and computer systems.

o   Tandem Computers: Computer systems for government, business, and industry.

New companies in technology-based industries need a higher level of assistance than someone starting a restaurant, health club or similar small business. Generally, they need large amounts of outside capital during the five to ten year period from their startup to their initial public offering of stock. Capital invested is high risk because it is being used to develop, manufacture, and sell "ahead of its time" technology. Markets for these products don't even exist and have to be created.

Money from venture capital sources pay employee salaries, fund research and build manufacturing capacity. High technology firms require expert managerial talent to survive the initial "make or break" period. Right from the beginning they face competition from overseas, particularly the Far East. You've heard about foreign corporate spies; well, these budding high technology companies are their targets. Security at such firms is generally poor or nonexistent. And, it's usually a race to the finish line -- the public release of the product -- between American and Far Eastern firms. The big difference can be the venture capital firm assisting these new companies bring their products to the marketplace.

WAVC capital usually comes from employee pension funds of major organizations, such as state and local governments, and from large corporations. These funds are supplemented by capital from financial institutions and college endowment funds. The venture capitalist's only compensation is a share of the profits only after their sponsored companies become successful. And, that doesn't always happen.

While the roster of members is provided at the end of this directory, you can obtain detailed information about each member's investment policies by telephoning or writing the association directly:
WAVC
The Western Association of Venture Capitalists
3000 Sand Hill Road, 1-190
Menlo Park, CA 94025
(415) 854-1322

VENTURE CAPITAL PROGRAM

Since 1972, the National Association for Female Executives (NAFE) has helped its entrepreneurial members by providing them information and moral support. They recently started a venture capital program to help women start a new venture or to help a member's existing business grow. NAFE invests in its members and becomes partners in their business. And, they're investing from $5,000 to $50,000 in each venture selected by their committee. For details on becoming a member and doing a joint venture with NAFE, you should write to:

NAFE VENTURE CAPITAL PROGRAM
4th Floor
127 West 24th Street
New York, New York 10011

VENTURE CAPITAL SOURCES

The best publication on the subject of finding venture capital sources is PRATT'S GUIDE TO VENTURE CAPITAL. In there you will find thousands of company listings. Most won't be suitable for you. Many will. Visit your local library's reference department. An extensive listing of venture capital sources has not been included in this book. Otherwise, it would cease to be THE ACTION GUIDE TO GOVERNMENT GRANTS, LOANS AND GIVEAWAYS. And, I would merely be duplicating another's effort.

An adequate number of venture capital firms have been included in the directory which follows. These have been culled from a variety of government sources and through private referrals. I cannot vouch for their reliability and do not promise that they won't ask for your first born as collateral. Use them as a starting point and develop your personal network of venture capital contacts.

**THE WESTERN ASSOCIATION OF VEN-
TURE CAPITALISTS (WAVC)
ROSTER OF MEMBERS**

ACCEL PARTNERS
One Embarcadero Center, Suite 3820
San Francisco, CA 94111
(415) 989-5656
Contact: Arthur C. Patterson

ADVANCED TECHNOLOGY VENTURES
1000 El Camino Real, Suite 360
Menlo Park, CA 94025
(415) 321-8601
Contact: Jos C. Henkens

ALAFI CAPITAL CO.
P.O. Box 7338
Berkeley, CA 94707
(510) 653-7425
Contact: Moshe Alafi

ALPHA PARTNERS
2200 Sand Hill Road, Suite 250
Menlo Park, CA 94025
(415) 854-7024
Contact: Brian J. Grossi

APPLE VENTURE CAPITAL
20525 Mariani Avenue, Mail Stop 38G
Cupertino, CA 95014
(408) 974-5686
Contact: Barry J. Schiffman

ASPEN VENTURES
3000 Sand Hill Road, Bldg. 3, Suite 105
Menlo Park, CA 94025
(415) 854-3330
Contact: David Crockett

ASSET MANAGEMENT CO.
2275 East Bayshore Road, #150
Palo Alto, CA 94303
(415) 494-7400
Contact: Craig C. Taylor

BANKAMERICA CAPITAL CORP.
555 California Street, Dept. #3908
San Francisco, CA 94104
(415) 622-2230
Contact: Patrick J. Topolski

BAY PARTNERS
10600 N. DeAnza Blvd., Suite 100
Cupertino, CA 95014-2031
(408) 725-2444
Contact: W. Charles Hazel

BAY VENTURE GROUP
One Sansome Street, Suite 2000
San Francisco, CA 94104
(415) 951-4674
Contact: William R. Chandler

BERLINER ASSOCIATES
535 Middlefield Road, #240
Menlo Park, CA 94025
(415) 324-1231
Contact: David L. Berliner

BESSEMER VENTURE PARTNERS L.P.
3000 Sand Hill Road, Bldg. 1, Suite 225
Menlo Park, CA 94025
(415) 854-2200
Contact: Neill H. Brownstein

BRENTWOOD ASSOCIATES
 MANAGEMENT PARTNERS
11150 Santa Monica Blvd., Suite 1200
Los Angeles, CA 90025
(310) 477-6611
Contact: B. Kipling Hagopian

BRYAN & EDWARDS
600 Montgomery Street, 35th Floor
San Francisco, CA 94104
(415) 421-9990
Contact: Alan R. Brudos

BRYAN & EDWARDS
3000 Sand Hill Road, Bldg. 1, Suite 190
Menlo Park, CA 94025
(415) 854-1555
Contact: William C. Edwards

BURR, EGAN, DELEAGE & CO.
One Embarcadero Center, #4050
San Francisco, CA 94111
(415) 362-4022
Contact: Brian Applegate

CAMPBELL VENTURE MANAGEMENT
375 Forest Avenue
Palo Alto, CA 94301
(415) 853-0766
Contact: Dean C. Campbell

CANAAN PARTNERS
2884 Sand Hill Road, Suite 115
Menlo Park, CA 94025
(415) 854-8092
Contact: John D. Chaparro

CHARTER VENTURE CAPITAL
525 University Avenue, Suite 1500
Palo Alto, CA 94302
(415) 325-6953
Contact: A. Barr Dolan

COMMUNICATIONS VENTURES
525 University Avenue, #600
Palo Alto, CA 94301
(415) 321-2900
Contact: Clifford H. Higgerson

CORNERSTONE MARKET
2420 Sand Hill Road, Suite 202
Menlo Park, CA 94025
(415) 854-2576
Contact: J. Michael Gullard

CROSSPOINT VENTURES PARTNERS
One First Street
Los Angeles, CA 94022
(415) 948-8300
Contact: Roger J. Barry

DAVID M. GOODMAN
4030 Palos Verdes Drive North, Suite 106
Rolling Hills Estates, CA 90274
(213) 377-2061
Contact: David M. Goodman

DELPHI BIOVENTURES, L.P.
3000 Sand Hill Road, Bldg. 1, Suite 135
Menlo Park, CA 94025
(415) 854-9650

DILLON READ & CO., INC.
555 California Street, Suite 4950
San Francisco, CA 94104
(415) 296-7900
Contact: Craig A. T. Jones

DONALD L. LUCAS
3000 Sand Hill Road, Bldg. 3, Suite 210
Menlo Park, CA 94025
(415) 854-4223
Contact: Donald L. Lucas

DOUGERY, WILDER & HOWARD
155 Bovet Road, Suite 650
San Mateo, CA 94402
(415) 358-8701
Contact: John R. Dougery

DRAPER ASSOCIATES
400 Seaport Court, Suite 250
Redwood City, CA 94063
(415) 599-9000
Contact: Timothy C. Draper

EL DORADO VENTURES
20300 Stevens Creek Blvd., Suite 395
Cupertino, CA 95014
(408) 725-2474
Contact: Gary W. Kalbach

ENTERPRISE PARTNERS
5000 Birch Street, Suite 6200
Newport Beach, CA 92660
(714) 833-3650
Contact: Charles D. Martin

EUROLINK INTERNATIONAL
950 Elm Avenue, #330
San Bruno, CA 94066
(415) 589-6477
Contact: Jacques Vallee

FIRST CENTURY PARTNERS
1111 Bayhill Drive, Suite 380
San Bruno, CA 94066
(415) 615-7915
Contact: David S. Heer

GLENWOOD MANAGEMENT
3000 Sand Hill Road, Bldg. 4, Suite 230
Menlo Park, CA 94025
(415) 854-8070
Contact: Dag Tellefsen

GLYNN CAPITAL MANAGEMENT
3000 Sand Hill Road, Bldg. 4, Suite 235
Menlo Park, CA 94025
(415) 854-2215
Contact: John W. Glynn, Jr.

HAMBRECHT & QUIST
One Busch Street
San Francisco, CA 94104
(415) 576-3300
Contact: William R. Hambrecht

HARVEST VENTURES, INC.
19200 Stevens Creek Blvd., Suite 220
Cupertino, CA 95014
(408) 996-3200
Contact: Cloyd Marvin

HEALTH ADVANTAGE VENTURES
2105 South Bascom, #390
Campbell, CA 95008
(408) 879-1800
Contact: Val Blanchette

HENRY & COMPANY
9191 Towne Centre Drive, Suite 230
San Diego, CA 92122
(619) 453-1655
Contact: James R. Everline

HMS GROUP
170 Middlefield Road, Suite 150
Menlo Park, CA 94025
(415) 324-4672
Contact: R. G. Grey

INDOSUEZ TECHNOLOGY
3000 Sand Hill Road, Bldg. 2, Suite 160
Menlo Park, CA 94025
(415) 854-0587
Contact: David E. Gold

INMAN & BOWMAN
4 Orinda Way, Bldg. D, Suite 150
Orinda, CA 94563
(510) 253-1611
Contact: D. Kirkwood Bowman

INSTITUTIONAL VENTURES PARTNERS
3000 Sand Hill Road, Bldg. 2, Suite 290
Menlo Park, CA 94025
(415) 854-0132
Contact: Reid W. Dennis

INTERWEST PARTNERS
3000 Sand Hill Road, Bldg. 3, Suite 255
Menlo Park, CA 94025
(415) 854-8585
Contact: W. Scott Hedrick

J. H. WHITNEY & CO.
3000 Sand Hill Road, Bldg. 1, Suite 270
Menlo Park, CA 94025
(415) 854-0500
Contact: William J. Harding

JAFCO AMERICA VENTURES, INC.
555 California Street, Suite 2450
San Francisco, CA 94104
(415) 788-0706
Contact: Bill Shelander

KLEINER PERKINS CAUFIELD & BYERS
Two Embarcadero Place, 2200 Geng Rd., #205
Palo Alto, CA 94303
(415) 424-1660
Contact: Brook H. Byers

KLEINER PERKINS CAUFIELD & BYERS
Four Embarcadero Center, Suite 3520
San Francisco, CA 94111
(415) 421-3110
Contact: L. John Doerr

LEONG VENTURES
146 Atherton Avenue
Atherton, CA 94025
(415) 327-1169
Contact: Helen C. Leong

MARATHON VENTURE PARTNERS
388 Market Street, Suite 900
San Francisco, CA 94111
(415) 989-1915
Contact: Thomas J. Bonomo

MATRIX PARTNERS
2500 Sand Hill Road, #113
Menlo Park, CA 94025
(415) 854-3131
Contact: Frederick K. Fluegel

MAYFIELD FUND
2200 Sand Hill Road
Menlo Park, CA 94025
(415) 854-5560
Contact: F. Gibson Myers

MBW MANAGEMENT, INC.
350 2nd Street
Los Angeles, CA 94022
(415) 941-2392
Contact: James R. Weersing

MEDICUS VENTURE PARTNERS
2180 Sand Hill Road, Suite 400
Menlo Park, CA 94025
(415) 854-7100
Contact: Fred Dotzler

MEDVENTURE ASSOCIATES
4 Orinda Way, Bldg. 4, Suite 400
Orinda, CA 94563
(510) 253-0155
Contact: Annette Campbell-White

MENLO VENTURES
3000 Sand Hill Road, Bldg. 4, Suite 100
Menlo Park, CA 94025
(415) 854-8540
Contact: H. DuBose Montgomery

MIP EQUITY FUND
3000 Sand Hill Road, Bldg. 4, Suite 280
Menlo Park, CA 94025
(415) 854-2653
Contact: Hans Severiens

MK GLOBAL VENTURES
2471 East Bayshore Road, Suite 520
Palo Alto, CA 94303
(415) 424-0151
Contact: Michael Kaufman

MOHR DAVIDOW VENTURES
3000 Sand Hill Road, Bldg. 1, Suite 240
Menlo Park, CA 94025
(415) 854-7236
Contact: Lawrence G. Mohr, Jr.

MONTGOMERY SECURITIES
600 Montgomery Street, 18th Floor
San Francisco, CA 94111
(415) 627-2000
Contact: Thomas Weisel

MORGAN STANLEY VENTURE CAPI
TAL FUND
555 California Street
San Francisco, CA 94104
(415) 576-2345
Contact: Virginia L. Turezyn

MORGENTHALER VENTURES
One Bush Street, 11th Floor
San Francisco, CA 94104
(415) 576-3332
Contact: Gary Morgenthaler

NEW ENTERPRISE ASSOCIATES
1025 Russ Bldg., 235 Montgomery St.
San Francisco, CA 94104
(415) 956-1579
Contact: C. Richard Kramlich

NEWTEK VENTURES
500 Washington Street, Suite 720
San Francisco, CA 94111
(415) 986-5711
Contact: John E. Hall

NIPPON ENTERPRISE DEVELOPMENT
3000 Sand Hill Road, Bldg. 4, Suite 235
Menlo Park, CA 94025
(415) 854-8760
Contact: Hirotaka Fujii

NORWEST VENTURE CAPITAL
MANAGEMENT, INC.
777 108th Avenue, N.E., Suite 2460
Bellevue, WA 98004-5117
(206) 646-3444
Contact: James R. Hanschen

OAK INVESTMENT PARTNERS
3000 Sand Hill Road, Bldg. 3, Suite 240
Menlo Park, CA 94025
(415) 854-8825
Contact: Catherine P. Goodrich

OLYMPIC VENTURE PARTNERS
2420 Carillon Point
Kirkland, WA 98033
(206) 889-9192
Contact: George H. Clute

ONSET
301 University Avenue
Palo Alto, CA 94301
(415) 327-5470
Contact: Terry L. Opendyk

OSCCO VENTURES
3000 Sand Hill Road, Bldg. 4, Suite 140
Menlo Park, CA 94025
(415) 854-2222
Contact: Stephen E. Halprin

OXFORD PARTNERS
16651 Cumbre Verde Court
Pacific Palisades, CA 90272
(310) 459-3610
Contact: Eric J. Schiffer

PACIFIC ASSET PARTNERS
650 California Street
San Francisco, CA 94108
(415) 352-6120
Contact: Robert M. Stafford

PALMER PARTNERS L.P.
3000 Sand Hill Road, Bldg. 4, Suite 145
Menlo Park, CA 94025
(415) 854-1293
Contact: William H. Congleton

PARTECH INTERNATIONAL
101 California Street, Suite 3150
San Francisco, CA 94111
(415) 788-2929
Contact: Thomas G. McKinley

PATHFINDER VENTURE CAPITAL FUNDS
3000 Sand Hill Road, Bldg. 3, Suite 255
Menlo Park, CA 94025
(415) 854-4706
Contact: Gene Fischer

PATRICOF & CO. VENTURES, INC.
One Embarcadero Place,
2100 Geng Rd., #220
Palo Alto, CA 94303
(415) 494-9944
Contact: Wilmer (Bill) Bottoms, Ph.D.

PAUL CAPITAL PARTNERS
2200 Sand Hill Road, Suite 240
Menlo Park, CA 94025
(415) 854-4653
Contact: Nick Harris

PEREGRINE VENTURES
1299 Ocean Avenue, #306
Santa Monica, CA 90401
(310) 458-1441
Contact: Gene Miller

PIERCE NORDQUIST ASSOCIATES
5350 Carillon Point
Kirkland, WA 98033
(206) 822-4100
Contact: John J. Rockwell

QUEST VENTURES
3000 Sand Hill Road, Bldg. 3, Suite 255
Menlo Park, CA 94025
(415) 989-2020
Contact: Lucien Ruby

R & D FUNDING CORP.
440 Mission Court, Suite 250
Fremont, CA 94539
(510) 656-1855
Contact: Richard E. Moser

ROBERTSTON, STEPHENS & COMPANY
One Embarcadero Center, Suite 3100
San Francisco, CA 94111
(415) 781-9700
Contact: M. Kathleen Behrens

ROSEWOOD GROWTH CAPITAL, INC.
4 Embarcadero Center, Suite 1580
San Francisco, CA 94111
(415) 362-5526
Contact: Ben Atkinson

SECURITY PACIFIC CAPITAL CORP.
2400 Sand Hill Road, Suite 100
Menlo Park, CA 94025
(415) 424-8011
Contact: Jim McElwee

SEQUOIA CAPITAL
3000 Sand Hill Road, Bldg. 4, Suite 280
Menlo Park, CA 94025
(415) 854-3927
Contact: Don T. Valentine

SIERRA VENTURES
3000 Sand Hill Road, Bldg. 4, Suite 210
Menlo Park, CA 94025
(415) 854-1000
Contact: Jeffrey M. Drazan

SIGMA PARTNERS
2884 Sand Hill Road, Suite 121
Menlo Park, CA 94025
(415) 854-1300
Contact: J. Burgess Jamieson

SONFINNOVA, INC.
One Embarcadero Center, Suite 4050
San Francisco, CA 94111
(415) 362-4021
Contact: Alain Azan

SPROUT GROUP
3000 Sand Hill Road, Bldg. 1, Suite 285
Menlo Park, CA 94025
(415) 854-1550
Contact: Keith B. Geeslin

SUNDANCE VENTURE PARTNERS,
L.P.
10600 North DeAnza Blvd., Suite 215
Cupertino, CA 95014
(408) 257-8100
Contact: Larry J. Wells

SUTTER HILL VENTURES
755 Page Mill Road, Suite A-200
Palo Alto, Ca 94304-1005
(415) 493-5600
Contact: David L. Anderson

TA ASSOCIATES
435 Tasso Street, Suite 200
Palo Alto, CA 94301
(415) 328-1210
Contact: Jeffrey T. Chambers

TAYLOR & TURNER
220 Montgomery Street, PH-10
San Francisco, CA 94104
(415) 398-6821
Contact: Marshall C. Turner, Jr.

TECHNOLOGY FUNDING
2000 Alameda de las Pulgas, #250
San Mateo, CA 94403
(415) 345-2200
Contact: Charles R. Kokesh

TECHNOLOGY PARTNERS
1550 Tiburon Blvd., Suite A
Belvedere, CA 94920
(415) 435-1935
Contact: William Hart

TECHNOLOGY VENTURE INVESTORS
2480 Sand Hill Road, Suite 101
Menlo Park, CA 94025
(415) 854-7472
Contact: Burton J. McMurtry

THE PHOENIX PARTNERS
1000 Second Avenue, Suite 3600
Seattle, WA 98104
(206) 624-8968
Contact: Stuart C. Johnston

THOMPSON CLIVE, INC.
3000 Sand Hill Road, Bldg. 4, Suite 240
Menlo Park, CA 94025
(415) 854-0314
Contact: Michael Elias

TRINITY VENTURES, LTD.
20813 Stevens Creek Blvd., Suite 101
Cupertino, CA 95014
(408) 446-9690
Contact: Lawrence K. Orr

U.S. VENTURE PARTNERS
2180 Sand Hill Road, Suite 300
Menlo Park, CA 94025
(415) 854-9080
Contact: William K. Bowes, Jr.

UNION VENTURE CORP.
445 South Figueroa, 12th Floor
Los Angeles, CA 90071
(213) 236-4092
Contact: Jeffrey A. Watts

VANGUARD ASSOCIATES
90 Middlefield, Suite 200
Menlo Park, CA 94025
(415) 324-8400
Contact: Douglas G. DeVivo

VENCA MANAGEMENT
2293 Washington Street, Suite 2
San Francisco, CA 94115
(415) 885-2100
Contact: Carolynn Gandolfo

WALDEN GROUP OF VENTURE
  CAPITAL FUNDS
750 Battery Street, 7th Floor
San Francisco, CA 94111
(415) 391-7225
Contact: Arthur Berliner

WEISS, PECK & GREER VENTURE
  PARTNERS, L.P.
555 California Street, 47th Floor
San Francisco, CA 94104
(415) 622-6864
Contact: Robert J. Loarie

WOODSIDE FUND
850 Woodside Drive
Woodside, CA 94062
(415) 368-5545
Contact: Vincent M. Occhipinti

XEROX VENTURE CAPITAL
3000 Sand Hill Road, Bldg. 3, Suite 140
Menlo Park, CA 94025
(415) 854-9635
Contact: Harold Shattuck

VENTURE CAPITAL LISTINGS

Alpha Venture Partners (See Note)
FUND MANAGER-Mr. Brian Grossi
TITLE-General Partner
2200 Sand Hill Road, Suite 250
Menlo Park, CA 94025
Tel. (415) 854-7024 FAX: (415) 854-7024

Brantley Venture Partners, L.P.
Bob Pinkcus, General Partner
20600 Chagrin Blvd., STE.520
Cleveland, OH 44122
Tel: (216) 283-4800
Fax: (216) 283-5324

Bus. Innovation/Equity Investm't Fund
Sandy Morganstein, Manager
100 W. Randolph, Ste., 3-400
Chicago, IL 60601
Tel: (312) 814-5246
Fax: (312) 814-6732

Claflin Capital Management, Inc.
Mr. Thomas M. Claflin II; General Partner
77 Franklin St.
Boston, MA 02110
Tel: (617) 426-6505
Fax: (617) 426-6505

Colorado Venture Management
Mr. Kyle Lefkoff, VP
4845 Pearl East Circle, Suite #500
Boulder, CO 80301
Tel: (303) 440-4055
Fax: (303) 440-4636

CT Seed Ventures Limited Partnership
Mr. Jonathan White, Member
200 Fisher Dr.
Avvon Park North, CT 06001
Tel: (203) 677-0183
Fax: (203) 677-0588

Enterprise Development Fund
Mary Campbell, General Partner
425 N. Mainstreet
Ann Arbor, MI 48104
Tel: (313) 663-3212
Fax: (313) 663-7358

First Stage Capital Fund
Mr. Gordon Baty, Gereral Partner
101 Main St.
Cambridge, MA 02142
Tel: (617) 876-5355
Fax: (617) 876-1248

Genesis Seed Fund, Inc.
Mr. Steve Economou, VP
2 Pen Center Plaza, Suite 410
Philadelphia, PA 19102
Tel: (215) 988-0010
Fax: (215) 568-0029

Geocapital Ventures
2115 Sinwood Ave.
Ft. Lee, NJ 07024
Mr. Stephen J. Clearman, Partner
Tel: (201) 461-9292
Fax: (201) 461-3563

Heartland Seed Venture Fund Co.
Lyle Honke, Manager
300 Walnut, Suite 215
Des Moines, IA 50309
Tel: (515) 282-5432
Fax: (515) 243-5948

Indiana Business Modernization and Tech
Mr. Delber Schuh, Acting President
1 North Capital Avenue
Indianapolis, IN 46204
Tel: (317) 635-3058
Fax: (317) 231-7095

Iowa Product Dev. Corp.
Mr. George Lipper, Investment Manager
200 East Grand Avenue
Des Moines, IA 50309
Tel: (515) 281-5292
Fax: (515) 242-4859

Kansas Seed Capital Fund Inc.
Mr. Tom Hyde, President
155 N. Market, STE 710
Wichita, KS 67202
Tel: (316) 262-8339
Fax: (316) 263-8151

Kansas Technology Enterprise Corp./Ad Astra
  Fund
Mr. Kevin Carr, VP
112 SW Sixth St.
Topeka, KS 66603
Tel: (913) 296-5272
Fax: (913) 296-1160

Kinship Partners II
Mr. Edward Tuck, Managing Partner
1900 W. Garvey Ave. South, Suite 200
West Covina, CA 91790
Tel: (818) 962-3562
Fax: (818) 962-0758

Massachusetts Technology Dev. Corp.
Ms. Marie Phaneuf, Public Info. Officer
148 State Street
Boston, MA 02109
Tel: (617) 732-4920
Fax: (617) 723-5983

Medical Sciences Partners, L.P.
Andre L. Lamotte, Man. Gerneral Partner
68 Harvard St.
Brookline, MA 02148
Fax: (617) 227-0113

Minnesota Seed Capital, Inc.
Pkdl. Piz., SU. 330W
Ray Allen, President
1661 South Highway 100
Minneapolis, MN 55416
Tel: (612) 545-5684
Fax: (612) 545-9549

Missouri Enterprise Business Assistance
 Center
Ms. Sheri Phelps, Director of Finance
800 West Fourteenth St., Suite 111
Rolla, MO 65401
Tel: (314) 364-8570
Fax: (314) 364-6323

Missouri Ingenuity, Inc.
Mr. Chip Cooper, Executive Director
T-16 Research Park
Columbia, MO 65211
Tel: (314) 882-2822
Fax: (314) 443-3748

Montana Science and Tech. Alliance
Mr. Carl Rusell, E.D.
46 N. Last Chance Gulch, Suite 2B
Helena, Mt 59620
Tel: (406) 449-2778
Fax: (406) 442-0788

Nebraska Research & Development Authority
Mr. Brad Edwards, President
660 NBC Center
Lincoln, NE 68508
Tel: (402) 475-5109
Fax: (402) 475-5170

NEPA Venture Fund, L.P.
Mr. Fred Beste III, Pres. - Gen. Partner
125 Goodman Dr.
Bethlehem, PA 18015
Tel. (215) 865-6550
Fax: (215) 865-6427

NY State Science & Tech. Foundation
Mr. John P. Ciannamea, President
99 Washington Avenue, Suite 1730
Albany, NY 12210
Tel: (518) 473-9741
Fax: (517) 473-6876

ONSET Enterprise Associates, L.P.
Terry L. Opdendyk, General Partner
301 University Ave., 2nd Floor
Palo Alto, CA 94301
Tel: (415) 327-5470
Fax: (415) 327-5488

Palmotto Seed Capital Fund L.P.
Richard F. Bannon, President and CEO
1330 Lady St. #607
Columbia, SC 29201
Tel: (803) 779-5759
Fax: (803) 779-4642

Sequoia Capital
Ms. Barbara Bergren, Administrative
 Manager
3000 Sandhill Rd., Bldg. 4, Ste. #280
Menlo Park, CA 94025
Tel: (415) 854-3927
Fax: (415) 854-2977

Sutter Hill Ventures
Ms. Maggie Beetlestone, Secretary
7545 Page Mill Rd., Suite A-200
Palo Alto, CA 94304-1005
Tel: (415) 493-5600
Fax: (415) 858-1854

Technologies Information and Publishing,
 Inc.
Mr. Frederick B. Bamber, General Partner
One Cranberry Hill
Lexington, MA 02173
Tel: (617) 862-8622
Fax: (617) 862-8367

Utah Technology Finance Corporation
Mr. Bob Brewer, Administrator
104 EVRO Bldg., University fo Utah
Salt Lake City, UT 84112
Tel: (801) 581-6348
Fax: (801) 581-5440

Utah Ventures
Mr. James C. Dreyfous, General Partner
419 Wakara Way, Suite 206
Salt Lake City, UT 84108
Tel: (801) 583-5922
Fax: (801) 583-4105

Zero Stage Capital Equity Fund
Paul Kelly, General Partner
101 Main St., 17th Floor
Cambridge, MA 02142
Tel: (617) 876-5355
Fax: (617) 876-1248

Zero Stage Capital II - Central and Northern PA, L.P.
Stan Fung, Managing General Partner
1346 South Atherton Street
State College, PA 16801
Tel: (814) 231-1330
Fax: (814) 231-1333

NON-SBIC VENTURE CAPITAL FIRMS

3i Capital Corp.
99 High St., #1530
Boston, MA 02110
(617) 542-0394

Advantage Capital Corp.
8630 Delmar Blvd., #218
St. Louis, MO 63124
(314) 993-8398

Allsop Venture Partners
2750 1st Ave., N.E., #210
Cedar Rapids, IA 52402
(319) 363-8971
FAX: (319) 363-9519
Branch Office
55 West Port Plaza, #575
St. Louis, MO 63146
(314) 434-1688
FAX: (314) 434-1688
Branch Office
7400 College Blvd., #302
Overland Park, KS 66210
(913) 338-0820
FAX: (913) 338-1019

Allstate Insurance Company
Venture Capital Division
Allstate Plaza South G5D
Northbrook, IL 60062
(708) 402-5681
FAX: (708) 402-0880

CID Venture Partners,LP.
201 Northe Illinois St., #1950
Indidanapolis, IN 46204
(317) 237-2350
FAX: (317) 237-2355

Capital Resource Partners
40 Beach St. #104
Manchester, MA 01944
(508) 526-8110
FAX: (508) 526-8070

Cardinal Development Capital Fund
155 E. Broad St., 20th Flr.
Columbus, OH 43215
(614) 464-5576
FAX: (614) 464-8706

Carolinas Capital Investment Corp.
6337 Morrison Blvd.
Charlotte, NC 28211
(704) 362-8222
FAX: (704) 362-8221

Centennial Funds (The)
1999 Broadway, #2100
Denver, CO 80202
(303) 298-9066
FAX: (303) 292-3512

Cherry Tree Ventures
3800 W. 80th St., #1400
Minneapolis, MN 55431
(612) 893-9012
FAX: (612) 893-9036

Command Security Corp.
P.O. Box 340, Lexington Park
LaGrangeville, NY 12540
(914) 454-3703
FAX: (914) 454-0075

Davis Venture Partners, LP.
One Willians Ctr., #2000
Tulsa, OK 74172
(918) 584-7272/0121
FAX: (918) 582-3403
BRANCH OFFICE
2121 San Jacinto St., #975
Dallas, TX 75201
(214) 954-1822
FAX: (214) 969-0256
BRANCH OFFICE
515 Post Oak Blvd., #250
Houston,TX 77027
(713) 993-0440
FAX: (713) 621-2297

El Dorado Ventures
800 East Colorado Blvd., #530
Pasadena, CA 91101
(818) 793-1936
FAX: (818) 793-2613
BRANCH OFFICE
20300 Stevens Creek Blvd., #395
Cupertino, CA 95014
(408) 725-2474
FAX: (408) 252-2762

Enterprise Management, Inc.
425 N. Main St.
Ann Arbor, MI 48108-1133
(313) 663-3213
FAX: (313) 663-7358

Forsyth Management Co.
4264 Brownsboro, Rd., #200
Winston-Salem, NC 27106
(919) 759-3005
FAX: (919) 759-2382

Fostin Capital Corp.
681 Andersen Dr., Bldg. 6, 3rd Flr.
Pittsburgh, PA 15220
(412) 928-1400
FAX: (412) 928-9635

Golder, Thoma & Cressey
120 S. LaSalle St., #630
Chicago, IL 60603
(312) 853-3322
FAX: (312) 853-3354

Horizon Partners, Ltd.
225 E. Mason, #600
Milwaukee, WI 53202
(414) 271-2200
FAX: (414) 271-4016

InverVen Partners
800 S. Figueroa St., #600
Los Angeles, CA 90017
(213) 622-1922
FAX: (213) 622-9035

Japan Associated Finance Co., Ltd.
 (JAFCO)
Toshiba Bldg. 10f,1-1-1 Shibaura, Minato-Ku
Tokyo, Japan 105
(03) 3456-4767
FAX: (03) 3456-4767

Kitty Hawk Capital, Ltd.
1640 Independence, Ctr.
Charlotte, NC 20246
(704) 333-3777
FAX: (704) 333-0603

Klotz Venture Capital Group
426 Essex St., #J
PO Box 586
Hackensack, NJ 07601
(201) 489-2080
(201) 447-3943

Louisiana Seed Capital Corp.
339 Florida St. #525
Baton Rouge, LA 70802
(504) 383-1508
(504) 383-1513

Mesirow Financial Private Equity Invest
ments
350 N. Clark St.
Chicago, IL 60610
(312) 670-6099
FAX: (312) 670-6211

Michigan Department of Treasury
Alternative Investments Division
430 W. Allegan
Lansing, MI 48922
(517) 373-4330
FAX: (517) 335-3668

NEPA Venture Fund, LP.
125 Goodman Dr.
Bethlehem, PA 18015
(215) 865-6550
FAX: (215) 865-6427

Nebraska Research & Development
 Authority
1248 O St., 660 NBC Ctr.
(402) 475-5109
FAX: (402) 475-5170

Nippon Investment and Finance Co., Ltd.
25-1 Nishi-Shinjuku 1-chome Shinjuku-ku
Tokyo, Japan 163
(03) 3349-0961
FAX: (03) 3349-0967

Oxford Partners
1266 Main St.
Stamford, CT 06902
(203) 964-0592
FAX: (203) 964-3192

Palmetto Seed Capital Corp.
1330 Lady St., #607
Columbia, SC 29201
(803) 779-5759
FAX: (803) 779-5759

Pathfinder Ventures Capital Funds
7300 Metro Blvd., #585
Minneapolis, MN 55439
(612) 835-1121
FAX: (612) 835-8389

Primus Venture Partners
1375 East Ninth St., #2700
Cleveland, OH 44114
(216) 621-2185
FAX: (216) 621-4543

Scientific Advances, Inc.
601 West Fifth Ave.
Columbus, OH 43201
(614) 424-7005
FAX: (614) 424-4874

TA Associates
45 Milk St.
Boston, MA 02109
(617) 574-6708
FAX: (617) 574-6789

Technology Funding, Inc.
2000 Alameda de las Pulgas
San Mateo, CA 94403
(415) 345-2200
FAX: (415) 341-1400

VEDCORP, Inc.
951 E. Byrd Street, #940
Richmond, VA 23219
(804) 648-4802
FAX: (804) 648-4809

Vencap Equities Alberta, Ltd.
1980, 10180 - 101 Street
Edmonton, Alberta
CANADA T5J 3S4
(403) 420-1171
FAX: (403) 429-2451

Venture Capital Fund of New England
(The)
160 Federal St., 23rd Fl.
Boston, MA 02110
(617) 439-4646
FAX: (617) 439-4652

Venture Investors of Wisconsin, Inc.
565 Science Dr., #A
Madison, WI 53711
(608) 233-3070
FAX: (608) 238-5120

WITECH Corp.
PO Box 2949
231 West Michigan St.
Milwaukee, WI 53201
(414) 347-1550
FAX: (414) 221-4668

Washington Resources Group, Inc.
11300 Rockville Pike, #1203
Rockville, MD 20852
(301) 816-7955
FAX: (301) 816-7961

William Blair Venture Partners
135 S. LaSalle St., 29th Flr.
Chicago, IL 60603
(312) 853-8250
FAX: (312) 236-1042

13.

DEPARTMENT OF HOUSING AND URBAN DEVELOPMENT PROGRAMS

****

Since 1965 the Department of Housing and Urban Development (HUD) has been the most important government agency overseeing the nation's housing needs. HUD superseded the Federal Housing Administration (FHA), which had been operating since 1934 as the national housing agency. While the FHA still exists, it now operates programs for mortgage and insurance for families who can fulfill their obligations but who, at the same time, require such insurance to obtain financing.

HUD oversees two of the most important federally sponsored real estate financing programs: the Federal National Mortgage Association (FANNIE MAE) and the Government National Mortgage Association (GNMA). One could also view HUD's activities as symptomatic of the nation's overall housing picture. And, from that point of view you might better understand the entire federal housing players.

HUD has increasingly concentrated its energies on providing mostly affordable housing for inner city residents. Where once the FHA financed single-family home ownership, HUD's emphasis has been in the construction of multi-family housing units and renovation of free-standing residences for the less well-to-do in inner-city neighborhoods. Other government agencies involved with real estate have filled the FHA's gap.

For instance, the Farmers Home Administration (FmHA), discussed at length in Chapter 15, serves rural America, where the bulk of the United States population once resided. After World War II, when greater Americans traded their country boots for city suits, the national housing market turned away its attention from small communities. FmHA filled that slack. As HUD concentrated more on inner city housing problems, particularly in helping overcome discrimination from lenders, FmHA actively supported outer-city folk.

The Federal National Mortgage Association raises private funds, independently from the federal government, and has nearly estranged itself from HUD. FANNIE MAE has been trading its shares, for some while, on the New York Stock Exchange as a public corporation, mentions the entirety of its name -- Federal National Mortgage Association -- insignificantly in its official brochures and annual report, and is, for all practical purposes estranged from HUD. Speculation has it that Fannie Mae will probably cease to be a federally sponsored before the decade is out. Their only concern is: "will it hurt our stock price?"

Meanwhile, Resolution Trust Corporation (RTC), discussed further in Chapter 14, disposes of properties created by the Savings and Loan association debacle. Behind that crisis was a little-known IRS loophole that S & Ls exploited for tax benefits and which caused them to wildly speculate in the real estate market. When Tax Reform arrived in 1986, the stock market responded with a resounding crash in October, 1987. First, the Federal Asset Disposition Association and then its successor, the RTC have acted as the nation's streetcleaner, picking up cow chips and trash from the thrift institution parade. Eventually, the RTC, itself, will be superannuated and its personnel merged with the Federal Deposit Insurance Corporation (FDIC).

Veterans Affairs (VA) provides housing for veterans with a loan guaranty program designed to market low-cost property and keep their foreclosure inventory at a steadily back-logged level. The VA Loan Guaranty program is the subject of Chapter 16. Without it, most beneficiaries would probably fit under the HUD umbrella and serviced with those programs. The VA loan guarantee limit often provides veterans with little more than marginal housing, but at least it does offer the veteran a housing opportunity preferable any HUD might comparably present him.

So, the American housing snapshot is complete. HUD serves minorities, FmHA deals with country folk, VA helps the veterans, FANNIE MAE services with the middle-class, and the RTC and FDIC purvey the waste products of the banking industry. Federal housing programs depend substantially on a less-than-benevolent banking industry, even one that is energetically guaranteed against loss. Federal regulators peer over lending officers' collective shoulders, demand that banks maintain proper asset to lending ratios and cause further languishing a banker's initiative to lend. At this writing, the American housing scene is dismal, but there is room for optimism.

Because there federal and state housing programs do exist, a complete collapse of the real estate industry has been prevented since the Tax Reform Act of 1986. The overall picture is less shaky than the way it was in 1989, before the Resolution Trust Corporation was created. HUD Secretary, Jack Kemp, has been a dynamic leader and has energized the Department of Housing and Urban Development. As he took over the reins, HUD was plagued with scandal and some whispers had it that HUD's days were numbers. Today, HUD has emerged from its tainted days and looks to a future of public/private housing partnerships -- where government and the private sector jointly work to create affordable and necessary housing.

But, as we can see, the overall real estate crisis is not yet behind us. HUD, as the nation's housing leader must assume its role as the stalemate-breaker between private lending institutions and federal regulators. Already, backstepping has occurred. In late 1991, HUD deleted its $100 down payment policy on selling HUD-foreclosed homes. In September, 1992 new FHA guidelines started bringing that federal mortgage insurance program closer to conventional guidelines: a larger down payment and a better credit record for borrowers. More changes are likely to occur in the "tight money decade" of the 1990's. But, because of the nature of the other federal housing programs, if HUD doesn't act as the backstop for urban America's housing needs, then our nation's major cities may soon be transformed into Calcutta-like ghettos.

In the next section of this chapter, the key individual HUD programs have been included for your review. Following those program descriptions and guidelines is the directory of HUD offices.

HUD PROGRAMS

ONE- TO FOUR-FAMILY HOME MORTGAGE INSURANCE
(SECTION 203(B) AND (I))

Federal mortgage insurance to finance homeownership and the construction and financing of housing.

Nature of Program: By insuring commercial lenders against loss, HUD encourages them to invest capital in the home mortgage market. HUD insures loans made by private financial institutions for up to 97 percent of the property value and for terms of up to 30 years. The loan may finance homes in both urban and rural areas. The maximum mortgage amounts are at least $67,500 in all areas, with higher limits in areas with higher median house prices up to a maximum of $124,875. Less rigid construction standards are permitted in rural areas.

HUD/FHA-insured homeowners threatened with foreclosure due to circumstances beyond their control, such as job loss, death, or illness in the family, may apply for assignment of their mortgages and adjusts the mortgage payments for a period of time until the homeowners can resume their financial obligations.

Legislation establishing this program was enacted in 1934.

Applicant Eligibility: Any person able to meet the cash investment, the mortgage payments, and credit requirements. The program is generally limited to owner- occupants.

Legal Authority: Section 203, National Housing Act (12 U.S.C. 1709 (b), (i)).

Administering Office; Assistant Secretary for Housing-Federal Housing Commissioner, Department of Housing and Urban Development, Washington, DC 20410-8000.

Information Source: HUD Field Offices.

Current Status: Active.

REHABILITATION MORTGAGE INSURANCE (SECTION 203(k))

Mortgage insurance to finance the rehabilitation of one- to four-family properties.

Nature of Program: HUD insures rehabilitation loans to (1) finance rehabilitation of an existing property; (2) finance rehabilitation and refinancing of the outstanding indebtedness of a property; and (3) finance purchase and rehabilitation of a property. An eligible rehabilitation loan must involve a principal obligation not exceeding the amount allowed under Section 203(b) home mortgage insurance. Legislation establishing this program was enacted in 1961.

Applicant Eligibility: Any person able to make the cash investment and the mortgage payments.

Legal Authority: Section 203(k), National Housing Act (12 U.S.C 1709(4k)).

Administering Office: Assistant Secretary for Housing-Federal Housing Commissioner, Department of Housing and Urban Development, Washington, DC 20410-8000.

Information Source: HUD Field Offices.

Current Status: Active.

HOMEOWNERSHIP ASSISTANCE FOR LOW-AND MODERATE INCOME FAMILIES
(Section 221(d) (2))

Mortgage insurance to increase homeownership opportunities for low-and moderate-income families, especially those displaced by urban renewal.

Nature of Program: HUD insures lenders against loss on mortgage loans to finance the purchase, construction, or rehabilitation of low-cost, one- to four-family housing. Maximum insurable loans for an owner-occupant are $13,000 for a single family home (up to $36,000 in high-cost areas). For a larger family (five or more persons), the limits apply to two- to four-family housing.

Legislation establishing this program was enacted in 1954.

Applicant Eligibility: Anyone may apply; displaced households quality for special terms.

Legal Authority: Section 221(d)(2), National Housing Act (12 U.S.C. 1715(d) (2)).

Administering Office: Assistant Secretary for Housing - Federal Housing Commissioner, Department of Housing and Urban Development, Washington, DC 20410--8000.

Information Source: HUD Field Offices.

Current Status: Active.

HOMES FOR SERVICE MEMBERS (Section 222)

Federal mortgage insurance enabling members of the armed services on active duty to purchase a home partially subsidized by the service.

Nature of Program: HUD allows the Departments of Transportation and Commerce to pay the HUD mortgage insurance premium on behalf of service members on active duty under their jurisdiction. The mortgages may finance single family dwellings and condominiums insured under standard HUD home mortgage insurance programs.

Legislation establishing this program was enacted in 1954

Applicant Eligibility: Service personnel on active duty in the U.S. coast Guard, or employees of the National Oceanic and Atmospheric Administration who have served on active duty for two years.

Legal Authority: Section 222, National Housing Act (12 U.S.C. 1715m).

Administering Office: Assistant Secretary for Housing-Federal Housing Commissioner, Department of Housing and Urban Development, Washington, DC 20410-8000.

Information Source: HUD Field Offices.

Current Status: Active.

HOUSING IN DECLINING NEIGHBORHOODS (Section 223(e))

Mortgage insurance of purchase or rehabilitate housing in older, declining urban areas.

Nature of Program: In consideration of the need for adequate housing for lower and moderate-income families, HUD insures lenders against loss on mortgage loans to finance the purchase, rehabilitation, or construction of housing in older, declining, but still viable urban areas where conditions are such that normal requirements for mortgage insurance cannot be met. The property must be in a reasonably viable neighborhood and acceptable risk under the mortgage insurance rules. The terms of the loans vary according to the HUD-FHA program under which the mortgage is insured. HUD determines if a project should be insured under Section 223(e) and become an obligation of the Special Risk Insurance Fund. This is not a separate program. It supplements other HUD mortgage insurance programs.

Legislation establishing this program was enacted in 1968.

Applicant Eligibility: Home or project owners ineligible for FHA mortgage insurance because property is located in an older, declining area.

Legal Authority: Section 223(e), National Housing Act (12 U.S.C. 1715n(e))

Administering Office: Assistant Secretary for Housing-Federal Housing Commissioner, Department of Housing and Urban Development, declining urban area.

Information Source: HUD Field Offices.

Current Status: Active.

CONDOMINIUM HOUSING (Section 234)

Federal mortgage insurance to finance the construction or rehabilitation of multifamily housing by sponsors who intend to sell individual units and to finance acquisition costs of individual units in proposed or existing condominiums.

Nature of Program: HUD insures mortgages made by private lending
institutions for the purchase of individual family units in multifamily housing projects under Section 234(c). Sponsors may also obtain FHA-insured mortgages to finance the construction or rehabilitation of housing projects which they intend to sell as individual condominium units under Section 234(d). A project must contain at least four dwelling units; they may be in detached, semi-detached, row, walk-up or elevator structures.

The maximum mortgage amount for a unit mortgage insured under Section 234(c) is the same as the limit for a Section 203(b) mortgage in the same area.

A condominium is defined as joint ownership of common areas and facilities by the separate owner of a single dwelling units in the project.

Legislation establishing this program was enacted in 1961.

Applicant Eligibility: Any qualified profit-motivated or nonprofit sponsor may apply for a blanket mortgage covering the project after conferring with his local HUD-FHA Field Office. Any creditworthy person may apply for a mortgage on individual units in a project; however, it is generally limited to owner-occupants.

Legal Authority: Section 234, National Housing Act (12 U.S.C. 1715y).

Administering Office: Assistant Secretary for Housing-Federal Housing Commissioner, Department of Housing and Urban Development, Washington, DC 20410-8000.

Information Source: HUD Field Offices.

Current Status: Active.

SPECIAL CREDIT RISKS (Section 237)

Mortgage insurance and homeownership counseling for low- and moderate income families with a credit history that does not qualify them for insurance under normal underwriting standards.

Nature of Program: HUD insures lenders against loss on home mortgage loans to low-and moderate-income families that are marginal credit risks. HUD is also authorized to provide budget, debt-management, and related counseling services to these families when needed. These services are performed by local services to these families when needed. These services are performed by local HUD-approved organizations. Applicants may seek credit assistance under most FHA home mortgage insurance programs. Insured mortgage limit is $18,000 ($21,000 in high cost areas).

Legislation establishing this program was enacted in 1968.

Applicant Eligibility: Low- and moderate income households with credit records indicating ability to manage their financial and other affairs successfully if given budget, debt-management, and related counseling.

Legal Authority: Section 237, National Housing Act (12 U.S.C. 1715z-2).

Administering Office: Assistant Secretary for Housing-Federal Housing Commissioner, Department of Housing and Urban Development, Washington, DC 20410-8000. Information Source: HUD Field Offices.

Current Status: Active as an insurance program.

HOUSING IN MILITARY IMPACTED AREAS (Section 238)

Federal mortgage insurance for housing in areas affected by military installations.

Nature of Program: Mortgage insurance for both single and multifamily housing is available under various insurance section of Title II of the National Housing Act. Projects are eligible where there is a military impact on a local economy to the extent that a mortgage would not normally be insured. This insurance is available in a community only if the Secretary of Defense certifies the need for additional housing; and if the HUD Secretary can show that the benefits of the insurance outweigh the risk of probable cost to the Government. Such mortgages will be the obligation of the special Risk Insurance Fund.

Legislation establishing this program was enacted in 1974.

Applicant Eligibility: Sponsor eligibility will be determined by the section of the National Housing Act under which applications are made, which is generally under the Section 221(d) program for multifamily projects. Tenant eligibility is open.

Legal Authority: Section 238(c), National Housing Act (12 U.S.C. 1715z-3(c)).

Administering Office: Assistant Secretary for Housing-Federal Housing Commissioner, Department of Housing and Urban Development, Washington, DC 20410-8000.

Information Source: HUD Field Offices.

Current Status; Active, however it is inactive with respect to multifamily programs.

SINGLE FAMILY HOME MORTGAGE COINSURANCE (Section 244)

Joint mortgage by the Federal Government and private lenders for homeownership financing.

Nature of Program: HUD offers an additional and optional method insuring lenders against losses on loans that they make to finance the purchase of one-to-four-family homes. In return for the right to expedited their own preliminary processing procedures, lenders assume responsibility for a portion of the insurance premium. Thus, coinsurance is expected to result in faster service to the buyer and to improve quality of loan origination and servicing.

For borrowers, the program operates like full insurance programs. The major differences affect the lending institution, which performs the property disposition functions normally carried out by HUD alone.

Legislation establishing this program was enacted in 1974.

Applicant Eligibility: Any mortgagee approved under the full insurance programs may apply for inclusion in this program. The coinsuring lender, based upon the characteristics of the property and the credit qualifications of the borrower, decides whether to make the loan.

Legal Authority: Section 244, National Housing Act (12 U.S.C. 1715z-9).

Administering Office: Assistant Secretary for Housing-Federal Housing Commissioner, Department of Housing and Urban Development, Washington, DC 20410-8000. Information Source: HUD Field Offices.

Current Status: Active.

GRADUATED PAYMENT MORTGAGES (Section 245)

Federal mortgage insurance for Graduated Payment Mortgages.

Nature of Program: HUD insures mortgages to finance early homeownership for households that expect their incomes to rise substantially. These "graduated payment" mortgages allow homeowners to make smaller monthly payments initially and to increase their size gradually over time.

Five different plans are available, varying in length and rate of increase. Larger than usual downpayments are required to prevent the total amount of the loan from exceeding the statutory loan-value ratios. In all other ways, the graduated payment mortgage is subject to the rules governing ordinary HUD insured home loans. Growing Equity Mortgages (GEM are insured under the same statutory authority.

Legislation establishing this program was enacted in 1974.

Applicant Eligibility: All FHA-approved lenders may make graduated payment mortgages; creditworthy owner-occupant applicants with reasonable expectations of increasing income may qualify for such loans.

Legal Authority: Section 245, National Housing Act (12 U.S.C. 1715z-10).

Administering Office: Assistant Secretary for Housing-Federal Housing Commissioner, Department of Housing and Urban Development, Washington, DC 20410-8000. Information Source: HUD Field Offices.

Current Status: Active.

ADJUSTABLE RATE MORTGAGES (ARM'S) SECTION 251)

Federal mortgage insurance for Adjustable Rate Mortgages (ARMs)

Nature of Program: Under this HUD-insured mortgage, the interest rate and monthly payment may change during the life of the loan. The initial interest rate, discount points, and the margin are negotiable between the buyer and lender.

The one-year Treasury Constant Maturities Index is used for determining the interest rate changes. One percentage point is the maximum amount the interest rate may increase or decrease in any one year. Over the life of the loan, the maximum interest rate may increase or decrease in any one year. Over the live of the loan, the maximum interest rate change is five percentage points from the initial rate of the mortgage.

Lenders are required to disclose to the borrower the nature of the ARM loan at the time of loan application. In addition, borrowers must be informed at least 25 days in advance of any adjustment to the monthly payment.

Legislation establishing this program was enacted in 1983.

Legal Authority: Section 251, National Housing Act (12 U.S.C. 1715z-16).

Administering Office; Assistant Secretary for Housing - Federal Housing Commissioner, Department of Housing and Urban Development, Washington, DC 20410-8000.

Information Source: HUD Field Offices.

Current Status: Active.

HOME EQUITY CONVERSION MORTGAGE (HECM)
INSURANCE DEMONSTRATION (Section 255)

Federal mortgage insurance to allow borrowers who are 62 years of age and older, to convert the equity in their homes into a monthly stream of income or a line of credit.

Nature of Program: Under the HECM Insurance Demonstration, FHA insures reverse mortgages that allow older homeowners to convert their home equity into spendable dollars Reverse mortgages provided a valuable financing alternative for older homeowners who wish to remain in their homes but have become "house rich and cash-poor." Any lender authorized to make HUD insured loans may originate reverse mortgages.

Borrowers may choose from among five payment options: (1) tenure -- the borrower receives monthly payments from the lender for as long as the borrower lives and continues to occupy the home as principal residence; (2) term -- the borrower receives monthly payments for a fixed period selected by the borrower; (3) line of credit -- the borrower can make withdrawals up to a maximum amount, at times and in amounts of the borrower's choosing; (4) modified tenure -- the tenure option is combined with a line of credit; (5) modified term -- the term option is combined with a line of credit.

The borrower retains ownership of the property and may sell the home and move at any time, keeping the sales proceeds in excess of the mortgage balance. A borrower cannot be forced to sell the home to pay off the mortgage, even if the mortgage balance, grows to exceed the value of the property. An FHA-insured reverse mortgage need not be repaid until the borrower moves, sell, or dies. When the loan is due and payable, if the loan exceeds the value of the property, the borrower (or the heirs)will owe no more than the value of the property. FHA insurance will cover any balance due the lender.

Applicant Eligibility: All borrowers must be at least 62 years of age. Any existing lien on the property must be small enough to be paid off at settlement of the reverse mortgage.

Legal Authority: Section 417 of the Housing and Community

Development Act of 1987, which added Section 255 to the National Housing Act.

Administering Office: Assistant Secretary and Urban Development,

Washington, DC 20410-8000.

Information Source: HUD Field Offices.

Current Status: Active.

MANUFACTURED HOMES (Title I)

Federal insurance of loans to finance the purchase of manufactured homes.

Nature of Program: HUD insures loans to finance the purchase of manufactured homes and/or lots. The loans are made by private lending institutions. The maximum loan amount is $40,500 for a manufactured home, $54,000 for a manufactured home and suitably developed lot, and $13,500 for a developed lot. The maximum limits for combination home and lot loans may be increased up to 85 percent in designated high-cost area. The maximum loan term varies from 15 to 25 years, depending on the type of loan.

Legislation establishing this program was enacted in 1969.

Applicant Eligibility: Any person able to make the cash investment and the loan payments; however, the program the program is limited to owner-occupants.

Legal Authority: Title I, Section 2, National Housing Act (12 U.S.C. 1703).

Administering Office; Assistant Secretary for Housing - Federal Housing Commissioner, Department of Housing and Urban Development, Washington, DC 20410-8000.

Information Source: See Administering Office

(Telephone: 1-800-733-4633).

Current Status: Active.

PROPERTY IMPROVEMENT LOAN INSURANCE (Title I)

Federal insurance of loans to finance property improvements.

Nature of Program: HUD insures loans to finance improvements,

alterations, and repairs of individual homes, apartment buildings, and nonresidential structures. Also, loans may finance new construction of nonresidential buildings. Loans on single family homes and nonresidential structures may be for up to $17,500, and may extent to 15 years and 32 days. Loans on apartment buildings may be as high as $8,750 per unit, but the total for the building may not exceed $43,750. The term may not exceed 15 years. Lenders process these loans. Loans for more than $5,000 require a mortgage to deed of trust on the improved property.

Legislation establishing this program was enacted in 1934.

Applicant Eligibility: Any person who is able to make the cash investment and the mortgage payments.

Legal Authority: Title I, Section 2, National Housing Act (12 U.S.C. 1703).

Administering Office: Assistant Secretary for Housing - Federal Housing Commissioner, Department of Housing and Urban Development, Washington, DC 20410-8000.

Information Source: See Administering Office (Telephone: 1-800-733-4663).

Current Status: Active.

COUNSELING FOR HOMEBUYERS, HOMEOWNERS, AND TENANTS
(Section 106)

Housing counseling for homebuyers, homeowners, and tenants under HUD programs and for homeowners with conventional mortgages or mortgages insured or guaranteed by other government agencies, including the Department of Veterans Affairs and the Farmers Home Administration.

Nature of Program: The Department is authorized to provide counseling to homebuyers, homeowners, and tenants under HUD programs and to homeowners with conventional mortgages or Department of Veterans Affairs (VA) guaranteed loans or Farmers Home Administration Mortgages. HUD provides the service through approximately 550 HUD-approved counseling agencies. For fiscal year 1991 HUD funded 331 agencies. These agencies are public and private nonprofit organizations with housing counseling skills and knowledge of HUD, VA, and conventional housing programs HUD awards housing counseling grants on a competitive basis to its approved agencies when the Congress appropriates funds for this purpose. The funding helps the approved agencies partially meet their operating expenses. Counseling consists of housing information, purchase and rental of housing, Home Equity Conversion Mortgage application guidance, money management, budgeting, and credit counseling to avoid mortgage default and rent delinquencies that lead to foreclosure or eviction,and home maintenance. The objective of the counseling is to help homebuyers, homeowner, and tenants to improve their housing conditions and to meet their responsibilities.

Legislation establishing this program was enacted in 1968 and subsequent years.

Applicant Eligibility: Homebuyers, homeowners, and tenants under programs indicated are eligible to receive the counseling services from HUD-approved housing counseling agencies.

Public and private nonprofit entities may apply through HUD office for HUD approval as a counseling agency.

Legal Authority: Section 106, Housing and Urban Development Act of 1968 (12 U.S.C. 1710x), as amended.

Administering Office: Assistant Secretary for Housing - Federal Housing Commissioner, Department of Housing and Urban Development,
Washington, DC 20410-8000.

Information Source: HUD Field Offices.

Current Status: Active.

MANUFACTURED HOME PARKS
(Section 207)

Federal mortgage insurance to finance construction or rehabilitation of manufactured home parks.

Nature of Program: HUD insures mortgages made by private lending institutions to help finance construction or rehabilitation of manufactured home parks consisting of five or more spaces. Mortgages are limited to $9,000 per individual manufactured home space within each park. In high-cost areas, this maximum may be increased to $15,750 per space. The park must be located in an area approved by HUD in which market conditions show a need for such housing.

Legislation establishing this program was enacted in 1955

Applicant Eligibility: Investors, builders, developers, cooperatives, and others meeting HUD requirements may apply to an FHA-approved lending institution after conferring with the local HUD office.

Legal Authority: Section 207, National Housing Act (12 U.S.C. 1713).

Administering Office Assistant Secretary for Housing-Federal Housing Commissioner,

Department of Housing and Urban Development, Washington, DC 20410-8000. Information Source: HUD Field Offices.
Current Status: Active.

MULTIFAMILY RENTAL HOUSING FOR MODERATE-INCOME FAMILIES (Section 221(d)(3) and (4))

Mortgage insurance to finance rental or cooperative multifamily housing for moderate-income households, including projects designated for the elderly. Single Room Occupancy (SRO) projects are also eligible for mortgage insurance.

Nature of Program: The Department insures mortgages made by private lending institutions to help finance construction or substantial rehabilitation of multifamily (five or more units) rental or cooperative housing for moderate-income or displaced families. Projects in both cases may consist of detached, semi-detached, row, walk-up, or elevator structures. SRO projects may consist of units that do not contain a complete kitchen or bath.

Currently, the principal difference between the programs is that HUD may insure up to 100 percent of replacement cost under Section 2221(d((3) for public nonprofit and cooperative mortgagors, but only up to 90 percent under Section 221(d)(4), irrespective of the type of mortgagor.

The Retirement Service Center (ReSC) program has been terminated, however, outstanding HUD Handbook procedures are still being applied to existing ReSC projects. Congregate rental projects for the elderly with central kitchens providing food services are no longer eligible.

Legislation establishing Section 221(d)(3) was enacted in 1954.

Legislation establishing Section 221(d)(4) was enacted in 1959.

Applicant Eligibility: Sections 221(d)(3) and 221(4) mortgages may be obtained by public agencies; nonprofit, limited-dividend, or cooperative organizations; private builders; or investors who sell completed projects to such organizations. Additionally, Section 221(d)(4)-mortgages may be obtained by profit-motivated sponsors. Tenant occupancy is not restricted by income limits. Legal Authority: Section 221(d)(3) and (4), National Housing Act (12 U.S.C. 1715(d)(3), (4)).

Administering Office: The Assistant Secretary for Housing-Federal Housing Commissioner, Department of Housing and Urban Development, Washington, DC 20410-8000.
Information Source: HUD Field Offices.

EXISTING MULTIFAMILY RENTAL HOUSING (Section 223(f))

Federal mortgage insurance under 207 pursuant to Section 223(f) for the purchase or refinancing of existing apartment projects; to refinance an existing cooperative housing project; or the purchase and conversion of an existing rental project to cooperative housing.

Nature of Program: HUD insures mortgages under Section 207 pursuant to Section 223(f) to purchase or refinance existing multifamily projects originally financed with or without Federal mortgage insurance. HUD may insure mortgages on existing multifamily projects under this program that do not require substantial rehabilitation. A project must contain at least five units, and must be at least three years old.

Legislation establishing this program was enacted in 1974.

Nature of Program: HUD insures mortgages under Section 207 pursuant to Section 223(f) to purchase or refinance existing multifamily projects originally financed with or without Federal mortgage insurance. HUD may insure mortgages on existing multifamily projects under this program that do not require substantial rehabilitation. A project must contain at least five units, and must be at least three years old.

Legislation establishing this program was enacted in 1974.

Applicant Eligibility: Investors, builders, developers, and others who meet HUD requirements.

Legal Authority: Section 223(f), National Housing Act (12 U.S.C. 1715(f)).

Administering Office: Assistant Secretary for Housing-Federal Housing Commissioner, Department of Housing and Urban Development, Washington DC 20410-8000.

Information Source: HUD Field Offices.

Current Status: Active.

MORTGAGE INSURANCE FOR HOUSING FOR THE ELDERLY (Section 231)

Federal mortgage insurance to finance the construction or rehabilitation of rental housing for the elderly or handicapped.

Nature of Program: To assure a supply of rental housing suited to the needs of the elderly or handicapped, HUD insures mortgages make by private lending institutions to build or rehabilitate multifamily projects consisting of five or more units, HUD may insure up to 100 percent of the Commissioner's estimate of value after completion for nonprofit and public mortgagors, but only up to 90 percent for private mortgagors. Congregate care projects with central kitchens providing food service are not eligible.

Legislation establishing this program was enacted in 1959.

Applicant Eligibility: Investor, builders, developers, public bodies, and nonprofit sponsors may qualify for mortgage insurance. All elderly (62 or older) or handicapped persons are eligible to occupy units in a project insured under this program.

Legal Authority: Section 231, National Housing Act (12 U.S.C1715v).

Administering Office: Assistant Secretary for Housing - Federal Housing Commissioner, Department of Housing and Urban Development, Washington, DC 20410-8000. Information Source: HUD Field Offices.

Current Status: Authorized, but not used. Multifamily housing for the elderly is now financed under the Section 221(d)(3), and(4) programs.

NURSING HOMES, INTERMEDIATED CARE FACILITIES, AND BOARD AND CARE HOMES
(Section 232)

Federal mortgage insurance to finance or rehabilitate nursing, intermediate care, or board and care facilities.

Nature of Program: HUD insures mortgages made by private lending institutions to finance construction or renovation of facilities to accommodate 20 or more patients requiring skilled nursing care and

related medical services, or those in need of minimum by continuous care provided by licensed or trained personnel. Board and care facilities may contain no fewer than five one-bedroom or efficiency units. Nursing home, intermediate care and board and care services may be combined in the same facility covered by an insured mortgage or may be in separate facilities. Major equipment needed to operate the facility may be included in the mortgage. Facilities for day care may be included. As of October 1988, existing projects already insured by HUD are also eligible for purchase or refinancing with or without repairs under Section 232.

Legislation establishing this program was enacted in 1969.

Applicant Eligibility: Investor, builders, developers, and private nonprofit corporations or associations, and public agencies (nursing homes only), or public entities that late licensed or regulated by the state to accommodate convalescents and persons requiring skilled nursing care or intermediate care, and /or board need care are eligible to live in these facilities.

Legal Authority: Section 232, National Housing Act (12 U.S.C. 1715w).

Administering Office: Assistant Secretary for Housing-Federal Housing Commissioner, Department of Housing and Urban Development, Washington, DC 20401-8000. Information Source: HUD Field Offices.

Current Status: Active.

SUPPLEMENTAL LOANS FOR MULTI-FAMILY PROJECTS
(Section 241)

Federal loan insurance to finance improvements, additions and equipment to multifamily rental housing and health care facilities. It provides owners of eligible low-income housing with an adequate return on their investment and the ability to finance the acquisition of eligible low-income housing.

Nature of Program: HUD insures loans made by private lending institutions to pay for improvements or additions to apartment projects, nursing homes, hospitals or group practice facilities that already carry HUD-insured or HUD held mortgages. Projects may also obtain FHA insurance on loans to preserve, expand, or improve housing opportunities, to provide fire and safety equipment, or to finance energy conservation improvements to conventionally financed projects. Major nonmovable equipment for nursing homes, group practice facilities, or hospitals also may be covered by a mortgage under this program.

Owners of eligible low-income housing who have filed a plan of action under HUD's mortgage prepayment programs may receive an equity take-out loan insured by HUD in order to enable them to receive an adequate return on their investment, while purchasers of

eligible low-income housing may receive HUD-insured acquisition financing.

Legislation establishing this program was enacted in 1968.

Applicant Eligibility: Qualified owners and purchasers of projects, including those who have filed a plan of action under HUD's mortgage prepayment programs, and owners of health care facilities (as specified above).

Legal Authority: Section 241, National Housing Act (12 U.S.C. 1715z-6).

Administering Office: Assistant Secretary for Housing-Federal Housing Commissioner, Department of Housing and Urban Development, Washington, DC 20410-8000.

Information Source: HUD Field Offices.

Current Status: Active.

LOW-INCOME HOUSING PRESERVATION AND RESIDENT HOMEOWNERSHIP
(Title VI)

A program that encourages low-income homeownership in dealing with the preservation of Section 221(d)(3) and Section 236 projects, whose low-income use restriction could otherwise expire after 20 years of the final mortgage endorsement.

Nature of Program: Provides financial incentives to owner retaining project or selling to a purchaser who will continue its low-income housing use. It allows an owner, under specific conditions, to prepay the mortgage and terminate the low-income affordability restrictions. It enables an owner to file a Notice of Intent within two years of prepayment eligibility. Further, an owner may only file a Plan of Action after agreement with HUD on the value of the project.

Under Title VI both the owner and the Department conduct appraisals of the property after the owner files a Notice of Intent. The statute specifies the values the appraisals must determine; (1) unregulated market rate rental housing for an owner who will retain ownership of the project; and (2) unrestricted highest and best use for an owner who intends to sell the project. Only if the appraisals agree that there is market value over and above the first mortgage debt is the owner eligible for incentives.

While Title II (see page 70) Plans of Action must be approved within affordable rent levels a determined by HUD, Title VI rents are constructed from the different required components of the program: first mortgage debt service, replacement reserves an owner's profit. If the project is sold, the rents must also include the debt service on the acquisition loan. In most instances rents must be approved which account for the sum of the component needs.

Unique to Title VI is its low-income homeownership component. Owners may sell only to priority purchasers (residents, nonprofits or agencies of State or local governments) for the first year the property is offered for sale. Thereafter, owners may sell to any qualified purchaser. If no purchaser comes forward under Title VI, the owner is free to prepay and terminate the affordability restrictions.

Title VI specifies to whom and when an owner can sell. Priority purchasers include: resident councils, nonprofits, or agencies of State and local governments. HUD's rule further restricts an owner's option for the first six months of the sales period to (1) resident councils seeking to convert the project to resident homeownership of (2) community based nonprofits.

An owner continuing ownership might receive the same incentives as in Title VI, except that Section 89 subsidy is also available to lower-income tenants, and loans under Section 241(f) may be insured only for 70 percent of equity. A project that is for sale may receive all these insured only for 70 percent of equity. A project that is for sale may receive all these incentives but the last one and, in addition, the purchaser may receive an acquisition loan (95 percent preservation equity) and priority purchaser can obtain grants for transaction costs and rent reductions, as well as additional up-front grants for technical assistance. Title VI owners continue the affordability restriction for the remaining useful life of the project, which may not be appealed by the owner for 50 years.

Legislation establishing this program was enacted under Title VI of the 1990 National Affordable Housing Act.

Applicant Eligibility: Owners of eligible low-income housing, resident councils organized to acquire projects, or nonprofit organizations or State or local agencies, or any entity that agrees to maintain low-income affordability restrictions for the remaining useful life of a project (50 Years) Legal Authority: Title VI of the National Affordable Housing Act of 1990 (U.S.C. 11)

Administering Office: Assistant Secretary for Housing-Federal Housing Commissioner, Department of Housing and Urban Development, Washington, DC 20410-8000. Information Source: HUD Field Offices.

Current Status: Active.

SECTION 8 RENTAL VOUCHER PROGRAM

Assists very low-income families in leasing privately-owned, decent, safe, and sanitary rental housing.

Nature of Program: HUD enters into contracts with local public housing agencies (PHAs) that administer the program. The PHA issues eligible very low-income families rental vouchers and the families are free to locate suitable rental units that meet their needs. The PHA makes assistance payments to the private owners who lease their rental units to assisted families. There are no rent limits in the rental voucher program, but the assistance payment on behalf of the family is fixed. The assistance payment makes up the difference between what a very low-income or 10 percent of gross income. A rental voucher holder may choose housing that rents more or less than the payment standard and therefore may pay more or less than 30 percent of adjusted income for rent. Rental units leased under this program must meet HUD housing quality standards.

In selecting applicants for assistance, the PHA must give a preference to families who are homeless or living in substandard housing, who pay more than half of their income for rent, or who are involuntarily displaced. If the assisted family decides to move after the first year of the lease term, the PHA terminates the assistance contract with the owner and the family may move to another unit with continued assistance.

Legislation establishing rental vouchers as a demonstration was enacted in 1983 and full program status was enacted in 1987.

Applicant Eligibility: Very low-income families with incomes not exceeding 50 percent of the median income for the area are eligible.

Legal Authority: Section 8(o), U.S. Housing Act of 1937 (42 U.S.C. 1437f(o)).

Administering Office: Assistant Secretary for Public and Indian Housing, Department of Housing and Urban Development, Washington, DC 20410-5000.

Information Source: Local Public Housing Agency or HUD Field Office.

Current Status: Active.

SECTION 8 RENTAL CERTIFICATE PROGRAM

Assists very low-income families in leasing privately-owned, decent, safe, and sanitary rental housing.

Nature of Program: HUD enters into contracts with local public housing agencies (PHAs) that administer the program. The PHA issues eligible very low-income families rental certificates and the families are free to locate suitable rental units that meet their needs. The PHA makes assistance payments to the private owners who lease their rental units to assisted families. The assistance payment makes up the difference between what a very low-income family can afford and the approved rent for the dwelling unit. Assisted families must pay toward rent the highest of 30 percent of adjusted income, 10 percent of gross income, or the portion of welfare assistance designated for housing. Rental Units leased under this program must meet HUD housing quality standards. Rents must be reasonable in relation to rents charged for comparable unassisted rental units in the market area, and at or below the fair market rent for the area as determined by HUD.

In selecting applicants for assistance, the PHA must give a preference to families who are homeless of living in substandard housing, who pay more than half of their income for rent, or how are involuntarily displaced. If the assisted family decides to move after the first year of the lease term, PHA terminates the assistance contract with the owner and the family may move to another unit with continued assistance. Project-Based Component.

APHA may choose to use up to 15 percent of its rental certificate assistance to implement a project-based certificate program. This component of the program encourages owners to construct or rehabilitate rental housing for very low-income families at rents within the HUD-established fair market rents for the area. Their assistance is tied to specific units under an assistance contract with the owner for a specified term, usually two to five years. A family that moves from a unit subsidized under the project-based certificate program does not have any right to continued assistance.

Applicant Eligibility: Very low-income families with incomes not exceeding 50 percent of the median income for the area.

Legal Authority: Section 8, U.S. Housing Act of 1937 (42 U.S.C. 1437f).

Administering office: Assistant Secretary for Public and Indian Housing, Department of Housing and Urban Development, Washington, DC 20410-5000
Information Source: Local public housing agency or HUD Field Office.
Current Status: Active

HOUSING AND URBAN DEVELOPMENT (HUD) DIRECTORY

REGION ONE BOSTON

Boston Regional Office
Room 375
Thomas P. O'Neill Jr. Federal Building
10 Causeway St.
Boston, MA 0222-1092
(617) 565-5234

FIELD OFFICES

Bangor Office
First Floor
Casco Northern Bank Building
23 Main St.
Bangor, ME 04401-6394
(207) 945-0467

Burlington Office
Room B-2B, Federal Building
11 Elmwood Avenue
PO Box 879
Burlington, VT 05402-0879
(802) 951-6290

Hartford Office
First Floor, 330 Main St.
Hartford, CT 06106
(203) 240-4523

Manchester Office
Norris Cotton Building
275 Chestnut St.
Manchester, NH 03101-2487
(603) 666-7458

Providence Office
330 John O. Pastore Federal Building
US Post Office-Kennedy Plaza
Providence, RI 02903-1785
(401) 528-5351

REGION II NEW YORK

New York Regional Office
26 Federal Plaza
New York, NY 10278-0068

FIELD OFFICES

Albany Office
52 Corporate Circle
Albany, NY 12203
(518) 464-4203

Buffalo Office
Fifth Floor, Lafayette Court
465 Main St.
Buffalo, NY 14203-1780
(716) 846-5755

Camden Office
The Parkade Building
519 Federal ST.
Camden, NJ 08103-9998
(609) 757-5081

Newark Office
Military Park Building
60 Park Place
Newark, NJ 07012-5504
(201) 877-1686

REGION 3 PHILADELPHIA

Philadelphia Regional Office
Liberty Square Building
105 South 7th Street
Philadelphia, PA 19016-3392
(215) 597-2560

FIELD OFFICES

Baltimore Office
Third Floor, The Equitable Building
10 North Calvert Street
Baltimore, MD 21202
(410) 962-2520

Charleston Office
Suite 708, 405 Capitol Street
Charleston, WV 25301-1795
(304) 347-7036

Pittsburgh Office
412 Old Post Office
Courthouse
7th Avenue and Grant Street
Pittsburgh, PA 15219-1939
(412) 644-6388

Richmond Office
First Floor, The Federal Building
400 North 8th Street
P.O. Box 10170
Richmond, VA 23240-0170
(804) 771-2575

Washington, DC Office
820 First Street, N.E.
Washington, DC 20002-4205
(202) 275-8185

Wilmington Office
Suite 850, 824 Market Street
Wilmington, DE 19801-3016
(302) 573-6300

REGION 4 ATLANTA

Atlanta Regional Office
Richard B. Russell Federal Building
75 Spring Street
Atlanta, GA 30303-3388
(404) 331-4739

FIELD OFFICES

Birmingham Office
Suite 300, Beacon Bridge Tower
600 Beacon Parkway West
Birmingham, AL 35209-3144
(201) 290-7617

Caribbean Office
New San Juan Office Building
159 Carlos Chardon Avenue
San Juan, PR 00918-1804
(809) 766-6121

Columbia Office
Stom Thurmond Federal Building
1835-45 Assembly Street
Columbia, SC 29201-2480
(803) 765-5592

Coral Gables Office
Gables 1 Tower
1320 South Dixie Highway
Coral Gables, FL 33146-2911
(305) 662-4500

Greensboro Office
415 North Edgworth Street
Greensboro, NC 27401-2107
(919) 333-5363

Jackson Office
Suite 910, Dr. A.H. McCoy
Federal Building
100 West Capitol Street
Jackson, MS 39269-1096
(601) 965-4738

Jacksonville Office
325 West Adams Street
Jacksonville, FL 32202-4303
(904) 791-2626

Knoxville Office
Third Floor
John J. Duncan Federal Building
710 Locust Street
Knoxville, TN 37902-2526
(615) 549-9384

Louisville Office
601 West Broadway
P.O. Box 1044
Louisville, KY 40201-1044
(502) 582-6255

Memphis Office
Suite 1200
One Memphis Place
200 Jefferson Avenue
Memphis, TN 38103-2335
(901) 544-3367

Nashville Office
Suite 200
251 Cumberland Bend Drive
Nashville, TN 37228-1803
(615) 736-5213

Orlando Office
Suite 270, Langley Building
3751 Maguire Blvd.
Orlando, FL 32803-3032
(407) 648-6441

Tampa Office
Suite 700
Timberlake Federal Building
Annex
501 East Polk Street
Tampa, FL 33602-3945
(813) 228-2501

REGION 5 CHICAGO

Chicago Regional Office
547 West Jackson Blvd.
Seventh Floor
Chicago, IL 60661
Attn: Property Disposition
(312) 353-5680

FIELD OFFICES

Cincinnati Office
Room 9002
Federal Office Building
550 Main Street
Cincinnati, OH 45202-3253
(513) 684-2884

Cleveland Office
Room 420
One Playhouse Square
1375 Euclid Avenue
Cleveland, OH 44114-1670
(216) 522-4065

Columbus Office
200 North High Street
Columbus, OH 43215-2499
(614) 469-7345

Detroit Office
Patrick V. McNamara Federal
Building
477 Michigan Avenue
Detroit, MI 48226-2592
(313) 226-6280/226-7144

Flint Office
Room 200
605 North Saginaw Street
Flint, MI 48502-2043
(313) 766-5109

Grand Rapids Office
2922 Fuller Avenue, N.E.
Grand Rapids, MI 49505-3499
(616) 456-2137

Indianapolis Office
151 North Delaware Street
Indianapolis, IN 46204-2526
(317) 226-7043

Milwaukee Office
Suite 1380
Henry S. Reuss Federal Plaza
310 West Wisconsin Avenue
Milwaukee, WI 53203-2289
(414) 297-3214

Minneapolis-St. Paul Office
20 Second Street South
Minneapolis, MN 55401-2195
(612) 370-3000

Springfield Office
Suite 206, 509 West Capitol Street
Springfield, IL 62704-1906
(217) 492-4085

REGION 6 FORT WORTH

Fort Worth Regional Office
1600 Throckmorton
P.O. Box 2905
Fort Worth, TX 76113-2905
(817) 885-5505

FIELD OFFICES

Albuquerque Office
625 Truman Street, N.E.
Albuquerque, NM 87110-6472
(505) 262-6472

Dallas Office
Room 860, 525 Griffin Street
Dallas, TX 75202-5007
(214) 767-8359

Houston Office
Suite 200, Norfolk Tower
2211 Norfolk
Houston, TX 77098-4096
(713) 653-3274

Little Rock Office
Suite 200, Lafayette Building
523 Louisiana Street
Little Rock, AR 72201-3707
(501) 378-5931

Lubbock Office
Federal Office Building
1205 Texas Avenue
Lubbock, TX 79401-4093
(806) 743-7276

New Orleans Office
Fisk Federal Building
1661 Canal Street, #3100
New Orleans, LA 70112-2887
(504) 589-7246

Oklahoma City Office
Murrah Federal Building
200 N.W. 5th Street
Oklahoma City, OK 73102-3202
(405) 231-5464

San Antonio Office
Washington Square
800 Dolorosa
San Antonio, TX 78207-4563
(512) 229-6758

Shreveport Office
Joe D. Waggoner Federal Building
500 Fannin Street
Shreveport, LA 71101-3077
(318) 226-5402

Tulsa Office
Suite 110, Boston Place
1516 South Boston Street
Tulsa, OK 74119-4043
(918) 581-7451

REGION 7 KANSAS CITY

Kansas Regional Office
Room 200, Gateway Tower ii
400 State Avenue
Kansas City, KS 66101-2406
(913) 236-2162
Information Number: (913) 236-2100

FIELD OFFICES

Des Moines Office
Room 259, Federal Building
210 Walnut Street
Des Moines, IA 50309-2155
(515) 284-4215

Omaha Office
Braiker/Brandeis Building
210 South 16th Street
Omaha, NE 68102-1622
(402) 221-3879

St. Louis Office
Third Floor, Robert A. Young
Federal Building
1222 Spruce Street
St. Louis, MO 63103-2836
(314) 539-6560

REGION 8 DENVER

Denver Regional Office
Executive Tower Building
1405 Curtis Street
Denver, CO 80202-2349
(303) 844-6518

FIELD OFFICES

Casper Office
(Note: Property handled by
Denver Regional Office, above.)
4225 Federal Office Building
100 East B Street
P.O. Box 580
Casper, WY 82602-1918
(307) 261-5252

Fargo Office
Federal Building
653 2nd Avenue North
P.O. Box 2483
Fargo, ND 58108-2483
(701) 239-5666

Helena Office
Room 340
Federal Office Building
301 South Park
Drawer 10095
Helena, MT 59626-0095
(406) 449-5283

Salt Lake City Office
Suite 220, 324 South State Street
Salt Lake City, UT 84111-2321
(801) 524-5216

Sioux Falls Office
(Note: Property handled by
Denver Regional Office, above.)
Suite 116, "300" Building
300 North Dakota Avenue
Sioux Falls, SD 57102-4223

REGION 9 SAN FRANCISCO

San Francisco Regional Office
Phillip Burton Federal Building
 and U.S. Courthouse
450 Golden Gate Avenue
P.O. Box 36003
San Francisco, CA 94102-3448
(415) 556-5900

Indian Programs Office Region IX
Suite 1650, 2 Arizona Center
400 North 5th Street
Phoenix, AZ 85004-2361
(602) 379-4156

FIELD OFFICES

Fresno Office
Suite 138, 1630 Shaw Avenue
Fresno, CA 93710-8193
(209) 487-5033

Honolulu Office
Prince Jonah Federal Building
300 Ala Moana Blvd.
P.O. Box 50007
Honolulu, HI 96850-4991
(808) 541-1343

Las Vegas Office
Suite 205
1500 East Tropicana Avenue
Las Vegas, NV 89119-6516
(702) 388-6500

Los Angeles Office
1615 West Olympic Blvd.
Los Angeles, CA 90015-3801
(213) 251-7136

Phoenix Office
Suite 1600, 2 Arizona Center
400 North 5th Street
P.O. Box 13468
Phoenix, AZ 85004-2361
(602) 379-4434

Reno Office
1050 Bible Way
P.O. Box 4700
Reno, NV 89505-4700
(702) 784-5356
Recorded message of properties,
call: (702) 784-5383.

Sacramento Office
Suite 200, 777 12th Street
Sacramento, CA 95814-1997
(916) 551-1351

San Diego Office
Room 5-S-3
Federal Office Building
880 Front Street
San Deigo, CA 92188-0100
(619) 557-5310

Santa Ana Office
Box 12850
34 Civic Center Plaza
Santa Ana, CA 92712-2850
(714) 836-2446

Tucson Office
Suite 410
100 North Stone Avenue
Tuscon, AZ 85701-1467
(602) 670-5223

REGION 10 SEATTLE

Seattle Regional Office
Arcade Plaza Building
1321 Second Avenue
Seattle, WA 98101-2058
(206) 553-1700

FIELD OFFICES

Anchorage Office
Federal Building-U.S. Courthouse
222 West 8th Avenue, #64
Anchorage, AK 99513-7537
(907) 271-4170

Boise Office
Federal Building-U.S. Courthouse
550 West Fort Street
P.O. Box 042
Boise, ID 83724-0420
(503) 326-2671

Portland Office
520 Southwest Sixth Avenue
Portland, OR 97204-1596
(503) 326-2671

Spokane Office
8th Floor East
Farm Credit Bank Building
West 601 First Avenue
Spokane, WA 99204-0317
(509) 353-2510

14.

THE RESOLUTION TRUST CORPORATION AFFORDABLE HOUSING DISPOSITION PROGRAM

****

On August 9, 1989, President Bush signed into law the historic Financial Institutions Reform, Recovery and Enforcement Act which created The Resolution Trust Corporation (RTC). The RTC's prime purpose was to dispose of the assets of the failed savings and loans institutions. I have covered this organization extensively in two earlier works: THE OFFICIAL GOVERNMENT AUCTION GUIDE (Crown Publishers) and DISTRESS SALE! Sonny Bloch's valuable book, HOW YOU CAN PROFIT FROM THE S & L BAILOUT (Putnam), reveals many of the inner workings of the Resolution Trust Corporation.

While the above books show you how to buy RTC properties at auction or directly from the RTC, this chapter shows you how to obtain financing for your RTC purchase. Financing is limited to properties you purchase from the Resolution Trust Corporation. You will not be able to purchase a home or property from someone other than the RTC and still obtain financing from the RTC.

That's not so bad. The Resolution Trust Corporation has several billion dollars worth of real estate properties up for grabs -- the exact number of properties has never been correctly calculated and appraisals have been inaccurate -- and will probably continue to have real estate properties available through the end of this century.

In case the Resolution Trust Corporation does finally close its doors, the Federal Deposit Insurance Corporation (FDIC) also has billions of dollars worth of properties -- roughly $4 billion at this writing. In that event, many experts believe the FDIC will step in and assume the duties the RTC currently performs. At their mammoth December 12, 1991 commercial real estate auction, the FDIC arranged financing for successful bidders. There was no indication that this was the last time they would do so.

What kind of properties does the RTC have available for financing? While a quick scan through their listings will show everything from parking garages to shopping centers, the Affordable Housing Disposition Program (ADHP) is strictly for lower-priced single-family properties. A portion of the bank-seized properties (seized by the Office of Thrift Supervision) are designated for this program. Because of the efforts of congressional lobbyists a large share of these single-family residences are now sold through this program.

QUALIFICATIONS FOR ADHP

Who qualifies to buy these homes? To participate in this program your income must be less than 115 percent of your area's median income. The exact maximum annual income can differ from one county to another, even in your area.

For instance, to qualify your income ceiling might be as low as $30,000 or as high as $50,000, depending on where you live. As you can see, it is designed to include the majority of eligible first-time home buyers in a given area.

Once you've financed your purchase through the RTC, you must occupy the home as your principal residence for at least one year. If you sell the home before residing there one full year, the RTC captures 75 percent of the profit for the sale of the property. When applying for financing, purchasers will be required to produce documents that verify income. Falsifying income and other program--qualifying data could lead to criminal prosecution.

Under the Affordable Housing Disposition Program, a nonprofit organization or public agency may purchase single-family residences by agreeing to rent or resell the properties to lower-income families. Lower-income families, as defined by the RTC, mean a family whose adjusted income is less than 80 percent of the area's median income. The purchaser must then agree to comply with occupancy, rental and resale restrictions.

FINDING THE PROPERTIES

The RTC sells these properties at auction, through sealed bids and by direct sales. Upcoming auctions in your area are usually advertised in newspapers and sometimes on radio and television. Crowds do show up but there are still good deals available. Sometimes buyers can even find fantastic deals. A recent consumer group study revealed that RTC real estate sold overall at greater than a 30 percent discount below appraised value. Farm properties sold for as much as 64 percent below appraised values; commercial real estate for as much as a 45 percent discount.

The RTC has set up clearinghouses in your state to facilitate your finding homes under this program. The RTC also publishes an Affordable Housing Calendar which lists special Affordable Housing sales nationwide. This calendar also includes affordable housing fairs and other special outreach events, including purchasing seminars on how to purchase a home through an auction or sealed bid under this program.

Your first step, if you wish to participate in this program is to contact your state clearinghouse to identify properties which are up for sale. A toll-free RTC Hotline phone number is your key to locating the properties. To find out about auction or sealed properties or RTC properties sold through a local real estate broker, contact the AFFORDABLE HOUSING HOTLINE:

1-800-624-HOME (1-800-624-4663)

If you don't wish to purchase your home at auction, ask the RTC to send you a list of properties available by direct sale. Some may also be advertised in newspapers. In the catalog or listing sheets you receive, find the contact person (usually a local real estate broker) under the listed property. Contact him or her and ask for a tour of the property. This broker can also answer any questions you may have about the financing or whether you qualify or not. Then, as with any real estate transaction, make an offer. If your offer is accepted, then your broker can assist you with the financing options available to you.

PRICE RANGE OF ADHP HOMES

Single-family homes and condominiums held by the RTC in the Affordable Housing Disposition Program (ADHP) have appraised values that do not exceed the following amounts:

Single (one-family unit) $67,500
Duplex (two-family units) $76,000
Triplex (three-family units) $92,000
Fourplex (four-family units) $107,000

Again, contact your state's clearinghouse for additional information about available properties in your area. Telephone the RTC AFFORDABLE HOUSING HOTLINE, mentioned above, to find the contact for your state. Not only will your state clearinghouse contact person provide you with lists of properties in your state, he or she can also identify alternative financing sources for you.

ADHP FINANCING REGULATIONS

If your family earns 80 percent of your area's median income (or less) and the property you acquire has a sales price of $50,000 or less, a minimum down payment of three (3) percent of the sale price is required. For example, if you purchase a $50,000 home, your down payment would be $1,500.

On homes that sell for more than $50,000, a down payment of $750 plus five (5) percent of the amount by which the sales price exceeds $25,000 is required. For example, if you purchase a $60,000 home, your down payment would be $2,500 ($35,000 x 5% = $1,750 + $750 = $2,500).

If your family earns greater than 80 percent, but 115 percent of less, of the area's median income, a minimum down payment of five (5) percent of the sale price is required. For example, if your area's median income is $40,000 and your income is between $32,001 and $46,000, your down payment would be five (5) percent. If you are buying a $50,000 home, under this restriction, your down payment would be $2,500.

For a family earning 80 percent of the area's media income or less, if the sale is to a family currently renting from the RTC, the down payment may be the lesser of two months current rental payments or the amounts described above. It is also possible under the "Tenant Purchase Program" to obtain an interest rate as low as seven (7) percent in order to avoid an increase from the purchaser's current housing cost.

RTC interest rates on their AHDP financing are based on the 60-day Federal National Mortgage Association (FNMA) mandatory delivery rate as published in the previous Wednesday's edition of *The Wall Street Journal*, rounded up to the nearest eighth of a point, plus an additional three-eighths of a percent.

ADDITIONAL ADHP FINANCING DETAILS

The loan term is not to exceed 30 years and the RTC may pay a portion of the closing costs. Borrowers must also participate in a home ownership and personal finance counseling program by a recognized community organization prior to the closing.

Your housing expense-to-income ratio (housing expense = principal, interest, taxes and insurance [PITI]) should not exceed 33 percent. For example, if your annual monthly income is $3,000, then your monthly housing expense, using the above formula, should not exceed $990.

You may be excluded from financing if you can qualify for conventional financing (such as Federal National Mortgage Association or Federal Home Loan Mortgage Corporation loans provided through your local bank) or Federal Housing Administration (FHA) loans.

Certain non-profit organizations and government entities may purchase one- to four-family RTC properties with a down payment as low as three (3) percent. The debt service coverage ratios must exceed 1:0:1. In addition, these organizations MUST AGREE to property use restrictions to ensure rental or resale to lower-income families.

COMMERCIAL REAL ESTATE FINANCING

You can also purchase land and commercial real estate, outside of the Affordable Housing Disposition Program, and obtain RTC financing for your purchase. If you cannot find acceptable conventional financing for your RTC purchase, then they will act as the lender of last resort for that property.

The RTC has a strong preference for 20 to 25 percent down payment but will consider a down payment as low as 15 percent. You can reduce the amount of your down payment to as low as five (5) percent, though, by placing funds into escrow for capital improvements. The RTC formula for this is a 50 cent decrease for every $1 deposited into escrow. For example, if you were purchasing a $200,000 property, your minimum down payment would be $30,000. However, if you placed $30,000 into an escrow account to improve the property, then you could lower your down payment to $15,000.

Financing is only good for seven years or less and the RTC will amortize the loan over a period of 30 years or less. Buyers must then face a large balloon payment after the loan term has expired and should expect to re-finance the loan elsewhere, pay it in full or be foreclosed. Payment frequency for land can be monthly or quarterly, whereas commercial real estate financing is repaid monthly.

The interest rate for financing is based on the U.S. Treasury Note Weekly Average Constant Maturity Index, as published by the Federal Reserve Bank. The margin above that interest rate index is based on one's down payment. The greater your down payment, the less of a margin above the interest index rate you will pay on your financing. Interest rates are normally locked in at the time of contract execution by the RTC and held until the sales contract expires. Here's the RTC breakdown on margins above the interest rate index compared to your down payment.

DOWN PAYMENT	MARGIN
30 percent or more	1.5%
25-29 percent	1.875%
20-24 percent	2.25%
15-19 percent	2.625%
15 percent or less	3.0%

Personal guarantees on RTC financing are negotiable, but personal liability is generally required when the down payment is less than 25 percent. No secondary liens are permitted without the prior consent of the RTC or any subsequent note holder. Bridge loan financing is also available, but terms may not exceed 18 months, and a 25 percent down payment and full personal guarantees are required.

The RTC may also provide for a second mortgage that allows for a rehab component when these conditions are met:

1. The combination of third-party first mortgage financing plus borrower equity total at least 65 percent of the total project cost;

2. The sum of the first mortgage and the RTC's mortgage do not exceed 95 percent of the total project cost; and

3. The sum of the first mortgage and the RTC's mortgage do not exceed 135 percent of the purchase price of the property. Total project cost includes the acquisition price of the property plus the cost of capital improvements and closing costs approved by the first mortgage lender.

CONCLUSION

The Resolution Trust Corporation has many benefits to both the residential home buyer and the commercial real estate investor. Properties have been discounted to sell quickly. There are terrific pricing opportunities and occasional "deals" the RTC offers.

For example, during the summer of 1992, the RTC offered an additional 10 percent discount on the purchase price of commercial real estate for those who obtained conventional financing. One large regional bank stepped in and provided financing to all buyers. After all, how could they lose?

The property had been discounted by approximately 40 percent at the auction; the RTC kicked in an additional 10 percent savings. Even if the investor defaulted on the loan, the potential resale value of the property would cover nearly all of the bank's exposure in that event.

Residential real estate auctions will be in high gear throughout 1993 and into 1994. So, there won't be any shortage of potential buying opportunities. And, RTC financing will be there for your use when you buy a home or commercial property.

RTC DIRECTORY INFORMATION

RESOLUTION TRUST CORPORATION

Main Operator:	202-416-6900
General Information	202-416-6900
Assets for Sale:	800-431-6900
S & L for Sale - Marketing Division	202-416-7119
Announcements on Scheduled Meetings	202-416-6985
Scheduled Meetings	202-416-6985
Consumers Affairs	800-934-3342
Becoming a Contractor or Broker for the RTC	202-416-7261
Press Office	202-416-7557
Inquiries About Assets for Sale	800-431-0600
Information on Rules and Policies	202-416-6940
Reading Room	800-842-2970
Freedom of Information Act Inquiries	703-908-6138
Announcements on scheduled Meetings	202-416-6985
Inquiries About Becoming a Contractor or Broker for an Agency	202-416-4182
Public Affairs	202-934-3342
Other General Information	202-416-6900

EAST REGION

Bayou Consolidated Office
100 St. James Street
Baton Rouge, LA 70802
(504) 339-1375
(800) 477-8790

Valley Forge Office
1000 Adams Avenue
Norristown, PA 19403
(215) 650-8500
(800) 782-6326

Southeast Consolidated Office
4200 West Cypress Street
Tampa, FL 33607
(813) 870-7000
(800) 283-1241

Mid-Atlantic Consolidated Office
100 Colony Square
Suite 2300 Box 68
(404) 881-4840
(800) 628-4362

CENTRAL REGION

Mid-Central Consolidated Office
Board of Trade Building II
4900 Main Street
Kansas City, MO 64112
(816) 531-2212
(800) 365-3342

Chicago Consolidated Office
25 Point Blvd. Northwest
Elk Grove, IL 60007
(708) 290-7300
(800) 284-6197

North Central Consolidated Office
3400 Yankee Drive
Egan, MN 55122
(612) 683-0036
(800) 873-5815

SOUTHWEST REGION

Metroplex Consolidated Office
3500 Maple Avenue
Dallas, TX 75219
(214) 443-2300
(800) 782-4674

Gulfcoast Consolidated Office
2223 West Loop South
Houston, TX 77027
(713) 888-2700
(800) 782-4221

Southern Consolidated Office
10100 Reunion Place, Suite 100
San Antonio, TX 78216
(512) 525-6500
(800) 283-9158

WEST REGION

Central Western. Consolidated Office
2910 North 44th Street
Phoenix, AZ 85018
(602) 224-1776
(800) 937-7782

Coastal Consolidated Office
4000 MacArthur Blvd.
Newport Beach, CA 92660
(714) 852-7700
(800) 283-9288

Intermountain Consolidated Office
1515 Arapahoe St., Tower 3, Suite 800
Denver, CO 80202
(303) 556-6500
(800) 542-6135

15.

FARMERS HOME ADMINISTRATION and FARM CREDIT LOAN ASSISTANCE
****

The Farmers Home Administration (FmHA) is an agency within the United States Department of Agriculture that grants loans for the purpose of providing rural housing. FmHA is administered by the Under Secretary for Small Community and Rural Development, who also heads the Rural Electrification Administration (REA) and the Federal Crop Insurance Corporation (FCIC). FmHA is directed by a national administrator, located in Washington, and has 250 district and 1,950 county offices. Farm and single-family housing loans are made by county offices; community facilities, multi-family housing, and business and industrial development loans are handled by district offices.

The Farmers Home Administration is the federal government's largest direct lender with a portfolio in excess of $63 billion. Nearly 2 million families now own their homes through rural housing loans from FmHA. FmHA has financed over 20,000 water and waste disposal systems in small towns (less than 10,000 population) throughout America. Despite the hard times farmers have had over the past years, FmHA has been able to help most of its borrowers stay in business.

Almost all FmHA farm loans are made to family-size farmers although the farm may be held by an individual, partnership, or a corporation. A "family farm" is defined by a local County Committee based on the general definition as a farm one family can operate and manage, performing the work with no more than occasional hired labor except in peak or emergency periods.

FmHA provides financial assistance to rural people and communities who cannot obtain commercial credit at affordable terms. To qualify for FmHA assistance, applicants must be unable to obtain credit from usual commercial credit sources. One of FmHA's farm credit goals is to help farmers attain self-sufficiency and to graduate to commercial credit as soon as possible.

This agency's number one priority, though, is to service the loans of borrowers already on the books. Local offices have technical and financial advice services counseling borrowers. More importantly, economic stress on the nation's farmers has called for reworking farm and home loan plans, rescheduling or reamortizing loans, and subordinating FmHA loans to commercial creditors. By taking a subordinate position and securing a second lien against property or chattels, the FmHA permits banks and other commercial lenders to make loans with a first lien.

FmHA PROGRAMS

There are many different types of loan and grant programs available from the Farmers Home Administration. Most of the funds come from private lenders for loans which are insured by FmHA. Let's discuss the main programs.

FARM OWNERSHIP LOANS

These are used to buy land; construct, repair or improve buildings; and improve farmland. Such loans facilitate farmers and ranchers to buy farms or give owners of insufficient or underdeveloped farms to enlarge or improve farms. Funding is limited to farms that are not larger than family size (see earlier definition at the beginning of this chapter).

Loans are usually scheduled for a 30-year repayment but when justified may be scheduled over period up to 40 years. FmHA may subsidize the rates on guaranteed loans up to four (4) percent depending on the borrower needs. During Fiscal Year 1991, 641 insured loans were made with an average insured loan amount of $89,000; 2,509 guaranteed loans were made that year with an average guarantee of $149,500.

FARM OPERATING LOANS

Such loans enable farm operators, who cannot get conventional financing, to acquire needed resources and to better use their land and other resources. Financing can be used to buy farm or non-farm equipment; livestock or other farm animals, provide operating expenses for farm, forestry, recreation, or non-farm enterprises; meet family subsistence needs and purchase essential home equipment; make minor real estate improvements; refinance secured and unsecured debts; pay property taxes; pay insurance premiums on real estate and personal property; plant softwood timber on marginal land; and support miscellaneous projects.

If you have had farm experience or training (one year's complete production and marketing cycle within the past five years), cannot get sufficient credit elsewhere at reasonable rates, possess the character and credit history, are a U.S. citizen, have the capacity to repay the loan, and have the industry and managerial capability to carry out the farm operation, then you are eligible for this loan. Loans are scheduled for repayment within seven years, but may be consolidated or rescheduled for up to 15 additional years. Applicants should file Form FmHA 1910-1, found at your local FmHA county office to apply; file Form FmHA 449-6 with your prospective lender for an FmHA guarantee.

Loans are insured up to $200,000 and guaranteed up to $400,000. For Fiscal Year 1991, the average insured loan was $46,000 and the average guaranteed loan was $101,000. During that same year, 10,679 insured loans and 10,745 guaranteed loans were made. Farm operating loans basically provide credit to establish beginning farmers, to assist farmers suffering from the price/cost squeeze so they can remain on the farm, and to help them expand their farming operations.

EMERGENCY LOANS

Funds are necessary to cover a farmer's losses when struck by natural disasters. These are available in counties named as eligible for disaster emergency loans by Presidential major disaster or emergency declaration, by a natural disaster determination from the Secretary of Agriculture, or by the FmHA Administrator's physical loss notification. Loan funds may be used to restore or replace damaged property, pay all or part of the production costs associated with the disaster year and/or the year following, pay delinquent debt installments, pay family living expenses, construct/repair/buy buildings, purchase machinery/equipment/foundation livestock, pay costs to reorganize a farming system when justified and/or to refinance short, intermediate and/or long-term debts when justified. Emergency loans carry a four percent interest rate and terms vary from seven to 40 years. Average estimated size of assistance for Fiscal Year 1992 was $42,300.

SOIL AND WATER LOANS

This type of loan is used to help farmers and ranchers develop, conserve and properly use land and water resources. Such loans can be used to drain farmland, establish or improve permanent pasture, development of pollution abatement and control facilities or the development of energy conserving measures. Funds may be used to level land, carry out basic land treatment practices, improve irrigation, acquire water rights, restore and repair ponds and similar tasks.

For Fiscal Year 1990, 236 direct and 11 guaranteed loans were made with an average financial assistance of $29,500. Loans range from $4,000 to $101,000. Loans made that year were used to drill wells, construct ponds, dig ditches and purchase and install irrigation equipment.

LIMITED RESOURCE LOANS

Limited resource loans exist to help low-income farmers and ranchers improve their operations. A "limited resource" farmer lacks equipment, capital, land, and/or adequate financing or farming methods. These are the obstacles faced by young and minority farmers who have been unable to develop farms than earn them an adequate living.

YOUTH PROJECT LOANS

Young people, between the ages of ten and twenty years, can borrow money to engage in income-producing projects. To be eligible you must live in the open country or in a town of less than 10,000 and be unable to get a loan from other sources. All projects must be part of an organized and supervised program of work connected with a school, 4-H club, or Future Farmers of America.

You can finance nearly any kind of income-producing project, including (but not limited to): lawn and garden service, livestock and crop production, repair shops, catering service, art and craft sales and roadside stands. You may use your loan proceeds to buy animals, equipment, and supplies; to buy, rent or repair needed tools and equipment; and to pay operating expenses for running the project.

Application forms are available from your FmHA county supervisor (at one of 1,900 offices throughout the country). Repayment will be worked out with the FmHA county supervisor, depending on what type of project is being financed. Sometimes, the county supervisor may require a cosigner on the loan. Your loan will be secured by liens on products produced for sale and on chattel property, including livestock, equipment, and fixtures purchased with loan funds.

RURAL HOUSING LOANS

These are called Section 502 Rural Housing Loans and exist to aid low- and moderate-income rural residents to purchase or to construct single-family housing or buy building sites. Farm home loans are restricted to rural communities with less than 10,000 population and rural towns with less than 20,000 population, where mortgage credit is hard to find. You don't have to be a farmer to qualify. Loans can be for as long as thirty-three years and the basic interest rate is determined each year, being adjusted according to the borrower's income level. The loan may be scheduled over 38 years if the applicant's adjusted annual income is less than 60 percent of the area median income.

Applicants must be without adequate resources to obtain housing, or related facilities. Loans may also be used to provide adequate sewage disposal facilities and/or safe water supply for the applicant's household; for weatherization; and for other similar reasons.

In Fiscal Year 1991, 32,700 new loans were made and a similar projection was made for Fiscal Year 1992. Financial assistance ranges from $1,000 to $105,000. Average construction loans were $52,363 and an average of $49,254 for existing structures.

RURAL RENTING HOUSING LOANS AND RENTAL ASSISTANCE PAYMENTS

For those who can afford to repay loans this program provides for individuals or organizations to establish apartments in rural areas for low- and moderate-income residents. For these loans to nonprofit corporations and cooperatives, assistance may be given to help defray some of the rental costs in housing low-income families. Subsequently, owners of FmHA-financed rental projects can reduce the rents paid by their tenants to no more than 30 percent of their incomes.

Applications are subject to an environmental impact study which is required when projects exceed 24 units. The application will be made on SF 424.2, Application for Federal Assistance, and submitted to your FmHA county office. Range of approval/disapproval time can be from 90 to 200 days. In fiscal year 1991, loans were made to provide 16,404 families with affordable housing. Average assistance to individuals providing this housing was $250,000; initial insured loans to organizations averaged $950,000. Regarding rural rental assistance 25,304 families received rent subsidies because of this program.

HOUSING REPAIR LOANS AND GRANTS

The objective of this program is to give very low-income rural homeowners an opportunity to repair or improve their dwellings. Maximum outstanding loan assistance is $15,000 to any eligible person and a maximum lifetime grant assistance to any eligible person 62 years of age or older is $5,000. The house must be located in a place which is rural in character and has a population that does not exceed 10,000. Loan recipients must have sufficient income to repay the loan. Very low-income limits range from $8,000 to $19,000 for a single person household, depending upon the area's median income.

In Fiscal Year 1991, 2,951 loans were made with assistance averaging $3,860; 3,695 grants were made and averaged $3,450. To participate in this program applicants must file Form FmHA 410-4 at their FmHA county office serving the county where the dwelling is located.

BUSINESS AND INDUSTRY LOAN GUARANTEES

The FmHA may guarantee loans to business owners with good business histories and who can supply as little as 10 percent of their capital needs. Business enterprises must be in cities or rural areas with less than 50,000 population; towns with less than 25,000 population will be given priority. Guaranteed loan rates are negotiated between the borrower and the lender. FmHA, like the U.S. Small Business Administration, requires extensive loan documentation. And, because this agency wants to increase rural prosperity by increasing business activity, they want to see a detailed description of jobs you will create and the overall impact the funding will have on the area's employment base.

FmHA generally wants projects that will either save existing jobs, help improve an existing business or industry, or create new jobs. Additionally, it will not make direct loans but will, instead, guarantee up to 90 percent of a bank loan to qualifying rural applicants. Loans can range from $500,000 to $2 million. Guarantees are 30 years for real estate purchases, 15 years for fixed asset financing and seven years for working capital loans. The lending institution sets the collateral requirements.

OTHER KEY FmHA PROGRAMS

The Farmers Home Administration also assists groups of six or more low-income families to construct homes. The groups must agree to work together until all homes are finished. Funds are used to buy materials and hire skilled labor.

Water and Waste Disposal loans and grants are available for the original installation or improvement of community water systems, sewer systems and solid waste disposal systems serving small towns and rural areas.

Other community facility loans are provided to build or improve public facilities such as hospitals, health clinics, fire and police stations, community centers, libraries, schools, roads and streets, and other essential community services.

FmHA is rural America's bright beacon. Without this agency a great deal of outer-urban America would be living in the Dark Ages. And, the rest of the country would be starving because it is the heartland that brings food to our tables and exports commodities overseas. Yet, there is another federally sponsored and independent agency that has an even greater impact on the United States.

THE FARMER CREDIT ADMINISTRATION

FmHA, the lender of last resort, provides only about 15 percent of the Nation's agricultural credit. The Farmer Credit Administration (FCA), an independent government agency, and commercial banks are the largest agricultural lenders, providing more than $350 billion in agricultural credit. FCA is an outgrowth of agricultural cooperatives, organized by farmers, from the 19th century. In order to establish Federal Land Banks, and further those farmers' original purpose, President Woodrow Wilson signed the Federal Farm Loan Act in 1916. This legislation set up 12 Federal Land Banks and was a major step in forming a credit system to meet the specific needs of agriculture.

The FCA was established as an independent agency in 1933 by Executive Order, was later shuffled in with the Department of Agriculture and by 1953 was given its independence and placed under the executive branch of the federal government.

Under the FCA the country is divided into twelve Farm Credit districts, each with Agricultural Credit Associations (ACAs), each operating under the name, "Farm Credit." Each regional office has many branch offices located in small towns and rural communities throughout the district.

Funding for the FCA's banks is raised primarily from the Federal Farm Credit Banks Funding Corporation, which manages and sells the Farm Credit System's securities. The Farm Credit Council is a trade association that lobbies for the interests of cooperative lenders in Washington.

Together, they help the FCA finance Farm Credit loans. The Farm Credit System is a financial intermediary, but its size, strength and status as a government sponsored agency helps attract investors at favorable rates.

There are a number of different Farm Credit loans and assistance programs available.

Farm Credit has long-term loans available for real estate acquisition, refinancing short- and intermediate-term indebtedness, construction of dwelling and facilities, farm improvements and grove development or rehabilitation. Loan are made for up to 20 years.

Intermediate-term loans are for one to ten years and are made primarily for machinery, equipment and vehicle purchases; refinancing short-term debts; or purchase of brood stock. Short-term loans are made to finance labor, seed, fertilizer, chemicals, equipment repairs, feed, veterinary costs, grove caretaking and family living expenses. Farmers can even turn to Farm Credit to send their children to college; build a country home; obtain crop, timber and credit life insurance; or lease equipment.

Loan rates are based on three primary factors: local competition, costs associated with obtaining loan funds and servicing the loan, and risks associated with the loan. Farmers and ranchers turn to Farm Credit because of the competitive interest rates and flexible terms available to them, but also because this agency specializes in agricultural lending.

One of the conditions is that loans are to be made for any purpose that is a direct or logical extension of a farmer's operation. This can include agriculture-related businesses that provide services and contribute to the overall well-being of the industry. Typical lending requirements prevail. Farm Credit wants to see that the borrower's financial position can meet the debt obligation and that his cash flow and projections are sufficient to warrant funding. Collateral is determined by the strengths or weaknesses of the borrower's capital and capacity to repay in a timely fashion.

Farm Credit has about 1,300 employees nationwide to serve over 70,000 farmers, ranchers and growers whose enterprises range from traditional farming and agribusiness to aquatic producers. Farm Credit institutions are organized as cooperative businesses. Each one is owned by its member-borrowers, i.e. its borrowers are its stockholders. Eligible borrowers purchase voting stock which gives them the right to not only elect directors but also to vote on issues affecting their association's operations.

FARMERS HOME ADMINISTRATION STATE DIRECTORY

ALABAMA
Dale N. Richey
Aronov Building, Room 717
474 S. Court St.
Montgomery, AL 36104
(205) 223-7077

ALASKA
Roger E. Willis
634 S. Bailey, Suite 103
Palmer, AK 99645
(907) 745-2176

ARIZONA
Clark R. Dierks
201 East Indianola
Suite 275
Phoenix, AZ 85012
(602) 640-5086

ARKANSAS
Robert L. Hankins
700 W. Capitol, P.O. Box 2778
Little Rock, AR 72203
(501) 324-6281

CALIFORNIA
Richard E. Mallory
194 West Main Street, Suite F
Woodland, CA 95695
(916) 666-3382

COLORADO
Judy A. Jaklich
655 Parfet Street
Room E-100
Lakewood, CO 802145
(303) 236-2801

CONNECTICUT
See Massachusetts

DELAWARE - MARYLAND
G. Wallace Caulk
4611 S. Dupont Highway
P.O. Box 400
Camden, DE 19934
(302) 697-4300

FLORIDA
Lewis Frost
4440 NW 25th Place
P.O. Box 147010
Gainesville, FL 32614-7010
(904) 338-3400

GEORGIA
Thomas M. Harris
Stephens Federal Building
355 E. Hancock Avenue
Athens, GA 30610
(706) 546-2162

HAWAII
Daniel K.J. Lee
Federal Building Room 311
154 Waianuenue Avenue
Hilo, HI 96720
(808) 961-4781

IDAHO
Michael A. Field
3232 Elder Street
Boise, ID 83705
(208) 334-1301

ILLINOIS
Jack L. Young
Illini Plaza, Suite 103
1817 S. Neil Street
Champaign, IL 61820
(217) 398-5235

INDIANA
George Morton
5975 Lakeside Boulevard
Indianapolis, IN 46278
(317) 290-3100

IOWA
Robert R. Pim
Federal Building, Room 873
210 Walnut Street
Des Moines, IA 50309
(515) 284-4663

KANSAS
John R. Price
1200 SW Summit
Executive Dr.
P.O. Box 4653
Topeka, KS 66683
(913) 271-2700

KENTUCKY
Mary Ann Baron
771 Corporate Ctr. Dr. - Suite 200
Lexington, KY 40503
(606) 224-7300

LOUSIANA
John C. McCarthy
3727 Government Street
Alexandria, LA 71302
(318) 473-7920

MAINE
Nathaniel A Churchill
444 Stillwater, Avenue
Suite 2
P.O. Box 405
Bangor, ME 04402-0405
(207) 990-9160

MARYLAND
See Delaware

MASSACHUSETTS -
RHODE ISLAND-CONNECTICUT
Theodore Fusaro
451 West Street
Amherst, MA 01002
(413) 253-4300

MICHIGAN
Calvin C. Lutz
1405 South Harrison Rd.
Room 209
East Lansing, MI 48823

MINNESOTA
Russ Bjorhus
Farm Credit Building
Room 410
375 Jackson Street
St. Paul, MN 55101
(612) 290-3842

MISSISSIPPI
Peter Johnson
Federal Building
Room 831
100 W. Capitol Street
Jackson, MS 39269
(601) 965-4316

MISSOURI
Gary L. Frish
601 Business Loop 70 West
Parkade Center, Suite 235
Columbia, MO 65203
(314) 876-0976

MONTANA
Eugene E. Coombs
900 Technology Boulevard
Suite B
P.O. Box 850
Boseman, MT 59771
(406) 585-2580

NEBRASKA
James L. Howe
Federal Building
Room 308
100 Centennial Mall N.
Lincoln, NE 68508
(402) 437-5551

NEVADA
See California

See Nevada Sub-State Office on
last page.

NEW HAMPSHIRE
See Vermont

NEW JERSEY
Takashi Moriuchi
Tarnsfield & Woodlane Roads
Transfield Plaza, Suite 22
Mt. Holly, NJ 08060
(609) 265-3600

NEW MEXICO
Vivian G. Cordova
Federal Building, Room 3414
517 Gold Avenue, S.W.
Albuquerque, NM 87102
(505) 766-2462

NEW YORK
James M. Hanley
Federal Building, Room 871
100 S. Clinton Street, P.O. Box 7318
Syracuse, NY 13261-7318
(315) 423-5290

NORTH CAROLINA
Larry W. Godwin, Sr.
4405 Bland Road, Suite 260
Raleigh, NC 27609
(919) 790-2731

NORTH DAKOTA
Marshall W. Moore
Federal Building, Room 208
220 East Roasser, P.O. Box 1737
Bismark, ND 58502
(701) 250-4781

OHIO
Allen L. Turnbull
Federal Building, Room 507
200 North High Street
Columbus, OH 43215
(614) 469-5606

OKLAHOMA
Ernest Hellwege
USDA Agricultural Center
Stillwater, OK 74074
(405) 624-4250

OREGON
Don Thompson
Federal Building, Room 1590
1220 S.W. 3rd Avenue
Portland, OR 97204
(503) 326-2731

PENNSYLVANIA
D. Eugene Gayman
1 Credit Union Place, Suite 330
Harrisburg, PA 17108-2996
(717) 782-4476

RHODE ISLAND
See Massachusetts

SOUTH CAROLINA
Nicholas P. Anagnost
Strom Thurmond Federal Bldg.
1835 Assembly Street
Columbia, SC 29201
(803) 765-5163

SOUTH DAKOTA
Don Scholten
Federal Building, Room 308
200 Fourth Street, S.W.
Huron, SD 57350
(605) 353-1430

TENNESSEE
Randle Richardson
3322 West End Avenue, Suite 300
Nashville, TN 37203
(615) 736-7341

TEXAS
Neal Sox Johnson
Federal Buildin, Suite 102
101 South Main
Temple, TX 76501
(817) 774-1301

UTAH
E. Lee Hawkes
Federal Building, Room 5438
125 South State Street
Salt Lake City, UT 84138
(801) 524-4063

**VERMONT-NEW
HAMPSHIRE-V.I.**
Bert McIntire
89 City Center
Montpelier, VT 05602
(802) 828-4472

VIRGINIA
Lloyd A. Jones
Federal Buildin, Room 8213
Richmond, VA 23240
(804) 771-2451

WASHINGTON
Earl F. Tilley
Federal Building, Room 319
P.O. Box 2427
Wenatchee, WA 98807
(509) 662-4352

WEST VIRGINIA
William Patton
75 High Street
Morganstown, WV 26505-7500
(304) 291-4791

WISCONSIN
Donald W. Caldwell
4949 Kirschling Court
Madison WI
(715) 345-7600

WYOMING
Michael F. Ormsby
Federal Building, Room 1005
P.O. Box 820
100 East B Sreet
Casper, WY 82602
(307) 261-5271

**NEVADA SUB-STATE
OFFICE**
Roger Van Valkenburg
1179 Fairview Drive, Suite C
Carson City, NV 89701
(702) 887-1222

DIRECTORY OF FARM CREDIT DISTRICT OFFICES

In each district you will find a Farm Credit Bank overseeing that entire zone. Farm Credit Banks oversee regional and branch offices in cities and counties throughout its area.

DISTRICT ONE
TERRITORY

Farm Credit
ME, NH, VT,MA,
67 Hunt Street
CT, NY, NJ
Agawam, Massachusetts 01001
Telephone: (413) 786-7600

DISTRICT TWO

Farm Credit
DE, DC, MD, PA,
14114 York Road
WV, Puerto Rico
Sparks, Maryland 21152
Telephone: (410) 329-5500

DISTRICT THREE

Farm Credit
FL, GA, NC, SC
1401 Hampton Street
Columbia, South Carolina 29202
Telephone: (803) 799-5000

DISTRICT FOUR

Farm Credit
IN, KY, OH, TN
Hillyard Lyons Center
501 4th Avenue
Louisville, Kentucky 40202
Telephone: (502) 566-3700

DISTRICT FIVE

Farmers Home Administration
AL, LA, MS
848 2nd Street
Gretna, Louisiana 70054
Telephone: (504) 361-4771

DISTRICT SIX

Farm Credit
AR, IL, MO
1415 Olive
St. Louis, Missouri 63103
Telephone: (314) 342-3200

DISTRICT SEVEN

Farm Credit
MI, MN, ND, WI
375 Jackson Street
St. Paul, Minnesota 55101
Telephone: (612) 282-8800

DISTRICT EIGHT

Farm Credit
NB, IA, SD, WY
206 S. 19th Street
Omaha, Nebraska 68102
Telephone: (402) 348-3333

DISTRICT NINE

Farm Credit
CO, KS, NM, OK
245 N. Waco
Wichita, Kansas 67202
Telephone: (316) 266-5100

DISTRICT TEN

Farm Credit Bank of Texas
Texas
6210 Highway 290 E.
Austin, Texas 78723-1037
Telephone: (512) 465-0400

DISTRICT ELEVEN

Farm Credit
CA, HI, NV, UT
3636 American River Drive
Sacramento, CA 95864
Telephone: (916) 485-6000

DISTRICT TWELVE

Farm Credit
ID, MT, OR, WA
North 2011 Hutchinson Rd.
Spokane, Washington 99212
Telephone: (509) 924-0944

16.

VETERAN'S AFFAIRS: GUARANTEED LOANS FOR VETERANS
****

The Department of Veterans Affairs (VA) administers the VA housing program by assuring all veterans are given an equal opportunity to buy homes with VA assistance. The VA loan program can offer important advantages over most conventional loans. These are the primary features:

o No downpayment unless required by the lender, the purchase price is more than the reasonable value of the property, or the loan is made with graduated payment features;

o An interest rate often lower than conventional mortgage interest rates;

o Long repayment terms;

o Limitations on closing costs;

o An assumable mortgage (for loans closed on or after March 1, 1988).

REQUIREMENTS FOR VA LOAN APPROVAL

To get a VA loan, the law requires that:
a) You must be an eligible veteran who has available home loan entitlement (except in the case of an interest rate reduction financing loan);

b) The loan must be for an eligible purpose;
c) You must occupy or intend to occupy the property as your home within a reasonable period of time after closing the loan;
d) You must have enough income to meet the new mortgage payments on the loan, cover the cost of owning a home, take care of other obligations and expenses, and still have enough income left over for family support; and
e) You must have a good credit record.

HOW TO ARRANGE A VETERAN'S GUARANTEED LOAN

There are six steps you should follow in arranging your VA-guaranteed loan.

1. Find a property suitable for your needs. Do a thorough search for your home.

2. Visit your bank, meet with the mortgage lending officer and apply for the loan.

3. Present your discharge or separation papers relating to the latest period of service and/or a Certificate of Eligibility.

4.   The bank will request an appraisal on your desired property from the VA and determine an estimate of the reasonable value of the property.

5.   The bank will then package up your loan application, verify your income and credit record and send the entire package to the VA for review.

6.   The bank will approve your loan and the VA will issue the lender a certificate of guaranty.

THE VA LOAN GUARANTY

The VA relies on private lenders, such as banks, savings and loan associations or mortgage companies, to lend you the money. You apply for the loan amount to the lender. If the loan is approved, Veteran's Affairs guarantees the loan at closing. The guaranty means the lender is protected against loss if you or a subsequent owner default on the loan.

Veteran's Affairs will guarantee up to 50 percent of a home loan for loans up to $45,000. Loans in excess of $45,000 can be guaranteed up to 40 percent of the loan amount to a maximum of $36,000. Based on these figures, the VA will only guarantee homes appraised at $90,000 or less.

The maximum amount of entitlement is presently $36,000. If some portion of that entitlement has been used before to get a VA loan, then the entitlement would, of course, be reduced. This entitlement is not cash; it is only the amount the VA will guarantee a lender against loss.

If you use up all or part of your entitlement, you can apply for and get it back by selling your property, repaying the loan and filling out VA Form 26-1880. Restoration of your entitlement is not automatic. You have to reapply each time you wish to have it restored.

The reason lenders will lend you money to purchase a home with no downpayment is because they accept a VA loan guarantee as the down payment. Your entitlement functions as the down payment for the loan. For instance, if you previously had a VA loan, you may still have "remaining entitlement" to use for another VA loan.

Most lenders require a combination of the guaranty entitlement and any cash down payment to equal at least 25 percent of the reasonable sales price of the property. If you have not fully used a portion of your entitlement, lenders may accept a combination of that entitlement along with a small cash down payment. Similarly, you can use your entitlement and cash to purchase a more expensive home.

WHAT YOU CAN PURCHASE WITH VA-GUARANTEED FINANCING

There are several different ways to approach the use of your entitlement funds for a real estate purchase. Below are the VA approved guidelines for use of the VA Loan Guaranty program:

o To buy a home.

o To buy a townhouse or condominium unit in a project that has been approved by the VA.

o To build a home.

o To repair, alter, or improve a home.

o To improve your home through installment of a solar heating and/or cooling system or other weatherization improvements.

o To refinance an existing home loan.

o To buy a manufactured (mobile) home and/or lot.

o To buy and improve a lot on which to place a manufactured home which you already own and occupy.

o To refinance a manufactured home loan in order to acquire a lot.

THE VA LOAN GUARANTEE APPLICATION PROCESS

As mentioned earlier in this chapter, you apply with a private lender for a loan to start the VA-guaranteed loan process. Contact lenders in your area by inquiring at local banks, savings and loan associations, mortgage companies real estate brokers' office and from your local chamber of commerce. Look them up in your telephone directory's yellow pages. Many mortgage lenders will already have the necessary forms so you may apply for a certificate of eligibility; if not, they can easily obtain them from the nearest VA regional office.

If you have a certificate of eligibility, you should present it to your lender when making your loan application. Some lenders may assist you in obtaining a certificate of eligibility if you don't have one. Apply for the loan anyway and then obtain one while the application is being processed.

If a lender is unwilling to accept your application for a loan, then find another lender. Just because one lender won't make the loan for veterans doesn't mean that all lenders in your area will not.

There are two ways a lender processes VA home loans. On a prior approval basis, the lender takes your application, requests the VA to appraise the property and verifies your income and credit record. Your application and other information are packaged and sent to the VA for approval.   Once approved, the VA sends a commitment to the lender, guaranteeing the loan. The lender then closes the loan and sends a report of the closing to the VA. If the loan complies with VA regulations, then the VA issues the lender a certificate of guaranty.

If your loan goes through automatic processing, the lender still orders an appraisal from the VA but can make the credit decision on the loan without the VA's approval. The biggest difference between prior approval and automatic processing is speed. The lender need not wait to get VA's approval before loan closing. Banks, savings and loan associations, and other designated lenders, which are approved by the VA, have the privilege of processing VA guaranteed loans using the automatic procedure.

You can reduce any loan processing delays with a few simple tips:

a) Obtain your certificate of eligibility before applying for the loan;
b) When applying, bring with you a list of the complete names, addresses, and telephone numbers of your past and present employers (covering a two year period). Include your employee identification numbers for each employer.
c) At that same time, bring with you the location and account numbers for savings and checking accounts where you bank.
d) At the same time, bring a list of all current indebtedness and financial obligations, as well as those you've recently paid off or closed.

LOAN REPAYMENT TERMS

The maximum VA home loan term is 30 years and 32 days; however the term may never be for more than the remaining economic life of the property as determined by the appraisal. You may partially or completely repay your VA loan at any time without a pre-payment penalty. Part payments may not be less than one monthly installment or $100, whichever is less.

It is possible to extend the loan maturity, provided the lender agrees and the extension period is within the maximum loan period.

period is within the maximum loan period. However, if you die, your spouse or other co-borrower must continue making the payments. If there is no co-borrower, then the loan becomes an obligation of the veteran's estate -- you can guard against this by obtaining mortgage life insurance.

There are four different, acceptable loan repayment plans. You should select the one suitable for yourself.

o Traditional Fixed-Payment Mortgage. This type of loan calls for equal monthly payments for the life or term of the loan. Each monthly payment reduces a certain portion of the principal owed on the loan and pays the accrued interest through that month.

o Graduated Payment Mortgage. This repayment plan calls for smaller- than-normal monthly payments for the first few years, usually five years, and then a gradual increase each year. Then, the repayment schedule calls for larger- than-normal payments. The reduction, in the early years, comes by delaying a portion of the interest due each month and adding it to the principal balance.

o Buydowns. The builder of a new home or seller of an existing home may "buy down" the veteran's mortgage payments by making a large lump-sum payment up front at closing that will be used to supplement the monthly payment for a certain period, usually one to three years.

o Growing Equity Mortgage. This repayment plan provides for a gradual increase in the monthly payments with all of the increase applied to the principal balance. The annual increases in the monthly payments may be fixed (for example, three percent per year) or tied to an appropriate index. The increases to the monthly payment translate into an early loan payoff -- knocking 14 to 19 years off a typical 30-year mortgage.

ADDITIONAL INFORMATION

On closing costs you won't be charged commission or brokerage fees for obtaining a VA loan. However, the lender may charge you a reasonable closing cost for the VA-guaranteed loan. Closing costs generally include charges for the VA appraisal, credit report, survey, title evidence, and recording fees, as well as a one (1) percent loan origination fee and a one (1) percent VA funding fee. Unless you are refinancing your VA loan, to obtain a lower interest rate, the closing costs and origination fee may not be included in the loan..

The VA funding fee is payable at the time of closing, but may be included in the loan and paid out from the loan proceeds. If you are receiving VA compensation for service-- connected disabilities, are a surviving spouse of a veteran who died in service or from a service-connected disability, or are receiving retirement pay instead of compensation, although you would be entitled to it, then no funding fee need be paid.

Veterans are not permitted to pay discount or "points" when receiving VA financing, unless they are paid in connection with the following types of VA loans:

o When refinancing an existing home loan on property you own;

o When repairing, altering, or improving your home;

o When building a home on land you already own or will buy from someone other than your builder; or

o In some cases, when you are purchasing a home from a seller which Veterans Affairs determines is legal precluded from paying such a discount.

VA DIRECTORY

If you are a veteran and are eligible for a Veterans Affairs Home Loan Guarantee, then please contact your nearest VA office for additional details and a copy of VA Pamphlet 26-5 (revised March, 1992) which includes valuable information about your benefits.

LOAN GUARANTY SERVICE REGIONAL OFFICE ADDRESS LIST

ALABAMA
VA Regional Office
474 South Court Street
Montgomery, AL 36104

ALASKA
VA Regional Office
235 East 8th Avenue
Anchorage, AK 99501

ARIZONA
VA Regional Office
3225 North Central Avenue
Phoenix, AZ 85012

ARKANSAS
VA Regional Office
P.O. Box 1280
Bldg. 65, Ft. Roots
N. Little Rock, AR 72115

CALIFORNIA
VA Regional Office
Federal Building
11000 Wilshire Boulevard
Los Angeles, CA 90024

VA Regional Office
211 Main Street
San Francisco, CA 94105

COLORADO
VA Regional Office
Box 25126
44 Union Boulevard
Denver, Co 80225

CONNECTICUT
VA Regional Office
450 Main Street
Hartford, CT 06103

DISTRICT OF COLUMBIA
VA Regional Office
941 North Capitol Street, NE
Washington, DC 20421

FLORIDA
VA Regional Office
P.O. Box 1437
144 First Avenue, South
St. Petersburg, FL 33731

GEORGIA
VA Regional Office
730 Peachtree Street, NE
Atlanta, GA 30365

HAWAII
VA Regional Office
P.O. Box 50188, 96850
PJKK Federal Building
300 Ala Moana Boulevard
Honolulu, HI 96813

IDAHO
VA Regional Office
Federal Building and U.S. Courthouse
550 West Fort Street
Box 044
Boise, ID 83724

ILLINOIS
VA Regional Office
536 S. Clark Street
P.O. Box 8136
Chicago, IL 60680

INDIANA
VA Regional Office
575 North Pennsylvania Street
Indianapolis, IN 46204

IOWA
VA Regional Office
210 Walnut Street
Des Moines, IA 50309

KANSAS
VA Medical and Regional Office Center
901 George Washington Blvd.
Wichita, KS 67211

LOUISIANA
VA Regional Office
701 Loyola Avenue
New Orleans, LA 70113

MAINE
VA Medical and Regional Office Center
Togus, Me 04330

MARYLAND
VA Regional Office
Federal Building
31 Hopkins Plaza
Baltimore, MD 21201

MASSACHUSETTS
VA Regional Office
John F. Kennedy Building
Government Center
Boston, MA 02203

MICHIGAN
VA Regional Office
Federal Building
477 Michigan Avenue
Detroit, MI 48226

MINNESOTA
VA Regional Office and Insurance Center
Federal Building
Fort Snelling
St. Paul, MN 55111

MISSISSIPPI
VA Regional Office
100 W. Capitol Street
Jackson, MS 39269

MISSOURI
VA Regional Office
Federal Building, Room 4705
1520 Market Street
St. Louis, MO 63103

MONTANA
VA Medical and Regional Office Center
Fort Harrison, MT 59636

NEBRASKA
VA Regional Office
Federal Building
100 Centennial Mall North
Lincoln, NE 68508

NEVADA
VA Regional Office
1201 Terminal Way
Reno, NV 89520

NEW HAMPSHIRE
VA Regional Office
Norris Cotton Federal Building
275 Chestnut Street
Manchester, NH 03101

NEW JERSEY
VA Regional Office
20 Washington Place
Newark, NJ 07102

NEW MEXICO
VA Regional Office
Dennis Chavez Federal Building
U.S. Courthouse
500 Gold Avenue, SW
Albuquerque, NM 87102

NEW YORK
VA Regional Office
Federal Building
111 West Huron St.
Buffalo, NY 14202

VA Regional Office
252 Seventh Avenue at 24th St.
New York, NY 10001

NORTH CAROLINA
VA Regional Office
Federal Building
251 North Main Street
Winston-Salem, NC 27155

OHIO
VA Regional Office
Anthony J. Celebrezze Federal Building
1240 East Ninth Street
Cleveland, OH 44199

OKLAHOMA
VA Regional Office
125 S. Main Street
Muskogee, OK 74401

OREGON
VA Regional Office
Federal Building
1220 Southwest 3rd Avenue
Portland, OR 97204

PENNSYLVANIA
VA Regional Office and Insurance Center
P.O. Box 8079
5000 Wissahickon Avenue
Philadelphia, PA 19101

VA Regional Office
1000 Liberty Avenue
Pittsburgh, PA 15222

SOUTH CAROLINA
VA Regional Office
1801 Assembly Street
Columbia, SC 29201

SOUTH DAKOTA
VA Medical and Regional Office Center
P.O. Box 5046
2501 West 22nd Street
Sioux Falls, SD 57117

TENNESSEE
VA Regional Office
110 Ninth Avenue, South
Nashville, TN 37203

TEXAS
VA Regional Office
2515 Murworth Drive
Houston, TX 77054

VA Regional Office
1400 North Valley Mills Drive
Waco, TX 76799

UTAH
VA Regional Office
P.O. Box 11500
125 South State Street
Salt Lake City, UT 84147

VERMONT
VA Medical and Regional Office Center
White River Junction, VT 05001

VIRGINIA
VA Regional Office
210 Franklin Road, SW
Roanoke, VA 24011

WASHINGTON
VA Regional Office
915 Second Avenue
Seattle, WA 24011

WEST VIRGINIA
VA Regional Office
640 4th Avenue
Huntington, WV 25701

WISCONSIN
VA Regional Office
P.O. Box 6
Milwaukee, WI 53295

WYOMING
VA Medical and Regional Office Center
2360 East Pershing Boulevard
Cheyenne, WY 82001

17.

STATE HOUSING AND REAL ESTATE MONEY
****

Your state may be very active in financing prospective homebuyers. State Housing and Finance Authorities (HFA) have been created to issue tax-exempt mortgage bonds so that first-time home buyers and low-income home buyers can purchase homes.

States have led the way with innovative home ownership programs, in which you can participate. Generally, if you have not owned a home during the past three years OR if you are willing to buy a home in an urban target area, you may qualify for state assistance. That assistance may include zero or low downpayment financing and a lower interest rate on your mortgage.

Each state has different programs available and exist to fill the void of national programs which preceded them. Guidelines are similar from state to state. Usually, your income can not exceed a certain level for the size of your family unit; this can reach as high as an annual income of $48,000. Prices of homes have a set ceiling, but the allowance for that limit is generous.

Depending on where you live, your state housing and finance authority can have neighborhood vitalization programs, financing for multi-family housing construction, environmental hazard removal programs, funds to make homes more energy efficient, and emergency mortgage funding. Each state has its own set of programs that change annually. Some states have special programs for disabled persons, the elderly, women, minorities, the handicapped, veterans, migrant farm workers, and/or Native Americans.

Because there are cooperative programs between the federal government and states or between states and local housing development corporations, you should inquire from your state's housing and finance authority about additional housing programs when you write or telephone.

STATE HOUSING AND FINANCE AUTHORITY DIRECTORY

STATE HOUSING FINANCE AGENCIES

ALABAMA
Alabama Housing Finance Authority, P.O. Box 230909
Montgomery, AL 36123-0909
Tel: (205) 244-9200

ALASKA
Alaska Housing Finance Corp.,
P.O. Box 1010205
Anchorage, AK 99510-1020
(907) 561-1900

ARIZONA
Arizona Department of Commerce
Office of Housing Development
3800 N. Central Ave. Ste. #1200
Phoenix, AZ 85012
(602) 280-1365

ARKANSAS
Arkansas Development Finance Authority
P.O. Box 8023
Little Rock, AR 72203
(501) 682-5900

CALIFORNIA
California Housing Finance Agency
1121 L Street, 7th Floor
Sacramento, CA 95814
(916) 322-3991

California Department of Housing
and Community Development
P.O. Box 952054
Sacramento, CA 94252
(916) 322-1560

COLORADO
Colorado Housing & Finance Authority
1981 Blake Street
Denver, CO 80202
(303) 297-7427

CONNECTICUT
Connecticut Housing Finance Authority
40 Cold Spring Road
Rocky Hill, Ct 06067
(203) 721-9501

DELAWARE
Delaware State Housing Authority
18 the Green
P.O. Box 1401
Dover, DE 19901
(302) 739-4263

DISTRICT OF COLUMBIA
DC Housing Finance Agency
1275 "K" Street Ste. #600 NW
Washington, DC 20005
(202) 408-0415

FLORIDA
Florida Housing Finance Agency
2574 Seagate Dr. Ste. #101
Tallahassee, FL 32301
(904) 488-4197

GEORGIA
Georgia Residential Finance Authority
60 Executive Parkway South, Suite 250
Atlanta, GA 30329
(404) 679-4840

HAWAII
Hawaii Housing Authority
P.O. Box 17907
Honolulu, HI 96817
(808) 848-3230

IDAHO
Idaho Housing Agency
60 W. Myrtle
Boise, Idaho 83702
(208) 336-0161

ILLINOIS
Illinois Housing Development Authority
401 N. Michigan Ave., Ste. 900
Chicago, IL 60611
(312) 836-5200
(800) 942-8439

INDIANA
Indiana Housing Finance Authority
115 W. Washington, Ste. #1350,
South Tower
Indianapolis, IN 46204
(317) 232-7777

IOWA
Iowa Finance Authority
100 East Grand Avenue, Ste. 250
Des Moines, IA 50309
(515) 281-4058

KANSAS
Kansas Office of Housing,
Department of Commerce
700 SW Harrison St., Ste. #1300
Topeka, KS 66603-3712
(913) 296-3481

KENTUCKY
Kentucky Housing Corporation
1231 Louisville Road,
Frankfort, KY 40601
(502) 564-7630

LOUISIANA
Louisiana Housing Finance Agency
200 La Fayette St., Ste. #300
Baton Rouge, LA 70808-2515
(504) 342-1320

MAINE
Maine State Housing Authority
353 Water St.
Augusta, ME 04330
(207) 262-4600
(800) 452-4668

MARYLAND
Department of Housing and Community De
 velopment
100 Community Place
Crownsville, MD 21032
(410) 514-7000

MASSACHUSETTS
Massachusetts Housing Finance Agency
50 Milk Street
Boston, MA 02109
(617) 451-3480

MICHIGAN
Michigan State Housing Development Authority
Plaza One-Fourth Floor
401 South Washington Square
P.O. Box 30044
Lansing, MI 48909
(517) 373-8370
(800) 327-9158

MINNESOTA
Minnesota Housing Finance
400 Sibley Street,. Ste. #300
St. Paul, MN 55101
(612) 296-9951

MISSISSIPPI
Mississippi Home Corporation
207 W. Amite # 13
3rd Floor
Jackson, MS 39201
(601) 354-6062

MISSOURI
Missouri Housing Development Commission
3770 Broadway
Kansas City, MO 64111
(816) 756-3790

MONTANA
Montana Board of Housing
2001 Eleventh Avenue
Helena, MT 59620
(406) 444-3040

NEBRASKA
Nebraska Investment Finance Authority
1033 O Street, Ste. 218
Lincoln, NE 68508
(402) 434-3900

NEVADA
Department of Commerce,
Housing Division
1802 N. Carson St., Ste. 154
Carson City, NV 89710
(702) 687-4258

Nevada Rural Housing Authority
2100 California Street
Carson City, NV 89701
(702) 687-5797

NEW HAMPSHIRE
Housing Finance Authority
P.O. Box 5087
Manchester, NH 03108
(603) 472-8623

NEW JERSEY
New Jersey Housing Agency
3625 Quakerbrige Road
Trenton, NJ 08650-2085
(609) 890-1300 or
(800) NJ-HOUSE

NEW MEXICO
Mortgage Finance Authority
P.O. Box 2047
Albuquerque, NM 87103
(505) 843-6880 or
(800) 444-6880

New Mexico State Housing Authority
1100 St. Francis Drive
Santa Fe, NM 87503
(505) 827-0258

NEW YORK
State of New York
Executive Department
Division of Housing and Community Re
newal
One Fordham Plaza
Bronx, NY 10458
(212) 519-5700

NORTH CAROLINA
North Carolina Finance Agency
3300 Drake Circle, Ste. 200
Raleigh, NC 27611
Also: P.O. Box 28066
Raleigh, NC 27611
(909) 781-6115

NORTH DAKOTA
Housing Finance Agency
P.O. Box 1535
Bismarck, ND 58502
(701) 224-3434

OHIO
Ohio Housing Finance Agency
77 S. High St., 26th Floor
Columbus, OH 43215
(614) 466-7970

OKLAHOMA
Oklahoma Housing Finance Agency
P.O. Box 26720
Oklahoma City, OK 73126-0720
(405) 848-1144 or
(800) 256-1489

OREGON
Oregon Housing Agency
Housing Division
1600 State St.
Salem, OR 97310
(503) 378-4343

PENNSYLVANIA
Pennsylvania Housing Finance Agency
2101 North Front St.
Harrisburg, PA 17110
(717) 780-3800

RHODE ISLAND
Rhode Island Housing and Mortgage Finance
Corporation
60 Eddy St.
Providence, RI 02903
(401) 751-5566

SOUTH CAROLINA
South Carolina State Housing Financing and
Development Authority
1710 Gervais St., Ste 300
Columbia, SC 29201
(803) 734-8836

SOUTH DAKOTA
South Dakota Housing Development Authority
P.O. Box 1237
Pierre, SD 57501
(605) 773-3181

TENNESSEE
Tennessee Housing Development Agency
404 James Robertson Parkway
Parkway Towers, Ste. #1114
Nashville, TN 37243-0900
(615) 741-4979

TEXAS
Texas Department of Housing and Community Affairs
P.O. Box 13941 Capital Station
Austin, TX 78711
(512) 475-3800

UTAH
Utah Housing Finance Agency
177 East 100 South
Salt Lake City, UT 84111
(801) 521-6950

VERMONT
Vermont Housing Finance Agency
One Burlington Sq.
P.O. Box 408
Burlington, VT 05402-0408
(802) 864-5743

VIRGINIA
Virginia Housing Development Authority
601 S. Belvedere Street
Richmond, VA 23220
(804) 782-1986

WASHINGTON
Washington State Housing Finance Commission
1111 Third Ave., Ste. 2240
Seattle, WA 98101-3202
(206) 464-7139

WEST VIRGINIA
West Virginia Housing Development Fund
814 Virginia St., East
Charleston, WV 25301
(304) 345-6475

WISCONSIN
Wisconsin Housing and Economic Development Authority
P.O. Box 1728
Madison, WI 53701-1728
(608) 266-7884, (800) 362-2767 or
(800) 544-3363

WYOMING
Wyoming Community Development Authority
123 Durbin St.
P.O. Box 634
Casper, WY 82602
(307) 265-0603

18.

FEDERAL EDUCATIONAL ASSISTANCE PROGRAMS
****

Were it not for the federal government a large share of the more than 13.6 million college and university students would have to find other ways to pay for their undergraduate and postgraduate educations. There are a number of different federal and related program that you should know about, either for your own benefit as a student or for your childrens' education.

While there are many different programs, from which one can choose, I will be first discussing the major areas where abundant federal and related grant or loan assistance will be found. Then, we will cover other types of financial assistance, including specialty, private-sector, minority or performance achievement awards which are possible. Additionally, reference works where you can find even more educational assistance can be found in the Suggested Reading Materials section in Section Four. The next chapter, Chapter 19, also covers private foundation grants and loans that may help supplement one's college and university expenses.

DEPARTMENT OF EDUCATION

During the 1991-2 school year, the Department of Education supported more than $19 billion in grants, loans and work-study aid. In this chapter's section, we will discuss the various grants and loans available to college student.

Later, in the co-operative education section, the college work-study program will be more fully explained.

Aid from most of the federal student financial assistance programs is awarded on the basis of financial need and on meeting the minimum student eligibility requirements. The Department of Education has certain eligibility requirements that include the following criteria:

o You are a student in financial need (see additional definition immediately following eligibility requirements);

o You have a high school diploma, a General Education Development (GED) Certificate, or has passed an independently administered test program approved by the U.S. Department of Education;

o You are a student enrolled in a program leading to a certificate or degree in a school participating in at least one of the federal student aid programs;

o You are enrolled at least half-time (usually means that you are taking one-half the normal course load each quarter or semester);

o You are a U.S. citizen or eligible non-citizen;

o You can demonstrate that you can make satisfactory academic progress;

o You will sign a statement of educational purpose/certification statement on refunds and default;

o You will sign an Anti-Drug Abuse Act Certification;

o You will sign a statement of updated information; and

o You will sign a statement of registration status.

EXPLANATION OF ELIGIBILITY REQUIREMENTS: There are certain points in the eligibility that need explanation. For instance, financial need does not mean your family is destitute. Financial need is determined by the cost of education at your school minus the amount your family expects to pay toward that cost; whatever the difference is becomes your financial need. Eligibility may be suspended or terminated by a court of law as part of a conviction for possessing or distributing illegal drugs. Non-citizens are eligible provided they meet certain U.S. Immigration and Naturalization Service (INS) designations (check with your local INS office). By signing a statement of educational purpose you are agreeing that you will only use your student aid for educational-related expenses. Regarding a certificate statement on refunds/defaults, you are stating that no refunds are due on a grant and that you haven't defaulted on a student loan. You must also certify that certain items on your Student Aid Report are correct and that you will agree to update any information on your Student Aid Report, if those items change.

FAMILY CONTRIBUTIONS: There are two different formulas used to determine the amount your family is expected to pay toward your college education. The Pell Grant Program is discussed below and has its own formula for deciding the size of your student grant. Other financial aid programs use a standard formula that can be obtained by writing to:

Federal Student Aid Information Center
P.O. Box 84
Washington, DC 20044

APPLICATION FORMS: Most students apply for federal student assistance by filling out one of five different forms: Application for Federal Student Air, Application for Pennsylvania State Grant and Federal Student Aid, Singlefile Form, Family Financial Statement or Financial Aid Form. Your school may assist you and, if available, let you use the school's computer to apply electronically (this is possible at approximately 2,000 schools). For assistance, you may also telephone: 1-800-FED AID. Most students make mistakes because they do not read the instructions on the application form. The highest number of errors occur on questions regarding your dependency status and income. Please read those instructions. Apply as soon as possible AFTER January 1st for the year you hope to receive student aid. Final deadlines for complete student aid applications are usually set for the first week in May.

STUDENT AID REPORT: Approximately four weeks after you apply for federal student aid, you will receive a Student Aid Report (SAR), which will contain the information you provided on your application and special numbers. On the SAR, look for the letters PGI and FC (PGI stands for Pell Grant Index and FC means Family Contribution). These letters will be followed by a number; that number determines your eligibility for a Pell Grant or for "campusbased" and Stafford Loan programs (more on that in this section). The SAR will state either that YOU MAY RE-

CEIVE A PELL GRANT or YOU'RE INELIGIBLE FOR A PELL GRANT. The next section will tell you about Pell Grant eligibility. However, if you're not eligible for a Pell Grant, contact your financial administrator to determine whether or not you're eligible another type of federal student aid. The deadline for submitting your SAR to your school's financial aid office is usually the end of June, or the last day enrollment, for the upcoming school year.

THE PELL GRANT PROGRAM

With your SAR you will receive instructions on how to review the SAR and ensure that it is correct or how and where to make changes, where necessary. Part 3 of your SAR is a Pell Grant Voucher. Take this to your financial aid administrator right away. He or she will determine the amount of your grant from the SAR information.

The Pell Grant is probably the most well-known federal educational assistance award. In terms of cost to the federal government, it is currently the largest federal student aid program. In 1992 more than 4 million Pell grants were awarded, costing the federal government more than $6 billion. It exists to help first-time undergraduates pay for their education after high school. A first-time undergraduate is one who has not earned a bachelor's or first professional degree, such as a degree in dentistry. Eligibility for those who receive a Pell Grant for the first time is usually limited to five or six years of undergraduate study, not including remedial coursework.

Half of the Pell grants go to people with incomes of less than $10,000. Most of the remaining ones go to those with incomes in the $10,000 to $40,000 range. A very few go to those with higher family incomes, but only in extraordinary circumstances. In 1992, Pell grants ranged from $200 to $2,400, with an average of about $1,440.

The hardest problem have with the Pell Grant is the Pell Grant Index (PGI). The lower the PGI, the greater the grant one receives. For example, a high PGI shows a family's greater financial strength and less need for such a grant. There is a large booklet (roughly 90 pages) that explains how to fill out the worksheets and how to calculate the amount of your eligibility. It contains a long and complex formula. You should obtain a copy of the booklet, THE PELL GRANT FORMULA, which is free of charge, by writing and requesting it:

FEDERAL STUDENT AID INFORMATION CENTER
P.O. Box 84
WASHINGTON, DC 20044

STAFFORD LOANS

Want a low-interest student loan? Your local lending institution (a bank, credit union or savings and loan association) or sometimes your school can lend you money for your college education. These loans are insured by your state's guarantee agency and then reinsured by the federal government.

Currently, loans are made at an interest rate of eight (8) percent for the first four years of repayment and ten percent after that. Depending on your financial need, as determined by your SAR (see above), you may borrow up to $2,625 if you're a first- or second-year undergraduate student, or if you are in a program that is normally completed in two academic years or less; $4,000 a year, if you've completed two years of undergraduate study and have achieved third-year status; or $7,500 each year, if you are a graduate or professional student.

The total amount of debt you may be permitted, as an undergraduate, is $17,250. Graduate or professional students may borrow up to $54,750, including Stafford Loans made at the undergraduate level. You cannot borrow more than your financial need level (cost of education at your school minus your family contribution).

You can get your application from a lender, any school accepting this program or your state's guarantee agency. Telephone 1-800-FED AID for the name, address and telephone number of your state's agency. After you fill out your part of the application, your school must complete its part, certify your enrollment, your cost of education, your academic standing, any other financial aid you will receive and your financial need.

If you are an undergraduate, your school must first determine your eligibility for a Pell Grant before you can receive this loan. Pell Grant eligibility must be considered in determining your overall financial aid.

Drawbacks to this program include the following: not every lender participates in the Stafford Loan Program, there is a five (5) percent loan origination fee deducted proportionately from each loan disbursement made to you, or your school can refuse to certify your loan application or certify you for less aid that you would be eligible for. Also, if you drop below half-time in your studies you may have to begin repayment within six months of doing so. Your repayment schedule can range between $50 and $200 monthly and you may be sending your payments to a servicing agency, other than your lender.

PERKINS LOANS

A Perkins Loan is a campus-based program and is administered by the financial aid administrator at your school. The school is your lender and loans you money through its financial aid office. This financial aid is a low-interest (five percent) loan for first-time undergraduates and graduate students with exceptional financial need, as determined by the school. Your school gives priority to Pell Grant recipients.

You can get $4,500 if you've completed less than two years of a program leading to a bachelor's degree, or if you are enrolled in a vocational program. If you have already completed two years of study toward a first bachelor's degree and have achieve third-year status, you can borrow $9,000. Graduate and professional students can get $18,000, including any amount borrowed under the Perkins program as an undergraduate.

Contact your school's financial aid administrator for further details. Do so quickly because these are limited and many apply for them.

SUPPLEMENTAL EDUCATIONAL OPPORTUNITY GRANTS

The Supplemental Educational Opportunity Grant (SEOG) is also a campus-based program. Your school awards these to first-time undergraduates with exceptional financial need, as determined by the school. A Pell Grant recipient is given priority over others.

Because it is a grant, you do not have to repay it. Depending on the restrictions you can get up to $4,000 each year. Your school only receives a certain amount of money each year for campus-based programs and awards on a first-come basis.

When you receive the SEOG, your school credits your account or pays you directly or uses a combination of both. Your school will pay you at least once per term, unless it uses a non-traditional term -- then the school will payout twice during the academic year. If SEOG aid is $500 or less, you may be paid just once during the academic year.

Contact your school's financial aid administrator for further details.

PLUS AND SUPPLEMENTAL LOANS FOR STUDENTS

To help pay for their children's education, a parent may want to borrow using a PLUS loan. Students can apply for Supplemental Loans for Students (SLS). Both SLS and PLUS loans are made by a private lender.

These loans have variable interest rates but will not exceed 12 percent. For example, the interest rate for 1991-2 was 9.34 percent. The servicing agency holding the loan, after it is made, must notify you of subsequent interest rate changes.

PLUS gives parents the opportunity to borrow up to $4,000 annually for a total of $20,000, for each child enrolled at least half-time and is a dependent student. SLS allows the graduate or professional student or an independent undergraduate student to borrow up to $4,000 per academic year for not more than $20,000. The same restrictions on course study apply with these loans as with other federal aid programs. Students applying under the SLS program may also borrow under the Stafford Loan Program.

Loan repayment with these is different from other programs. PLUS and SLS borrowers must begin repaying both principal and interest within 60 days after the final loan disbursement. There are no grace periods with these loans, as with the Perkins or Stafford Loans. The borrowers must continue paying interest even if a deferment for being in school occurs.

Contact your financial aid administrator for additional information about these loan program.

R.O.T.C.

Reserve Officer Training Corps (ROTC) programs offer young men and women to qualify for commissions in the Armed Forces while attending college. This is a scholarship training program that was established to educate and prepare college students for service as commissioned officers. Through a highly competitive national selection process, students are awarded scholarships for tuition and other financial benefits worth as much as $70,000 at more than 800 colleges and universities throughout the United States. Two-, three- and four-year scholarship programs are offered.

Eligibility requirements are stiffer than for many other college scholarship programs. Applicants must be U.S. citizens; be between 17 years and 21 years old and younger than 25 years old in the year of their graduation; be high school graduates or possess equivalency certificates; be physically qualified by Armed Forces standards; have no moral obligations or personal convictions preventing one from bearing arms; apply for and gain admission to a R.O.T.C. college; achieve qualifying entrance examination scores on the Scholastic Aptitude Test (SAT) or American College Test (ACT); and generally score in the top ten percent nationally on those tests (usually an ACT comp score of 24 or an SAT total score of 1,000 or over). Depending on the branch of the Armed Forces, one may also be excluded if one is a single parent or if one has already enrolled previously full time at a college or a university.

Scholarship selection boards interview applicants to discover officer potential and determine this through a diligent investigation procedure. They review your high school academic records, college entrance examination results, leadership and work experience, extracurricular activities, and the results of your personal interview, questionnaire and evaluation by your high school officials.

Boards usually meet three times each year. Apply to the earliest one since selection opportunities may be greater then.

To activate your scholarship you must pass a physical fitness test, which includes running, push-ups, sit-ups, a standing long jump and pullups (men) or flexed arm hang (women). You must qualify within a maximum allowable weight limit. Your entire body will be given a thorough inspection and your eyes, heart, joints and teeth must be in normal order. Depending on the service branch, there may be other physical requirements.

Once you've completed your education and receive a commission, your minimum active duty obligation is four years. If you discharge from the R.O.T.C. program for academic or personal reasons after beginning your sophomore year, you may be required to fulfill two years of active enlisted service.

There are seven steps you need to take when applying for the four-year scholarship program after obtaining an application form.

Step One: Complete and mail the application form.

Step Two: Take the SAT or ACT and authorize release of your scores to the R.O.T.C. scholarship program, as indicated on your test registration form.

Step Three: Apply to your first three R.O.T.C. college or university choices.

Step Four: Upon written notification from the Recruiting Command indicating you are "board eligible," contact the R.O.T.C. coordinator at your designated recruiting office to complete the final application process. (You may have to take the college entrance tests again to improve your test scores if you are deemed "non-board eligible.")

Step Five: The R.O.T.C. coordinator will schedule you for an officer interview and assist you in completing the R.O.T.C. Application Forms Booklet. He will also direct you to where the officer interview will take place.

Step Six: Your formal application package will be forwarded to a selection board for final consideration.

Step Seven: Depending on your application status, you will be scheduled for a physical examination by the Department of Defense Medical Review Board. There are additional programs available from each service branch. Contact your local recruiting office for details, an information package and application form.

THE FULBRIGHT PROGRAM

Since it began in 1946, more than 181,000 have participated in the Fulbright Program: 64,000 from the United States and 117,000 from overseas. This is the United States Government's international educational exchange program and was designed "to increase mutual understanding between the people of the United States and the people of other countries." Grants are awarded to U.S. students, teachers and scholars to study, teach, lecture and conduct research abroad. Foreign nationals are given grants to do the same in the United States. About 5,000 grants are awarded annually.

The United States Information Agency (USIA) administers this program through its 207 posts in 127 countries around the world. Final candidates for these awards are selected by the J. William Fulbright Foreign Scholarship Board, which is composed of 12 educational and public leaders appointed by the President of the United States. Commissions and foundations propose the annual country programs. These establish the numbers and categories of grants available. In 1991, Congress appropriated $95 million for this program while foreign governments contributed an additional $18 million.

Most of the programs bring foreign students, teachers and scholars to the United States. However, U.S. research scholars, lecturers, teachers and graduate students can also participate in this program. These are the groups one should contact for additional information and how to participate in their programs.

If you are a researcher, scholar or lecturer, write or telephone:

Council for International Exchange of Scholars
3007 Tilden, N.W., Suite 5-M
Washington, DC 20008-3009
Telephone: (202) 686-4000

If you are a U.S. graduate student and want to pursue your studies overseas, write or telephone:

Institute of International Education
809 United Nations Plaza
New York, New York 10017
Telephone: (212) 984-5314

If you are a teacher and wish to participate in the teacher's exchange program, write or telephone:

Teacher Exchange Branch (E/ASX)
United States Information Agency
301 Fourth Street, S.W., Room 353
Washington, DC 20547
Telephone: (202) 619-4555

EDUCATIONAL ASSISTANCE FROM YOUR STATE

The U.S. Department of Education and your state jointly provide financial assistance for your higher education. Your state's higher education agency also provides state aid. Each have their own names for those programs. Let's discuss the federal-state programs here.

Paul Douglas Teacher Scholarships are given to outstanding high school graduates who want to pursue teaching careers after they finish college. A Douglas scholarship provides up to $5,000 annually to students who graduate from high school in the top 10 percent of their class and who meet other selection criteria that their state agency may establish. Generally, students are required to teach two years for each year of scholarship assistance they receive.

The Robert C. Byrd Honors Scholarship Program will give students $1,500 for their first year of education after high school. Applicants must demonstrate outstanding academic achievement and show promise of continued excellence in order to receive funding.

The National Science Scholars Program gives two students in every congressional district up to $5,000 for each year of undergraduate study (or the cost of education, whichever is less). Graduating high school seniors, or those who will obtain the equivalent of a certificate of graduation, should apply for this program to finance their postsecondary education. To qualify, you must have demonstrate excellence and achievement in mathematics, engineering, or the physical, life or computer sciences.

For details on federal/state educational assistance programs and for the name of your state's higher education agency, please telephone:

1-800-4-FED AID   (1-800-433-3243)

COOPERATIVE EDUCATION PROGRAMS

Cooperative education, from its beginnings at the University of Cincinnati in 1906, is now offered in one form or another by approximately 1,000 colleges and universities around the country. These programs bring together your classroom studies with actual professional experience in your field. This work/study program gives you the chance to test out various career options. And, if you do know the field you wish to pursue, you can begin working up the organizational ladder before you graduate from college.

The co-op program is found mainly in two- and four-year college programs, but is also available in five-year programs. You will find co-operative education available in virtually every type of college subject and including all levels from an associate degree to a PhD. A four-year college might make provisions for you to spend to or three semesters or quarters in work assignments during your regular academic program. Two-year schools usually offer programs where you spend part of the day in class and part on a work assignment.

Every college and university has a different and limited number of placements available in each curriculum. For example, Rochester Institute of Technology had 1,132 engineering placements during 1991/1992 but only 61 health openings. During that same period, Pace University had 0 available engineering placements but 760 business placements. Determine if there are enough openings at your school for your major, or any at all, to avoid a letdown.

Co-op programs can be centralized or not, depending on the school. Many have a contact person you may write or speak to, in order to find out more about available placements in your major. It is important that you find out the specific details of the program before enrolling in that school.

For many the important benefit is the income one receives on the work/study program. A Co-op education allows you to earn money toward college tuition and living expenses. It could make your college education possible.

NATIONAL COMMISSION FOR COOPERATIVE EDUCATION
360 Huntington Avenue
Boston, Massachusetts 02115

PRIVATE SECTOR SOURCES OF FINANCIAL ASSISTANCE

There are other areas where you should also look for educational assistance, aside from those sources found in Chapter 19.

Private sector financial aid has been very important in assisting students and their families meet college costs. Over the past five years, private aid was increased by nearly 75 percent. Private sector groups allocate approximately $10 billion annually for financial assistance. Many companies and labor unions have programs to help pay for the educational cost of their employees or members or for their children. Some will give small grants, usually under $1,000, for outstanding or promising students. Others will offer special loans, some even deductible from the employee's paycheck. You should contact your human resources for benefit details. Often, such notices are thumb-tacked on employee bulletin boards.

Also, the College Financial Planning Service, a fee-based research service, tracks private sector aid and maintains a database of 180,000 awards in scholarships, fellowships, grants and loans. Many of these awards are UNCLAIMED each year because most students are not aware of them; in 1986, for example, according to the National Commission on Student Financial Assistance approximately $5.6 billion went unclaimed! Various sources of private sector financial aid can include corporations, memorials, trusts, foundations, religious groups and other philanthropic organizations. For a $45 fee they will research every available grant and loan opportunity for you. They have a fantastic guarantee -- if you do not receive a minimum of $100 in financial service, they will refund their fee. Write or telephone for details and their application form:

College and Financial Planning Service
Administration and Research
3455 Commercial Avenue
Northbrook, Illinois 60062
Telephone: (800) 933-3100
            (708) 559-0954

Another firm you may wish to also contact is:

Student College Aid
2525 Murworth, Suite 207
Houston, Texas 77054
Telephone: (713) 796-2209
Toll-Free: (800) 245-5137

Or another:

National Scholarship Research Service (NSRS)
Telephone: (707) 546-6781

Corporations can offer grants for special interest categories. Ralston Purina Company gives out $750 to incoming juniors or seniors in a college of agriculture at all of the 65 Land-Grant college each year. (Write to Ralston Purina Co., Checkerboard Square, St. Louis, Missouri 63164.) High school students who have been with a Chick-fil-A franchise for at least two years and maintain a grade average of C or better are eligible for a one-time $1,000 scholarship. Ben and Jerry's Ice Cream also have a foundation that provides financial assistance. There are thousands of company grant and loan programs available. Many desire to help their employees and get wonderful publicity for doing so, an advertising dollar well spent.

Religious organizations provide financial assistance. Lutherans, Presbyterians and other religious institutions and associations award grants and scholarships to their church members. Contact your local minister for assistance in locating the national agency that assists its members.

Fraternal organizations and veterans organizations have private foundations that offer college scholarships. Each year, the Elks Lodge offers more than 1,500 college scholarships with assistance ranging from $1,000 to $6,000 annually. The American Legion offers scholarships, grants and loans as an alternative source of funds for creditworthy parent borrowers (Call 1-800-LOAN USA). Check with your local fraternal organization's club office for more information.

Trade Unions help their members with a wide variety of scholarship programs. Nearly all of these awards are available to union members and their families. The AFL-CIO as a no-cost guide for its members. Send away for it by writing to the AFL-CIO, Department of Education, 815 - 16th Street, N.W., Washington, DC 20006. The Communications Workers of American (CWA) also assists members and their families through scholarships and grants for undergraduate and graduate students. Write for details to: Communications Workers of America, 1925 K Street, N.W., Washington, DC 20006

Look at your current or past activities and groups to which you belonged. For instance, if you were a Boy Scout or Explorer, there are numerous opportunities available to you. Scholarship foundations or endowment funds at sixteen colleges and universities, including Stanford University, may give you awards or scholarships for having been a Boy Scout, particularly an Eagle Scout. Even three preparatory schools and military academies have scholarships available annually for Scouts and Explorers. Write for an updated directory of scholarship information for Scouts and Explorers to:

Boy Scouts of America
Education Relationships
1325 West Walnut Hill Lane
P.O. Box 152079
Irving, Texas 75015-2079

One private foundation makes unrestricted, interest-free and non-collateralized loans to students entering their senior year of college. You start repaying after graduation, based on your income capacity. Write to:

Hattie M. Strong Foundation
1625 Eye Street, N.W.
Washington, DC 20006
Telephone: (202) 331-1619

SPECIALTY EDUCATIONAL ASSISTANCE

Check with your school's guidance counselor about national scholarship programs. The National Honor Society and the National Merit Scholarship provide outstanding high school students with financial assistance each year. These are achievement programs and limited to a certain number of qualified high school students each year.

If you are already in an undergraduate program, you may qualify for scholarships, grants or awards. In my final year of college I was once handed a small check by my Classics professor from an honors society, having been awarded for excellence and achievement in Classical Literature. This was completely unexpected. However, to obtain financial assistance, you can't always hope for a surprise; you have to apply. Check with the dean at your college for available assistance programs and find out if you qualify. You may also be able to obtain financial support from your college or university before matriculating. Find out from the college of your choice before filing your application.

In 1993 up to 85 Truman Scholarships will be awarded by the Harry S. Truman Foundation to outstanding junior level students at four-year colleges and universities and to sophomore level students at two-year colleges. Applicants should have extensive records of public and community service, have out-standing leadership potential, possess intellectual strength and analytical abilities, and wish to influence public policies through a career in government or elsewhere in the public sector (such as military, educational or public-service oriented, non-profit organizations). Only one scholarship is available to each qualified state resident in each of the 50 states, the District of Columbia and Puerto Rico. These scholarships can provide up to $3,000 for one's senior year and up to $27,000 for postgraduate studies. At-large scholarships are also offered annually. Students who wish more information about this program should contact:

The Harry S. Truman Scholarship Foundation
712 Jackson Place, N.W.
Washington, DC 20006
Telephone: (202) 395-4831
Fax: (202) 395-6995

Veterans Affairs can assist veterans in pursuing their education. Contact your Veterans Affairs office in the directory section of Chapter 16 for addresses, phone numbers and additional programs. There is a demand for undergraduate and graduate students in health care shortage categories, such as nursing and physical therapy. Scholarships and Reserve Member Stipends are awarded annually for those already studying in those fields. In return for these awards, participants are required to provide professional service for one year, for each year of support, in a VA medical center. Last year, scholarship recipients receive tuition, educational expenses and a monthly stipend of $621. Reserve Stipend recipients get $400 monthly while enrolled in full-time course work. For more information about this program, telephone or write to:

The Health Professionals Educational Assistance Programs
Department of Veterans Affairs
Office of Academic Affairs
810 Vermont Avenue, N.W.
Washington, DC 20402
Telephone: (202) 535-7528

The National Sciences Foundation (NSF) seeks to improve the human resource base of science, mathematics and engineering in the United States. In 1993 they will award approximately 1,000 graduate and minority graduate fellowships. About ten percent of those applying annually are granted a fellowship. NSF will provide graduate students with $14,000 for 12-month tenures, prorated at $1,167 for lesser periods. Prospective applicants can request initial application materials by writing or telephoning:

The Fellowship Office
National Research Council
2101 Constitution Avenue
Washington, DC 20418
Telephone: (202) 334-2872

One can look to their career objective and find financial assistance. The Club Managers Association of America offers scholarships for students enrolled at colleges and universities that have Hotel Restaurant and Institutional Management programs. If you are interested in a private club management career, write to:

Club Manager's Association of America
7615 Winterberry Place
Bethesda, Maryland 20817

Let's say you are interested in graphic arts. The Education Council of the Graphic Arts Industry awards scholarships for studies in printing management, printing technology and graphic arts education. For further details, write to:

The Education Council of the Graphic Arts Industry, Inc. Attention: NSTF
4615 Forbes Avenue
Pittsburgh, Pennsylvania 15213.

The above are just a few of the specialty assistance programs. Let your career objective help lead you to your educational financing source. Find out if there is an association, foundation or educational council that provides financial assistance for your desired profession or vocation. Check with your vocational school or college or university. Ask someone who is already pursuing that career about a professional organization to which he belongs; inquire with that association for details.

ASSISTANCE FOR WOMEN AND MINORITIES

The American Association of University Women (AAUW) have helped nearly 6,000 women with American Fellowships, professions fellowships, international fellowships, and research and project grants. Last year this educational foundation awarded more than $2 million in fellowships and grants for community action projects. Fellowship stipends can range from $2,000 to $25,000; professions fellowships can award between $5,000 and $9,000; international fellowships award $14,000; career development grants can give you between $1,000 and $5,000; and community action grants provide up to $5,000 in seed money grants to AAUW branches or individual women for community action work. For more details, telephone or write:

AAUW EDUCATIONAL FOUNDATION
1111 Sixteenth Street, N.W.
Washington, DC 20036-4873
Telephone: (202) 728-7603

See the Suggested Reading Materials in Chapter 23 for additional reference works regarding women's funding programs.

In annual competition, 700 scholarships worth over $2 million are awarded through the National Achievement Scholarship Program for Outstanding Negro Students. For further information, write to:

National Achievement Scholarship Program
 for Outstanding Negro Students
One American Plaza
Evanston, Illinois 60201.

Minority students may also find funding from the American Fund for Dental Health. Scholarships range between $2,000 and $4,000. Students must be U.S. citizens who are also Native Americans, Mexican-Americans, Puerto Ricans or Black Americans. Write to:

Director of Programs
American Fund for Dental Health
211 E. Chicago Avenue
Chicago, Illinois 60611.
Telephone: (312) 787-6270

The United Negro College Fund (UNCF) awards scholarships to students attending its member institutions. Eligibility requires that you have an unmet financial need as verified by the financial aid office; you must have a 2.50 Grade Point Average; you must be recommended by the financial aid office at the UNCF institution where enrolled; you must file a Financial Aid Form (FAF) of the College Scholarship Service (CSS), or a Family Financial Statement (FFS) with the American College Testing Program (ACT); and you must request that the FAF or FFS report be sent to the financial aid office at the UNCF college where you plan to enroll. For additional details and the names of UNCF colleges and universities, please write or telephone:

UNITED NEGRO COLLEGE FUND, INC.
500 East 62nd Street
New York, New York 10021
Telephone: (212) 326-1328

Additional grants and loans are available through national and state minority and women's organizations or associations. Check with your desired college or university, your high school's guidance counselor, local professionals or religious leaders and others for further assistance. Chapter 19 also includes foundations who assist select individuals.

CONCLUSION

There really is not a scarcity of funding sources for students, or parent of children, who wish educational assistance. Most give up before trying; others close their minds and don't look. Aggregately, between public and private sector, approximately $30 billion is earmarked each year to assist college students with undergraduate and postgraduate studies. No conceivable reason exists, other than an unwillingness to look, why any student cannot pursue a college education. Often, a student can combine a grant or scholarship program with a loan or work-study program to pursue his or her education. Paperwork, time, and effort are involved and sometimes try one's patience, but it is certainly not for a lack of outside financing that someone could not pursue a vocational, academic or professional training and education.

If you are still stumped, review your options. Which groups or organizations do you or your parents belong to? What are your hobbies or student activities? What is your career choice? Could you obtain an athletic scholarship? Are you a member of a minority? Are you or your parents handicapped? Of what heritage, ethnic group, or religious persuasion are you? Do you have a special talent? Where do your parents work? Simple questions like those above can help direct you to college financial assistance sources. When you've answered those questions, you'll be on your way to additional educational assistance sources. The next chapter, Foundation Grants for Education, may also be of further use to you.

DIRECTORY OF
STATE FINANCIAL AID AGENCIES

Please use this directory to contact your state's educational financial aid agency. There may be different types of state available for you.

Alabama: Alabama Commission on Higher Education; One Court Square, Suite 221; Montgomery, AL 36104; 205-269-2700

Alaska: Alaska Commission on Postsecondary Education; P.O. Box 11050; Juneau, AK 99811; 907-465-2962

Arizona has no central aid agency, but information on state programs is available from the financial aid office of any college in the state.

Arkansas: Arkansas Department of Higher Education; 114 East Capitol Street; Little Rock, AR 72201; 501-324-9300

California: California Student Aid Commission; Box 510845; Sacramento, CA 94245; 916-4450880

Colorado: Colorado Commission on Higher Education; Colorado Heritage Center; 1300 Broadway, 2nd Floor; Denver, CO 80203; 303-866-2723

Connecticut: Connecticut Department of Higher Education; 61 Woodland Street, Hartford, CT 06105; 203-566-2618

Delaware: Delaware Higher Education Commission; Carvel State Office Building; 820 North French Street, 4th Floor; Wilmington, DE 19801; 302-577-3240

District of Columbia: Office of Postsecondary Education; DC Department of Human Services; 2100 Martin Luther King, S.E., Suite 401; Washington, DC 20020; 202-727-3688

Florida: Office of Student Financial Assistance; Department of Education; 325 West Gaines Street, Room 1344; Tallahassee, FL 32399; 904-488-4095

Georgia: Georgia Student Finance Authority; 2082 East Exchange Place, Suite 200; Tucker, GA 30084; 404-493-5444

Hawaii has no central aid agency, but information on state programs is available from the financial aid office of any college in the state.

Idaho: Idaho Scholarship Program; Office of State Board of Education; 650 West State Street, Room 307; Boise, ID 83720; 208-334--2270

Illinois: Illinois State Scholarship Commission; 106 Wilmot Road; Deerfield, IL 60015; 708-948-8500

Indiana: State Student Assistance Commission; 150 West Market, 5th Floor; Indianapolis, IN 46204; 317-232-2350

Iowa: Iowa College Aid Commission; 201 Jewett Building; 914 Grand Avenue; Des Moines, IA 50309; 515-281-3501

Kansas: Kansas Board of Regents; Capitol Tower, Suite 609; 400 Southwest 8th Street; Topeka, KS 66603; 913-296-3517

Kentucky: Kentucky Higher Education Assistance Authority; 1050 U.S. 127 South, Suite 102; Frankfort, KY 40601; 502-564-8121

Louisiana: Louisiana Office of Student Financial Assistance; Box 9102; Baton Rouge, LA 70821; 504-922-1038; 800-259-5626 ext. 1038

Maine: Finance Authority of Maine; Maine Education Assistance Division; State House Station 119; One Weston Court; August, ME 04330; 207-289-2183

Maryland: Maryland State Scholarship Administration; 16 Francis Street; Annapolis, MD 21401; 301-974-5370

Massachusetts: Board of Regents Scholarship Office; 330 Stuart, 3rd Floor; Boston, MA 02116; 617-727-9420

Michigan: Michigan Department of Education; Student Financial
Assistance Services; Box 3008; Lansing, MI 48909; 517-373-3394

Minnesota: Minnesota Higher Education Coordinating Board; Capitol
Square, Suite 400; 550 Cedar Street; St. Paul, MN 55101-2292; 612-296-3974

Mississippi: Board of Trustees of State Institutions of Higher Learning, Student Financial Aid Office, 3825 Ridgewood Road; Jackson, MS 39211-6453; 601-982-6570

Missouri: Missouri Coordinating Board of Higher Education; 101 Adams Street; Jefferson City, MO 65101; 314-751-3940

Montana has no central aid agency, but information on state programs is available from the financial aid office of any college in the state.

Nebraska has no central aid agency, but information on state programs is available from the financial aid office of any college in the state.

Nevada has no central aid agency, but information on state programs is available from the financial aid office of any college in the state.

New Hampshire: New Hampshire Postsecondary Education Commission;
Two Industrial Park Drive; Concord, NH 03301; 603-271-2555

New Jersey: New Jersey Department of Higher Education; Office of
Student Assistance; 4 Quakerbridge Plaza, C.N. 540; Trenton, NJ 08625; 800-962-4636 College Info; 800-792-8670 Scholarships, Grants, Loan; 609-292-4310 General Info.

New Mexico: New Mexico Educational Assistance Foundation; Box 27020; 3900 Osuna Avenue, N.E.; Albuquerque, NM 87125; 505-345-3371

New York: New York State Higher Education Services Corp.; Student Information; 99 Washington Avenue; Albany, NY 12255; 800-642-6234 (New York only, out of state inquiries must be made by mail.)

North Carolina: North Carolina State Education Assistance Authority; Box 2688; Chapel Hill, NC 27515; 919-549-8614

North Dakota: North Dakota Student Financial Assistance Program;
State Capitol, 10th Floor; Bismarck, ND 58505; 701-224-4114

Ohio: Ohio Board of Regents; Student Assistance Office; 3600 State Office Tower; 30 East Broad Street; Columbus, OH 43266-0417; 614-466-7420

Oklahoma: Oklahoma State Regents for Higher Education; 500 Education Building; State Capitol Complex; Oklahoma City, OK 73105; 405-525-8180

Oregon: Oregon State Scholarship Commission; 1445 Willamette Street; Eugene, OR 97401; 800-452-8807 (in Oregon only); 503-346-3200

Pennsylvania: Pennsylvania Higher Education Assistance Authority; 660 Boas Street; Harrisburg, PA 17102; 800-692-7435 (in Pennsylvania only); 717-257-2800

Rhode Island: Rhode Island Higher Education Assistance Authority; 560 Jefferson Blvd.; Warwick, RI 02886; 401-277-2050

South Carolina has no central aid agency, but information on state programs is available from the financial aid office of any college in the state.

South Dakota: Office of the Secretary; South Dakota Department of Education and Cultural Affairs; 700 Governors Drive; Pierre, SD 57501; 605-773-3134

Tennessee: Tennessee Student Assistance Corporation; 1950 Parkway Towers; 404 James Robertson Parkway; Nashville, TN 37219; 800-342-1663 (in Tennessee only); 615-741-1346

Texas: Coordinating Board; Texas College and University System; Box 12788, Capitol Station; Austin, TX 78711; 512-483-6340

Utah: Utah System of Higher Education; Utah State Board of Regents; 355 West North Temple; 3 Triad Center, Suite 550; Salt Lake City, UT 84180; 801-538-5247

Vermont: Vermont Student Assistance Corporation; Champlain Mill; Box 2000; Winooski, VT 05404; 802-655-9602

Virginia: State Council of Higher Education; Financial Aid; James Monroe Building; 101 North 14th Street; Richmond VA 23219; 804--225-2141

Washington: Higher Education Coordinating Board; 917 Lakeridge Way; Olympia, WA 98504; 206-753-3571

West Virginia: Central Office of the State College and University System; Higher Education Grant Programs; Box 4007; Charleston, WV 25364; 304-347-1266

Wisconsin: Wisconsin Higher Education Aids Board; 7885; Madison, WI 53707; 608-266-2578

Wyoming has no central aid agency, but information on state programs is available from the financial aid office of any college in the state.

Puerto Rico: Council on Higher Education; Box 23305, UPR Station; San Juan, PR 00931; 809-758-3356 or -3328

Guam: University of Guam; UOG Station; Mangilao, Guam 96913; 671-734-2921

Virgin Islands: Virgin Islands Board of Education; Box 11900; St. Thomas, Virgin Islands 00801; 809-774-4546

American Samoa: American Samoa Community College; Box 2609; Pago Pago, American Samoa 96799; 684-699-9155

Northern Mariana Islands: Northern Marianas College; Board of Regents; Box 1250; Saipan, Central Mariana 96950; Saipan 670-234-7642/5498/5499

Federated States of Micronesia/Marshall Islands/Palau: College of Micronesia; Box 159, Kolonia: Ponape, Federated States of Micronesia 94941; phone Ponape 480 or 479; or Micronesian Occupational College; Box 9; Koror, Palau 96940; phone Ponape 471

19.

FOUNDATION GRANTS FOR EDUCATION
****

There are many different grants available from private foundations to assist you in achieving you educational objectives. While looking through the directory, which comprises all but introduction to this chapter, please remember that because of the way foundations are setup, each have specific limitations.

Rarely are foundations established with anything but a fixed purpose in mind. That purpose might be very specific (i.e., scholarships only to current or former member of the Order of Demolay of Bethel, Wisconsin). If that is the case and you are outside that limitation, then please don't waste your time and postage applying for a grant from that foundation. There are plenty of other from which to choose.

Each year many foundations don't give out all the funds they have allocated for grants. Not enough qualified individuals apply. It is sad that someone might not go to college or struggle to make ends meet when a grant was available to him or her. Please carefully research this directory for possible foundation sources.

Stick primarily to your own state or region. Many foundations were created to serve their local area. The size of that geographical area frequently depends upon the endowment size of that foundation. Some are national foundations, with a large endowment, so don't pass those by. Please read the limitations. If you have questions, write or telephone for their guidelines. You are almost always required to file a foundation's particular application so it won't cost you additional funds to request guidelines while you are doing a search.

Every single foundation that provides educations assistance was not included in this directory. The large volume of foundations precluded such an attempt. Hundreds were intentionally omitted because they were overly specific in their geographic limitations with only a tiny endowment available. I recommend you contact your school's guidance counselor and inquire about you local area's specific grants. There is another valuable method for you to pursue.

At the end of this chapter, I have also included a list of Foundation Center libraries. Visit them and continue to look for foundation grantmakers in they might have on educational funding sources. There are many around the country and probable one near you.

FOUNDATION GRANTS DIRECTORY

Mary M. Aaron Memorial Trust
 Scholarship Fund
P.O. Box 241
Yuba City, CA 95992
Contact: W.D. Chipman, Trustee
Limitations: Undergraduate scholarships to
residents of California to attend schools
within the state of California.

Nancy Jo Abeles Scholarship Fund, Inc.
1055 Bedford Road
Pleasantville, NY 10570
Phone: (914) 769-0781
Contact: Sophia Abeles, President
Limitations: Higher education scholarships
for students from New York or students
attending college in New York.

George Abrahamian Foundation
945 Admiral Street
Providence, RI 02904
Phone: (401) 831-2887
Contact: Abraham G. Abraham, Treasurer
Limitations: Scholarships to local students of
Armenian ancestry to attend colleges and
universities primarily in Rhode Island.

Adelphic Educational Fund, Inc.
c/o United Bank & Trust Co., Tax Dept.
101 Pearl Street, P.O. Box 31317
Hartford, CT 06103-7317
Application Address: One Edwards Road,
Portland, CT 06480; Phone: (203) 342-2607
Contact: Herbert A. Arnold
Limitations: Scholarships primarily to
undergraduate students at Wesleyan University, CT, based on financial need and scholastic aptitude.

AEI Scholarship Fund
c/o Citizens Trust
100 South Main Street
Ann Arbor, MI 48104
Phone: (313) 994-5555
Contact: B. Todd Jones, Trust Officer
Limitations: Educational loans only to female
Students accepted at or attending accredited
medical schools in the U.S.

Edith K. Eyre Ainsworth Scholarship
 Trust, No. 2
c/o Bankers Trust Company
P.O. Box 829, Church Street Station
New York, NY 10008
Application address: Bankers Trust,
280 Park Avenue, New York, NY 10017.
Contact: Mary Hughes, Trust Officer
Limitations: Awards scholarships to people of
Irish heritage for higher education.

Ida and Benjamin Alpert Foundation
31275 Northwestern Highway 234
Farmington Hills, MI 48018
Application address: c/o David Caplan, 27600
Northwestern Highway, No. 214, Southfield,
MI 48034.
Contact: Myron Alpert, President
Limitations: Scholarships to Michigan resi-
dents accepted by or enrolled in an accredited
law school.

America's Junior Miss Scholarship Foundation
(Formerly California's Junior Miss Scholarship
 Foundation)
P.O. Box 1863
Santa Rosa, CA 95402
Phone: (707) 576-7505
Contact: "Ting" Guggiana
Limitations: Educational scholarships only to
contestants of California's Young Women of
the Year. Contestant must apply within five
years of having been in the pageant.

Educational Fund of the Honolulu Branch of the American Association of University Women
1802 Keeaumoku Street
Honolulu, HI 96822
Phone: (808) 537-4702
Contact: Chairperson
Limitations: Graduate and undergraduate college scholarships to residents of Hawaii; Awards to professional foreign Asian and Pacific working women for specific two-to six-month projects or graduate study in Hawaii

American Otological Society, Inc.
c/o Dr. Robert Kohut
300 South Hawthorne Road
Winston-Salem, NC 27103
Application address:
c/o Dr. Arnold Duvall III,
Box 396, Univ. of Minnesota Hospitals,
420 Delaware St., S.E., Minneapolis, MN 55455; Phone: (612) 373-8607.
Limitations: Grants are awarded to U.S. and Canadian citizens only for research in the field of otosclerosis.

Americans for Middle East Understanding, Inc.
475 Riverside Drive, Room 241
New York, NY 10115
Phone: (212) 870-2053
Contact: John F. Mahoney, Executive Director
Limitations: Grants to support studies, research, and other projects concerning the Middle East.

Ameritec Foundation
760 Arrow Grand Circle
Covina, CA 91722
Phone: (818) 915-5441
Contact: John Watson, President
Limitations: Awards prized to individuals to promote medical (not clinical) research toward the goal of finding a cure for spinal chord functional impairment (paralysis).

Arnold Foundation
c/o Jim Arnold, Jr.
406 Sterzing Street
Austin, TX 78704
Application address:
University of Texas, Office of Student Financial Affairs, 2608 Whitis St.,
Austin, TX; Phone: (512) 471-4001
Contact: Mike Novak
Limitations: Scholarships to working students attending the University of Texas at Austin.

Atherton Family Foundation
c/o Hawaii Community Foundation
222 Merchant Street, Second Floor
Honolulu, HI 96813
Phone: (808) 537-6333
Contact: Caroline Sharman, Scholarship Admin.
Limitations: Scholarships to Hawaii residents who are children of Protestant ministers, graduate theological students at a Protestant seminary, or ministers seeking further education.

The Aurora Foundation
P.O. Box 1848
Bradenton, FL 34206
Phone: (813) 748-4100
Contact: Anthony T. Rossi, Chairman
Limitations: Scholarships for education and training of Christian ministers, missionaries, or those otherwise engaged in Christian service.

William H. F. S Austin Trust
Maiden Trust Company
94 Pleasant Street
Malden, MA 02148
Application address: P.O. Box A, Malden, MA 02148; Phone: (617) 321-1111
Contact: Robert M. Wallask, Trust Officer
Limitations: Non-interest bearing educational loans to students with deceased fathers who are in pursuit of a college degree and who are residents of Massachusetts.

The Bagby Foundation for the
 Musical Arts, Inc.
501 Fifth Avenue
New York, NY 10017
Phone: (212) 986-6094
Contact: Eleanor C. Mark, Executive Director
Limitations: Musical study grants based on talent and need.

The Bill Baldwin Fund, Inc.
c/o Louis Rubin
176 Third Street
Troy, NY 12180-4459
Phone: (518) 252-8420
Limitations: Grants for people in the periodical industry.

Ruth Eleanor Bamberger and John Ernest
 Bamberger Memorial Foundation
1201 Walker Building
Salt Lake City, UT 84111
Phone: (801) 364-2045
Contact: William H. Olwell, Secretary-Treasurer
Limitations: Undergraduate scholarships to Utah residents, with preference given to student nurses. Occasional loans awarded for medical education.

Bank of America - Giannini Foundation
Bank of America Center, Department 3246
Box 37000
San Francisco, CA 94137
Phone: (415) 953-0932
Contact: Caroline O. Boitano, Administrator
Limitations: Fellowships to individuals for post-doctoral research done at one of the eight medical schools in California.

The Bankhead Foundation Educational &
 Charitable Trust
P.O. Box 702
York, SC 29745
Limitations: Awards scholarships to residents of South Carolina.

Bantly Charitable Trust
1578 Crestline Drive
Atlanta, GA 30345
Contact: Thomas W. Bantly, Trustee
Limitations: Award scholarships for religious study and medical research.

The Barker Foundation, Inc.
P.O. Box 328
Nashua, NH 03061
Phone: (603) 889-1763
Contact: Allan M. Barker, President
Limitations: Scholarships primarily to residents of New Hampshire.

Augustus & Kathleen Barrows Memorial
 and Trust Fund
271 South Union Street
Burlington, VT 05401
Phone: (802) 863-4531
Contact: Maureen T. McNeil
Limitations: Scholarships for women residing in Vermont who are under the age of 25.

Lyle P. Bartholomew Scholarship
 & Loan Fund
P.O. Box 2808
Portland, OR 97208
Application address: University of Oregon,
School of Architecture, Lawrence Hall, Room
202, Eugene, OR 97403
Phone: (505) 606-3656
Contact: George M. Hodge
Limitations: Awards scholarships for the
study of architecture at the University of
Oregon.

Dr. Mary E. Bates Trust Fund
2201 South Holly Street, No. 5
Denver, CO 80222-5613
Phone: (303) 757-0147
Contact: Mabel Wolfe, Trustee
Limitations: Grants for Women in Medicine
in Colorado.

E. Perry & Grace Beatty
 Memorial Foundation
c/o Dollars Savings & Trust Company
P.O. Box 450
Youngstown, OH 44501
Limitations: Awards scholarships to students
in OH.

Charles and Els Bendheim Foundation
One Parker Plaza
Fort Lee, NJ 07024
Limitations: Grants to Jewish individuals for
religious study.

The James Gordon Bennett Memorial Corporation
c/o New York Daily News
220 East 42nd Street
New York, NY 10017
Contact: Denise Houseman
Limitations: Scholarships to children of journalists who have worked in New York City on
a daily newspaper for ten years or more.

Frank and Lydia Bergen Foundation
Philanthropic Services Group
c/o First Fidelity Bank, N.A. and N.J.
765 Broad Street
Newark, NJ 07102
Phone: (201) 430-4533
Contact: Mr. James S. Hohn,
Assistant Vice President, First Fidelity Bank
Limitations: Educational support to aid worth
music students in New Jersey in securing a
complete and adequate musical education.

Beta Theta Pi Fraternity Founders Fund
208 East High Street
P.O. Box 111
Oxford, OH 45056
Phone: (513) 523-7591
Contact: Thomas A. Beyer,
Administrative Secretary
Limitations: Scholarships only to members of
Beta Theta Pi fraternities around the country.

BF Foundation
114 North San Francisco Street, Suite 107
Flagstaff, AZ 86001
Phone: (602) 774-1094
Contact: David Chase, Secretary-Treasurer
Limitations: Individual undergraduate student
awards made through the financial aid offices
of designated institutions.

Mary E. Bivins Foundation
P.O. Box 708
Amarillo, TX 79105
Application address:
6214 Elmhurst, Amarillo, TX 79106
Contact: Lindy Ward, Director
Limitations: Scholarships for post-secondary
education to residents of Texas whose field
and institution are religious.

James Hubert Blake Trust
c/o Beldock, Levine & Hoffman
99 Park Avenue
New York, NY 10016-1502
Phone: (212) 490-0400
Contact: Elliot Hoffman, Esquire
Limitations: Music scholarships, particularly for students interested in traditional American ragtime music.

Grace T. Blanchard Trust f/b/o Flora T. Blanchard Scholarships
c/o Easton Bank & Trust Company
225 Essex Street
Salem, MA 01970-3728
Phone: (617) 599-2100
Contact: Gary A. Peterson
Limitations: Scholarships for Massachusetts residents attending either Harvard University or Radcliffe College.

Violet Bohnett Memorial Foundation
16149 Redmond Way, Suite 220
Redmond, WA 93052
Contact: James N. Bohnett, Managing Trustee
Limitations: Scholarships to individuals in WA, OR, CA, AZ and HI based on demonstrated ability and financial need.

Charles H. Bond Trust
c/o The First National Bank of Boston
P.O. Box 1861
Boston, MA 02105
Contact: Sharon Driscoll, Trust Officer
Limitations: Scholarships to Massachusetts high school seniors who will be attending college the following year.

Ethel N. Bowen Foundation
First National Bank of Bluefield
500 Federal Street
Bluefield, WV 24701
Phone: (304) 325-8181
Contact: R.W. Wilkenson, Secretary-Treasurer
Limitations: Scholarships for students from the coal mining areas of southern and southwestern Virginia.

Ella Frances Brisley & Noma Brisley Phillips Scholarship Loan Fund
c/o Third National Bank
P.O. Box 351
Sedalia, MO 65301
Phone: (816) 827-3333
Contact: Carol Scrimager, VP,
Third National Bank
Limitations: Scholarships to needy medical and nursing students attending accredited schools and deserving and needy students attending Methodist colleges.

The Eva H. Brown Foundation, Inc.
405 Lexington Avenue
New York, NY 10017
Limitations: Scholarships only to residents of upstate New York.

Joe Q. & Dorothy Dorsett Brown Foundation
1801 Pere Marquette Building
New Orleans, LA 70112
Phone: (504) 522-4233
Contact: D.P. Spencer, Vice President
Limitations: Scholarships primarily to Louisiana and Mississippi residents.

Annette M. Brown Trust
49 Pineland Street
Lewistown, ME 04240-5650
Phone: (207) 784-6566
Contact: Richard Bernier
Limitations: Educational loans to Maine residents.

Florence H. Brown Trust
c/o Bank of Delaware, Trust Department
300 Delaware Avenue
Wilimington, DE 19899
Limitations: Scholarships to current Delaware residents, who were born in Delaware, who are studying chemistry, law, medicine or dentistry, and who demonstrate financial need.

Gabriel J. Brown Trust
112 Avenue E West
Bismarck, ND 58501
Phone: (701) 223-5916
Limitations: Student loans to residents of North Dakota.

The Bush Foundations
East 900 First National Bank Building
332 Minnesota Street
St. Paul, MN 55101
Phone: (612) 227-0891
Limitations: Fellowships to residents of Minnesota, North Dakota and South Dakota, and specified counties of western Wisconsin for career advancement; and fellowships to Minnesota residents who are physicians currently practicing in MN, ND, SD and western WI.

James F. Byrnes Foundation
P.O. Box 9596
Columbia, SC 29290
Phone: (803) 776-1211
Add. Phone: (803) 776-3372
Contact: Margaret Courtney, Executive Secretary
Limitations: Scholarships to young South Carolina residents who have lost one or both parents by death.

California Masonic Foundation
1111 California Street
San Francisco, CA 94108
Phone: (415) 776-7000
Contact: Scholarship Committee
Limitations: Scholarships for full-time undergraduate students in California who are U.S. citizens.

Callejo-Botello Foundation Charitable Trust
4314 North Central Expressway
Dallas, TX 75206
Phone: (214) 741-6710
Contact: William F. Callejo, Trustee
Limitations: Scholarships primarily to students planning to attend educational institutions in TX.

Francis L. Calvi Memorial Foundation
14 South California Avenue
Atlantic City, NJ 08401-6413
Phone: (609) 345-0151
Contact: George Brestle, Trustee
Limitations: Tuition aid for New Jersey residents.

Ruth A. Cantrall Trust
c/o Bank IV Olathe
P.O. Box 400
Olathe, KS 66061
Phone: (913) 782-3010
Limitations: Financial assistance only for needy students attending the Kansas State School for the Deaf.

Cape Foundation, Inc.
550 Pharr Road, N.E., Suite 605
Atlanta, GA 30305
Phone: (404) 231-3865
Contact: S. G. Armstrong, Trustee
Limitations: Scholarship grants to undergraduates.

Marjorie Sells Carter Boy Scout
 Scholarship Fund
P.O. Box 527
West Chatham, MA 02669
Contact: Mrs. B. Joan Shaffer
Limitations: College scholarships only to former Boy Scouts who are residents of the New England area.

Arthur H. Carter Scholarship Fund
c/o American Accounting Association
Sarasota, FL 33581
Application address: c/o American Accounting Association,
Sarasota, FL 33581.
Phone: (813) 921-7747
Contact: Marie Hamilton
Limitations: Scholarships for students who have completed two years of accounting courses and wish to pursue the accounting field in college or graduate school.

CENEX Foundation
5500 Cenex Drive
Inver Grove Heights, MN 55075
Phone: (612) 451-5129
Limitations: The foundation operates scholarship programs for students attending a participating vo-tech or community college and for students attending an agricultural college and enrolled in courses of cooperative principles.

Charleston Scientific and Cultural Educational
 Fund
C & S Trust Company
P.O. Box 10608
Charleston, SC 29411
Application address: Wade H. Logan, III, P.O. Box 1090, Charleston, SC 29402
Phone: (803) 722-1634
Limitations: Awards grants to South Carolina natives for scientific, cultural or educational pursuits.

Judge C. C. Chavelle Foundation
123 Third Avenue
Seattle, WA 98104
Limitations: Scholarships for residents of WA.

Chesed Avrhom Hacohn Foundation
c/o Gateway Bancorp, Inc.
1630 Richmond Road
Staten Island, NY 10304
Application address: 5422 14th Avenue, Brooklyn, NY 11219;
Israel application address: P.O. Box 91130, Jerusalem, Israel 13042
Phone: (718) 948-7643
Contact: A. Romi Cohn, Chairman
Limitations: Grants for the continued education of rabbinical scholars.

China Times Cultural Foundation
43-27 36th Street
Long Island City, NY 11101
Phone: (718) 392-0995
Contact: Jame N. Tu
Limitations: Scholarships for undergraduate, graduate, and Chinese language studies.

Chinese American Citizens Alliance Found-
dation
1910 West Sunset Blvd., No. 460
Los Angeles, CA 90026
Phone: (213) 483-8561
Contact: BIlly W. Lew, Vice President
Limitations: Scholarships for students
matriculating in the south California area.

Churches Homes Foundation, Inc.
c/o Bank South, N.A. - Personal Trust Depart-
ment
P.O. Box 4956
Atlanta, GA 30302
Application address: 706 West Conway Drive,
N.W.,
Atlanta, GA 30302.
Contact: Duncan G. Peek, President
Limitations : Scholarships to Georgia residents
with evidence of financial need and satisfacto-
ry prior academic performance.

Charles I. and Emma J. Clapp Scholarship
Fund
First of America Bank-Michigan, N.A.
Kalamazoo, MI 49007
Application address: First of America Bank--
Michigan N.A.,
Otsego Office, 110 East Allegan St.,
Otsego, MI 49078.
Contact: Jim Yankoviak
Limitations: Non-interest-bearing student
loans to non-drinkers. Female applicants
must, in addition, be non-smokers.

Ty Cobb Educational Fund
c/o Trust Company Bank
P.O. Box 4655
Forest Park, GA 30051
Application address: P.O. Box 725,
Forest Park, GA 30051.
Contact: Rosie Atkins, Secretary
Limitations: Scholarships limited to Georgia
needy and deserving residents who have completed on year in an accredited institution of
higher learning;
graduate school scholarships available to law,
medical or dental students only.

Deo B. Colburn Education Foundation
63 Saranac Avenue
Lake Placid, NY 12946
Phone: (518) 523-3231
Contact: Deo B. Colburn, President
Limitations: Scholarships for post-secondary
education for residents of Northern New York
state.

The James W. Colgan Scholarship Fund
c/o Bank of New England-West, Trust Depart
ment
P.O. Box 9003
Springfield, MA 01101
Phone: (413) 787-8562
Contact: Thea K. Katsounakis, Trust Officer
Limitations: Undergraduate loans only to
residents of Massachusetts who are needy,
deserving and under 30 years old.

Joseph Collins Foundation
c/o Wilkie, Farr & Gallagher
153 East 53rd Street
New York, NY 10022
Phone: (212) 935-8000
Contact: Mrs. Augusta L. Packer, Secretary -
Treasurer
Limitations: Scholarships to needy students
attending accredited medical schools in pursuit
of the M.D. degree.

Paul and Mary Collins Trust No. 2
c/o Lyon County State Bank
Rock Rapids, IA 51246
Phone: (712) 472-2581
Limitations: Scholarships to individuals to pursue college education.

Colorado Masons Benevolent Fund Association
1770 Sherman Street
Denver, CO 80203
Application address: 1130 Panorama Drive, Colorado Springs, CO 80904;
Phone: (719) 471-9589
Limitations: Scholarships only to graduating seniors of high schools in Colorado planning to attend institutions of higher learning in Colorado; Educational loans only to children of Master Masons of Colorado Lodges, who are either juniors or seniors in colleges.

The Commonwealth Fund
One East 75th Street
New York, NY 10021-2692
Phone: (212) 535-0400
Contact: Adrienne A. Fisher,
Grants Manager
Limitations: Graduate grants in nursing and management and fellowship program in academic medicine for minority students.

Community Hospital Foundation, Inc.
P.O. Box 24183
Houston, TX 77229
Contact: Dr. Loren Rohr, President
Limitations: Grants to graduate students seeking a degree in medical-related education.

Continental Grain Foundation
277 Park Avenue
New York, NY 10172
Contact: Dwight C. Coffin, Vice President
Limitations: Grants to students for exchange programs between the U.S. and other countries.

Viola Vestal Coulter Foundation, Inc.
c/o United Bank of Denver
1700 Broadway
Denver, CO 80274-0081
Phone: (303) 863-6023
Contact: Charles H. Myers, Vice President
Limitations: Scholarships to students at specifically designated colleges and universities in the western United States for graduate and undergraduate degree programs.

Council on Library Resources, Inc.
1785 Massachusetts Avenue, N.W.
Washington, DC 20036
Phone: (202) 483-7474
Contact: Warren J. Haas, President
Limitations: Grants are generally limited to librarians for research grants, and the Academic Library Management Intern Program.

The Cultural Society, Inc.
P.O. Box 1374
Bridgeview, IL 60455
Phone: (312) 434-6665
Contact: Mohammad Nasr, MD, Treasurer
Limitations: Scholarships to Muslim students.

Daughters of the Cincinnati
122 East 58th Street
New York, NY 10022
Phone: (212) 319-6915
Contact: Scholarship Administrator
Limitations: Scholarships only to high school seniors who are daughters of regular commissioned officers (on active duty or retired) in the Army, Navy, Air Force, Coast Guard or Marines.

Carl and Virginia Johnson Day Trust
108 West Madison Street
Yazoo City, MS 39194-1018
Phone: (601) 746-4901
Contact: J.C. Lamkin, Manager
Limitations: Interest-free student loans only for residents of Mississippi attending Mississippi schools.

The Gladys Krieble Delmas Foundation
c/o Reid and Priest
40 West 57th Street, 27th Floor
New York, NY 10019
Phone: (212) 603-2302
Contact: Joseph C. Mitchell, Trustee
Limitations: Predoctoral or postdoctoral grants for research in Venice, Italy.

Deloittle and Touche Foundation
 (Formerly Deloitte Haskins & Sells Foundation)
Ten Westport Road
Wilton, CT 06897-0820
Phone: (203) 761-3000
Contact: Gerald A. Sena, President
Limitations: Fellowships and research grants to doctoral and graduate accounting students.

Emma Fanny Dietrich Trust
240 Third Avneu West
Hendersonville, NC 28739
Contact: Boyd B. Massagee, Trustee
Limitations: Awards scholarships to male students in North Carolina.

Dog Writers Educational Trust
Kinney HIll Road
Washington Depot, CT 06794
Application address: 47 Kielwasser Road, Washington Depot, CT 06794;
Phone: (203) 868-2863
Contact: Sara Futh
Limitations: Awards scholarships to students with background in dog activities, planning to major in journalism or veterinary medicine.

E. John Dolan Foundation
c/o Herbert Susser
370 Seventh Avenue
New York, NY 10001
Limitations: Grants only for study for the Roman Catholic priesthool.

Herbert A. Mike Donovan Scholarship Fund
c/o Sovran Bank
One Commercial Bank
Norfolk, VA 23510
Application address: Rector of Christ Church, Charlottesville, VA
Contact: Rector of Christ Episcopal Church
Limitations: Scholarships for further studies in the field of religion.

Dougherty Foundation, Inc.
3620 North Third Street
Phoenix, AZ 85012
Phone: (602) 264-3751
Contact: Mary J. Maffeo, Secretary
Limitations: Scholarships and loans based on financial need only to Arizona residents who are U.S. citizens and enrolled in an accredited college-degree program.

The Dow Jones Newspaper Fund, Inc.
P.O. Box 300
Princeton, NJ 08543-0300
Phone: (609) 452-2820
Contact: Thomas E. Engelman, Executive Director
Limitations: Journalism programs and scholarships for college and high school students, including programs for minorities. There is also a fellowship program for inexperienced high school jounalism
teachers and newspaper advisers.

Dunkin Donuts Charitable Trust
c/o Dunkin Donuts, Inc.
Pacella Park Drive, P.O. Box 317
Randolph, MA 02368-1756
Phone: (617) 961-4000
Contact: Office of the President
Limitations: Scholarships awarded to students in New England.

John J. Dwyer Scholarship Fund, Inc.
P.O. Drawer 524
St. Louis, MO 63166
Contact: John K. Travers, President
Limitations: Scholarships to deserving individuals in Missouri.

John P. Eager Educational Trust
P.O. Box 150
Manchester, NH 03101
Application address: 875 Coleville Road, Silver Springs, MD 20910
Contact: William Martin, Director of Finance
Limitations: Grants for U.S. citizens of the continental U.S. with an interest in micrographics.

Earhart Foundation
2200 Green Road, Suite H
Ann Arbor, MI 48105
Phone: (313) 761-8592
Contact: David B. Kennedy, President
Limitations: Fellowship grants are awarded to individuals who have distinguished themselves professionally, generally in such disciplines as economics, history, international affairs, and political science.

Ebell of Los Angeles Scholarship Endowment Fund
743 South Lucerne Blvd.
Los Angeles, CA 90005
Phone: (213) 931-1277
Contact: Ebell Scholarship Chairman
Limitations: Undergraduate scholarships to unmarried, full time students who are U.S. citizens and residents of Los Angeles County, CA, attending colleges and univesities in Los Angeles County.
Students must be of at least sophmore standing, in financial need, and with a GPA of at least 3.25.

Royal A. and Mildred D. Eddy Student Loan Trust Fund
P.O. Box 209, Trust Department
Gary, IN 46402
Application address: 2999 McCool Road, Portage, IN 46368.
Contact: Joseph N. Thomas, Attorney-at-Law
Limitations: Loans to students throughout the U.S. who have completed at least two years of college and are within two years of graduation.

Education Communication Scholarship Foundation
721 North McKinley Road
Lake Forest, IL 60045
Phone: (708) 295-6650
Contact: Maureen O'Connor
Limitations: Scholarships to high school students throughout the U.S.

Educational Foundation of the National Restaurant Association
250 South Wacker Drive, Suite 1400
Chicago, IL 60606
Phone: (312) 715-1010
Add. Phone: (800) 522-7578
Contact: Scholarship Department
Limitations: Scholarships available for undergraduate studies in the food service area and graduate degree fellowships and work-study grants to teachers and administrators.

Christ & Anastasia Eftimoff Scholarship Fund
564 Sturgeon Avenue
Akron, OH 44319
Phone: (216) 644-7686
Contact: Michael Hadgis, Trustee
Limitations: Awards scholarships to students who are members of the young Macedonian Patriotic Organization, or whose parents are members of the Macedonian Patriotic Organizations.

Charles and Anna Elenberg Foundation,
 Inc.
c/o Jack Scharf
P.O. Box 630193, Spuyten Duyvil Station
Bronx, NY 10463
Application address: 3133 Brighton Seventh
Street, Brooklyn, NY 11235;
Phone: (718) 769-8728
Contact: Rabbi David B. Hollander
Limitations: Scholarships to needy students of
Hebrew faith who are attending high school or
college, with preference given to orphans. No
grants to married students.

Ralph Waldo Emerson Memorial Association
c/o J.M. Forbes and Company
79 Milk Street, 10th Floor
Boston, MA 02109
Phone: (617) 423-5705
Contact: Roger L. Gregg, Treasurer
Limitations: Awards contributions to well-
recognized scholars and editors.

The Eppley Foundation for Research, Inc.
c/o Turk, Marsh, Kelly & Hoare
575 Lexington Avenue
New York, NY 10022
Phone: (212) 371-1660
Contact: Huyler C. Held, Secretary
Limitations: Grants primarily for postdoctoral
research in advanced scientific subjects
through recognized educational and charitable
organizations.

The Ernst & Young Foundation
 (Formerly The Ernst & Whitney Foundation)
277 Park Avenue
New York, NY 10172
Contact: Bruce J. Mantia, Chairman
Limitations: Grants to doctoral candidates in
the U.S. and Canada for dissertation work in
accounting or auditing.

Kittie M. Fairey Educational Fund
c/o The South Carolina National Bank
101 Greystone Blvd., Unit 9344
Columbia, SC 29226
Application address: South Carolina National
Bank,
1401 Main Street, Columbia, SC 29226.
Limitations: Scholarships to residents of
South Carolina, attending four-year college or
university within the state.

Family Health Foundation
P.O. Box 18469
Raleigh, NC 27619-0146
Limitations: Loans to medical students in
North Carolina.

Felid Co-Operative Association, Inc.
P.O. Box 5054
Jackson, MS 39296
Phone: (601) 939-9295
Contact: Ann Stephenson
Limitations: Educational loans only to Missis-
sippi residents.

Files Foundation
c/o Security State Bank
P.O. Box 429
Anahuac, TX 77514-0429
Phone: (409) 267-3171
Contact: Douglas Cameron, President
Limitations: Scholarships for residents of
Texas.

Maud Glover Folsom Foundation, Inc.
P.O. Box 151
Harwinton, CT 06791
Phone: (203) 485-0405
Contact: Leon A. Francsico, President
Limitations: Scholarships to men of American
ancestry and of Anglo-Saxon or German
descent to the age of thirty-five. Initial grants
limited to males between the ages of fourteen
and twenty.

The Ford Foundation
320 East 43rd Street
New York, NY 10017
Phone: (212) 573-5000
Contact: Barron M. Tenny, Secretary
Limitations: Fellowships, professorships or internships for advanced research, training and other activities related to urban poverty, human rights, rural poverty, education and culture, public policy and international affairs. No loans to individuals.

Hamilton M. & Blanche C. Forman Christian Foundation
1850 Eller Drive, Suite 503
Fort Lauderdale, FL 33316
Limitations: Grants for education to residents of Florida.

Charles Le Geyt Fortescue Graduate Scholarship Fund
c/o Westinghouse Electric Corporation
Westinghouse Building, Gateway Center
Pittsburgh, PA 15222
Application address: Forescue Fellowship Committee, Institute of Electrical and Electronics Engineers, Inc.,
345 East 47th St.,
New York, NY 10017.
Limitations: Scholarships for post-graduate work or other work in the field of electrical engineering.

Foundation for Nutritional Advancement
600 New Hampshire Avenue, N.W., No. 720
Washington, DC 20037
Phone: (202) 337-4442
Contact: Curtis Cutter, Executive Director
Limitations: Grants primarily for research on micronutrition and health and nutrition in the treatment and prevention of diseases.

Foundation for the Carolinas
301 South Brevard Street
Charlotte, NC 28202
Phone: (704) 376-9541
Contact: Marilyn M. Bradbury,
Vice President
Limitations: Limited scholarships only to students residing in North Carolina or South Carolina.

Foundation of Westchester Clubmen, Inc.
20 Perry Lane
White Plains, NY 10603
Contact: Marian S. English, Treasurer
Limitations: Scholarships for higher education.

Four Shra Nish Foundation
c/o Arcanum Lions Club
P.O. Box 72
Arcanum, OH 45304
Contact: Craig Dynes, Trustee
Limitations: Award scholarships to Ohio residents.

Fuchs-Harden Educational Fund
c/o The Bank of California, Trust Department
Seattle, WA 98114
Limitations: Scholarships for residents of Washington.

Fukunaga Scholarship Foundation
900 Fort Street Mall, Suite 500
Honolulu, HI 96813
Application address: Scholarship Selection Committe, P.O. Box 2788, Honolulu, HI 96803.
Phone: (808) 521-6511
Limitations: Scholarships to residents of Hawaii for a minimum of one year to study business administration at the University of Hawaii or other accredited universities.

C. G. Fuller Foundation
c/o NCNB South Carolina
P.O. Box 2307
Columbia, SC 29202
Phone: (803) 758-2317
Contact: R. Westmoreland Clarkson
Limitations: Scholarships to incoming freshmen who are residents of South Carolina, attending South Carolina colleges and universities.

Rev. Edmond Gelinas Foundation, Inc.
603 Stark Lane
Manchester, NH 03102-8515
Contact: Gerald Rheault, Treasurer
Limitations: Awards scholarships to New Hampshire students who are Catholic and of French or Canadian ancestry.

General Educational Fund, Inc.
c/o The Merchants Trust Company
P.O. Box 1009
Burlington, VT 05402
Contact: David W. Webster, President
Limitations: Undergraduate scholarships only to residents of Vermont.

Ben & Lucille Gentry Endowment Scholarship
 Fund
c/o Union Bank & Trust Company
P.O. Box 748
Kokomo, IN 46904-0748
Limitations: Awards scholarships to residents of Indiana.

German Marshall Fund of the United States 11 Dupont Circle, N.W., Suite 750
Washington, DC 20036
Phone: (202) 745-3950
Contact: Frank E. Loy, President
Limitations: Postdoctoral fellowship program for U.S. scholars for research concerned with contemporary problems of industrial societies; also provides professional fellowship to U.S. and European environmentalists as well as short-term travel awards, for participation at conferences only, as a discussant or presenter of papers.

GFF Educational Foundation, Inc.
P.O. Box 826
Norcross, GA 30091
Phone: (404) 447-4254
Contact: F. Roy Nelson, Secretary
Limitations: Scholarships primarily for residents of Georgia.

Jake Gimbel Trust
c/o Wells Fargo Bank
525 Market Street, 17th Floor
San Francisco, CA 94163
Application address: 555 South Flower, Sixth Floor,
Los Angeles, CA 90071;
Phone: (213) 253-7216
Contact: Ms. Minh Lee
Limitations: Loans to male students studying for graduate degrees in selected colleges and universities in California.

Gravity Research Foundation
41 Kirkland Circle
Wellesley Hills, MA 02181
Application address: 7920 Rolling Knolls Drive,
Cincinnati, OH.
Contact: Dr. Louis Witten, Vice President
Limitations: Awards to individuals for essays on the subject of gravitation.

Sidney H. & Mary L. Langille Gray Family
Scholarship Fund
c/o The Massachusetts Company, Inc.
99 High Street
Boston, MA 02110
Limitations: Awards scholarships to residents
of MA who are members of middle-income
families.

Carl M. Hansen Foundation, Inc.
1600 Washington Building
Spokane, WA 99204
Contact: Scott B. Lukins, Trustee
Limitations: Scholarships awarded to students
in the field of engineering.

Dane G. Hansen Foundation
P.O. Box 187
Logan, KS 67646
Phone: (913) 689-4832
Contact: Dane G. Bales, President
Limitations: Scholarships to graduates of
high schools in central or northwest KS; post-
graduate scholarships for theology, medical
and dental students from other areas.

Phil Harden Foundation
c/o Citizens National Bank
P.O. Box 911
Meridian, MS 39302
Application address: P.O. Box 3429, Merid-
ian, MS 39301;
Phone: (601) 483-4282
Contact: C. Thompson Wacaster, Vice Presi-
dent
Limitations: Limited to student loans only to
residents of Mississippi.

The Harding Foundation
Harding Foundation Building
P.O. Box 1130-Fifth and Hidalgo
Raymondville, TX 78580
Phone: (512) 689-2706
Contact: Glenn W. Harding, President
Limitations: Scholarships primarily to
seminary students after the student is enrolled
in the seminary school.

H. H. Harris Foundation
200 West Adams Street, Suite 2905
Chicago, IL 60606-5208
Phone: (312) 346-7900
Contact: John Hough, Manager
Limitations: Scholarships and other forms of
educational aid to students and professionals in
the metallurgical and casting of metals field.

Harvey Foundation, Inc.
First Federal Building, Suite 507
1519 Ponce de Leon Avenue
Santurce, PR 00909
Contact: Arthur J. Harvey, Jr, President
Limitations: Scholarships only to residents of
Puerto Rico.

Health Careers Foundation
c/o Amcore Bank
P.O. Box 1537
Rockford, IL 61110
Application address: 6729 Millbrook Drive,
Rockford, IL 61110.
Contact: Carolyn Kobler
Limitations: Educational grants to residents of
Illinois pursuing a career in health care.

Heed Ophthalmic Foundation
c/o First National Bank of Chicago
One First National Plaza, Suite 0111
Chicago, IL 60670-0111
Phone: (312) 732-5771
Contact: Margaret Venables
Limitations: Fellowships to men and women of exceptional ability who desire to further their education in the field of diseases of the eye and surgery, or to conduct research in ophthalmology.

Heily Foundation
c/o Security Pacific Bank Washington
777 108th Avenue, N.E., Suite 360
Bellevue, WA 98004
Contact: John Heily
Limitations: Scholarships and interest-free and low-interest student loans for attendance at a post-secondary educational institution.

The Hellenic Foundation
P.O. Box 7224
York, PA 17404
Contact: John F. Grove, Jr., Trustee
Limitations: Scholarships for needy students to pay tuition, cost of books, and living expenses at any school, college or university.
Fannie and John Hertz Foundation
P.O. Box 5032
Livermore, CA 94551-5032
Phone: (415) 373-1642
Contact: Dr. Wilson K. Talley, President
Limitations: Graduate fellowships for students in engineering, applied science, the physical sciences and all other fields of science at specified nationwide institutions; also provides scholarships to high school graduates from the San Francisco Bay Area.

Charles F. High Foundation
1520 Melody Lane
Bucyrus, OH 44820
Phone: (419) 562-2074
Contact: John R. Clime, Secretary-Treasurer
Limitations: Scholarships only to male residents of Ohio to attend Ohio State University.

Historical Research Foundation, Inc.
700 South Fourth Street
Harrison, NJ 07029
Phone: (201) 481-4800
Contact: Arthur Anderson, President
Limitations: Grants for historic or philosophic research and studies.

Cynthia E. & Clara H. Hollis Foundation
100 Summer Street
Boston, MA 02110
Application address: 35 Harvard Street, Brookline MA 02146.
Contact: Walter E. Palmer, Trustee
Limitations: Scholarships are for Massachusetts area residents, with preference given to students of the helping professions, such as nursing, social work, dental or medical technicians, etc., and vocational education students. Adult education and graduate study are also funded.

Esther Gowen Hook Music Fund
c/o Mellon Bank (East) N.A.
P.O. Box 7236
Philadelphia, PA 19101
Phone: (212) 553-3208
Contact: Pat Kiling, Manager
Limitations: Scholarships to local students attending music school.

The Horbach Fund
c/o National Community Bank of New Jersey
P.O. Box 896
Maywood, NJ 07607
Limitations: Scholarships to needy, gifted, young people under the age of 20, residing in Connecticut, Massachsetts, New Jersey, New York or Rhode Island.

Jessie R. Horton Trust
P.O. Box 678
Portland, ME 04104-5017
Phone: (207) 774-8221
Contact: Gregory Maynard, Trust Department
Limitations: Educational assistance to Maine residents.

Howard Memorial Fund
500 East 62nd Street
New York, NY 10021
Contact: Gayle F. Robinson, Chairman, Scholarship Committee
Limitations: Scholarships only to residents of the greater Metropolitan New York area who are at least 14 years of age.

Huguenot Society of America
122 East 58th Street
New York, NY 10022
Phone: (212) 755-0592
Limitations: Awards scholarships for undergraduate education to descendants of Huguenots.

Humane Society of the Commonwealth of
 Massachusetts
177 Milk Street
Boston, MA 02109
Application address: 195 Dedham Street, Dover, MA 02030;
Phone: (508) 785-0071.
Contact: Charles F. Adams, Secretary
Limitations: Fellowships to residents of MA for medical education and research.

Ed E. and Gladys Hurley Foundation
c/o NCNB Texas National Bank
P.O. Box 830241
Dallas, TX 75283-0241
Phone: (214) 508-1935
Contact: John P. McKenna, Trust Officer
Limitations: Scholarships to theological students who are residents of Arkansas, Louisiana or Texas to attend the institution of their choice.

The Institute for Aegean Prehistory
c/o The Millburn Corporation
1270 Avenue of the Americas
New York, NY 10020
Contact: Malcolm H. Wiener
Limitations: Research grants to study Aegean preshistory with expectation of research and publication under the direct supervision and control of the Institute.

Institute for World Understanding of Peoples,
 Cultures & Languages
939 Coast Blvd., No 19DE
La Jolla, CA 92037
Phone: (619) 454-0705
Contact: Dr. B.W. and Dr. F.G. Aginsky
Limitations: Grants for research and education of "anthropological events affecting interrelationships in societies."

Institute Francais de Washington
380 Tenney Circle
Chapel Hill, NC 27514-3112
Phone: (919) 942-5271
Contact: Prof. Edouard Morot-Sir
Limitations: Award fellowships and prized to professors and students involved in topics of French literature and culture, and Franco--American literary, historical and cultural relations.

Institute of Current World Affairs, Inc.
 (also known as The Crane-Rogers Founda
 tion)
Four West Wheelock Street
Hanover, NH 03755
Phone: (603) 643-5548
Contact: Peter Bird Martin, Executive Director
Limitations: Fellowship to persons 35 years or younger for minimum two-year fellowship outside the U.S.

Agnes and Sophie Dallas Irwin Memorial
 Fund
Provident National Bank
1632 Chestnut Street
Philadelphia, PA 19103
Phone: (215) 585-5695
Limitations: Grants to teachers in private girls' schools who have earned the right to retire and to provide opportunities for travel, study and research.

Maria C. Jackson-Gen. George A. White
 Student Aid for Children of War Veterans
 Foundation
c/o U.S. National Bank of Oregon,
Trust Group
P.O. Box 3168
Portland, OR 97208
Phone: (503) 275-4456
Limitations: Scholarships and student loans only to U.S. Armed Forces veterans or children of veterans who are high school graduates or long time residents of Oregon and are studying at institutions of higher learning in Oregon.

Jehovah Jireh, Inc.
P.O. Box 795
Clifton Park, NY 29721
Phone: (518) 383-1864
Contact: Larry Deason, Director
Limitations: Scholarships to theological students.

Jewish Foundation for Education of Women
330 West 58th Street
New York, NY 10019
Phone: (212) 265-2565
Contact: Florence Wallach,
Executive Director
Limitations: Scholarships and loans to women who are legal residents of the greater New York City metropolitan area (a 50-mile radius which includes Long Island and New Jersey, but not Connecticut) and who are attending undergraduate or graduate school on a full-time basis.

Dexter G. Johnson Educational & Benevolent
Trust
900 First City Place
Oklahoma City, OK 73102
Phone: (405) 232-0003
Contact: Phil C. Daugherty, Trustee
Limitations: Educational loans limited to residents of Oklahoma.

Barbara Piasecka Johnson Foundation
c/o Danser, Balaam and Frank
Five Independent Way
Princeton, NJ 08540
Phone: (609) 921-1200
Contact: John Peach, Director
Limitations: Grants to defray expenses of scientific or artistic endeavors, including costs of equipment, supplies, tuition, basic living expenses, and related costs.

Myrna M. Johnson Memorial Trust
 Scholarship Fund
1515 Charleston Avenue
Mattoon, IL 61938
Contact: Michael Hagen, Vice President
Limitations: Scholarships to students who want to further their education in music, art or nursing.

David W. Jones Scholarship Fund
321 North Spring Avenue
St. Louis, MO 63108
Contact: Art Baebler
Limitations: Scholarships are available for students interested in pursuing a printing education.

Kaiulani Home for Girls Trust
c/o Hawaiian Community Foundation
222 Merchant Street, Second Floor
Honolulu, HI 96813
Phone: (808) 537-6333
Contact: Caroline Sharman, Scholarship Admin.
Limitations: Undergraduate scholarships to girls who are legal residents of Hawaii, with preference to those of Hawaiian or part Hawaiin ancestry, to attend colleges and universities in the United States, with emphasis on Hawaiin institutions.

The Kaltenborn Foundation
349 Seaview Avenue
Palm Beach, FL 33480
Contact: Rolf Kaltenborn, Trustee
Limitations: Research fellowships only to individuals conducting scholarly written publishable research in the theory and practice of communication-press, radio, TV, magazines, etc.

Kawabe Memorial Fund
 (also known as Harry S. Kawabe Trust)
c/o Seattle First National Bank, CSC-9
P.O. Box 3586
Seattle, WA 98124
Phone: (206) 358-3388
Contact: Rod K. Johnson, Vice President, Seafirst Bank
Limitations: Scholarships to residents of Alaska.

Lucille R. Keller Foundation
c/o Irwin Union Bank & Trust Company
500 Washington Street
Columbus, IN 47201
Limitations: Awards scholarships for higher education to Indiana residents.

Korean Cultural Center
10801 Main Street, Suite 200
Bellevue, WA 98004
Application address: The Korea Times,
426 Yale Avenue North,
Seattle, WA 98109;
Phone: (206) 622-2099.
Limitations: Higher education scholarships for students of Korean descent.

Kosciuszko Foundation, Inc.
15 East 65th Street
New York, NY 10021
Phone: (212) 734-2130
Fax: (212) 628-4552
Contact: Joseph E. Gore, President
Limitations: The foundation offers: domestic scholarships for Americans of Polish descent and study/research programs for Americans in Poland.

Samuel H. Kress Foundation
174 East 80th Street
New York, NY 10021
Phone: (212) 861-4993
Contact: Dr. Marilyn Perry, President
Limitations: The Kress Foundation administers Kress Fellowships for pre-doctoral candidates in the history of art and for independent advanced training in art conservation.

Milton and Hattie Kutz Foundation
Jewish Federation of Delaware
101 Garden of Eden Road
Wilmington, DE 19803
Phone: (302) 478-6200
Contact: Executive Director, Jewish Federation of Delaware.
Limitations: Scholarships only to Delaware residents who are freshmen; possible renewal of grant until completion of undergraduate program.

Albert and Mary Lasker Foundation, Inc.
865 First Avenue, Apt. 15E
New York, NY 10017
Phone: (212) 421-9010
Contact: Mary W. Lasker, President
Limitations: Awards to medical researchers.

Lillibridge-Grimson Rainbow Memorial
 Loan Fund Trust
2811 Cherry Street
Grand Forks, ND 58201
Contact: Maynard A. Morrison
Limitations: Student loans to females between the ages of 17 and 24 who have been members of the Order of Rainbow.

The Lincoln Foundation, Inc.
233 West Broadway, Suite 400
Louisville, KY 40202
Limitations: Scholarship loans for graduate study.

Franklin Lindsay Student Aid Fund
Texas Commerce Bank of Austin,
Trust Division
P.O. Box 550
Austin, TX 78789-0001
Phone: (512) 476-6611
Contact: Rebecca Gassenmayer,
Admin. Officer
Limitations: Undergraduate and graduate loans to students attending Texas colleges and universitites.

John D. and Catherine T. MacArthur Foundation
140 South Dearborn Street, Suite 700
Chicago, IL 60603
Phone: (312) 726-8000
Contact: Ruth Adams, Director
Limitations: Research and writing grants to individuals to explore peace and cooperation issues.

The Magale Foundation, Inc.
First National Bank of Shreveport
P.O. Box 21116
Shreveport, LA 71154
Phone: (318) 226-2382
Contact: Mary J. Fain, Treasurer
Limitations: Student loans only to residents of Arkansas, Louisiana and Texas.

Arthur & Ann Marciano Scholarship and
 Charity Trust
18 Baldwin Farms North
Greenwich, CT 06830
Phone: (203) 867-9127
Contact: Arthur & Ann Marciano
Limitations: Grants for higher education.

Masonic Educational Foundation, Inc.
1309 Masonic Temple Building
333 St. Charles Street
New Orleans, LA 70130
Contact: Jack Crouch, Grand Secretary
Limitations: Scholarships to residents of Louisiana.

Ernestine Matthews Trust
P.O. Box 39070
Washington, DC 20016-9070
Limitations: Scholarship awards granted only to applicants from the District of Columbia, Maryland, Pennsylvania, Virginia and West Virginia based upon financial need.

The Mayne Educational Fund
205 Oxford Place
Louisville, KY 40207
Application address: c/o Mayne Educational
Fund, P.O. Box 716, Swannanoa, NC 28778
Contact: K. Bartlett, Treasurer
Limitations: Awards scholarships for higher
education.

McDonald Memorial Fund Trust
c/o First National Bank of Warsaw
P.O. Box 1447
Warsaw, IN 46580
Limitations: Loans for high school, college or
professional studies.

Arthur B. & Anna McGlothlan Trust
American National Bank, Trust Department
St. Joseph, MO 64501
Phone: (816) 233-2000
Limitations: Scholarships are given to students who will attend a church related or affiliated college.

The McKnight Foundation
410 Peavey Building
Minneapolis, MN 55402
Phone: (612) 333-4220
Contact: Michael O'Keefe,
Executive Vice President
Limitations: Grants only to researchers in plant biology.

Herbert T. McLean Memorial Fund
c/o Allen Gibson
1012 East Front
Bloomington, IL 61701
Contact: Allen Gibson
Limitations: Awards scholarships for higher education to residents of Illinois.

William J. McMannis and A. Haskell McMannis Educational Fund
c/o Marine Bank Trust Division
P.O. Box 8480
Erie, PA 16553
Phone: (814) 871-9204
Contact: Sister M. Lawreace Antoun, SSJ,
Executive Director
Limitations: Scholarships for higher education only to students who are U.S. citizens.

Alexander & Ilse Melamid Charitable Trust
32 Washington Square West
New York, NY 10011
Limitations: Awards scholarships to students in NY unable to provide for their own financial needs.

Edward Arthur Mellinger Educational
Foundation, Inc.
1025 East Broadway
Monmouth, IL 61462
Phone: (309) 734-2419
Contact: Scholarship Committee
Limitations: Scholarships to undergraduate students and student loans primarily to graduate students residing in or attending institutions in the Midwest.

Michigan Agri-Business Educational Trust
2500 Kerry Street, Suite 104
Lansing, MI 48912-3657
Application address: Michigan State University, Ag. Hall, Room 1,
East Lansing, MI 48824; Phone:
(517) 353-9780
Contact: Dr. Clifford Jump
Limitations: Scholarships to students studying agri-business or a related field.

Mikesell Scholarship Fund
P.O. Box 1387
Warsaw, IN 46580
Contact: Robert Gephart, Trustee
Limitations: Awards scholarships for higher education for IN residents.

Nettie Millhollon Educational Trust Estate
309 West Saint Anna Street
P.O. Box 643
Stanton, TX 79782
Contact: Ed Lawson, Chairman
Limitations: Educational loans to needy residents of Texas.

Milwaukee Music Scholarship Foundation
c/o First Wisconsin Trust Company
P.O. Box 2054
Milwaukee, WI 53201
Phone: (414) 765-5908
Contact: M. Grefig
Limitations: Financial assistance to residents of Wisconsin who are needy, worthy, and talented , and wish to pursue training and education in the field of music.

Minnesota Foundation
1120 Norwest Center
St. Paul, MN 55101
Phone: (612) 224-5463
Contact: Paul A. Veret, President
Limitations: Scholarships to residents of Minnesota. Grants are limited by fund agreements.

The Berkeley Minor and Susan Fontaine
 Minor Foundation
c/o John L. Ray
1210 One Valley Square
Charleston, WV 25301
Limitations: Scholarships only to residents of West Virginia.

John Miskoff Foundation
665 North East 58th Street
Miami, FL 33137
Phone: (305) 754-5169
Limitations: Scholarship loans for students who have completed their sophmore year of college.

Morris Traveling Fellowship Fund
c/o First Interstate Bank
Trust Division, Tax Department
Logan, UT 84142
Application address: Landscape Architecutral Department, Utah State University
Logan, UT 84322
Contact: Dr. Richard E. Toth
Limitations: Awards traveling fellowships for architectural students.

The Mull Foundation
c/o Wachovia Bank & Trust Company, N.A.
P.O. Box 3099
Winston-Salem, NC 27150
Application address: The Mull Foundation, c/o Reverand Julian M. Aldridge, Jr., P.O. Box 923,
Morganton, NC 28655.
Limitations: Awards scholarships for college education to residents of NC.

The Mercedes M. Murphy Foundation
6550 Fannin, Suite 2323
Houston, TX 77030
Phone: (713) 795-4300
Limitations: Scholarships for educational purposes.

Mustard Seed Foundation, Inc.
2700 Hospital Trust Tower
Providence, RI 02903
Contact: Philip Barr, Esquire
Limitations: Awards scholarships for higher education to residents of RI.

The Native American Scholarship Fund, Inc.
3620 Wyoming Blvd., N.E., Suite 208-C
Albuquerque, NM 87111
Phone: (505) 275-9788
Limitations: Awards scholarships to Native Americans for the study of math, engineering, science, business, education and computers.

The Nehemiah Foundation
230 Wilson Pike Circle, P.O. Box 2036
Brentwood, TN 37027
Phone: (615) 373-1560
Contact: William Z. Baumgartner, Jr., President
Limitations: Grants to parents for their children's education.

Sarah S. Ollesheimer Fund, Inc.
c/o A. Kurtz
21 Wensley Drive
Great Neck, NY 11021-4916
Application address: Vivian Bartetta, 236 Sarles Street,
Mt. Kisco, NY 10549;
Phone: (914) 241-3848.
Contact: Vivian Bartetta, Secretary
Limitations: Awards scholarships to residents of NY.

Matred Carlton Olliff Foundation
P.O. Box 995
Wauchula, FL 33873
Application address: Box 385,
Wauchula, FL 33873;
Phone: (813) 773-4131
Contact: Mr. Doyle E. Carlton, Jr., Trustee
Limitations: Grants for scholarships primarily in Florida.

Panwy Foundation, Inc.
Greenwich Office Park, No. 9
10 Valley Drive
Greenwich, CT 06831
Phone: (203) 661-6616
Contact: Ralph M. Wyman, Vice President
Limitations: Scholarships for higher education.

Alicia Patterson Foundation
1001 Pennsylvania Avenue, N.W., Room 1250
Washington, DC 20004
Phone: (202) 393-5995
Add. Phone: (301) 951-8512
Contact: Margaret Engel, Executive Director
Limitations: Fellowships to U.S. citizens who are working professionally as print journalists. Must have at least five years experience as a print journalist.

Marion D. & Eva S. Peeples Foundation
c/o Bank One, Franklin
Franklin, IN 46131
Phone: (317) 736-2498
Contact: Michael Ramsey, Asst. Vice President
Limitations: Scholarships primarily to graduates of Indiana high schools to pursue studies in nursing or dietetics, or to obtain training in teaching industrial arts.

Willis & Mildred Pellerin Foundation
c/o A.A. Harman & Company
311 Baronne Street, 1st Floor
New Orleans, LA 70112
Phone: (504) 586-0581
Limitations: Scholarships for residents of Louisiana who are enrolled in a college or university in that state.

The Greg Persson Memorial
 Scholarship Fund
P.O. Box 731
Upton, NY 11973-0731
Limitations: Awards and scholarships for
college education.

The Endowment Fund of Phi Kappa Psi
 Fraternity, Inc.
510 Lockerbie Street
Indianapolis, IN 46202
Phone: (317) 632-5647
Limitations: Scholarship grants and awards
for higher education for undergraduate and
graduate students. Preference is given to
members of the Fraternity for equally qualified
applicants.

Phi Kappa Theta National Foundation
c/o Reverend J. Raymond Farret
6531 Beechmont Avenue
Cincinnati, OH 45230
Limitations: Scholarships only to members of
Phi Kappa Theta Fraternity.

Minnie Stevens Piper Foundation
GPM South Tower, Suite 200
800 NW Loop 200
San Antonio, TX 78216-5699
Phone: (515) 525-8494
Contact: Michael J. Balint, Executive Director
Limitations: Student loans for undergraduate
juniors or seniors, or graduate students who
are residents of Texas attending Texas
colleges, universities, or graduate schools.

The Piton Foundation
511 Sixteenth Street, Suite 700
Denver, CO 80202
Phone: (303) 825-6246
Contact: Mary Gittings or Phyllis Buchele
Limitations: Scholarships to residents of CO,
WY, UT, MT, ND and SD, with emphasis on
CO.

Poncin Scholarship Fund
c/o Seattle-First National Bank, Charitable
Trust Administration
P.O. Box 3586
Seattle, WA 98124
Phone: (206) 358-3388
Contact: Rod Johnson, Vice President
Limitations: Grants awarded to individuals
engaged in medical research in a recognized
institution of learning within the state of WA.

Stephen J. Potter Memorial
 Foundation, Inc.
R.D. 1, P.O. Box 376
Queensbury, NY 12804
Phone: (518) 793-3712
Contact: John Austin, Jr., Secretary-Treasurer
Limitations: Awards scholarships for higher
education to residents of NY state.

Herschel C. Price Educational Foundation
P.O. Box 179
Huntington, WV 25706
Phone: (304) 529-3852
Contact: E. JoAnn Price, Trustee
Limitations: Scholarships primarily to
undergraduates residing in West Virginia and/-
or attending West Virginia colleges and uni-
versities.

Price Foundation, Inc.
P.O. Box 672
Upland, CA 91786
Application address: c/o Barbara Biane, 190 West 14th Street,
Upland, CA 91786
Phone: (714) 985-7338.
Contact: Barbara Biane
Limitations: Awards student loans for higher education.

Quad City Osteopathic Foundation
c/o ERA Associate Counselors
6236 North Brady Street
Davenport, IA 52806
Phone: (319) 386-5204
Contact: Eugene Holst, President
Limitations: Scholarship awards to students in Iowa and Illinois pursuing a degree in the field of osteopathy.

Randolph Memorial Scholarship Trust
c/o Farmers Bank & Trust Company
301 Second Street
Henderson, KY 42420-3139
Limitations: Awards scholarships to residents of Kentucky.

The Bill Raskob Foundation, Inc.
P.O. Box 4019
Wilmington, DE 19807
Phone: (302) 655-4440
Contact: Patricia M. Garey,
1st Vice President
Limitations: Student loans to American citizens currently enrolled at accredited institutions as upperclassmen for the upcoming school year.

Spence Reese Scholarship Fund
c/o Security Pacific National Bank
P.O. Box 3189, Terminal Annex
Los Angeles, CA 90051
Application address: Boys & Girls Clubs of San Diego,
3760 Fourth Avenue, Suite 1,
San Diego, CA 92103;
Phone: (619) 298-3520
Contact: John W. Treiber,
Executive Director
Limitations: Scholarships awarded only to males currently attending their senior year in high school who are majoring in medicine, law, engineering or political science.

Betsy Barter Richardson Scholarship Fund
P.O. Box 38
Stonington, ME 04681
Phone: (207) 367-2781
Contact: Gordon A. Richardson, Trustee
Limitations: Scholarships to students enrolled in colleges or vocational schools in the state of Maine.

Rinker Companies Foundation, Inc.
1501 Belvedere Road
West Palm Beach, FL 33406
Phone: (407) 833-5555
Contact: Frank S. LaPlaca,
Assistant Secretary
Limitations: Scholarships to Florida residents with business or construction industry-related majors.

William G. Rohrer, Jr. Educational Foundation
c/o First Peoples Bank of New Jersey
P.O. Box 300
Haddon Township, NJ 08108
Phone: (609) 858-7561
Contact: James C. Ayrer, Vice President
Limitations: Financial assistance for higher education to those demonstrating financial need.

The Roothbert Fund, Inc.
475 Riverside Drive, Room 252
New York, NY 10115
Phone: (212) 890-3116
Contact: Jacob Van Rossum, Admin. Secretary
Limitations: Scholarships to students who are primarily motivated by spiritual values, with preference to those considering teaching as a profession; Applicants must be available for an interview in New York City.

John M. Ross Foundation
c/o Bishop Trust Company, Ltd.,
Hilo Branch
P.O. Box 397
Hilo, HI 96721
Limitations: Scholarships only to residents of the Island of Hawaii (Big Island).

Rotch Travelling Scholarship, Inc.
c/o Fiduciary Trust Company
175 Federal Street
Boston, MA 02110
Application address: Shepley & Bullfinch, 40 Broad Street, Boston, MA 02110
Phone: (617) 482-5270
Contact: Hugh Shepley, Secretary
Limitations: Grants to architects under thirty-- five years of age, with educational or professional experience from Massachusetts for foreign travel and study in architecture.

C. L. Rown Charitable & Educational Fund, Inc.
1918 Commerce Building
Fort Worth, TX 76102
Phone: (817) 332-2327
Contact: Elton Hyder, Jr., President
Limitations: Grants to Texas residents for higher education.

Julius Rudel Award Trust Fund
1800 West Magnolia Blvd.
Burbank, CA 91506
Application address: General Director, New York City Opera, State Theater, Lincoln Center, New York,
NY 10023.
Limitations: Scholarships for the study of opera.

Sachs Foundation
90 South Cascade Avenue, Suite 1410
Colorado Springs, CO 80903
Phone: (719) 633-2353
Contact: Morris A. Esmiol, Jr., President
Limitations: Graduate and undergraduate scholarships to black residents of Colorado.

Sapelo Island Research Foundation, Inc.
P.O. Box 1373
Brunswick, GA 31521
Application address: Sapel Island Research Foundation, 547 Broyles Street, S.E., Atlanta, GA 30312.
Phone: (404) 525-6444
Contact: Allan McGregor
Limitations: Scholarships only to Georgia residents for study in marine biology and marine research.

Scarborough Foundation
P.O. Box 1536
Midland, TX 79702
Phone: (915) 682-0357
Contact: Evelyn Linebery, President
Limitations: Scholarships primarily to residents of West Texas and southeast New Mexico.

Leopold Schepp Foundation
15 East 26th Street, Suite 1900
New York, NY 10010-1505
Phone: (212) 889-9737
Contact: Mrs. Edythe Bobrow, Executive Secretary
Limitations: Scholarships to students who are U.S. citizens enrolled on a full-time basis at an accredited college or university. Only one member of a family may apply at the same time. Under-graduate scholarships to individuals under 30, graduate scholarships to individuals under 40, and a limited number of postdoctoral fellowships to individuals in the arts and literature, medicine and oceanography.

Helen Martha Schiff Foundation
c/o Bank of California, N.A.
P.O. Box 3123
Seattle, WA 98114
Limitations: Scholarships primarily for residents of Washington.

Scholarships for Children of American Military Personnel
c/o Stanley Sloman Accountancy Corp.
16633 Ventura Blvd., Suite 1140
Encino, CA 91436
Application address: 136 South Fuller Avenue, Los Angeles, CA 90036;
Phone: (213) 934-2288.
Contact: Leora M. Ostrow, Secretary
Limitations: Awards scholarships to children whose parent served in the military forces in Southeast Asia and was missing-in-action, killed-in-action, or a prisoner-of-war.

The Scholarships Foundation, Inc.
Davies & Davies
50 East 42nd Street
New York, NY 10017
Application address:
P.O. Box 170, Canal Street,
New York, NY 10013.
Limitations: Scholarships to undergraduate and graduate students with priority given to those who do not fit into defined scholarship categories.

Gus Schultz Scholarship Foundation
Sandra S. Russell
117 West Rosette Avenue
Foley, AL 36535
Limitations: Awards scholarships to residents of Alabama.

Byron S. Schuyler Child Educational Fund Trust
c/o State Bank of Albany
One East Avenue
Rochester, NY 14638
Limitations: Awards scholarships to residents of New York.

Scripps Howard Foundation
P.O. Box 5380
Cincinnati, OH 45201
Phone: (513) 977-3035
Contact: Albert J. Schottelkotte, President
Limitations: Scholarships to professional print and broadcast journalists or students pursuing careers in same.

The Second Chance Foundation
c/o Cummings & Lockwood
3001 Tamiami Trail North, Suite 400
Naples, FL 33940-4196
Phone: (813) 267-8311
Contact: Lloyd S. Taylor, Trustee
Limitations: Awards scholarships primarily to residents of Florida.

The Abe and Annie Seibel Foundation
c/o United States National Bank,
Trust Dept.
P.O. Box 179
Galveston, TX 77553
Phone: (409) 763-1151
Contact: Judith T. Whelton, Trust Director,
United States National Bank
Limitations: Interest-free student loans to graduates of Texas high schools attending Texas colleges and universities.

Select Educational Trust
2424 Old Bullard Road
Tyler, TX 75701
Application address: P.O. Box 6580,
Tyler, TX 75701
Phone: (214) 595-98355.
Contact: Eleanor Stringer, Trustee
Limitations: Scholarships to residents of Texas.

Ben Selling Scholarship Loan Fund
c/o First Interstate Bank of Oregon, N.A.
P.O. Box 2971
Portland, OR 97208
Phone: (503) 225-2368
Contact: Charles K. Woodcock, Trust Officer
Limitations: Low-interest student loans to Oregon residents attending Oregon schools.

William A. and Mary A. Shreve
 Foundation, Inc.
c/o Robert M. Wood, Esquire
2640 Highway 70, Building 1
Manasquan, NJ 08736
Application address: Route 1, Box 408,
Wallingford, VT 05773; Phone: (802) 446-2513.
Contact: Dr. Clifford G. Pollock
Limitations: Scholarships primarily to students in New Jersey, Pennsylvania and Vermont.

Skidmore, Owings & Merrill Foundation
33 West Monroe
Chicago, IL 60603
Phone: (312) 641-5959
Contact: Lisa Westerfield,
Administrative Director
Limitations: Fellowships for research relating to architecture and/or architectural engineering.

Slocum-Lunz Foundation, Inc.
c/o South Carolina Marine Resources Research Institute
217 Fort Johnson
Charleston, SC 29412
Phone: (803) 762-5003
Contact: Dr. Victor G. Burrell, Jr., Chairman,
Scholarship Committee
Limitations: Scholarships, fellowships and research grants only to students of marine biology and closely related natural science.

Somerville Rotary Educational Fund
482 Broadway
Somerville, MA 02145
Phone: (617) 625-7604
Contact: Paul S. Kaufman, Clerk
Limitations: Awards scholarships to Massachusetts residents.

Special People in Need
500 West Madison Street, Suite 3700
Chicago, IL 60606
Phone: (312) 715-5000
Contact: Gary H. Kline, Secretary
Limitations: Awards scholarships to residents of Illinois

Antoinette J. St. Martin Humanitarian Trust 78
Lowther Road
Framingham, MA 01701
Application addresses: Arthur H. Jackson,
Univeristy of Massachusetts, Amherst, MA
01003; Phone: (413) 545-0801;
Linda DeGrassi, Elms College, Chicopee, MA
01005; Phone: (413) 598-8351.
Limitations: Scholarships for Massachusetts
residents.

Donald A. and Jane C. Stark
 Charitable Trust
5036 Willow Leaf Way
Sarasota, FL 33583
Contact: B. Wade White, Trustee
Limitations: Grants for student scholarships.

State Industries Foundation
P.O. Box 307, Old Ferry Road
Ashland City, TN 37015
Phone: (615) 244-7040
Contact: Joseph P. Lanier
Limitations: Awards scholarships to students
in TN.

The Statler Foundation
Statler Towers, Suite 508
Buffalo, NY 14202
Phone: (716) 852-1104
Contact: Peter J. Crotty, Chairman
Limitations: Scholarships to students of hotel
or food service management.

Steinbach Foundation
c/o U.S. National Bank of Oregon
P.O. Box 3168
Portland, OR 97208
Limitations: Awards scholarships and loans to
residents of Oregon.

Emanuel Sternberger Educational Fund
P.O. Box 1735
Greensboro, NC 27402
Phone: (919) 275-6316
Contact: Ms. Brenda Henley,
Executive Director
Limitations: Educational loans only for legal
residents of North Carolina, for use by juniors,
seniors and graduate school students.

J. C. Stewart Memorial Trust
7718 Finns Lane
Lanham, MD 20706
Phone: (301) 459-4200
Contact: Robert S. Hoyert, Trustee
Limitations: Scholarships and student loans to
Maryland residents.

Ann Bradshaw Stokes Foundation
P.O. Box 29707
Dallas, TX 75229
Phone: (214) 528-1924
Contact: William S. Stokes, Jr.
Limitations: Scholarships to students majoring
in theater and drama at colleges and universi-
ties in Texas.

Straub Family Foundation
3100 Grand Avenue, Unit 71
Des Moines, IA 50312
Phone: (515) 255-3397
Limitations: Scholarships for residents of the
State of Iowa.

Gertrude S. Straub Trust Estate
c/o Hawaiian Trust Company, Ltd.
P.O. Box 3170
Honolulu, HI 96802
Application address: c/o
Hawaiian Community Foundation,
212 Merchant Street, Suite 300,
Honolulu, HI 96813; Phone: (808) 538-4540
Contact: Caroline Sherman, Administrator
Limitations: Scholarships to Hawaii high school graduates to attend mainland U.S. colleges or universities, with a major relating to international understanding and cooperation, and world peace.

Hattie M. Strong Foundation
Paramount Building
1735 I Street, N.W., Suite 705
Washington, DC 20006
Phone: (202) 331-1619
Contact: Barbara B. Cantrell, Secretary-Treasurer
Limitations: Non-interest-bearing college loans to American students who are within one year of completing their studies in a degree program from an accredited four-year college or graduate school.

Student Aid Foundation
c/o First National Bank of Atlanta
Trust Tax Department
P.O. Box 4148, MC705
Atlanta, GA 30302
Application address: 2190 Kinridge Road, Marietta, GA 30062.
Contact: Catherine W. Reynolds
Limitations: Student loans to women and girls who are legal residents of Georgia.

Sunnyside Foundation, Inc.
8609 Northwest Plaza Drive, Suite 201
Dallas, TX 75225
Phone: (214) 692-5686
Contact: Mary Rothenflue,
Executive Director
Limitations: Educational aid to underprivleged children residing in Texas to provide for their intellectual needs.

Otto Sussman Trust
P.O. Box 1374
Trainsmeadow Station
Flushing, NY 11370-9998
Contact: Edward S. Miller
Limitations: Education expenses to residents of New York, New Jersey, Oklahoma and Pennsylvania who are in need due to illness or death in their immediate family or some other unusual or unfortunate circumstance.

Sweet Foundation, Inc.
P.O. Box 9089
Winter Haven, FL 33883
Application address: 25 Spirit Lake Road, Winter Haven, FL 33880.
Contact: Richard W. Martineau
Limitations: Scholarships to students enrolled in an accredited college; "restricted as to upper income limits."

J. T. Tai & Company Foundation, Inc.
18 East 67th Street
New York, NY 10021
Contact: Managing Director
Limitations: Grants for medical education expenses.

Jewell L. Taylor Family Trust
America Bridge Bank
P.O. Box 2050
Fort Worth, TX 76113
Phone: (713) 884-4153
Contact: Suzanne Jennings
Limitations: Award scholarships to Texas residents for the study of home economics.

Teacher's Appreciation Grant, Inc.
 (also known as T.A.G., Inc.)
P.O. Box 540, Court & Third Streets
Brookhaven, MS 39601
Contact: Dr. George Brumfield
Limitations: Awards scholarships for postgraduate study to Mississippi teachers.

Teamsters BBYO Scholarship Fund
225 Park Avenue South
New York, NY 10003
Phone: (212) 254-8424
Contact: Martin Adelstein
Limitations: The purpose of the fund is to maximize opportunities for individuals in the Northeast region to attend B'nai Brith Youth Organization Summer Programs.

The John Edgar Thomson Foundation
The Rittenhouse Claridge, Suite 318
Philadelphia, PA 19103
Phone: (215) 545-6083
Contact: Gilda Verstein, Director
Limitations: Grants for education and maintenance of the daughters of deceased railroad employees until they are twenty-two years of age.

Treacy Company
Box 1700
Helena, MT 59624
Phone: (406) 442-3632
Contact: James O'Connell
Limitations: Scholarships for undergraduate study only to residents of, or students attending institutions of higher education in the northwest, including ID, MT, ND, SD and WA.

Elizabeth Tuckerman Foundation
Wells Fargo Bank
P.O. Box 63954
San Francisco, CA 94163
Application address: Wells Fargo Bank,
323 South Grand Street,
Los Angeles, CA 90071.
Contact: Ms. Jenkins, Administrator
Limitations: Scholarships for students who demonstrate scholastic ability and financial need.

Sam and Ida Turken Charitable Foundation
929 Fee Fee Road, Suite 200
Maryland Heights, MO 63043
Contact: Mark Turken, VP
Limitations: Awards scholarships for higher education, primarily to residents of Missouri and Tennessee.

Tyson Foundation, Inc.
2210 Oaklawn
Springdale, AR 72764
Contact: Cheryl J. Tyson
Limitations: Scholarships to students attending accredited colleges and universities and majoring in business, agriculture, engineering, computer science, or nursing.

Ullery Charitable Trust
c/o First National Bank & Trust Company of
 Tulsa
P.O. Box 1
Tulsa, OK 74193
Phone: (918) 586-5845
Contact: Marilyn Pierce, Trust Officer
Limitations: Scholarships awarded primarily
for study at Presbyterian theological semi-
naries.

The Vatra's Educational Foundation
c/o Bank of Boston
P.O. Box 1861
Boston, MA 02105
Application address: 517 East Avenue,
New York, NY 10017.
Contact: Peter D. Peterson, Chairman
Limitations: Scholarships only to students of
Albanian lineage or descent.

James M. Vaughn, Jr. Foundation Fund
MTRUST
P.O. Box 2266
Austin, TX 78780
Application address: 2235 Brentwood, Hous-
ton, TX 77019.
Contact: James M. Vaughn, Jr., President
Limitations: Fellowships only to scholars
pursuing research or publishing work in the
field of mathematical research format con-
jecture.

W. E. Walker Foundation
c/o Edward L. Brunni, Trustee
1675 Lakeland Drive, Riverhill Tower, Suite
400 Jackson, MS 39216
Phone: (601) 362-9895
Contact: W.E. Walker, Trustee
Limitations: Scholarships only to local residents attending graduate school, with a focus
on theology and human service.

Wenner-Gren Foundation for Anthropological
 Research, Inc.
220 Fifth Avenue, 16th Floor
New York, NY 10003
Phone: (212) 683-5000
Contact: Dr. Sydel Silverman, President
Limitations: Fellowships and research grants
to anthropology scholars, anywhere in the
world, affiliated with accredited institutions or
organizations.

James L. & Nellie M. Westlake
 Scholarship Fund
c/o Mercantile Bank, N.A.
P.O. Box 387
St. Louis, MO 63166
Application address: Local high school
counselor or the foundation at 111 South
Bemiston, Suite 412,
Clayton, MO 63105;
Phone: (314) 725-6410
Contact: Gary Clark
Limitations: Scholarships only to high school
seniors who are residents of Missouri.

Barbara Thorndike Wiggin Fund
c/o Maine National Bank, Trustee
400 Congress Street
Portland, ME 04104
Application address: P.O. Box 3555, Portland,
ME 04104;
Phone: (202) 775-1000.
Contact: Wil Sirois
Limitations: Loans to women pursuing careers
in nursing or teaching.

Milton L. Williams Trust
18 Brown Street
Salem, MA 01970-3728
Contact: Robert W. Welch
Limitations: Awards scholarships to residents
of MA.

J. B. & Garnet A. Wilson Charitable Trust
854 Howard Road
Waverly, OH 45690
Contact: J.B. Wilson, Manager
Limitations: Scholarships for studies only at Ohio colleges and universities.

Mark and Catherine Winkler Foundation
1900 North Beauregard Street, No. 308
Alexandria, VA 22311
Contact: Lynne Bromley, Assistant Treasurer
Limitations: Scholarships primarily to residents of Virginia.

David H. Winton Foundation, Inc.
Merrily Farm
South Woodstock, VT 05071
Contact: David H. Winton, President
Limitations: Scholarships based on financial need to students attending colleges and universities throughout the U.S.

Women's Seamen's Friend Society of
 Connecticut
74 Forbes Avenue
New Haven, CT 06512
Phone: (203) 467-3887
Contact: Rev. Henry Burdick III,
Executive Director
Limitations: Scholarships for the study of marine sciences in Connecticut or by Connecticut residents in schools out-of-state, and for dependents of Connecticut merchant marine seamen pursuing any course of study.

The Frank and Bea Wood Foundation
2304 South State Route 202
Tipp City, OH 45371
Phone: (513) 667-2222
Contact: John H. Holtvoigt, President
Limitations: Awards grants for research and preceptorships in homeopathic medicine.

William & Laura Younger Memorial Fund
354 Cherry Street
Denver, CO 80220
Phone: (303) 333-8126
Contact: Hyman A. Coggan
Limitations: Grants and loans for scholarships are restricted to needy adn qualified Jewish children seekin an education.

Youth Foundation, Inc.
36 West 44th Street
New York, NY 10036
Contact: Edward F.L. Bruen,
Vice President
Limitations: Scholarships for undergraduate study.

Hans and Clara Davis Zimmerman Foundation
c/o Hawaii Community Foundation
222 Merchant Street, Second Floor
Honolulu, HI 96813
Phone: (808) 537-6333
Contact: Caroline Sharman, Scholarships Admin.
Limitations: Scholarships to full-time students who are legal residents of Hawaii to complete studies at an accredited two- or four-year college or university that would lead to a careerin the field of medicine, nursing or a related health field.

THE FOUNDATION CENTER DIRECTORY

The Foundation Center is an independent national service organization established by foundations to provide an authoritative source of information on private philanthropic giving. The New York, Washington, DC, Cleveland and San Francisco reference collections operated by the Foundation Center offer a wide variety of services and comprehensive collections of information on foundations and grants. Cooperating Collections are libraries, community foundations and other nonprofit agencies that provide a core collection of Foundation Center publications and a variety of supplementary materials and services in areas useful to grantseekers.

REFERENCE COLLECTIONS OPERATED BY THE FOUNDATION

The Foundation Center
8th Floor
79 Fifth Avenue
New York, NY 10003
(212) 620-4230

The Foundation Center
Room 312
312 Sutter Street
San Francisco, CA 94108
(415) 397-0902

The Foundation Center
1001 Connecticut Avenue, N.W.
Washington, DC 20036
(202) 331-1400

The Foundation Center
Kent H. Smith Library
1422 Euclid, Suite 1356
Cleveland, OH 44115
(216) 861-1933

ALABAMA

Birmingham Public Library
Government Documents
2100 Park Place
Birmingham 35203
(205) 226-3600

Huntsville Public Library
915 Monroe Street
Huntsville 35801
(205) 532-5940

University of South Alabama
Library Reference Dept.
Mobile 36688
(205) 460-7025

Auburn University at
 Montgomery Library
7300 University Drive
Montgomery 36117-3596
(205) 244-3653

ALASKA

University of Alaska
Anchorage Library
3211 Providence Drive
Anchorage 99508
(907) 786-1848

Juneau Public Library
292 Marine Way
Juneau 99801
(907) 586-5249

ARIZONA

Phoenix Public Library
Business & Sciences Dept.
12 East McDowell Road
Phoenix 85257
(602) 262-4636

Tucson Public Library
101 North Stone Avenue
Tuscon 85726-7470
(602) 791-4393

ARKANSAS

Westlark Community College
 Library
5210 Grand Avenue
Fort Smith 72913
(501) 785-7000

Central Arkansas Library System
Reference Services
700 Louisiana Street
Little Rock 72201
(501) 370-5950

Pine Bluff-Jefferson County
 Library System
200 East Eighth
Pine Bluff 71601
(501) 534-2159

CALIFORNIA

Ventura County Community
 Foundation
Community Resource Center
1357 Del Norte Road
Camarillo 93010
(805) 988-0196

California Community
 Foundation
Funding Information Center
606 S. Olive Street, Suite 2400
Los Angeles 90014-1526
(213) 413-4042

Community Foundation for
 Monterey County
177 Van Buren
Monterey 93942
(408) 375-9712

Riverside Public Library
3581 7th Street
Riverside 92501
(714) 782-5201

California State Library
Reference Services, Room 301
914 Capitol Mall
Sacramento 94237-0001
(916) 654-0261

Nonprofit Resource Center
Sacramento Central Library
Downtown Plaza South Mall
Sacramento 95812-2036
(916) 449-2131

San Diego Community
 Foundation
101 West Broadway, Suite 1120
San Diego 92101
(619) 239-8815

Nonprofit Development Center
1762 Technology Drive, Suite 225
San Jose 95110
(408) 452-8181

Peninsula Community Foundation
1700 South El Camino Road
San Mateo 94402-3049
(415) 358-9392

Volunteer Center Resource Library
1000 East Santa Ana Blvd.
Santa Ana 92701
(714) 953-1655

Santa Barbara Public Library
40 East Anapamu
Santa Barbara 93101-1603
(805) 962-7653

Santa Monica Public Library
1343 Sixth Street
Santa Monica 90401-1603
(213) 458-8600

COLORADO

Pikes Peak Library District
20 North Cascade Avenue
Colorado Springs 80901
(719) 473-2080

Denver Public Library
Sociology Division
1357 Broadway
Denver 80203
(303) 640-8870

CONNECTICUT

Danbury Public Library
170 Main Street
Danbury 06810
(203) 797-4527

Hartford Public Library
Reference Department
500 Main Street
Hartford 06103
(203) 293-6000

D.A.T.A.
70 Audubon Street
New Haven 06510
(203) 772-1345

DELAWARE

University of Delaware
Hugh Morris Library
Newark 19717-5267
(302) 451-2432

FLORIDA

Volusia County Library Center
City Island
Daytona Beach 32014-4484
(904) 255-3765

Nova University
Einstein Library-Foundation
 Resource Collection
3301 College Avenue
Fort Lauderdale 33314
(305) 475-7497

Indian River Community College
Learning Resources Center
3209 Virginia Avenue
Fort Pierce 34981-5599
(407) 468-4757

Jacksonville Public Libraries
Business, Science & Documents
122 North Ocean Street
Jacksonville 32206
(904) 630-2665

Miami-Dade Public Library
101 West Flagler Street
Miami 33130
(305) 375-2665

Orlando Public Library
Orange County Library System
101 East Central Blvd.
Orlando 32801
(407) 425-4694

Selby Public Library
1001 Blvd. of the Arts
Sarasota 34236
(813) 951-5501

Tampa Hillsborough County
 Public Library System
900 North Ashley Drive
Tampa 33602
(813) 223-8865

Community Foundation of Palm
 Beach and Martin Counties
324 Datura Street
West Palm Beach 33401
(407) 659-6800

GEORGIA

Atlant-Fulton Public Library
Foundation Collection-Ivan
  Allen Department
1 Margaret Mitchell Square

Atlanta 30303-1089
(404) 730-1900

HAWAII

Hawaii Community Foundation
Hawaii Resource Room
222 Merchant Street
Honolulu 96813
(808) 537-6333

University of Hawaii
Thomas Hale Hamilton Library
2550 The Mall
Honolulu 96822
(808) 956-7214

IDAHO

Boise Public Library
715 South Capitol Blvd.
Boise 83702
(208) 384-4024

Caldwell Public Library
1010 Dearborn Street
Caldwell 83605
(208) 459-3242

ILLINOIS

Belleville Public Library
121 East Washington Street
Belleville 62220
(618) 234-0441

Donors Forum of Chicago
53 W. Jackson Blvd., Room 430
Chicago 60604
(312) 431-0265

Evanston Public Library
1703 Orrington Avenue
Evanston 60201
(708) 866-0305

Sangamon State University
  Library
Shepherd Road
Springfield 62794-9243
(217) 786-6633

INDIANA

Allen County Public Library
900 Webster Street
Fort Wayne 46802
(219) 424-7241

Indiana Univesity Northwest
  Library
3400 Broadway
Gary 46408
(219) 980-6582

Indianapolis-Marion County
  Public Library
40 East St. Clair Street
Indianapolis 46206
(317) 269-1733

IOWA

Cedar Rapids Public Library
Funding Information Center
500 First Street, N.E.
Cedar Rapids 52401
(319) 398-5123

Southwestern Community
  College
Learning Resource Center
1501 West Townline Road
Creston 50801
(515) 782-7081 ext. 262

Public Library of Des Moines
100 Locust Street
Des Moines 50308
(515) 283-4152

KANSAS

Topeka Public Library
1515 West Tenth Street
Topeka 66604
(913) 233-2040

Wichita Public Library
223 South Main
Wichita 67202
(316) 262-0611

KENTUCKY

Western Kentucky University
Helm-Cravens Library
Bowling Green 42101-3576
(502) 745-6125

Louisville Free Public Library
301 York Street
Louisville 40203
(502) 561-8617

LOUISIANA

East Baton Rouge Parish Library
Centroplex Branch
120 St. Louis Street
Baton Rouge 70802
(504) 389-4960

Beauregard Parish Library
205 South Washington Avenue
De Ridder 70634
(318) 463-6217

New Orleans Public Library
Business and Science Division
219 Loyola Avenue
New Orleans 70140
(504) 596-2580

Shreve Memorial Library
424 Texas Street
Shreveport 71120-1523
(318) 226-5894

MAINE

University of Southern Maine
Office of Sponsored Research
246 Deering Avenue, Room 628
Portland 04103
(207) 780-4871

MARYLAND

Enoch Pratt Free Library
Social Science and History
  Department
400 Cathedral Street
Baltimore 21201
(301) 396-5320

Carroll County Public Library
Government and Funding
 Information Center
50 East Main Street
Westminster 21157
(301) 848-4250

MASSACHUSETTS

Associated Grantmakers of
 Massachusetts
294 Washington Street
Suite 840
Boston 02108
(617) 426-2608

Boston Public Library
666 Boylston Street
Boston 02117
(617) 536-5400

Western Massachusetts Funding
 Resource Center
Campaign for Human Development
65 Elliot Street
Springfield 01101
(413) 732-3175

Worcester Public Library
Grants Resource Center
Salem Square
Worcester 01608
(508) 799-1655

MICHIGAN

Alpena County Library
211 North First Avenue
Alpena 49707
(517) 356-6188

University of Michigan-
 Ann Arbor
209 Hatcher Graduate Library
Ann Arbor 48109-1205
(313) 764-1148

Battle Creek Community
 Foundation
One Riverwalk Centre
34 West Jackson Street
Battle Creek 49017
(616) 962-2181

Henry Ford Centennial Library
16301 Michigan Avenue
Dearborn 48126
(313) 943-2330

Wayne State University
Purdy-Kresge Library
5265 Cass Avenue
Detroit 48202
(313) 577-6424

Michigan State University
 Libraries
Reference Library
East Lansin 48824-1048
(517) 353-8818

Farmington Community Library
32737 West 12 Mile Road
Farmington Hills 48018
(313) 553-0300

University of Michigan-Flint
 Library
Reference Department
Flint 48502-2186
(313) 762-3408

Grand Rapids Public Library
Business Department
60 Library Plaza, N.E.
Grand Rapids 49503-3093
(616) 456-3600

Michigan Technological
 University Library
1400 Townsend Drive
Houghton 49931
(906) 487-2507

Sault Ste. Marie Area Public
 Schools
Office of Compensatory
 Education
460 West Spruce Street
Sault Ste. Marie 49783-1874
(906) 635-6619

MINNESOTA

Duluth Public Library
520 West Superior Street
Duluth 55802
(218) 723-3802

Southwest State University
 Library
Marshall 56258
(507) 537-7278

Minneapolis Public Library
Sociology Department
300 Nicollet Mall
Minneapolis 55401
(612) 372-6555

Rochester Public Library
11 First Street, S.E.
Rochester 55902-3743
(507) 285-8000

St. Paul Public Library
90 West Fourth Street
Saint Paul 55102
(612) 292-6307

MISSISSIPPI

Jackson-Hinds Library System
300 North State Street
Jackson 39201
(601) 968-5803

MISSOURI

Clearinghouse for Midcontinent
 Foundations
University of Missouri
Block School of Business
5110 Cherry Street, Suite 310
Kansas City 64112
(816) 235-1176

Kansas City Public Library
311 East 12th Street
Kansas City 64106
(816) 221-9650

Metropolitan Association for
 Philanthropy, Inc.
5615 Pershing Avenue
Suite 20
St. Louis 63112
(314) 361-3900

Springfield-Greene County Library
397 East Central Street
Springfield 65801
(417) 866-4636

MONTANA

Eastern Montana College Library
1500 North 30th Street
Billings 59101-0298
(406) 657-1662

Bozeman Public Library
220 East Lamme
Bozeman 59715-3579
(406) 584-4787

Montana State Library
Reference Department
1515 East 6th Avenue
Helena 59620
(406) 444-3004

NEBRASKA

University of Nebraska
106 Love Library
14th & R Streets
Lincoln 68588-0410
(402) 472-2848

W. Dale Clark Library
Social Sciences Department
215 South 15th Street
Omaha 68102
(402) 444-4826

NEVADA

Las Vegas-Clark County Library
 District
1401 East Flamingo Road
Las Vegas 89119-6160
(702) 733-7810

Washoe County Library
301 South Center Street
Reno 89501
(702) 785-4012

NEW HAMPSHIRE

New Hampshire Charitable Fund
One South Street
Concord 03302-1335
(603) 225-6641

Plymouth State College
Herbert H. Lamson Library
Plymouth 03264
(603) 535-2258

NEW JERSEY

Cumberland County Library
800 East Commerce Street
Bridgeton 08302-2295
(609) 453-2210

The Support Center
17 Academy Street, Suite 1101
Newark 07102
(201) 643-5774

County College of Morris
Masten Learning Resource Center
Route 10 and Center Grove Road
Randolph 07869
(201) 328-5296

New Jersey State Library
Governmental Reference
185 West State Street
Trenton 08625-0520
(609) 292-6220

NEW MEXICO

Albuquerque Community
 Foundation
6501 America's Parkway, N.E.
Suite 665
Albquerque 87110
(505) 883-6240

New Mexico State Library
325 Don Gaspar Street
Santa Fe 87503
(505) 827-3824

NEW YORK

New York State Library
Cultural Education Center
Humanities Section
Empire State Plaza
Albany 12230
(518) 474-5355

Suffolk Cooperative Library System
627 North Sunrise Service Road
Bellport 11713
(516) 286-1600

New York Public Library
Bronx Reference Center
2556 Bainbridge Avenue
Bronx 10458
(212) 220-6575

Brooklyn in Touch
One Hanson Place
Room 2504
Brooklyn 11243
(718) 230-3200

Buffalo and Erie County Public
 Library
Lafayette Square
Buffalo 14202
(716) 858-7103

Huntington Public Library
338 Main Street
Huntington 11743
(516) 427-5165

Queens Borough Public Library
89-11 Merrick Blvd.
Jamaica 11432
(718) 990-0700

Levittown Public Library
One Bluegrass Lane
Levittown 11756
(516) 731-5728

SUNY/College at Old Westbury
 Library
223 Store Hill Road
Old Westbury 11568
(516) 876-3156

Adriance Memorial Library
93 Market Street
Poughkeepsie 12601
(914) 485-3445

Rochester
Business Division
115 South Avenue
Rochester 14604
(716) 428-7328

Onondaga County
 at the Galleries
447 South Salina Street
Syracuse 13202-2494
(315) 448-4636

White Plains
100 Martine Avenue
White Plains 10601
(914) 422-1480

NORTH CAROLINIA

Asheville-Buncomb Technical
 Community College
Learning Resources Center
340 Victoria Road
Asheville 28802
(704) 254-1921 ext. 300

The Duke Endowment
200 South Tryon Street
Suite 1100
Charlotte 28202
(704) 376-0291

Durham County Library
300 North Roxboro Street
Durham 27702
(919) 560-0100

North Carolina State Library
109 East Jones Street
Raleigh 27611
(919) 733-3270

The Winston-Salem Foundation
310 West 4th Street, Suite 229
Winston-Salem 27101-2889
(919) 725-2382

NORTH DAKOTA

North Dakota State University
The Library
Fargo 58105
(701) 237-8886

OHIO

Stark County District Library
715 Market Avenue North
Canton 44702-1080
(216) 452-0665

Public Library of Cincinnati and
 Hamilton County
Education Department
800 Vine Street
Cincinnati 45202-2071
(513) 369-6940

Columbus Metropolitan Library
96 South Grant Avenue
Columbus 43215
(614) 645-2590

Dayton and Montgomery County
 Public Library
Grants Information Center
215 East Third Street
Dayton 45402-2103
(513) 227-9500 ext. 211

Toledo-Lucas County Public
 Library
Social Science Department
325 Michigan Street
Toledo 43623-1614
(419) 259-5245

Ohio University-Zanesville
Community Education and
 Development
1425 Newark Road
Zanesville 43701
(614) 453-0762

OKLAHOMA

Oklahoma City University Library
2501 North Blackwelder
Oklahoma City 73106
(405) 521-5072

Tulsa City-County Library System
400 Civic Center
Tulsa 74103
(918) 596-7944

OREGON

Oregon Institute of Technology
 Library
3201 Campus Drive
Klamath Falls 97601-8801
(503) 885-1772

Pacific Non-Profit Network
Grantsmanship Resource Library
33 North Central, Suite 211
Medford 97501
(503) 779-6044

Multnomah County Library
Government Documents Room
801 S.W. Tenth Avenue
Portland 97205-2597
(503) 248-5123

Oregon State Library
State Library Building
Salem 97310
(503) 378-4277

PENNSYLVANIA

Northampton Community College
Learning Resources Center
3835 Green Pond Road
Bethlehem 18017
(215) 861-5360

Erie County Public Library
3 South Perry Square
Erie 16501
(814) 451-6927

Dauphin County Library System
101 Walnut Street
Harrisburg 17101
(717) 234-4961

Lancaster County Public Library
125 North Duke Street
Lancaster 17602
(717) 394-2651

The Free Library of Philadelphia
Logan Square
Philadelphia 19103
(215) 686-5423

University of Pittsburgh
Hillman Library
Pittsburgh 15260
(412) 648-7722

Economic Development Council
 of Northeastern Pennsylvania
1151 Oak Street
Pittston 18640
(717) 655-5581

RHODE ISLAND

Providence Public Library
Reference Department
150 Empire Street
Providence 02903
(401) 521-7722

SOUTH CAROLINA

Charleston County Library
404 King Street
Charleston 29403
(803) 723-1645

South Carolina State Library
Reference Department
1500 Senate Street
Columbia 29211
(803) 734-8666

SOUTH DAKOTA

Nonprofit Grants Assistance Center
Business and Education Institute,
 East Hall
Dakota State University
Madison 57042
(605) 256-5555

South Dakota State Library
800 Governors Drive
Pierre 57501-2294
(605) 773-5070
(800) 592-1841 SD Residents

Sioux Falls Area Foundation
141 North Main Avenue, Suite 500
Sioux Falls 57102-1134
(605) 336-7055

TENNESSEE

Knoxville-Knox County Public
 Library
500 West Church Avenue
Knoxville 37902
(615) 544-5750

Memphis & Shelby County Public
 Library
1850 Peabody Avenue
Memphis 38104
(901) 725-8877

Public Library of Nashville and
 Davidson County
8th Avenue North and Union Street
Nashville 37203
(615) 862-5843

TEXAS

Community Foundation of Abilene
Funding Information Library
500 North Chestnut, Suite 1509
Abilene 79604
(915) 676-3883

Amarillo Area Foundation
700 1st National Place One
800 South Fillmore
Amarillo 79101
(806) 376-4521

Corpus Christi State University
 Library
6300 Ocean Drive
Corpus Christi 78412
(512) 994-2608

Dallas Public Library
Grants Information Service
1515 Young Street
Dallas 75201
(214) 670-1487

El Paso Community Foundation
1616 Texas Commerce Building
El Paso 79901
(915) 533-4020

Texas Christian University Library
Funding Information Center
Fort Worth 76129
(817) 921-7664

Houston Public Library
Bibliographic Information Center
500 McKinney Avenue
Houston 77002
(713) 236-1313

Lubbock Area Foundation
502 Texas Commerce Bank
 Building
Lubbock 79401
(806) 762-8061

Funding Information Center
507 Brooklyn
San Antonio 78215
(512) 227-4333

UTAH

Salt Lake City Public Library
Business and Science Department
209 East Fifth South
Salt Lake City 84111
(801) 363-5733

VERMONT

Vermont Dept. of Libraries
Reference Services
109 State Street
Montpelier 05609
(802) 828-3268

VIRGINIA

Hampton Public Library
Grants Resources Collection
4207 Victoria Blvd.
Hampton 23669
(804) 727-1154

Richmond Public Library
Business, Science &
 Technology
101 East Franklin Street
Richmond 23219
(804) 780-8223

Roanoke City Public Library
 System
Central Library
706 South Jefferson Street
Roanoke 24016
(703) 981-2477

WASHINGTON

Seattle Public Library
1000 Fourth Avenue
Seattle 98104
(206) 386-4620

Spokane Public Library
Funding Information Center
West 906 Main Avenue
Spokane 99201
(509) 838-3364

Greater Wenatchee Community
 Foundation at the Wenatchee
 Public Library
310 Douglas Street
Wenatchee 98807
(509) 662-5021

WEST VIRGINIA

Kanawha County Public Library
123 Capital Street
Charleston 25304
(304) 343-4646

WISCONSIN

University of Wisconsin-Madison
Memorial Library
728 State Street
Madison 53706
(608) 262-3242

Marquette University Memorial
 Library
1415 West Wisconsin Avenue
Milwaukee 53233
(414) 288-1515

WYOMING

Laramie County Community
 College Library
1400 East College Drive
Cheyenne 82007-3299
(307) 778-1205

Teton County Library
Community Resource Library
320 South King Street
Jackson 83001
(307) 733-2164

AUSTRALIA

ANZ Executors & Trustees Co., Ltd.
91 William Street, 7th Floor
Melbourne VIC 3000
(03) 648-5764

CANADA

Canadian Centre for Philanthropy
1329 Bay Street, Suite 200
Toronto, Ontario M5R 2C4
(416) 515-0764

ENGLAND

Charities Aid Foundation
114/118 Southampton Row
London WC1B 5AA
(71) 831-7798

JAPAN

Foundation Library Center
 of Japan
Elements Shinjuku Bldg, 3F
2-1-14 Shinjuku, Shinjuku-ku
Tokyo 160
(03) 350-1857

MEXICO

Biblioteca Benjamin Franklin
American Embassy, USICA
Londres 16
Mexico City 6, D.F. 06600
(905) 211-0042

PUERTO RICO

University of Puerto Rico
Ponce Technological College
 Library
Box 7186
Ponce 00732
(809) 844-8181

Universidad Del Sagrado
 Corazon
M.M.T. Guevarra Library
Correo Calle Loiza
Santurce 00914
(809) 728-1515 ext. 357

20.

FEDERAL ASSISTANCE FOR THE ARTS AND HUMANITIES

****

There are two federal endowment agencies for the arts and the humanities. By far, the largest is the National Endowment for the Arts. We will discuss this federal agency first and then examine the other, The National Endowment for the Humanities, later in this chapter.

An independent federal government agency, the National Endowment (NEA) for the Arts was created by Congress to encourage and support American art and artists of all aesthetics. It awards grants and provides leadership and advocacy activities for artists. Funding supports art activities, American arts organizations and individual artists.

The Mission Statement of the NEA is as follows:

o   to foster the excellence, diversity and vitality of the arts in the United States; and
o   to help broaden the availability and appreciation of such excellence, diversity and vitality.

Part of this mission is, of course, to not impose any singular aesthetic viewpoint, under any circumstance, upon an artist or attempt to direct his or her content. In recent years, one artist was publicly dragged through the press regarding this matter as one Senator imposed his judgement upon the artist's work and attempted to re-direct funding because of its content.

Subsequently, this became a matter of editorial concern at hundreds of newspapers and talk shows across America. Now, I neither advocate nor condone pornographic work, whether it is considered art or not, but either the NEA must narrow its mission statement or it should aggressively challenge any vote-seeking politician on the basis that it is, indeed, fulfilling its congressional imperative through its funding practices.

An artist is not usually a normal or average person. Take aside the fact that artists have exceptional talent in one or more areas, something that immediately places them a cut above the typical individual. Artists usually struggle through their lives successfully or unsuccessfully communicating a point of view or vision. While hobbyists might enjoy writing a poem or painting a bowl of fruit, the artist might often be driven or obsessed with the communication of an ideal. The NEA has existed and should exist to help the artist communicate his or her dream or ideal. If that dream or ideal happens to be a perverse abomination, then it will probably die through public negligence on its own; this can take several forms, of which most prominently, of course, is commercial unviability. The public will either buy it or not. The NEA's job is to assist the artist to survive while communicating that viewpoint. Art generally outlasts politics in the long run, anyway. Go to any museum or library, if you don't believe me, and see for yourself.

Further, whenever politics has taken the form of censorship, it fails. Threats of cutting off funding, in order to propel an opinion into the media spotlight, fall between threatening one's child for being bad (and grounding him or her) and Nazi book-burning. The artist is already suppressed in a society. He or she will succeed or fail, whether an NEA exists or not. Historically, artists have been funded by patrons, not a government agency. But, American artists have been repressed since the 17th century and have lagged behind their European, African and Oriental counterparts. (If not, why have so many artists sought to study overseas?) The NEA does exist, does provide funding for artists and should continue to do so without political interference.

Far worse investments of taxpayer money have been made to bail out the savings and loan associations, to cover losses on federally guaranteed housing and student loans, and on defaulted SBA-loan guarantees. And, those financial losses have been far greater that the NEA has collectively ever seen since its formation. Don't let one mistake, if it is or was one, become an attempt to bring the American artist into line with, and gain approval from, a special interest group. Artists work faster, perhaps even better, in a nurturing environment. They are already struggling with a vision. Need they also contend with politicians who play a children's game of "you can have it, no can't; here it is, oops, you can't have it"? It may sound like a silly game, but try working under that kind of insanity!

BACKGROUND INFORMATION

The NEA awards grants to individual American artists and arts groups through artistic programs and different fundings. Private /public partnerships provide arts organizations; every federal dollar awarded must be matched with one non-federal dollar. In most cases, artist fellowships are awarded on a non-matching basis.

In 1965 there were five state arts agencies with combined appropriations of $2.7 million. By 1990 arts agencies were available in all states and territories, with a combined appropriation of $285 million. Seven regional organizations, with combined budgets of $18 million, blanket the U.S. and provide multi-state support. There are approximately 3,000 arts councils, 600 of which have full-time staff. While the NEA awarded organization grants of $119 million in 1989, private sector funds generated $1.36 billion for arts organizations. Overall private-sector funding grew to $7.49 billion in 1989.

Since 1965 fifty-six professional nonprofit theatres have grown to more than 400 today. Professional dance companies jumped from thirty-seven in 1965 to more than 250 today; the dance audience today has reached over 16 million. Over the past two decades the NEA has supported hundreds of museum exhibitions, has established approximately 300 visual arts organizations and more than seventy Media Arts Centers, and has encouraged the growth in the operatic field, jazz, small press book publishers, public television and multidisciplinary arts presentations.

TYPES OF ENDOWMENTS

The NEA provides the following financial assistance:

1.   Fellowships to artists of exceptional talent and who are citizens or permanent U.S. residents.

2.   Matching grants to nonprofit, tax-exempt organizations and projects of the highest artistic level and merit. By matching is meant that the

organization must independently raise at least half the cost of the project and match the NEA's Funding on at least a one-to-one basis.

3.   Matching grants to state and local arts agencies and regional arts groups.

There are some restrictions with the NEA's funding policies. Program guidelines show a preference for existing, rather than new, organizations, and for organizations that have demonstrated a value to their communities and their ability to attract private-sector funding. The NEA does not award grants to cover your deficits. Grants are awarded generally for one year; getting an award does not mean subsequent support.

Additionally, organizations must be tax-exempt and nonprofit. They must comply with various federal discrimination laws; must pay professional personnel, laborers and mechanics not less than minimum wage; and comply with the Drug-Free Workplace Act of 1988.

THE APPLICATION PROCESS

When applying for a grant, you should determine your basic eligibility from a description of the programs that follow. After deciding which program best describes your aesthetic activity, you should contact the appropriate NEA office in the directory at the end of this chapter and request the applicable application guidelines. These guidelines contain instructions, application forms and other important information about the NEA funding.

Once you've applied, your application proceeds through a six to eight month review process. As soon as it is received, your submission is sent, along with other applications in your category, to an advisory panel for review and recommendation. After reviewing your application, the panel either recommends

funding or does not. It may fund your project for less than the amount you requested. Panel recommendations for or against funding are passed on to the National Council on the Arts. This council makes final recommendations to the Chairman. On the basis of recommendations for funding, the Chairman makes the final decision on grant actions. Applicants are advised to not seek information about the status of their applications until they hear from the NEA.

Below are the various NEA funding programs, grants and contact telephone numbers for applications forms and instructions following each section. Remember, fellowships are generally awarded to those with exceptional talent and ability; grants are usually given to proven and outstanding organizations. At the end of this chapter is a directory of State Art Agencies, which you may contact for additional assistance and guidance.

Dance

Fellowships are available for choreographers who have shown work professionally for at least three years and have choreographed at least five works during his or her professional career, or for choreographers working in traditional forms, staged or adapted at least five works based on the treatment of traditional material. Most grants will be awarded for a two-year period at $10,000 per year; fewer grants of $7,000 will be awarded for a one-year period. The panel may also recommend a limited number of three-year fellowships at $15,000 per year.

Dance company grants are available to support a dance company's season, creative work, rehearsal time, touring, administrative projects and similar activities. Eligibility includes having a paid professional artistic and managerial staff, at least 20 weeks of rehearsals and/or performances per year and a three-year history of continuous operation as a professional company. Matching grants usually range between $10,000 and $300,000.

Dance companies can also obtain grants for touring and presentation through state and regional arts agencies.

Experienced sponsors can obtain grants of between $5,000 and $20,000 to present a dance company. Sponsors must have guaranteed fees to dance artists/companies for at least three years prior to application, must present a series of three or more professional dance companies or dance artists or a long-term engagement of two or more weeks during the current and upcoming seasons and have paid professional, administrative and technical staff. Your dance company may not apply on its behalf, but may, instead, apply to present other companies or dance artists.

For additional information, please contact the Dance Office of the NEA at (202) 682-5435.

Design Arts

Design arts can include architecture, landscape architecture, urban design and planning, historic preservation, interior design, industrial and product design, and graphic design.

USA fellowships of between $5,000 and $20,000 are granted to designers and other individuals working in design-related professions to study and travel independently within the United States. Applicant are considered either for outstanding contributions to the design field or if they demonstrate the potential for outstanding work in the future.

Individuals can also receive $5,000 to $10,000 grants for Design Innovation. These grants support professional designers who challenge the status quo, who through their project can advance design aesthetics, utility and/or economics by demonstrating an ability to improve the quality of life. Project grants, of up to $15,000, are also

available to individuals to advance design practice, theory, research and communication. These can include originating an exhibit or producing films on design or other similar projects.

Organizations are also eligible for the above project grants, as well as project grants for design education, conservation of heritage, and for design assistance for rural and small communities. Depending on the project grant, the size can range from $5,000 to $50,000.

For additional information, please contact the Design Arts office of the NEA at (202) 682--5437.

Expansion Arts

The Expansion Arts Program funds professionally directed arts organizations that reflect culturally diverse, inner-city, rural, or tribal communities. Only arts organizations that employ or serve artists are eligible. Matching grants are available for up to $50,000. Programs have different operational requirements, such as two or three years, and must have programs that benefit primarily artists.

Rural arts organizations may receive matching grants of up to $40,000 for more than three years when done in collaboration with state arts agencies. State arts agencies should apply as they then regrant the funds to approximately three to six rural arts organizations within each state. Approximately thirty Expansion Arts Organizations for specific arts education activities can receive up to $30,000 over a two year period for programs providing instructional activities to preschool and school-aged youths, kindergarten through twelfth grade.

For additional information, please contact the Expansion Arts office of the NEA at (202) 682-5443.

Folk Arts

Folk art grants are available for organizations and individuals. Folk arts can include music, dance, poetry, tales, oratory, crafts and various types of visual art forms. The program's main objectives are to preserve and enhance America's multicultural heritage and to make it more available to a wider public.

Exemplary master folk artists and artisans can receive one-time-only National Heritage Fellowships of $5,000. The panel reviews nominations on the basis of authenticity, excellence and significance within a particular artistic tradition. You must be nominated for this fellowship, worthy of national recognition, should have a record of ongoing artistic accomplishment and be actively participating in that art form.

Organizations can receive up to $40,000 in grants to help offer celebrations, festivals, exhibits instructional workshops, concerts, residencies and tours that present traditional arts and artists of the highest quality. Grants are also available to help produce radio or television programs or series, recordings, slide/tape presentations, and small publications for public distribution.

For additional information, please contact the Folk Arts office of the NEA at (202) 682-5449.

INTER-ARTS

The Inter-Arts Program supports multi-disciplinary arts presenting organizations which offer events to broad audiences, artists collaborating in the development of new inter-disciplinary work, and nationally significant projects which provide services and support the development of this field.

Presenting Organizations can receive matching grants of up to $50,000. The presenter must have at least two years of experience and full-time, paid professional administrative staff whose primary responsibility is presenting professional artists to the general public in a balanced seasonal format with events in two or more art forms.

Matching grants are also available for up to $50,000 to national service organizations and regional arts organizations that help presenters improve their ability to provide diverse, high-quality arts programming.

Individual artists can explore the boundaries between arts disciplines, traditions, and/or cultures with projects that receive non-matching grants of between $7,000 and $15,000. Projects should involve more than one art form. Organizations can receive matching grants for up to $30,000

Your organization can be funded up to $25,000 in matching grants to provide an artists' community or work place that provides studios and living space for artists. You must have rigorous policies and procedures for selecting and rotating artists, have a full-time, year-round professional staff, and have been in business for at least two years. Two or more organizations can also apply for matching grants up to $50,000 for the commissioning and presentation of new interdisciplinary works and related residency activity.

For additional information, please contact the Inter-Arts office of the NEA at (202) 682-5449.

Literature

Fellowships are available for published creative writers and literary translators of exceptional talents to set aside time for writing, research, travel or advancing their careers in various ways. Creating Writing Fellowships of $20,000 are available to poets and authors of fiction and creative non-fiction. Translators' fellowships of $10,000 or $20,000 (depending upon the length and scope of the project) are available for specific translation projects from other languages into English.

Matching grants are available to help fund and market literary magazines and provide assistance to noncommercial literary and university small presses. Magazines must have a history of publishing contemporary creative writing of the highest quality and must have published at least three issues in the two calendar years prior to the application deadline. Matching grants range between $2,000 and $10,000 with the stipulation that 10 percent of the grant funds are paid to writers. Small presses must have published at least four volumes, of 24 pages or more, of poetry, fiction, plays, translation, or creative non-fiction during the past three years. Matching grants range from $2,000 to $25,000 depending on the past publishing volume. Funds for both of these programs have a restricted publishing use and may not be used to pay for office space, travel, or equipment.

Nonprofit organizations, literary centers and audience development projects can receive up to $20,000 in matching grants to help develop audiences, provide residencies or in other ways assist writers. Distribution projects can also receive from $4,000 to $65,000 for activities that increase public access to works of contemporary creative writing.

For additional information, please contact the Literature office of the NEA at (202) 682-5451.

Media Arts

Regional fellowships for independent film and video artists are available with grants up to $10,000 through the Independent Film and Videomaker Program. The NEA, the American Film Institute, state arts agencies, and private foundations and corporations contribute to this program. Fellowships are administered by regional media arts centers. At the end of

this chapter, please look for the directory of regional media arts centers.

Individual and organizations can compete, respectively for non-matching and matching funds, to fund the creation or completion of high quality film/video artworks. Projects can include documentary, experimental, animated and narrative works. Organizations can receive up to $75,0009 and individuals up to $35,000. However, the production assistance category is highly competitive and ten percent or less of all applicants are recommended for funding. You should have a history of critical recognition and support for your media work at the state, regional or national level.

Individuals and organizations involved in a single production or series for radio broadcast, or those who provide services such as conferences, workshops, seminars and publications can receive funding for their projects. Individual radio producers can receive a grant as large as $15,000. Organizations can receiving up to $50,000 in matching funds.

Matching fund grants are available to organizations for institutional film/video art support; to organizations that contribute to the support of media arts centers and artists; to help organizations locate, restore, preserve, and catalogue films of artistic and cultural value; to help organizations promote the growth and development of the media arts field.

For additional information, please contact the Media Arts office of the NEA at (202) 682--5452.

Museums

Museum professionals can receive fellowships up to $25,000 to conduct arts-related independent research or to travel, write, or in some other way improve their professional credentials. Fellowships can last from one month to a year, but do not cover study or research directed toward a degree. You must be currently employed full-time as a museum professional and have served on the staff of a museum for at least one year.

Museum grants are available to museums for various special projects. These can include helping museums preserve their collections by solving problems in climate control, security or storage; presentation of collections, educational programs; cataloguing of permanent collections; and special exhibitions. Grants may be as low as $5,000 for an exhibition or as high as $200,000 to implement a collection maintenance project.

For additional information, please contact the Museums office of the NEA at (202) 682-5442.

Music

Different fellowships are available in the music field. Fellowships are offered to help individual composers create or complete new work, for composers and their collaborators, for jazz musicians in their creative development, for jazz composers, for jazz study, for jazz special projects and for solo recitalists.

Individual composers can receive fellowships up to $25,000 to pay for their time, costs of copying and reproducing scores, studio expenses and other direct project costs. Composers and their collaborators, such as librettists, video artists, filmmakers, poets, and choreographers, can receive fellowships up to $35,000 to help create or complete collaborative works (the composer must submit the application). Professional jazz musicians can get fellowships up to $15,000 for rehearsals, performances, workshops and related expenses. Jazz composers may be eligible for up to $10,000 for the creation or completion of their new works, including arrangements and the reproduction of scores or parts of completed works. Aspiring jazz performers and composers can receive fellowships of up to $5,000 to

study with recognized professional artists of their choice in non-institutional settings. Individuals with innovative and exemplary projects of national or regional significance that benefit the jazz field but who are not eligible under other Jazz Fellowship categories may receive grants for not less than $5,000. Solo recitalists may receive grants for up to $15,000 to assist them with preparation and presentation costs, accompanist fees, management fees or expenses involved in the preparation of demonstration recordings.

Presenting organizations can receive matching grants up to $50,000 (most fall into the $5,000 to $10,000 range) to present chamber music ensembles; new music ensembles, soloists and duos; jazz ensembles, soloists and duos; solo recitalists and duos; any combination of the above; or with choruses or orchestras in a multi-music presentation.

Organizations supporting music festivals, with a track record of at least four different concerts in the past two seasons may be eligible for matching grants of between $5,000 and $50,000. Festivals must involve tow or more of these music genres: chamber music or new music, chorus, jazz, orchestra, opera-musical theater, or solo recitalists/duos.

Matching grants are also available to professional music ensembles. Chamber and Jazz ensembles can receive up to $20,000. Choruses can get up to $50,000. Orchestras may receive up to $300,000 as long as the matching grant does not exceed five percent of the organization's total budget.

Scholarships are available to support a musician's advanced training and education and applicant organizations can receive matching grants up to $65,000. Music organizations can receive matching grants up to $25,000 to help pay for a composer in residence while in collaboration with the music performing organization. Nonprofit organizations, soloists and duo performers can receive music recording grants up to $50,000 if they have a proven history of producing records or have letters of commitment from recording companies. Organizations devoted to the professional career development of solo music artists can receive matching grants of up to $60,000, provided they have at least ten artists on their roster and book at least three recitals annually for each.

Additional music special projects are available, especially those that serve the career development of artists, or provide services of a national scope to the field.

For additional information, please contact the Music office of the NEA at (202) 682-5445.

Opera-Musical Theater

Independent producers may find support in the development of new work through the New American Works/Individuals as Producers program. Matching grants can range has high as $45,000. Applicants must have demonstrated they are capable of producing opera-musical theater and also be U.S. citizens or permanent residents.

Organizations can receive matching grants up to $145,00 to create, develop, rehearse and produce new American opera and musical theater works. Professional companies can receive matching grants of at least $5,000 to provide support for their seasons of originally produced opera-musical theater. Regional touring companies can receive matching funds of up to $100,000 to present multiple performances in several geographic regions.

Special projects and services to the arts can obtain funding of at least $5,000 in matching grants. These projects are designed to support creative projects that enhance the development and growth of opera and musical theater or, in some other way, assist this area.

For additional information, please contact the Opera-Musical Theater office of the NEA at (202) 682-5447.

Theater

Fellowships are available to solo theater artists, playwrights, directors and stage managers.

Solo theater artists can receive up to $12,500 for activities that contribute to an individual's artistic growth. A solo theater artist can perform in these areas: puppeteering, mimes/movement theater artists, storytellers, monologists, clowns, new vaudevillians or in a similar solo artistic capacity.

Professional playwrights may be eligible to receive up to $35,000 (over a two year period) if they have had a play produced by a professional theater company within the past five years. Grantees may also receive $2,500 to defray the costs of a residency at a professional theater of the playwright's choice. Funds are to be used to enable the playwright to set aside time for writing, research, travel, or other activities that helps enhance their artistic vision.

Early career stage directors and stage managers of exceptional talent who work in not-for-profit theater may receive fellowships for direct support for work with senior professionals or for independent fellowship activities.

Professional not-for-profit theater companies, which produce high quality work of national or regional significance, may be eligible for up to $300,000 in matching grants. The applicant organization must have operated as a professional theater for at least three of the four years prior to the proposed grant period. Grants may be use to pay not more than half of the total artists' compensation.

Matching grants are also available for not-for-profit theaters, educational organizations and publishers to enhance national art resources. Presenters, state arts agencies, and regional arts organizations can obtain up to $75,000 in matching funds for tours and presentations.

Educational organizations can receive matching funds of $10,000 to $70,000 for professional theater training programs. Other organizations and publishers can receive more than $2,000 in matching grants for projects and/or specific services that assist professional not-for-profit theater on a national scale.

For additional information, please contact the Theater office of the NEA at (202) 682-5425.

Visual Arts

National Visual Artists Fellowships are available up to $15,000 to encourage the creative development of practicing professional artists of exceptional talent with demonstrated ability working in a wide range of styles and a variety of media. Such media can include: painting, sculpture, photography, crafts, printmaking, drawing, artists books, video, performance art, conceptual art, and new genres. A complementary program of regional fellowships award $5,000.

Visual artists organizations can receive matching grants of up to $50,000 (usually from $5,000 to $30,000) to support exhibitions, installations and other presentations of contemporary visual artists' work. Groups may also be funded to provide artists with access to working facilities, information and advisory services, lectures, seminars, and publications.

Forums such as noncommercial publications, visiting artists programs, residencies, conferences and symposia can be supported with matching grants for $25,000 or less. Organizations may also apply for matching grants up to $50,000 for public art projects; funding can be used to pay artists to create new works for specific sites or to plan for public art projects. Other special projects may be considered but interested organizations should fIrst contact the NEA's Visual Arts office.

For additional information, please contact the Visual Arts office of the NEA at (202) 682--5448.

State and Regional Programs

You will find a state arts agency in all 50 states and in six special jurisdictions, such as Guam and the District of Columbia. Nearly all are state government agencies. Your state arts agency provides a wide range of grants and services to artists, art organizations and the general public. Regional arts organizations advise states on providing a greater variety of arts programs and services to their state residents.

To help the state arts agencies carry out their approved state plans, the NEA awards block grants on a formula basis. By law, not less than 25 percent of the Art Endowment's program funds are allocated to state and regional arts agencies. Three-quarters of this amount is divided to each state in equal amounts. Half of the remainder is divided among the regional groups, with most of the other half divided among the states on the basis of their population level.

Many states award grants to assist the struggling and creative talent. You should contact your state arts agency and regional arts organization regarding any funding you or your organization may desire on a local level, found at the end of this chapter. For additional assistance, contact the NEA's state and regional program office at (202) 682-5429.

THE NATIONAL ENDOWMENT FOR THE HUMANITIES

In 1965 Congress enacted the National Foundation on the Arts and the Humanities Act of 1965, which also established the National Endowment for the Humanities (NEH), as an independent grant-making agency of the federal government. Its purpose is "to promote progress and scholarship in the humanities" and the NEH does this by supporting research, education and public programs in the humanities. Grants are made for educational programs, for fellowships and seminars, for research programs, to state programs, for preservation and access programs, and for public programs.

Basically, the NEH includes support for these disciplines: history, philosophy, languages, linguistics, literature, archaeology, jurisprudence, art history, ethics, comparative religions and social sciences. The NEH does not fund projects that are undertaken to obtain an academic degree (see Department of Education); projects that are covered by the National Endowment for the Arts, such as musical composition, dance, painting, sculpture, poetry, or short stories and novels; projects that persuade an audience to a particular political, philosophical, religious, or ideological point of view; projects that advocate a particular program of social action or change; or projects that examine controversial issues without taking into account competing perspectives.

Eligibility

Individuals, nonprofit associations, institutions and organizations may apply to the NEH for grants. Foreign nationals who have been legal residents in the United States for a period of at least three years immediately preceding the submission of the application may also apply.

You should obtain the NEH's current guidelines and descriptive materials regarding their programs two months in advance of the application deadline date. Deadline dates for receipt of applications vary throughout the year, depending on the program.

How Applications Are Evaluated

Find out about the program which describes your project. Get the appropriate guidelines and literature describing the program, its requirements and application form. Submit your proposal for a project to the correct Endowment funding category. The final decision can take up to six months.

Each application is evaluated by a knowledgeable person outside the NEH. He or she is asked for their judgement about the quality and significance of the proposed project. About 1,200 scholars, professionals in the humanities, and other experts serve on approximately 225 panels throughout the course of the year. In some cases a panelist's judgement may be supplemented by individual reviews solicited from specialists who have extensive knowledge of the specific subject area or technical aspects of the application under review.

NEH staff assemble the evaluators' advices, make comment on the significant issues of the project, fill in any remarks that may assist in a final decision and present the project proposal and review to the National Council on the Humanities. This twenty-six member board, nominated by the President and confirmed by the U.S. Senate, meet four times each year to advise the Chairman of the Endowment on various proposals submitted to them. The Chairman, a four-year presidential appointee, makes the final decision about funding, by taking into account the information provided by this review process.

ENDOWMENT PROGRAMS

As mentioned earlier, there are several areas supported by the NEH: education, fellowships and seminars, preservation and access, public programs, research programs, and state programs. Let's look at the individual programs within those categories.

Higher Education

These grants support national conferences, curriculum development efforts, core curriculum projects, and faculty study programs. Acceptable projects are those meant to foster the reinvigoration of teaching, especially those that improve the humanities preparation of new teachers at all levels, enhance foreign language teaching and promote the study of humanities in two-year institutions. Eligible applicants are two- and four-year colleges and universities, nonprofit academic associations, and cultural institutions, such as libraries and museums.

For further information, telephone: (202) 606-8380.

Elementary and Secondary Education in the Humanities

These grants are designed to improve teaching of the humanities in elementary and secondary school projects. Grants usually go programs to support national and regional summer institutes, state and local collaborative projects and other special projects. The NEH encourages projects about Western and world civilization, English and American literature, and foreign language study. Eligible applicants are public and private elementary and secondary schools, school systems, colleges and universities, museums and other nonprofit educational and cultural organizations.

For further information, telephone: (202) 606-8377

Other Educational Programs

Teachers can also apply to the NEH for various humanities and foreign language study programs. The Reader's Digest Teacher-Scholar Program offers teachers for an academic year of full-time independent study in one discipline of the humanities. Telephone: (202) 606-8377.

Elementary and secondary school teachers can also apply for a six week fellowship of $3,000 for independent study in the humanities. School principals and librarians may also apply. Call or write to:

Independent Study in the Humanities P.O. Box 135 Ashton, Maryland 20861 Telephone: (202) 347-4171

Elementary and secondary school teachers may also apply for a foreign language fellowship, which provides six weeks of overseas summer study. Grants have been awarded to Connecticut College to support this program. Applicants must have at least three years of prior teaching experience to obtain these $3,750 grant. Call or write to:

NEH Fellowships Program for Foreign Language Teachers K-12 Connecticut College 270 Mohegan Avenue New London, Connecticut 06320 Telephone: (203) 439-2282

Fellowships and Seminars

There are several fellowship programs available to help individual scholars, teachers and other interpreters of the humanities. Study and research opportunities can range from several weeks to one year.

University Teachers, College Teachers and Independent Scholars

Grants are available for faculty members of and teachers to help them undertake full-time independent study and research in the humanities. This program is also open to individuals employed by schools, museums and libraries, or for independent scholars and writers. For further information, telephone: (202) 606-8466

Dissertation Grants, Study Grants and Young Scholars

College and University teachers, doctoral candidates in the humanities, college students and high school students may apply humanities study and research grants. Awards, depending on the category, can range from six weeks to twelve months. For further information, telephone: (202) 606-8463.

Faculty Graduate Study Programs for Historically Black Colleges and Universities

Faculty at these colleges and universities may apply for grants that support one year of full-time study leading to a doctoral degree in the humanities. Preference is given to those who are at the dissertation stage of their work. For further information, telephone: (202) 606-8466.

Other Fellowship Programs

In the past, individual scholars, who wished to travel to use research collections of humanities materials in libraries, archives, museums or other repositories in the United States or overseas, applied for a "Travel to Collections" grant. This program was recently merged with the Summer Stipends program, which includes that program and also provides support for postsecondary teachers, and individuals employed by schools, libraries, museums, etc. to undertake full-time independent study and research in the humanities for two consecutive months. Applicants can also apply for a travel supplement to this stipend, if significant travel is required to complete the project. For further information, telephone: (202) 606-8466.

NEH grants also fund summer seminars for all levels of education, from accomplished teachers and scholars to kindergarten teachers. These seminars focus on significant texts in the humanities. Both teachers who attend them and scholars who may direct them are funded by the NEH. For further information about this program, telephone: (202) 606-8463.

Preservation and Access Programs

The National Endowment for the Humanities supports many projects that preserve and increase the availability of resources important for research, education and public programming in the humanities. Such projects can include books, journals, newspapers, archives and manuscript collections, maps, photographs, film, sound recordings, and objects of material culture held by libraries, archives, museums, historical organizations, and other repositories.

Library and Archival Materials

NEH grants support preservation projects to reformat the intellectual content of nationally important collections of brittle books, archival materials, sound recordings, and film held by single institutions or a consortium of institutions. Funds are available for cataloguing materials, the arrangement of archives and manuscript collections, archival surveys, microfilming important non-U.S. collections and projects that assist libraries and other repositories can improve ways to make available information about research materials. For further information, telephone: (202) 606-8570.

Other Preservation Programs

Nonprofit museums and historical organizations, universities and state agencies get NEH funding to stabilize material culture collections important to the humanities. This usually includes support for housing and storage, improved climate control, and the installation of security, lighting, and fire-prevention systems.

Similarly, grants are available to preserve and develop bibliographic control of U.S. newspapers. Grants fund the cataloguing of newspapers, the entry of bibliographic information and holding records in the Library of Congress CONSER data base, and the preservation microfilming of endangered newspapers considered important to humanities research.

For further information, eligible institutions may telephone: (202) 606-8570.

Public Programs

The National Endowment for the Humanities also supports projects that increase public understanding and appreciation of the humanities. They fund those projects that bring significant insights to general audiences through radio and television programs, exhibitions, lectures, symposia, printed materials, etc.

Grants are available to support the planning, writing, or production of television and radio programs in the humanities, especially those that reach general audiences. They are particularly interested in broadcast media projects on the lives of historically significant Americans. For further information, please telephone: (202) 606-8278.

Museum and historical organization exhibitions are also funded. Awards are made for institutional self-study, seminars, symposia and other special projects that present the humanities. For information, please telephone: (202) 606-8284.

Other public programs are available, generally to nonprofit organizations, colleges and universities and other similar institutions interested in the humanities. To find out more about these programs, please telephone: (202) 606-8271.

Research Programs

One of the most important areas funded by the NEH is research. Grants in this division provide up to three years of support for the preparation for publication of editions, translations, and other important works in the humanities; the preparation of reference materials; research conferences; an research opportunities offered through independent research centers and scholarly organizations.

Grants are available to support various stages in the preparation of authoritative and annotated editions of works and documents of value to humanities scholars and general readers. Translations into English of various projects that are of important historical, artistic, philosophic or literary interest also NEH-funded. Individuals, educational institutions, associations and nonprofit organizations are eligible for these grants. For further information, please telephone: (202) 606-8207.

Other research programs may include the publication and dissemination of excellent books in all fields of the humanities by small or scholarly presses; projects for the preparation of reference works that will enhance the availability of information and research materials; for interpretive research that will advance knowledge in various disciplines of the humanities; postdoctoral fellowship programs at independent centers for advanced study; and international research grants for American scholars who wish to pursue research in the United States or overseas. For further information about these programs, please telephone: (202) 606-8210 or (202) 606-8358.

State Programs

The National Endowment for the Humanities supports humanities councils throughout the United States. Each council establishes its own grant guidelines and sets its own application deadlines. State councils support many different projects. These may include library reading programs, speaker-discussion series, conferences, seminars, media presentations, and museum and traveling exhibitions. A directory of your state's humanities council follows at the end of this chapter. You may also contact the NEH office administrating this program at (202) 606-8254.

Additional NEH Information

You should write or telephone for additional information, deadline dates on grant programs and for application forms for the submission of your project to:

PUBLIC INFORMATION OFFICE NATIONAL ENDOWMENT FOR THE HUMANITIES 1100 Pennsylvania Avenue, N.W. Washington, DC 20506 Telephone: (202) 606-8438

National Endowment for the Arts Program: Regional Fellowships

Fellowships are administered by regional media arts centers. For information and application forms, contact:

GREAT LAKES
 Illinois, Inidana, Michigan, Ohio

Center for New Television
1440 North Dayton Street
Chicago, IL 60622
(312) 951-6868

Pittsburgh Film Makers, Inc.
3712 Forbes Avenue, 2nd Floor
Pittsburgh, PA 15213-3409
(412) 681-5449

NEW ENGLAND
 Connecticut, Maine Massachusetts,
 New Hampshire, Rhode Island, Vermont

Boston Film/Video Foundation, Inc.
1126 Boylston Street
Boston, MA 02215
(617) 536-1540

SOUTHEAST
 Alabama, Florida, Georgia, Kentucky,
 Louisiana, Mississippi, North Carolina, South
Carolina, Tennessee, Virginia

Appalshop, Inc.
306 Madison Street
Whitesburg, KY 41858
(606) 633-0108

SOUTH CENTRAL
Arkansas, Kansas, Missouri, Nebraska, Oklahoma, Texas, Puerto Rico, Virgin Islands

South West Alternate Media Project
1519 West Main
Houston, TX 77006
(713) 522-8592

UPPER MIDWEST
Iowa, Minnesota, North Dakota, South Dakota, Wisconsin

Film in the Cities
2388 University Avenue
St. Paul, MN 55114
(612) 646-6104

WEST
Alaska, Arizona, California, Colorado, Hawaii, Idaho, Montana, Nevada, New Mexico, Oregon,
Utah, Washington, Wyoming, Pacific Territories
Northwest Film and Video Center
Oregon Art Institute
1219 S.W. Park Avenue
Portland, OR 97205

STATE ART AGENCIES

Alabama State Council on the Arts
One Dexter Avenue
Montgomery, AL 36130
(205) 242-4076

Alaska State Council on the Arts
411 West 4th Avenue
Suite 1E
Anchorage, AK 99501-2343
(907) 279-1558

American Samoa Council on Culture,
Arts and Humanitites
Office of the Governor
P.O. Box 1540
Pago Pago, American Samoa 96799
9011-684-633-4347
9011-684-633-2059

Arizona Commission on the Arts
417 West Roosevelt
Phoenix, AZ 85003
(602) 255-5884 or 255-5882

Arkansas Arts Council
1500 Tower Building
323 Center Street
Little Rock, AR 72201
(501) 324-9150

California Arts Council
2411 Alhambra Blvd.
Sacramento, CA 95817
(916) 739-3186

Colorado Council on the Arts
 and Humanities
750 Pennsylvania Street
Denver, CO 80203-3699
(303) 894-2617
TDD/894-2664

Connecticut Commission on the Arts
227 Lawrence Street
Hartford, CT 06106
(203) 566-4770

District of Columbia Commission
 on the Arts and Humanities
410 8th Street, N.W.
Washington, DC 20004
(202) 724-5613 or 727-9332

Florida Department of State
 Division of Cultural Affairs
The Capitol
Tallahassee, FL 32399-0250
(904) 487-2980

Georgia Council on the Arts
 and Humanities
530 Means Street, N.W., Suite 115
Atlanta, GA 30318
(404) 651-7920

Guam Council on the Arts
 and Humanities
P.O. Box 2950
Agana, Guam 96910
(9011) 671-477-1454 or
 472-8059

State Foundation on Culture
 and the Arts
335 Merchant Street
Room 202
Honolulu, HI 96813
(808) 586-0300

Idaho Commissiono on the Arts
3404 West State Street
c/o Statehouse Mail
Boise, ID 83720
(208) 334-2119

Illinois Arts Council
State of Illinois Center
100 West Randolph Street
Suite 10-500
Chicago, IL 60601
(312) 917-6750
TDD/814-4831

Indiana Arts Commission
402 West Washington Street
Room 072
Indianapolis, IN 46204
(317) 232-1268
TDD/233-3001

Iowa Arts Council
Capitol Complex
1223 East Court Avenue
Des Moines, IA 50319
(515) 281-4451

Kansas Arts Commission
Jayhawk Towers, Suite 1004
700 Jackson
Topeka, KS 66603
(913) 296-3335
TDD/800-766-3777

Kentucky Arts Council
31 Fountain Place
Frankfort, KY 40601
(502) 564-3757

Division of the Arts
Louisiana Department of Culture,
 Recreation and Tourism
P.O. Box 44247
Baton Rouge, LA 70804
(504) 342-8180

Maine Arts Commission
55 Capitol Street
State House Station 25
Augusta, ME 04333
(207) 289-2724

Maryland State Arts Council
601 North Howard Street
Baltimore, MD 21201
(301) 333-8232
TDD/301-333-4519

Massachusetts Cultural Council
80 Boylston Street, 10th Floor
Boston, MA 02116
(617) 727-3668
TDD/338-9153

Michigan Council for the Arts
1200 Sixth Avenue
Detroit, MI 48226
(313) 256-3735
TDD/256-3734

Minnesota State Arts Board
432 Summit Avenue
St. Paul, MN 55102-2624
(612) 297-2603
TDD Relay/612-297-5353

Mississippi Arts Commission
239 North Lamar Street, Suite 207
Jackson, MS 39201
(601) 359-6030

Missouri State Council on the Arts
Wainwright Office Complex
111 North Seventh Street
Suite 105
St. Louis, MO 63101
(314) 340-6845

Montana Arts Council
316 North Park Avenue
Helena, MT 59620
(406) 444-6430

Nebraska Arts Council
1313 Farnam-on-the-Mall
Omaha, NE 68102-1873
(402) 595-2122

Nevada State Council on the Arts
329 Flint Street
Reno, NV 89501
(702) 688-1225

New Hampshire State Council on the Arts
Phenix Hall
40 North Main Street
Concord, NH 03301
(603) 271-2789

New Jersey State Council on the Arts
4 North Broad Street, CN 306
Trenton, NJ 08625
(609) 292-6130
TDD/609-984-7025

New Mexico Arts Division
228 East Palace Avenue
Santa Fe, NM 87501
(505) 827-6490

New York State Council on the Arts
915 Broadway
New York, NY 10010
(212) 387-7000 Reception
(212) 387-7055 Alternate Number
(212) 387-7049 TDD

North Carolina Arts Council
Department of Cultural Resources
Raleigh, NC 27601-2807
(919) 733-2821

North Dakota Council on the Arts
Black Building
Suite 606
Fargo, ND 58102-4998
(701) 239-7150

Commonwealth Council for Arts
 and Culture
Convention Center
Commonwealth of the Northern
 Mariana Islands
P.O. Box 553, CHRB
Saipan, MP 96950
(9011) 670-322-9982/83

Ohio Arts Council
727 East Main Street
Columbus, OH 43205
(614) 466-2613 Reception
(614) 466-4494 Fax
(614) 466-4541 TDD

Oklahoma State Art Council
P.O. Box 18154
Oklahoma City, OK 73154-0154
(405) 842-0890

Oregon Arts Commission
550 Airport Road, S.E.
Salem, OR 97310
(503) 378-3625

Commonwealth of Pennsylvania
 Council on the Arts
Finance Building
Suite 216
Harrisburg, PA 17120
(717) 787-6883

Institute of Puerto Rican Culture
Apartado Postal 4184
San Juan, PR 00905-4184
(809) 723-2115

Rhode Island State Council on the Arts
95 Cedar Street
Providence, RI 02903
(401) 277-3880
Voice/TDD/401-277-3880

South Carolina Arts Commission
1800 Gervais Street
Columbia, SC 29201
(803) 734-8696

South Dakota Arts Council
230 South Phillips Avenue
Suite 204
Sioux Falls, SD 57102
(605) 339-6646

Tennessee Arts Commission
320 Sixth Avenue, North
Suite 100
Nashville, TN 37243-0780
(615) 741-1701

Texas Commission on the Arts
P.O. Box 13406
Capitol Station
Austin, TX 78711-3406
(512) 463-5535

Utah Arts Council
617 East South Temple Street
Salt Lake City, UT 84102
(801) 533-5895/6
TDD/533-6196

Vermont Council on the Arts, Inc.
136 State Street
Montpelier, VT 05602
(802) 828-3291

Virginia Commission for the Arts
223 Governor Street
Richmond, VA 23219-2010
(804) 225-3132
TDD/Voice/804-225-3132

Virgin Islands Council on the Arts
41-42 Norregade
St. Thomas, VI 00802
(809) 774-5984

Washington State Arts Commission
110 9th and Columbia Building
P.O. Box 42675
Olympia, WA 98504-2675
(206) 753-3860
(800) 833-6388 TDD
(206) 586-5351 Fax

Arts & Humanities Section
Division of Culture & History
West Virginia Department of
 Education & the Arts
Charleston, WV 25305
(304) 558-0225

Wisconsin Arts Board
101 East Wilson Street
1st Floor
Madison, WI 53703
(608) 266-0190

Wyoming Council on the Arts
2320 Capitol Avenue
Cheyenne, WY 82002
(307) 777-7742
TDD/307-777-5964

Regional Arts Organizations

Arts Midwest
Hennepin Center for the Arts
528 Hennepin Avenue, Suite 310
Minneapolis, MN 55403
(612) 341-0755
 Illinois, Indiana, Iowa, Michigan,
 Minnesota, North Dakota, Ohio,
 South Dakota, Wisconsin

Consortium for Pacific Arts
 and Cultures (CPAC)
2141C Atherton Road
Honolulu, HI 96822
(808) 946-7381
 American Samoa, Guam,
 North Marianas

Mid-America Arts Alliance (MAAA)
912 Baltimore Avenue
Suite 700
Kansas City, MO 64105
(816) 421-1388
 Arkansas, Kansas, Missouri,
 Nebraska, Oklahoma, Texas

Mid-Atlantic Arts Foundation (MAAF)
11 East Chase Street
Baltimore, MD 21202
(301) 539-6659
 Delaware, District of Columbia,
 Maryland, New Jersey, New York,
 Pennsylvania, Virginia, West Virginia

New England Foundation for
  the Arts, Inc. (NEFA)
678 Masschusetts Avenue
Cambridge, MA 02139
(617) 492-2914
  Connecticut, Maine, Massachusetts
  New Hampshire, Rhode Island, Vermont

Southern Arts Federation (SAF)
1293 Peachtree Street, N.E.
Atlanta, GA 30309
(404) 874-7244
  Alabama, Florida, Georgia, Kentucky,
  Louisiana, Mississippi, North Carolina,
  South Carolina, Tennessee

Western States Arts Foundation (WSAF)
236 Montezuma Avenue
Santa Fe, NM 87501
(505) 988-1166
  Alaska, Arizona, California, Colorado,
  Idaho, Montana, Nevada, New Mexico,
  Oregon, Utah, Washington, Wyoming

National Service Organizations

**Arts for America/National Assembly
  of Local Arts Agencies**
927 15th Street, N.W.
12th Floor
Washington, DC 20005
(202) 371-2830

**National Assembly of State
  Arts Agencies (NASAA)**
1010 Vermont Avenue, N.W.
Suite 920
Washington, DC 20005
(202) 347-6352

STATE HUMANITIES COUNCILS

ALABAMA
Alabama Humanities Foundation
2217 Tenth Court South
Birmingham, AL 35205
(205) 930-0540

ALASKA
Alaska Humanities Forum
430 West Seventh Avenue, Suite 1
(907) 272-5341

ARIZONA
Arizona Humanities Council
The Ellis-Shackleford House
1242 North Central Avenue
Phoenix, AZ 85004
(602) 257-0335

ARKANSAS
Arkansas Humanities Council
10816 Executive Center Drive
Suite 310
Little Rock, AR 72211-4383
(501) 221-0091

CALIFORNIA
California Council for the Humanities
312 Sutter Street, Suite 601
San Francisco, CA 94108
(415) 391-1474

COLORADO
Colorado Endowment for the Humanities
1836 Blake Street, #200
Denver, CO 80202.
(303) 292-4458

CONNECTICUT
Connecticut Humanities Council
41 Lawn Avenue
Wesleyan Station
Middletown, CT 06457
(203) 347-6888

DELAWARE
Delaware Humanities Forum
2600 Pennsylvania Avenue
Wilmington, DE 19806
(302) 573-4410

DISTRICT OF COLUMBIA
D.C. Community Humanities Council
1331 H Street, N.W.
Washington, DC 20005
(202) 347-1732

FLORIDA
Florida Endowment for the Humanities
1718 East 7th Avenue
Ybor City, FL 33605
(813) 272-3473

GEORGIA
Georgia Humanities Council
1556 Clifton Road, N.E.
Emory University
Atlanta, GA 30322
(404) 727-7500

GUAM
Guam Humanities Council
House 6, Dean's Circle
University of Guam
UOG Station
Mangilao, Guam 96923
(671) 734-1727

HAWAII
Hawaii Committee for the Humanities
First Hawaiin Bank Building
3599 Waialae Avenue, Room 23
Honolulu, HI 96816
(808) 732-5402

IDAHO
Idaho Humanities Council
217 West State Street
Boise, ID 83702
(208) 345-5346

ILLINOIS
Illinois Humanities Council
618 South Michigan Avenue
Chicago, IL 60605
(312) 939-5212

INDIANA
Indiana Humanities Council
1500 North Deleware Street
Indianapolis, IN 46202
(317) 638-1500

IOWA
Iowa Humanities Board
Oakdale Campus N210 OH
University of Iowa
Iowa City, IA 52242
(319) 335-4153

KANSAS
Kansas Committee for the Humanities
112 West Sixth Street, Suite 210
Topeka, KS 66603
(913) 357-0359

KENTUCKY
Kentucky Humanities Council, Inc.
417 Clifton Avenue
University of Kentucky
Lexington, KY 40506-0414
(606) 257-5932

LOUISIANA
Louisiana Endowment for the Humanities
1001 Howard Avenue, Suite 3110
New Orleans, LA 70113
(504) 523-4352

MAINE
Maine Humanities Council
P.O. Box 7202
Portland, ME 04112
(207) 773-5051

MARYLAND
Maryland Humanities Council
516 North Charles Street, #102
Baltimore, MD 21201
(301) 625-4830

MASSACHUSETTS
Massachusetts Foundation for the
 Humanities
One Woodbridge Street
South Hadley, MA 01075
(413) 536-1385

MICHIGAN
Michigan Council for the Humanities
Nisbet Building, Suite 30
1407 South Harrison Road
East Lansing, MI 48823
(517) 355-0160

MINNESOTA
Minnesota Humanities Council
26 East Exchange Street
Lower Level South
St. Paul, MN 55101
(612) 224-5739

MISSISSIPPI
Mississippi Humanities Council
3825 Ridgewood Road, Room 508
Jackson, MS 39211
(601) 982-6752

MISSOURI
Missouri Humanities Council
911 Washington Avenue
Suite 215
St. Louis, MO 63101-1208
(314) 621-7705

MONTANA
Montana Committee for the Humanities
P.O. Box 8036
Hellgate Station
Missoula, MT 59807
(406) 243-6022

NEBRASKA
Nebraska Humanities Council
Suite 225 Lincoln Center Building
915 Centennial Mall South
Lincoln, NE 68508
(402) 474-2131

NEVADA
Nevada Humanities Committee
P.O. Box 8029
Reno, NV 89507
(702) 784-6587

NEW HAMPSHIRE
New Hampshire Humanities Council
19 Pillsbury Street
P.O. Box 2228
Concord, NH 03302-2228
(603) 224-4072

NEW JERSEY
New Jersey Committee for the Humanities
73 Easton Avenue
New Brunswick, NJ 08901
(908) 932-7726

NEW MEXICO
New Mexico Endowment for the
 Humanities
Onate Hall, Room 209
University of New Mexico
Albuquerque, NM 87131
(505) 277-3705

NEW YORK
New York Council for the Humanities
198 Broadway, 10th Floor
New York, NY 10038
(212) 233-1131

NORTH CAROLINA
North Carolina Humanities Council
425 Spring Garden Street
Greensboro, NC 27401
(919) 334-5325

NORTH DAKOTA
North Dakota Humanities Council
P.O. BOx 2191
Bismarck, ND 58502
(701) 255-3360

THE NORTHERN MARIANA ISLANDS
Council for the Humanities
P.O. Box 1250
Saipan, MP 96950
(670) 234-7642

OHIO
The Ohio Humanities Council
P.O. Box 06354
Columbus, OH 43206-0354
(614) 461-7802

OKLAHOMA
Oklahoma Foundation for the Humanities
Festival Plaza
428 W. California, Suite 270
Oklahoma City, OK 73102
(405) 235-0280

OREGON
Oregon Council for the Humanities
812 S.W. Washington, Suite 225
Portland, OR 97205
(503) 241-0543

PENNSYLVANIA
Pennsylvania Humanities Council
320 Walnut Street, Suite 305
Philadelphia, PA 19106
(215) 925-1005

PUERTO RICO
Fundacion Puertorriquena de las
 Humanidades
Box S-4307
Old San Juan, PR 00904
(809) 721-2087

RHODE ISLAND
Rhode Island Committee for the
 Humanities
60 Ship Street
Providence, RI 02903
(401) 273-2250

SOUTH CAROLINA
South Carolina Humanities Council
1610 Oak Street
Columbia, SC 29204
(803) 771-8864

SOUTH DAKOTA
South Dakota Committee for the
 Humanities
Box 7050, University Station
Brookings, SD 57007
(605) 688-6113

TENNESSEE
Tennessee Humanities Council
1003 18th Avenue South
Nashville, TN 37212
(615) 320-7001

TEXAS
Texas Committee for the Humanities
Banister Place A
3809 South Second Street
Austin, TX 78704
(512) 440-1991

UTAH
Utah Endowment for the Humanities
Ten West Broadway
Broadway Building, Suite 505
Salt Lake City, UT 84102-2002
(801) 531-7868

VERMONT
The Vermont Council on the Humanities
Grant House, P.O. Box 58
Hyde Park, VT 05655
(802) 888-3183

VIRGINIA
Virginia Foundation for the Humanities
 and Public Policy
145 Ednam Drive
Charlottesville, VA 22901-3207
(804) 924-3296

VIRGIN ISLANDS
Virgin Islands Humanities Council
GERS Building, 3rd Floor
Kronprindsens Gade
P.O. Box 1829
St. Thomas, VI 00803
(809) 776-4044

WASHINGTON
Washington Commission for the
 Humanities
Lowman Building, Suite 312
107 Cherry Street
Seatte, WA 98104
(206) 682-1770

WEST VIRGINIA
West Virginia Humanities Council
723 Kanawha Blvd., East
Suite 800
Charleston, WV 25301
(304) 346-8500

WISCONSIN
Wisconsin Humanities Committee
716 Langdon Street
Madison, WI 53706
(608) 262-0706

WYOMING
Wyoming Council for the Humanities
P.O. Box 3643-University Station
Laramie, WY 82071-3643
(307) 766-6496

21.

FOUNDATION GRANTS FOR THE ARTS
****

There are additional private foundation sources to assist artists of nearly every aesthetic creation. Private foundations exist to fill a particular need, as expressed by the individual(s) or group that provided the funding. Some will specify funding a special discipline; others will include more than one. Rarely, will you find a broad range of financial assistance.

Foundation funding divides into three separate types. A private foundation may award a fellowship that grants funds to assist the artist with a create project. It may also provide relief assistance or emergency aid to a needy artist in a specified geographic area or discipline. Finally, the grantmaker may provide the artist with a studio, work or living space, equipment, materials or other similar assistance.

Additional artistic awards from foundations do exist, in the form of prizes, contests and awards. As mentioned in Chapter 19, visit your local Foundation Center library (that directory information is also at the end of Chapter 19) and find out about supplemental programs. Your local library may also have current publications that will direct you to a contest for your discipline.

Please carefully read the limitations for each private foundation listed in this directory. It is unnecessary to waste your time and money applying to a private foundation that does not include your discipline or geographical area in its limitations. They are very strict about their regulations.

Nearly all require that you complete and mail them an application form. Write or telephone the foundation and ask that you be sent an application and their guidelines. Follow their instructions and refer to Chapter 2 of this book, as necessary.

FOUNDATION GRANTS FOR THE ARTS

Edward Albee Foundation, Inc.
c/o A. Kozak Company
468 Park Avenue South, Suite 1407
New York, NY 10016
Application address: William Flanagan Memorial Center for Creative Persons, 14 Harrison Street, New York, NY 10013; Phone: (212) 226-2020.
Limitations: Grants for free room only to artists and writers seeking studio space.

The American Society of Journalists and
 Authors Charitable Trust
1501 Broadway, Suite 1907
New York, NY 10036
Phone: (212) 997-0947
Fax: (212) 768-7414
Contact: Murray Teigh Bloom, Chairman, Board of Trustees
Limitations: Relief assistance to needy, established, professional freelance writers who are 60 years of age or older or disabled.

Art Matters, Inc.
P.O. Box 40818
Washington, DC 20016
Phone: (202) 966-1699
Limitations: Project support and fellowship to individuals in the arts, including the fine arts, film and performance art. AMI does not fund publications, music or art students of any kind.

Artists Fellowship, Inc.
c/o Salmagundi Club
47 Fifth Avenue
New York, NY 10003
Contact: Richard Plonk
Limitations: Emergency aid to American professional visual artists and their families.

Athena Foundation, Inc.
P.O. Box 6259
Long Island City, NY 11106
Contact: Anita Contini, President
Limitations: Grants generally for visual or performing artists in New York City.

The Bagby Foundation for the Musical
 Arts, Inc.
501 Fifth Avenue
New York, NY 10017
Phone: (212) 986-6094
Contact: Eleanor C. Mark
Limitations: Relief assistance to aged needy individuals who have aided the world of music and are in need of financial support in order to survive.

The Bush Foundation
East 900 First National Building
332 Minnesota Street
St. Paul, MN 55101
Phone: (612) 227-5222
Limitations: Fellowships to selected writers, choreographers, composers, and visual artists residing in Minnesota, North Dakota, South Dakota and 26 counties in western Wisconsin.

Ella Lyman Cabot Trust, Inc.
109 Rockland Street
Holliston, MA 01746
Contact: Mary Jane Gibson, Executive Secretary
Limitations: Grants for individual projects sometimes involving a departure from one's usual vocation or a creative extension of it, with a promise of good to others.

Carnegie Fund for Authors
330 Sunrise Highway
Rockville Center, NY 11570
Phone: (516) 764-8899
Limitations: Emergency assistance to needy writers who have commercially published at least one book of reasonable length which has received reader acceptance.

Cintas Foundation, Inc.
c/o William B. Warren
101 Park Avenue, 5th Floor
New York, NY 10178
Application address: Arts International, Institute of International Education, 809 United Nations Plaza, New York, NY 10017-3580; Phone: (212) 984-5564.
Contact: Rebecca Sayles, Program Officer
Limitations: Fellowships to individuals of Cuban citizenship or lineage for continuing work outside Cuba in the arts, including fine arts, music and literature. No fellowship students pursuing academic programs.

Blanche E. Colman Trust
c/o Boston Safe Deposit & Trust Company
One Boston Place
Boston, MA 02106
Phone: (617) 722-7341
Contact: Ms. Sylvia Salas, Trust Officer
Limitations: Grants by recommendation to worthy artists residing in New England (including CT, NH, ME, MA and VT).

Fleishhacker Foundation
One Maritime Plaza, Suite 830
San Francisco, CA 94111
Phone: (415) 788-2909
Contact: Christine Elbel, Executive Director
Limitations: Fellowships to assist individual artists, 25 years of age or older, in the San Francisco Bay, CA area.

The Foundation for the Jan Mitchell Prize, Inc.
595 Madison Avenue
New York, NY 10022
Phone: (212) 755-9760
Contact: Jan Mitchell, President
Limitations: Prizes for writers who win a competition of art history books. Books must be submitted for entry. Only art history books in English accepted.

Fund for Investigative Journalism, Inc.
1755 Massachusetts Avenue, N.W., No. 324
Washington, DC 20036
Phone: (202) 462-1844
Contact: Anne Grant, Executive Director
Limitations: Fellowships to journalists doing investigative work who have a statement of intent to publish from a suitable outlet.

Adolph and Esther Gottlieb Foundation, Inc.
380 West Broadway
New York, NY 10012
Phone: (212) 226-0581
Contact: Sandford Hirsch, Secretary
Limitations: Grants for painters, sculptors and printmakers who have at least 20 years in a mature phase of their art. Emergency assistance available for same visual artists who have at least 10 years in a mature phase of their art and are in need as a result of an unexpected, catastrophic event.

John Simon Guggenheim Memorial Foundation
90 Park Avenue
New York, NY 10016
Phone: (212) 687-4470
Contact: Joel Conarroe, President
Limitations: Fellowships to published authors, exhibited artists and others in the fine arts.

ISE Cultural Foundation
750 Airport Road
Lakewood, NJ 08701
Application address in Japan: ISE Cultural
Foundation, Inc., Negishi, 2-1-4, Paito,-Ku,
Tokyo 110, Japan
Contact: Jared Lubarsky
Limitations: Awards grants for activities
related to cultural exchange between Japan and
the U.S.

Jerome Foundation
West 1050 First National Bank Building
332 Minnesota Street
St. Paul, MN 55101
Phone: (612) 224-9431
Contact: Cynthia Gehrig, President
Limitations: Grants for film and video projects by artists residing in New York City, and
for travel and study for individuals in dance,
literature, media arts, music, theater and the
visual arts residing in the Twin Cities metropolitan area.

John Anson Kittredge Educational Fund
c/o Key Trust Company of Maine
P.O. Box 1054
Augusta, ME 04330
Application address: P.O. Box 2883, Cam-
bridge, MA 02238; Phone: (617) 495-1109
Contact: Ernest R. May
Limitations: Grants awarded to artists and
scholars in very special circumstances. No
scholarships are awarded.

Koussevitzky Music Foundation, Inc.
200 Park Avenue
New York, NY 10166
Phone: (212) 351-3092
Contact: Ellis J. Freedman, Secretary
Limitations: Provides commissions based on
merit to composers of serious music who are
over 25 years of age, have completed formal
conservatory studies or have a B.A. from a
recognized conservatory, college or university, or demonstrated equivalent, and whose
music has been published, recorded and/or
performed in public and are sponsored by a
performing organization.

The Bascom Little Fund
34750 Cedar Road
Gates Mills, OH 44040
Phone: (216) 442-0360
Contact: Richard A. Manuel, Treasurer
Limitations: Grants to cover expenses in
connection with promotion, through the media
of concerts, publications, recordings, etc., of
serious and semi-popular music, newly composed by Ohio composers per formed in or
near Cleveland, Ohio.

Lotta Theatrical Fund
294 Washington Street, Room 636
Boston, MA 02108
Phone: (617) 451-0698
Contact: Claire M. McCarthy,
Trust Manager
Limitations: Grants to deserving, needy mem-
bers of the theatrical profession.

Israel Matz Foundation
14 East Fourth Street, Room 403
New York, NY 10012
Phone: (212) 673-8142
Contact: Dr. Milton Arfa, Chairman
Limitations: Relief assistance to indigent
Hebrew writers, scholars, public workers and
their dependents.

Money for Women Barbara Deming Memorial Fund, Inc.
P.O. Box 40-1043
Brooklyn, NY 11240-1043
Phone: (718) 499-0190
Contact: Pam McAllister, Administrator
Limitations: Grants to individual feminists in the arts.

Musicians Emergency Relief fund-Local 802
30 West 42nd Street
New York, NY 10036
Phone: (212) 239-4802
Contact: Carl Janelli, Secretary
Limitations: Welfare assistance in the form of interest-free loans to sick, distressed, or indigent musicians who have been union members for a minimum of three years and are in good standing (membership dues paid-up).

Musicians Foundation, Inc.
200 West 55th Street
New York, NY 10019
Phone: (212) 247-5332
Contact: Brent Williams, Secretary-Treasurer
Limitations: Emergency financial assistance to professional musicians and their families.

Peninsula Community Foundation
1204 Burlingame Avenue
P.O. Box 627
Burlingame, CA 94011-0627
Phone: (415) 342-2477
Contact: Bill Somerville, Executive Director
Limitations: Grants to artists, including painters, dancers, photographers and poets who are residents of San Mateo County and northern Santa Clara County, CA.

Poetry Society of America
15 Gramercy Park South
New York, NY 10003
Phone: (212) 254-9628
Limitations: Awards and prizes to professional and student poets. Except as noted below for entries in the Cane, Farber, Williams and DiCastagnola contests, all poems must be unpublished. Poems accepted for publication prior to the bestowal of awards must be withdrawn from the publication.

The Pollock-Krasner Foundation, Inc.
725 Park Avenue
New York, NY 10021
Application address:
P.O. Box 4957,
New York, NY 10185.
Phone: (212) 517-5400
Contact: Charles C. Bergman, Executive Vice President
Limitations: Grants based on financial need to talented visual artists in the U.S. and abroad to further their careers and their personal well-being. Emergency aid is also given in cases of serious illness or personal catastrophe. Only visual artists, those working in painting, sculpture, graphic and
mixed media, will be considered.

The Martha Boschen Porter Fund, Inc.
White Hollow Road
Sharon, CT 06069
Contact: Robert Terrall
Limitations: Grants for artistic and cultural projects for needy artists.

488 FOUNDATION GRANTS FOR THE ARTS

Evelyn W. Preston Trust
One Constitution Plaza
Hartford, CT 06115
Application address: Connecticut Bank
and Trust Company, P.O. Box 3334,
Hartford, CT 06103.
Phone: (203) 244-4330
Contact: Norman E. Armour, Senior Vice
President
Limitations: Grants to musicians to perform
free band and orchestral concerts in Hartford,
CT, from June through September.

The Shifting Foundation
8000 Sears Tower
Chicago, IL 60606
Contact: Pat Culver
Limitations: Grants to artists who have distinguished themselves or shown promise in the
fields of literature, contemporary music with
an improvisational element, and less frequently, visual or multi-media forms. Grants are
made for tuition expenses at an educational
institution or for a career or project development.

John F. and Anna Lee Stacey
Testamentary Trust
c/o Security Pacific National Bank
P.O. Box 3189, Terminal Annex
Los Angeles, CA 90051
Application address:
Stacey Award Committee,
P.O. Box 448, Sonoita, AZ 85637.
Contact: Mrs. R. Brownell McGrew
Limitations: Fellowships and scholarships to
artists between the ages of 18 and 35 who are
U.S. citizens and whose work is devoted to the
classical or conservative tradition of western
culture.

William Matheus Sullivan Musical
Foundation, Inc.
251 West 89th Street, Suite 10-B
New York, NY 10024
Phone: (212) 874-2373
Contact: David Lloyd, Executive Director
Limitations: Financial assistance to gifted
professional singers in the early stages of their
careers. Applicants must have future engage-
ments with a full orchestra.

Gladys Turk Foundation
9777 Wilshire Blvd., Suite 700
Beverly Hills, CA 90212
Phone: (213) 273-6760
Contact: Max Fink, President
Limitations: Grants only for voice culture
training, primarily to vocalists residing in
southern California. Funds extremely limited.

Ludwig Vogelstein Foundation, Inc.
P.O. Box 4924
Brooklyn, NY 11240-4924
Contact: Frances Pishny,
Executive Director
Limitations: Grants to individuals in the arts
and humanities. No scholarships, student aid
or faculty assistance granted.

Marguerite Eyer Wilbur Foundation
P.O. Box 3370
Santa Barbara, CA 93130-3370
Contact: Gary Ricks,
Chief Executive Officer
Limitations: Resident fellowships, research
grants, and support for writing projects to
individuals in the areas of humane literature.

SECTION FOUR:

CONCLUSION AND APPENDICES
****

22.

CONCLUSION

****

Conclusions to books in contemporary non-fiction often make it a habit of not really bringing matters to a conclusion. A conclusion's normal function is to allow the author to ponder the future, declare a particular aspiration, encourage that others join a new trend, or something like that. Sometimes, the author does all of these. And so will I.

Where lies the future of many grants and loans programs? Since 1965 emphasis has been placed on helping the economically disadvantaged, often at the expense of the middle class. At this writing, that class has increasingly become a disadvantaged peoples. Who is to bail them out? The federal government itself needs bailed out. Aggravating this problem is the fact that banks are having a rough time of it. Federal regulators snooping over their shoulders, looking for illiquidity, hinders them from loosening their purse strings. Federal government dependence upon banks for billions in business, real estate and educational loan guarantees makes for a bleak future for those programs.

Banks basically cut off the broad, general credit spigot to individual Americans in the early months of 1990. At that time, there was a world-wide pullback of the credit flow. Simultaneously, major Far Eastern nations restrained themselves in financing real estate and corporate acquisitions, U.S. banks induced a credit crunch, consumers stopped spending, and the American economy came to a standstill. I remember a conversation I had with a British business associate, during March and April, 1991. Both of us compared notes on our respective economies and concluded that "people weren't buying." When people don't buy goods and services, companies cannot pay their bills; employees are laid off. The downward spiral continues until credit is loosened.

How long will it take for a broad and general credit loosening? Some estimates -- especially one from an article published in a July, 1992 issue of a World Bank newspaper -- have it that the global economy won't pick up until 1996. In a conversation I had several years ago with Dr. Ravi Batra, author of THE GREAT DEPRESSION OF 1990, he predicted that if an economic depression occurred in 1992, instead of 1990, that it would last through 1996.

Unfortunately, the "tight money" situation is going to make life tough. Consumers must buy an increasing amount of goods and services to create an economic revitalization on a national scale. The actual purchasers of goods and services are themselves unable to continue doing so with their limited resources. Spending habits over the past generation have been transformed from one of reluctantly buying on the installment plan to a revolving credit society. Just as a drug addict ordinarily goes through a series of traumatic withdrawal symptoms to kick the habit, the American credit-oriented society is likely to pass through some form of tumultuous adventure in learning to purchase primarily with cash instead of credit. Banking institutions, responding to federal guidelines rather than political pressure, are abruptly forcing that lesson upon us.

If there were aspiring trends that I might encourage, it would be first the cancellation of the Tax Reform Act of 1986, which in itself might have led us to this current economic belt-tightening. Through its repercussions federal programs have suffered and that has trickled down to state, local and private programs. No economic overhaul could be complete without the elimination of the present income tax system. A substitute tax system is probably our only long-term national solution. That alternative would be a National Sales Tax replacing the present income taxing and collection system -- one that taxes consumption instead of taxing an individual's savings.

Such a consumption tax would create an overabundance of investment capital, flood our banking institutions with savings accounts, and skyrocket the national average of monies stored in savings accounts. Then, we might really see fireworks. Banks, now hesitant to lend money even when federally guaranteed, would subsequently have an increased cash-to-loans ratio. Flush with cash to lend, businesses would be financed at a record pace and level. And, much of the recent economic misery would be relegated to textbook fodder instead of continuing as a painful reality to many.

Because a great many federal programs are dependent upon banks, a national consumption tax might also be the only solution to not only growth in our country's grant and loan programs but, most likely, the very survival of many of these programs. One organization that you should contact for information about this idea is:

CITIZENS FOR AN ALTERNATIVE TAX SYSTEM
100 N. Brand Boulevard
Glendale, California 91203
Telephone: (818) 548-1394
Toll-Free: (800) 767-7577

So much for pondering the future, declaring aspirations or encouraging you to join a trend. Use this book wisely and with the purpose of bettering not only yourself, but your family and the nation. Use the money that you receive from sources listed in this book to produce valuable goods and services, or to create or develop the highest quality art, whether directly from the business and arts programs, or indirectly through the educational and real estate programs available to you. The money you receive from a government- or private-funded program was often hard-won and not so easily disbursed. Make it easier for the next man or woman by supporting that program's fundamental intention.

23.

SUGGESTED READING MATERIALS
****

You can enhance your understanding of each of the preceding chapters through additional reading. One can always improve a business plan or grant proposal by getting more information. There are many books and pamphlets, published either privately or by a government agency, that have more data on each of the subjects covered in this book. The more information you are armed with, the greater your chances of success. Often, the more you know and understand, the more you will be able to do in that area.

I have listed suggested reading materials so they correspond with the chapter which may interest you. The government agency's local office usually has many of these materials available to you at no charge or at nominal costs. Where suggested reading is privately published, I will include the publisher's name; these can usually be found at your local bookstore or library (where possible I have enclosed the telephone number where you can obtain the publication). Unless it is specifically noted otherwise, you can obtain the item from the government agency under the chapter category in which that publication is listed.

There are also numerous publications from America's largest publisher: The Government Printing Office. You can find out more about government publications by writing or calling to:

U.S. GOVERNMENT BOOKS
Superintendent of Documents
P.O. Box 371954
Pittsburgh, PA 15250-7954
Telephone: (202) 783-3238
Fax: (202) 512-2550

Chapter 2:   Writing a Grant Proposal

Getting a Grant in the 1990s by Robert Lefferts (Prentice-Hall).

Chapter 3:   How to Write a Business Proposal

How to Write a Winning Business Plan by Joseph R. Mancuso (Prentice-Hall).
How to Really Create a Successful Business Plan by David E. Gumpert (Inc. Magazine).
Buying a Business by Joseph R. Mancuso (Prentice-Hall).
The Small Business Survival Guide by Bob Coleman (Norton).
Growing a Business by Paul Hawken (Simon & Schuster)
The Entrepreneur's Guide to Preparing a Winning Business Plan and Raising Venture Capital by W. Keith Schilit (Prentice-Hall).

*The Complete Small Business Loan
Kit* by Arnold Goldstein (Bob Ad-
ams Publishers).
Business Loans by Rick Stephan
Hayes (Wiley).
How to Get a Business Loan by
Joseph R. Mancuso (Prentice-Hall)

Chapter 5:   Small Business Administration

*Women's Business Ownership
Major Laws Administered by U.S.
Department of Labor
Which Affect Business* (Department of
Labor)
*U.S. Government Purchasing and
Sales Directory
The Facts About ....* (individual
brochures describing
each SBA program in detail).

Chapter 6:   Small Business Development
Centers/SCORE

*Informational Packet for Small
Business Men and Women:
Some Advice* by Bill Manck (SBDC,
Tampa: 813-974-4274)

Chapter 8:   U.S. Department of Commerce:

*Federal Assistance for Export.
Export Programs: A Business
Directory of U.S
Government Resources.
A Basic Guide to Exporting.
CIMS: Commercial Information
Management System*
("We Put the World at Your
Fingertips.")
*Export Management System:
Summary of Guidelines.*

The OEL Insider (Export Administra-
tion magazine).
*Summary of Export Controls.
Business America* (official house
magazine).
Overseas Private Investment
Corporation packet.
*United States and Foreign Commercial
Service: Special Brief.
Eximbank and the Environment.
Export-Import Bank Credit Insurance.
Export-Import Bank Program
Selection Guide.
A Resource Guide for Exporting
Energy-Efficient
Products* (Alliance to Save Energy:
(202) 857-0666).
*U.S. Trade and Development
Program: Annual Report.
The World Is Your Market: An
Export Guide for Small
Business* by William A. Delphos
(Braddock Communications).

Chapter 10:   Small Business Innovation
Research

*SBIR: Office Of Innovation,
Research and Technology.
The NIST/DOE Energy-Related
Inventions Program.
SBIR Program Solicitations.
The Entrepreneur's Guide to Doing
Business with the
Federal Government* by Bevers,
Christie, and Price.

Chapter 11:   Minority Business Development Agency

National Initiatives at a Glance
(MBDA).
Grants for Minorities (Foundation
Center).

Chapter 12:   Venture Capital Sources

The Bankers' Handbook by William H.
   Baughn and Charles E. Walker (Dow
   Jones-Irwin)
Guide to Venture Capital Sources
   (Stanley Pratt).
Who's Who in Venture Capital
   (David Silver).
National Venture Capital Association
   brochure
   (703-528-4370).

Chapter 13:   Department of Housing and
   Urban Development

*A Home of Your Own: Helpful
   Advice from HUD on Choosing,
   Buying, and Enjoying a Home.*
Wise Home Buying.
The Programs of HUD.
Regulatory Barriers.
*Guide to Single Family Home
   Mortgage Insurance
   Programs.*
HUD USER.
*Not In My Back Yard: Removing
   Barriers to Affordable
   Housing.*
*Homeownership and Affordable
   Housing: The
   Opportunities.*
*Grants for Community Development,
   Housing & Employment*
   (Foundation Center).
Retirement Income on the House
   (National Center for
   Home Equity Conversion:
   (800) 247-6553

Chapter 14:   The Resolution Trust
                  Corporation

*General Financing Guidelines for
   Real Estate*

(RTC Sales Center).
How to Buy Real Estate (RTC Sales
   Center).
*Buying and Financing a Single-Family
   Home: Affordable Disposition
   Program* (RTC Sales Center).
*How You Can Profit from the S & L
   Bailout* by Sonny Bloch and Carolyn
   Janik (Bantam).

Chapter 15:   Farmers Home Administration

ASCS Conservation Programs.
*The Great Plains Conservation
   Program.*
*Farm Credit: How it Operates
   Farmers Home Administration
   Program Aid:*
   (Numbers 62, 977, 990, 1002, 1059,
   1400, 1441)

Chapter 16:   Veterans Affairs

*Doing Business with the Department
   of Veterans Affairs
   Pointers for the Veteran Homeowner*
   (VA Pamphlet 26-5).
*VA-Guaranteed Home Loans for
   Veterans* (VA Pamphlet 26-4).
Investing in Real Estate by Andrew
   James McLean.

Chapter 18:   Federal Education Programs

*The Student Guide: Financial Aid
   from the U.S.
   Department of Education.*
On Your Own from the Office of
   Student Financial
   Assistance.
Need A Lift? (American Legion
   Education Program).
The Pell Grant Formula.

College Scholarship Information Booklet:
Air Force ROTC, NAVY ROTC.
Profile: A Guide to Military Lifestyles (Army, Navy, Marine Corps, Air Force, Coast Guard).
Young Scholars Program (National Science Foundation).
United States Information Agency Fact Sheet.
Health Professionals Educational Assistance Programs by the Department of Veterans Affairs.
Cooperative Education Undergraduate Program Directory.
Special Programs for Disadvantaged Student: TRIO.
The College Cost Book (The College Board).
The Scholarship Book.
Putting Your Kids Through College by Scott Edelstein (Consumer Reports Books).
Peterson's College Money Handbook.
How to Pay for Your Children's College Education (The College Board).

Chapter 19:   Foundation Grants for Education

Foundation Grants to Individuals (Foundation Center).
Grants for Higher Education (Foundation Center).
Grants for Scholarships, Student Aid & Loans (Foundation Center).
Grants for Women & Girls (Foundation Center).

Chapter 20:   National Endowment for the Arts

Guide to the National Endowment for the Arts.
Arts in America.

Chapter 21:   Foundation Grants for Artists

The National Guide to Funding in Arts and Culture (Foundation Center).
Grants for Film, Media & Communications (Foundation Center).
Grants for Arts, Culture & the Humanities (Foundation Center).

You may also order the federal government's Consumer Information Catalog by writing to:

R. Woods
Consumer Information Center-2D
P.O. Box 100
Pueblo, Colorado 81002

24.

GLOSSARY, ACRONYMS AND ABBREVIATIONS

****

A glossary is a list of specialized, or uncommon words, with their definitions. It accompanies the text in a book, is usually at the end of the book, and assists the reader in quickly understanding what was meant by the use of certain special words, known as "glosses." That's what a glossary means: a collection of glosses or special words.

Because I expect that the educational range of individuals reading this book is going to vary widely, I have included terms that may already be familiar to some readers. In many cases, this glossary also includes words that you may expect to come across when going through the loan or grant procedure. Every effort has been made to provide an "action" definition, one that is easy to understand and which can be used immediately. Many basic terms are defined here. An ample glossary has been provided to help you quickly read and understand this book, as well as future loan or grant applications. If you cannot find a word

in this glossary, please use a regular dictionary. Please consult your attorney or accountant where legal or financial definitions need further clarification.

ACRONYMS AND ABBREVIATIONS

At the end of this chapter, after the glossary, you will find a special section unscrambling the acronyms and abbreviations used in this book. An acronym is a new word formed by combining the first letters or syllables in a series of words. It differs from an abbreviation (or the words) because you can pronounce the acronym. Because of the quantity of government agencies and government acronyms and abbreviations, I wanted to reduce confusion and increase understanding of what these letters meant, either during your reading of this book or later when you receive government agency literature.

THE GLOSSARY

Abstract: A summary of your grant proposal.

Accounting: A system that provides quantitative data about a person's or business' finances, i.e. the amount of money a person or business really has.

Accounts Payable: A list of debts that a person or business currently owes. Such debts mainly include purchases of services, inventory or supplies which have been billed but not paid. Normally, this list does not include unpaid salaries, interest or rent that have accumulated. A person or business can and should keep this list to know how much is owed and to whom.

Accounts Receivable: A list of monies owed for goods delivered and services rendered for which a person or business has not yet been paid.

Accounts Receivable Financing: A method a business uses to borrow working capital by pledging monies owed from others. A business uses the accounts receivable as collateral to borrow funds so it can continue producing goods and delivering services.

Accounts Receivable Turnover: A ratio derived by dividing the total credit sales of a business by its accounts receivable. This ratio shows how many times a receivable portfolio has been collected during a certain accounting period. A low turnover can spell trouble.

Accredited Investor: In a private placement deal, also known as a private limited partnership, a wealthy investor who does not count as one of the maximum 35 individuals permitted to invest in the deal. He has either a high net worth, a proven high income over a period of years, or both and is familiar with this type of investing.

Active Corps of Executives (ACE): This is an association of volunteers who assist small businesses, under the SBA, and who supplement the SERVICE CORPS OF RETIRED EXECUTIVES (SCORE). While they are volunteers, these are still active business people.

Actual Cost: The amount paid for an asset (see asset), not its resale value or worth. An item's cost can also include the freight charges and installation cost.

Adjustable Rate Mortgage (ARM): A mortgage loan that has a changeable interest rate over the length of the loan.

Appraisal: An opinion or estimate of a property, usually performed by an expert who compares the value of one property to that of other similar properties.

Appreciation: The condition or state where something's value increases over a period of time.

Arrears: This refers to a debt or obligation that was not paid by a specified date.

As is: The condition in which something is agreed by a purchaser to buy it.

Asking Price: The price at which something is offered for sale.

Assess: The act of determining something's value or pricing it for the purpose of taxing it.

Assessment: The amount of tax due, based on something's value.

Asset: Anything an individual or business owns that has value and can be used for payment of debts; something that can be used to purchase goods, services, labor or is transferrable into cash. Something you can exchange for something else. In common use it is a valuable resource.

Assign: To transfer ownership from one to another.

Auction: A method of marketing property by asking for bids and awarding the property to the highest bidder.

Audit: To inspect the accounting records and procedures of a business or organization in order to verify whether or not they are accurate and complete. An internal audit is done by a member of the organization whose records are being inspected. An independent audit is done by someone outside of the organization.

Balance: The amount shown in an account, normally the difference between a debit and a credit.

Balance Sheet: A financial statement that gives a snapshot of the property owned by a company and of claims against that property as of a certain date.

Balloon: Also known as a balloon payment. This is an unusually large final payment on a loan and which pays the loan in full. It is called a balloon because the final payment is greater that the normal installment payment.

Bank: A government-regulated business that maintains savings and checking accounts, issues loans and credits, and deals in negotiable corporate and government securities.

Base Period: A time period used to measure an activity.

Beneficiary: The name of a business, organization or individual to whom the proceeds of an insurance policy are paid when a specific condition is met.

Benefit: Something that increases the profitability of a business or improves an individual's lifestyle.

Bill: An account submitted and demanding payment for goods sold, services rendered and/or work completed or in progress.

Bond: An interest-bearing or discounted government or corporate IOU. Its issuer pays the holder a specified sum of money at certain intervals in addition to paying the principal by a specific date.

Book Value: The actual value of individual assets minus any depreciation allowances.

Bottom Line: The net profit or loss on an activity.

Break-Even: Also known as the break-even point. The point at which income is equal to the cost in producing that income.

Bridge Loan: A short-term loan that is made when one is expecting intermediate- or long-term financing. Short-term can mean weeks or months, not years.

Budget: One's estimate of income and expenses over an interval of time, whether daily, weekly, monthly, annually, etc.

Bureau: Referring to a particular department, agency or office, usually (but not always) referring to a particular task or duty performed by government agents in that office or department.

Business: An enterprise, profession or trade that provides a product or service and operates for a profit-making purpose.

Business Plan: The strategy a business uses to achieve its continued survival through the entire cycle of developing a product or service to delivering it to an individual consumer or another business or organization.

Buyer: An individual or another business who purchases the goods or services produced by you or your business and who pays or promises to pay for those.

Call Loan: A loan which either the borrower or lender can terminate at will. Also known as a demand loan.

Capital: The money and other assets of an individual or business used to produce and market its goods or services.

Capital Asset: Something of value with a relatively long life.

Capital Improvement: Something that improves an asset's value and extends its life.

Carnet: A permit allowing one to bring samples of product into a foreign country without paying duty on those samples, provided they are not sold in that country.

Cash: The asset on a balance sheet that represents currency, negotiable checks and money orders, and bank balances.

Cash Basis: A common accounting method used by individuals and which notes when income is received and debts or deductions are paid.

Cash Flow: The cash earnings of an operation, either net income before or with depreciation and noncash charges.

Cash Ratio: The percentage of cash and marketable securities compared to current liabilities.

Cash Reserves: The amount of surplus cash a business or individual owns, above one's debts or liabilities.

Certificate of Deposit: A certificate issued by a bank whereas it borrows your money and pays you competitive interest on the loan. Also known as a CD. Maturities vary.

Check: A draft authorizing the withdrawal of money from previously deposited funds, paying a specific amount to a specific person on demand.

Closing Costs: The expenses involved when real estate is transferred from a seller to a buyer and which usually include attorney's fees, survey costs, title searches, insurance and filing fees.

Collateral: An asset that is pledged to a lender until the loan is repaid.

Collection Ratio: A comparison of a company's accounts receivables to its average daily sales.

Common Stock: A share of ownership of a public corporation.

Company: An business organization organized as either a proprietorship, partnership or corporation.

Consolidation Loan: Normally, this is an installment loan that combines and refinances all previous loans and debts to reduce the amount of one's installment payments.

Construction Loan: A short-term real estate loan used to finance building costs with the funds disbursed in stages on a prearranged plan and is repaid when the project is completed.

Consumption Tax: In its pure form, a sales tax is paid by the end consumer user, unlike a Value-Added Tax (VAT) which taxes each stage of the production and distribution cycles.

Contract: An agreement between two or more parties that creates an obligation to do or not do something.

Contract Award: The amount one receives to perform a service for or delivered finish goods to an end user; the individual or business receiving this award is legally bound to perform an exact function resulting in a result. When a
government agency makes a contract award, it is giving an assignment, usually to a private firm, to produce goods or perform services, as stipulated in the agreement.

Corporate Bond: A certificate given to an investor in exchange for borrowed money, which has interest usually repaid over intervals and the principal at the expiration of the loan.

Corporation: A legally created artificial person, chartered by the federal or a state government, for the purpose of doing business in the place of a real person or group of persons and which is separate and different from them. This entity is legally treated as a real person but with a potentially longer life span and the ability to sell off parts of it through stock transfer.

Cost of Goods Sold: The amount it costs to buy raw materials and produce finished goods.

Credit: The unused amount available for one to borrow from a lending institution.

Credit Rating: An independent and formal investigation, analysis and maintenance of an individual's or business' responsibility to repay debt. A history is kept showing one's past performance, often for a number of years.

Credit Risk: An evaluation of the possibility that an obligation will not be repaid or that a loss will occur.

Current Ratio: One's current assets divided by current liabilities; current defined as usually being within a one-year period.

Debt: Something one is obligated to pay another through an expressed or implied agreement. This can be secured or unsecured and can be money, goods or services. Amounts are payable on a certain date or on demand, as specified by the agreement.

Debt-to-Equity: The total liabilities divided by the total shareholders' equity.

Deed: A written contract transferring the legal title of real estate from one to another.

Default: The failure of a debtor to pay an obligation by a certain date.

Deficit: More liabilities and debts than income and assets or an excess of expenditures above a budget.

Demand Loan: A loan that has no set expiration date but which a lender can ask for repayment at any time, usually when certain conditions fail to be met.

Depreciation: The wearing out of plant equipment, machinery, etc. and which reduces taxable income.

Direct Loan: Funds that are lent from one party to another without an intermediary.

Direct Payment: Funds that are given, without an expectation of, or as, repayment, from one party to another.

Distribution: The movement of goods from a manufacturer to the consumer or another business.

Dividend: The amount decided by a corporation's board of directors to be paid to shareholders as a distribution of earnings produced by the business.

Draft: A signed, written instruction by one party to another to pay a third party a specified sum. Commonly called a bank check.

Due Diligence: A meeting where company representatives are interrogated about its background and use of stock offering or loan proceeds by an investment company or lending institution prior to raising or lending funds; or the act of this investigation.

Duty: A tax usually imposed when goods are imported or exported between countries.

Earnings: Earned income that comes about by producing goods and services.

Eligibility: Conditions which must be met by an applicant for a grant or loan.

Endowment: A gift of money or property from one to another, usually of a government agency or private foundation to another organization or an individual. It can also mean the permanent fund from which these gifts are drawn.

Entrepreneur: An individual who starts a new business.

Equity: The amount a property can be sold minus the claims against it.

Equity Financing: The act of raising money by selling shares in a company. It is best done when the company or its products are in demand.

Escrow: Money, securities or property held by a third party until a contract can be executed.

Execution: Completing a contract or agreement.

Exercise: To make use a legal right in a contract.

Expenses: The laying out of money, time, labor, resources and/or thought for the purpose of receiving a benefit or to bring about a result.

Export: Something produced in one country and then shipped and sold in another; or the act of doing this.

Factoring: The act of selling one's accounts receivables to a third party for cash at a discounted rate.

Feasibility Study: An analysis and projection of future income, expenses and profitability of business or investment.

Fiduciary: A person, company or association who holds assets in trust for a beneficiary with the responsibility of investing wisely on behalf of the beneficiary.

Finance Charge: The cost of borrowing money.

Finance Company: A lending institution that does not receive deposits to lend, but instead borrows from banks and others and re-lends that money at a higher rate.

Financial Statement: A written statement describing the financial status of an individual, business or organization.

Firm: Another way of describing a business.

Fiscal Year: An accounting period over twelve consecutive months but which can be measured in consecutive weeks, quarters or days. It is not always the same as a calendar year. For example, the United States government's fiscal year begins on October 1 and ends on September 30 of the following calendar year.

Fixed Asset: The tangible property of a business used in its operation but not expected to be converted into cash unless the business is liquidated.

Fixed Rate Loan: A loan whose interest rate does not change.

Fluctuation: A change in price or interest rates, either upward or downward.

Foreclosure: The act of losing one's property when debt has not been honored on time.

Foundation: An institution or association organized to contribute money, or some other form of assistance, for benevolent, charitable, educational, religious, or research purposes.

Franchise: The legal right or privilege to sell another's product or perform a service.

Fraud: One's intentional misrepresentation or deception of or about an action or activity that causes loss to another party.

Full Disclosure: The requirement that one disclose all the important details about a transaction.

GAAP: Generally accepted accounting principles. These are the rules of procedures that define how accounting should be practiced.

General Partner: The managing partner of a limited partnership who is responsible for running the operation and who is liable for debts incurred.

Going Public: The act of offering a company's shares to the general public.

Grace Period: A loan period where payment is past due but when default or cancellation does not occur.

Grant: To give money or property to another, usually without a direct compensation. The gift itself.

Grantor: The person who transfers or gives property to another.

Gross Income: The total income actually received before deducting expenses.

Gross National Product: The market value of all goods and services produced within a country in a year which is determined without doublecounting.

Guarantee: To take upon the responsibility of honoring an obligation if the person or business fails to repay the debt by a specified date.

Guaranty: The promise to pick up a dropped ball, i.e. the first party failed to repay an obligation so the second party performs that duty.

Holding Period: The time between when one has acquired property and not yet developed it or between acquisition and resale of that property.

Hypothecation: The act of pledging property to secure a loan.

Income: The amount of money received by a business or individual.

Initial Public Offering: The moment a company's shares are being offered to the public for the first time.

Import: To bring into a country or the commodity itself which is brought into a country from or by another.

Income Statement: A profit and loss statement, i.e. the summary of the income, costs and expenses during a certain accounting period.

Insurance: A scheme where individuals and companies pay a certain amount over a period of time to another (an insurance company) as protection against a loss and which then reimburses them for that loss, if it occurs.

Insured Loan: A loan indirectly guaranteed by a government agency through an insurance program.

Interest: A right, claim, participate, title or legal share in something. In a loan, it is the money paid for the privilege of borrowing funds. There can be many forms of interest.

Interest, accrued: earned but not paid; accumulated interest: due or past due but not yet paid; compound interest: interest upon interest.

Interest Rate: A percentage of a loaned amount of money which is paid for its use over a certain period.

Interim Financing: A short-term loan borrowed to cover costs until longer-term financing is obtained.

Interim Statement: A financial statement issued, in accounting, for a period between the regular accounting period.

Intermediary Loan: A third party loan where the lender first borrows money from another to lend out to the end borrower.

Inventory: A company's raw materials, supplies used in its operations or finished goods or an individual's list of assets and their cost or market value.

Investment: Money or property spent to acquire property or other assets to produce income.

Joint Venture: A project undertaken by more than one investor acting as one organization.

Judgement: The final and public determination of a court, usually placing a debt upon an individual or organization.

Kickback: An illegal payoff for favors by one individual to another.

Letter of Credit: A document issued by a bank and guaranteeing the payment of a customer's drafts up to a certain limit for a specified time period, whereby a bank substitutes its credit for the buyer's and eliminates the seller's risk. In international trade it is drawn in the name of the third party.

Leverage: The relation of one's debt to one's worth. Over-leveraged refers to one who is deeply in debt; under-leveraged to one who is capable of additional borrowing.

Liability: Money owed. It can also be a claim on the assets of a company or individual, with an obligation to transfer assets or services at a later specified date.

Lien: A creditor's claim against the property of an individual or business. There are different types of liens, all which basically make one's property and possessions security or collateral for a debt or obligation.

Loan: A transaction where the owner of property allows another to use that property, usually for a certain period of time and with an added payment for having used that property. This can apply to money as well as another commodity or real estate.

Loan Guarantee: The act of a government or a third party promising to repay a loan if the borrower defaults. The third party is also liable for the debt.

Market: Also known as the marketplace. In this sense it means the public place where goods and services are sold, either directly or through brokers.

Market Value: The sales value of something.

Maturity: The time when the lending period expires and the remaining balance of the loan is due. It also commonly refers to the entire lending period, i.e. the loan has a maturity of seven years (the lending period expires after seven years).

Micro Loan: A loan that is smaller than average. An SBA Loan Guarantee averages about $100,000; a micro loan averages less than $25,000, usually for $15,000.

Mortgage: A certificate, or some other written proof, that a borrower gives a lender a lien on a property, which is used as security for or as a collateral against the loan. A mortgage normally indicates a real estate transaction.

Negotiable: Two entirely different definitions. (1) Something that can be sold or transferred to another person or business in exchange for money or to settle an obligation. (2) A transaction that requires mutually satisfactory conditions to occur between two or more parties.

Net Income: The leftover amount after all expenses have been paid. The difference between all sales or income and the cost or expense in producing that income or sales.

Net Loss: What is owed to another or others after one has calculated income and expenses.

Net Present Value: The method of evaluating investments by comparing the cash outlays against the future income of that expense and determining if it will be profitable or not.

Net Profit: The amount an individual or business owns after subtracting expenses from income.

Pledge: To transfer the right to sell property if a default occurs on a debt obligation.

Prepayment: Paying a debt for the loan period expires. Sometimes one is penalized for this because a lender does not receive the expected return on that investment.

Price/Earnings: The ratio of a company's share price divided by its reported or future earnings.

Prime Rate: A key interest rate which banks charge their most credit worthy customers to lend them money. It is determined by how much it costs the bank to borrow these funds and how much borrowers are willing to pay for the use of those funds.

Principal: The basic amount of a debt on which interest is earned or owed.

Present Value: Today's value of a future payment which is discounted at a certain rate.

Pre-tax Earnings: Net income before taxes.

Profit: The amount one gets to keep after expenses.

Profit Margin: Also known as margins of profit or just margins. The relationship between one's total sales and the amount one gets to keep.

Project Grant: An amount of money given to complete a specific project by a certain time. The funds are normally paid in stages as phases of the project are completed.

Property: Something which belongs exclusively to an individual or group.

Return: The profit on an investment, expressed as an annual percentage rate.

Return on Investment: Also known as return on investment capital. Basically, what comes back after investing money into something. This commonly is expressed as a percentage of the amount earned on a company's total capital. It is calculated by dividing total capital by earnings before interest, taxes and dividends.

Security: The collateral a debtor offers to a lender against which funds are borrowed.

Seed Money: The first contribution to a start-up business.

Share: Participation in a corporation as measured in units or the percentage of ownership of that corporation or venture.

Stock: Ownership of a corporation, in part or whole, represented by shares or units and which act as a claim against its earnings and assets.

Surety Bond: A contract promised by a third party guaranteeing that party will fulfill the financial obligations of the first to the second party if the first defaults in performing one's responsibility.

Tax: The compulsory contribution made to support a government.

Value: The estimated worth of property, calculated in terms of money, when offered to a buyer.

Variable Rate Mortgage: A mortgage loan which fluctuates and is based upon a specific indicator, such as the prime rate.

Venture: A business enterprise, especially referring to one where one risks time and money for a reward.

Venture Capital: Also known as risk capital. An external source of funds provided by one company for a start-up or turnaround company in exchange for future profits and potential or immediate ownership in that company.

Work: The effort one does that results in actual goods or services developed, manufactured or sold.

Working Capital: The funds which keep a company operational by financing the conversion cycle of the company, from the time it takes to convert raw materials into delivered and paid-for finished goods which bring cash back to the company.

Yield: The return on money or property invested into something. It is calculated by dividing the net income plus any capital gains by the amount one invested.

ACRONYMS AND ABBREVIATIONS

ACE: Active Corps of Executive

AFL-CIO: American Federation of Labor-Congress of Industrial Organizations

AID: Agency for International Development

A/P: Accounts Payable

APR: Annual Percentage Rate

A/R: Accounts Receivable

CATS: Citizens for an Alternative Tax System

CD: Certificate of Deposit

CD-ROM: Compact Disk - Read Only Memory

COD: Cash on Delivery OR Collect on Delivery

CPA: Certified Public Accountant

CUST: United States Customs Service

D & B: Dun and Bradstreet

DOC: United States Department of Commerce

DOD: United States Department of Defense

DOE: United States Department of Energy

DOI: United States Department of the Interior

DOJ: United States Department of Justice

DOS: United States Department of State

DOT: United States Department of Transportation

ED: United States Department of Education

EEB: Economic Bulletin/Board

EEOC: Equal Employment Opportunity Commission

ELAN: Export Legal Assistance Network

EOM: End of Month

EPA: Environmental Protection Agency

ERLC: Export Revolving Line of Credit

Exim: Export-Import Bank of the United States

EXIMBANK: Export-Import Bank of the United States

FAS: Foreign Agricultural Service

FCIA: Foreign Credit Insurance Association

FDIC: Federal Deposit Insurance Corporation

FEMA: Federal Emergency Management Assistance

FHA: Federal Housing Administration

FHLMC: (also Freddie Mac) Federal Home Loan Mortgage Corporation

FmHA: Farmers Home Administration

FNMA: (also Fannie Mae) Federal National Mortgage Association

FOB: Free on Board

FOIA: Freedom of Information Act

FPM: Flexible Payment Mortgage

FTC: Federal Trade Commission

GAAP: Generally accepted accounting principles

GAO: General Accounting Office

GATT: General Agreement on Tariffs and Trade

GEM: Growing Equity Mortgage

GNMA: (also Ginne Mae) Government National Mortgage Association

GNP: Gross National Product

GPM: Graduated Payment Mortgage

GPO: Government Printing Office

GSA: General Services Administration

HFA: Housing Finance Agency

HHS: Department of Health and Human Services

HUD: Department of Housing and Urban Development

ICC: Interstate Commerce Commission

IDB: International Data Base

IPO: Initial Public Offering

IRS: Internal Revenue Service

ITA: International Trade Administration

JTPA: Job Training Partnership Act

LBO: Leveraged Buyout

LTV: Loan to Value Ratio

MBDA: Minority Business Development Agency

MPP: Market Promotion Program

NAIC: National Association of Investment Clubs

NASA: National Aeronautics and Space Administration

NAV: Net Asset Value

NEA: National Endowment for the Arts

NIH: National Institutes of Health

NCV: No Commercial Value

NTDB: National Trade Data Bank

NPV: Net Present Value

NYSE: New York Stock Exchange

OEL: Office of Export Licensing

OMB: Office of Management and Budget

OPIC: Overseas Private Investment Company

OSDBU: Office of Small and Disadvantaged Business Utilization

PASS: Procurement Automated Source System

P & I: Principal and Interest

P & L: Profit and loss statement

PE: Price-earnings ratio

PITI: Principal, Interest, Taxes and Insurance

PV: Present Value

R & D: Research and Development

ROI: Return on Investment

RTC: Resolution Trust Corporation

SBA: U.S. Small Business Administration

SBDC: Small Business Development Centers

SBDU: Office of Small and Disadvantaged Business Utilization

SBIC: Small Business Investment Company

SBIR: Small Business Innovation Research

SCORE: Service Corps of Retired Executives

SEC: Securities and
              Exchange Commission
SEM: Shared Equity
              Mortgage
SEOG: Supplemental Educa-
              tional Opportunity
              Grant
S & L: Savings and Loan
              Association
SLMA: Student Loan Marketing
              Association (also known
              as Sallie Mae)
TAPO: United States Trade
              Assistance and
              Planning Office
TDP: Trade and
              Development Program
TIN: Taxpayer Identifying
              Number
TPCC: Trade Promotion
              Coordinating
              Committee
TREA: United States
              Department of the
              Treasury
UCC: Uniform Commercial
              Code

USDA: United States
              Department of
              Agriculture
US & FCS: United States and
              Foreign Commercial
              Service
USIA: United States
              Information Agency
USITC: United States
              International Trade
              Commission
USPS: United States Postal
              Service
USTR: United States Trade
              Representative
USTTA: United States Travel
              and Tourism
              Administration
VA: U.S. Department of
              Veterans Affairs
VC: Venture Capital
WCGP: Working Capital
              Guarantee Program
XIS: Export Information
              System
YTD: Year-to-date
YTM: Yield to maturity